Employee Surveys in Management
Theories, Tools, and Practical Applications

About the authors

Ingwer Borg is Scientific Director at the GESIS-ZUMA academic survey research institute in Mannheim, Germany, Professor of Psychology at the University of Giessen, Germany, and Executive Consultant at the Kenexa Research Institute. He studied experimental psychology (MSc, Tulane), applied psychology (Dipl.-Psych., Dr. phil., University of Munich), and mathematical psychology (postdoctoral research, University of Michigan). A veteran of some 30 years in employee surveys, mostly in German-headquartered companies of all sizes, he has been involved in all conceivable aspects of employee surveys as a cofounder and former partner of HRC (now Kenexa, Germany). He has authored or edited sixteen books and hundreds of articles on survey methodology, data analysis, scaling, theory construction, and various substantive topics of psychology.

Paul M. Mastrangelo, PhD, specializes in the transformation of employee data into insightful pathways to change. He has over 15 years of experience in psychological assessment, organization development, and adult education. Paul works as a Senior Consultant and Director of New Service Development at Genesee Survey Services, where he has facilitated survey driven change efforts for companies such as Apple, Cisco Systems, Hewlett Packard, Johnson & Johnson, Lyondell, Raytheon, and Polaroid. Paul has over 20 original publications and is a regular presenter at the Society for Industrial and Organizational Psychology's annual conference. Paul received his PhD in Industrial and Organizational Psychology from Ohio University in 1993 and his BA in Psychology from the University of Rhode Island in 1989, where he was inducted into the Phi Beta Kappa Honor Society. He cheers for the Boston Red Sox from Rochester, NY, with his wife, Kim, and his two children, Ally and Marc.

Employee Surveys in Management

Theories, Tools, and Practical Applications

Ingwer Borg
with
Paul M. Mastrangelo

Library of Congress Cataloging in Publication

is available via the Library of Congress Marc Database under the
LC Control Number 2008931542

Library and Archives Canada Cataloguing in Publication

Borg, Ingwer
    Employee surveys in management : theories, tools, and practical
applications / Ingwer Borg, Paul M. Mastrangelo.

Includes bibliographical references.
ISBN 978-0-88937-295-5

    1. Employee attitude surveys. 2. Organizational effectiveness--Evaluation.
I. Mastrangelo, Paul M. II. Title.

HF5549.5.A83B66 2008   658.30072'3   C2008-903805-3

© 2008 by Hogrefe & Huber Publishers

PUBLISHING OFFICES
USA: Hogrefe & Huber Publishers, 875 Massachusetts Avenue, 7th Floor, Cambridge, MA 02139
          Phone (866) 823-4726, Fax (617) 354-6875; E-mail info@hogrefe.com
EUROPE: Hogrefe & Huber Publishers, Rohnsweg 25, 37085 Göttingen, Germany
          Phone +49 551 49609-0, Fax +49 551 49609-88, E-mail hh@hogrefe.com

SALES & DISTRIBUTION
USA: Hogrefe & Huber Publishers, Customer Services Department,
          30 Amberwood Parkway, Ashland, OH 44805
          Phone (800) 228-3749, Fax (419) 281-6883, E-mail custserv@hogrefe.com
EUROPE: Hogrefe & Huber Publishers, Rohnsweg 25, 37085 Göttingen, Germany
          Phone +49 551 49609-0, Fax +49 551 49609-88, E-mail hh@hogrefe.com

OTHER OFFICES
CANADA: Hogrefe & Huber Publishers, 1543 Bayview Avenue, Toronto, Ontario M4G 3B5
SWITZERLAND: Hogrefe & Huber Publishers, Länggass-Strasse 76, CH-3000 Bern 9

Hogrefe & Huber Publishers
Incorporated and registered in the State of Washington, USA, and in Göttingen, Lower Saxony, Germany

No part of this book may be reproduced, stored in a retrieval system or transmitted, in any form or by
any means, electronic, mechanical, photocopying, microfilming, recording or otherwise, without written
permission from the publisher.

Printed and bound in the USA
ISBN 978-0-88937-295-5

Content

Preface xv

1 Characteristics and Types of Employee Surveys 1
1.1 Current Usage of Employee Surveys in Industry 1
1.2 Some Typical Cases of Employee Surveys 3
1.3 General Characteristics of Employee Surveys 5
1.4 The Purposes of Employee Surveys 6
1.5 Some Basic Types of Employee Survey 8
    Employee Polls 8
    Benchmarking Employee Surveys 9
    Climate Employee Surveys With Feedback 11
    Unfreeze-and-Involve Management Programs 12
    Systemic Employee Surveys 13
    Employee Surveys for Measurement and Change 15
1.6 On the Evolution of Employee Survey Types 17
1.7 Potentials and Risks of an Employee Survey 19
1.8 Employee Surveys and Naïve Models of the Employee 21
    Five Models about the Employee 21
    The Five Employee Models and their Corresponding Employee Surveys 23
    Employee Models and Employee Surveys 25

2 Positioning an Employee Survey 27
2.1 Positioning the Employee Survey 27
    Total Package Designs 27
    Stakeholders, Explicit Goals, and Hidden Agendas 30
2.2 The Context of an ES 31
    Project Antecedents and Apparent Needs 31
    Introducing General Information about Employee Surveys 33
    Considering the Benefits of an ES 35
    First Thoughts on the Costs of an Employee Survey 37
    Readiness of an Organization for an ES 38
    Finding the Right Time to Administer the ES 41
2.3 Positioning the Employee Survey through Top Management 43
    Goals 44
    Risks and Dealing with Risks 44
    Defining Minimal Requirements for Managers and Non-Managers 45
    Top Management's Own Public Commitment 46
2.4 Further Facets of Positioning an ES 47
    Content Considerations 47
    Dissemination of ES Results 49
    Comparing Employee Survey Results across Organizational Units 49
2.5 Ethical and Legal Use of Individual Employee Data 51
    Anonymity 52
    Confidentiality 55
    Allowing for Demographic Item Non-Response 55
    Data Protection 56
    Inadmissible Questions 57

	2.6	Census and Sample Surveys 57
		Statistical Considerations..57
		Cost Considerations 58
		Psychological Considerations 59
		Usability for Organizational Decision Making 60

3 Coordinating and Planning the ES Project 61
    3.1   Architecture 61
           Architecture of the Coordination Team 61
           Tasks of ES Coordinators 63
           Recruitment and Selection of ES Coordinators 64
           ES Coordinators and ES Consultants...66
           Time Consumed by Coordinators in an ES Project 67
    3.2   ES Project Plan 67
           The ES Master Plan 68
           Differentiating Roles in the ES Project...69
           Phases, Activities, and Roles of an ES Project 71

4 Content of Questionnaire 77
    4.1   Approaches for Defining the Content of an ES 77
           Existing Questionnaires and Instruments..78
           Interviewing Senior Leaders to Create Survey Content.............................79
           An ACE Hierarchy to Guide Questionnaire Construction 81
           Using ACE to Construct Indices..83
           From ACE to RACER 84
           The Performance-Satisfaction Motor...85
           Using Company Scorecards to Identify Measurement Fields....................88
           The Various Functions of ES Items...89
    4.2   Standard ES Questions: The Individual Employee's Perspective 91
    4.3   Extending Standard ES Topics: Performance and Strategy 95
    4.4   Extensions II: Further Psychological Topics.. 97
    4.5   Topics Not Suited for an ES 100
    4.6   Facets of ES Items 101
    4.7   Importance as a Judgment Criterion... 103
    4.8   Typical Item Compilations 106
    4.9   Demographic Items 107

5 Item and Questionnaire Design 109
    5.1   Closed Items with Rating Scales 109
           Number of Categories in a Likert Response Scale 111
           The Middle Category of a Likert Response Scale 111
           Using "Don't Know" Categories and no Middle Categories 113
           Numerical Labels for the Categories of the Response Scale 114
    5.2   Response Criteria in Items.. 115
    5.3   On the Psychology of Answering Survey Items...................................... 117
    5.4   Items with Qualitative Response Scales 120
    5.5   Comments 123
    5.6   Open-Ended Questions with a Focus 126
    5.7   Formulating ES Items 128
    5.8   Scales and Single Items 132

	5.9	Items in Different Languages 133

- Back-Translations 133
- Further Criteria for Questionnaire Translations 134
- The TRAPD Approach 134

5.10 Collecting Demographic Information 135
5.11 The Structure of the Questionnaire 136
- Reasons for a Questionnaire Structured by Content 137
- Criteria for Sorting Items 138

5.12 Layout of Questionnaire 139
- Cover Page and Introduction 139
- Design and Layout of Demographic Items 140
- Layout of the Blocks of Content Items 141
- Alternative Layouts of ES Questionnaires 141
- Total Design Method 146

5.13 Prognosis Questionnaires 146
5.14 Electronic Questionnaires 148

6 Processes of Questionnaire Development 153

6.1 Developing an Early Version of the Questionnaire 153
6.2 The ES Project Team's Role in Questionnaire Development 155
- Coordinating Language Adaptation and Translations 155
- Coordinating the Development of Group-Specific Items 156
- Coordinating the Development of Demographic Items 158

6.3 Involving Stakeholders into Questionnaire Development 160
- Involving Rank-And-File Employees 161
- Involving the Organization's Executive Board 161
- Involving the Works Council 162
- Involving Middle Management and ES Advisory Boards 163

6.4 Pre-Testing and Pilot-Testing the Questionnaire 163
- A Simple Pre-Testing Approach for Employee Surveys 164
- Cognitive Pre-Testing 165
- How Many Pre-Tests? 166
- Pilot-Testing the Questionnaire 167

7 Sampling 169

7.1 The Population 169
7.2 Non-Random Samples 170
- Convenience Samples 170
- Typical Cases, Extreme Cases, Experts 171
- Cut-Off Samples 171
- Snow-Balling 171
- Quota Sampling 172

7.3 Random Samples 173
- Simple Random Samples 174
- Systematic Random Sampling 174
- Stratified Random Samples 174
- Cluster Samples 176
- Multi-Stage Sampling 176

7.4 Sampling Errors 177
- Sampling Errors in Samples of Different Size 177
- Sampling in Small Populations 179

		Sampling Errors for Means and Other Statistics	179
		Sampling Errors under Different Sampling Methods	180
	7.5	Sample Size	180
	7.6	Response Rates and Nonresponse	183
		Nonresponse Bias	183
		Dealing with Nonresponse	184
		Item Nonresponse	186
	7.7	Sample Construction in Practice	187
8		**Information Campaign Before the Survey**	**191**
	8.1	Phases and Steps of an ES Information Campaign	191
	8.2	Activities in Phase I of the Information Campaign	192
		Informing Employees About the Survey	192
		Motivating to Participate	193
		Informing About Survey Administration	198
		Bridging the Time of "No Action" After the Survey	198
	8.3	Planning the Information Campaign	200
	8.3	Style of the Information Campaign	200
	8.4	Typical Questions and Answers	201
9		**Data Collection**	**207**
	9.1	Survey Administration and Survey Logistics	207
	9.2	Data Collection in Group Sessions	208
		The Polling Station Method	208
		Organizing a Polling Station Setting	212
		Polling Station Data Collection and Other Group Sessions	213
		Special Participation Requests for Unavailable Employees	214
		Monitoring Response Rates and Using Reminders	215
	9.3	Data Collection by Postal Mail	216
		Monitoring Response Rates and Using Reminders	218
	9.4	Online Data Collection	220
		General Advantages of Online Surveys	220
		Challenges of Online Employee Surveys	221
		Online Data Collection and Anonymity	221
		Monitoring Response Rates and Using Reminders	224
		Combining Online and Traditional Methods of Data Collection	225
	9.5	Alternative Methods of Data Collection	226
	9.6	Summary Comparison of Data Collection Methods	227
	9.7	Measures to Increase Response Rates	228
		What Response Rates can be Considered High Response Rates?	229
		Persuasive Positioning	229
		Reducing Anonymity and Confidentiality Concerns	231
		Transparency and Visibility	231
		Incentives	232
		Monitoring Response Rates and Reminders	234
		Questionnaire Design and Personal Invitation Letter	236
	9.8	Data Entry and Data Coding	237
	9.9	Data Cleaning	238

10 Standard Data Analysis 241
10.1 Elementary Analysis of ES Data 241
Survey Results for Single Items...241
Comparisons of the Focal Group with Other Organizational Units...............245
Placing Absolute Scores in the Context of Several Standards 246
Items, Indices, and Indicators 248
Using Interrelationships among Items to Determine Importance 251
10.2 Standard ES Reports... 252
10.3 Focal Reports... 253
The General Introduction of a Focal Report...253
Turning to the Focal Group 255
Tables of the Focal Report...256
Alternative Ways to Organize the Items in a Focal Report 257
Reporting Demographics in a Focal Report..258
Appendices of a Focal Report..259
10.4 Cross-Comparison Reports... 259
Cross-Comparison Tables..260
Who Should Get Cross-Comparisons? 261
10.5 Prognoses Reports 262
10.6 Standard Reporting of Answers to Open Questions................ 263
10.7 First-Results Reports for Employees..................................... 265
10.9 How to Organize Report Ordering 266
Specifying Selection Rules 266
Automated Report Ordering 268

11 Designing Follow-Up Processes.. 271
11.1 Basic Components of the Follow-Up Processes..................... 271
Actions and Busy Work...271
Monday Morning Actions: Starting Small..272
Avoiding Unnecessary New Initiatives or New Goals 273
Types of Responses to ES Results..274
11.2 Approaches to Designing Follow-Up Processes 275
The Top-Down Approach..275
The Bottom-Up Approach 277
The Task-Force Approach 279
The Big-Bang Approach..280
Soft Varieties of the Top-Down Approach 280
11.3 Communicating the Organization's Official Response to ES Results 282
11.4 Creating Dialogue as a Response to Survey Results 284
11.5 Cultivating Individual Responses to Survey Results............... 286
11.6 The 7+7 Approach for Rolling-Out the Follow-Up Processes................ 289
11.7 Response Sequences for Individual Managers 291
11.8 Criteria for Planning and Evaluating Follow-Up Processes.................... 292

12 Nonstandard Data Analysis 295
12.1 Interpreting ES Results... 295
12.2 Experience-Based Hypotheses and ES Results 297
12.3 Benchmarking... 298
Types of Benchmarks 298
Benchmarking Single Items and Indices..300

On the Validity of Benchmarks 300
Benchmarks from Different Countries...301
Benchmarking Against Industry and Job Norms 303
Benchmarking by Cross-Comparisons within the Organization..............................304
Upward and Backward Benchmarking 305
Benchmarking Against Prognoses 306
Benchmarking Correlations and Patterns..306
12.4 Using Theory to Interpret ES Data 307
12.5 Deep Statistical Analyses 310
The Psychological Map of the Respondents 310
Dependent Variables within MDS...312
External Dependent Variables and Linkage Research...313
Relating Internal Dependent Variables to Demographic Information 316
Interpretations and the "More is better" Fallacy..317
12.6 Business-Oriented Frameworks for ES Data Interpretation..................... 318
ES Data and the Balanced Scorecard 318
SWOT Analysis..319
12.7 Triangulation and Other Views onto the Data... 321

13 Presenting Survey Results to Management 323
13.1 Structuring an ES Presentation... 323
Introduction of an ES Presentation..323
Facets/Dimensions of the Organization Climate 325
The Performance-Satisfaction Network: Core and Extension 327
A Simpler Alternative: ACE or RACER Structuring 327
Further Break-Downs of the Statistics..328
Empirical Structure of Items..329
Special Topics...329
Business Perspectives 329
Monday Morning Action Platforms..330
Summary and Recommendations 330
Still Other Forms of Structuring an ES Presentation 331
13.2 The ES Presentation Process 332
Aligning the Final Presentation with Key Managers...332
Global Management Decisions as Input to the Follow-Up Processes 334
Overcoming Typical Psychological Barriers..334
13.3 Adding Punch to the Presentation 336
Positioning the Presentation in the Context of the Follow-Up Processes 336
Avoid Wasting Time on Side Issues..336
Avoid Over-Interpretation..338
13.4 Motivating Managers to Act.. 339
Motivating Managers to Get Involved..339
Building Platforms for Immediate Actions...340

14 Employee Survey Workshops 343
14.1 Foundations of ES Workshops 343
The Basic Goals of an ES Workshop..343
Feedback, Discussion, and Explanations 344
Proposals for Solutions 345
Alignment..346
14.2 Typical Design of an ES Workshop 347
Phase I: Introduction..347

		Phase II: Discussing and Structuring the Results	350
		Phase III: Action Fields and Ideal Scenarios	354
		Phase IV: Outlook on Next Steps	356
		Phase V: Wrapping Things up After the Workshop	356
	14.3	The Participants of an ES Workshop	357
	14.4	The Facilitator of an ES Workshop	357
	14.5	Organizing and Preparing an ES Workshop	359
		Participants, Time, Location, and Invitation	360
		Room	360
		Materials	360
		Preparing an ES Workshop: the ES Coordinator's Role	361
		A Facilitator's Personal Preparation for the ES Workshop	362
	14.6	Discussing ES Results	363
		Workshop Activities for a Particular Item Block	364
		An Illustrative Item Block	364
		Another Illustration with Items on the Supervisor	366
	14.7	Tips and Hints for Facilitating an ES Workshops	368
		Timing	368
		Role and Behavior of the Facilitator	369
		Presenting the Survey Results	370
		Discussing the ES Results	370
		Behavior of the Participants in the Discussions	372
		Discussing the Items on the Direct Supervisor	373
		Brainstorming on the Fields of Action	374
		Behavior of Managers in ES Workshops	375
		Giving Feedback to the Supervisor after the ES Workshop	375
	14.8	Variants of the Traditional ES Workshop	376
		ES Workshops with Managers Only	376
		ES Workshops under Tight Time Constraints	377
	14.9	Alternatives of the Traditional ES Workshop	378
	14.10	Planning Batteries of ES Workshops	382
	14.9	Additional Follow-Up Work on ES Workshop Results	383
		Additional Statistical Analysis of the Survey Data	383
		Consulting Additional Theory in the Literature	384
		Understanding Opportunities	384
		Cause-And-Effect Analyses for Problem Areas	384
		Testing the Strategic Value of Possible Areas of Action	385
		Summarizing how Workshop Participants Interrelate the Topics	386
15	**Action Management**		**389**
	15.1	Developing Ideas for Actions	389
	15.2	Organizing Actions	392
		Level of Action	392
		Roles in Action Management	393
		Selecting Action Directors and Action Team Members	393
		Action Management vs. Line Management	394
		The Action Mission Contract	395
		Defining the Action Director's Action Space	396
		When to Begin Action Planning	397
	15.3	Foundations of Action Planning	398
		Planning Actions Hierarchically	398
		The Timeline of an Action	399

15.4 Simple Action Planning Tools 399
"W" Action Forms 400
"W" Action Forms with Status Indicators 400
15.5 Planning Complex Actions 401
Planning Milestones 401
Planning Activities 403
15.6 Controlling Action Implementation 404
Principles of Action Controlling 405
Reporting 406
Simple Reporting Forms 406
Reporting in Complex Actions 406
Adjusting an Action Plan 407
Online Action Planning Tools 409
15.7 Soft Factors in Action Management 409
Selecting the Right People 410
Delegating Actions Away 411
Remaining Open to Clarify the Action's Goals and Conditions 411
Accepting and Endorsing the Action Plan 411
Insisting on Discipline 411
Leading Action Team Members 412
Planning Realistically 412
Controlling Action Progress Constructively 412
Thinking About the Politics of the Action 413
Turning the Action Team into a Team 413
Keeping Technical Gimmickry Minimal 414
Showing Commitment to the Action and its Tasks 414

16 Information Campaign after the Survey 415
16.1 Information on Results and Management's Responses 415
16.2 Information on Actions 416
16.3 Planning and Organizing the Information Campaign 419
Architecture and Roles 419
Publications and Time Line 421
Communication Politics 423
16.4 Communication as Part of Planned Change Management 425
Creating Perceptions of what most People are Doing 425
Communicating what Employees are Ready to Hear 426

17 Evaluating Employee Survey Projects 427
17.1 Project Evaluation and Learning 427
17.2 Evaluating ES Projects 428
Positioning the Evaluation of an ES Project 428
Evaluation Criteria 429
Objective Business Criteria 431
Finding the Right Time for Evaluations 432
17.3 Evaluation Methods 433
Analyzing the Quality of the Survey Data 433
Studying Documentation Materials 434
Collecting Observations on the ES Project 435
Interviews to Evaluate the ES Project's Results and Processes 436
Surveys to Evaluate the ES Project's Results and Processes 439

17.4 The Practice of ES Evaluations 439
    Sample 439
    Organization 440
    Items and Survey Design 441
    Data Analysis and Interpretation 443

References **447**

Author Index **463**

Subject Index **469**

Preface

Arnold Palmer once described golf as "deceptively simple and endlessly complicated." Such is the employee survey (ES). At the simplest level, to survey employees is to ask, to listen, and to respond. Yet the complexity of each of these tasks only becomes apparent when one thoughtfully attempts to achieve them or, unfortunately, when one recognizes the attempt was not thoughtful enough.

Although employee surveys today are commonplace, with millions of employees being surveyed around the world year after year, it is not uncommon to be asked for help from respected organizations in a surprisingly naïve way. For example, one nonprofit organization with several thousand employees recently called the first author at his university office and asked whether he knew a student who would be interested in running an ES as part of his or her thesis project. Apparently, that organization did not realize that letting someone run an ES means turning over a major element of leading and managing an organization to an outsider, and that one should make sure that this is done with extreme care, coordination, and expertise. In another case, an ES project manager from a large company who had been doing employee surveys for almost 20 years asked one of the authors to evaluate their questionnaire, identifying poor items, suggesting additional good items, and generally optimizing the questionnaire. When asked back about the purpose of the ES, its criteria of success, its quality requirements, its usual follow-up processes, management's role in the ES, etc., confusion set in, because many of these issues had never been systematically discussed, decided, or developed in this company. Under these conditions it is, of course, hard to optimize a questionnaire, except in a very narrow technical sense (e.g., eliminating ambiguous items).

Those who have done employee surveys can typically attest that an ES process is far more than simply conducting a survey. Here we describe various approaches to design and run the "total package." It includes the survey, but it also includes the follow-up processes, for example. Indeed, we here suggest that just doing a survey is, from a managerial point-of-view, almost with certainty bound to be a suboptimal project, because it does not systematically take into account what goals the survey is supposed to serve and under what constraints (resources, culture, politics, etc.) it must operate. In this book, therefore, we look at the whole ES process, not just at how to construct a questionnaire and or how to analyze the data.

We show at least one concrete way for doing each phase and step of an ES project. For example, it is common rhetoric in the context of employee surveys to say that the survey results should (or even *must*) lead to actions. However, exactly how one manages to get from ES results to actions, is typically left open. We here describe in detail how this can be done. Although we do not suggest that our proposals are necessarily the best solutions under all circumstances, we do present what we found to be both efficient and effective in many concrete survey projects over the last 25 years. Similarly, our proposal for running ES workshops is but one approach, although one that has been used successfully in many ES projects. Still, we suggest that readers take our proposals only as springboards for designing their own methods that optimally take the particular strengths and weaknesses of their own organization into account. Moreover, what works well in one country may not be optimal in another, because employees are used to different methods. ES coordinators should consider how they can adapt an approach as a chef modifies a recipe to suit the dinner guests.

If you are preparing to manage an ES for the first time, this book should be of particular interest to you because of its comprehensive scope. We recommend that you start with a simple approach and then power up the ES process systematically over several cycles. Doing so is not just a technical matter, but an effective way to maximize the benefits-costs ratio. All stakeholders have to learn first, and they should not be overtaxed with a design that absorbs too many resources. Measure the eternal variables job satisfaction and commitment, the conditions that are necessary for the employees to be productive, the clarity of goals and strategy. Interpret results to identify one to three main issues where action appears necessary or most promising. Finally, collaborate with stakeholders to proceed concretely, building quick successes that can be leveraged to attain even more improvements. Sometimes the results will call for action and other times simply reaction, but they always call for a response. Keep everyone informed about progress, and remind them how the survey served as a catalyst.

If you have managed ES projects previously, you will appreciate the depth of knowledge from our 40 years of combined experience in the field of employee surveys. Much of the advice given here is based on practical experience that we collected over all these years in literally hundreds of survey projects all over the world. However, we also keep an eye on scientific research, where we both have contributed books, articles, journal papers, and conference presentations. In this book, we present a fairly large number of new developments and research that have never been published before or that appeared in scientific journals that most survey practitioners have never read. These developments and this research have always been driven by practical requirements. For example, managers often find the results of an employee survey "obvious." But are they? And, if not, what can be done to avoid this cognitive fallacy? Likewise, it is common practice not to report scale means, but "percent favorable" scores. The percentage of employees with favorable perceptions is widely understood, but it seems that it would ignore information that is captured by a mean value. Under close examination, we see that there is no loss of information: Percent favorable scores correlate almost perfectly with mean values. And how should one interpret a survey with a "low" participation rate? Is this survey worthless? Research shows that this is most likely not so, because most non-respondents are "passive" ones: They simply did not participate for one reason or another, but they have the same attitudes and opinions as respondents. Thus, survey results are typically meaningful despite disappointing participation. Facts like these are useful to know in practice, because they maximize the survey's impact.

In this book, we also introduce other innovations and proposals that have not been described before. One example is the RACER model, a system of indices that extend the focus on employee engagement by adding further essential macro-variables that could be considered in employee surveys. Such models are also useful in benchmarking and in guiding data analysis. In data analysis, we cover a wide scope of standard and non-standard methods, introducing a variety of new methods to represent the survey results in frameworks that have been found highly effective in management presentations. Examples are MDS plots that show the correlations of survey items, and that allow data-based and action-oriented discussions on what drives what with management. Other examples are showing the survey results as they relate to a balanced scorecard or within the network of the satisfaction-performance motor, another model that relates a host of core constructs usually measured in employee surveys. Then, we discuss in detail the "7+7" design for rolling out the follow-up processes of an ES. More generally, we introduce the notion of "total package designs" to optimize not just the questionnaire, but all processes of the ES project.

We should also mention that this book is based on the 3rd edition of the first author's German book "Führungsinstrument Mitarbeiterbefragung." The idea was to combine what was written there, and what was based primarily on German (or European) companies, with what the second author had learned about US (or US-headquartered) companies. This should make the book more useful for the "global" ES researcher or practitioner, and it should help to avoid the unfortunate mistakes that survey vendors sometimes make when exporting their "proven" solutions to other countries or cultures. What works in one culture, may not work in another. Sometimes it could work if it was set up differently (e.g., by involving different stakeholders in particular ways). We hope to have made a contribution here to the important field of organizational assessment and development, helping those who design or run employee surveys to achieve stronger effects with less risk and at reduced costs.

Finally, at this point, we like to express our thanks to a number of persons who have substantially contributed to this book in one way or another. Our thanks go to Julia Khorshed (GESIS; Mannheim, Germany), Patty Langdon (Rochester, USA), and Christiane Spitzmüller (University of Houston; Houston, USA).

1 Characteristics and Types of Employee Surveys

Employee surveys are tried and tested instruments of organization development. Karl Marx (1880) used them to establish "precise and reliable knowledge about the conditions under which the working class works" in order to "show the world how things present themselves for the worker" (quotes from Pauli, 1992). For Marx, an employee survey (ES) was social science research for political purposes. Today, an ES almost always is set up to serve economic purposes, to yield data needed to manage the organization, or to support strategic change directly by involving employees and managers into working towards innovation and improvement. While survey researchers and practitioners tend to see today's ES as more than merely a "job satisfaction survey," even this outdated understanding can lead managers to discover how to improve outcomes for both the organization and the employee.

1.1 Current Usage of Employee Surveys in Industry

Employee surveys have become popular instruments during the last decades. Gallup (1988) published a survey where 70% of 429 American companies report that they had run a least one ES in the last ten years, and 69% indicated that they planned to conduct further employee surveys. Delany et al. (1988) found in a study of some 7,000 managers of American companies that between 38% and 51% of them had used employee surveys in their areas of responsibility. Kraut & Freeman (1992) report that a survey of the HR directors from 75 "large well-managed" American companies showed that 78% of them had conducted employee surveys. Bungard et al. (1997) found that some 50% of the 100 largest German companies had conducted employee surveys, and that they planned to also run such surveys in the future. Today, these percentages tend to be even greater. Hossiep et al. (2008) report that 80% of the 820 largest industrial companies in the German-speaking countries had conducted employee surveys and that 64% run such surveys "regularly". Kraut (2006) describes a poll of leading ES firms and writes "Their estimates vary but indicate that about three of four larger firms survey their employees—for example: Mercer Human Resource Consulting polled 2,600 respondents in the U.S. workforce. Sixty-four percent said their firms conducted employee surveys. In Watson Wyatt's 2002 survey of 13,000 employees in the U.S. workforce, 53% said their companies had conducted an ES in the past three years. Watson Wyatt's 2001 Human Capital Index Survey of HR practices in 500 publicly traded companies showed that 79% surveyed employees regularly" (p. 2). Kraut (2006) also concludes that "survey use is higher among Fortune 1000 companies" (p. 2).

Employee surveys are clearly popular in Western countries. While we are unaware of any comparable study from other regions, from our own experience in the ES business in the last 30 years, we know that employee surveys are at least "exported" into those regions via globalization. International companies usually run their surveys in all the regions and countries where they have subsidiaries or employees. That does not mean, though, that the ES is exactly the same. For example, when running a global ES for a large German power group with a German headquarter, we used paper-pencil methods in all plants in Eastern Europe, but online methods in the West. Apart from such technical adjustments, the follow-up processes (e.g., presenting the results to management or running workshops to discuss the results with employees) also had to be designed in such a way that they would fit into the respective local culture. That is even true in companies with many professional and highly educated employees. For example, when running an ES for a large IT company, the employees in Japan did not easily discuss items that assess the employees' satisfaction with their supervisors—a situation made worse if the supervisor was present.

Company size is another variable that influences an ES. Small companies generally do not run employee surveys on a regular basis. Large companies, in contrast, have learned that strategic people management and informed leadership decisions call for systematic data on employees' attitudes and perceptions, on how such indicators change over time, and how they compare to internal units and other companies. Employee surveys are the foundation of data-guided organization development.

Another sign for the spreading interest in employee surveys is the growing number of publications on this topic (e.g., Borg, 1995; Bungard, Müller, & Niethammer, 2007; Church & Waclawski, 2001; Deitering, 2006; Domsch & Ladwig, 2006; Folkman, 1998; Freimuth & Kiefer, 1995; McConnell, 2003; Töpfer & Zander, 1985; Smith, 2003). The reasons for this interest are manifold, but their main driver is no doubt the conviction that an ES can have positive effects on the business bottom line if it is done right.

What an ES is supposed to accomplish, in the end, is to accelerate and align change processes by focusing the employees' attention on new goals; by inducing awareness for new directions and the need for behavioral changes; by aligning employees' awareness and understanding; by supporting the creation of structures and systems that reinforce certain directions in an organization's behavior; or by measuring progress on important criteria—to name just a few related issues. Hence, in times of an increasingly global environment where change has become a major challenge, employee surveys have become ever more important.

In regions such as Eastern Europe, the growing interest in employee surveys is closely related to the new role that the employee (and the manager, in particular) must fill in their massively changed economic environment. When running an ES in such regions, one typically meets an environment with little experience in "democratic" people management despite lots of hope and expectations for quick change and improvements. This requires special efforts to carefully position the ES as a change instrument and to gradually move from a simple survey to a sophisticated change instrument. This transition should occur over a few repetitions rather than attempting too much in one single shot.

The experience with employee surveys in Eastern Europe and in other non-Western regions of the world repeats, in a sense, what has happened before in the Western world. Originally, an ES was more a social-science instrument, a method to assess public opinion and, in particular, a tool to measure job satisfaction, morale, and organizational climate (Neuberger & Allerbeck, 1978; Rosenstiel, Falkenberg, Hehn, Henschel, & Warns, 1983). The goal was only to collect data; the ES was not embedded into a system of processes aimed at transforming these data into change effects. These processes can become rather wide and deep, involving all managers and employees in various roles, and requiring lots of skills, experience, and motivation to become cost-effective. When moving to regions where employee surveys are used for the first time, one quickly learns that many of these factors have to be built first. Yet, today one knows what it takes and, therefore, creating this environment can be accomplished more efficiently than what it took historically in the West.

1.2 Some Typical Cases of Employee Surveys

Let us begin by first looking at some rather typical cases of employee surveys in practice. They will serve to derive and illustrate general properties of employee surveys.

Case 1. The reunification of Germany in the early '90s also led to a merger of the West and the East German railroads. This merger went along with restructuring the organization from a state-owned company with civil servants to a profit-oriented firm that was planned to become a public corporation. Hence, many changes were necessary. Indeed, no integrated personnel information system existed at that time, but rather numerous local systems that differed vastly from each other and that were, in part, just card files with unknown quality. Indeed, not even the exact number of employees was known. Top management was eager to get the facts, and so they decided to also run an ES to get *a reliable and valid picture* of how the employees perceived the situation, what they were concerned about, what they were hoping for, what their attitudes were, and what their commitment was. An ES was therefore conducted as a *mail survey* that was sent to a *representative random sample* of 15,000 employees of all regions, functions, and levels of the company.

Case 2. Companies in the IT industry pay close attention to changes in their markets and their technological environments. Many trends are closely monitored by watching sophisticated indicators, including those on *soft factors* such as employee engagement, turnover tendencies, or attitudes towards innovations. About a dozen leading IT companies from both North America and Europe gathered in 1992 to found a *consortium* on employee surveys. The basic rule was that each company would regularly conduct an ES, using a certain number of common items, and then feed its data into a common data pool. These data would then be used to generate industry-specific *benchmarks*. For example, if one finds that only 40% of one's middle managers in Japan are satisfied with their salary, one can compare this value against what is average, worst, or best in the Japanese IT industry in general.

Case 3. The business results of a mid-sized Dutch company that made printing devices looked rather good. At the occasion of a major anniversary of the company, the CEO felt that he should do something for the company's *organizational climate*. He decided to conduct an ES as a census survey and ask the employees about their *job satisfaction* and about possible *problems* that needed to be fixed. The survey data were fed back to every working group for discussion and action. The idea was that the anonymous survey would help to identify problems and involve all employees and their supervisors in an effort to improve the present situation.

Case 4. The top management of a large automobile production plant had formulated new guiding principles for management that aimed at giving the shop-floor employee more decisional freedom and more responsibilities. This meant a major cultural change because management in this plant used to be command oriented. An ES was designed as a *vehicle for this organizational change*. The ES focused on a wide scope of issues such as the employees' satisfaction with their working conditions, their supervisors, and their pay and benefits, but also on a set of issues related to the new guiding principles. The survey results were fed back in a *top-down process*, beginning with top management and ending with each working group. Data analysis focused, in particular, on how various attitudes and opinions were related to the "dependent variables" such as understanding and endorsing the guiding principles. The results were discussed on all levels of the organizational hierarchy, and certain *strategic areas of focus* and *task assignments to take action* were defined by top management for all subordinate managers.

Case 5. A business group had decided to concentrate its portfolio to two of its business lines only, selling all other businesses, and acquiring new companies that would fit into their strategy to become the world leader in its new business field. Some of the companies of this group had conducted their own employee surveys before, but now things had changed and the group's top management emphasized the notion of one common company. The various employee surveys were thus integrated into one *common* one, with some room for *local* issues. Moreover, feedback began at the group's executive board, and this board defined a few *areas of focus* that were passed on to lower levels. Managers were *expected to act* if improvements were required in some cases, or if opportunities could be realized in others. Because the ES was found to be an effective intervention, top management decided to run it *annually*. It was also decided to construct a *people-management index* from the ES data and use this index as one criterion for *allocating bonuses* to managers. To measure this index more often, sample surveys were run in between the large census surveys. The ES, thus, became part of the group's measurement and management systems.

1.3 General Characteristics of Employee Surveys

The five cases above show that an ES is not always the same. It can serve completely different purposes; it can be administered in different modes; it can ask each member of the population to participate or just a sample; it can be interlaced with other management instruments or just be a stand-along HR project; it can be conducted regularly or in an ad-hoc way; it can put top management into the driver's seat or focus on the shop-floor working groups only. With that many differences, what defines an ES? The following lists some characteristics that all employee surveys satisfy. An ES asks

1) *employees* (either at all levels, functions, subsidiaries, and regions or of specially selected subgroups; in the entire population or in a sample),
2) using *methods* from the empirical social sciences (questionnaires, interviews, focus groups),
3) *systematically* (i.e., according to a well-defined plan)
4) about their *attitudes, opinions, and perceptions* (i.e., about their observations, hopes, assessments, concerns, memories, and emotions),
5) regarding different issues that are directly or indirectly *important for reaching the organization's goals,*
6) with the intent to *aggregate* their answers over various groups of employees (e.g. those in particular departments, regions, or workgroups) and to map them into statistics, indicators, and indices,
7) in order to *help achieve the goals* of the organization.

With respect to facets #5 and #7 above, one should add that the term "goals" encompasses the goals of all stakeholders of the organization. That is, the goals of the organization are not just the goals of "the company" (which, often, is essentially the goals of top management or the goals of the owners of the company), but also those of middle managers, of professionals in research & development, or of female employees. Note, though, that we always mean groups and not single individuals.

Besides employee surveys there are other methods to systematically survey the employees of an organization. One example is the yearly *performance appraisal* sessions where a supervisor discusses each subordinate's performance during the past year. The results of these appraisals and discussions lead to goals and targets for the next year for each single individual. Performance appraisals are not special cases of employee surveys because usually no attempt is made to aggregate such data systematically to arrive at statistics for groups of employees.

An upward appraisal (often part of a multi-rater 360-degree feedback system) is different from an appraisal in that employees are asked to assess the performance of supervisors or managers. Because such data are typically aggregated over employees to yield overall scores for a supervisor or manager ("This is how you are seen by your subordinates...."), upward appraisals are special cases of an ES that focus on just one particular job aspect.

Another example is the *exit interview* where employees who leave the company to work somewhere else are asked for the reasons that motivated them to quit their jobs. Here, too, we have an example of an ES (with a special focus) because it is not the

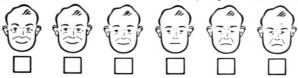

Figure 1.1. Kunin's (1955) faces scale for measuring job satisfaction.

reasons of each single individual that is of interest but the more general trends that show up in the interview data.

1.4 The Purposes of Employee Surveys

Employee surveys are done for two major reasons: Measurement and change. Historically, the emphasis was on measurement. An ES was designed to measure attitudes and opinions in a cost-effective and psychometrically acceptable way while little attention was paid to how to make use of the data thus collected.

A classic example of the measurement approach is the *Kunin scale* (Figure 1.1) which now often uses *smiley faces* to avoid representing only one gender or ethnicity. It consists of one single item that measures overall job satisfaction (Kunin, 1955). The item is a Likert-type item with a bipolar answer scale. The scale recognizes that satisfied employees are typically more frequent than dissatisfied employees by providing three response categories in the satisfied range but only two in the dissatisfied range of the scale.

Job satisfaction remained the main issue in the 1960s and '70s. However, single item measurements were replaced by multi-item scales. Psychometrics became popular, and everything had to be measured *exactly* and in a *differentiated* way. *Standard instruments* were developed based on mathematical-statistical models. They were required to be *objective* (lead to the same results across researchers), *reliable* (generate consistent results), and *valid* (produce results that allow one to predict external variables such as performance or withdrawal behavior). Examples for such instruments are the JDI (Cranny, Smith, & Stone, 1992), the ABB (Neuberger & Allerbeck, 1978), or the MSQ (Weiss, Dawis, England, & Lofquist, 1967). For these instruments empirical *norms* (reference statistics, benchmarks) were established. These norms served to help the user interpret the ES results by answering the question "What does one *usually* get when asking these questions?" If one finds, for example, that 65% of the employees of company ABC endorse an item as the one in Figure 1.1, the normative value establishes whether this is a good or a bad result.

> *The opportunity for independent thought and action in my position:*
>
> - How much <u>is</u> there now? .... (min)   1 2 3 4 5 6 7 (max)
> - How much <u>should</u> there be? 1 2 3 4 5 6 7
> - How <u>important</u> is this for me? 1 2 3 4 5 6 7

Figure 1.2. An is/should/importance item.

The ideal of standardizing ("one size fits all") and simple models of cognitive processes were characteristics of this era. In hindsight, however, the psychology often remained shallow, using mathematical composition rules that, from today's perspective, appear far too simple and premature. Figure 1.2, for example, illustrates a "triple" item that estimated a respondent's dissatisfaction with one job aspect by plugging the three ratings into the formula $\mid is - should \mid \times importance$. The employee's overall job (dis)satisfaction was calculated by averaging the results of this formula over all items (Haire, Ghiselli, & Porter, 1966)[1].

A different type of perspective on employee surveys began to emerge in the 1970s. It put a lot less emphasis on measurement, but stressed the ES's potential as an *intervention* method. Nadler's book "Feedback and Organization Development: Using Data-Based Methods" was particularly influential in this direction. Its core idea was to feed the survey data back into the organization in special *workshops*. Figure 1.3 illustrates how this is done. The members of a workgroup are informed by a facilitator about the survey results. They then discuss these results, explain them further by adding qualitative comments and concrete explanations, sort the data into meaningful clusters and structures, and possibly generate action plans to fix problems or to respond to newly discovered opportunities for improvements. Today, this *survey feedback approach* is one of the most important methods for organization development.

The two basic approaches—measurement and intervention—led to a number of developments in the 1980s. The ideal of a standard instrument (e.g., Litwin & Stringer's (1968) climate survey) that fits all needs and circumstances was essentially dropped in favor of the notion of instruments that have to be *tailored* to the particular needs of the particular organization while still maintaining a core of common items for benchmarking. In addition, the substantive focus of employee surveys was shifted away from job satisfaction to business issues. In other words, issues important to the organization (such as performance, strategy implementation, or innovation) began to complement issues that were important to the individual employee (such as his or her satisfaction with various aspects of work).

---

[1] To illustrate the rule, If a respondent answers the item by *is*=3, *should*=7, and *importance*=6, then his or her dissatisfaction with this work aspect is computed as $|3-7| \times 6 = 4 \times 6 = 24$. This rule is based on the assumptions that all ratings are made on the same (ratio) scale and that "too much" of a property is the same as "too little" of it.

1.5 Some Basic Types of Employee Surveys

In the nineties, various different types of employee surveys emerged. Borg (2003) described five such types (Table 1.1). This classification is by no means the only one that is possible, and depending on the facet that is given particular emphasis, different classifications can be easily derived. One such facet is the purpose of the ES: It can be an attempt to reliably and validly measure what the employees think and feel about their work and the company, or it can be an intervention that serves to bring about or to accelerate change. Then, an ES can be a stand-alone project that is conducted once or in an ad-hoc fashion or it can be an integral part of the management systems that is carried out every year at a certain time because it generates data that are needed to run the systems (e.g., performance appraisals and bonus allocation). An ES, moreover, can be employee-centered, emphasizing topics such as job satisfaction and organizational climate, or it can be strategy-oriented with topics such as performance, customers, innovation, and productivity.

In today's practice, an ES typically is not either just employee-centered or just strategy-centered, but almost always serves both of these perspectives. It also attempts to measure a variety of constructs as precisely as possible, but it also intends to promote improvements and strategic progress by planning the ES as a total package that reaches far beyond the mere survey. These various functions of an ES may, nevertheless, become clearer and easier to understand by describing the five types of employee surveys from Table 1.1.

Employee Polls

To take a somewhat closer look at employee polls, let us return to Case 1 in Section 1.2. Here, the German railroads had no reliable information on the psychology of their employees. Yet, a merger of that magnitude cannot be intelligently planned without data on how employees and managers see the situation, what they expect, what they are concerned about, etc. In a large organization that is geographically spread out, the CEO cannot simply talk to his or her employees in one or a few meetings. To manage such an organization, one needs reliable survey data.

Because the purpose of an employee poll is to yield a differentiated picture of the psychology of the company, one typically needs a relatively large random sample that is representative with respect to important characteristics, such as organizational function, hierarchical level, geographic location, job type, and gender. This enables the statistician to break down the data so that one can infer the population parameters of various subgroups (e.g., middle managers of function X in county Y) with acceptably small errors of estimation.

Employee polls can also be less ambitious. An example is a survey of the employees about their company cafeteria. For such a survey one might choose just a quota sample that makes sure that employees who regularly visit the cafeteria, for example, are interviewed on how they like the food, while those who do not visit the cafeteria are asked why they do not go there. Such a poll is a survey where the precision of the results is less important. Indeed, the survey may be done with many open-

Figure 1.3. A scene from an ES workshop.

ended questions where it matters more to get qualitatively interesting answers rather than precise parameter estimates for standard variables. This "cafeteria survey" is also an example of an ad-hoc survey project. Its design is not based on sophisticated theory, nor does it plan wide and deep follow-up processes with many workshops and action planning. This is typical for employee polls in general. For example, in Case 1 above (the ES for the German railroads), no follow-up processes were planned. Rather, the results were presented in detail to the executive management, and everything else was left open ("wait and see").

Another example of an employee poll is a *pulse survey*, which is often used to bridge the gap between the annual or biennial ES that is common in many companies today. While the regular ES typically is run as a census survey (i.e., as a survey that invites every employee to participate), the pulse survey measures important issues with small random samples of the workforce in order to keep track of vital business statistics.

Benchmarking Employee Surveys

A benchmarking ES is a survey project that almost always comes with a long-range perspective. A snap-shot comparison with data collected only at time t generally holds little value because it is unclear how much the results depend on particular context factors that were valid only at time t. Benchmarking surveys are, therefore, typically repeated several times to see trends over time. Certain variables improve, others go down, and still others oscillate up and down, with more or less scatter.

Table 1.1. A classification for main types of employee surveys.

Type	Purpose	Embedding
Employee poll	Understand how employees/groups see things	Wait and see, then decide on further actions
Benchmarking ES	Compare employees' attitudes and opinions with those in other organizations	Repeat regularly to see trends
Climate ES (of the "shop floor") with feedback	Improve climate and satisfaction, fix "local" problems	None, the ES is a stand-alone, singular project that is run from time to time
Unfreeze-and-involve management program (UIMP)	Improve satisfaction and performance, involving all employees and levels	Repeat regularly, build follow-up processes, empower managers and employees to use results
Systemic ES	Measure soft factors to improve management	Integral part of the management systems (e.g., bonus allocation), linked with other business data

In a benchmarking ES, external benchmarks are of immediate interest. The question is how the company is doing relative to other companies, in particular those in the same industry. Because other companies are often interested in the same information, they sometimes form ES consortia as described in Case 2 above. They thus agree to run employee surveys regularly, with a core set of similar items, and feed the data into a common data pool administered by an external vendor who, in turn, delivers anonymous statistics to the various participants of the consortium (Johnson, 1996). Hence, company X may find that its employees are quite satisfied with their salary compared to how satisfied the employees in this industry are on average.

A benchmarking ES emphasizes a particular method to evaluate the survey results, i.e., comparing them with norms. In practice, one usually compares one's values with the industry's average values. In the USA and in Western Europe, many survey firms offer such norms, but even though they can be based on huge numbers of employees, they are often not representative. The reason is that they are typically based on those companies for whom the vendor happened to run or analyze employee surveys and not on true random samples. Yet, if the norms include an interesting set of contributing companies, these norms may be all that is needed.

There are other norms that may be even more important. Comparing one's survey results with the results of previous surveys in the same company, for example, shows what changed and what did not. Another benchmark approach that is always possible consists in comparing certain groups within the particular organization. For example, one can compare the results among the different functions of a company (although one should take into account typical differences among such functions). A third example is comparing similar organizational units. Managers are often interested to cross-compare the organizational units that directly report to them. In that case, each unit is benchmarked against the distribution of its "sister" units.

Benchmark employee surveys do not plan particular follow-up processes. They simply collect data and provide norms. They may also deliver some help on how to read such statistics, but it remains up to management what to do with the results.

Climate Employee Surveys With Feedback

A climate ES with feedback is the traditional ES. Its design goes beyond questionnaire construction, administration, and data analysis by explicitly planning a phase of "survey feedback" to the organization, in particular to the working groups at the shop floor. The working groups are expected to discuss the results and complement the statistics with qualitative information. For example, if the survey shows that the employees are dissatisfied with the information they need to do a good job, it should be clarified exactly what the problem is. Is it the quality or the quantity of the information, its timeliness, its relevance, its precision, its reliability, its accessibility, or what? What information is really needed? What is it that the employees want? Obviously, one cannot turn to action planning before such questions have been answered, and so survey feedback serves to enrich the quantitative results of the survey with additional qualitative details. Additionally, the survey feedback processes also aim at involving everyone into action planning, in particular into considering what can and what cannot be accomplished given the various goals and constraints.

The "official" purpose of a climate ES is typically to improve the conditions for employee satisfaction. For management, however, the real motivation to spend money on a climate survey is their belief that higher employee satisfaction leads to better performance (Hinrichs, 1991). As we later show (see Figure 4.5), this belief is too simple, although not wrong. However, it usually suffices to generate a survey that focuses on topics that are at least indirectly related to performance, and so management also gets what it wants, although often in an inefficient and indirect way.

In a climate survey, top and senior top management typically plays no major role by design. They see the results, but then leave everything else to the working groups at the shop floor. The focus is on local issues, but the climate survey has no explicit strategy for aligning local actions with the company's strategy.

In some countries (but not in the US), managers may not expect to be involved in a climate ES. If they receive a questionnaire, they assume that it was erroneously sent to them and do not fill it out. In Germany, for example, the term employee ("Mitarbeiter") means, first of all, rank-and-file employee, and *not* manager. There is no term that refers to "any" employee. Hence, an "employee survey," by semantics, suggests that the target group is rank-and-file employees, not managers. This is especially true if one communicates that the survey is about "employee satisfaction," about "what the employee thinks" and similar topics characteristic for a climate survey. Hence, if one also wants to interview managers, one must clearly communicate this extension of the target group to all persons on the organization's payroll and invite or ask everyone explicitly to participate in the survey.

Unfreeze-and-Involve Management Programs

A pure measurement notion of an ES is the exception. Even in employee polls, the data are not collected just to have data, but rather to use them for business purposes. The problem, however, is the perception that the ES project is over when the results are presented. Frequently, the survey design does not include preparations and plans for follow-up processes. Under these circumstances the outcomes resulting from the survey are hardly ever optimal. Often, the ES results simply disappear from attention in a short time because new business data and requirements are coming in day by day and quickly push aside complex issues that require more than quick-fix responses. To avoid that the ES leads to no responses—which is commonly seen as the major problem in employee surveys (Kraut, 2006)—one must design the ES project as a total package in which the survey is but one step in an intervention process that involves all functions, levels, and employees of the organization. The unfreeze-and-involve management program (UIMP) is one approach to achieve this goal (Borg, 1995, 1997).

Many elements of an UIMP are also relevant in other types of employee surveys, but the particular characteristics of an UIMP are not always that obvious. For example, in the questionnaire of a UIMP, one might use some items that do not intend to measure the employee's attitudes or opinions, but serve as "Trojan horses" that carry certain notions deep into the organization so that they can be pursued further in the follow-up processes. In employee polls, in contrast, using items where the respondents have no opinion is considered a major problem (Bradburn & Sudman, 1991).

The four main phases of an UIMP are depicted in Figure 1.4, and the steps within these phases are further described in Table 1.2. Overall, the four main phases are designed to accomplish the following:

1) The first phase serves to position the ES project, to design the instruments and processes of the ES, to plan the project, to organize its logistics, its survey administration, its data analysis and report generation, and its utilization of the ES results.
2) In the second phase, top management deals with the results of the ES. That means that management first learns about the results in special presentations, interprets the findings, evaluates their meaning, and defines certain areas of focus ("You must pay attention to issue X and consider action if it seems promising or necessary") or task assignments ("You must act on issue Y!") that all managers and organizational units must respond to. Top management may also decide directly to plan and implement some actions for the entire organization or parts of it.
3) In the third phase, the ES results—together with top management's reactions and decisions—are fed back into the organization in a top-down fashion, starting with the senior management teams of the large organizational units and cascading down to the shop-floor working groups. At each level,

Figure 1.4. Phases and steps of employee surveys.

the results are discussed, evaluated, interpreted, and screened for needs and for opportunities to act so that a few powerful action plans can be developed.

4) In the fourth phase, the action plans are implemented, monitored, controlled, and then marketed towards the employees. Finally, a UIMP is concluded with an evaluation of its processes and/or its results. However, in contrast to normal project management, a UIMP has no clear-cut end-point because many actions (and other responses) that follow an ES become part of normal management or are supposed to become an integral part of continuing change and improvement processes. The survey thus becomes a 365-day process where the actual survey administration is just the beginning of the next cycle.

Today, a usual UIMP cycle takes about nine months, although it often remains somewhat arbitrary to define an end-point because evaluations are either skipped completely or incorporated into the next survey administration. Some companies add survey questions that are specific to the previous post-survey actions or they maintain most of the survey questions from the previous survey administration to track changes in attitudes and perceptions.

Systemic Employee Surveys

Case 5 in Section 2 above shows how an ad-hoc ES can develop into a systemic ES. A systemic ES is not a project or program anymore because the ES has ceased to

Table 1.2. Phases and steps of an UIMP.

No.	Activities
Phase 1	
1	The ES is positioned re goals, side constraints (timing, budget, quality, risks), expectations, roles of stakeholders, anonymity and data protection, rules, etc.
2	The ES is concretely designed and planned with respect to its questionnaire, its survey administration, its data analysis and data reports, the recipients of data reports, and its processes. Managers are empowered to make the most of an ES.
3	The survey is administered to the employees. The data are analyzed and the results are documented in ES reports for managers. Deeper statistical analyses are conducted and presentations of ES results are prepared.
Phase 2	
4	The ES results are presented to the executive officers. Their meaning and their potentials are discussed with these officers.
5	The executive officers decide on areas of focus and/or on task assignments for all managers ("You must pay attention/must act on issue X!"). The officers may also directly decide on certain actions.
Phase 3	
6	The ES results, together with decisions made by top management, are fed back into the organization in a top-down cascade. This information is discussed, evaluated, complemented with qualitative information, structured, etc. In the end, a few areas of response are defined and ideal scenarios are developed for these areas ("If things were ideal, this is what this area would look like...").
7	Responses on the ES results—mostly in the form of improvement actions—are considered and planned.
Phase 4	
8	The plans for the responses/actions are implemented, monitored and controlled, and marketed to the employees.
9	The success of the responses/actions is evaluated.

become a special activity. Rather, a systemic ES is an integral part of an organization's management systems. In Case 5, the systemic ES is linked, for example, to the bonus allocation system and so one does not have a choice to run or not run the ES in a particular year. The ES *must* be run, because the data that it yields are needed by the bonus system. That does not mean that the ES must be carried out in exactly the same way year after year. One can, for example, alternate between a census ES with wide and deep follow-up processes in even years and a sample survey that yields reliable people-management indices for top managers in odd years (if this information is needed for top managers only). Similarly, a systemic ES may be linked with customer satisfaction surveys; with hard-fact measurements such as turnover data, productivity indices, sickness rate statistics, etc.; or, more generally, with balanced scorecards that systematically show how strong or weak the company is on important hard and soft domains.

Good indices of the strengths of a company's soft factors are typically the weakest components in company scorecards. The usual scorecards do not directly show what employees feel or think but typically exhibit only certain (cheap or easy to get) "objective" measurements that are deemed to be proxies of the psychological variables one is really interested in. Yet, if one wants to measure a company's strength with respect to innovation and learning, for example, the number of improvement suggestions or the number of action plans would be poor indicators of things to come. What one should assess is the employees' perception of the extent to which suggestions for improvements are generally encouraged, quickly and competently discussed, effectively implemented if possible, and perhaps even rewarded. Instead of using survey response rates as a metric of "engagement" or even survey scores themselves (which unscrupulous managers can attempt to influence), we are seeing the beginning of a trend toward measurements of appropriate action.

At a macro level, some organizations are including at least one survey question regarding the effective use of the previous survey data (see Figure 1.5) that can be analyzed according to various demographic cuts or used as a demographic cut in itself to show what areas have not progressed since the last survey administration. Online action planning systems are increasingly used as a part of the survey process, allowing actions to be entered, tracked, and evaluated by management.

Once certain scorecards are introduced, they become strategic instruments that cannot be easily changed without threatening long-range measurements. Systemic employee surveys, thus, once established, cannot be easily changed, but should be continuously developed together and in coordination with all other management systems.

Employee Surveys for Measurement and Change

Designing an ES first requires one to answer one basic question: Does the survey primarily serve as a measurement ("a report card") or a particular change purpose ("action oriented")? In the first case, the success criterion of the ES is the quality of its measurements, which is evaluated primarily by reliability, validity, and sample representativeness. Employee surveys for change are interventions in organizations that require involving employees and managers with the intent that the respondents and the circumstances around them are different after the ES. These effects may, in turn, affect the attitudes and opinions that were measured in the first place. Hence, a pure measurement-oriented ES (as in Case 1 above) should be constructed in such a way that it does *not* lead to changes of attitudes and opinions. Otherwise, the inferences from the sample to the population would be biased because the sample would not be the same anymore after the ES. In practice, however, managers rarely consider such scientific standards (e.g., the Solomon Four Group Design) to be necessary.

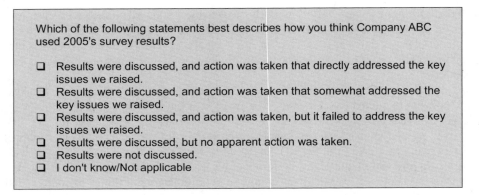

Figure 1.5. A survey item for tracking the perceived ES effectiveness.

When it comes to change, measurement is really quite irrelevant, as long as change results. This does not mean that the quality of measurement can be ignored, however, and that one can work with bad questionnaires, poor analyses, or improper statistical methods; too many people would notice such deficits and the ES project would get stuck in endless discussions, counter-arguments, and objections to rely on such results. However, one should always ask about the contributions of each element of an ES project to the project's end goals. For example, in an intervention-oriented ES one can include (a few) items that do not really measure anything, but that serve to put certain issues on the agenda for further discussion in the follow-up processes. Such items make no sense in a measurement-oriented ES.

The typical steps of a measurement-oriented ES (ES/m) can be understood from the loop in the upper right-hand corner in Figure 1.4. Their prototype is the employee poll or the benchmarking ES of Table 1.1. Their beginnings are (formally) similar to the first steps of an UIMP. That is, one starts by positioning the project, continues with designing its instruments and processes, and so on (see Table 1.2). However, an ES/m ends with the presentation of the ES results to management and then leaves the rest to line management. This does not mean that the results do not lead to concrete responses or actions, but it is simply not an element of the ES project and its project team anymore.

An effective intervention-oriented employee survey (ES/i) needs good measurement, as we have seen, but a measurement-oriented ES can also induce change effects. For example, in the time period between two regular employee surveys with an UIMP emphasis, one sometimes uses an *interim survey* that is set up as census surveys of middle and top management. Such a survey often contains an item such as "I believe that the employees in my area of responsibility endorse the company's strategy." This item not only measures the managers opinions on an important issue, but also serves to remind them that it is their task to ensure that their subordinates know the strategy and believe in it. Because the next regular ES is likely to contain items that ask all employees directly to what extent they endorse the strategy, the interim survey may drive managers to launch extra efforts selling the company's strategy to their subordinates to make sure that the results of the next ES are positive for them.

1.6 On the Evolution of Employee Survey Types

From a historical point-of-view, the UIMP and benchmarking ES are relatively modern types, whereas a climate ES or an employee poll are older approaches. Systemic employee surveys are the most recent developments. No ES type is obsolete, however. Most employee surveys today are really mixtures of different types. It therefore makes little sense to order different ES types along an "evolution" dimension (Higgs & Ashworth, 1997). What is true, though, is that many progressive organizations have led the ES through an evolution from a passive monitor of mood to a proactive tool for implementing HR strategy (Hinrichs, 1991, p. 301).

In the literature, employee surveys are mostly positioned as instruments of organization development (Moorehead & Griffin, 1989; Nadler, 1977), change management (Hellriegel, Slocum, & Woodman, 1992), or as "survey-guided development" (Pacific Gas and Electric Company, 1991). This perspective is appropriate even if the ES officially only serves diagnostic purposes because the survey's results will always influence management's action—even without a step-by-step model of how the survey results are systematically transformed into such activities. Hence, it makes sense in any case to at least consider what needs to be done to feed back the results easily and reliably. What works in one organization, however, may not work elsewhere because the managers in one company, for example, may not have the skills to read a standard ES report or because the established reward systems in another company prevent using the ES results in certain ways.

Taking an organization's specific context into account rather than using a standard questionnaire has become the normal approach not only in employee surveys, but in surveys in general. Indeed, in the 1970s the focus was almost completely on designing the measurement instrument, and a variety of standard instruments were developed and used over and over again in many different contexts. Little was done to optimize even the most immediate survey processes, such as methods of achieving a high response rate. In public opinion surveys such topics were first picked up by Dillman (1978) in what he called the *total design method*. The TDM simply studied the effects that different seemingly trivial design elements (e.g., the layout of the questionnaire or the letter of invitation) have on the total response rate. With the new survey administration possibilities, the TDM was extended to a *tailored design method* (Dillman, 2000). In the context of employee surveys, a tailored design perspective extends to a much wider action field, covering multiple processes for designing, participating in, and acting upon the survey. The way a tailored approach began in the 1970s was by carefully adapting the language of standard questionnaires to the specific jargon of the particular company under study, by adding company-specific items (e.g., on the company's strategy or on certain hot topics), and by computing company-specific indices from the ES data.

Design considerations were quickly extended beyond the survey instrument to cover all processes, resulting in what we call the *total package design method*. The term comes from car racing where the experts know that the total package wins the race, not necessarily the car with the most horsepower or the best driver. This means that *everything* that has an effect on the outcome—including the factors that can have an effect if they do not work—must be considered and optimized within the given constraints of time, budget, and other context factors.

ES professionals do not, of course, have to rediscover all the relevant factors in each new project. Rather, they have long check lists that they can systematically work through to arrive at optimal designs. This includes, for example, the questionnaire and its items; various formats for the feedback of results in ES reports; different methods to run workshops with managers and non-managers to work with the ES results; effective approaches to administer the survey in different environments; proven methods to increase the response rates; tools to empower managers to effectively work with ES results; methods to plan and implement actions on the basis of ES results; and many other methods, tools, and recipes.

Contrary to this trend for tailored employee surveys and for diversification, recent years have also witnessed some *counter-movements* reverting towards simplicity or perhaps over-simplification[2]. An example in this direction is Gallup's *Q12* questionnaire (Buckingham & Coffman, 1999). Gallup advocates this questionnaire for all purposes. This promise is supported by a number of "discoveries" that are essentially correlations of these twelve items with other variables such as employee retention, customer loyalty, and performance. The items of the *Q12* are interesting and often important for an ES (even though they all load heavily on general job satisfaction and, hence, in effect do not differ much from Kunin's "*Q1*" in Figure 1.1). Whether these items are always necessary or sufficient for good diagnoses and interventions is another matter. Moreover, from a cross-cultural perspective, some of these items are problematic, politically incorrect in some cultures, and very difficult to translate with culturally equivalent meanings (Borg, 2002b). On the other hand, such standard instruments come with many benchmarks and may be sufficient to show where one has to dig deeper by conducting focus group discussions or other data gathering techniques. Standard surveys are also easy to run because one does not need to go into the complicated process of constructing tailor-made questionnaires that all of an organization's stakeholders can live with.

In general employee surveys have become quite sophisticated over the years. The focus has shifted from merely focusing on the ES questionnaire to considering the ES project as a whole. Questionnaire content, items, and data analysis are no longer treated as psychometric issues but as change management tools. Indeed, the object of interest today is not the questionnaire, but the entire ES project. It is this object that needs to be optimized, not the alpha coefficients of survey scales or the R square values of predictive models. This higher-order perspective is open to many methodologies and, thus, one needs a general rule that guides the design process. One such rule

---

[2] Simple mathematical modeling is one example. It keeps resurfacing in "magic" formulas that supposedly work everywhere and, thus, can be programmed so that the computer grinds out hundreds of "meaningful" results in seconds.

is the total package design method which requires considering all elements of the ES project as a systemic whole, and not simply combining proven elements and best practices in an additive fashion[3]. The car that wins the race is not necessarily the one with "golden spark plugs" or exceptional torque, but the one where car, driver, mechanics, and other elements are optimal for the race track, weather conditions, and competition of the day. What is true in car racing is also true in designing and running an ES: Any ES must be planned in an integral way, with all of its instruments and processes harmonizing with each other and serving the project's goals.

One of the challenges that have become ever more important in recent years is conducting cross-cultural employee surveys. They make simple best-practice thinking quite risky because what is the best practice in one culture is not always best in another culture. The differences are sometimes surprising and dramatic. Gomez-Mejia (1994) showed, for example, that what seems a natural reward strategy with positive benefits on organizational commitment can have exactly the opposite effects in other countries: Pay for performance leads to higher commitment in American companies, but to higher turnover in Mexico because the Mexican workers (in the production sites studied by Gomez-Mejia) were aiming at certain amounts of total earnings and once they had made that much, they simply left the plant. More generally, work value research (Elizur, Borg, Hunt, & Magyari-Beck, 1991; Borg, 1986; Borg & Braun, 1996; Liu, Borg, & Spector, 2004; Harzing, 2006) has made sufficiently clear that one cannot simply export standard approaches to other cultures. This makes it difficult to conduct employee surveys in global organizations because culture affects not only the content of the questionnaire, but all other elements of an ES project. No one philosophy can address cultural differences in the anonymity concerns of employees, the use of certain answer scales when responding to survey questions ("response styles"), the local management's attitudes toward ES results, or the effective use of focus groups that deal with ES results.

1.7 Potentials and Risks of an Employee Survey

Managers typically underestimate the potentials of an ES, but overestimate its risks. Their major concern is that an ES leads to expectations on the side of the employees that cannot be satisfied (Fritz, 1992). That is, when asking about satisfaction with pay, for example, the employees would answer that they are not satisfied so that they get more money. However, such notions assume that the employees do not understand that the organization cannot satisfy all their wishes immediately and unconditionally. Experience shows that the opposite is true: An open and honest discussion on what is possible and what is not is good for an organization's success (Alper, Pfau, & Sirota, 1986; Hinrichs, 1996). What one should not do, however, is to censor the results of an ES or to simply lock them away and not feed them back and discuss

---

[3] We note here that this is not a problem for the *Q12* because it is not a stand-alone questionnaire but an element of an integrated management process termed "The Gallup path" (see www.gallup.com/management).

them. This can damage the organizational climate and lead to a loss of trust because it violates the psychological contract of such a project ("My honest answers for management's responses").

Managers usually know this danger. Viteles (1953, p. 394) reports one executive as saying: "An attitude survey is like a hand grenade—once you pull the pin you have to do something with it." Less drastically, the personnel director of a big German company once argued: "I want to run an employee survey in the near future in our company, but not before management has accepted the idea that it must do something with the results and respond with visible actions." This assessment appears basically correct, but upon closer inspection, it reflects the notion that management becomes, in a sense, the victim of an ES. No ES forces management to do anything. Rather, what management should do is to publicly position itself with respect to the results. Action is not always needed. The results may, for example, be excellent and show that everything is running smoothly. Then, a perfectly reasonable response by management is to communicate that what the organization is doing is the right thing, and that it will therefore continue doing what it is doing. Management might even feel that the ES does indeed identify certain problems that need attention and action. Yet, the organization may not have the resources for appropriate actions at that time. It may also be true that solving the particular problems does not contribute to the given strategic goals. In that case, management may simply communicate its decision and the reasons that led to it. If the arguments are transparent and convincing, then this response is all that is needed in terms of action.

Any ES, moreover, can be positioned in such a way that it prepares follow-up activities and responses in certain ways and with certain nuances. For example, rather than asking "How satisfied are you with your pay?" one could ask "Do you feel that your pay is adequate for your performance?" This latter option legitimizes (or even requires) follow-up activities that focus not simply on pay, but on pay in relation to performance.

Managers often know that "something" must be done in response to the survey results, and some may even know what needs to be done. Yet, many do not initiate corrective action because they already have too much work to do or because they feel that they cannot handle yet another issue. So, attempts at improvement are frequently postponed or allowed to die. In reality not all actions need to be shouldered by one manager or even a few managers. Rather, most actions turn out to require the work of special action teams, specialists, or even all employees in an entire organizational unit or working group. Managers, however, have to be prepared to make the necessary decisions and monitor its consequences. This means that one should always design an ES in such a way that it becomes clear that it serves to coordinate and focus work that needs to be done and not as a Christmas wish list where the employees simply indicate what they want from others (i.e., management) to make them happy.

1.8 Employee Surveys and Naïve Models of the Employee

The types of employee surveys discussed above are not the only ones that are conceivable. Another classification results from distinguishing different naïve models that managers have about their employees and then asking which sort of ES each such model implies. By "naïve employee model" we mean the set of assumptions a manager has about "the employee." For example, each manager has latent beliefs regarding what motivates employees such as "money motivates all employees," "only satisfied employees are good employees" or "employees are truly engaged only if they are given enough freedom to do their work." Qualifiers such as "all," "only" or "truly" point towards the theoretical content of such statements, to the assumed underlying lawfulness that practice has proven to be true ("that is the way it is," "I know from experience," "no doubt about that").

Naïve theories (McGregor, 1960; Hofer, 1985) arise naturally, unnoticed, and unavoidably as rules that structure the social world around us. Most such theories are quite simple so that the outside observer can group them into various prototypes. So, while each statement above would seem to indicate a manager's model, the manager may not be consciously aware of his or her categorization. We are suggesting that there are models ascribed by outside observers to explain a manager's behavior in the sense that the manager behaves "as if" he or she uses this rule.

Five Models about the Employee

One model of the employee is the *machine model* typical for the early decades of the 20th century. Similar to a machine, the employee's behavior at work can be analyzed and optimized by methods of "scientific management" (Taylor, 1912, 1947). Motivation plays the role of a constant that is given. What counts are processes. In German, for example, one speaks of employees who function just as "the wheels in a gear box" or of a company that runs as if it had been "well oiled." A similar mechanical notion underlies the idea that if things do not work well, they must be "repaired." Weber (1922) thought of the bureaucratic organization with its discipline, order, planning, hierarchy, functional specialization, standardization and routines, and with its impersonal and fact-oriented management style as the generally best form of organization. This model was successful for its time because values such as discipline and order were generally accepted, and because the economic environment was so stable that a company could produce and sell the same products and services with the same employees year after year.

The Hawthorne studies of the 1930 brought another model to everyone's attention, the *child model*. The studies showed the importance of organizational climate, of respecting subordinate employees and recognizing their contributions, of status, of informal structures and networks—things that McGregor (1960) summarized under the notion "The human side of enterprise." Having a say or co-determination, however, had no place in this model. Rather, the child model believes in patriarchic leadership where the employees are well-treated as if they were the children of the big boss, but this boss is the only one who really knows what is right or wrong and, thus, makes the decisions. The child model emphasizes the importance of emotions such as belongingness, status, recognition, status, prestige, pride in the company, affective commitment to the company, job security, and general attitudes towards work and towards the company. Its major topic, job satisfaction, dominated organizational psychology for decades and produced over 3,000 scientific publications up to the 1970s (Locke, 1976). The major reason for this interest was the assumption that satisfied employees are also "good" employees (Katzell, Thompson, & Guzzo, 1992; Porter & Lawler, 1968) .

Not much later than the discovery of the social-emotional side of an organization, the psychology of learning and cognition became strong. This led to the *robot model*. Robots, in contrast to machines, are intelligent, although this intelligence is constrained by the quality of their software that the robots cannot change themselves. To the extent that their software allows it, robots can solve problems and reach their goals on new paths. Robots learn on the basis of their experience of success and failure ("law of effect"). For their behavior, special interests or particular motives are not important: It suffices to use some incentives to make the robot move. What is important, though, is that rewards and punishments must be given close in time, differentially and consistently, to have an effect on the robot's behavior. Hence, the robot model for HR management requires that goals are specific, clear, and related to points in time, and that feedback is "smart" (specific, motivating by setting higher but achievable goals, relevant, time-related, etc.). Management, in addition, must provide the necessary environment for performance (e.g., proper working conditions, the right tools, clear job description, adequate role descriptions, good feedback on performance, or excellent training).

Stressing the employee's particular motivational set-up has been a popular naïve model for a long time. It is mostly based on Maslow's (1954) widely cited need hierarchy theory. In addition, the 1980s witnessed the rise of interest in work values and value change away from material values and towards post-material values such as self-actualization (Inglehart, 1977, 1995; Pawlowsky & Flodell, 1984). These perspectives are represented in the *individual model,* which assumes that every employee has his or her own profile of interests, values, and motives. The individual employee assesses things from his or her own point-of-view and attempts to pursue his or her own interests and goals, within work (pay, advancement, interesting work, etc.) and outside of work (family, spare time interests, friendships, etc.). With their individual value profiles, employees each fit differently into the normative values of the organization (O'Reilly III, Chatman, & Caldwell, 1991; Borg, 2006b). Yet, in contrast to robots, individuals are not just victims of their environment. Rather, they can attempt to change this environment in a critical, creative, or innovative way—if they are interested in the outcomes or in the change activities themselves. Individuals can also decide to leave the company to work somewhere else.

With the rise of systems thinking, some managers also began to think of the employee as a *business partner.* Management—and the company as a whole—is dependent on its subordinates and employees, just as the employees depend on management and the company. Ideally, the employee knows and endorses the company's goals and strategy, expecting to get his or her fair share of the total outcomes. However, this employee also identifies with the company and behaves as an organizational citizen (Organ, 1984) who contributes—in a discretionary way—to reaching common goals. A business partner contributes to the organization's overall success and does not ask for immediate compensation or rewards for each single behavior. Rather, entrepreneurship and the joy of making real contributions can be major motives for high performance. In the business-partner model, there is no "one best way" in the sense of Taylor's "art and science of using a shovel" (1912).

The Five Employee Models and their Corresponding Employee Surveys

Under the machine model, employee surveys are measurement-focused. The employee takes on the role of a measurement device that objectively delivers data on his or her work and working environment. These data are then analyzed, without further involvement of the employee, by an "engineer." The goal is to find solutions that are ideal, not context-specific, workarounds, or quick fixes. The ES is part of a strategy to become better and better, moving towards an ideal final state, rather than adapting to a constantly changing environment that leads to new and often unexpected challenges all the time. Examples for such employee surveys often focus on working conditions (tools, machines, maintenance, support, etc.), on work safety (climate, noise, lighting, etc.) and on work processes (flow of work, production of parts, responsibilities, etc.). The questions posed to the employee are typically rather technical ones, not questions phrased in everyday language.

Under the child model, employee surveys focus on job satisfaction. A simple proposal for such an ES is the single item by Kunin (1955), shown in Figure 1.1. Many proposals with batteries of items exist for job satisfaction, many of them with explicit manuals, norms, and interpretation schemes. Examples are the JDI ("Job Descriptive Index"; Smith, Kendall, & Hulin, 1969; Smith, 1992), the ABB ("Arbeitsbeschreibungsbogen"; Neuberger & Allerbeck, 1978), the MSQ ("Minnesota Satisfaction Questionnaire"; Weiss et al., 1967) or the SAZ ("Skala zur Messung der Arbeitszufriedenheit"; Fischer & Lück, 1972; Fischer, 1989). Such scales assess job satisfaction on different facets such as satisfaction with work itself, satisfaction with supervisor, and satisfaction with pay. General job satisfaction is then estimated as the average of a person's facet satisfactions[4]. All these questionnaires focused primarily on the employee's psychology (satisfaction, climate, mood, morale), not on the facts of his or her working environment or on business topics, so that "pulse measurement" (York, 1985) or "temperature measurement" (Schiemann, 1992) are appropriate terms for such employee surveys. Feedback workshops on the ES results became a normal component of ES projects. These workshops were not only meant to inform the employees about the results and to complement the statistics with qualitative input on

---

[4] Scarpello & Campell (1983) analyze a variety of single items on general job satisfaction. They argue that the best single item for that purpose is "Overall, how satisfied are you with your job?", an item similar to Kunin's original item. Wanous et al. (1997) and Nagy (2002) show that such single items are not only reliable and valid, but that they may measure overall satisfaction even better than summing an employee's answers over the different job facets. Hence, Kunin's one-item approach is by no means outdated.

their "background" (what, who, why, when, etc.), but they were also believed to have a cathartic function. The role of the employee in an ES, thus, changed from being a measurement device to a person who reveals his/her feelings and perceptions. The patriarch listens respectfully, tries to understand, shows understanding, decides what needs to be done, and then attempts to convince the employees that his/her decisions are the right ones.

Under the robot model, an ES becomes an important tool to deliver the data needed to "program" the robot. Management is programming and, therefore, it holds that "You can't manage what you don't measure" (Globerson, Globerson, & Frampton, 1991). The ES is supposed to show the problems and obstacles that prevent efficient and effective behavior. The focus is not limited to working conditions and to the technical-organizational environment, but it includes goals, goal settings, contingencies of goal achievements and its consequences, and strategies. The role of the employee in such surveys is not only that of a measurement device, but that of a diagnostician. That is, one wants the employee's judgments about possibly complex systems, not just statements of how far "the needle" moves on a single dimension. Decisions on what to do with the ES results, however, are made by management alone. On the other hand, the employees are typically actively involved in further diagnostics within survey feedback workshops. The goal is to understand the details—and possibly even the reasons—for the ES statistics, and then structure and prioritize the data. This information is then used in a coordinated process of action planning, action implementation and monitoring, and evaluation.

Under the individual model, an ES is conducted to reveal individual points-of-view and values. What one wants to know is how the employees see the situation, what expectations they have, what they are concerned about, what they are hoping for, what they plan to do. For management, this is important to know because it determines where to "pick them up" and "what road to take" when striving for business goals or change. In an ES with that emphasis, the role of the employee is not to provide measurement values or to diagnose a problem, but to articulate his or her point-of-view. This is not without risk for the employees, and so they must have reasons to trust the integrity of the ES project. There should be no anonymity concerns, for example, and the purpose and the steps of the ES project should be clear and reliable. Under such circumstances, one can ask directly for personal value judgments. The typical value item begins with the question: "How important is [X] for you personally?" Such questions also appear in older instruments such as the "Need Satisfaction and Role Perception Questionnaire" by Porter & Lawler (1968) discussed above (see Figure 1.2), but in these instruments the value scores are simply used as weights in an attempt to measure satisfaction more precisely. More relevant for the individual model are value items or statistical models that allow one to tell what the employee really wants, a question that is especially important in cross-cultural surveys. For example, do East Germans have the same goals and the same personal guiding principles as West Germans, after forty years of socialism? The answer is No (Borg &* Braun, 1992, 1995), although the structure of work values seems to be the same across the world (Elizur et al., 1991; Schwartz, 1999, 2004). However, the issue is complicated because one needs to understand to what extent certain differences are merely due to different response styles and not due to different feelings. Employees in research & development, for example, typically appear less satisfied than employees in marketing, but the former are generally more introverted than the latter, and to simply compare their ratings may therefore be too simplistic (Judge, Martocchio, & Thoresen, 1997; Judge, Heller, & Mount, 2002; Roccas, Sagiv, Schwartz, & Knafo, 2002). What one needs to do is to study the network of their answers and determine what other variables (e.g., turnover tendency, commitment, endorsing the strategy) their satisfaction scores allow one to predict.

Under the business-partner model, the emphasis of an ES shifts from wanting to understand to wanting to get together to promote the business. The employees, in particular, may have many good ideas that remain hidden in the normal day-to-day activities. They need to be brought to the surface, where they can be discussed and pursued further. More generally, the intent is to involve every employee as much as possible into promoting such business essentials as customer orientation, working on productivity, promoting new ideas and innovation, or evaluating every action and decision in terms of costs and benefits or profitability. If the employee is seen as a business partner, then the ES becomes an element of a *continuous* effort to build a culture where every employee wants to—and is given the opportunity to—contribute as much as possible to the company's well-being. These contributions are effective only to the extent that they are aligned with the business goals and the company's strategy. Hence, the alignment issue—as well as the strategy itself—also becomes an emphasis under this model. Schiemann & Morgan (2006) stress this perspective in their notion of "strategic employee surveys" that are "focused on the people issues that make the greatest difference in business performance" (p. 76).

Employee Models and Employee Surveys

The different types of employee surveys that result from the five different types of employee models are compared in a compact way in Table 1.3. In practice, of course, no ES ever corresponds to exactly one of these prototypes, although most employee surveys have a definite accent in the sense of these models.

With respect to the different roles of the employee in these surveys, there is a certain order from the machine to the business partner model in the sense that the employee is taken more and more seriously as a source of potentially important contributions. The business partner is an active contributor to the company's long-range success, whereas the machine simply functions mechanically and the robot executes, with more flexibility, the system's programs. The individual, on the other hand, has the freedom to develop his or her own stance with respect to the strategy, but this does not affect the strategy itself. The business partner also not only learns how to work around obstacles (as the robot does), but he or she also learns in the sense of the "double loop" (Argyris, 1994), where the employee is actively rethinking old paths and actively developing entirely new solutions. In the business-partner context, one can thus request from managers that they *empower* their subordinates as much as possible to maximize their opportunities for bottom-line contributions.

Table 1.3. Five employee models with the corresponding employee surveys.

Employee model	ES content	Purpose of ES	Role of employee in ES	Role of manager in ES
Machine	Techn.-org. working conditions	Optimize work and work processes	Deliver measurement scores	Adjust, repair, lubricate, optimize
Child	Climate, satisfaction	Increase job satisfaction	Speak up	Show interest, compassion, see what you can do for employees
Robot	Efficiency, effectiveness	Optimize person-system functioning	Diagnose functioning in system	Set up systems, program robots accordingly
Individual	Values, points-of-view	Understand differences	Articulate what you really want	Understand where to pick them up
Business partner	Contributions to business goals, strategy	Strengthen business culture	Contribute ideas, get involved	Involve everyone into business and strategy

2 Positioning an Employee Survey

Employee surveys are often conducted without spending much time and effort to design the project first in a comprehensive manner. Consequently, the survey does not yield optimal results. Indeed, without a clear definition of the project goals and its side constraints, one cannot even say what would be "optimal." Even so, managers and employees are sometimes disappointed that the survey does not satisfy their private expectations. To avoid such situations, one has to make these expectations explicit. One should also make clear what it takes to satisfy them. However, even the survey sponsor him- or herself may not really know what can and what cannot be accomplished with an ES project, and under what conditions. To lay out the possibilities, ponder about different design packages, and possibly even build a strategy to develop the ES project systematically over a number of replications into a tool that is fully coordinated with other business metrics and processes, is what we mean by positioning the ES.

2.1 Positioning the Employee Survey

There exists no off-the-shelf ES design that is applicable in all organizational settings. Even where a standard design can be used, it is rarely optimal. To make it optimal, one has to design a comprehensive package that satisfies a set of requirements as much as possible.

Total Package Designs

The casual auto-racing fan might believe that the car with the most powerful engine will win the race, but this is rarely true. There are many other important factors besides horsepower: a host of motor characteristics (e.g., torque, fuel consumption), the driver (e.g., skills, experience, motivation), the car (e.g., aerodynamics, tires), the crew (e.g., mechanics, technicians, tacticians), or the fit of the car to its driver and team, to name just a few. What leads to victory on a given race track with certain weather conditions is the best total package.

So, what is the best total package for an ES? Obviously, one can only begin to answer this question in any detail when it is clear how to assess "best." In car racing, this is easy: Best means being the first to cross a particular line after a certain number of laps. However, what is best when running an ES? To answer this question, one

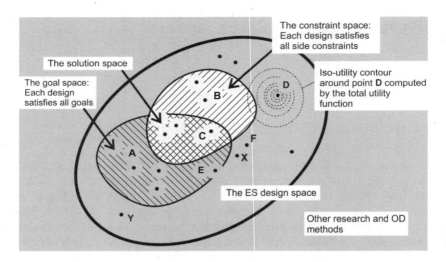

Figure 2.1. Positioning an ES in design space.

first needs to specify the goals of the ES and the basic requirements that it must satisfy. This is the first step in positioning the ES or, more realistically, it often is but the beginning of a complex design process that may come back several times to the goal definitions.

Positioning an ES is really an iterative process, where an optimal solution is found in a sequence of considerations and decisions. One begins with (a) a *preliminary* definition of the survey project's goals and (b) a *first* specification of the project's side constraints (time, budget, available resources, etc.). This defines the goal space and the constraint space, respectively: All ES designs that satisfy all goals are elements of the goal space, and all ES designs that satisfy all side constraints lie in the constraint space. Both spaces may be empty, because one may request goals that are contradictory or specify constraints that are so demanding that no ES design exists that can satisfy all of them. For example, a typical unrealistic demand is that the ES should lead to major strategic improvements without management having to commit itself to anything. This would be like washing one's hands without getting wet, an impossible undertaking.

The union of the goal space and the constraint space is the total-package design space. Their intersection is the solution space (Figure 2.1). It too can be empty, but if it is not, then it contains all feasible designs. The design problem is solved by picking the feasible design that has the highest utility.

Yet, "picking" the best design is easier said than done. Even standard designs are never completely ready to go. Indeed, any concrete ES project must pay attention to so many requirements, it must satisfy so many stakeholders, and consider so many context factors that standard designs only reduce the work that needs to be done.

What is typical for a project design phase is that it involves *numerous trade-off considerations*. For example, one may want to measure a particular attitude with an established multi-item attitude scale. However, using this scale consumes a lot of time of the survey, and so one may also consider using a shorter scale or just a single item to measure this attitude. The trade-off is precision and measurement quality at the expense of time and space for other content issues. Other examples for trade-offs are comparing the benefits and the costs of running a sample or a census survey; or carefully translating and back-translating the questionnaire in other languages or offering the questionnaire in, say, English only. Trade-offs can also extend over different facets of the project. For example, deep analysis of the survey results by expert statisticians can lead to interesting insights, but a simple standard data analysis is possible overnight and, thus, preserves the momentum of the survey. One may also wonder if the limited personnel resources one has in the survey project team should better be spent on optimizing the questionnaire, or on informing employees about the survey, or on empowering managers on how to later work with the survey results, or, indeed, what particular *mixture* of efforts would lead to the best overall results of the ES project.

What also makes positioning complex is that neither the goal space nor the constraint space are really fixed, because both goals and constraints can be changed, in particular if one finds designs that nearly satisfy the initial goals and constraints (such as X or F in Figure 2.1), and that promise to have a higher utility in a somewhat modified utility function. Consider, for example, the budget constraint. The project team may have a seemingly fixed amount of money for the ES project, but we have seen it more than once that a CEO was willing to double this amount quickly if he feels that the more expensive design is likely to have a much stronger impact on achieving crucial strategic goals.

Positioning may seem complex, and indeed, it is. It has many parameters and it involves different people and groups. It requires an ES expert who knows what is possible and what is takes to get there. It also needs capable managers and articulate stakeholders who are willing to explore and to compromise. The expert and the organizational decision makers have to enter some kind of ping-pong process, where different sets of constraints, utility functions, and various ES packages are defined, discussed, and adapted until one finds a package that appears optimal.

The practical problem is that only a good ES expert really knows all the possibilities. It would be useless to ask top management (or the sponsors of the ES) to specify exactly what they want from the ES. Managers often respond to this question with vague answers, because they usually do not know what one can accomplish with an ES, and under what conditions. Hence, the expert has to first study the project's context and conditions—e.g., by interviewing top managers and other stakeholders—and suggest specifications that the ES should satisfy in this organization. She can then look for a best-possible ES in that solution space. If there is none, she must go back to the drawing board of positioning the ES with specifications that are less demanding.

Stakeholders, Explicit Goals, and Hidden Agendas

A good total package design (TPD) must be tailored to the organization and its current situation. It most likely will not be found in a prepackaged survey design; it might not be found in an organization's previous survey either.

The survey project must be positioned to adequately satisfy the needs of many stakeholders with diverse and sometimes conflicting needs and demands. These stakeholders comprise senior managers, boards, and regulators (Halamaj, 2007), but also middle and lower line managers, rank and file employees, and union representatives or the works council, plus special functions such as the legal department or the data protection officer. Moreover, changes within and outside the organization (e.g., reliance on new technology, globalization, increased focus on corporate governance/compliance, more stringent requirements for data security and protection) can lead to changes in the number and types of stakeholders that must be considered (Barbera, Beres, & Lee, 2007).

Most stakeholders, if asked, would name obvious purposes for the survey (e.g., assess employee satisfaction, improve alignment with organizational goals), but all ES projects are always connected to a large number of less obvious intentions. Many of these may not be discussed in the open, nor may they be fully known even to those who have them. Examples for such hidden agendas include a vice president of HR's ambitions to move towards a position on the executive board by developing a strategically oriented ES. In another case, a member of the works council strongly advocated the ES project to gain popularity for the next election by demonstrating how strongly he was working for employees to get a voice. Other project experience demonstrates that individuals may also lobby against the survey to push their political motives. For example, one new HR director remained skeptical about the survey and wanted long explanations for even small details, but it became clear that his resistance was due to the fact that the ES had been installed by his predecessor—he wanted to position himself as the "new guy" and not as a mere successor with no new ideas. Hidden agenda items of this sort can be significant obstacles or drivers of an ES. Naturally, they are not always easy to understand, but one should be aware that these hidden agendas do exist. Some of their issues can possibly be resolved, but others will remain present and potentially thwart project progress in different manners. Yet, if the ES project team succeeds at defining the ES project so that the hidden personal ambitions of key players are served by the project, then the project can only benefit from these efforts. Indeed, it may be better for the project's success to leave these ambitions hidden.

What Block (1999) observes for consulting work also applies to the ES: there will be cognitive aspects, which are rational and explicit, and there will be affective aspects, which are steeped in feelings and trust. When positioning the ES, working at only the cognitive level is just as dangerous as considering only half of the stakeholders. There are politics and taboos, expectations and agendas. Failure to navigate these successfully when they appear can mean failure to achieve the goals of the survey process later on. Moreover, since the ES project is a series of accomplishments that build on each other, stakeholder needs should be discovered early in the process to accommodate, because otherwise the consequences are either delays and redundant work, or dissatisfied stakeholders and withheld support.

2.2 The Context of an ES

Positioning an ES is always a challenging task even for an experienced ES expert. Thinking about what is needed for the survey to have real impact, an important requirement is to have strong commitment—indeed, *informed commitment*—of top management to the ES. The executives should not only emotionally support the ES, but they should also clearly understand what can be done with the survey, and what it takes to unlock its potentials. The task of the ES expert is to present the theory, illustrative examples, cases, anecdotes, etc., and make the suggestions that generate this informed commitment. Often, this means moving beyond the stated reasons for considering an ES. If it can be demonstrated how the ES can promote important goals that top management never really associated with "a survey," then a constructive discussion about the right TPD becomes easy. Executives are no survey experts, and typically they are not even experts on soft factors. However, they do not know what they do not know, and so the expert's task is it to inform them about the potentials of ES projects.

Successful TPD discussions are not driven by academic lectures about employee surveys in general. Rather, they require relating the ES to the organization's specific needs and resources. Against this background, the expert can present recommendations to top management in the sense of "What would I do?" or "What a good friend of the organization would suggest to do." Executives are usually quite interested to learn about such opportunities. Once they understand properly what is possible, they often find the necessary budget. In fact, the survey expert may have to rein in the project so that management does not attempt to do too much with one ES.

Project Antecedents and Apparent Needs

Most ES projects get started similarly: A survey consultant is contacted by a company for advice on how to conduct an ES or to discuss possibilities for collaboration on an ES. In many cases, the individual who contacts the consultant is not inherently interested in the ES. Instead, he or she frequently works on getting multiple bids for a survey, or on establishing contact with the actual promoters of the ES. At this stage, little information about the organization's rationale for wanting to conduct an ES is likely to be revealed. Often, one hears the following initial reasons:

1) The promoter has been requested (by the HR director, the new CEO, the board of directors, etc.) to prepare and conduct an ES.
2) The organization has experienced problems relating to employee morale or work behavior such as high levels of absenteeism or turnover. The promoter is interested to identify the causes for these problems so that they can be fixed.

3) The promoter wants to identify obstacles and barriers to employees' efficiency and effectiveness, and then find solutions with maximal effects.
4) The promoter is attempting to improve the company's communication culture. The ES is meant to measure attitudes of different stakeholder groups, and serve as a basis for data-driven dialogue after completion.
5) The promoter believes that happy employees make productive employees, leading to satisfied customers. The ES thus focuses on job satisfaction and on actions that change things that make employees dissatisfied.
6) The promoter wants a survey to involve employees in strategic planning and thinking by asking them questions that focus on various aspects and implications of the strategy.
7) The promoter is aware of an ES conducted in some other organization that has led to substantial improvement. The hope is that similar results can be achieved here by running a similar ES.
8) The promoter is interested in getting his organization certified according to some quality standard or ranked in some "best company" competition. Many such awards require that employee surveys—mostly assessing job satisfaction—are done regularly (Becker, 1997).

It is important to understand these initial reasons. They must be addressed before the ES can be optimized for this organization. It makes little sense to position the ES based on someone else's preconceived notion of how an ES should be designed.

Reason number 1 above is a mere trigger. The promoter is confronted with a task that he or she wants to fulfill by finding competent external ES consultants. Reason number 2 demands a diagnostic ES that can generate in-depth insights into the problems the company is experiencing. Reason 3 is another classic drive. It is similar to reason 2, but its emphasis is more the organizational and the technical working environment, and not so much psychology. Reason 4 is the motive behind most ES projects, namely to alleviate communication problems. Likewise, reason 5 is fairly prevalent in organizations, although the underlying motivational theories are in most cases overly simplistic. However, it at least opens the door for a theory-based ES with a longer time perspective. Similarly, reason 6 focuses on strategic objectives as well and, thereby, opens the door to discussions of how to use the survey results in systematic follow-up processes. Practically speaking, however, both reasons 4 and 5 tend to underestimate the potential of an ES for improving organizational performance and engagement. Reason 7 may be indicative of a false hope that some specific set of survey questions in itself is an answer to the organization's maladies, disregarding what needs to be done with the results. Reason 7 might also hint at the promoter's desire for career advancement, assuming favorable outcomes will be attributed to the survey and its promoter. Conversely, if the ES is somehow judged a failure, the promoter may fear detrimental career consequences.

Reason 8 highlights a difference between Europe and the USA. Quality awards are frequently cited in Europe as an organization's initial reason for considering an ES. One prominent example is the EFQM award (European Foundation for Quality Management, 1994) which is based on the "model" displayed in Figure 2.2. This model is believed to provide guidance to success. Its components are separated into two

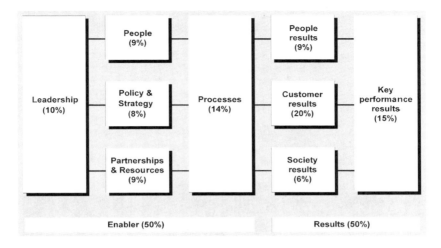

Figure 2.2. The EFQM model.

groups, *enablers* and *results*, where enablers are necessary antecedents of results. Both enablers and results contain criteria that can only be measured by directly asking employees, customers, or others for their opinions or attitudes. For example, "people results" is typically understood as "employee satisfaction," and an ES is the only instrument accepted by the EFQM to measure this component. Moreover, to be certified with an EFQM, an organization has to provide evidence for positive trends in ES data. Hence, a series of surveys is needed. Indeed, if one begins to think about the EFQM model further, it is easy to see that an ES is not just useful to measure employee satisfaction, but that almost any other box in Figure 2.2 has a "soft" side. Customer satisfaction, for example, is certainly driven by the customer orientation of the organization and its employees, and leadership can be measured from the perspective of subordinates. Hence, starting from this entry, it is easy to find a springboard for positioning an ES project.

In the US, surveys are frequently seen as one necessary step toward corporate recognition by business magazines and evaluating agencies. Typically, an organization pays to be ranked based on several criteria, one of which is employee responses to a "copyrighted" set of survey questions (e.g., Gallup's Q12 items). Sometimes this experience leaves organizational leaders wanting a more customized survey solution with more actionable content and follow-up activities, either because they failed to be ranked highly enough or because the cookie-cutter process disillusioned them. In this situation the organization seems to realize that there must be something more to the ES process, but they may not know what that potential is or how to achieve it.

Introducing General Information about Employee Surveys

The organizational representative approaching an ES expert frequently does not know much about employee surveys. Hence, the expert must provide some answers on sim-

Figure 2.3. Plant manager communicating ES results in a works meeting at a German automobile plant; slide says "Actions begin now!"

ple questions such as these: "What forms of employee surveys are there? What types of employee surveys have other organizations in our industry conducted? What experiences and problems have other organizations faced?" Chapter 1 answers most of these questions by characterizing major types of employee surveys. In addition, chapter 1 also demonstrates the phases and steps of a typical ES, even if the initial objective of the survey is to be "merely an employee opinion poll."

For a novice making decisions about the organization's ES, illustrative material and demonstrations of processes from various survey projects are particularly informative. For example, a picture of a survey results feedback session as in Figure 2.3 shows that conducting an ES will eventually lead to the question "Given these results, what do we do now?" Contemplating this question early on encourages backwards thinking—planning for the intended outcome. One should have a plan that optimizes the project's impact on relevant goals. The picture also shows that the power is not in the survey itself, but in the survey process. The desired organizational impact of an ES will require an investment beyond the creation of a good questionnaire and intelligent reports. Indeed, issuing survey reports is rarely the end of the survey project. It typically also includes communication of results and leaders' reactions, results interpretation workshops for managers receiving their own reports, listening sessions to let employees react to results and interpretations, action planning workshops to develop organizational responses, coaching sessions to guide line leaders through action planning and execution, tracking execution of plans, and the design of follow-up survey items for action evaluation.

Other survey show-and-tell elements include brochures from different ES projects, posters used to motivate employees to participate in the survey, survey reports for managers, demonstration presentations to top management, action-planning tools, procedures that empower managers to make the most use of the results, and so on. Yet, while the use of these materials can be very effective, the materials have to be carefully selected and assembled—otherwise, they can lead to the impression that an ES is a highly complex project that is too risky to initiate. As stated earlier, an organization's first survey should have modest goals. Our point here is to make sure that the organization is aware of what lies beyond the initial survey project.

Considering the Benefits of an ES

An organization's decision to conduct an ES is dependent on the benefits and costs of an ES. To be more precise, the organization should ask "Do we need the benefits provided by this ES? Are we willing to invest the required resources for those benefits?"

For top management, business considerations are always most important. Thus, ES experts are frequently asked to discuss the effects of an ES on "the bottom line." Because an ES focuses on attitudes and opinions, it is relevant to know, for example, that Hinrichs (1989) estimates the "typical dollar impact" of attitudes and opinions to range between 30% and 50% of the total revenues. Mirvis & Lawler (1977) provide impressive demonstrations of the cost benefits of increasing employee job satisfaction by one standard deviation. Similarly, Cascio's (1982) behavioral accounting models suggest that even small changes in employee behavior can have massive consequences if groups of individuals engage in the same behaviors. Then, Harrison et al. (2006) show statistically that the "individual effectiveness" of employees—their role performance, their discretionary context performance, and their lack of withdrawal behaviors combined—correlates with .50 with "overall job attitude," an index that combines job satisfaction and organizational commitment. Thus, when doing an ES, one is indeed focusing on important drivers of organizational success.

Empirical studies on the effects of soft factors on the bottom line are often not particularly convincing to management. Indeed, they always depend on numerous context factors that may or may not hold for the particular situation and organization. Hence, models that are based on logical reasoning and strong arguments often find more acceptance from managers. The EFQM model (Figure 2.2) is an example of an intuitive, easily understood explanation of how organizational results depend on a set of enabling factors that include people and leadership. By using a logical framework in presenting the benefits of an ES to organizational leaders, a survey consultant likely will not need empirical evidence as proof. An ES process that measures and improves these *necessary* conditions of success *must* have an effect on the bottom line, at least in the long run. Furthermore, the impact of a successful survey process on the bottom line may not be visible because of other factors that affect business success. If external factors (e.g., cost of raw material) or internal factors (e.g., the company's products in a changing market) are squeezing profits, improvements in morale and organizational climate might help the company cope over time, but they will not provide a sudden turnaround.

When presenting the case for implementing an ES, its bottom-line benefits cannot be evaluated as easily as some would like. For this reason, we suggest focusing more on rational arguments and more on the immediate consequences of morale and climate improvement (e.g., the relationship between low employee satisfaction and high turnover and absenteeism). An ES can also address hot topics or problem issues, but they should always be embedded into a set of standard "eternal" topics (e.g., immediate supervision, organizational commitment). This approach provides better understanding of the current problems within an established theoretical framework, and it supports the development of a system of conditions that enables and motivates employees to perform well.

Another good argument for an ES is to show some typical "hot" results from such surveys. For example, when using an item that asks the employees whether they have "concrete ideas" on what can be done in their immediate work environment to help them to be personally "substantially more productive," experience (in German companies) shows that some 80% of the employees can be expected to at least partially endorse this item. Any experienced manager recognizes immediately that such a result is an invitation to discuss productivity, improvements, and innovation with managers and non-managers. However, one manager once said: "Great if it comes out this way. But what if it doesn't? Then, we are in trouble!" Of course, the answer is that completely different results are not likely, but if scores are markedly different, then management has the opportunity to ask why this company does not see the same degree of improvement potential as almost any other company does. Hence, they end up in the same situation where they discuss with the employees the issues of productivity and how to improve it.

Related arguments are the old "You can't manage what you don't measure" (Globerson et al., 1991) and the "You get what you measure" adages. The former requires one to make clear what one wants and to keep track of progress. The latter says that aligning managers and employees to focus on certain outcomes (e.g., customer satisfaction), and supporting this focus with good data and with proper recognition and rewards will promote progress in the desired direction. An ES can certainly help not only measuring important variables, but also focusing everyone's attention onto these variables, particularly if the survey results have noticeable consequences for managers.

Besides such reasoning, a convincing argument in favor of an ES is simply pointing out what leading companies are running such surveys and for how long they have been doing this. It is easy to generate long lists of companies that are running census or sample surveys of their employees every year or every other year. Furthermore, attitude assessment and management is one of the HR practices that are associated with lower turnover, increased sales, and increased market value (Huselid, 1995). In some cases, such surveys have become integral parts of the company's HR or even management systems. That is, they are needed to yield an index value on each manager's people management performance (as viewed from their subordinates) that is associated with their bonus allocation. In other cases, indexes of employee satisfaction, commitment, or the employees' attitudes towards innovation and change are used to complement the company's scorecards.

It is easy to show that using ES data for such purposes makes sense by simply pointing out how interesting such data would be to the company's competitor or to an external investor. If the investor, for example, learns that the employees in the company are highly dissatisfied with their pay, he or she will certainly look differently at the company's business figures. This company seems to have a latent problem, and business profitability can go down quickly once this problem surfaces and the employees demand more money. You could imagine that the investor would not be as eager to buy stocks from this company. Why then would management not want to have this information?

Obviously, there are many potential benefits of an ES. In the initial phases of positioning an ES, it is important to point out some of these benefits and how the survey should be designed to generate them. The danger is to list benefit after benefit without making clear that desired outcomes do not come automatically from simply conducting a survey. Rather, what is needed is a well-designed survey process that includes management's commitment to support both the assessment and the corresponding actions.

First Thoughts on the Costs of an Employee Survey

For presenting the idea of an ES to top management, one needs a fairly reasonable estimate of how much the project will cost the organization. The most obvious costs are those for *external* vendors, perhaps including survey designers, data analysts, consultants, and facilitators. *Internal* costs are more difficult to estimate because many activities related to the ES surely consume working hours of managers and non-managers. However, many of these activities would have to be conducted anyway—with or without a survey. One can argue that the survey addresses problems at the organizational level and therefore *reduces* the costs that would have accumulated if each unit attempted to solve these problems separately. That even holds for an ES that has no strategic orientation but that is solely designed to fix a particular HR problem (e.g., high turnover or low morale), because such problems often cannot be solved at the level of single organizational units, and attempting this means wasting resources.

Initially, the calculation of external costs is only possible in the sense of model computations and rule-of-thumb estimates. It is fairly easy to calculate the costs of administering the survey itself. Sample surveys are less expensive (and less useful) than census surveys, and web surveys are somewhat less expensive than paper surveys. Translation costs for the survey add to the costs, but not as much as the translation costs for open-ended comments (e.g., translating suggestions from 10 languages into the one language spoken at corporate headquarters). Costs also increase if certain groups within the organization receive survey items that other groups do not receive (i.e., questions specific to business unit, function, or management level). How participants are identified and invited (e.g., PIN invitations from an HR feed versus completely anonymous, unlimited access) also has internal and external cost implications.

In contrast, the costs of the follow-up processes are more difficult to estimate. These activities vary across companies. Sometimes, all that is done is a presentation of the survey results to top management, and possibly some similar presentations to a few large business units. The rest is then left to line management, where the ES process can help to actually reduce costs, as discussed above. However, follow-up processes can be very labor-intensive—training, presentations, discussions, workshops, and action planning sessions across all levels of the organization. While these activities are typically cut out of external consulting budgets, it may be more economical for companies to have them planned and executed by an outside vendor than to leave everything to internal managers who are already strapped for time.

We often find that business units are willing to pay for follow-up processes that corporate headquarters did not budget for. Perhaps they have a better sense of the scope of the problems or the work necessary to solve them. Even with all of the "bells and whistles" added to the costs of the survey process, the endeavor is relatively inexpensive. There is no other continuous improvement intervention that can measure and promote strategic alignment for all employees and organizational units in such a short timeframe and at a comparable budget. The survey process is a bargain.

Moreover, when thinking about the costs of an ES, one should not focus too narrowly on the particular ES project, but also take into account its various spillover effects. For example, training managers in action management or facilitation skills may be necessary for effective ES follow-up processes, but such trainings surely empower managers with skills that are applicable in many other contexts. Even learning to see things from the employees' point-of-view is a worthwhile investment in managerial skills. In a very real way, the successful survey program is the execution of what management should always be doing. The survey process is effective leadership.

Readiness of an Organization for an ES

ES packages with deep follow-up processes are usually too demanding for an organization that has no previous experience with surveys. The necessary skills to optimally use the data are simply not available yet. Developing these skills during the company's first ES project is a time-consuming endeavor, especially if the company expects action from top to bottom. As an alternative, it would be better to position the ES more as a survey with some feedback that focuses on larger subunits only. However, one may extend the positioning perspective to later surveys, and design a learning strategy that evolves the ES instrument systematically from replication to replication. Starting with a simple opinion polling approach, it typically takes two to three surveys to reach a stage where the ES can deliver its maximum impact as an OD tool without overtaxing the organization's resources.

Previous experience is just one variable that influences an organization's readiness for employee surveys of different types. Table 2.1 lists a set of other reasons that one should routinely consider when positioning an ES. One such facet is "key players." To illustrate what this means, consider the following case. The executives of one company had heard that an ES was successfully run by major competitors, leading to

Table 2.1. Some factors of the readiness of an organization for an ES.

Factors	Facets and questions
Resources	Willingness and ability to provide the resources (money, people, time) needed for a particular ES package
Skills	Skills and availability of skills of individuals who can run an ES project as coordinators, managers, and non-managers
Timing	Possible conflicts of ES time plan with other important activities of the organization (e.g., vacations, trade fairs, end of business year)
Circumstances	Special circumstances that speak against an ES (downsizing, new executive board, tariff negotiations with unions, etc.)
Culture	Values, norms, taboos, traditions that exclude particular forms of processes, content areas, questions etc.
Fear	Requirements for guaranteed anonymity and/or confidentiality, data protection, concerns about data abuse, fear of retaliation for criticism
Openness	Openness of organization to try out new things, to take advice from externals, to learn, to innovate
Expectations	Level of expectations concerning the ES and its effects
Needs	Strength of need for the effects that an ES can deliver
Key players	Commitment of key player to reach the goals of the ES, even if it means that they personally have to get involved
Resistance	Amount and kinds of resistance, power of obstructing persons or groups, accessibility of resisters to arguments
Enthusiasm	Persons (missionaries, supporters, change champions) who support the ES project; intensity, kind of support
Strategic compatibility	Extent to which the ES project supports the strategy; extent to which this is understood by stakeholders

higher engagement of their employees. They thus decided to "try out" this instrument. Yet, when the results were presented, the executives remained passive because they did not understand that simply running a survey is not enough. It is like washing your hands; you cannot do that successfully without getting yourself wet. Hence, if the ES expert feels that management does not really understand its role in the project, or if management is not committed to take on an active role in the ES process, then it may be better to run the survey as a diagnostic sample survey only—or not at all.

A company's readiness for an ES also depends on the attitudes of influential members of the works council and/or union representatives. Occasionally, such persons feel that only they are entitled to represent the employees' interests. So, if an ES is launched by HR or by top management, it can be perceived as a threat. Sometimes works council members or union representatives will argue that there is no need for an ES because they already know what the employees think or feel: "We speak with them all the time!" On other occasions, these representatives may make it clear that they might agree to allow an ES, but only under certain circumstances that give them a special role in the process or that guarantee that management will act on whatever the employees are not satisfied with. In these situations, running an ES is difficult because it involves a power struggle with management, often for circuitous reasons. In one case, a works council member insisted that participating in the survey needed to be rewarded with an incentive or else the works council would not recommend participating. The problem was that management had already communicated that no material incentives would be used. The works council member, however, used exactly management's public commitment as an opportunity to stand up to management and position himself as the person with no fear who should be elected as chairman of the council.

To prevent such political struggles, one should be careful not to communicate anything to the employees about a proposed ES before having talked to the unions or the works council. By involving them in survey planning as early as possible, perhaps having them meet with an external survey consultant, unions and works councils can better understand how the survey can work for all of the organization's stakeholders. Representatives from unions and works councils may want to talk to their colleagues in other companies about their experiences with employee surveys and their roles in these projects.

One simple way to involve the union or works council in an ES is to include a representative in the ES project team. This person would serve as a linking pin and represent labor's points-of-view in this steering team. However, care must be taken to clearly define this person's role. He or she should not be just an "observer" on the team, but a regular member whose duty it is to bring the project to a successful ending.

Resistance can come from other stakeholders as well. Managers from different geographical regions and countries often resist a highly centralized plan from headquarters. Different functions that have historically conducted surveys in the organization (Communication, Organization Effectiveness, etc.) can also pressure the sponsor of this survey project.

"Fear of feedback" (Jackman & Strober, 2003) is often strong among managers in the sense that they are concerned that the survey will lead to negative assessments from their subordinates. To reduce such concerns, managers have to be well informed about the utility of an ES. "Negative" feedback from subordinates can be very useful information for the individual manager on where to improve. Moreover, such feedback is rarely meant to be destructive. Rather, it typically is uttered with the hope that it leads to positive change. And then, the survey results of each workgroup are accessible only to this workgroup, and to the manager to whom the supervisor of this workgroup reports. That means, in particular, that negative feedback "from below" for a particular manager will never be shown to his or her peers. The feedback processes usually are set up in such a way that this manager will have a one-on-one discussion on the survey results with the manager to whom he or she reports. In this discussion, the survey data are put back into a larger context, and a plan is developed on how to improve.

Other employees may also resist an ES because they are afraid that they may not be able to answer all items of the questionnaire "correctly." This would damage their self-esteem or, if it gets known to others, could lead to ridicule or the inquisitive questions from their supervisors ("What exactly did you mean by that?"). So, employees should know that an ES normally asks almost exclusively about attitudes and opinions, not about facts. It is the employees' *subjective* perceptions that are of interest, and so they should tell how they feel, what they think, and what they perceive to be true. Besides, if an employee feels too uncertain about an answer, or simply does not know what to answer, the item can be skipped.

Employees may also avoid (i.e., not participate) or even resist an ES, because they are afraid to provide answers that are wrong in another sense. For example, shop-floor employees may have learned in the follow-up processes of previous surveys that it can backfire for them to say in the survey that they "have good ideas for improvements," because this can easily lead to considerable extra work after the survey (e.g., workshops, task assignments etc., all aimed at improving the work environment). This concern can only be reduced if it is made clear that management is committed to deliver its fair share in any improvement activities after the survey, and not delegate everything back to the shop floor.

Although many of the above reasons that speak against an ES could be argued away, one may find it ineffective to deal rationally with each argument because the resistance is often more an emotional reaction. One might hear, for example, that it is "not the right time" for an ES. The intent of this argument may simply be to postpone the ES indefinitely. Nevertheless, one must answer the timing question carefully.

Finding the Right Time to Administer the ES

Picking the right time for its administration is a cardinal design issue for any ES. This decision is made, above all, by finding time periods when the largest majority of employees is present at work to fill out the questionnaire. In the US and Europe employees usually take time off in July and August. In countries such as France, entire plants may shut down for the month of August. A similar vacation time is near Christmas and New Year's Day. Chinese, Hindu, Jewish, Muslim and similar customs must also be considered when planning the start and the duration of the administration phase, in particular in international surveys.

However, data collection is just one issue; the timing of feeding back the results, top level presentations, and distribution of reports are just as important. The ideal situation would be to ask employees to fill out the questionnaire shortly before vacation times, and then communicate results and responses when they get back. For European Union countries, the time before school summer vacations and late November or early December are usually good data collection times. These times mean that the follow-up processes can be started after vacation times without employees perceiving the time between data collection and follow-up processes as particularly long. In the US, springtime and the summer months may be the best time of the year to conduct employee surveys. Dates around the major holidays (e.g., July 4, Thanksgiving and Christmas) should be avoided. We find that most multinational and global companies administer surveys in the spring or autumn months. Likewise, certain industries have particularly busy times that need to be accommodated; November and December employee surveys would be impossible for most retail stores, for example.

Cyclical employee surveys should preferably be conducted during the same month every year. Some organizations have even decided to conduct their employee surveys on the exact same day every year to make that day "ES day" or even "employee day" (filled with other HR activities) for the entire organization. However, one may not want to brand the organization's ES as an HR activity, because both HR and line leadership ultimately make the process successful.

Once a time has been set and plans have been worked out for data collection and for the follow-up processes, it becomes difficult to change the major milestones. Management sometimes wants to postpone the ES right before data collection is supposed to begin, but this only shows that management is not aware of what it means to delay such a complex project. Besides recreating coordinated plans and printed announcements, there is also psychological damage that such postponements can cause ("They probably found out that the results will be negative!"). Indeed, requests to delay the survey often reflect management's fear of feedback. Sometimes they prefer to wait for times when they expect to receive "better" results. If so, it shows that management has not yet understood the purpose and the potentials of an ES.

However, sometimes there are good reasons to consider postponing an ES. Special circumstances or events within the organization, such as a serious accident, a product recall, or major job cuts, probably warrant a delay. Catastrophic world events, such as natural disasters or terrorism, might also justify a postponement. The events of September 11, 2001, for example, had a detectable, although small, general effect on ES data collected at the time (Genesee Survey Services, 2002), but they markedly affected some attitudes (e.g., those towards management) for many months after the events (Ryan, West, & Carr, 2003; Brooks, Wiley, Hause, & Moechnig, 2002).

A more common reason for postponing an ES is an ongoing major restructuring of the organization. If organizational structures change a lot after or during the survey, then employees may be regrouped into different workgroups with new supervisors, new working conditions, and new business processes. The results of the ES, therefore, would be based on data that describe obsolete circumstances and that relate to organizational units that do not exist anymore.

One may also ask to what extent particular events before or during the survey substantially alter the results of the ES. For example, consider the case where a production plant was to decide whether the plant would be shut down and all labor was to be outsourced outside the country. Would that "limbo" have an effect on the survey results? Clearly, attitudes related to perceived job security, intentions to leave the organization, or trust in management are most likely substantially affected by the pending decision. However, employees' opinions about working conditions were fairly unaltered in comparison to an ES conducted two years later at the same plant. This example suggests that managers' frequent concern about *all* survey items being influenced may be unwarranted. In other words, employees do not necessarily evaluate all aspects of their job negatively just because the organization is in transition or other events are occurring (Nadler, 1977; Folkman, 1998).

Finding a good date for an ES is more difficult if it is the first survey conducted within a particular company. For the second survey this is less of an issue, in part because organizational stakeholders grow more confident about the survey process having been through it once. However, when consecutive ES projects are conducted, one has to ensure that the time between the first administration and the second administration is sensible. If too much time has passed, then backward comparisons become dubious. Moreover, managers forget the skills they acquired during the first survey. If not enough time has passed, then actions taken in reaction to the prior survey are not yet visible. This time span should be no more than two years. One year is more typical, especially when employee surveys are done for the first time and the intention is to build a continuous assessment and change management process.

Survey data provide leading indicators of organizational success, and so an annual metric is prudent. One year may not be enough time to evaluate the effects of actions implemented after the previous survey, but any organization keeps changing all the time, and the accuracy of an evaluation improves with more data, not less. It is better to know, for example, that scores continue to drop one year later so that one can better assess one's action plan two years later. If one's scores level off in the third year, an action plan could be considered at least a partial success because it prevented a further drop; however, without that second year of survey data, the action plan would seem a failure because the scores will have dropped below the first set of scores. Even more important than the accuracy of the evaluation is the responsibility that leaders have to monitor a situation that caused them concern.

If the organization cannot afford to survey all of its employees on an annual basis, we suggest alternating between a census survey and a sample survey to maintain an annual metric while cutting costs. Sample surveys may not allow for reports at all levels of the company, but they will give feedback for the total company and its major divisions.

Whatever the cycle is, the survey administration should be kept at a fixed time of year so that comparisons from one cycle to the next become easier. If the survey is always administered after 3rd quarter sales figures are announced, during budget planning, and before annual bonuses are calculated, then these constant conditions make interpreting survey trends fairly easy. However, if the survey administration changes with each cycle, or if each part of the organization is allowed to administer the survey at a different time, then interpreting trends becomes difficult.

Consistent administration not only improves the usefulness of survey results, but also makes the survey a part of the organization's culture. Managers and employees can make plans around these dates. The survey gains a rhythm, and the organization stays in beat with its assessment-action two-step.

2.3 Positioning the Employee Survey through Top Management

The positioning of any ES should at least be officially accepted by the team of managers who make the ultimate decisions in the particular organization. In most organizations it is sufficient if the ES consultant communicates with that part of the management team that takes responsibility for the project (decider, sponsor, HR director). The more strategic components there are to an ES, the more important is it that the CEO and the entire management team become involved.

Goals

The survey consultant has to ensure that the goals for the survey remain structured, focused, and realistic. This is not an easy task, because management often produces long wish lists of vague goals. Scholtes (1998) reports a case where executives were asked to reduce a long list of goals they had compiled. When the executives returned the reduced list, they had taken out the most specific goals and had left overarching goals that encompassed the original list. Simply reducing the number of goals is, therefore, not sufficient. A more intelligent approach is to sort the various goals into a hierarchy first, and then retain the super goals that are most promising (Borg & Staufenbiel, 1992; Borg, Staufenbiel, & Pritchard, 1995). This hierarchy need not be newly invented for each ES project. Rather, one could start with an established theory (e.g., ACE, RACER, or the PS motor; see chapter 4) to structure the goals into meaningful categories. Such a theory can then be adapted to the specific demands of the particular organization[5]. To make the goals realistic often requires to point out what can and what cannot be accomplished with an ES project, and what it requires in terms of resources and commitment.

Risks and Dealing with Risks

An ES always comes with certain risks. Some are real ones, and others are only perceived risks. One common perception is that if employees express considerable dissatisfaction with pay, then this puts pressure on management to increase salaries. However, representative population surveys show that considerably more employees rate themselves as satisfied with their pay than as dissatisfied in all West European countries and in North America (Sirota, Mischkind, & Meltzer, 2005; Kenexa Research Institute, in press). Worldwide, there are few countries where this ratio is tipped in favor of the dissatisfied (e.g., some East European countries such as Hungary or Bulgaria). Yet, in these cases, low pay satisfaction is a general phenomenon and so it does not put special stress on the management of a particular company. Moreover, pay satisfaction depends on a number of factors, not just the level of pay but, most of all, on social comparisons ("What do others get for the same work?"; Lawler, 1981), and on perceived fairness and procedural justice in pay policies (Spector, 1997). Hence, relatively low pay satisfaction does not necessarily mean that the employees want more money. Often, what they want is more justice, or even entirely different things. For example, in one large German manufacturing company, only about 25%

---

[5] The focus of the super goals can also be translated into a "motto" for the entire ES project. One example comes from SAP's global survey project, where the motto was "satisfaction and performance." The objective of this motto (besides playing on the company name) was to communicate to everyone what the employee survey was all about.

of the employees were satisfied with their pay. Yet, all stakeholders, including the works council, agreed that there was no need for "more money." Instead, everyone felt that actions should focus on securing the future (e.g., better utilizing all opportunities for improvement, better customer orientation, clearer contingencies of individual performance and rewards in general).

Many concerns about the potential risks of an ES can best be clarified if they are eliminated proactively, before they are even voiced. For instance, in many organizations it is unclear who the beneficiary of the ES is. In Europe, an ES is often believed to be primarily a tool to enhance the well-being of the rank-and-file employees, because, unfortunately, the term "employee" is some European languages also means "non-manager" or "subordinate." To position an ES in this sense is possible, but rarely appropriate. Most often, it is better to design the ES from the start as a win-win project *for all stakeholders* of the organization, not just as a project for the benefit of certain groups. This emphasis also reduces the risk to stir up conflict among stakeholder groups that will grind progress on survey planning to a halt.

Resistance can come, nevertheless, from certain groups or persons. Kiresuk & Lund (1979) recommend dealing with the "force of greatest resistance" first by pacifying them through addressing concerns by making "technical" modifications to the ES design. It also helps if key individuals from various locations and functions are given a say in the ES project from the start (e.g., by becoming involved in the ES project team or in an ES advisory board) so that they can support the project in a "missionary" role.

Another risk worth considering is being naively optimistic about the organization's readiness for a particular ES package. An ES can easily consume substantial organizational resources, and if these resources are unrealistically planned, the survey project will run into problems.

A related issue is the commitment of the individual manager to the ES project. The survey and its activities are often seen by middle managers as yet another distraction from their "real" jobs. Hence, the survey sponsor, the ES project team and, most importantly, top management should stress how the survey benefits each manager by helping him or her to reach the given goals more effectively. By design, one should also provide resources that will make managers feel reassured and prepared for what they are being asked to do.

Defining Minimal Requirements for Managers and Non-Managers

Top management and/or the CEO should always express what they expect from their managers and non-managers when it comes to the ES. One way of doing this is to formulate certain *minimal requirements*. Here are some examples:

- Every manager is expected to actively promote the ES among his or her subordinates. Promotion should be done in positive ways—convincing people of the benefits of the project, motivating them to get involved—rather than pressuring them and asking who has yet to participate.

- All employees are expected to participate in the ES and voice their opinions openly and honestly. The company needs these data. The survey is done for everyone's benefit.
- All employees must be given the opportunity to review at least a summary of the results of the ES.
- All employees must be given an opportunity to discuss the results of the ES.
- Every manager is expected to carefully analyze the results of the employee survey and to respond to them in an adequate manner.
- Every manager is expected to inform his or her subordinates about the ES.
- Top management will define areas of focus for taking action, and every manager is expected to carefully study the survey results that pertain to these areas of focus in his or her report.
- If needed, actions are expected primarily in the focus areas, but may include other areas where the results indicate a need for improvement or an opportunity for advancement.
- Action plans must be implemented systematically, and all employees have to be informed regularly about their status.
- All rules of the ES project (e.g., anonymity, confidentiality, cross-comparing results) have to be strictly adhered to.

The above formulations are somewhat vague, and they would have to be tailored to the organization's needs, but they still manage to show some bounds and the seriousness of the ES project. It is clear, for example, that a manager who meets his or her boss in the elevator should be prepared to have a good answer to the question "So, what have you done with the survey?" before the elevator reaches an upper level floor. A legitimate answer could be: "I have studied the results carefully. They showed me that we are on the right track. There is no need for any extra actions. I discussed this with my subordinates and we agree on that. I can explain this to you in more detail any time." A poor answer would be: "So far, I have not done anything with these results. I have not really thought about this issue either." This manager would be in trouble.

Top Management's Own Public Commitment

Top management should not only define its expectations for other groups in the organization, but also make a public commitment to its own contribution toward a successful outcome, making the ES a "fair deal." Employee surveys are rarely successful if top management is unwilling to commit to anything and is content to let others do the work. However, even if top management assumes full responsibility for the ES project, it should recognize and communicate that the survey process exists to benefit all employees—not just serve top management's objectives.

Practical experience shows that in many cases executives prefer to delegate as much responsibility for the ES project as possible. If this is done excessively, the psychological contract of the employees with their organization can be damaged. When employees make a contribution, they want the executive officers to build on this foundation by facilitating the necessary follow-up processes. Furthermore, employees expect the results of the survey to be shared openly within a reasonable amount of time; they usually resent if results are not publicized within a couple of months from the close of the survey administration. Therefore, in exchange for employees' commitment and willingness to participate, the executives at least need to make the following minimum commitments:

- Top management will take visible responsibility for the ES project.
- Top management will carefully analyze the results of the survey and take these results seriously.
- Top management will inform employees about the survey results in an open, timely, and honest manner.
- Top management will make use of the results of the survey to benefit the overall organization.

Commitments of this sort have to be well thought out. They mean that top management has to list the ES among its priorities and recognize the responsibility for delivering results. The commitments stated above are more binding than they may seem at first glance. They empower employees (as well as the board of directors, the union, the works council, etc.) to follow up with top management on the specific means they have taken to accomplish the objectives. For example, on bullet point number 4, employees are entitled to ask what top management has actually done with the results. On the other hand, top management is not too tightly restricted to respond with particular actions. An answer such as "We have decided to do (or focus on) this, and not to do this" is a feasible response. The point is that asking the question "What have you done?" has been made legitimate and top management should not want to give an answer that is meaningless when this question comes up.

2.4 Further Facets of Positioning an ES

After going through a first positioning of the ES with the project's sponsor, top management, and other key players or groups, the ES project team can work out a more detailed proposal for the ES.

Content Considerations

Managers typically first assume that an ES is on employee satisfaction. Since most managers also believe that employee satisfaction drives performance, running an ES is generally okay with them, although it does not get much attention if its focus remains on satisfaction. Employees, on the other hand, are often concerned about the survey's content: "What questions will be asked? Are they personal ones? Will I be able to answer these questions?"

The ES project team, in either case, must provide an answer to why the survey needs to focus on certain topics and not on others. The answer must be convincing and transparent so that managers as well as employees accept these topics as legitimate and worthy of a response. What one does not want is a never-ending process where question after question is suggested for inclusion in the survey. Moreover, the impression that the questionnaire's content is based on arbitrary decisions must be eliminated. Rather, all stakeholders should feel that the survey does indeed cover the crucial issues in a balanced way.

One way to answer questions on content is to say that the survey addresses the "standard" topics that are also asked in many other organizations. It includes standard scales or items that have been previously validated and for which there are external benchmark values.

Another answer is that the survey content is based on strong theories about employee work attitudes and behavior. If employee interests (some might call this "satisfaction") and organizational interests ("performance") can be connected through theory, then the core survey components are interrelated to the benefit of all parties involved. A strong theoretical emphasis can also serve to avoid additional topics being pushed into the survey last minute. In many cases, these topics are rather unrelated to the overall ES goals. They only seem "interesting" to certain individuals or groups, or they are simply motivated politically (Church, Desrosiers, & Oliver, 2007).

Most employee surveys are similar in terms of the content they cover. They typically assess perceptions of company leadership, immediate supervision, working conditions, compensation, development, ethical behavior, strategy, goals, and execution. Note that some survey items ask about the employees' degree of satisfaction, but many ask the participants what they are observing. Indeed, the state-of-the-art for employee surveys is beyond merely asking about "job satisfaction." The rationale for this accepted approach to survey assessment is based on a *system* of interrelated organization issues that must be *fully covered*. It is like maintaining a car: You need to pay attention to *every important part*, not just to some.

The system perspective also suggests that it is problematic to leave out particular topics. In one case, the survey sponsor wanted to leave out all questions pertaining to employee compensation because he was afraid that this would lead to expectations that could not be satisfied. Yet, leaving out such a salient aspect of the employees' work experience only increases the likelihood that remuneration will receive an extra-heavy emphasis. Employees would notice the "conspicuous" absence of this topic and start to make assumptions about why management wants to avoid it. Moreover, not knowing how employees feel about their pay—not just its amount, but also its other facets such as fairness or performance-relatedness—makes it difficult to understand engagement or performance behavior. Hence, a systemic model (relating satisfaction, environment, and performance) helps to argue what topics need to be covered by the survey, and what topics are not necessary.

The rest of the questionnaire is open for ad-hoc topics. Such topics can be "hot topics" at the time of the survey, questions that special groups would like to survey (e.g., how the company newsletter is received by the employees), or strategic business issues that the executive board is focusing on (e.g., to what extent the employees understand the company's new "we first" initiative). To identify such issues, the ES project team may interview top managers and other key players, if possible. Such an involvement also helps to generate commitment to the ES in general.

Dissemination of ES Results

Data from employee surveys have to be handled carefully and cautiously. Consider the story of one company that conducted an ES that included questions about employees' perception of the company's future. The majority of the employees judged the company's future as not very promising. Because the organization had agreed not to censor the survey results, written reports were distributed to all employees. A few days later, the local newspaper reported that the company's employees saw the future in a rather somber light. Obviously, neither the company nor the employees benefited from this type of media coverage. Thus, in their subsequent employee surveys, only a few written reports were generated, and they were distributed as confidential information, which prohibited further reproduction. Most employees were given feedback about results through workshop meetings.

This survey "war story" is a common one. Journalists make a living by finding interesting stories. Media coverage of an organization, especially one already in the media spotlight, is likely in this era of 24-hour news channels and investor publications. If there is media interest surrounding an organization, then the handling of sensitive survey information needs to be conducted even more carefully. In addition, the company's competitors are always interested in the employee survey data, and so are analysts. Whether various measures of protecting the ES information are effective is not certain, but their implementation at least ensures that employees on all levels are aware of the sensitivity of these data. Employees should be given some information about survey results, but they should understand that inappropriate sharing of this information can harm the organization.

Positioning an ES, therefore, has to include planning for how results will be communicated within the organization. The early planning stages need to outline the process of who gets access to what material on what time schedule. Most organizations will use a top-down process of disseminating survey results. This top-down process implies that information is first presented to the executive board, then to upper and middle management, and finally to rank and file employees. At each stage in this process, the information is likely less detailed and more combined with general interpretations.

This top-down communication of survey results ensures that managers have the opportunity to reflect on the meaning without having to react right away. In addition, discussions with managers' supervisors or coaches can help managers reevaluate the results of the ES. If managers are not granted sufficient time to deal with the survey results, they may react defensively or aggressively, preventing constructive discussions from occurring.

Comparing Employee Survey Results across Organizational Units

An important question that must always be addressed as part of positioning the ES pertains to the types of comparisons that should be allowed between any parts of the organization. Naturally, the manager of organizational unit X is interested to see the results of his or her colleagues, the managers of "peer" units Y and Z. Similarly, the employees in unit X are often quite interested in the results of Y and Z. Yet, whether

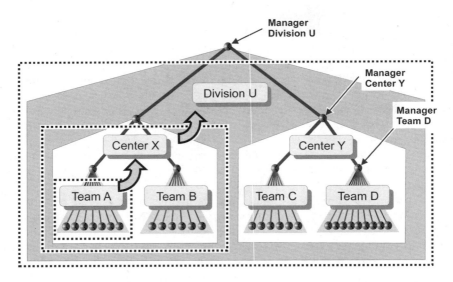

Figure 2.4. Typical rules for upward comparisons.

these results should be made available is not so clear. If, for example, the manager of X is harshly criticized, disseminating this result to everyone can make improvements very difficult for this manager. Moreover, negative feedback from employees may have different reasons. One possibility is that the manager is doing a poor job, while another is that the manager is trying to turn a reluctant team around.

More generally, turning an ES into a competition between different units puts too much emphasis on being a winner or a loser rather than concentrating on improvement and organizational development. For this reason, comparisons across units on the same level typically are not allowed. Other comparisons, such as comparing the organizational unit to the entire company are possible. This rule reduces fear while still providing benchmarks. Its disadvantage is that outstanding units may not get the praise they deserve, as Townsend & Gebhardt (1992) remark. Whether these units really deserve such praise is not obvious from survey scores alone; in order to properly evaluate the meaning of these statistics, you need to consider the context and the circumstances of the units being compared. For example, workgroup X might consist primarily of hourly workers, who tend to have relatively low survey scores, while workgroup Y consists of white-collar employees only, and these are generally more satisfied. Hence, comparing the ES results of different workgroups is not that simple.

Figure 2.4 illustrates the usual rule for "who will see what results." Each employee in Team A will see the results of his or her own team (A), compared to the results of the larger unit to which the team belongs (here called "Center X"), and compared to the results of the whole organization, for example (here "Division U"). In Figure 2.4, the results are always based on all employees excluding the manager who is responsible for the respective unit.

In addition to what is shown to all employees, higher-level managers will also be given a cross-comparison of the organizational units within their areas of responsibility. For example, the manager of Center Y in Figure 2.4 will get a cross-comparison of the results of Team C and Team D. The usual additional restriction is that these cross-comparisons are only made for the units that *directly* report to a manager, but not for units deeper down in the organizational hierarchy. So, the manager of Division U would get a cross-comparison of Center X and Center Y, but not of the teams A to D. This latter information is still available, but the manager of Division U is asked to access it via the Center managers. This rationale prevents higher managers from looking at scores deep down in the hierarchy without first discussing them with the manager responsible for those lower units.

An exception to this rule must often be made for top management. Executives are typically not only responsible for a particular division or function of the organization, but also, as members of certain boards, for the entire company. Hence, they must not only see their own results, but also get the picture of the entire company and its parts in terms of similarities and differences.

We also do not recommend comparisons across different areas of the organization. Some managers may argue that ranking organizational units on survey scores encourages healthy competition that ultimately benefits the entire organization, but the competition is not on an even playing field. Even when comparing units on changes from the previous survey (i.e., most improved, least improved), differences in job type, group size, local history, and countless other variables are often overlooked. The competition creates enormous pressure on managers even though differences may not be attributable to their actions. If the organization's culture is based on competition, then ranking units on survey results may be a natural occurrence, and the survey consultant will need to remind managers what an unfair competition this is. In most cases, the competition will needlessly yield negative consequences. Why risk resignations, resentment, or reduced collaboration?

2.5 Ethical and Legal Use of Individual Employee Data

Protecting individual data is not only an ethical issue, but also a legal issue in many countries. In Germany, for example, any ES must be set up in such a way that *personal* and potentially *sensitive* data (a person's responses to the questionnaire or information about his or her participation in the survey) are protected from abuse. Abuse means that the data are used for a purpose different from the one that has been officially defined. The purpose, in turn, is closely associated with the company's interest in certain information. This interest must be clearly work-related and must not intrude into the person's private affairs. What that means is often a matter of negotiation between the company and some form of employee representation such as, in many countries, the works council. It also means that sensitive questions are to be avoided, if at all possible.

Anonymity

In any ES, one has to closely consider to what extent the questions ask about personal and sensitive information for participants. This issue partly depends on whether the survey will be anonymous or confidential. Surveys where no one can tell which person gave what answers to the survey's questions are *anonymous*. However, whether a particular survey is anonymous or not, is not always easy to say. Obviously, if printed questionnaires are marked with identification codes, then it is possible to identify the individual participant directly. Similarly, if an online survey is accessed through personal identification numbers (PINs), then once again the survey is not anonymous (if the respondents' answers are stored together with their PINs in the same data file). On the other hand, if an online survey uses one login and password for all participants and the survey can be accessed from anyone's computer via any internet connection, then the survey seems anonymous. Yet, *particular* persons may still be able to identify some individuals *indirectly* through their demographic profile. For example, if the computer says that some particular survey answers were provided by (a) a woman with (b) less than two years at the company who (c) works for the marketing team in (d) Toronto, it may be clear for the manager of the marketing team in Toronto that these data must come from "Jane Miller"—given that the demographics are correct[6]. Hence, this survey is not completely anonymous for every participant, and additional constraints must be specified to make it anonymous. One possibility that at least reduces the identifiability of single respondents is to keep the number of demographic variables small. In addition, one must report only survey results that are based on a certain minimum number of respondents (*cutoff value*).

Typical rules that serve to protect the participant's anonymity include the following:

1) Participation is voluntary.
2) The respondent's name is not recorded in the questionnaire.
3) Only [three] demographic items are assessed (to make focused feedback possible): Organizational tenure (containing five answering options), organizational unit of the respondent, and position of the respondent in the hierarchy (from executive board to shop floor, containing five answering options).
4) Respondents can skip any item they do not want to or cannot answer.
5) The results of the survey are only reported as summary statistics (e.g., percentages, means).
6) The answers to any survey item are reported only if at least [seven] respondents answered this item.

The third statement says that the number of demographic variables is kept at a minimum. Here, it could even be reduced further by dropping the tenure variable,

---

[6] Many employees and, in particular, their representatives typically grossly underestimate how difficult it is to identify employees using such "police techniques," because data analysis is typically done outside the organization and the outside analysts have no knowledge about the persons behind certain demographic profiles. Yet, such concerns must be taken seriously, because they may lead to low participation rates.

because tenure most likely will be used for some general analyses but is not essential for the survey feedback process. The most important variable is the name of the organizational unit of the respondent. It is critical for the follow-up processes, because they heavily rely on focused feedback. This should be easy to see for any employee but it cannot hurt to explain the function of such a variable in addition to underlining why such information is needed.

In contrast, assessing the number of years employees have worked for the organization is not as obvious. Instead, one has to explain why new and old employees may differ from each other in satisfaction or attitudes. The pattern that occurs in most organizations is that employees who are new to the company have the highest survey scores. Mid-career employees' scores tend to be lower, and employees with the longest tenure frequently have scores that are almost as high as the newcomers' scores. This U pattern is so prevalent that it is worth investigating when it does not appear in an organization's survey.

Managers frequently push to include gender and, in the US, ethnicity as demographic questions. While it may be important for some companies that seek a diverse employee workforce to review survey scores by gender and ethnicity, this is typically an issue for the corporate staff rather than for line managers. Thus, if these demographics are used, it may not be necessary to include results by gender and ethnicity in all managers' reports. Survey consultants should meet with an organization's legal representative to explore how survey results by gender and ethnicity might be used as part of lawsuits against the company. As a means of providing legal protection, some organizations refuse asking these demographic questions.

The last bullet point above states that a certain cutoff criterion is used to protect the individual respondent's anonymity. There may also be separate anonymity rules for showing a group's results by demographics (e.g., tenure, gender). Thus, a unit may get a report (possibly with some items suppressed), but they may not get a breakout by demographics unless separate rules are met (e.g., no demographic group smaller than 7 will be displayed in a report).

For surveys that allow open-ended comments, yet another rule might exist to determine which reports will include these data (e.g., units with 50 or more participants get comments in their reports).

Anonymity rules such as these should be communicated before and during the survey administration so that employees understand how they are being protected and what managers will and will not see in the reports. These rules are necessary, but they have consequences that can upset managers and employees alike. Managers may be dismayed when they realize that there were not enough participants from their unit to allow a report to be generated. Employees can become upset that their written comments were not read by their supervisor because the anonymity rules did not allow that supervisor to see comments. Indeed, if the cutoff values are set too high, then many mangers fail to receive a report, and the employees from units deemed "too small" lose their chance to get specific actions generated from the survey. We have seen stakeholder groups (works councils and corporate leaders alike) argue for large cutoff values without realizing the disadvantages of their argument until it was too late. If one requires 100 participants to generate a focal report, for example, this will upset a lot of managers and employees because their units are being left out of post-survey data-based actions. Once a rule is communicated to employees, the organization has to stick to that rule or else the psychological contract will be broken and the integrity of the survey will be lost.

The question remains why pick $N=7$ and not, say, $N=10$? The answer depends on the typical number of employees who work in small workgroups, and on the expected participation rate. If the latter is 66%, and typical small workgroups have some 12 employees, then one arrives at $N=7$. In small organizations or in organizations with many project teams, it may even make sense to set the minimum N to values as small as 5. However, in these situations managers can be tempted to pressure all employees in these smaller units to participate so that the unit gets a report.

If multiple employee surveys are planned for one organization, then it may make sense to start out with a larger cutoff value. This can help eliminate concerns about anonymity for the first employee survey. Once employees become familiar with the follow-up processes and have established confidence in the survey, then it is usually less difficult to justify smaller group sizes. If everything works well, then it is even likely that employees and managers will later request analyses based on smaller groups to allow for more focused diagnostics. Hence, organizations involved in ES projects tend to find their own balance between protection of employee privacy, and accomplishment of project objectives through specific feedback.

Surveys that contain open-ended questions are harder to protect against concerns about privacy violations. Both content and formulation of an employee's comments may allow his or her identification. Thus, summarizing comments is a good means of circumventing problems pertaining to privacy violations.

Occasionally, another form of anonymity that is often overlooked and that can later lead to complaints is the anonymity of managers that are objects of the questions in the survey. For example, a questionnaire may contain the item "Are you satisfied with your supervisor?" When analyzing the data of a particular workgroup, it is clear that this supervisor is a particular person. In an online survey, this can be made even more unambiguous by displaying the name of that individual in the questionnaire. More generally, there are always questions in the survey that pertain to topics supervisors or managers are responsible for. The ES project team has to clarify whether this level of specificity is desired, and whether supervisors can deal effectively with this feedback. In addition, when making a decision about supervisory feedback, considerations pertaining to the organizations' general feedback culture may prove useful in evaluating whether individual supervisor feedback will be more beneficial than harmful. If organizations are unsure as to whether they want every supervisor to receive individual feedback, they choose a large cutoff value (e.g. larger than 30). If groups are this large, there are usually multiple supervisors, diffusing the impact of the feedback on individual supervisors. Furthermore, supervisors can also be provided with help and recommendations as to what they can do with their feedback data. In addition, many supervisors feel less threatened by results of employee surveys if they know that the upward feedback they receive through the ES will not directly affect their performance evaluation. For surveys with open-ended comments, one may want to consider removing references to names and titles so that managers are not helpless victims of libelous statements. Their careers may be damaged by false accusations that they themselves might not be aware of. On the other hand, employees may feel cheated if their use of specific names is censored.

Confidentiality

A confidential survey satisfies different criteria than an anonymous survey. The individual respondent's survey data are stored together with personal identifiers such as the respondent's name and address, but only a sharply defined group of researchers—typically from outside the organization—archives these data and has access to them. These researchers may use the survey data only for research purposes (defined as identifying patterns and trends that hold for *groups* or *types* of people), never releasing any *individual* data to the outside. Indeed, a particular individual's data are really not interesting to the research questions; what counts is being able to discover lawful relations by linking individual survey data to other individual data such as education level, trainings received, answers to previous surveys, entry interview information, level of pay, etc. This research can lead to invaluable insights into correlations and even causal relationships of key variables of organizational functioning.

Obviously, a confidential survey is highly desirable, and so the number of requests to run surveys that include identifying codes or demographics is rising. However, confidential surveys need to be carefully prepared, and often cannot be run because of legal constraints (data protection laws, co-determination laws) unless the employees agree to such a survey. To get this agreement, management has to negotiate with the employee representatives (often the works council) to arrive at a contractual agreement that specifies the requirements the survey (including data storage, data access, data processing etc.) must satisfy. To reach such an agreement is often very difficult or simply impossible, in particular if the company does not have much experience with surveys.

Allowing for Demographic Item Non-Response

Another consideration regarding personal data is whether the participating employee can withhold information on demographic items. Can the employee, for example, not answer a question on his or her gender? For paper questionnaires, which are not typically coded and designated for a specific individual, each employee controls what information he or she wants to supply or omit (item non-response). Many web questionnaires are set up in a similar manner. Participants can skip demographic questions or even misrepresent themselves (e.g., a sales representative claims to be from manufacturing). However, web questionnaires can be designed to force participants to answer each question, and so the respondents not wishing to respond to a particular item are forced either to fabricate an answer or to opt out of taking the survey. Web questionnaires can also be designed to match demographic data to the employees' individual data maintained by HR—someone would be able to decipher how you responded and if you responded. Some survey professionals consider this "forced" data matching unethical, even if the employee is made aware of what is going on in the background (which we consider a requirement). Others consider this approach to be the path toward more accurate data collection and reporting.

Data Protection

In various European countries, an important role (required by law) in any ES is played by the *data protection officer*. This person must make sure that the data are processed in such a way that they serve only the intended purpose. Hence, the data protection officer must be informed about the survey, how the data will be collected, how they will be stored, who has access to them at what time, how they will be used, and how they are protected from abuse. Better still is to involve the data protection officer as early as possible into efforts to design an optimal ES. The data protection officer can then help to design the ES project properly so that it satisfies all the requirements that he or she must pay attention to.

Data protection is to ensure that the individual employee's survey responses and participation data are used *solely* for the *explicitly defined purpose*s of the ES. To make sure that this objective is reached, different measures must be taken and communicated to the employees. Some typical examples are:

- The data protection officer and a member of the works council are actively involved into planning the ES. (This increases confidence on the side of the employees that things are in order.)
- The questionnaire only addresses work-related issues, not personal matters.
- All data protection regulations are strictly followed and enforced. For instance, the external data entry institute encrypts data, and no personal data (e.g., access codes) are stored together with an individual's answers to the survey questions.
- The raw data (i.e., the ES data of every individual participant) are archived only at the external vendor; the raw data are not stored anywhere else, and no one in the company has access to the raw data.
- The survey vendor only delivers reports with summary statistics.
- During data collection, measures are taken to ensure that technical and organizational regulations for data and privacy protection are enforced.
- Data collection is done such that
    o each employee can submit only one questionnaire
    o some follow-up actions to enhance participation rates remain possible
    o data can be transferred reliably and easily to the data entry vendor

These specifications are still rather generic, but they show to every employee that a lot of thought went into the issue of data protection. Most importantly, if trustworthy persons such as the data protection officer, a works council member, a professional ES project team, and a renowned survey vendor commit themselves to do a first-rate job, suspicion is replaced by trust.

Depending on the mode of data collection (online, paper-pencil by mail, polling station, or other), one can be more specific on the rules used during survey administration. For example: "In the polling station, when an employee returns a questionnaire, then a member of the ES project team uses a list containing all employee names to check off the name of the individual handing in the survey. The purpose of the list is to prevent employees from participating multiple times. The list is only accessible to the ES project team, and is destroyed when data collection is completed." Such rules are set up to make sure that data collection is done orderly, not violating anybody's rights, and convincing each employee that it is safe to participate in the ES.

Inadmissible Questions

The final consideration regarding the sensitivity of personal data is the content of the question. An item such as "I have a best friend at work" that is used in Gallup's Q12 questionnaire is problematic in many countries. A company is granted a legitimate interest to learn about its employees' attitudes and opinions only as long as they are clearly job-related and as long as this does not negatively affect the individual employee's personal rights. This means that a decision has to be made what is and what is not clearly job-related. This decision leaves room for judgment, and its boundaries can be stretched by negotiating about borderline items with the works council. What must be shown is why this question is asked and what purpose it serves. This makes it virtually impossible to include, say, a personality inventory into an ES in Europe because it would be hard to convince many employee representatives why a question such as "Do you like to go to parties?", for example, is relevant. Apart from legal restrictions some employees might refuse to answer this question ("Why do you want to know this? This is none of your business!"), and this would cause negative sentiment and taint the ES.

2.6 Census and Sample Surveys

Positioning an ES always also includes considerations on whether the survey should be conducted as a census survey (asking every employee to participate) or whether it makes more sense to only draw a small sample of employees from the population. This decision is a complex one, with many implications on the ES project.

Statistical Considerations

Lay people are usually surprised to see that relatively small samples are sufficient to estimate population parameters with high precision. Samples as small as 1,000 persons allow one to predict the voting behavior of tens of millions of voters. However, this is true only if these samples are representative random samples (i.e., samples that match the population in many variables that are important predictors for voting behavior such as gender, religion, income, and geographical region), and samples that are truly randomly drawn from the population. In that case, following Gallup (Kagay & Elder, 1992), the sample is like a sample of blood: It is sufficient to make a judgment about the individual's health, and there is no need to draw a person's whole blood for that purpose. The problem is that constructing representative random samples can be time consuming and expensive.

Moreover, statistics computed from samples are only *estimates* of the population parameters of interest. They always come with a statistical margin of error. Thus, in an ES context, we end up with statements such as this: "55% of the employees are satisfied with their pay, plus/minus 3%, with 95% probability" (see Chapter 7). Hence, the results of an ES become somewhat fuzzy, and one needs enough expertise to explain this properly to non-statisticians. We have seen companies that did not want to live with this fuzziness and the statistical "gimmicks." For that reason alone, they decided to run the ES as a census survey.

Another drawback of sample surveys is that they may provide reliable estimates of certain parameters of the whole population, but not necessarily of similar parameters of smaller subgroups of the population (e.g. all managers or certain subsidiaries of the organization). For each such subgroup, there must be enough cases in the sample for a reliable estimate. So, when constructing a sample, one must first list all subgroups of interest, and then define the overall sample size so that the smallest subgroup can be reliably estimated. An alternative is to oversample certain subgroups and later down-weight the resulting subgroup data when computing aggregate statistics. However, this makes understanding the statistics even more difficult. To illustrate the problem, consider a case. When planning a survey for the German railroads with its (then) 320,000 employees, we first had to take into account that the railroads consisted of several divisions of vastly different size. The smallest division, railroad stations, had only some 8,000 employees. Yet, an average statistic for railroad stations obviously is not very interesting. The stations are spread out all over Germany, and regional differences were most likely. When a top manager expressed that he was interested to see the results for station managers in one of the smallest German states, it became clear that sampling would become complex, because our initial sample of 15,000 employees showed only 2 station managers in that state. Naturally, the data of two managers (assuming that they both participate in the ES) is no reliable basis for any conclusions or actions. Clearly, an organization that wants reports for many units and analytical cuts for demographics needs a census, not a sample survey.

Cost Considerations

In large organizations, using a sample and not a census survey can reduce costs substantially. Yet, the exact definition of costs of an ES is partially a definitional question. Surely, there are costs for data collection, in particular when running an ES in a traditional mode such as mailing paper questionnaires to every employee and paying the postage for each returned questionnaire. If the data are collected during working hours in a production site, then production is slowed down and a controller can compute how much that costs. In the administration department, on the other hand, one may classify the "time lost" for filling out the questionnaire as "opportunity costs." However, if an ES succeeds to identify problems that are then addressed and eliminated, these costs are really investments. Ultimately, they may be less costly than ignoring existing problems or than attempting to find individual solutions to each problem. However, the benefits of an ES are only a promise for the future, while the costs for running the survey must be paid for today. If employees, managers, or the works council feel that the ES is expensive, then there is a problem, particularly in organizations where cost savings is an important issue. In that case, using a cheaper sampling-based strategy may lead to a higher acceptance of the ES.

On the other hand, organizations frequently fail to recognize that constructing a representative sample is costly in itself. Samples can also lead to considerable costs later on in the project's course that were unanticipated at the beginning. For example, one may find that no reports can be generated for important subgroups, because there are too few respondents in the realized sample. Then, a complicated and costly process of deliberations on how to combine various subgroups to form larger ones that at least satisfy the minimal requirements for anonymity sets in.

If resources are scarce, however, then a sample survey is often the only feasible way of data collection. This is particularly true if data collection is done by traditional paper-pencil methods. Indeed, investing some of the available money into carefully constructing a representative sample may be better than attempting to collect "many" data without investing enough into informing and involving employees into the ES.

The smaller number of respondents in a sample can also *speed up* data entry and data cleaning. Again, this is particularly true for traditional ways of data collection. When running an ES online, data entry is automatic.

Psychological Considerations

Census surveys typically lead to higher response rates than sample surveys. A census approach also leads to more involvement, because it affects every employee. Even those employees who opt not to participate are, nevertheless, approached in the preparation phases or in the follow-up processes. From an organizational development perspective, thus, census surveys clearly create more momentum for change in the follow-up processes. However, for some projects with more specific objectives, it may not be desirable *not* to create this type of momentum. If the project's sole objective is the assessment of opinions while not "disturbing" the organization by raising expectations on deep follow-up activities, then a sample survey is to be preferred.

When running a sample survey, however, it can also be quite difficult to explain convincingly why certain individuals were selected to participate, and others were not. Few employees understand random sampling, and many employees develop their own theory for the selection logic. For example: "I know why I was not selected: They don't want to hear critical voices, and I am known as a critical person!" Or, another typical explanation: "They want to get rid of critical people. Now they are running this survey to find out who is negative." Obviously, such theorizing can make it difficult to collect open and honest answers.

Another problem with sampling occurs when an employee explicitly requests to participate. Due to statistical concerns pertaining to the representativeness of the sample, wishes of this sort cannot be granted. So, in the end, one must reject those people who are particularly motivated to cooperate and get involved. The only way to alleviate this problem is to offer them special involvement in the follow-up processes.

Then, the results based on samples are always less persuasive than census-based results. Hence, one must find a way to "sell" these statistics to managers and employees. They should at least accept the reasons why a sample is used, and not a census survey. Also, some empirical measurements are better than none.

Finally, anyone can argue that sample results are biased because the sample only contains a particular fraction of the employees, and it just happens that these people are particularly positive or negative. In a random sample, this is not very likely, but not impossible. This means, for example, that supervisors receiving negative upward feedback can always point out that the sample may be biased, and the results contradict their own experience. Consequently, they do nothing with the feedback.

Usability for Organizational Decision Making

Sampling-based ES results provide sufficient information to diagnose issues pertaining to larger organizational units. From a top-management perspective, this broad view is frequently sufficient. For the remaining managerial employees, such overall trends are less interesting. Census surveys are therefore required if every manager is supposed to receive a report pertaining to his or her organizational unit. These detailed reports are often more meaningful and more "binding" for the individual manager than broad overall results.

Census surveys are also needed to see similarities and differences among smaller organizational units. This information is particularly relevant for middle managers, because it is an excellent basis for discussions with subordinate managers. If all they get from a survey is a general trend result, no one feels responsible for poor results, because everyone would argue that he or she is an exception and that others cause these negative results.

Hence, if an ES is not just a measurement device, but also a tool for developing leadership and management, a census survey is the right choice—if the necessary resources for conducting a census survey are available. If the budget is too tight, then a high quality sample survey is always the better option over an underfinanced census survey.

3 Coordinating and Planning the ES Project

People who know little about employee surveys sometimes believe that preparing one is just a matter of writing a questionnaire and distributing it to employees. Those with a bit more experience in running surveys know that constructing a questionnaire is a fairly complex undertaking in itself. Moreover, the questionnaire is by no means the only necessary ingredient for an ES. As we have already seen in Chapter 2, the ES first needs to be positioned and this requires many thoughtful decisions. These decisions are the foundations for planning all the processes surrounding the ES. In this chapter, we concentrate on the major elements of planning an ES.

3.1 Architecture

An ES is never fully run by one person, even if that person is supported by an external vendor. There is always a group of people from within the company that is needed to appropriately coordinate various activities, to involve different stakeholders, and to provide the information necessary to properly position the ES. The key person in this context is, of course, the ES project director, but this person is usually supported by a project team that is often called the ES project team or the *ES coordination team* (CT).

Architecture of the Coordination Team

The architecture of the CT depends on the requirements defined by the organization. In the simplest case the organization is a production plant or a subsidiary where all employees are situated at one site. In such an environment the CT can be a small group that runs all activities out of a central office. If, however, the organization operates in many different locations with a complex organizational structure of business units, regions, and functions, then a centralized CT is far too simple. Although there is no general rule for structuring a CT for a complex environment, the model shown in Figure 3.1 can be used as a convenient starting point. This model, with some tailoring, has been used to run several global ES projects successfully.

The central element of the CT is the core coordination team (CCT). It usually consists of no more than about five persons. Their task is planning and steering the ES project in all its phases. Within the CCT, the work is organized such that different CCT members take over different responsibilities as ES subproject directors. For ex-

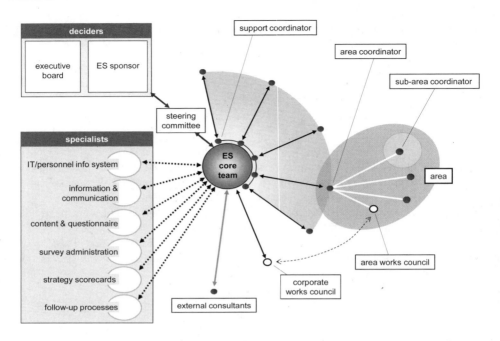

Figure 3.1. Architecture of a global ES project.

ample, one person might be assigned to coordinate all communication activities. He or she would present plans to the entire CCT for discussion and decision making. Another person might work on making sure that the IT infrastructure for running an online survey is in place and will be aligned with the logistics for any paper-pencil surveys. He or she might verify that the personnel information system yields correct access codes and addresses of those employees who will be invited to participate. Our point is that much of the work can be done outside the CCT by specialists. The main task of the ES subproject director is coordinating this work—managing all subproject activities, assuring that important milestones are reached, and otherwise keeping the survey project on track.

When assembling a CCT, it is important to take the time to find the right combination of people with the right mix of skills. The subproject director for "information & communication" should be a person who belongs to the corporate communication department, knows the structure of the media used in the organization, and has connections to other specialists in the field of communication and advertising. In a complex organization, having a CCT member with an informal network of experts within the organization and across countries or regions can help assure that corporate decisions will work in local settings.

In the lower left-hand corner of Figure 3.1, we display an example for subdividing the work so that it can be assigned to different subproject directors and special teams. Naturally, a particular person can also take on more than one subproject, and the ES project director can also lead a subproject (typically the design of content and questions).

The CCT in the model shown in Figure 3.1 extends into the organization via *support coordinators,* who are well informed if not actually involved in designing and planning the ES. Support coordinators are ideally situated "just down the hall" from the CCT members. Their main task is to provide the operational support that is needed to carry the ES into the various branches of the organization via the *area coordinators.* Support coordinators and area coordinators serve as linking pins between the CCT and the organization's areas, functions, or regions. Each area coordinator supports one *sub-area coordinator* who manages all ES activities within the particular sub-area to which he or she belongs.

To illustrate, assume an ES is run in a global group with a Swedish headquarter. Then, you would have a CCT in Sweden and area coordinators in Sweden as well as (for example) in Asia-Pacific, in Africa, and in North America. Most area coordinators would be located far away from the CCT, and therefore they need a partner in the headquarter-located ES project team. This partner is the support coordinator who keeps them informed of decisions, transmits support material, gives advice, listens to problems and complaints, and seeks solutions from the CCT.

An element of the architecture in Figure 3.1 that is sometimes useful in very large ES projects is a *steering committee.* This is a group of influential people (such as the HR director, some senior managers, some middle managers, and strategists) who occasionally sit down with the ES core team to discuss plans and progress. The steering committee can serve as a sounding board where the ES core team checks out how important decisions are viewed from different perspectives. Management often does not have time to consider all the implications of setting up an ES in a particular way; thus, they appreciate knowing that the ES core team was guided by a steering committee whose strategic judgment they can trust.

Tasks of ES Coordinators

The various tasks of ES coordinators can vary a lot from one project to another, but Table 3.1 displays what we consider to be typical activities. Note the range and the importance of these activities. They go far beyond the usual notion that all that coordinators do is to distribute and collect questionnaires! Consider the first task: To inform managers about the potential uses of an ES requires that the area coordinator really understands the ES project and, in particular, its positioning. Another challenge is Task #10. Since the area coordinator certainly cannot support all such workshops personally, he or she must see that good workshop coordinators are found (inside or outside the organization) and/or get trained in working with the ES results.

Task #11 also shows how the CCT, the support coordinators, the area coordinators and further coordinators in the areas would cooperate in practice. In a global organization, it is not always possible to have all coordinators "fly in" for a central training on how to facilitate ES workshops. Even if the situation allows such a centralized meeting, language barriers may limit its usefulness. A more realistic plan is to hold two or three meetings of the area coordinators, the support coordinators, and the CCT

Table 3.1. Some tasks of ES area coordinators

1. *Inform* management about the potentials of an ES in management
2. *Build, lead* information team that informs all employees well about the ES (purpose, timing, anonymity, action plans, implementation, etc.)
3. *Drive* input of regional items for the questionnaire (content items)
4. *Check, supplement* demographic items for region (completeness, logic, spelling, compliance to legal and political norms)
5. *Check* translations of questionnaire (meaning, easy to understand).
6. *Specify* which reports are needed in region
7. *Set up, lead* survey administration team for region (organizes, manages data collection)
8. *Identify, build* skills in region for competent feedback of survey results
9. *Identify, build* skills in region for competent action management following the ES
10. *Support* (facilitate, coach, empower) workshops on all levels that discuss the ES results
11. *Support* managers and non-managers in action planning
12. *Observe* follow-up processes and inform the CCT regularly on how they run

during an ES project for instructions, empowerment, discussions, and trainings. The area coordinators then build the necessary skills in their areas. Another alternative is to have a group of experienced trainers travel to various regions to conduct professional trainings for all area and sub-area coordinators. This approach often yields the best cost-benefit ratio, especially if the meetings can be part of an existing regional conference that many coordinators attend. On-site meetings consistently led by knowledgeable support coordinators are the best way to attain tightly aligned ES processes.

Most of the work of an ES coordinator lies in the first third of the ES project (i.e. in the planning and preparation steps before survey administration), in helping to administer the survey, and in getting the right survey reports to the various managers. In later phases of the ES project, the role of the ES coordinator shifts to an auxiliary role, supporting line managers in making optimal use of the ES results or reporting the actions that result from the ES to the CCT.

Recruitment and Selection of ES Coordinators

ES coordinators are not hired by an organization to serve in this capacity. Rather, they have to be selected from among the organization's employees. The ES project director is usually chosen ahead of time by the organization itself, but all other coordinators must be picked "by hand" according to some criteria. The success of the project very much depends on thorough specification of such criteria and appropriate recruitment of available employees. In practice, what often happens is that the survey project director specifies profiles that coordinators should have only to see a group of extremely inexperienced trainees fly in for the first coordinator training meeting. It is too late then to change plans. The ES project director must work hard on communicating the importance of the coordinator positions and may need to help identify qualified candidates. Furthermore, the project director may have to persuade the candidates, their supervisors, or both that the survey project is a worthwhile assignment.

As we have seen above in Figure 3.1, the architecture of a coordination team can be quite complex, with different positions and roles for its members. Hence, there is no single list of requirements that all coordinators must satisfy. However, some positions are particularly crucial, and so particular care must be taken to fill them. This is especially true for area coordinators because they have to run the ES project for large parts of the organization out of a decentralized position where they often have little formal power. However, it is desirable for all non-specialists in the coordination team to score high on all of the following criteria:

- *Experience in project work*: An ES can be a huge project and the persons who work together to run such a project should have at least some experience coordinating the activities of multiple people.
- *Knowing the organization and its culture*: Coordinators are often decisive in providing the information needed to properly set up the survey, the feedback of survey results, and the follow-up processes so that they fit their particular parts of the organization. The CCT cannot know, for example, what can and cannot be done in a "remote" location.
- *Familiarity with basic HR systems:* An ES always touches on numerous issues that are related to an organization's HR tools and systems such as the organizational structure, the pay system, or the personnel information system.
- *Familiarity with basic management tools:* An ES can be run more efficiently if it uses tools that are available in the organization rather than inventing everything anew. For example, many organizations have certain methodologies for planning and implementing action plans, and they may be just right for the ES follow-up processes.

Project experience and knowing the organization is most important, while familiarity with HR systems and management tools can be acquired or filled differently during the ES project. The coordinator, for example, can simply find out the answers to the latter two issues by talking to the local HR department.

In terms of the personal characteristics, coordinators should satisfy the following requirements:

- Be intrinsically *motivated* to work on the ES project
- Be able to *endure pressure and stress* to deliver results under sometimes complex and demanding circumstances (within short timeframes, under changing requirements, with little support from managers, etc.)
- Be *resourceful* in finding ways to get things done, even if they do not have a strong formal power basis
- Work *systematically* towards reaching the milestones of a master plan, with the ability to plan their own activities early and realistically, and with the discipline to pursue this plan *conscientiously* but flexibly

- Have sufficient *social skills* to bring together and involve the various stakeholders into the ES project without alienating anyone or damaging the organizational climate
- Be *perceived* as competent, honest, and worthy of employees' and managers' trust

Effective teams need not consist of members who are all very similar. Often, a good mix of different talents is better. For a coordination team, one should consider not only drawing HR people, but also line managers who are more action-oriented or analytic minds from the R&D function. Yet, in the more general roles of ES coordinators, such "outside" talents typically do not work well. They also make work in the coordination team more complicated. Line managers do not want to spend much time on the project, and R&D employees can slow down the project with too much attention to detail. We have found in many ES projects that it is better to select coordinators that come from HR.

For the specialists who support the CCT (see Figure 3.1, lower left-hand corner), the above criteria are not all that relevant. For them, what counts, in particular, is their special talent.

A question that usually comes up when running an ES in Europe is whether a member of the works council should or may become a coordinator. Our answer is no. We recommend inviting one or two members of the works council to participate in a few cardinal meetings of the entire coordination team where they can voice their perspective and learn of survey plans in order to communicate them to the entire works council. The coordination team has nothing to hide, but the works council should not be given a special role in the ES. We recall one case where the works council wanted to send an "observer" to all meetings of the coordination team. In another, they wanted to have the final say on all decisions of the coordination team. Such special roles are inappropriate for the works council, whose purpose is to review sensitive questions and defend employees' privacy rights. They are not a decision maker or a censor. Senior leadership, not the works council, ultimately owns the ES. The CCT should reach out to the works council as early as possible, but only as one of many stakeholders.

ES Coordinators and ES Consultants

The success of any project depends to a large extent on the quality of the people on the project team. It is equally true that getting the best possible people is difficult because they are usually the busiest people in an organization. When recruiting coordinators the project director should distinguish between work that is procedural but requires few special skills versus work where expertise is most valuable. While ES coordinators from within the company can most effectively execute routines and processes, an ES consultant—typically from outside the organization—can perform certain specialized roles more efficiently.

The value of ES consultants is most apparent during the follow-up processes, when survey data become the catalyst for improvement efforts. ES consultants ideally are seasoned HR professionals or managers who know how to turn soft factors into hard results. They can support line management to turn the ES reports into responses that positively affect the bottom line. Such support is critical because line managers often find it difficult to turn ES results into actions that make sense. There is a tendency for managers either to do nothing or to fall into the "actionitis" trap where many activities are planned just to show everyone that they did something. A competent ES consultant, however, can provide advice and recommendations that are both independent from internal perspectives and constraints, and based on experience with many different organizations. Managers, in turn, may be able to discuss problems more easily with an outsider than with a member of the CCT. With the right combination of internal and external insights, the organization benefits from creative yet realistic responses to survey results.

The ES project director has to prepare the ES consultant in order to achieve this level of synergy. The consultant needs to be aware of the survey's goals, the structure and the timeframe for the follow-up processes, and the results as displayed in the reports that reach the individual managers. In addition, ES consultants should be trained on how to use models, instruments, tools, and recipes developed by the CCT to support activities in the follow-up processes (see the hints and tips shown in Tables 11.1 to 11.3). Because so much of what happens after survey administration depends on the preparation before survey administration, however, the effectiveness of working with an ES consultant increases with his or her early involvement in survey design and planning.

Time Consumed by Coordinators in an ES Project

Those assigned to an ES project typically do not work exclusively for this project. Hence, these individuals and each of their supervisors must get a reliable estimate of how much time the ES project is going to require. The answer to this question depends on the individual's role, skills, and experience. Of course, the answer also depends on the organization's readiness for the survey. An organization embarking on a new survey process will certainly require more time than if it were launching the survey for the nth time in essentially the same way.

Nevertheless, for the survey coordinators who work primarily on preparing the survey, a coarse estimate amounts to some three weeks of work exclusively devoted to the ES project. The time needed for the follow-up processes is impossible to estimate without first designing what the coordinators (or the consultant) are to do.

3.2 ES Project Plan

An employee survey is a large endeavor. Depending on the scope and the depth of the follow-up processes, the survey may be the largest project that the HR function leads. Such projects not only require an adequate project architecture, but also careful planning of the various milestones and activities.

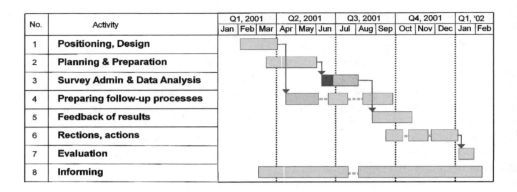

Figure 3.2. Master plan of an ES project in a global company.

The ES Master Plan

A coarse overview of the main components and timelines of an ES master plan is shown in Figure 3.2. Although this example shows a real ES case, it still adequately describes the typical ES project. All ES projects involve the same eight basic components from positioning to informing, even though they do not always surface in a project plan. To lay them out explicitly from the start elucidates what needs to be done in a rational manner.

The pivoting element for designing a first sketch of an ES master plan is the time period when the employees are given the opportunity to fill out the questionnaire (shown as a black bar segment in row #3 of Figure 3.2). As discussed in Section 2.2, this time window must be set so that it offers a maximal number of employees the opportunity to participate in the survey. Hence, there should be no major vacation times, holidays, or pre-holiday times where people are focusing on other things. However, even if almost all employees are present, business requirements (such as a major trade fair or the end of the business year where business results have to be reported to shareholders) may be consuming so much of the employees' working time that an ES would not capture enough attention.

An additional consideration for setting the time window for administering the survey is how the survey's momentum can be transferred into the follow-up processes. When running a survey in November, for example, one can use the month of December and the beginning of January for data analysis and feedback to top management. When the employees come back from their end-of-the-year vacations, the follow-up processes can start with full thrust on all levels. Psychologically, this does not lead to a particularly noticeable gap between survey and actions. Rather, it seems that survey feedback and action planning begins without much delay. Similarly in the master plan in Figure 3.2: Although there is a greater time gap between survey administration and the follow-up processes, this gap is filled up with summer vacations and everyone can easily see that it would not make sense to begin any earlier. The summer, of course, is not wasted. Rather, it is filled with data analysis, computing data reports for all managers, preparing and conducting ES results presentations to top managers, and working out top management's responses to the ES results (i.e.: "How we see these results," "What we intend to do," "What we expect managers to do," "What we expect all employees to do").

Figure 3.2 also shows that the various elements of an ES project do not and should not run one after the other. On the contrary, proceeding sequentially would be too slow, and some *interactions* do exist among the various activities. When positioning the ES, for example, one can begin preparing the questionnaire and the survey administration as soon as the directions and time line become clear. On the other hand, positioning is often greatly helped if the ES project team provides some concrete and realistic proposals regarding the questionnaire or the time line rather than remaining in relatively abstract discussions only.

The master plan in Figure 3.2 also shows a few arrows that lead from one activity to another. These arrows denote logical dependencies. For example, one cannot provide any feedback on the ES results before one has completed the necessary analysis of the survey data. Other activities overlap without having such strict dependencies.

Finally, some bars in Figure 3.2 are split into a number of pieces. For example, the activity "Survey Administration & Data Analysis" first shows a two-week data collection window (dark section of bar), directly followed by five weeks for data entry, data cleaning, and data analysis[7]. The activities of planning the follow-up processes, on the other hand, are split into three sectors that are not contiguous. In this case, the first sector comprises the activities related to planning the follow-up processes and empowering ES coordinators/consultants accordingly. The second section needs certain results from the survey for training facilitators to run ES workshops and other meetings where the ES results are discussed. The third section, finally, describes the activities planned to logistically organize ES workshops and other meetings in the follow-up processes (when, where, who).

Differentiating Roles in the ES Project

Not everyone has the same role in an ES project. Coarse role assignment such as "Mr. Miller is responsible for the project" can lead to confusion that can be avoided by more differentiated role assignments. Some roles can also be overlooked, especially in complex projects. For example, it is easy to forget to inform a particular person or group on time about a project milestone because this person/group does not explicitly appear in the project plan in the role "must be informed."

Andersen et al. (1984) distinguish among eight different roles in projects: "Executes the work; takes the decision solely or ultimately; takes the decision jointly or partly; manages work and controls progress; provides tuition on the job; must be consulted; must be informed; available to advise." These roles can be reduced to the five roles shown in the MIDEX scheme in Table 3.2.

---

[7] The survey of this ES master plan was partly run in a paper-pencil mode. In online surveys, the time period for data analysis can be a lot shorter.

Table 3.2. MIDEX roles of persons/groups in projects.

code	role
M	= <u>m</u>anages progress (assigns work, controls progress, finds solutions, gets resources, leads action team, etc.)
I	= must be <u>i</u>nformed/involved
D	= <u>d</u>ecides
E	= <u>e</u>nables (gives expert advice, makes proposals, suggests solutions, is available for help, etc.)
X	= e<u>x</u>ecutes work

A person or group can take on several roles simultaneously in any part of a project. Indeed, the simple "is responsible for" assignment that is typical for so many task assignments is one example for assigning multiple roles to one person at the same time. Yet, it leaves open the question "Responsible for what?" Responsible for doing the work, for keeping the project on course in terms of its dates, for reaching the project's goals, for staying within the limits of the budget, or for what else? When planning an ES project, it often pays to carefully disentangle the main responsibilities for each activity and assign each of them to one person or group only. Conversely, when considering different activities in a project plan, one will find that almost all of them involve different people or groups in one role or another.

Some persons have relatively stable roles in an ES project. One of them is the ES consultant. In the planning phase of an ES, this individual plays primarily an *E*-role (Enables) because he or she supports the ES core team by providing information, by recommending appropriate instruments and process, and by empowering the coordinators to fulfill their respective tasks. This role changes to an *X*-role (Executes) when the survey data are in because then the survey consultant (or the external vendor) is expected to generate the various reports for managers and teams. The core ES project team and the ES project director, in particular, often have *M*-roles (Manages) in the various activities. This role in itself has many facets: It ranges from setting clear goals, defining reasonable timelines, coordinating the work that is delegated to (capable) others, motivating others to do that work, to supporting or coaching them to reach their goals. Top management has primarily *D*-roles (Decide). It decides which of various proposals should be implemented or changed so that it satisfies certain criteria. Top management typically does not have an *X*-role in the sense that it does execute any work. The works council, on the other hand, is most often in *I*-roles (i.e., this group must be informed at certain times about the status of the ES project and about decisions made by top management). The works council must also be involved in planning an ES design that takes care of anonymity concerns and that satisfies data protection requirements. However, if a member of the works council also serves as a coordinator on the project team, then this person takes on an *X*-role, not an *I*-role.

Phases, Activities, and Roles of an ES Project

The reader will be able to plan an ES in more detail as he or she learns more about its potential and its pitfalls. In Tables 3.3a-3.3d we offer a generic skeleton plan for running an ES that can serve as a guideline or starting point when designing one's own survey. This skeleton plan should also help clarify the *MIDEX* roles by listing stakeholders' typical activities in an ES project. We distinguish seven different stakeholders: 1) The consultant (who could be internal, but is likely independent of the client), 2) the combination of the ES promoter and the core coordination team (as their roles are so similar), 3) the other coordinators (support, area, sub-area), 4) top management and the ES sponsor, 5) line managers at all levels of the hierarchy, 6) the works council, and 7) the employees. Each reader may want to specify other stakeholders, of course, but our distinctions should serve many situations.

To better understand the role assignments, consider the task "define architecture" in the activity "Planning & Preparation" in Table 3.3a. Here, the ES consultant is expected to first propose a reasonable model (e.g., a modification of the model shown in Figure 3.1). The ES consultant explains his or her model and then supports the CCT in fine-tuning this proposal to the needs and context of the particular organization. The consultant may also decide to propose and discuss a set of different models. The CCT, then, has to understand the strengths and weaknesses of these models and then merge their features into one design that appears optimal for the organization. At this point specific individuals have to be identified to fill the various positions in the ES architecture. The CCT has to get in touch with these persons, recruit them for their role in the ES project, and discuss the time required and the benefits of collaborating with the team. At the same time, the CCT must also contact the supervisors of the potential ES coordinators and check whether they would agree to release these persons to the ES project. Moreover, the CCT must inform top management about the project architecture and the persons who will fill its various positions.

Table 3.3b shows some elements of a summary activity called "Informing." Informing comprises two sets of activities: One set is concerned with communicating what will happen throughout the survey process, and the other set of activities deals with the survey results and the follow-up processes. The first set serves the goal of informing all employees about the ES and, in particular, its positioning (purpose, goals, timing, content, follow-up processes, rules regarding anonymity and confidentiality, rules regarding data analysis, expectations of top management, etc.). All these activities are meant to motivate each employee to participate in the survey, and they may be complemented by other direct "advertising" measures (e.g., posters, brochures, letters), too. The second set of activities is more dependent on the results of the survey, such as the employee responses that primarily concern top management and a proposed course of action.

Table 3.3c shows a number of important (and potentially concurrent) activities of the summary activity "Survey Administration & Data Analysis." Once again this general skeleton plan belies the complexity of what needs to be done. For example, "administering the survey" can be an extremely demanding logistical undertaking, in particular if the administration is at least partly a traditional paper-pencil format using various languages. The survey administration also has implications for subsequent activities in the summary activity "Data entry and data cleaning." If, for example, one runs an online survey, then data entry is automatic and needs no extra planning. Data cleaning—in the sense of eliminating or correcting wrong entries on demographic variables—may also be superfluous if these data are automatically inserted into each employee's questionnaire out of a well-tested personnel information system (PIS) that is up to date at the time of survey administration. (The PIS can also be used to simplify data collection in traditional paper-pencil modes; see "sticker method" in Section 5.10). This means that an activity such as "Data cleaning" can be shifted, effectively, into the earlier activity "Instruments" because the work is front-loaded into assuring the accuracy of the PIS in providing demographic information.

Regarding training activities in this skeleton, we only listed training sessions on how to conduct ES workshops. Whether one also wants to empower managers in one way or another (e.g., on how to read survey reports or on how to plan actions) must be decided on the basis of the apparent needs and interests as well as the available resources of the organization.

"Data analysis" in the skeleton plan in Table 3.3c is fully associated with the ES consultant, assuming the typical case that this person comes from the vendor who is generating the survey reports and that the analysis is done externally. This procedure is becoming more common for a few reasons. First, it is the preferred choice for visibly protecting the respondent's anonymity. Second, few organizations are willing to maintain an internal staff that supplies survey expertise anymore. Third, generating and distributing thousands of accurate reports within a matter of days requires special software and data processing skills that are rarely available within any organization.

Finally, Table 3.3d summarizes some activities that take place after data analysis. Presenting the results of an ES to top management is standard in any ES, but the other activities very much depend on the purpose of the ES.

Table 3.3a. Phases, activities, roles in an ES project (1 of 4).

Phases/Activities	ES Consultant	Promoter/CCT	CT, Special	TM/Sponsor	Line Mnmgt.	Works Council	Employee
Design & Positioning							
Positioning							
Clarify context, side constraints	E	X					
First positioning with TM	X			D			
Involve the works council	X				I	I	
Fine-tune positioning, decide	E	X		D			
Planning & Preparation							
Planning							
Define architecture	E	X		D			
Work out ES project plan	E	X		D			
Trainings							
Introduction to ES for coordinators	E	X	X				
Training for generating special items	E	X	X				
Training on how to order reports	E	X	X				
Training on how to organize survey administration	E	X	X				
Training on how to motivate employees	E	X	X				
Instruments							
Questionnaire: Items, demographic items, layout	X	X	X				
Translations in other languages	E	M	X				
Collect and improve special items	X	M	X		X	X	X
Pretest questionnaire(s)	X	I	I				X
Construct prognosis questionnaire	X	I	I				
Produce questionnaire for field application	E	M	I	D		I	
Organizing I (Data Collection)							
Admin of survey: Time, rooms, materials, processes, rules, electronic polling stations, help desks, support at survey sites	E	M	X	I		I	

Legend. For roles, see Table 3.2; CCT=Core coordination team, CT=Coordinator not in the CCT; Special=Special teams (see Figure 3.1), TM=top management.

Table 3.3b. Phases, activities, roles in an ES project (2 of 4).

Phases/Activities	ES Consultant	Promoter/CCT	CT, Special	TM/Sponsor	Line Mnmgt.	Works Council	Employee
Informing							
Informing I (before survey)							
First announcement by Board, senior managers	E	M		D	I	I	I
Statement on ES by works council	E	M			I	X	I
Media plan for company, functions, areas	E	M	X				
Letter of TM to managers	E	M		X	I	I	
Q &A on ES, anonymity, data protection	E	M	X	D	I	I	I
Info: When, where, who, how	E	X	I	I	I	I	I
Posters, e-mail, call for participation	E	M	X	X	X	X	I
Informing II (after survey)							
Thank you for participating, info on return rates	E	M	X	D	I	I	I
Info on feedback of results, ES workshops	E	M	X	I	I	I	I
Info on action planning and action plans	E	M	X	D	X	I	I
Status reports on progress of actions	E	M	X	X	X	I	I

Table 3.3c. Phases, activities, roles in an ES project (3 of 4).

Phases/Activities	ES Consultant	Promoter/CCT	CT, Special	TM/Sponsor	Line Mnmgt.	Works Council	Employee
Survey Administration & Data Analysis							
Data collection							
Prognosis survey	E	M	X	X	X	X	
Administration of survey to employees	E	M	X	X	X	X	X
Following up on participation	E	M	X	X	X	X	X
Data entry and data cleaning							
Data entry (scanning, manual)	X						
Data cleaning	X						
Cleaning up free-format comments	X						
Data analysis							
Reports (Focal reports, comments, prognoses)	X						
Summaries of results (text)	X						
Producing presentations, recommendations	X						
Preparing Follow-up Processes							
Organizing II (Workshops)							
Organizing ES workshops (when, who, where, how, facilitated by whom, ...)	E			I		I	
Training for Follow-Up Processes							
Train-the-Trainer-Trainings on ES workshops	X	M		I			
Training facilitators to run ES workshops		M	X				

Table 3.3d. Phases, activities, roles in an ES project (4 of 4).

Phases/Activities	ES Consultant	Promoter/CCT	CT, Special	TM/Sponsor	Line Mnmgt.	Works Council	Employee
Feedback							
Results to Executive Board							
Present, agree with sponsor on presentation	X			X			
Presentation to executive board	X			X			
Derive, decide on areas of focus, responses	E			X			
Results to Works Council, Senior/Area Mngmt.							
Presentation to works council	X					X	
Presentation to ES coordinators	X	X					
Presentation to Senior/Area managers	X				X		
ES Workshops							
Workshops with middle managers	E	M	X		X		
Workshops with employees of workgroups	E	M	X				X
Actions							
Action planning							
Planning actions: Company-wide, global	E	M		X			
Planning actions in functions, areas, subsidiaries…	E	M			X		
Planning actions locally, in workgroups	E	M			X		X
Implementing actions							
Monitoring, controlling of action implementation	E			X	X		
Reporting within management lines	E			X	X		I
Evaluation							
Positioning the evaluation (goals, timing, criteria…)	E	X		D			
Decide on mix of methods	E	X					
Construct, pick measurement instruments	E	X					
Collect data, analyze	E	M	X	X	X	X	X
Present results	X	I	I	X	I	I	I
Conduct follow-up processes of evaluation	E			X	X		

4 Content of Questionnaire

An ES can address many, but obviously only a limited number of different topics and issues. Hence, one must carefully consider what is and what is not important. In order to do this, it helps to look first at the great variety of questions that are "usually" used in an ES. One can then select those questions that yield the information that is needed to promote the goals that the ES is positioned to serve. In some organizations, the ES is called "the employee satisfaction survey," and so in this case it obviously is important to measure all the issues that are important indicators and drivers of employee satisfaction and dissatisfaction. However, unless the purpose of the organization is non-profit, employee satisfaction hardly ever is the ultimate goal. Rather, managers typically believe that employee satisfaction drives employee performance, which drives customer satisfaction that, in turn, drives business results. Hence, even if the ES is officially an "employee satisfaction survey," employee satisfaction is not the end goal. The team that compiles an appropriate ES questionnaire, therefore, has to look beyond the immediate and the apparent issues by utilizing a comprehensive theory or even a set of comprehensive theories and models that relate the different issues to the end goals of the ES, even if management believes in a much simpler theory.

4.1 Approaches for Defining the Content of an ES

An ES questionnaire typically contains some 50 to 60 *content items* and a small set of *demographic items*. Content items ask for the employees' opinions or perceptions regarding various substantive issues. An example is the item that consists of the question "How satisfied are you with your pay?" and some appropriate answer scale such as a 10-point rating scale from "not at all" to "very much." Demographic items classify the employees into the categories of a *background variable* that serves to break down the data into strata or subgroups. Examples include job type, location, tenure, and organizational unit, although gender and ethnicity are also frequently included.

Finding or constructing appropriate content items is one of the biggest challenges of any ES. It first requires identifying which *content domains* should be covered by the questionnaire. Once this is clear, one can then formulate appropriate items that measure these content domains.

There are two broad methods for arriving at definitions of the content domains of an ES. One method is working from one's desk, looking at questionnaires used elsewhere, studying relevant books, considering the goals of the ES, pondering relevant scientific theories on employee satisfaction, commitment, engagement and performance, and then picking the content domains that appear most relevant for the situation. The other is to go out and interview various persons and groups from the organization on what they think should be covered by the ES questionnaire. Frequently, questionnaire development proceeds with a combination of both approaches. For example, before conducting management interviews, an outline of the questionnaire is crafted based on previous work.

Existing Questionnaires and Instruments

Beginning by looking at the questionnaires used previously elsewhere (e.g., in other companies or in some parts of the organization) is never a bad start. External consulting firms specializing in employee surveys can frequently provide multiple samples of such questionnaires, at least in an anonymous form. Some questionnaires are even published, more or less completely, in the literature (e.g., Borg, 2003; McConnell, 2003; Wallner, 2000). Yet, simply copying such questionnaires generally makes little sense because good ES questionnaires need to be *tailor-made* for a particular organization. However, what one quickly learns from screening large samples of questionnaires is that there is considerable substantive overlap of the topics that they cover. These topics are important for employee satisfaction and performance.

The academic literature also provides many *standard instruments* that have been meticulously developed and validated in the past. They focus on many issues and constructs such as organizational commitment, job characteristics (e.g., work overload, monotonousness, job control, empowerment at work, social support), job stress, job roles (e.g., conflict, ambiguity, role justice, goal and process clarity), organizational justice, person-organization fit, workplace behaviors (e.g., taking charge, citizenship behavior, influence factors), or work-family conflicts (see Fields, 2002, for a collection of such scales). Most instruments probably exist for measuring job satisfaction. Examples are the JDI (Cranny et al., 1992), the JSS (Spector, 1997), the MSQ (Weiss et al., 1967), the SAZ (Fischer & Lück, 1972), and the ABB (Neuberger & Allerbeck, 1978).

For employee surveys, such standard instruments are rarely directly suited, however, because they almost always use many items for each construct they measure. The goal is to get a reliable and precise score for each individual, not to get scores for groups of people in a minimum of time, as in an ES.

Moreover, standard instruments are often not formatted in the same way as the typical ES items (i.e., as five-point Likert items), and thus there are no direct benchmarks for their scores. For example, the JDI contains items such as the following: "Think of your present job. In the blank beside each word or phrase, write Y for 'yes' if it describes your job, N for 'no' if not does not describe your job, and '?' if you cannot decide." After this introduction, the actual questions are formulated as "Work ____ Routine"; "Work ____ Satisfying"; "Pay ____ Bad"; or "Pay ____ Less than I deserve." One could argue that items such as "Work ____ Routine", together with the "Y/N/?" answer categories, are not that different from a Likert item with a 3-point answer scale, but to what extent the two formats cause differences in the survey results is not really known. On the other hand, the JDI items suggest topics that are certainly worth considering. For example, to what extent employees consider their work "routine" may be of interest in an ES, although one would probably want to be more specific with regard to what is really meant by "routine" (Always the same? Too often monotonous? Too easy, no challenge? Etc.).

What standard instruments also provide is insight into the psychological structure of the constructs of interest (such as job satisfaction or commitment). By knowing the academic research related to these constructs, one can avoid overlooking relevant aspects of those content areas in the survey or focus more clearly on the subdimension of greatest interest. For example, in academic research on organizational commitment, one typically distinguishes three components of organizational commitment: affective, normative, and continuance commitment (Meyer & Allen, 1997). Knowing this component structure, and knowing the items that make up the various commitment scales, the survey methodologist can pick or formulate items that focus sharply on what she really wants to measure.

Items from standard instruments almost always must be re-written for usage in ES questionnaires. Indeed, they often should be re-written to fit better to the jargon of the current company, or to serve better the purpose of the ES project. This is even truer for items that were used before in a different organization. Indeed, for such items, it is not always easy to see what they are supposed to measure. If that is the case, they should not be used: Just because they seem "interesting" or just because company X has used them before, is not a sufficient reason for adopting an item. There should always exist an underlying content theory and a strategic framework guiding the selection of items from existing instruments. It is easier not to begin questionnaire construction by copying existing instruments, or by culling items from them on the basis of what seems to make sense, but by first thinking about the survey content and the issues that one wants to address in the survey. After one has arrived at clearer ideas about the questionnaire's content, one may still look for existing scales or items that can be used or that could complement the items one has.

Interviewing Senior Leaders to Create Survey Content

One basic approach to building survey content is to conduct interviews with organizational stakeholders, such as senior leaders, managers, and employees. Historically, the interviewer or group facilitator would present potential survey items and then ask "What items would you want us to use in the ES?" This often encourages considerable debate over matters that are better addressed by survey experts (e.g., the wording of items, the number of normative items). We have found that everyone's time is better utilized when stakeholder groups discuss important issues for inclusion in the survey, and not survey items.

When working with companies that are developing their first questionnaire, we have successfully used "Blue Sky Sessions" to guide content development and increase top-level commitment. Senior leaders, for example, would be introduced to a tablet resembling Figure 4.1. This scheme is based in part on business practices that

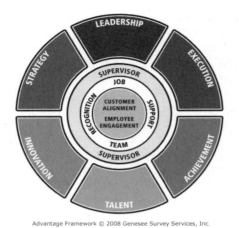

Advantage Framework © 2008 Genesee Survey Services, Inc.

Figure 4.1. A strategic framework for considering survey content.

have been found to be important for lasting business success (Collins, 2001; Joyce, Nohria, & Roberson, 2003): A clearly stated, focused strategy; flawless operational execution; a performance-oriented culture; a fast and flexible organization; recruitment and development of talented employees; leaders committed to the business; innovative products and procedures; and company growth. The framework reduces these to six broad, macro-level practices and links them to the individual employee level using the immediate supervisor as the conduit. Employees directly observe the effects of these practices on their job, including the support they receive, teamwork they experience, and recognition they receive. It is within this context that employees evaluate their own level of engagement and contribution to pleasing customers.

After briefly explaining the diagram, a facilitator guides discussion of these issues within the company at this time, much like a SWOT analysis. Each leader writes out ideas for each of the practices, and after reviewing the ideas, they vote for what they consider the two most important practices. By the end of the session, the facilitator has recorded specific input on each critical element of the framework and the voting results for which elements are most important for the company's success at this time. This format can be repeated with other stakeholder groups. From this process, the survey designer can create survey items to reflect the priorities of the stakeholder groups.

The outcomes of such sessions depend, however, on the quality of the facilitator. What is needed is a facilitator who is successful in "muddling with a purpose" (Wrapp, 1967). That is, the facilitator must have a clear notion of a balanced ES questionnaire in mind when he or she enters the session, and must be striving to reach this goal in a flexible way. At the same time, he must be open for interesting topics or ideas that are generated by the session's participants; in particular those that promise to support the goals of the ES project. The facilitator may even suggest ideas that can stimulate the participants' thinking, in particular if the discussion tends to become unproductive. For example, Lowenstein (2006) reports a surprising, but consistent gap between employees' perceptions and their customers' perceptions of customer service. Companies often waste effort by focusing their customer service efforts on functionality of the product or service, which customers consider basic and expected. In contrast, customers remain loyal to a brand or service based on trust, communication, anticipation of needs, and collaboration/interaction with the company—all of

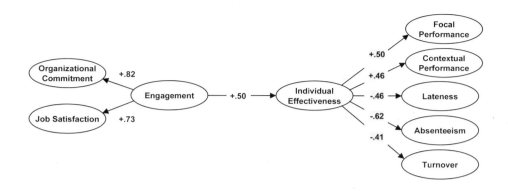

Figure 4.2. A model relating engagement and individual effectiveness (after Harrison et al., 2006)

which can be addressed via customer and employee surveys. Thus, this framework builds a survey that assesses two measures of success and employees' perceptions of contextual issues, including issues that directly affect employees and broad issues that correspond with senior level interests.

An ACE Hierarchy to Guide Questionnaire Construction

A less customized method for content development is to approach item construction through empirically supported research models. Consider the model shown in Figure 4.2, which shows the (slightly reworded) main result of a large meta-analytic study by Harrison, et al. (2006) on the relationship of two core constructs of I/O psychology, job satisfaction and performance. A sheer endless number of studies on these two constructs and their relationship had found no consistent relationships and often small correlations. The obvious way to explain this disappointing result is to point out that one needs to measure and relate the right indicators of satisfaction and performance, in particular those that are not restricted by various external context variables not under the employee's control. Harrison, et al. (2006) suggested just the opposite approach to more differentiation, i.e., to look at *larger* constructs that cover job satisfaction and performance comprehensively. Their final model (i.e., the one that best explained the data) shows two core constructs, engagement[8] (called "overall job attitude" by Harrison, et al.) and "individual effectiveness" (i.e., the difference that an individual makes in an organization). The former has two indicator constructs, job satisfaction and (affective) organizational commitment. The latter has three types of indicators: in-role performance, contextual performance, and three forms of with-

---

[8] Engagement is here understood as a notion that blends several familiar constructs such as job involvement or organizational commitment into one "higher order job attitude construct" (Newman & Harrison, 2008, p. 32). Engagement can be defined as the employee's *attitude* to promote the organization's goals through any behavior within and beyond his or her work roles.

drawal behavior (lateness, absenteeism, and turnover). One notes that engagement strongly predicts individual effectiveness ($r=.50$).

The construction of an ES questionnaire can start from here. Find, in particular, items that measure job satisfaction and commitment. They are *known* to predict individual performance in its widest sense ("individual effectiveness"), incorporating in-role performance as well as context performance and withdrawal behaviors. You may also consider adding some items that directly assess one or more constructs on the right-hand side, such as the employee's turnover intention. In any case, you end up with items that need no further justification.

Yet, the Harrison, et al. (2006) model is still too narrow. As we have seen above, engagement as such is not sufficient for performance that makes strategic sense. Indeed, every employee can be highly engaged, but if everyone pursues different goals, the overall productivity can be null.

Schiemann & Morgan (2006) proposed a wider model they call the *ACE model*, where the E stands for engagement in the sense of organizational commitment and work involvement, A means alignment (with the business strategy), and C stands for capabilities (to deliver customer value). The idea is that these three components, in a proper mix, capture "people equity," i.e., what is important to make a company successful from an HR perspective. If we combine the A and the E, we arrive at the notion of *aligned engagement*, where alignment can be interpreted in the sense that the individual employee has incorporated or is in agreement with the company's business goals, customer orientation, quality standards, and corporate values (O'Reilly III et al., 1991; Schwartz, 1999; Borg, 2006b). The ACE model can be used to identify important content domains that the ES should cover.

One can combine the Harrison, et al. (2006) model with the ACE model in the sense that two more constructs, E and C, are added to Figure 4.2, both pointing at individual effectiveness. Then, A, C, and E can each be related to indicators (subconstructs, scales, indices, or items) and, indeed, to a *hierarchy of indicators* that measure the core constructs in more or less differentiated ways, whatever appears sensible and actionable. Figure 4.3 shows an example that sketches how one could embed the ACE notions into a hierarchy of constructs and items. Where one wants to use items to measure a construct rather globally, or where one wants to split up a construct into smaller subconstructs, depends on the positioning of the survey. Sometimes, particular topics need to be measured in detail, and sometimes a few items or just one item yield sufficient information. Job satisfaction, for example, can be subdivided into such subscales as satisfaction with working conditions, supervisor, coworkers, pay, and company, respectively, and each subscale can be build from a set of individual items (see, e.g., Liu et al., 2004). In other cases, a single item on overall job satisfaction (as, e.g., the Kunin item in Figure 1.1) is sufficient. If so, one has room to measure the topics in more detail. However, what one should *always* measure (reliably and validly), is alignment, engagement, and capabilities.

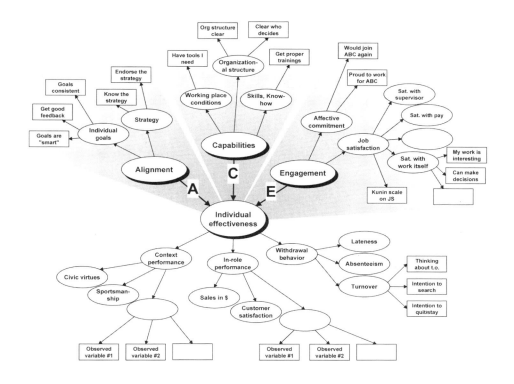

Figure 4.3. A hierarchy of constructs (ellipses), ES items (rectangles in upper half), and dependent external variables (rectangles in lower half)

Using ACE to Construct Indices

The ACE formula and hierarchy are useful in practice, because they bring some order into the usual survey topics and, thus, make it easier to design (and to interpret!) the survey. However, it is not always easy to agree on the indicators of A, C, and E. The C category, in particular, is a rather wide notion. It encompasses everything that employees who know their goals and who are motivated to achieve them cannot control or cannot change easily but that can be decisive for goal achievement. One can argue, for example, that C depends on the employees' skills and know-how; their technical working conditions; their organizational working conditions (clear work processes, access to needed information, amount of bureaucracy, etc.); but also on the cooperation and the cohesion within the workgroup and across workgroups; and the opportunities for them to implement ideas and change. Thus, C can have many facets. An overall C-index is, therefore, not easy to interpret if it is computed in the usual additive-compensatory way, because poor scores on some facets can be compensated for

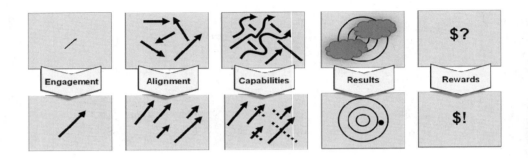

Figure 4.4. The five constituents of the RACER model and their goal states.

by good scores on other facets. Of course, this can be changed by constructing the overall C-score so it jumps to "red" if one or more of its sub-dimension scores are below predefined minima. The disadvantage of this approach is that it makes the ACE notion more complicated and more difficult to explain and to work with.

From ACE to RACER

Simplification always comes at a price, and the ACE formula may be a bit too condensed. It captures essential elements that "get the employees going," but it does not measure that clearly how employees keep track of the effects of their behavior and what keeps them going: Do they see the results of their efforts? Do they receive proper feedback from supervisors, from customers, and from other sources? Do they get proper rewards for good performance? Does poor performance lead to negative consequences? Since these questions are important for effective people management, it is worthwhile to extend the *Performance = f(ACE)* notion to the RACER model, where the R's stand for *recognizing results* (feedback on one's work, seeing the results of one's efforts) and for *receiving rewards* (material rewards, social-emotional rewards, additional opportunities, more interesting work, etc.), respectively. These five constituents of performance and the conditions one wants them to be in can be represented in a pictorial form that helps in communicating and discussing them (Figure 4.4). The formula expression is S*ustained Performance = f(RACER)*. Expressed in words: Aligned engagement, combined with the necessary capabilities, that generates behavior whose effects are clearly seen by the employee him- or herself (and by others), and that is rewarded appropriately. This would translate into ACERR, but RACER is not only easier to memorize, but it also expresses that the R elements—at least the rewards—feed back onto both E and A. Hence, embracing ACE with two R's adds a systemic flavor to the formula. This, finally, leads us to the *PS motor*, a more differentiated theory of work performance and job satisfaction, which we discuss in the following.

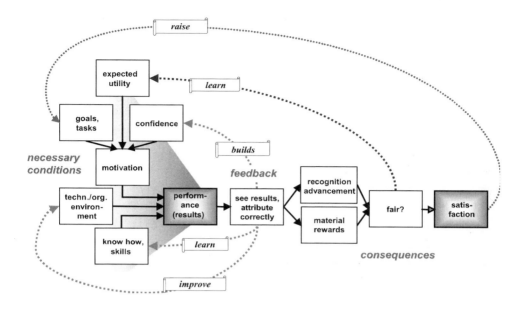

Figure 4.5. The simple performance-satisfaction motor.

The Performance-Satisfaction Motor

Most employee surveys cover a common core of standard issues. These issues are the "eternal" topics of employees working in a job and of managing people to do what they are supposed to do. To make sure that one covers what needs to be covered, one needs a comprehensive theory on these core issues. Figure 4.5 shows such a theory, the *performance-satisfaction motor* (PSM; Borg, 2003). The PSM is particularly suited as a foundation for an ES because it builds on topics that are of interest to different stakeholders: Performance, of course, is the prime interest of managers, and satisfaction is the main concern of employees and works councils. Moreover, almost everyone believes that satisfaction and performance are related in some way, and most think that satisfaction drives performance. So, to justify one's content selection by recurring to such "obviously" important foundations makes it easier to convince the various stakeholders that the issues were not picked arbitrarily but rather for solid theoretical reasons.

The PSM combines a number of psychological laws into one system of interdependencies (e.g. Thorndike's Law of Effects (1911) or Locke & Latham's goal setting theory (1990)). To explain the PSM to managers, one can start with the element they are most interested in, namely the box "performance (results)" in Figure 4.5. The flow-chart shows that there are three types of components that lead to this box and that are, therefore, the necessary conditions for (in-role) performance: Skills and competencies (Do the employees have the necessary skills and competencies to deliver the results that are expected of them?), the organizational and technical environment (Do they have the equipment they need? Is work organized such that they can be productive?), and the effort that they put into their work. Performance will be low if either of these preconditions is deficient. Hence, it makes sense to ask a few questions that allow one to diagnose the state these domains are in and whether there are any problems that need to be fixed. Such questions are easy to find for the organizational and technical working environment, and a bit more difficult for skills and competencies—here, the emphasis could be more on trainings and education—and quite difficult for effort. It would make little sense to simply ask "Are you willing to work hard?", because most employees would probably answer "Yes, but it is not my fault that …," pointing to the circumstance that make results difficult. However, what one can do is ask about the conditions that generate work effort: Do they understand what is expected of them? (If not, the desired results would only happen by chance.) Do they believe that they can do it? (If not, they would not even try.) Do they believe that working hard or not hard has consequences of some value? (If not, why work, unless the work itself is intrinsically rewarding.)

The measurement of performance results itself is usually not part of an ES. One could only ask the respondents to self-rate their own performance, but this is almost never done, because the validity of such ratings is dubious and, in particular, since such ratings would change the climate of the survey. However, one may consider whether other data sources exist that could be linked to the aggregated survey statistics (e.g., sales performance statistics for groups of employees in sales or withdrawal statistics such as sickness rates for workgroups in production sites).

What an ES should address, on the other hand, is whether the individual employee can see the results of his or her own work, and whether these results are correctly understood as the outcomes of his or her work. Indeed, many surveys have shown that this is by no means guaranteed. Employees often complain about not getting any feedback on their efforts, because, for example, they never see the final product or because their supervisor does not provide "smart" feedback (specific, motivating and constructive, on achievable goals, relevant with respect to their goals and tasks, and close in time). Being able to adequately assess one's own results is necessary for learning, for building realistic self-efficacy beliefs, and for seeing what needs to be improved in one's work environment.

The issues that follow work results and seeing work results in the PSM are the consequences related to these outcomes, positive consequences (rewards) or negative consequences (punishments). There are intrinsic rewards and extrinsic rewards (material, social-emotional, and cognitive ones). All of them can be measured in the ES questionnaire. One can ask, for example, how interesting the employee finds his goals and tasks (intrinsic rewards), how satisfied he or she is with his pay or with job security (material rewards), or whether he or she feels that better performance leads to better chances for professional trainings and for getting more interesting tasks (cognitive rewards). One can also ask to what extent the employees feel that rewards and punishments depend on performance. Such beliefs, in turn, influence the effort they put into their work, which is shown by the feedback loop termed "learn what to expect" in Figure 4.5.

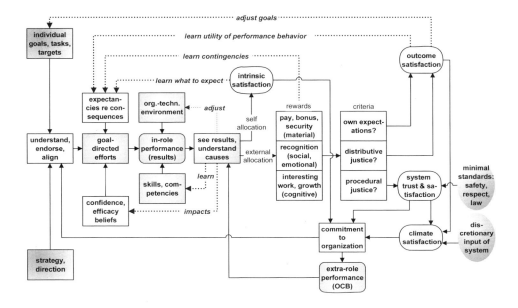

Figure 4.6. The extended performance-satisfaction motor.

Next, the PSM shows that all consequences are evaluated in terms of appropriateness, fairness, and justice. Many questions can be asked on these issues. If employees feel, for example, that their pay is commensurate with the type of job they have, similar to what they would get elsewhere for the same type of work, and fair in comparison to what others are getting, then they would arrive at an overall positive assessment of their pay. In the end, more or less satisfaction with pay (or other job facets) will result, and this satisfaction can, in turn, lead to employees setting new goals for themselves.

The PSM in Figure 4.5 does not cover some issues that are important for employee surveys such as the employees' organizational commitment. One way to augment the PSM with such variables is by throwing them into the PSM's "background." Another approach is to expand the PSM so that these extra variables become part of an enlarged PSM (Figure 4.6). Doing this, the notion of "satisfaction" from Figure 4.5 now becomes *outcome satisfaction*, because it builds on the rewards given for the work outcomes produced by the employee. However, in the expanded PSM, three additional forms of satisfaction arise. One of them is *system satisfaction*. It results from the employee's assessment of how the organizational systems work: Are rewards distributed fairly? Are procedures and rules transparent, reliable, and are they handled in a just way? Are "psychological contracts" kept or are they violated? System satisfaction also depends on a number of variables that are not related to work and performance, namely certain minimal standards that the organization is expected to adhere to such as making sure that work is safe or not asking employees to break the law.

System satisfaction together with *climate satisfaction* generates (affective) organizational commitment that, in turn, leads to a second form of performance, i.e., extra-role performance (also called context performance, pro-social behavior, or organizational citizenship behavior). This type of performance is discretionary performance such as behaving altruistically (e.g., voluntarily helping others even if you get "nothing" for it), carrying out task assignments conscientiously and even going beyond the call of duty, exhibiting courtesy, showing sportsmanship and fairness, and living civic virtues such as responsible participation. These behaviors are obviously important for the functioning of an organization and should not be overlooked. The PSM approach makes sure that one does not miss them by error.

The PSM also shows a number of feedback loops. For example, if high work efforts reliably lead to better results, and these then to better rewards, employees develop enhanced self-confidence and higher outcome satisfaction, leading them to set higher goals. Mealiea & Latham (1996) refer to this phenomenon as the "high-performance cycle."

It is easy to see how the PSM can be useful in guiding the definition of content domains that the ES should address. It is like wanting to tune a motor for better performance. In order to do this, one must *focus on the whole system*, not just on a particular subset of its components. Just installing "golden spark plugs" into a motor would not help: Rather, one should make sure that no single component is poor and that all components together generate the highest possible performance. In order to do this, you must know how well the essential components function. If you forget an important component, you may never be very successful.

Using the PSM to define the content domains for the ES also anticipates a particular way of analyzing the survey results. The results should serve to show where the performance-satisfaction system needs to be fixed and where it can be tuned. The PSM also shows what leads to what. For example, if the feedback component in the center of the PSM is weak, then the performance of the entire system will be negatively affected. Hence, it is easy to see that good functioning of this element is vital. One does not need to ask the employees, for example, whether they feel that performance feedback is "important" or not. Rather, the survey results are like the lab results in medicine: The doctor knows how to interpret the various pieces of information within a well-researched theory that shows what is important for what, and that thus gives the information its meaning.

Using Company Scorecards to Identify Measurement Fields

In today's competitive market economy, it becomes increasingly important to compare ES data to strategic scorecards that guide a company in its longer-range efforts. A popular approach for assessing a company's strategic strengths and weakness is the Balanced Scorecard (Kaplan & Norton, 1996). The BSC not only measures a company's financial strength, but also customer satisfaction, the shape the company's business processes in (efficiency, productivity), and the company's strength on innovation and learning. The BSC argues that managers must keep an eye on all these measurement fields, not just on the "bottom line" (i.e., profit). However, the measurements that are typically collected for the BSC remain one-sided and focus mainly on hard facts (e.g., EBIT or earnings before interests and taxes to measure financial strength; number of complaints about products and market share to measure customer satisfaction; products per employee and time period to measure productivity in production sites). Typically, the only exception is customer satisfaction, where market share or the number of complaints are complemented by directly asking the customer in market research studies. There are also attempts to somehow map employee satisfaction into the measurement fields of the BSC (Kaplan & Norton, 1996), or to add a fifth measurement field for that purpose (Olve, Roy, & Wetter, 1997). Yet, doing this it has been essentially overlooked that *every* one of the four measurement fields of the BSC has two sides—one with *hard* facts and one with *soft* facts. This is easy to see if one takes the perspective of an investor. Assume you consider buying stocks from company ABC. You would be pleased to learn that the company makes money, but how would you react if you learned that the employees were highly dissatisfied with their pay? You probably would be hesitant to buy stocks from this company because the employees are likely to demand more money at some time, which has obvious implications for the company's earnings. It may also happen that the best employees decide to leave the company, which has the same effects. Similarly, customer satisfaction has an employee side: Do the employees actually know who is their customer? Do they know about customer satisfaction? Do they have the means to satisfy customer needs? Do they feel that the organization is customer-oriented? In addition, when it comes to efficiency, an ES offers a way to ask the employees about problems, bottlenecks, red tape, and inefficiencies in their working environment. Innovation/learning also has its soft side; the ES may show that employees feel that suggesting ideas does not pay, that it is difficult to suggest innovative ideas, or that new ideas are not readily accepted by their supervisors. Indeed, this soft side may provide better *leading indicators* (i.e., indicators that predict the future rather than measuring what happened in the past).

The measurement fields of a company strategy card such as the BSC can thus be used as a springboard for constructing the content of an ES questionnaire. As with any of the models discussed, picking content domains on the basis of such a system also anticipates a particular method to later look at the results of the survey. What one wants to know from these results is what they say about the strength of a company with respect to the measurement fields of its scorecard—viewed from the perspective of those who are key in producing the hard data.

The Various Functions of ES Items

The items in most social science surveys have just one function: They are there to measure an issue. In an ES, an item can have many more functions. While measurement is the dominant function, additional functions should be considered when assembling an ES questionnaire, and some items may not even have a measurement role at all.

Measurement items assess perceptions and attitudes with a maximum level of scientific rigor, in a reliable and valid way. For instance, the item "I am seriously considering leaving the company within the next twelve months" is frequently used in an ES to assess the employees' turnover intentions. The percentage of employees endorsing the item should be predictive of the percentage of employees leaving the organization within a 12-month timeframe, provided they are marketable and no particular efforts are made to retain them. The item "I am interested in working part-time if program X is offered" is also a measurement item. Through its use, the HR department can gain information about the number of employees who would consider working part-time if certain programs were in place. This information can then be used to estimate the organizational consequences of offering particular part-time programs.

Placement items convey a message or simply put an issue on the agenda. In one French automobile company, for example, we used the item "I would support having our sales organization restructured into profit centers." We used the item even though it was clear before the survey that few would know what that statement meant. Indeed, after the survey employees complained that this item was unclear and that no one really knew what "profit center" meant. Management apologized and proceeded to explain what they had in mind, finding an attentive audience that was eager to listen. Although the item seemed inappropriate in gathering information from employees, it was quite successful as a means of conveying information to employees.

Action items prepare employees for involvement in a particular issue later in the follow-up processes. A classic action item is "Given certain changes in my working environment, I could be substantially more productive." In most employee surveys, some 50-60% of the employees endorse this item, and another 20-30% partially supports it. Hence, from a measurement point-of-view, the item is useless because its results are predictable. However, it is easy to see that such a result empowers management to discuss later with their subordinates possibilities for enhancing productivity: "Most of you endorsed this statement, at least partially! So, let us discuss what can be done to enhance your productivity." Paradoxically, even if the result should be different and few employees actually do endorse the item (which is not likely), one could still embark into the same follow-up activity by simply pointing out that "Normally some 80% of the employees at least partially support this item, but not here. So, is there nothing that can be done to enhance your productivity?"

Reminder items ask a question in a way that conveys a message regarding who is responsible for a specific duty. Consider, for example, the following items from a manager survey: "I believe that ____% of my subordinates identify with the division's strategy." Although the item seems to assess the employees' identification with strategy, it also reminds the respondents of their responsibility to ensure their subordinates' identification with the company's strategy. The reminder function of an item can be even more subtle. Compare the item "I get the information I need to do a good job" with the similar item "I can get the information I need to do a good job." While the former item suggests that the employees can lean back and wait for someone else to provide information to them, the latter item makes it the employees' responsibility to seek this information on their own. This second item has a built-in reminder function or, possibly a placement function if an active role in obtaining information is a new emphasis for the organization.

De-biasing items are designed to reduce or eliminate an opinion bias. Most people feel that they could have predicted the results of any survey with a fair amount of accuracy. They are "not surprised" by the results, and may even find them obvious or trivial. The illusion is closely related to the hindsight bias, where any outcome seems obvious after it has occurred. To de-bias the minds of any skeptical managers, one can ask them to predict the results of some items: "Please predict what percentage of your subordinates will support this statement: I am satisfied with my pay." The predicted percentage can then be compared with the results, a method that can be shown to reduce the "I knew it all along" impression and make the results appear more interesting.

Placement items, action items, reminder items, and de-biasing items are item forms unique to employee surveys. Indeed, most of them make little sense in the social sciences or in market research where good measurement is the only thing that matters. In contrast, the ultimate purpose of employee surveys is improvement, not measurement. Thus, the traditional psychometric criteria may not be as relevant.

4.2 Standard ES Questions: The Individual Employee's Perspective

To make these points more concrete, it often helps to review a list of typical ES questions. They come from content domains that are usually covered in an ES, either because they yield the information requested by a theory as in Figure 4.5, or simply because they are important to employees. Leaving any of these issues out of the survey may be perceived as an attempt to suppress a sensitive topic ("Naturally, they don't ask about satisfaction with pay, because they want to avoid this issue.")

In the following, we show a (non-exhaustive but hopefully suggestive) collection of ES items that emphasize the perspective and concerns of the individual employee. These items come primarily from the vast research on job satisfaction, and one or more questions on each of these topics is often included in an ES. Such a "single item" would then be phrased, for example, as "Overall, I am satisfied with my [working conditions]." A single item might be complemented by one or a few specific questions that take a closer look at particular issues within the given content domain. The standard domains are detailed below.

Working conditions, addressing such issues as these[9]: Do you (i.e., the employee) have all the materials, tools, and supplies needed to perform your tasks adequately? Are these materials, tools, and supplies replenished as often as needed? Is your office or workspace sufficient? Is the level of noise in your working environment acceptable? Is the illumination of your working area appropriate? Are health and safety re-

---

[9] All of the questions in the following can be turned into questionnaire items by adding a "definitely yes, yes, undecided, no, definitely no" answer scale. It is also easy to reformulate them into statements to generate the usual Likert items that are typically used in an ES. For example, in case of the first question, one gets "I have all the materials, tools, and supplies I need to perform my tasks adequately", with the "Agree … Disagree" answer scale.

quirements observed in your working environment? Is your workspace kept clean? Are the working hours and the flexibility of working hours appropriate for you?

Goals and tasks: Are your work goals and tasks clearly defined? Do you know what is expected of you in your job? Do you find your job tasks interesting? Do you like what you are doing? Do you have sufficient authority to make the normal decisions needed to do a good job? Are your work goals in agreement with your personal values? Can you utilize your abilities and skills in your work? Are your tasks compatible with each other (or are your tasks in conflict with each other)? Are your goals realistic (or: achievable, motivating, specific, time-related, etc.)? Do you have a say in setting your goals? Do you actually set goals regularly with your supervisor? (Hackman & Oldham, 1976; Locke & Latham, 1990).

Advancement: How satisfied are you with your opportunities for advancement? Are you satisfied with the trainings offered for new tasks? Do you get sufficient opportunities to learn on a personal and task level? Are you given the chance to make an occasional mistake? Do you know what additional competencies you need to perform your job well in the future? Do you know what competencies you have to acquire to have a fair chance to be promoted? How do you assess the corporate training and development center? Does the company offer you the training you need? Does the quality of training meet your expectations? Are the training programs offered useful for you to better perform in your everyday tasks? Do you feel that better performance is increasing your chances for advancement? Are you satisfied with the opportunities for promotion in this function/area/subsidiary/company? Do you think that the promotion policies and practices in your work environment are fair and just? Do you believe that the advancement opportunities in this company are comparable to other workplaces? (Warr, 1987; Farr, 1993; Woehr & Roch, 1996).

Compensation and benefits: Are you satisfied with your pay? Do you feel your pay is adequate for the type of work you do? Do you believe that your pay is commensurate to what is being paid by other companies for similar jobs? Do you feel that pay is fair when working night shifts/in physically challenging tasks? Do you believe that other companies pay more money for the type of work you are doing? Do you feel that exceptional performance is rewarded accordingly? Is your performance appraisal transparent/fair/reliable/objective? Are you satisfied with the relationship between base pay and bonus pay? Are you satisfied with the benefits (health insurance, corporate retirement system, etc.) that you get? Do you know what benefits you are entitled to? Do you understand how your pay is allocated? (Lawler, 1971; Lambert, 2000).

Coworkers, workgroup, co-operation: Are you satisfied with your coworkers? Are you satisfied with the climate in your workgroup? Are there frequent conflicts within your workgroup? Do the members in your workgroup help each other if necessary? Can you rely on your coworkers when you work on a common project? Are your coworkers technically competent? Are your coworkers socially competent? Do all of your coworkers work as hard as you to reach your workgroup's goals (or are some of them free riders)? Do high-performers have a high status in your workgroup (or are they cut down by others)? Are individuals with different ethnic and religious backgrounds accepted as equal members of the workgroup? Is discrimination prevalent?

Does your workgroup receive sufficient support from other workgroups? Do the various workgroups in this company collaborate well with each other? (John & Mannix, 2001).

Supervisor: Do you know what your supervisor expects of you in your job? Does your supervisor sit down with you regularly to discuss and set "smart" (specific, motivating, achievable, realistic, time-related) goals for you?[10] Do you get good/smart performance feedback from your supervisor? Does your supervisor normally delegate task assignments in such a way that you know what he or she wants you to do? Do you feel that your supervisor is doing a good job on planning and organizing? Are your supervisor's attitudes/instructions/requirements/actions consistent (or are they contradictory)? Does your supervisor support his or her subordinates? Are you looking up to your supervisor as a role model? Do you like your supervisor? Is your supervisor treating you with respect? Does your supervisor encourage new ideas and suggestions for improvement? Is your supervisor actively committed to the workgroup's cohesion? Do you perceive your supervisor as an effective leader? Does your supervisor give his or her subordinates sufficient say in decisions? Do you get sufficient leeway to do your work (or do you feel the supervisor is micro-managing)?

Management: Do you feel that the executive management is pursuing a clear strategy? Do you feel that top management is competent to lead the company into a successful future? Do you feel that upper management cares about the company's employees? Does upper management clearly communicate corporate strategy in a persuasive, comprehensible way? Would you be able to explain the company's strategy to a new coworker? Do you feel that higher-level managers are really committed to the company? Is upper management encouraging innovation and improvement suggestions? Do you believe that the managers in this company act ethically and with high levels of integrity at all times? Do you perceive upper managers as role models? Do you trust the executive board? Do you feel that the top management is competent and knows the business? Do you feel that upper management is listening to employee concerns? Do you usually agree with management's decisions? Is management willing and able to correct decisions quickly if they need to be corrected? Does management provide the environment that your workgroup needs to be successful (possibly explain: sufficient resources/effective organizational structure/good work tools)?

Information: Do you feel sufficiently informed about corporate matters (e.g. policies/practices/decisions/strategy)? Are important decisions within the corporation/department/org unit quickly communicated to all employees? Is information normally communicated in a timely manner? Do you have easy access to information that is important for your work? How do you evaluate corporate newsletters/corporate TV/other corporate media? What are your primary sources of information concerning the company/department/your workgroup? To what extent is important information in this company/department/org unit communicated through the grapevine?

Company: Do you feel that your company is a good employer to work for? Do you feel that the different people and groups in this company cooperate ethically and reli-

---

[10] The way this question is formulated may serve as a transportation item. If the notion of "smart goals" has been introduced before in the particular organization, then explanations such as those shown here in parentheses can be dropped.

ably? Does this company keep its promises? Are employees treated in a fair and just way? Does everyone get the same chances and rights? Do you find the current climate in this company pleasant? Is your workplace safe? Do you think that your company is really concerned about employee well-being? Are you confident that your company has a bright future? Is your company a responsible corporate citizen? Do you think that your company has a positive image?

Organization: Are the organizational structures in your work environment transparent to you? Are the business processes transparent to you? Do they make sense? Are they lean? Do these business processes serve the customer? Do you know which persons you have to get in touch with if you need to get decisions? Do you frequently experience role conflicts (e.g., based on having multiple supervisors or based on working in multiple departments)? Do you believe that the recent restructuring efforts are beneficial for productivity/customer orientation/efficiency? Do you feel that employees have enough say in restructuring efforts?

Organizational commitment: Do you identify with this company? If you had a second chance, would you join this company again? Do your values match the values of this company? Do you feel that you owe it to this company to continue working for it? Do you continue to work here mainly to avoid negative consequences (such as loss of benefits, vacation time, or salary)? Are you concerned about the company's well-being? Would you recommend the company as an employer/the company's products to friends, family, and acquaintances? (Allen & Meyer, 1990; Meyer, Stanley, Herscovitch, & Topolnytsky, 2002; Macey & Schneider, 2008).

Job involvement, work engagement: To what extent is your job the center of your life? Do you derive prestige and motivation from your job? Is your job of central importance to your self-esteem? Do you look forward to going to work in the morning? Do you feel inspired by your job? Is your work challenging to you? At your work, do you feel strong and vigorous? Are you proud of the work you do? Can you continue working for long periods at a time? Do you feel 'enthusiastic' about your job? (Reeve & Smith, 2001; Schaufeli, Bakker, & Salanova, 2006; Shirom, 2003; Downey, Wefald, & Whitney, 2007).

The above set of questions is by no means comprehensive. Cook et al. (1981), for example, have collected about 3,000 items related to job satisfaction published in the literature (see also Fields, 2002; Silberman, 2002). However, even these 3,000 items are only a small fraction of all possible items. Indeed, it is easy to show that there exist an almost infinite number of such items (see Section 4.6, below). That does not mean, however, that it necessary to start from scratch each time one is planning an ES. The huge variety of potential ES items stems largely from the fact that one can modify any item in many facets that are often irrelevant (see Section 4.6). Hence, it always makes sense to consider using a set of "seasoned" items first, i.e., items which probably have normative data from other companies, industries, or countries.

4.3 Extending Standard ES Topics: Performance and Strategy

Most of the questions presented above represent topics connected to employees' motivation and job satisfaction. These topics have been a common part of employee surveys for over 35 years, and empirical evidence shows that these constructs are positively correlated with employee performance and negatively correlated with employee withdrawal behaviors (Judge, Thoresen, Bono, & Patton, 2001; Harrison et al., 2006). Yet, one can also address various issues related to performance and productivity more directly. Some examples are listed in the following, but this list does not exhaust all possibilities simply because many management topics come and go, often in new clothes. Thus, the following topics are not nearly as durable as the ones discussed above. They cannot be repeated year after year, but should be changed or adapted to support the present management initiatives and programs. Furthermore, some of these issues might be included for only some parts of the organization, but not in the part of the survey that goes to all employees.

Productivity: Is it common practice in your workgroup to base decisions on both costs and benefits? Do you understand the organizational structure well enough to be able to explain it to a new coworker? Do you know whom to contact if important decisions have to be made? Do these decisions come quickly? Are complicated rules and unnecessary bureaucracy making it difficult for you to perform well? Is the organizational structure supporting your tasks and goals? Do you think that this company's org structure is customer oriented? Do you have easy access to the information you need to do your job? Are performance standards supported by organizational and workgroup norms? Are meetings generally well prepared in advance? Are meetings generally efficient and effective? Do you think that resources are often wasted unnecessarily in your working environment? Do you feel that the present way to evaluate employee performance leads to higher performance? Is the culture in your work environment supporting high individual performance? Do you perceive that everyone in your work environment is truly committed to avoid unnecessary costs? Is there sufficient feedback on your workgroup's success to reduce costs? (Pritchard, 1990; Boyett & Conn, 1995; Lepsinger & Lucia, 1997).

Quality: Do you believe that this company/your department/your workgroup is really committed to high quality standards? Do you endorse the present TQM programs? Do you believe that the present TQM programs are reaching their objectives? Was quality (or just quantity) an important issue in your last performance appraisal? To what extent is your work output systematically monitored for high quality? In your working environment, is performing at levels of high quality rewarded? Does your supervisor pay attention that your workgroup produces high-quality work?

Change management: As you see it, is change in your working environment generally managed in a well-organized and systematic way? Do you feel that employees affected by organizational change are informed in a timely manner? Do you feel that you have enough say in decisions that affect your work? Do you understand the reasons for the [recent] change program [X]? Are you endorsing the [recent] change program [X]? If not, why not? (open question) (Kanter, Stein, & Jick, 1992; Howard & Associates, 1995).

Customers: What is your opinion: How do customers think about this company? Do you know who is your primary (internal/external) customer? Do you know the needs of your customers? Do you know any recent measures for improving the satisfaction of your customers? Do you believe that this company is doing all it can do for the customer? Are you doing everything you can do for the customer? Do you feel treated as an internal customer [by the HR department]? (Whiteley, 1991).

Strategy: Do you know the company's strategy well enough to explain it to a new coworker? Do you feel sufficiently informed about the company's strategy? Do you know what the strategy means for your work? Could you name one or two strong reasons why the strategy is as it is? Do you endorse the company's strategy? If not, why not? (open question) Can you name one or two things that could be done to make the strategy more effective? Can you name one or two things that could be done to accelerate the implementation of the strategy? Do you know what you can do to contribute to achieving our strategic goals? Do you believe that engaging in behaviors supporting the corporate strategy will be beneficial for you?

Innovation: Is the climate in your working environment encouraging innovation and new ideas? In your department/workgroup, are new ideas quickly accepted and turned into practice? Are new ideas encouraged in your working environment? Are you satisfied with the internal suggestion system? If not, why not? (open question) Are new ideas encouraged by your direct supervisor/middle management? Do you feel that this company is doing enough for innovation? Are you expected to take a calculated risk if necessary? Do you feel that it is often better not to voice new or innovative ideas? Would you get proper recognition for suggesting innovative ideas and improvements? Do you feel constrained by too many rules and regulations in your working environment? Would you describe your working environment as rule-oriented and predictable rather than as risk-taking and open to experimentation? (Amabile, Conti, Coon, Lazenby, & Herron, 1995; Amabile & Conti, 1999).

Projects: Do you feel that projects are managed professionally in your working environment/by your supervisor/by management? Are the project's objectives usually clearly defined? Are project teams usually equipped with the necessary competencies and resources? Does upper level management provide sufficient support for projects? When project teams are staffed, is recruiting and staffing a transparent process? Are project team members instructed adequately? Are they compensated fairly for their work? Do you consider working in a project a chance or extra-work? Is communication and cooperation among project team members normally working well? (Brown & Eisenhardt, 1995; Lewis, Welsh, Dehler, & Green, 2002).

Networking: Are you well-networked within the organization? Do you personally know colleagues who work in different organizational units and hierarchical levels? Do you know at least one person in the organization who is usually well-informed and can provide up-to-date information informally? Are you well-connected interpersonally (e.g., do you have personal friendships at work, have you cooperated with others in the past)? Is relevant information exchanged quickly in your working environment? In your workgroup, are employees normally willing to help each other adequately? Do you feel that your workgroup is sufficiently cohesive? Are there different interest groups within your working environment who are confrontational towards each other? (Adler & Kwon, 2002; Seibert, Kraimer, & Liden, 2001).

Mergers and restructurings: Are you concerned that the merger/restructuring can make your job obsolete? Do you trust management to handle the merger/restructuring to the best of the company? Would you be willing to relocate and move to another city if this is necessary to keep your job? Do you feel that you have sufficient opportunity to contribute to the changing organization? Do you know what is expected of you during/after the merger/restructuring? (Mirvis, 1990).

4.4 Extensions II: Further Psychological Topics

When running an ES, it can be useful to check whether the academic research in industrial/organizational psychology is focusing on "new" topics. Such topics can be interesting in their own right, but they also can anticipate topics relevant in corporate HR work and soft factor management of tomorrow. Care must be taken, of course, not to adopt too many of such new topics: The bulk of an ES questionnaire should always cover "eternal" topics (and not become too faddish), but new research may also lead to new accents for these basic issues. Here are some examples of "newer" topics that are not as central as those discussed above. They may lead to a few extra questions in the questionnaire.

Employee empowerment: Are you encouraged/enabled to make more/bigger decisions more often without having to refer to someone more senior? Are you encouraged to play a more active role in your work? Are you involved in taking responsibility for improving the way that things are done? Do you have sufficient autonomy in your job? Are you satisfied with the freedom you have to execute your work? Did you receive enough training to do what you are supposed to do? Do you feel that you should not risk anything and avoid making mistakes under all circumstances? Do you believe that your supervisor would support you in case you make a mistake? (Conger & Kanungo, 1988; Kanungo & Mendonca, 1992; Spreizer, 1995; Pfeffer, 1995)

Stress, strain, and burnout: Do you feel permanently overloaded with work? Do you feel burnt out by your job? Is your present job living up to what you expected it to be? Were the expectations that you had on your job disappointed? Do you feel you have good control over your duties, tasks, and schedules? Do you suffer from physical symptoms relating to job stress, such as chronic fatigue? Are you confident that you exactly know what your roles are? (Warr, 1987; Locke & Taylor, 1990; Nelson & Sutton, 1990; Kahn & Byosiere, 1992).

Organizational citizenship behavior (pro-social behavior, extra-role behavior): In your workgroup, is it always easy to find volunteers for things that need to be done on top? Are you satisfied with the extent everyone in your workgroup exhibits sportsmanship and fairness? Is helping others the norm (or an exception) in your working environment? Is volunteering for committee or project work the norm (or an exception to the rule) in your working environment? Are there coworkers in your working environment who feel entitled? Does everyone in your working environment treat corporate property with due respect? Are all of your coworkers willing to engage in behaviors they do not directly benefit from, but that may benefit others? Do all of your coworkers pass on necessary information (or do they tend to keep it to themselves)? Do your coworkers tend to complain about every detail? Does everyone in your workgroup attend important meetings that are not mandatory? (Organ, 1984; Brief & Motowidlo, 1986; Tsui, Pearce, Porter, & Tripoli, 1997; Van Dyne & LePine, 1998; Morrison & Phelps, 1999).

Job- and task-specific self-esteem: Do you feel that you are recognized as someone who counts in your working environment? Do you feel that others listen to you and take your opinions seriously? Do you get sufficient respect and acknowledgement from your supervisor/from managerial personnel? Do you feel overly controlled by your supervisor? (Pierce, Gardner, Cummings, & Dunham, 1989; Duffy, Shaw, & Stark, 2000; McAllister & Bigley, 2002; Judge & Bono, 2001).

Task-specific self-efficacy: Do you believe that you can make a difference in your work environment? Do you feel that you can influence what is happening around you (or do you feel like a "puppet")? Do you feel that there are too many obstacles that prevent you from being more effective in your job? Can you generally cope with the challenges of your job (or do you feel that too much is expected of you)? Do you frequently feel that you may not be able to reach your work goals? Do you often feel overloaded with work? Do you frequently face doubts about your global self-worth? (Thomas & Velthouse, 1990; Bandura, 1997; Judge & Bono, 2001).

Trusting the systems: Do you think that your performance is evaluated fairly? Is your supervisor trying to be as objective as possible in evaluating the performance of subordinates? Is high performance rewarded adequately (e.g., bonus payments, promotion, more interesting work)? Are you satisfied with the transparency of the reward systems? Do you have sufficient access to information about the reward systems? Do informal and subjective criteria play a major role in performance appraisals? Are voluntary contributions (e.g. voluntary extra-work in projects) adequately recognized and rewarded? Are decisions made so that all shareholders are fairly treated? Do you consider the administrative processes reliable and fair? Is the company's internal suggestion system considering every employee's suggestions independently of his or her status in the organization? Do you trust HR to keep your personal data as confidential? (Moorman, 1991; Mayer & Gavin, 2005)

Justice and fairness: Do you feel that your pay is fair? Is similar work performed within the organization compensated for similarly? When it comes to performance appraisals, do you think that circumstances you cannot influence are adequately taken into account? Are promotion opportunities the same for everyone (or are they discriminatory)? Do you feel that you are normally getting the recognition for good work that you deserve? Do you receive honest performance feedback from your supervisor? (Folger & Konovsky, 1989; Fryxell & Gordon, 1989; Greenberg, 1990; Moorman, Blakely, & Niehoff, 1998; Masterson, Lewis, Goldman, & Taylor, 2000).

Psychological contracts: Do you feel that in this company all explicit and implicit agreements between the employees and the company are considered binding for both sides? Can oral agreements reached with your supervisor/management be trusted? Is management committed to securing employees' jobs? Does management normally deliver on its promises? Are the things you were promised when you started working in this workgroup kept? Do you feel that the company is paying you adequately for the kind of work you are doing? Is it necessary in this company to make sure one is getting everything in writing? (Robinson & Rousseau, 1994)

Trust in leadership: Do you fully trust the executive board/senior management/middle management? Do you feel that top management has the vision and competency to lead this company into a successful future? Do you feel that top management has high ethical standards and high integrity? Do the managers in [your organizational unit/department/in this company] stick with their word? Are managers role models for employees' behavior? (Oswald & Wendt, 1993; Borg & Braun, 1995; Rousseau, Burt, & Camerer, 1998; Wicks, Berman, & Jones, 1999).

Winning-team perception. Do you feel that the company [your workgroup, your division, your subsidiary, etc.] can successfully compete with other companies in the same industry? Are your company's products and services really competitive? Do you feel that this company has a bright future?

Mobbing: Are you scared of your supervisor? Are your coworkers behaving inadequately (e.g., with sexually or racially discriminating or harassing behaviors)? Do your coworkers make your work more difficult than it needs to be? Are your coworkers, your supervisor, or your managers intentionally limiting your performance? Do you feel mobbed in your working environment? Do you feel you can turn to the HR department for help in case you are being treated unfairly? (Leymann, 2002).

Discrimination: Do you believe this company is ensuring equal chances for everyone? As far as you know, are the employees in this company protected according to the Civil Rights Act and the Americans with Disabilities act experiencing the same treatment as all other employees? Do you think that diversity is valued within this company? Have you experienced acts of discrimination from coworkers or supervisors, or have you observed others being discriminated against? If discrimination occurs, are sanctions enforced immediately or are discriminatory actions covered up? Do stereotypes threaten productive collaboration between members of protected and non-protected groups? (Woehr & Roch, 1996; Hall & Parker, 1993; Roosevelt Thomas, 1996).

Job security: Are you concerned about job loss? Are you concerned about losing certain positive features of your present job? Are you concerned about your skills becoming obsolete in the near future? Do you feel that the company cares if the employees are concerned about their job security? Do you think that you and your workgroup can increase the security of your jobs by high-quality work (or is this a management decision that has nothing to do with your work)? (Hartley, Jacobson, Klandermans, & Van Vuuren, 1991; Borg, 1992b; Staufenbiel, Kroll, & König, 2006)

Work-family and work-life balance: Are you satisfied with how you can balance your work life and your personal life? Do you feel permanently overloaded with work? Is your personal life suffering from extensive work commitments (e.g., long work hours, shift work)? Do you feel that the pressures at work lead to problems you are experiencing at home? Are you able to adequately plan your time to balance personal and work life? Does this company adequately support child care, telecommuting, and dual careers? (Thomas & Ganster, 1995; Lambert, 2000).

Again, the above list is by no means exhaustive and could be extended by various other topics. Moreover, many of the above topics overlap. Still, the number of possible questions is almost endless. Thus, in most employee survey projects, the challenge is not to find a sufficient number of topics, but to identify the topics and questions that cover issues that are currently most pressing.

4.5 Topics Not Suited for an ES

A useful criterion when thinking about a possible content domain for an ES is not whether or not that content is "interesting," but whether it promises to yield information that serves the goals of the ES or that can bring about positive change. While there may be some interest in the attitudes of gay and lesbian employees, for example, asking about a person's sexual orientation is not advisable. Not only might this question be illegal and politically incorrect, it also is not actionable. Similarly, it is common in the US to ask for an employee's ethnicity as part of the ES. Such a question is illegal in many countries, but even if legality allows the question, we do not recommend its inclusion unless the company is reacting to specific and recent racial issues. Likewise, we can think of few situations where an ES should include personality items (e.g., "Do you prefer going to a crowded party or reading a book alone?"). Personality constructs have been found to predict job satisfaction and various dimensions of performance (see, e.g., Warr, 2007). For example, extroverts are more satisfied with their jobs than introverts, perhaps explaining why sales representatives typically have more positive survey scores than R&D employees. Yet, personality questions may seem intrusive to employees, union representatives, and works councils. Unless these items yield *actionable* information, it is not worthwhile to include them.

Still, deciding whether an item is actionable or not is not always obvious. Some items become actionable in combination with other items. For instance, perhaps knowing employees' predispositions to change (i.e., openness to experience) can help determine how a company should induce buy-in for a new business strategy.

There are also cases where the action is less obvious. A production site might ask employees about their satisfaction with the current parking situation, not because they intend to solve the parking problem, but because they want to illuminate reasons why the issue is not a top priority. The item's purpose is to give management a chance to respond to the constant complaining, even if that response is only an explanation of why *no* action will occur.

Some topics should also be avoided because they are too sensitive at the given time of the ES. For instance, in times of recession, items asking employees about their perceived job security may be misinterpreted and lead to unnecessary concerns and mistrust ("Things are probably much worse than they tell us! Why else would they ask me whether I am concerned about losing my job?"). If, on the other hand, decisions—in particular, hard decisions such as downsizing the company—have been made by the company's leaders and top decision makers, then it makes little sense—

indeed, it is even unethical—to ask employees whether they are concerned about layoffs.

In the European context, where works councils and unions are strong, one needs to show why the company wants to know what it is asking. If the employee representatives can be convinced that this is ultimately related to work and the company's mission and strategy, then almost any question can be admitted. If not, it will be blocked. Of course, in some cases, it may be arguable whether a particular question does indeed relate to the employees' work context or not. For instance, questions pertaining to the employee's family situation or childcare may be directly relevant to job performance and satisfaction, but in many cases employees would perceive them as a threat to privacy. Thus, if there is no clear prerogative for including such an item, they should not even be discussed. One should avoid making the works council suspicious for no serious reason.

It is also necessary to avoid all control items. Control items are items similar or equivalent to previously asked items. Their purpose is to check the respondent's reliability or consistency. In most cases, employees detect such control items and react negatively. They either feel that this is an attempt to check their honesty or that the survey is a waste of valuable time. Either reaction can ruin the climate for follow-up change processes. Because the consistency of the employees' answers can be tested by other statistical means (e.g., by meaningful and predictable correlation patterns) or by content analyses (e.g., by asking whether the various results "make sense" together), there is really no reason to include the same or very similar item at multiple points in the survey. In addition, the large number of topics to be covered by an employee survey also prohibits wasting items on control questions. The biggest problem of those who construct an ES questionnaire is always how to keep it reasonably short, and any convincing argument to delete an item should therefore be welcomed.

4.6 Facets of ES Items

An ES questionnaire may contain both questions and items. Technically speaking, its typical item is formatted as a statement together with an agree-to-disagree rating scale. The respondent must pick a category of this scale as his or her answer. Any other answer (e.g., writing a comment on this statement onto the questionnaire) is considered inadmissible. Even if the item is formulated not as a closed item, but as an open item (e.g., "Is there anything else you want to say on that issue? If so, please comment in your own words."), there may be answers that would not be considered relevant and therefore not considered in further data analysis. What is and what is not relevant is usually only implicitly defined, but if the respondents properly understand the intended meaning of the question, they will normally try to provide only relevant answers. This follows from the logic of conversation (Grice, 1975; Schwarz, 1996).

To formulate content items more systematically and open-eyed, one can first consider the facets that such items should or could address. One can then decide in each case, whether the item should explicitly refer to each facet or not (Borg & Shye, 1995). The four major facets of ES items are:

- *Content domain.* Which content domain is the item geared towards (e.g., pay, work itself, or working conditions)? The definition of the item's content domain is the most important part of item development, and most items will be centered on a specific content domain.
- *Reference person/group.* Which person or group does the item focus on (e.g., the respondent him- or herself, his/her supervisor, or upper management)? An item can ask, for example, about the particular respondent's own satisfaction with pay, or it can ask about their coworkers' satisfaction with pay. In an ES, one usually focuses on the respondent him- or herself, not on other persons or groups.
- *Mode of evaluation.* Does the item ask primarily about emotions, cognitions, or behaviors? Questions that ask about the respondent's satisfaction with an object typically focus heavily on emotions (e.g., "How to you feel about X? Positively or negatively? Good or bad?"). Questions may also ask about the respondent's cognitive evaluation of an object (e.g., "Do you think that our strategy is the right strategy? If not, why not?") or their awareness of a particular issue (e.g., Do you understand our strategy?). ES items can also ask about behavior (typical behavior, past behavior, behavioral intentions, etc.). For example, one may ask the employees whether they had a one-on-one performance appraisal meeting with their direct supervisor last year. An example for a behavioral intention item is the classic question "I am seriously considering leaving this company within the next 12 months", together with an agree-disagree answer scale.
- *Timeframe.* An item's timeframe reflects whether its question refers to a point in time that lies in the past, the present, or the future.

Reflecting upon other, minor facets can provide further help in item development in the sense that one may or may not decide to stress these facets:

- *Responsibility allocation.* Which person or group is responsible for the issue that the item focuses on? For example, when asking "Do you get good feedback on your performance from your supervisor?", then obviously the supervisor is the person who is responsible for this issue. In the case of asking "Do you know the company's strategy?", then it may be "management" that is primarily responsible for what the employee knows.
- *Function of item.* What primary function does the item serve? ES items most often are there to measure something. Yet, ES items sometimes are also used in order to get employees to think about a certain issue or problem (e.g., "How to you like the plan for the new organizational structure?"). Then, items can serve to prepare a particular action (e.g., by involving employees into an issue), or their purpose can be to remind a certain group of people (e.g., supervisors) of their responsibilities.
- *Strategic aspect.* Is the item aligned with the company's strategic objectives? Does the item provide information relevant for assessing the current strength of

the company or for predicting future developments on strategically important issues (e.g., financial strength, productivity, customer satisfaction, or innovation)?

Each of the facets can be combined with other facets in generating items, leading to a theoretically huge number of items or, more precisely, item types. For example, by combining seven facets, Borg (2002b) generated a blueprint for ES items that distinguishes some 500,000 item types. For each such type (e.g., an item on content domain X, with reference person P, stressing mode M), many specific items can be formulated as the lists above demonstrate. Thus, it is easy to see that an ES will *never be able to address all issues that might be of interest*. Instead, the ES questionnaire design team needs to choose items that are most important and, if possible, items that can serve a number of *different goals at the same time*.

One way of doing this is to ask more comprehensive items rather than items that have a very narrow focus only. For example, instead of asking employees about their satisfaction with their supervisors, their coworkers, their pay, and their job tasks, they could be asked to just answer one item reflecting their overall satisfaction (e.g. "How satisfied are you currently with your job?"). Such an item specifies the reference group (="you," the individual employee), the time frame (="currently"), the evaluation mode (=emotions), while leaving the content domain very general (="your job").

4.7 Importance as a Judgment Criterion

Many employee surveys do not only ask how satisfied the employee is with a particular aspect of his or her work, but also how important this aspect is to him or her. Some surveys ask employees to make both a satisfaction and an importance judgment for each item. This not only doubles the number of items, but empirical research has found that—surprisingly—importance scores do not improve the validity of the results (Quinn & Mangione, 1973; Neuberger, 1974). The reasons for this finding are somewhat intricate, but they give us some useful insights into the psychology of responding to an ES.

Satisfaction and importance judgments are not independent of each other. Statistically, the two are slightly but reliably positively correlated (Borg & Galinat, 1987). That is, persons who are satisfied with a certain work aspect judge this particular aspect as more important than persons dissatisfied with the aspect. More detailed analyses reveal, however, that this positive correlation only holds true for individuals who are satisfied, slightly to strongly. For those who are dissatisfied, there are two different trends: A positive relationship and a U-shaped relation, depending on the content domain (see Figure 4.7). With the U-shaped relation, importance increases with both high satisfaction and high dissatisfaction. Mobley & Locke (1970) suggest that extreme satisfaction/dissatisfaction is possible only for content domains that are subjectively highly important. Thus, diagrams of both importance and satisfaction mean ratings are U-shaped because highly important job aspects allow for more scatter of the satisfaction scores. This would explain the left-hand panel of Figure 4.7. The right-hand panel needs an additional explanation: The person who experiences

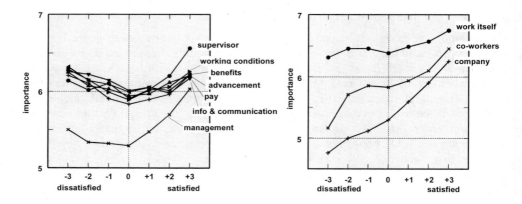

Figure 4.7. Average importance ratings for persons in different categories of a 7-point satisfaction scale (Borg, 1991b).

high dissatisfaction with something that he or she considers very important is forced to cope with an unpleasant dissonance. One solution is to solve the problem objectively; another one is to downgrade importance (e.g., "I never really wanted to be a millionaire anyway. Money is really not that important to me, after all."). Psychological research has found ample evidence supportive of this explanation (Borg & Noll, 1990; Borg, 1994).

Based on the above observations and considerations one can formulate a parsimonious model for these phenomena. The model assumes, first of all, that the answers an employee gives to the survey items are based on judgments that are generated, at least in part, in response to the researcher's question. Expressed conversely, the responses to the "How important?" and "How satisfied?" questions are not a mere reporting of crystallized attitudes that are directly available to the respondent, nor are they opinions taken from a "mental file drawer" (Wilson & Hodges, 1992). Rather, the model assumes that items such as "How satisfied are you with your pay?" and "How important is it to you to make a lot of money?" first lead to *cognitive activities* related to the object of the question. Expressed differently, the respondent would ask him- or herself: "What thoughts come to my mind when I think of my pay and of making money?" The thoughts, memories, and associations constitute a *mental representation* (Tourangeau, Rips, & Rasinski, 2000) of the object "pay/money." The simplest possible model of this representation is a feature set of affectively loaded ("signed") and affectively neutral elements. Figure 4.8 illustrates a case. It shows a feature set with twelve elements: Three elements are affectively neutral and nine elements are signed, five positively and four negatively. The model claims that a satisfaction judgment is a monotone function f of the difference of the number (#) of positive and negative elements in the feature set of the respective object: Satisfaction = f(# of positive elements - # of negative elements). The importance judgment, in con-

Figure 4.8. The mental representation of "pay" as a feature set (Borg, 2006).

trast, results from a monotone function g of the number of signed elements in the same set: Importance = g(# of positive elements + # of negative elements). The details of this model are less important here (Borg, 2006a). What matters is that one realizes that a survey response is not just a Pavlovian reflex. Rather, it involves cognitive processes and judgments. These processes may lead, for example, to a mental representation of the object where negative and positive elements are balanced. The answer, then, can be expected to be "mixed" but not "neutral." A "neutral" answer should result if no signed elements come to mind.

The interdependencies of satisfaction and importance judgments demonstrate how difficult interpretations of importance scores can be. Thus, one should not hope that asking the employees what is and what is not important to them will lead to an easy answer to the eternal question: "What is really important?" Rather, it often makes more sense to answer this question using multivariate statistics, for example, where one regresses certain dependent variables on a set of predictors. Another approach is to map the ES results into a theory such as the PSM (Figure 4.6). This is what a doctor does when he or she looks at the patient's lab results: For the patient, they are a mere array of numbers, but the doctor embeds these data into a knowledge network based on medical research and practical experience. Only in this context, the numbers acquire meaning and show what is and what is not important. Either of these first two approaches works well if the goal of the survey is to maximize satisfaction, engagement, or commitment. A third approach is to have importance determined by senior leaders before the survey is administered. As part of the design of the survey, senior leaders can evaluate content domain based on the business context (i.e., mission, five-year objectives, opportunities, threats). This approach works best for surveys assessing employee perceptions of the company's business and management practices (alignment, wasteful activities, understanding of strategy, etc.).

4.8 Typical Item Compilations

How many items should an ES consist of? There is certainly no one right answer to this question, but practical experience shows that most employee surveys consist of between 12 and 300 items. On average, employee surveys include about 60 to 70 items. Colihan (1999) reports a study with 31 international corporations, all conducting employee surveys regularly. On average, the companies included about 64 items, with the number of items ranging from 31 to 100. These numbers need to be interpreted cautiously, however, because they do not reflect the item type used. That means that 70 Likert items correspond to a relatively short questionnaire (in terms of the time required to answer it), while a questionnaire with the same number of items but with varying answer formats and many open-ended items would be a long one. Therefore, a general rule of thumb for the number of items is difficult to obtain. In case one uses mostly Likert items, as most employee surveys do, the following numbers of items can be taken as a first orientation:

- 50 items for measuring the most important performance and satisfaction topics
- 10 items for current topics
- 10 items for topics relevant on a regional level
- 5-10 items for managers only

Again, the number of items is not a good indicator of survey length. What matters is the actual *time* spent on questionnaire completion. For this time, one should not allocate more than 20 or, at most, 30 minutes. Obviously, whether a questionnaire satisfies this criterion can only be checked by empirically pre-testing the questionnaire with a sample of typical respondents.

The availability of benchmarks is another factor to consider when compiling item batteries. If annual versions of employee surveys are planned, the items chosen for inclusion on an annual basis need to be carefully selected and phrased independently of current trends.

Some employee surveys also use items to cover current "hot" topics. Other surveys include questions that are geared towards specific subgroups of the workforce only, such as the "for managers only" items above. Electronic questionnaires provide considerable opportunities to generate tailor-made surveys for different employee groups, while traditional paper questionnaires have only very limited capacities for group-specific items. In an electronic questionnaire, one can, for example, use demographic information collected at an earlier point to lead employees to follow-up questions that are unique for particular demographic groups. For instance, if an employee indicates he or she is part of a French sales unit, the electronic questionnaire can be programmed such that the employee is presented some items specific to the French sales unit (e.g., about the particular distribution channels used in the area). Thus, one can easily build *lean* "adaptive" questionnaires for each employee. They ask specific items but do not bother the individual respondent with a complex questionnaire layout with many "if's" (e.g., "if .. then go to item No. x" or "Answer this item only if…").

4.9 Demographic Items

Most items of an ES are content items. Demographic items (as illustrated in Figure 4.9) should be used only with restraint. There must always be a clear plan for using this information in analyzing the ES data. Demographic items make it possible to:

- *break down* the ES results by certain strata (e.g., showing the difference of attitudes and opinions of men and women, or of newer and older employees, or of managers at different levels and rank-and-file employees);
- *drill down* into the ES results to identify what the employees of particular focal groups said in the survey (e.g., employees in country X only, or in subsidiary Y, or in workgroup Z).

What must be decided ahead of time is whether such breakdowns and drilldowns are really needed. What we have found important is to be able to stratify the data by hierarchical level to arrive at manager vs. non-manager differences, and to drill down the data to any organizational unit where a certain minimum number of employees participated in the survey. Typically, such drill-downs are done hierarchically, beginning with the company as a whole, then moving on the major divisions, regions, countries, and so on, and ending with the individual workgroups. Hence, the position of the respondent in the organization's hierarchy and its organizational unit should be considered the minimum of what is needed in terms of demographic information.

The demographic variable that classifies the respondent's organizational unit needs to be *detailed*, *exhaustive*, and *reliable*. Thus, variable #5 in Figure 4.9 may be too coarse for a data analysis that satisfies even a minimum degree of differentiation. In large organizations, there are thousands of workgroups, and one must make sure that one knows to which workgroup each respondent belongs. This requires a methodology for collecting this information, because, obviously, one cannot offer the respondent a questionnaire with thousands of categories (see Section 5.10 for a solution). One must also make sure every demographic variable exhaustively covers all possibilities. The gender variable (#1 in Figure 4.9) is obviously exhaustive (for all practical purposes), while variable #3 may leave out some respondents in some organizations. To make sure that the demographic variable is indeed exhaustive, often requires a lot of attention. Regarding reliability, self-completion formats for collecting demographic information is not the optimal approach. Employees sometimes do not know the (current) "official" name of the organizational unit to which they belong. They may also make simple errors when filling out the questionnaire. They also sometimes fill out a category incorrectly on purpose in order to make sure they remain anonymous or because they are trying to be "funny" by indicating they belong to the company's executive board, for example. Yet, these technical problems can be avoided (see Section 5.10). What matters at the initial stages of drafting a questionnaire is to first decide on the demographic variables one needs for data analysis and for effective follow-up processes, and not be concerned with how to collect this information concretely.

1. What is your gender?
   - ○ Male
   - ○ Female
2. How many years have you been working for company ABC?
   - ○ Less than 2 years
   - ○ 2-5 years
   - ○ 6-10 years
   - ○ more than 10 years
3. Which of the following categories best describes your position?
   - ○ Manager with subordinate managers, board of directors
   - ○ Supervisor
   - ○ Exempt professional, without personnel responsibility
   - ○ Exempt employee, without personnel responsibility
   - ○ Tariff worker, clerk
   - ○ Apprentice
4. In which department do you work?
   - ○ Research and development
   - ○ Production/Quality control
   - ○ Marketing/Sales/Order processing
   - ○ Logistics/Warehouse
   - ○ Repair service/Technical training
   - ○ Support/Service
   - ○ Finances/Controlling
   - ○ Buying Department
   - ○ HR
   - ○ Administration/IT
   - ○ Company management
5. At which location do you work?
   - ○ Main Office
   - ○ Subsidiary

Figure 4.9. Some demographic items used in a small company.

5 Item and Questionnaire Design

After deciding on the substantive topics that the survey must address, the actual instruments for collecting the data have to be constructed. This means, first of all, that items have to be set up (i.e., particular questions together with devices that capture the respondents' answers to these questions). The most common type of an ES item is the Likert item, where the respondents are asked to rate a statement such as "I like my job" on a scale from "fully agree" to "fully disagree." Sometimes, an ES also uses open-ended items, where the respondents provide answers in their own words. For example, the item "What would be your one suggestion for improving the company this year?" would be accompanied by space for the respondents to write down their answers. The various items are typically sorted into item blocks that address different aspects of one particular topic. These item blocks are then embedded into a questionnaire that is formatted so that the respondents can answer it efficiently and reliably.

5.1 Closed Items with Rating Scales

One way of formulating questionnaire items is to ask a question and offer a scale of response categories. For example, one such ES item could be "To what extent are you informed about the company's strategy?", together with an 11-point rating scale ranging from "not at all" (coded as 0) to "very much" (coded as 10). Another item could be "How satisfied are you with your pay?" together with the rating scale "very dissatisfied" (-3) to "very satisfied" (+3). The first answer scale is *unipolar*, assuming that "not at all" is the least level one can be informed about something. The second answer scale is *bipolar*, assuming that satisfaction lies on one dimension that ranges from high dissatisfaction to high satisfaction (with "mixed" in between).

Items like these are common in public opinion surveys, but they are seldom used in employee surveys. Rather, almost all employee surveys use *Likert items*. Likert items first make a *statement* and then ask the respondents to position themselves with respect to this statement on an agree-to-disagree scale. For example, the above question on satisfaction with pay can be formatted as "I am satisfied with my pay", together with the 5-point answer scale "Fully agree – agree – undecided – disagree – fully disagree."

Various forms of Likert items exist. Some authors prefer 7- or 9-point agree-to-disagree scales; others use a 3-point answer scale. Different authors also label the categories of the answer scale in different ways. Other authors prefer to use a real question instead of a statement (Trost, Bungard, & Jöns, 1999). That is, instead of "My work is interesting" they ask "Is your work interesting?" together with a "YES – yes – mixed – no – NO" answer scale.

Virtually any question that aims at measuring the respondents' attitudes and opinions can be expressed in a Likert format. That means that most items of the ES can be formatted in such a way that they use exactly the same answer scale. This makes it easier to produce comparatively *thin* questionnaires than using items with many different answer scales. Thin questionnaires increase the likelihood of high participation rates and they also reduce the probability that items are skipped, particularly those at the end of the questionnaire. Moreover, using a Likert format throughout reduces the time needed to fill out the questionnaire or, expressed differently, allows to ask many items in a time window that is typically restricted to a maximum length of 20 to 30 minutes. Finally, Likert items lead to better data because they do not require as much reading and attention as items with specific answer scales: The respondents quickly get used to the agree-disagree answer scale and are then able to reliably answer many items in a short time.

Likert items, however, also come with some drawbacks. They produce results that can be questioned in the survey feedback processes (particularly, of course, if the results are "negative" and managers try to discredit the data). For example, one can discuss whether checking "strongly disagree" on the statement "I am satisfied with my supervisor" means that the respondent is simply "not satisfied" or that he or she is "strongly dissatisfied." Indeed, the respondent only strongly rejected the statement that he or she is satisfied with the supervisor. Nothing was said about dissatisfaction. Yet, these problems are really not as serious as they might appear to armchair theorists. To see this, consider the following case that not only illustrates this problem but also throws some light on what goes on when a respondent answers a survey item. In an ES conducted in a German company in the 80's, one of the authors used the item "I am very satisfied with my chances for advancement in this company" with the usual agree-disagree response scale. In a feedback workshop after the survey, one employee said this: "When reading this item, I thought that I should answer it by checking 'Fully disagree' because I am not 'very satisfied' but only 'satisfied' with my chances for advancement. However, I knew what you wanted to know, namely the extent to which I am satisfied or dissatisfied with my chances for advancement. Therefore, I checked 'agree' in the end."[11]

This anecdote also suggests that one should not word the statement in an extreme way. If one uses a graded answer scale, the respondent can adequately express the intensity of his or her response agreement by checking the relevant answer category. Items such as "I am extremely satisfied with…" or "I could not agree more…" are not needed.

Empirical research shows that unipolar items and Likert items on the same issue typically lead to similar results (e.g., similar mean scale values after adjusting the

---

[11] Occasionally, the opposite can also occur, however. The respondent may interpret the item very differently from what the questionnaire's author intended. To reduce this risk, items must not only be carefully formulated but also empirically pretested on a sample of persons similar to those for whom the survey is made (see Section 6.4).

results for scale length). Hence, they corroborate what the anecdote says: The respondents do not read the items literally and strictly logically. Rather, they *interpret* the items in the sense "What exactly do they want to know from me?" and "How can I express what they want to know on the given answer scale?" The item, thus, is really just an element of the *communication process* between the interviewer and the employee. This communication is normally governed by a certain *logic of conversation* (Grice, 1975; Levinson, 1983), a set of tacit rules that regulate the behavior of people in conversations. According to this logic, conversations proceed according to a "cooperativeness" principle. This principle can be expressed in the form of four maxims or ideals: Speakers are supposed to be truthful, relevant, informative, and clear. As a result, the recipients would assume that "communicated information comes with a guarantee of relevance" (Sperber & Wilson, 1986, p. vi), and listeners normally interpret the speaker's utterances "on the assumption that they are trying to live up to these ideals" (Clark & Clark, 1977, p. 122).

Number of Categories in a Likert Response Scale

Likert items most often use five or, sometimes, seven categories for their response scales. Using more categories than seven does not help to make the responses more reliable or more valid (Krosnik & Fabrigar, 1997). More categories unrealistically assume that individuals can make very finely graded distinctions, but there are definite limits to the number of categories humans can distinguish in general. The best known rule-of-thumb in this regard is the "Magical 7±2 Principle" which claims that humans cannot distinguish more than about seven categories at a time (Miller, 1956). Offering more categories (e.g., in a questionnaire where each respondent quantifies agreement or disagreement numerically with a number between +100 or -100) would lead to data that only seem more precise. Indeed, experiments show that respondents do not really use such a long scale, but rather pick from its categories only certain "simple" numbers such as 0, 25, 50, 75, or 100 and, thereby, effectively reduce the 100-category scale to a scale with only a few categories (Sudman, Bradburn, & Schwarz, 1996).

Conversely, reducing the number of categories to just three can cause other problems. Respondents may feel that this format forces them to express their judgments in an overly simplistic way or that it even attempts to manipulate them. This can lead them to quit participating. Hence, five categories is a good choice.

An additional and very important argument for using five-point Likert scales is that most employee surveys use this format. Therefore, almost all benchmark values available today are based on this scale.

The Middle Category of a Likert Response Scale

Likert items sometimes use four or six response categories, thus omitting the middle category. The respondents are therefore *forced* to decide whether they tend to agree or to disagree. Hence, if they have a true middle positions on such an item, they can either incorrectly express their opinion by choosing the mildest possible agree or disagree category, or they must skip the item. However, a respondent can choose the middle category also if he or she is not sure what to say or the item requires too much brainwork. This response offers a convenient way of *avoiding* the issue while still appearing cooperative in the survey (called "satisfycing" by Krosnick, 1991). Answering "undecided" is, after all, a legitimate response if this category is explicitly offered in the questionnaire. On the other hand, an avoidance answer adequately represents those respondents who have truly *no opinion* on the issue that the item focuses on. For the organization, however, there is no chance to find out whether picking the middle category represents a truly mixed opinion, an escapist response, no opinion, or merely uncertainty of the respondent.

Asking relevant questions that the employee can answer should reduce such ambiguities, but omitting the middle category does not solve the problem. It is also problematic in another sense: Employees should not feel that they are forced into giving certain answers. If they feel *manipulated*, they will complain and stop participating. Hence, it seems better to accept the possibility of receiving some possible avoidance answers on some items than risk a lower overall response rate.

On the other hand, "according to many seasoned survey researchers, offering a no-opinion option should reduce the pressure to give substantive responses felt by respondents who have no true opinions" (Krosnick et al., 2002, p. 371). This additional answer category is usually labeled as "don't know". It seems to offer a way that allows one to distinguish "undecided" positions—which can be strong relations as, for example, a love-hate attitude—from a "no opinion" position where the respondent is not able to generate any relevant thoughts or judgments.[12]

The labeling of the middle category should, in any case, clearly distinguish a response that belongs to this category from a "don't know" response. Good labels for the middle category are "neither agree nor disagree", "mixed", or "undecided", but not "?", for example. In case of attitudes, "mixed" seems to be optimal, because it describes one possible attitude composition (see Figure 4.8). The often-used label "neutral", in contrast, if taken literally, would characterize a "no attitude" situation, because attitudes are, by definition, affective dispositions, and "neutral affects" are really no affects. However, since not every item of an ES measures an attitude, using "undecided" or "neither-nor" are probably the labels that are optimal in general. Likert (1932) suggested using "neither agree nor disagree", and this category seems common in normative data sets in the US. Ultimately, either wording option is likely to work equally well if the employee population is used to seeing closed-ended survey questions.

There are also more practical reasons for using a middle category. It captures a set of employees who can be swayed with the right post-survey response, and seeing a large percentage of employees "sitting on the fence" between a favorable and an unfavorable response suggests that this area provides a substantial opportunity to improve the organization. One multinational producer of healthcare products has its survey leaders review changes in annual survey scores by their "migration" from one response to another to assess the level of decline or improvement.

---

[12] If one wants to admit such a "don't know" option, then it should be placed *outside* the Likert answer scale, because it does *not* belong to the agree-disagree continuum that the Likert scale uses.

Further, consider an item such as "In my working environment, there is much potential for improving the quality of work." Normative data suggest that at least 50% of employees will endorse this statement and 30% will give an "undecided" answer. Hence, one can tell the leadership team that only 20% of the respondents see no potential for improvement, while the rest of the workforce sees *at least some* potential. This interpretation helps to generate momentum for actions. More generally, the middle category offers a certain leeway for interpreting or at least discussing the results in a way that can help the follow-up processes. Thus, the right interpretation of a middle point can add an extra dimension when the ES is used as an instrument for change management.

Using "Don't Know" Categories and no Middle Categories

Some authors (e.g., Converse & Presser, 1986) recommend skipping the middle category, but adding a "Don't Know" (DK) answer category to capture "no opinions." However, experimental research by Krosnick et al. (2002) shows that the DK category may play a more complex role in surveys: "Attraction to no-opinion options was found to be greatest among respondents lowest in cognitive skills ..., among respondents answering secretly instead of orally, for questions asked later in a survey, and among respondents who devoted little effort to the reporting process. The quality of attitude reports obtained ... was not compromised by the omission of no-opinion options. These results suggest that inclusion of no-opinion options in attitude measures may not enhance data quality and instead may preclude measurement of some meaningful opinions." (p. 371).

Offering DK categories may also change the meaning of the entire response scale because it suggests—in particular if it is actually labeled with a "know"—that the respondent should be reasonably sure to give the "right" answer: if not, then choose the DK category! However, in an ES, most items assess opinions and attitudes, not facts. There are no right or wrong answers, but only honest answers. Hence, a better label for the DK category in an ES is often "not applicable".

DK responses remain difficult to interpret so one should not use them indiscriminately for all items. Rather, one should try to make sure that most items measure issues where almost any employee has an opinion or attitude, and that the items are formulated so that most employees are able to answer. Careful item construction and pretesting are the best methods for achieving this goal. Moreover, the instruction sheet of the questionnaire ("How to fill out the questionnaire?") and the general information about the ES should make clear what the respondent is expected to do in case he or she has a "tentative" opinion only (e.g., in case where he or she is asked to judge a new supervisor). The organization is interested to hear about this opinion too, of course, because first impressions, for example, also determine what people do. Only if the respondent has really no opinion at all, should he or she skip the item.

If one wants to know how crystallized the various judgments are, additional items (e.g., "How confident are you about your judgment?" or "To what extent have you thought about this issue before?") could be added. However, such additional items are almost never utilized in an ES because this issue is not important enough to merit additional items. After all, time is limited and each item for one purpose comes at the expense of an item for another purpose.

Note also that if DK categories are offered, respondents are likely to choose them more frequently than simply skipping items. In one survey that included DK categories, their frequency of use was as high as 30%. When the survey was repeated without the DK responses, but allowing the respondent to skip an item "in case you really have no opinion at all," non-response rates went down to about 5%. Weisberg et al. (1996) report similar results for surveys in general. Since an ES is supposed to involve the employees, promoting no responses or avoiding responses is not desirable. Indeed, an ES may even use some items that focus on issues where the employees do not have a stable or even no opinion. The purpose of such "transportation items" is not measurement, but putting an issue on the agenda to start a discussion. This purpose is thwarted if DK categories are offered.

Numerical Labels for the Categories of the Response Scale

The categories of a response scales often are given numerical labels, sometimes in addition to verbal labels, sometimes without such verbal labels. Such numerical labels may be necessary as, for example, in cases where the respondent must express his or her scale value numerically as in a telephone interview. In paper questionnaires, however, one can easily provide check boxes for the answers. There, numbers often serve only to make life easier for the data typists.

Psychologically, Guilford (1954) argues that such (integer) numbers help "to achieve greater equality of psychological intervals between categories" (p. 264). However, newer research shows that numbers *can change the meaning* of the scale categories. In a public opinion survey, Schwarz et al. (1991) asked "How successful would you say you have been in life?" This question was combined with an 11-point response scale that was labeled at the end points with "not at all successful" and "extremely successful", respectively. In addition, the scale categories were also labeled with numbers from 0 to 10 for one group of respondents, and with -5 to +5 for the other group. In the first group, 34% endorsed a category between 0 and 5, while in the other group only 13% endorsed one of the first six categories of the scale. The interpretation of this marked difference seems obvious: The minus signs apparently affects the meaning of the scale categories. In one case (=0), it suggests the total absence of success, in the other (=-5), it turns the meaning of the category "not at all successful" into an expression of complete failure. This example clearly shows that numerical codes can affect the scale's meaning.

Hence, not using numbers in addition to verbal labels is the proper choice, but if numbers become necessary, Hippler et al. (1991) recommend bringing "the numerical scale values in agreement with the intended uni- or bipolarity of the underlying dimension: Judgments on a bipolar dimension should be assessed with a bipolar scale that employs numbers ranging from minus to plus. Judgments that merely assess the intensity of a property without addressing its opposite should be assessed with unipolar scales whose values should preferably start with '0' to clearly denote absence of the property" (p. 61). In contrast, Guilford (1954, p. 264) suggests not using negative category codes: "This may be a more natural scale to some [persons] who are versed in algebra but it may be unnatural, if not bewildering, to less sophisticated [persons]."

We tend to side with this second point of view. There are many commonly used survey items with scales that are clearly bipolar even though they do not use negative scale values. For example, one sometimes uses a rating scale (akin to school grade scales) that ranges from "1=very good" to "5=poor" with a mid-point of "3=satisfactory." Employees (at least the ones from the US and Germany) know the meaning of these answers, and they provide a good bipolar scale despite the lack of negative numbers.

The coding of scales is complicated further by the fact that it is not always clear whether the scale is bipolar or not. For example, if the respondent rejects the statement "It is important to me that my work is interesting," one should conclude that he or she puts no particular value on "interesting" work, but not that he or she is *against* interesting work. In this case the agree-reject Likert response scale is only bipolar on the surface, but not in the context of this substantive judgment. Determining exactly what employees meant when responding to this item might be difficult. For this reason, someone with survey expertise should review new items as this person often can spot interpretation problems before the survey is administered.

In the great majority of cases, the formatting of the numerical codes seems to have little effect on employees' responses. However, this issue becomes more relevant when changing the format of a questionnaire from one survey to the next. Experience shows that such changes do not make much difference, provided the respondent understands what the survey is assessing. However, format changes may lead to lengthy discussions with the survey's recipients about the meaning of the results, especially if these results are not so positive for them.

5.2 Response Criteria in Items

Any item asks a respondent to assess an object or issue with respect to some criterion. For example, the object can be the respondent's pay, and the criterion is the respondent's satisfaction with pay. Another criterion can be the importance that the respondent puts on pay. Satisfaction and importance, in particular, are prominent criteria in employee surveys, but many other criteria are conceivable. For example, one can extend the notion of importance by not stressing "importance for the respondent" but by asking about "importance for the wellbeing of the organization." One can also consider different criteria such as "present state of object/issue," "desirable state of object/issue" or the "apparent improvability of object/issue." Obviously, there are many more criteria that can be combined with additional facets such as a particular time perspective (e.g., last year, now, next year, in the longer-range future).

Figure 5.1 provides an example where each of the survey items has two response formats: one for satisfaction and the other for importance. An obvious disadvantage of such a double rating is that it doubles the number of judgments. Because the questionnaire cannot be arbitrarily long, this means that overall one can address few topics

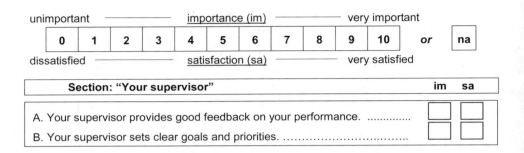

Figure 5.1. Excerpts from a rather complex questionnaire with importance and satisfaction scales awkwardly combined.

of interest. This is a serious problem because in practice one almost always is confronted not with a lack of interesting topics but rather with far too many. Importance items, moreover, are quite difficult to interpret (see Section 4.8) and yield little "actionable" information.

If one wants to ask importance questions, one should carefully consider how to format such items. The format shown in Figure 5.1 is one practical example that lends itself to discuss various issues involved in designing a proper format. Here, the respondents are asked to rate each statement both in terms of satisfaction and importance, and write their answers numerically into the "im" and "sa" boxes. In addition, a "not applicable" category is offered, whose meaning remains ambiguous (it could mean "not relevant for me", "don't know" or "don't want to answer here").

The example shows some technical problems. The satisfaction judgments reach from "dissatisfied" to "satisfied," creating a bipolar scale. The importance judgments, on the other hand, reach from "not important" to "important," creating a unipolar scale. In spite of this difference, the same "0 to 10" coding is used to express both judgments. The coding also begins with "0", which brings in semantic connotations, as was discussed above.

Another problem is using the criterion "satisfaction" for expressing all sorts of opinions and attitudes. The issue of whether the supervisor sets clear goals and priorities or not, for example, should better be assessed on the criterion "true or not true", and not on "satisfaction". Moreover, by repeating the criterion "satisfaction" over and over again in every item, the entire survey acquires an emotional overtone which can reinforce an overall *affective halo* (see Section 5.3) that affects all items.

Finally, one can critically remark on the format used in Figure 5.1 that responding by writing numbers into boxes means more work for the respondents than simply checking response boxes. In addition, such handwritten numbers are more difficult to scan and tend to differ over cultures. For example, Germans and Americans typically write the numbers 1 and 7 differently. While the Germans write the number 1 with a long upward line (1), the American write the same number typically as a single vertical line (|); for the number 7 one typically gets a seven with a cross-bar in Germany and a plain 7 (i.e., two strokes) in the USA. Hence, a German 1 can easily be read as

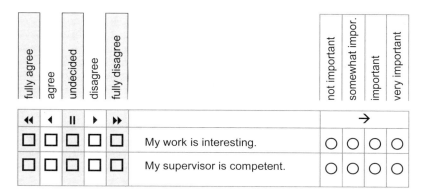

Figure 5.2. Excerpts from a questionnaire with a less complex combination of importance and satisfaction criteria.

a 7 by an American data typist or by an American scanner, and an American 7 is coded as a 1 in Germany. The example shows how easy it is to make simple technical mistakes when setting up items in a questionnaire.

Ideal solutions for all these problems are hard to find, but the format shown in Figure 5.2 appears to offer a better compromise. Here, the usual 5-point Likert scale is used on the left-hand side to assess opinions and attitudes with respect to the issues that the items address. On the right-hand side, a unipolar 4-point scale is used to grade importance judgments. A certain effort is made to also design the scales differently in their graphical appearance, so that the respondents more clearly see that they are dealing with different criteria.

5.3 On the Psychology of Answering Survey Items

Those who develop employee surveys seldom spend much time considering how the employees generate their answers to the survey. One common assumption is expressed by Tourangeau et al. (2000, p. 12) as follows: "Most attitude research seems to take it for granted that having an attitude means having a preexisting judgment about an issue or a person and that people automatically invoke these judgments when answering a relevant question..." Expressed differently, the tacit assumption is that attitudes exist somewhere in "crystallized" form. When asked for one's attitude toward an object, this attitude is directly activated by the question or the respondent has to find it in a "mental file drawer", and then simply reports it (Fazio, 1989; Wilson & Hodges, 1992).

A different theory claims the item asks for a judgment that is *generated* on the spot in response to the question. One way of generating such a judgment is to average the various positive or negative emotions associated with the components that make up the attitude object (Ajzen, 1988; Feger, 1980). To illustrate, consider the question

"How satisfied are you with your supervisor?" Once the respondent understands the question, she could be psychologically modeled as if she is going through a consideration process like this: "OK, I understand the question. Let me think. My supervisor? This person is quite nice. So, that is good. However, when it comes to clear goals, I am often lost, so, that is not so good... (other issues are reviewed). So, summarizing, I come to conclude that ..."

These two theories can be seen as extremes of one continuum (Fischoff, 1991). There certainly exist issues in an employee's work environment where he or she can produce a judgment almost instantaneously. Other issues may require some pondering before a reliable judgment can be given. Yet, even in the first case, the answering process cannot be understood too mechanically: It should not be conceived in the sense that a coin (i.e., the question) is inserted into a coke machine (i.e., the respondent) that then mechanically throws out a can (i.e., the answer). Certain cognitions are always involved:

- *Understanding the task.* The logical first step in responding to an item is to understand the question and its intent. The respondents should first read the instructions of the questionnaire, activate what they remember from the information communicated in the pre-administration campaign, add their assumptions regarding the ES, and so on. When the respondents consider the content of an item, they must first read it and form an opinion about what the item is assessing. It is quite possible for the employee's reading to be imprecise so that this person forms a faulty opinion about what the survey designer really wants to know. In any case, an item usually leaves a certain leeway for how one reads it. One reason is semantics, where the respondents can wonder about the item's words and meaning ("What does this mean? What do they mean by 'supervisor'? Who is this person?"). Another reason is pragmatics ("What does the interviewer really want to know?")
- *Activating relevant cognitions.* If the respondents want to give "honest" answers to the items—answers that truly express how they feel or think instead of just "some" answers—they must activate relevant memory traces. This means that some of the abovementioned mental file drawers are accessed to take out relevant pieces of information, or that a process of thinking about the item is triggered off in the sense of "What comes to my mind regarding this issue?" However, this memory search is limited, fallible, and carried out only as long and as deep as necessary to allow a satisfactory judgment, given the time constraints and the respondents' motivation.
- *Generating an overall judgment.* The pieces of the mental representation activated by an item are then sorted, prioritized, evaluated, and condensed into an overall judgment (see Section 4.7 for a model on how this could be conceived).
- *Reporting the judgment in the given format.* Finally, the respondents must somehow express their judgments. In case of an open-ended item, they can use their own words to do this, but in the much more common case of a closed item, they must map their judgments into the categories of the response scale of the item. Naturally, additional considerations may also come into play here. The respondents may *edit* their judgments and express them, for example, in particularly "drastic" terms because they hope that this might cause certain desirable effects.

Another possibility is that the respondents censor their judgments (reporting them in an overly positive way or not answering sensitive items at all), because they are concerned about anonymity.

Because employee surveys today always use more than just one item, the above processes become more complicated due to the order in which the respondents read or answer the various items. If the items are presented strictly one after the other (e.g., in a telephone interview or in an online questionnaire that shows only one item at a time), then the order of the items can make a major difference. For example, if the respondent first encounters the item "My pair is fair" and then "Overall, I am satisfied with my pay", he or she may infer (by the rules of the logic of conversation) that the second item means "everything concerning pay, except for fairness, because fairness has been covered already" (Strack, Martin, & Schwarz, 1988). Similarly, a series of "negative" items can induce a negative mood that affects answers to later items. What comes to the respondent's mind is a function of the content of the previous items and the emotions generated by them because they may increase the cognitive accessibility of certain information. Conversely, items perceived as overly optimistic can generate reactance: The respondents then become suspicious that this is some trick to generate positive survey results and react with extra-negative answers—or quit altogether.

The employees, moreover, bring a certain general mood to the survey. This overall mood depends to some extent on the employee's job satisfaction, but also on a lot of other things outside of work. Even the weather can have an influence (Schwarz & Clore, 1983). On the other hand, job satisfaction depends on his or her satisfaction with pay satisfaction, for example, and pay satisfaction is a function of how the employee feels about the pay's amount, its fairness, and on how it is related to performance, for example. There is a hierarchy of attitude objects, as shown in Figure 5.3.

Judgments on objects on higher levels of this hierarchy are formed by the respondent by aggregating over the things that come to his or her mind when thinking about this object (Figure 4.8). Yet, this bottom-up formation of a final judgment is not the whole story. Judgments on objects are also influenced by what "rains down on them from above." The rays emanating from the "general mood" cloud illustrate this. Similar top-down rays could be drawn from "general job satisfaction" to "satisfaction with pay" and to "fair", with decreasing intensity. The more general objects therefore form *affective halos* that radiate down on all elements in lower levels. This *sandwich model* (Borg, 2003) predicts that if general mood or general job satisfaction goes up, satisfaction with every single job aspects goes up too, and that this effect is the stronger the wider the scope of these job aspects. For example, if an employee is in a good overall mood, then all of that person's judgments of the supervisor (particularly on broad criteria) should be more positive than if the employee was in a bad mood. This sometimes leads to seemingly paradoxical findings. For example, satisfaction with pay may be quite positive, even though the employees are not particularly positive about any concrete aspect of pay (e.g., amount, fairness, increases). The halo model also explains why satisfaction judgments on the different job dimensions are always positively correlated among each other in a typical ES (Borg, 2001a; Spector, 1997).

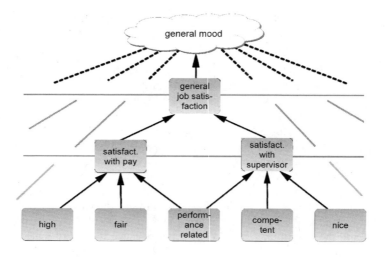

Figure 5.3. Scheme of the sandwich model for judgments on attitude objects.

When constructing the items for an ES, the sandwich model suggests not overloading the questionnaire with affective items. The widespread practice of formulating ES items in a "How satisfied are you with...?" format is an example of what not to do, because such item formats generate answers that are loaded with a strong general halo component and, thereby, yield information *blurred* by overall emotions.

That is not to say, of course, that one cannot ask questions on satisfaction. What should be avoided, though, is an overabundance of satisfaction items. Other criteria should be considered. For example, some items should have a cognitive focus, asking the respondent for rational judgments on specific and concrete aspects of his or her work ("factual items"). Other items can ask about behavioral intentions, about past behavior, or about events in the past. If only satisfaction is stressed, one should not be surprised if the various items tend to be highly intercorrelated.

5.4 Items with Qualitative Response Scales

Items with qualitative response scales are also used occasionally in employee surveys, particularly those that focus more deeply on a specific issue. An example for such an item is provided in Figure 5.4 (Domsch, 1985). Here, the respondent is expected to provide an answer by checking up to three statements concerning his or her professional advancement. The statements are not ordered in the sense that category x is "stronger" than category y. Formally, Coombs (1964) calls such an item a "pick-n" item (with $n<4$ here). They belong to a class of items that lie between closed items with rating scales and open items where the respondents provide an answer in their own words.

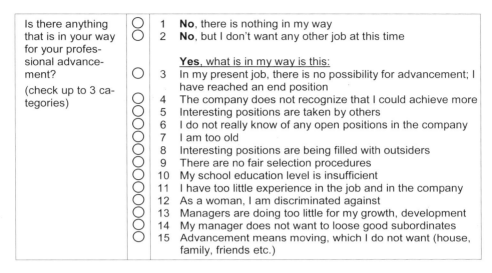

Figure 5.4. Item with a qualitative response scale (a German ES consortium).

Figure 5.4 shows the typical semantic chaos of a pick-*n* qualitative item. To answer this item can be quite a burden for the respondents. To reduce work, the respondents often proceed sequentially and check whatever seems correct until they either reach the end of the category list or until they run out of answers. Thus, the first categories in the list are more likely to be chosen, but the last ones also have an advantage because they too are relatively prominent when the respondent first screens the item to understand what it is asking.

The example in Figure 5.4 also illustrates another issue. It does not offer an "other" category or an "open" category where the respondent can specify further reasons for non-advancement in his or her own words. Such categories are not needed if the categories that are offered are *exhaustive*, but this condition is typically difficult to satisfy. In the example in Figure 5.4, an employee might feel that his/her advancement is hindered by lack of time for trainings or because he/she feels discriminated against in terms of religion (not gender, as in category 12). For this employee, the categories are not exhaustive, and there is therefore no way for this person to properly answer the item. However, the problem is easily solved by extending the answer scale as shown in Figure 5.5.

One should know, though, that providing answer categories is associated with an additional problem: They can strongly influence the results. Bishop et al. (1988) report a telephone survey where the respondents were asked what they find important in a job. The categories offered were well-paid work, secure job, good chances for advancement, and so on. A second group answered the same question without any answer categories by using their own words. Results showed that both groups reported about the same number of job values, but the group without a qualitative response scale specified different work values. If analyzed in the categories of the qua-

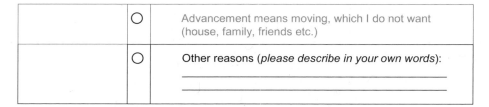

Figure 5.5. Extending the answer scale of Figure 5.4 with an "other" category.

litative scale offered to the first group, the differences in frequency were in some cases larger than 30%. Hence, concluding that X or Y is or is not important for a group of respondents is risky as the answers depend on how one formulated the importance item.

Survey researchers often request that pick-n lists should not only be exhaustive, but also *relevant* for the respondents, a requirement that is also difficult to satisfy. In an ES, however, relevancy can be looked at differently. It may indeed make sense under certain circumstances to offer some categories that the respondents are very unlikely to use on their own, or that they do not really understand. This is sometimes done on purpose in a survey that serves as a platform to place such issues on the agenda, or to set the stage for focused discussions in the follow-up processes.

Apart from the categories themselves, their order is also of some importance for the statistical distribution of the responses. What one observes here are both *primacy* and *recency* effects (Noelle-Neumann & Petersen, 1998). The primacy effect makes a response category more likely to be chosen if it appears early in the list. The recency effect makes a response category more likely to be chosen if it appears at the end of the list. In typical employee surveys, primacy effects are more likely. The respondents often feel a certain time pressure (e.g., onsite group administrations) or they do not want to spend much time on the questionnaire (e.g., taking the survey during personal time). Hence, they would not first read all response alternatives but proceed sequentially and check whatever seems plausible until n answers are given or until the end of the list has been reached. This is why Schuman & Presser (1996) and Sudman & Bradburn (1974) recommend that in "long" lists the alternatives that are probably most preferred should be presented at the beginning. This assumes, however, that the respondents do indeed proceed from top to bottom in the list. Schwarz et al. (1989) showed, however, that in long lists it is the categories in the middle of the list that have the lowest likelihood to be picked. This suggests that the respondents do not strictly proceed top-down but more randomly, possibly beginning at the top and then jumping to the end, in an attempt to screen the list quickly.

The responses to the categories of a pick-n item are also influenced by how the respondents feel that they are related in terms of *content*. For example, if employees are asked for the reasons why former coworkers have left the company, and if one offers a plausible reason next to an unlikely reason, then the probability that the plausible category gets many endorsements is increased—a *contrast effect* (Noelle-Neumann, 1970). Inversely, some response category X may profit in terms of the frequency of endorsements from having "something" in common with a preferred response category (*assimilation effect*).

These considerations lead to a number of recommendations for setting up qualitative items for an ES. The response categories of these items should be ...

- ... *distinct* to enable simple analyses—a fuzzy set of overlapping super- and subcategories leads to ambiguities
- ... *exhaustive* for the topic addressed by the item's question (in case of doubt, add the category "other")
- ... *relevant* for the respondents (which makes sure that they are at least understood by the respondents, and also in the sense in which they were intended by the interviewer)
- ... *limited in their number*—typically not more than about ten response categories are used; if more are needed, then the answer categories should be structured into subsets with proper headlines, or more than just one item should be used

Thus, the requirements for good pick-*n* items are quite demanding. Formulating such items requires a lot of preparatory work. What one needs, most of all, are clear ideas about the many response possibilities. Such ideas can be generated, for example, in brainstorming sessions of the ES coordination team; or by conducting focus group interviews with different samples of employees; or by studying the answers that were provided in other surveys that used open-ended questions on the same issue; or by interviewing specially selected employees or experts; or by carefully pretesting the item prototypes, in particular with respect to missing categories. If one is still not certain after all this whether the item really offers the most important answer categories, the list can be expanded by an "other" option or by an additional "other, please describe" option (see Figure 5.5).

Too little effort is often invested in constructing pick-*n* items in practice. Such items, then, are not much more but a potpourri of "bullet points", supplemented by a bashful "other" category. Using such items, however, will only save resources when constructing the questionnaire: When it comes to data analysis, any such savings will prove illusory because data analysis becomes difficult and no one will buy the results in the follow-up processes or be able to work with them.

5.5 Comments

Online employee surveys, in particular, offer the possibility to not only use closed items (such as Likert items), but also open-ended items. The most common type is a question of the *"Anything else?"* type. It typically follows a battery of closed items that measure opinions and attitudes on various aspects of a particular topic such as pay. The comment item then asks, for example: *"If there is anything else you want to remark on pay and related issues, please do so by writing in the field below what you want to say."* Occasionally, comment items may also be placed at the end of the questionnaire, with an instruction like this: *"If you feel that this questionnaire missed something important, then please tell us about it in the following window. Use your own words."* Or, with a hint at suggestions: *"In the following, you have the opportunity to tell us about problems, ideas, or suggestions in your own words."*

The purpose of such comment items is simply to give the respondent a chance to complement the information collected by the closed items with further detail and additional issues. This can reduce the risk that the ES misses important issues. Comments can also help to understand what the respondents "really mean" (Kulesa & Bishop, 2006) with their scores on the closed items. Some authors argue that comments can "confirm" the findings of the closed items (Smith, 2003, p. 42). Moreover, most textbooks agree that the frequency of comments on a particular issue is an indicator of the relative importance of that issue (Church & Waclawski, 2001).

Before using comment items, one should carefully consider their draw-backs and risks, and set up proper rules in case one decides to use them. The most obvious problem is that comments are expensive items in a traditional paper-and-pencil survey. The respondents usually provide their comments by writing into an answer field in the questionnaire, and their handwritings must then be deciphered, corrected, or transcribed by data entry specialists. This process can be expensive and it usually takes a lot of time. In case of an online survey, though, these problems vanish because the respondents type their comments directly into the computer. That is why comments have grown in popularity over recent years.

A number of challenges and risks remain. The most obvious ones are related to reporting and interpreting the comments. The easiest solution is to reproduce the comments *verbatim* in the survey reports and leave it to the respective managers and workgroups how to interpret and use them. Typically, however, the comments are edited to eliminate politically incorrect ones. Racial slander, insults, and foul language are often censored. One may also want to eliminate names of persons (supervisors, in particular). There exist computer programs that do these jobs quite well, but not perfectly. The text material always has to be screened by intelligent persons for sensitive text missed by the computer. Even so, some unacceptable comments are likely to remain. Irony, sarcasm, euphemisms, jargon, and allusions to specific events will not be obvious to an editor who does not know the particular context. Text passages that involve typos and new forms of "creative" spelling ("This is 4U, BTW") will also be difficult to edit, as will statements formulated as questions ("Am I really supposed to …?"). In addition, international surveys often require editors with multiple language skills. There may also be comments that violate the norms of one culture, but not of other cultures.

Where anonymity is a big issue, reporting comments verbatim can be risky. People have certain habits in their choice of words and expressions so that one can often tell (or think that one can tell) who made the comment if one knows that it was a co-worker or a subordinate. Hence, some employees may complain that reporting comments verbatim is jeopardizing anonymity. This form of feeding back comments, therefore, needs to be communicated *before* the survey, as part of the survey's rules. Also, what needs to be stressed before the survey is that comments must be politically correct, because "editing" comments may otherwise be perceived as censorship.

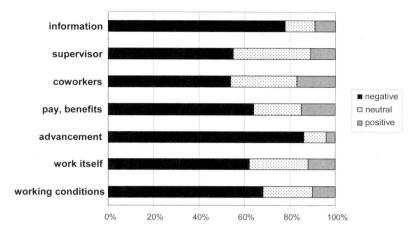

Figure 5.6. Proportions of negative, neutral, and positive comments in an ES.

Another problem that needs to be considered ahead of time is that comments can distort the interpretation of the survey's results. Managers typically like to read comments, and if one gives them the comments before one presents the survey statistics, their interest in the statistics is likely to drop dramatically. Managers also tend to generalize single comments as evidence for what "the" employee "really" thinks (Grabner, 1985; Jolton, 2004). The problem is exacerbated by the fact that the majority of comments tends to be negative. To illustrate, Figure 5.6 (Borg, Zuell, & Beckstette, 2007) shows the proportions of some forty thousand positive, neutral, and negative comments on seven job facets provided by 45% of the employees of a European IT systems support organization. One notes that the proportion of positive comments is relatively small (17% at most) for each job facet. Positive comments also tend to be brief ("Nice guy!", "I like my work"), while negative comments tend to be much longer. Moreover, the number and length of negative comments is negatively correlated with the respondents' general job satisfaction, job facet satisfaction, and organizational commitment. However, that does not mean that negative comments are useless! On the contrary, they usually contain detailed descriptions of problems that need to be solved. The ES user must understand the apparent paradox that comments tend to suggest that the work situation is terrible while survey statistics typically indicate the opposite. This finding is *not* contradictory. Normally, only 30-50% of those you participate in the survey write comments, and more so those who are less satisfied and less committed (Borg et al., 2007; Jolton, 2005; Suckow, 2005). The question of why these persons write comments can be explained as a sign that they have not given up completely on their jobs or on the organization. Rather, they are willing to deliver this effort and incur a certain risk of exposure as an *investment* that hopefully will lead to improvements. Employees with extremely low commitment would not even participate in the survey.

One alternative to supplying managers with verbatim comments is to report common themes with only a few explanatory quotes. Church & Waclawski (2001, p. 197) suggests reducing costs by considering a sample of the comments only: "the general rule of thumb here is a 20 percent sample of the total responses." The comments in this sample are then sorted into the content categories or themes that are used to structure all other survey feedback. The frequencies of the comments in each category is tabulated "so that the relative importance of each issue can be determined" (p. 198) by the simple rule that more comments mean that the category is more important. Finally, the authors recommend reporting for each category some "representative sample quotes," while other authors (Edwards, Thomas, Rosenfeld, & Booth-Kewley, 1997; Folkman, 1998; Sirota et al., 2005) recommend reporting "particularly interesting" or "typical" comments.

These suggestions are all based on a convincing arguments or on content analysis methodology (Früh, 2001; Krippendorff, 2004). However, no justification is offered for the 20% sample, nor is it clear how the substantive categories can be generated and how reliable and valid they are. Moreover, it is not clear how a "typical" comment is defined. Recent research (Borg et al., 2007) also shows that the number of comments on a topic is *not* related to the importance of an issue (as measured by asking the employees directly to rate "How important is [X] to you?").

Thus, analyzing and interpreting comments remains challenging under any methodology. From our experience, we recommend reporting comments verbatim for organizational units with a certain minimum number of respondents (e.g., greater than 75). This generates more anonymity, but still feeds back the information to groups that are likely to understand what the comments mean. Some preprocessing of the comments is necessary. At the very least, names should be suppressed by checking the comments against a list of names taken from the personnel information system. Politically incorrect comments can be much reduced in their frequencies by clearly communicating the rules for comments before the survey and possibly even in the questionnaire. Given such rules, editing comments may not be necessary, which demonstrates a willingness to hear employees' thoughts and emotions without judgment or censorship.

5.6 Open-Ended Questions with a Focus

Comment items are not the only type of item that can be used to collect qualitative information in an ES. Open-ended questions can avoid many of the problems of comment items if they are more focused in both their question and their answer parts. This can best be illustrated by two prototypical items of that class of items (asked in company ABC):

- "What are the top 1-2 actions that ABC can take to improve our rate of profitable growth?"
- "What are the top 1-2 actions that your manager can take to increase productivity and contribution of your workgroup?"

In contrast to a comment item, these items are much more focused. Rather than inviting any type of comment related to growth or productivity, this format specifically

Your code	Your suggestion

Code	Major focus area
1	Business Strategy Execution
2	Client Services Improvements
3	Staffing & Deploying Resources
4	Process & Bureaucracy Simplification
5	Employee Development
6	Marketing Effectiveness
7	Cost Containment
8	Paying & Rewarding Employees
9	Employee Involvement/Respect-based Practices
10	Communication
11	Managing Performance

Figure 5.7. Theme codes and answer fields (top) for item "Actions to improve productivity?"

asks for two actionable ideas. This requires respondents to first sort and evaluate their ideas instead of reporting just about anything that comes to their minds in a spontaneous way.

Yet, the question alone does not solve the problem of how to report the text material thus collected. With items like these, this is an even more challenging task than sorting broad comments because the answers to such focused questions tend to be more technical (e.g., "The X3 needs to be upgraded by T code"; "The XPS approach is inappropriate for my kind of work"). Coding these answers correctly poses an almost insurmountable challenge for the data analyst. This problem can, however, be substantially reduced if the respondents are asked to *self-theme* their answers by using a code from a list of relevant categories. An example for the answer fields of the "improving productivity" item from above is shown in Figure 5.7 (a case from a U.S. IT company). The respondents are guided here by the item's answer format to produce up to two different answers, write or type them into two separate answer fields, and assign a code from the category list to each answer field.

The list of codes can be understood as part of the item's question. The categories for coding the answers make the question clearer and even more focused. They tell the respondent what kinds of answers are expected. They can also *prime* answers that the respondent would not think of without such hints.

For the category lists, the rules set up above in Section 5.4 apply. That is, the answer categories should be disjoint, exhaustive, relevant, and limited in their number. To set up such lists requires expertise and possibly a number of focus groups with various groups of employees. To invest some time and effort into the construction of such items is always worthwhile because the quality of the category lists largely determines the quality of the data that the item delivers in the end. The questionnaire itself could use different category lists for different workgroups. This is particularly easy to implement in an electronic questionnaire.

In terms of their content, open-ended items with more focus than "Anything else?" items can be phrased differently. In particular, they can stress more cognitive or more affective assessments. For example, asking *"What could be done to make you more satisfied with your job?"* obviously aims at emotions. However, an open-ended question that asks about satisfaction may seem focused, but it will likely yield responses resembling a wish list ("More money! Hire more people! More time for training!" and so on). Such wish lists are often quite simplistic and not oriented on the organization's goals. Better to focus on performance, such as *"Please describe the one action that would be most effective in improving your productivity."* With such an item, an answer such as "More money!" is really quite inappropriate and, therefore, excluded by the way the item poses the question. In addition, the popular request to hire more personnel would have to be explained more clearly: What people, with what qualifications, to do what, and why? In any case, answers that appear too vague can be discussed in the follow-up processes. The item "legitimizes" such discussions, so that the facilitator of later workshops is "entitled" to poke into the answers and ask how, for example, "more money" would lead to higher productivity.

5.7 Formulating ES Items

Despite a long history of research, there are no simple formulas for developing survey items, partly because there are so many criteria for optimal items. For example, there is no best answer scale because the answer options must harmonize with the question part of the item. In addition, what is optimal in one context may not be optimal in another. While unipolar items may be clearer, using only unipolar items would require more items (and time) to cover the same breadth possible with bipolar items, potentially raising administration costs and lowering participation rates. Nevertheless, split sample research, lab experiments, practical experience from running many surveys, and sheer logic have produced a set of general rules for formulating survey items (Brislin, 1986; Converse & Presser, 1986; Rea & Parker, 1992; Schuman & Presser, 1996; Spector, 1992; Borg, 2002b). While most of these rules hold for surveys in general, some of them are special for the context of employee surveys.

Survey items should ...

1. *be as short as possible*
   "If I think about it, I do come to the conclusion that my job is really quite satisfactory." → "I like my job." [The short version measures the same thing.]
2. *be understandable (for all respondents in the same sense)*
   "The ROI in our industry..." → "The profits in our industry..." [ROI? Would everyone understand what ROI means? Seems too academic.]
3. *address only one topic at a time*
   Not: "My supervisor is nice and competent." [The answer is ambiguous. What does a 'No' mean? He/she is not nice, not competent, or both?]
4. *be free of negations*
   "It is not good if work is finished late" or even "It is not good if work is not finished on time" [Unclear exactly what a 'Yes' or a 'No' means as an answer to these items.]
5. *have the right level of precision*
   (a) The item can be too imprecise as "My supervisor seldom talks with me." [Seldom? Talks? About what? What is that supposed to mean?] (b) The item can also be over-precise as "In the last 12 months, my supervisor has talked with me in detail about my work goals at least once every month." [Who can really answer this question?]
6. *not be too extreme*
   "I am very satisfied with my job." → "I am satisfied with my job." [The respondent can give a graded answer on the rating scale!]
7. *not contain questionable premises*
   "To avoid conflict, my coworkers should..." [What if there are no conflicts?]
8. *avoid faddish expressions*
   "My supervisor is really cool." [Fads change quickly. Such items often cannot be used in replications of the ES.]
9. *be uniquely interpretable*
   "My work is very repetitive, but it seems impossible to change that." [A 'no' means what? Not repetitive? Impossible to change that? Both?]
10. *change their directions from time to time*[13]
    "My work goals are clear." → "My work goals are vague." [Reason: Avoid mechanical response tendencies such as acquiescence, i.e. the tendency to answer each item with a 'Yes', regardless of its content.]
11. *use the survey time efficiently*
    So, e.g., do not change the response scale all the time without good reasons.

---

[13] Negations are a poor device for reflecting an item, and using the word "not'" is the worst of all possibilities. What one needs to find are *semantic* opposites. For example, "I love my job" should not be reversed by saying "I do not love my job", but rather by "I hate my job".

ES survey items should ...

12. *be answerable by all employees to whom they are posed*
    Items that cannot be answered by the large majority of the employees to whom they are posed should not be used in an ES (except in a few specialized sections). Pretest the items. Do not try to solve the problem by offering "Don't know" answer categories: Once offered even respondents who have an attitude often choose DK, because it is more convenient.
13. *be relevant for the goals of the ES*
    Items must serve the goals of the ES. That the items satisfy this criterion should be obvious to all respondents. It must, at least, be explainable.
14. *avoid duplications*
    Do not use "control items" in an ES. They may lead to suspicion and to employees terminating the survey. Group similar/related items into blocks of items so that the respondents can see the differences.
15. *not ask about personal or private matters*
    Only ask about things related to the person's work.
16. *use jargon that will be understood throughout the organization*
    "My immediate supervisor..." or "My direct manager..." or ...? [What expression is normal in this organization?]
17. *not promote a passive and finger-pointing attitude*
    "I am not well informed here." → "I can easily get the information that is important for doing my job well." [The ES is not a wish list, where the employee simply checks what management must then deliver!]
18. *refer to the respondent personally rather than to generic people*
    "People are being well informed in this company." → "I can easily get the information I need to do a good job." [Results in more involvement and in more commitment to the answers. Everyone should answer for him- or herself. Who, in any case, is "people"?]
19. *choose "positive" wordings whenever possible*
    "In our workgroup, we have conflicts all the time." → "The atmosphere in our workgroup is good." [Management may mind that the survey is ruining the work climate by repeatedly asking about problems and negative aspects of work life.] But: "I am seriously considering leaving the company within the next 12 months." [Not everything can be expressed positively! For example, "Thou shall not kill" cannot be expressed positively either.]
20. *not appear manipulative*
    "I would also work on weekends if the economic situation of the company made it necessary." [This seems to be a trap. If the employees feel manipulated, the organizational climate will be damaged. Hence, if one is interested in the employees' willingness to work on weekends, simply ask this: "I am willing to work on weekends." If Saturday and Sunday may be seen differently, then two questions would be needed, one for Saturday and one for Sunday.]

21. not focus on emotions only
"I often dislike my job." → "I am seriously considering leaving the company within the coming 12 months." [Behavioral intentions are more concrete. They better predict real behavior.]

These rules cannot be applied mechanically. They require interpretation and often a compromise is needed (Fowler, 2001). For example, if one formulates an item very compactly, Rule 1 is satisfied. However, a few more words and explanations can make an item more understandable, thus satisfying Rule 2. Rule 5 requires finding the right balance between fuzziness and over-precision. Even Rule 3, which is the classic of all item formulation rules, may appear simpler than it is. Consider the item "Overall, I am satisfied with my supervisor." The item actually asks the respondent to aggregate a variety of different evaluations into one overall judgment. Therefore, it seems that the item contradicts the requirement that one should address only one topic at a time[14]. However, compare this item with the item "My supervisor is nice and competent." The difference is that the former item addresses *one natural psychological object* (i.e., the supervisor), even though this object has *many facets*. The latter item, in contrast, asks for a judgment on two issues that are neither logically nor psycho-logically related to each other. Rule 3 is meant to focus the survey participant on one meaningful object in order to simplify the process of answering the question and standardizing what people mean when they respond. Adhering to the intended spirit of each rule is the best way to negotiate the potential conflict among the list of rules.

Pure "placement items" (see Section 4.1) violate, by definition, a number of rules. Above all, they are not truly answerable by all employees. Similarly, action and debiasing items serve special goals. For them, the above rules are also less important. Their quality depends primarily on their *functionality*.

All rules are *technical* in nature. That is, they are meant only to control and modify items, but they cannot generate any items by themselves. This requires content considerations, theoretical and empirical knowledge, and reflections on the role of the items within the ES project. When non-experts formulate ES items, they tend to make similar mistakes. They produce items that are ...

- technically problematic, violating the above rules (e.g., containing a "not")
- too academic or business-oriented in language and content so that many employees do not understand these items
- unclear in their purpose and merely "interesting"
- relevant only to those who proposed it
- not useful or even counter-productive for the goals of the survey program (the items can, for example, damage the organizational climate by being too negative)

Hence, when non-experts provide suggestions for items, one must take extra care to check them.

---

[14] Truly one-dimensional items are rather abstract notions. Almost anything is, at closer inspection, a conglomerate of different components, as a "mixed bag".

5.8 Scales and Single Items

On almost all relevant issues, one can find relevant items in the literature and even entire item batteries that form scales (Bearden, Netemeyer, & Mobley, 1993; Fields, 2002; Silberman, 2002). Items form a scale if they possess certain formal properties (Borg & Staufenbiel, 2007; DeVellis, 1991). The answers to such items are intercorrelated in the sense that respondents tend to answer them similarly: Knowing a person's answer to one item allows one to predict the person's response tendency to the other items. For example, a person who endorses an item above its average is also likely to endorse the other item above its average, and vice versa. The items, thus, measure the *same dimension* or construct[15], although generally with items that have *different levels of difficulty*[16]. Scales are often used instead of single items, because using a battery of related items allows one to average the answers, thereby arriving at a scale value that is more differentiated and more reliable than the answer on just one 5-point response scale (Nunnally & Bernstein, 1994).

For employee surveys, such scales are rarely useful for the simple reason that they use many items to measure one issue. For example, the scale to measure subjective job insecurity by Ashford et al. (1989) uses 56 items, just for this one construct! Moreover, in an ES, one wants to measure attitudes and opinions of groups, and not of individuals, and so one always gets a certain data-smoothing and error-reducing effect from aggregating the answers of different persons. Finally, single item measurements are not necessarily poor either. Wanous et al. (1997) showed, for example, that single item measurements of general job satisfaction (e.g., using a Kunin scale item as in Figure 1.1) arrive at similar results as large item batteries such as the JDI or the MSQ. The scores of the single item and the scale scores are highly correlated ($r=+.70$). Nagy (2002) finds similar results for different job dimensions, such as satisfaction with work itself, pay, and supervisor. These job dimensions were assessed with the relevant multi-item scales of the JDI[17] and with discrepancy-based single items (e.g., "How does the amount of pay that you currently receive compare to what you think it should be?") together with the response scale "not at all satisfactory" to "very satisfactory." Single items and scales correlated from +.62 to +.72 for the different job dimensions. Even more importantly, results suggested that the single items can be even *better* predictors of some dependent variables, such as turnover tendency, than the corresponding JDI scores. Nagy (2002) believes that the reason for this result may be that the scales with their averaging-over-items composition rule may not correctly reflect how the respondent arrives at an overall judgment. Using a single item,

---

[15] Scales can also be multidimensional. In that case, its items form subgroups in the sense that items within a subgroup correlate substantially with each other, while items that belong to different subgroups are uncorrelated. Each such subgroup is a "dimension".

[16] The difficulty of an item refers to the item's extremity. If many respondents endorse an item, the item is considered "easy," if few agree with the item, it is "difficult."

[17] The JDI consists of 72 items that comprise five sub-scales or facets: Work itself, pay, opportunities for promotion, supervision, and co-workers. The JDI has been used to measure job satisfaction in over 400 studies (Smith et al., 1969) and has documented evidence of convergent and discriminant validity (e.g. Gillet & Schwab, 1975; Johnson, Smith, & Tucker, 1982; Jung, Dalessio, & Johnson, 1986).

in contrast, does not make a particular assumption on how a judgment is made, neither in terms of content issues, not in terms of cognitive composition rules.

Thus, using single items may not be as bad as suggested in the traditional psychometric literature. In applied research, the set of relevant criteria is larger than in science anyway. In almost any ES, one has to assess too many issues to be able to use scales for all or even many of them. Moreover, one is never interested in the attitudes and opinions of single individuals, but only in groups. In the ES context, it is therefore normal practice to consider using scales where they exist, but to use only some of their items that appear particularly interesting (clear, relevant, important, etc.). They lead to thin questionnaires with high participation rates, and are still valid in predicting important dependent variables.

5.9 Items in Different Languages

Cross-cultural employee surveys are becoming ever more important as companies become more global. In addition, online data collection makes such surveys feasible in terms of cost and speed. However, such surveys also lead to new challenges, most notably translating the questionnaire into many different languages.

The main requirement for translating a questionnaire is that the items should be *equivalent* in the different language versions. Taking a closer look, one notes that the notion of equivalency has surprisingly many facets. Johnson (1998), for example, distinguishes no less than 51 varieties of item equivalency.

Back-Translations

Of the many different types of item equivalency, only one has dominated applied research: Equivalency in the sense of back-translation. This means that translator A translates an item from English into German, for example, and then translator B translates the item back from German into English. The translation of the original item into German is considered equivalent, if the back-translated item matches the original item (Van De Vijver & Leung, 1997).

However, back-translation requires that the translators pay sufficient attention to the context of the questionnaire. Harkness (2005) illustrates this issue with a bizarre example. There is an idiomatic German expression for saying that one lives life to the fullest: "Das Leben in vollen Zügen geniessen." A formally correct but semantically wrong translation[18] says "To enjoy life in full (railway) trains," while the item really means "in full draughts". This sentence back-translates exactly into the original item. Hence, the example shows that even if the back-translated item matches the original item 100%, the translation may still be wrong and completely miss what the item wants to assess. A *blind* translation (e.g., by computer) and back-translation is, therefore, insufficient. The translator must be aware of the items' intentions and about the goals of the survey, and the decision maker should be able to read or speak the lan-

---

[18] "Zug" in German can mean train, draw, draft, trait, move, drag etc.--depending on the context!

guage into which the questionnaire is translated. In practice, this often means that the translation is not given to some translation bureau. Rather, a committee (e.g., the ES project team) that at least supervises and checks the translations, and that knows the company jargon and the positioning and context of the survey typically coordinates it.

Further Criteria for Questionnaire Translations

When considering translations of a questionnaire, a host of criteria has to be taken into account. For example, translating the questionnaire into certain languages may be legally required as, for example, in case of running an ES in Canada where English and French is a must (Johnson, 1996). Yet, as soon as two languages appear, other languages typically become unavoidable. For example, when running a survey in a global IT company, having a version in Canadian French immediately led the French in France to request "their" version of the questionnaire—in "proper" French, of course. In addition, when the Brazilians requested their version, the Portuguese insisted on a version in "proper" Portuguese. Moreover, there were two English versions, one for the UK, and one for North America. Much sensitivity is typically associated with such language issues.

In a global survey, however, not all languages are technically easy to implement. Languages such as Arabic, Chinese, Cyrillic, or Hebrew need fonts that are not always available on older computer platforms. This may not be obvious from the beginning. For example, if a Turkish questionnaire is run on a computer that is configured to a German windows environment, the special Turkish fonts will be displayed incorrectly on the computer screen. The analogous is true for German umlauts within an English environment. Thus, one must check and double-check the questionnaire not only on one computer, but also on the typical computer of the respective employee.

For such technical reasons it is often argued in a global ES that the survey should be run in English only because "almost everybody speaks English around here anyway." However, when carefully pretesting an English-only questionnaire, one often finds that many employees speak English very well in a technical sense, but when it comes to finer judgments on attitude objects or to more differentiated opinions on facts and directions, they become insecure. Even translators are often experts on a particular vernacular only. In one computer company, for example, questionnaire translation was given to a group of professionals (all of them bi- or multilingual) who normally translate the company's manuals and user interfaces into other languages. The result was terrible because the translations required expertise in psychology rather than in computer science. To find the one and only expression for "attitude" in German, Spanish, or Russian is apparently not that easy.

The TRAPD Approach

Harkness (2005) described basic steps for producing a final version of a questionnaire under the name TRAPD, where T=translation, R=review, A=adjudication (deciding on a version), P=pretesting, and D=documentation. She argues that "all or some of these procedures may need to be repeated at different stages. For example, pretesting and debriefing sessions with fielding staff and respondents will lead to revisions; these then call for further testing of the revised translations. Even if a committee approach is not employed, any strict compartmentalization of procedures and people involved (for example, leaving translators out of assessment stages or reviewers out of adjudication stages) is counterproductive and not recommended" (p. 38).

The step of the TRAPD procedures that is most often missing in practice is pretesting the translated questionnaire with a sample of typical respondents. The translation committee should make sure that this step is not overlooked. Even a simple pretesting (e.g., an interviewer goes through the questionnaire with some respondents) may detect flaws. Furthermore, documenting this step can prevent situations where management rejects the survey results because of a "poor" questionnaire ("No one understood these items!", "Too abstract!", "Ambiguous!").

5.10 Collecting Demographic Information

Every ES needs to collect some demographic information about the respondent. For example, what one absolutely must know is the organizational unit of the respondent, because without this information only "average trends" can be reported. Such statistics do not generate much momentum for the follow-up processes.

For companies administering the survey online, the technology enables demographic information from the HR system to be loaded automatically when an employee enters a unique code (i.e., Personal Identification Number or PIN) assigned to him or her, often via an emailed invitation. This increasingly popular option results in a confidential survey rather than anonymous one; someone can indeed link the person's name to his or her answers. Hence, this approach can be a disadvantage for companies whose employees believe that the survey will become a witch-hunt for dissenters. In these situations, third party vendors offer the advantage of being independent from the company. Carefully worded contracts with the client organizations help assure employees that their survey answers will be anonymous to the employer.

The biggest advantage of using an HR feed to automatically supply demographic information is that employees will be placed into their correct units and departments rather than relying on employees' responses, which can be intentionally or unintentionally inaccurate. Moreover, the questionnaire itself is not as lengthy or time-consuming when demographic questions are not necessary.

Collecting demographic information is more difficult with paper questionnaires. The main problem is that typically there are thousands of organizational units. Obviously, the questionnaire cannot offer all these units as categories in one questionnaire (as shown, e.g., in Figure 4.9). This would turn a printed questionnaire into a book. One solution is to print different versions of the questionnaire or separate "slip sheets" with codes for each unit that can be entered onto the actual questionnaire or response page. With this approach a limited number of demographic categories can be listed in each version. Of course one must make sure that each version of the questionnaire reaches its target respondents.

A different solution is to print the *essential* demographic information on self-adhesive *demographic stickers*. Such a sticker typically exhibits the respondent's organizational unit, his or her position in the organizational hierarchy, and the country where he or she works. This information is shown in full text rather than as a numerical or graphic code in order to reduce concerns that the coding may jeopardize anonymity. The sticker comes within the survey packet together with the questionnaire, the return envelope, the instruction sheet etc. The respondent is asked to attach this sticker in a special field on the questionnaire.

The sticker method presupposes that a personnel information system exists that is differentiated and up-to-date. If so, one can pull out the information one needs and store it in an Excel sheet for sticker production and for generating focal reports[19].

Demographic stickers have been used with great success in many companies. The respondents appreciate that such stickers make it easy for them to fill out the questionnaire. Few respondents omit the sticker from their questionnaires. Demographic item nonresponse tends to be lower than using traditional ways to collect this information, probably because the sticker method leads to higher degrees of attention so that unintentional omissions are lower. The sticker method can also help to improve the quality of the demographic information collected by the questionnaire. Not all employees are always sure exactly how their organizational unit, for example, is officially called at the time they fill out the survey. Using a sticker reduces such uncertainties and produces the best-possible data.

In organizations where anonymity concerns are high, the sticker method can be modified in such a way that the respondents can choose to either use the sticker, copy the information by hand, or leave the space blank for each demographic item. Another variant would be to print onto the sticker only those demographic items that are *essential* for effective follow-up processes (e.g., the organizational unit or the department to which the respondent belongs). Any additional "nice-to-have" but "risky" demographic items (such as gender or tenure level) could be offered as items that the respondents can fill out by checking an appropriate category box in the questionnaire. Respondents such as the newly hired female trainee can thus decide to skip the item on tenure and/or the item on gender to protect her anonymity, but still opt to identify herself as an employee of the particular organizational unit so that her answers will become part of the feedback report of this unit.

5.11 The Structure of the Questionnaire

In any questionnaire, the items must be ordered in some way, either *randomly* or in *blocks of similar content*. The random order design comes from psychometrics. Its purpose is to prevent respondents from answering the items is a schematic way, whatever their content. For example, a respondent may form a response set after ans-

---

[19] In an electronic survey, one can automatically link the questionnaire with this data file. The respondent is identified by his or her particular access code or user code.

wering the first few items, and then proceed mechanically by answering "agree" to whatever item that follows ("acquiescence").

The content blocks design, in contrast, builds on findings from cognitive psychology: Its purpose is to allow the respondents to arrive at better judgments by allowing them to think more deeply about the item content. One can sort the items into blocks, the items within the blocks, and the blocks themselves by similar principles. One usually begins with the items that focus on concrete issues such as the working conditions, and then continues with work itself, advancement, pay and benefits, coworkers, supervisor, management etc. up to relatively abstract issues such as the company as a whole or strategy. Within the content blocks, a similar order can be followed, beginning with more concrete issues and ending with an "All in all, I am satisfied with [X]" item. This makes it easier for the respondent first get used to the item formats and the answering scale. Moreover, the overall satisfaction judgment is presented as some kind of bottom line that sums everything up into a global attitude statement.

Reasons for a Questionnaire Structured by Content

Questionnaires structured into content blocks rather than those that sort their items randomly are typical in ES research. There are good reasons to prefer such a questionnaire. The respondents must find an answer to each item by either reporting attitudes or opinions that exist and that are accessible to them, or, more likely, by thinking about the issue and forming a judgment on the issue raised by the item. If a completely "crystallized" judgment is simply reported on an item, the context of the other items—in particular those that precede the item—is not relevant, provided the respondents truly attempt to provide *optimal* answers and do not simply resort to a mechanical response set that only formally does the job (e.g., by always choosing the middle category "undecided"). Krosnick (1991) termed the latter type of answer "satisfycing" which means that the respondent chooses a legitimate but not substantively empty answer that merely satisfies the requirements of the interviewer and the norms of conversation. If the efforts required to fill out the questionnaire in an optimal way become demanding, and the respondent is not highly motivated, then satisfycing answers or answers that build on just "some" thinking become quite likely.

If no ready-to-report response is available to the respondent, and if he wants to give an optimal rather than just a satisfycing answer, he must find an answer to the question of the item. This requires first reading and understanding the item, and then searching his memory: "What comes to my mind regarding this issue? How do I evaluate this information? How can I aggregate these pieces into one judgment? How can I express this in the format of the answer scale of the item?" All of these cognitive processes require time and effort (Sudman et al., 1996). If the context changes from item to item, because the items are randomly ordered, one may assume that the respondents will arrive at a final rating in a less stable and detailed manner: As soon as he feels that he can give an adequate answer, he should give that answer (Tourangeau et al., 2000). If the items are sorted into groups of similar content, however, the answers are generated within a similar context that contains more cognitions and richer information. Moreover, the accessibility of relevant memory information is facilitated by the general context and by the priming effect of the related items. That should be particularly important for general questions, where the richer mental representation should help to improve the reliability and validity of such judgments. This also provides a rationale for sorting the items within the content blocks from concrete and narrow to more abstract and general.

Edwards et al. (1997, S. 54) point out, moreover, that the respondents can become disenchanted if an entirely new issue is addressed by each new item: "What a carelessly assembled questionnaire! They could have done a better job." This could entice the respondents to stop filling out the questionnaire, because if the questionnaire is already that "poor", then the whole ES surely cannot be a serious project.

An additional argument for sorting the items from concrete-specific to abstract-general is the need to transform judgments into the format of the answer scale. The respondent has become familiar with this scale first. Research shows that answering the first few items of the questionnaire typically takes considerably more time than answering items that come later in the questionnaire. Borg (2002a) has found that the items in the first content block of an online survey require some 22 seconds each, while the items in later content blocks consume just about 10 to 15 seconds on average. That is the response latency drops after the first item block, even though the item content tends to become more abstract. To get used to the answer scale seems easier if the required judgment is relatively simple as in case of judgments on different aspects of the respondent's working environment.

Random sorting of items is, therefore, rarely used in employee surveys. It is, nevertheless, still popular in scientific research, where costs and time do not seem to matter that much. The various standard questionnaires and scales that come from science are often randomly sorted (see, e.g., Spector, 1997)

Criteria for Sorting Items

The items of an ES can be sorted into different classes. For example, one may sort them into categories by *semantic* or by *logical* criteria. Yet, if one wants to group the items in such a way that this grouping somehow matches *psychological* categories, then the sorting should help to generate more reliable and more valid judgments, according to the above considerations on survey responses. Natural categories can be derived from research on job satisfaction, in particular, or from statistical analyses of former surveys in the particular company. Items that form interpretable scales, factors or clusters could be considered homogeneous. Usually, what one finds in an ES are categories such as the following:

- Working conditions
- Pay and benefits
- Advancement
- Coworkers, collaboration, team
- Direct supervisor
- Management, strategy, future of company
- Information

Items that fall into these content classes are typically one-dimensional or at least positively intercorrelated. In contrast, items that focus on tasks and goals are often two-dimensional, where the two dimensions are

- Clarity of goals and tasks
- Enjoying one's work

Since statistical uni-dimensionality is but an auxiliary criterion, one may still group items that relate to goals and tasks into one item block. What counts, in the end, is whether the items form a meaningful complex of issues that mirrors what comes to the typical respondent's mind when he or she thinks about an aspect of work. If that is the case, the item groupings should make it easier for the respondent to generate good answers.

An ES, however, often has goals in addition to just measurement. In particular, it may want to change things by asking questions, and grouping items under some "new" headlines may stimulate thinking in certain ways. For example, assume that a certain number of items are grouped into categories labeled as "productivity thinking" or "cost-conscious behavior." Such concepts may be part of a strategic language-creation plan of the company. By using such categories, the survey lays a seed for systematically promoting certain behaviors by first identifying them under certain names. Therefore, it is common that an ES questionnaire contains not only item blocks related to job satisfaction dimensions, but also "strategic" categories that may even have novel labels.

5.12 Layout of Questionnaire

An important factor for promoting participation in an ES is the appearance of the questionnaire. A questionnaire that looks cheap or even sloppy does not signal to the employee that the ES is a serious project, potentially reducing the participation rate. A proper layout should lead to a questionnaire that looks professional, offers a transparent structure of the questionnaire, provides easy readability, and accommodates the employee as well as the data entry person.

Many companies design a comprehensive communication concept that includes graphical and textual elements. For example, at SAP, the employee survey was positioned under the motto "SAP = Satisfaction and Performance." A logo was developed for the "S and P" notion, which worked both on paper and in an animated way on the PC or on the company TV. In addition, a catalogue of further design elements that was consistent with corporate design criteria was defined, so that the questionnaire—both online and paper—could be embedded into this system. This gave the questionnaire a professional appearance.

Cover Page and Introduction

A questionnaire usually begins with a cover page. It contains text elements such as "Employee Survey 2008," the company name and/or the function or the country, and the motto of the survey. Everything should be graphically laid out in an attractive way (although an overly glossy appearance can make the survey seem costly and wasteful in some organizations). For the graphical design, one should always consult experts in advertising and communication. Rarely does the ES coordination team have these skills itself, and their attempts to produce a professionally looking ES questionnaire often miss the mark.

Following the cover page, a new page explains how to fill out the questionnaire (see Figure 5.8 for an example). It may also briefly answer important questions, such as how anonymity is guaranteed. An important piece of information for the potential respondent is also an estimate on how long it takes to fill out the questionnaire. A proper time estimate can be based on tests in the pretesting phase of the questionnaire. This helps to reduce uncertainty on the side of the respondents also by setting a target on how deeply they are expected to think about their answers.

Design and Layout of Demographic Items

Demographic items should be ordered by their importance. The respondent's answers to *essential* demographic items should be collected first, and preferably automatically if possible (e.g., by inserting this information into an online questionnaire). Other demographic items can be offered to the respondent for self-completion. So, the respondents are given the option to strengthen the anonymity of their responses by skipping some demographics, although this option should not be promoted too strongly so that these demographics are not left unanswered because the information appears totally unimportant.

Figure 5.9 shows an example for collecting demographics in a paper questionnaire. On this page, one first recognizes a headline. It says "demographic information" in this example, but one must carefully consider what the best expression is in the particular company. For example, in one company we wanted to use the term "personal data" but pretests showed that this would not work. Some individuals felt that this information had no place in an anonymous survey, and others even remarked that "personal" matters had no place in any ES at all. Therefore, in the end, we used the term "statistical data" in this company.

The first demographic item asks the respondent to place the demographic sticker into the field reserved for it. This sticker, of course, contains the essential demographic data (i.e., those that are needed to produce focal reports for workgroups and other subgroups of the organization). The two items that follow collect nice-to-have demographics. They are offered here for discretionary self-completion.

In older paper-pencil surveys, demographic items often appeared at the end of the questionnaire, not at its beginning. This has the advantage that when the respondents come to these items, they have already seen the content items. This can reduce concerns about anonymity because the respondents see that the items make sense, that they are not too risky, and that the information they collect can be useful to improve their work environment. However, placing the demographic items at the end also has disadvantages. Some respondents feel that the survey is essentially over after the last content item, or they never even get that far because the topics tend to get ever more abstract in the usual ordering of content blocks. These respondents thus do not provide any demographic information, limiting the utility of their data.

On the other hand, respondents do not always proceed in a strictly sequential manner, and what information hits them first is not always clear. They may page through the questionnaire in order to form a first impression, and look at the questionnaire's front cover but also its back cover, before providing their answers. Salant & Dillman (1994), therefore, suggest not putting any sensitive questions onto the back cover to avoid an "unfavorable first impression" (p. 108).

Layout of the Blocks of Content Items

Figure 5.10 shows excerpts of a page with content items. On this page, a headline indicates that the items belong to a section that is common to all employees of the company ("general section"). Then, one notes some item blocks, each one beginning with a headline and ending with an "Overall, I am satisfied with [X]" item.

The layout of this example is compact so that many items can be placed on one page. Esthetically, a less condensed display may be more pleasing, but this may also lead to higher printing and mailing costs in case of a paper questionnaire, and a perception that the survey is "wasteful." In addition, a less compact layout generates questionnaires which appear "longer" and, thereby, lead to lower response rates. The layout in Figure 5.10 also lends itself to efficient data entry by scanning devices.

Using a constant format for all items is not only economical: It also has the important advantage that the respondents, after getting used to this format, are enabled to fill out the questionnaire rather quickly. They thus can answer relatively many items in a given time windows. Moreover, the constant format reduces the likelihood of response errors so that the answers become more reliable.

Alternative Layouts of ES Questionnaires

The layout shown in Figure 5.10 is not the only one that is conceivable. Many other formats are used in practice. We illustrate this by a page from a "standard questionnaire" used by a former German survey consortium (Domsch, 1985). The items here (Figure 5.11) are formulated as questions, with Likert-like response scales. All response scales—with the exception of question 36—contain a "Don't know" category[20]. The obvious disadvantage of this layout is that it leads to a long questionnaire.

The literature shows many further examples for designing an ES questionnaire (e.g., Domsch & Schneble, 1991; Töpfer & Zander, 1985). However, it is not always clear which criteria they attempt to optimize. Similar to the example in Figure 5.10, they often contain a mixture of Likert items, with or without middle categories, with

---

[20] The example in Figure 5.11 demonstrates a number of technical errors. For example, it is not good to integrate a "Don't Know" category both optically as well as numerically as category "6" into the answer scale, because this category is *qualitatively* different from the categories 1 to 5. Another example is the wording of the answer scales of questions 40 and 41 are semantically unclear: A natural answer scale to the question if pay is seen as fair is "Yes, fair" to "No, not fair", and not "I am satisfied" to "I am dissatisfied". Although the respondent probably understands what the interviewer wants to know, such little errors add up and make responding unnecessarily slow and strenuous.

Preface

What to do

This questionnaire is on your personal opinions and attitudes. Your answers are "correct" if they truly reflect what you think or feel.

Please read each question carefully. Then, answer honestly. Do not ponder too long about your answer.

Try to answer all questions. Note that on some issues, you have strong opinions, on others you may have tentative opinions only. Please report any opinion, strong or weak. Pretests have shown that it is unlikely that you have absolutely no opinion on any item. However, if you really cannot answer a question, skip it.

Anonymity

Your questionnaire will be send directly to XYY, the company that is doing the survey. YYZ will scan the questionnaires and destroy them afterwards.

The survey will be analyzed only for **groups** that consist of **at least seven participants**. Your answer will therefore be pooled with those of at least six other persons. The results will describe what all the persons of the group think, on average. Each single individual remains **anonymous**.

How to fill out the questionnaire?

Please use a pen with black or blue ink!

	Fully agree	Somewhat agree	Undecided	Somewhat disagree	Fully disagree
Check a box like this:	☒	■	☐	☐	☐
Corrections are made like this:	☐	☐	☐	☒	☐

Filling out the questionnaire takes about 20 minutes.

Thank you for your cooperation and support!

Figure 5.8. Introduction page for an ES paper questionnaire.

Item and Questionnaire Design 143

Demographic information

In the following, you are asked to provide some information about the organizational unit you belong to, about your job level, your gender, and your tenure. This information makes it possible to do a more focused data analysis. The information on the sticker is particularly important for effective action planning.

Please glue the sticker from your personal letter of invitation into this box. The sticker shows the team you belong to and the position you have.

attach your sticker here

1. Your gender?

☐ male
☐ female

1. How many years have you been working for ABC?

☐ less than 2 years
☐ 2-5 years
☐ 6-10 years
☐ more than 10 years

Figure 5.9. Example for collecting information with a demographic sticker and with self-completion items.

Part I: General topics

	Fully agree ⏪	Somewhat agree ◀	Undecided ‖	Somewhat disagree ▶	Fully disagree ⏩
Working conditions					
I have the tools and the equipment that I need to do a good job.	☐	☐	☐	☐	☐
I am satisfied with service and support for the equipment I work with.	☐	☐	☐	☐	☐
All in all, I am satisfied with my working conditions.	☐	☐	☐	☐	☐
Work itself, tasks, goals					
I know exactly what is expected of me in my job.	☐	☐	☐	☐	☐
My present tasks and goals motivate me to do my best.	☐	☐	☐	☐	☐
My work makes me feel I can make an important contribution to the ABC.	☐	☐	☐	☐	☐
All in all, I am satisfied with the actual work I have.	☐	☐	☐	☐	☐
Advancement					
During the last 12 months, I was able to learn a lot of additional things in my work.	☐	☐	☐	☐	☐
...					

Figure 5.10. Excerpts from the content part of an ES paper questionnaire.

Please mark your answer here
↓

Question		
36. How do the co-workers **in your workgroup** cooperate with you?	○ ○ ○ ○ ○	1 very good 2 good 3 average 4 bad 5 very bad
37. How do the colleagues in **other departments/groups** cooperate with you?	○ ○ ○ ○ ○ ○	1 very good 2 good 3 average 4 bad 5 very bad 6 have nothing to do with other dept./groups
38. How are the tasks of your department/group coordinated with those of other departments/groups?	○ ○ ○ ○ ○ ○	1 very good 2 good 3 average 4 bad 5 very bad 6 cannot tell
39. If you consider all payments you receive from your company (salary, Christmas bonus, vacation money, profit shares), how would you assess this? How does XY pay you in comparison to what you would get in other companies?	○ ○ ○ ○ ○ ○	1 very good 2 good 3 average 4 bad 5 very bad 6 cannot tell
40. Do you feel that you are paid fairly in comparison to what your **co-workers** get?	○ ○ ○ ○ ○ ○	1 I am very satisfied 2 I am satisfied 3 mixed 4 I am dissatisfied 5 I am very dissatisfied 6 cannot tell
41. Do you feel that you are paid according to your **performance**?	○ ○ ○ ○ ○ ○	1 I am very satisfied 2 I am satisfied 3 mixed 4 I am dissatisfied 5 I am very dissatisfied 6 cannot tell

Figure 5.11. A page of an ES questionnaire (translated from Domsch, 1985, S. 123).

or without "Don't Know" categories, uni- and bipolar response scale, and no obvious blocking of items by content. In addition, they also tend to be unnecessarily thick and force the respondent to read a lot of convoluted text.

As we showed, when constructing a questionnaire, a host of criteria—such as semantics, psychology, psychometrics, practical-economical issues—have to be taken into account. Not all of these criteria are always compatible. For example, the semantics of an item may be better if the item is unipolar, but such scales often require more text, which requires more time to fill out the questionnaire. More time, in turn, means that the survey becomes more expensive if data collection is conducted during paid time. Hence, one has to carefully consider the trade-offs in such decisions.

Total Design Method

Dillman (1983) has collected various factors that need to be considered when constructing a survey questionnaire under the roof of a theory he calls the *Total Design Method* (TDM). TDM aims at designing all elements of the survey in such a way that participation and data quality is as high as possible. The guiding principle for reaching this goal is to maximize the ratio of (tangible or expected) benefits that the respondent perceives in each element relative to their subjective costs and risks.

To illustrate this principle, consider a case. Assume we produce a questionnaire printed on thick paper with many pages. Such a questionnaire looks like more work than the same questionnaire printed on thinner paper and with a more compact layout. The same effect is caused by items that are unnecessarily verbose. Higher costs are also caused by difficult answer scales, items that are grouped in a random fashion, items that do not tap important issues, items that address personal matters, and poor readability of the print and an unclear arrangement of the items on the page. Even the printing quality is relevant as it suggests that the survey is an important or a not so important project in the company.

Other aspects of the survey process influence respondents' perceptions of the survey's costs and benefits. The quality of the rules for protecting the respondent's anonymity, for example, is an important factor in many companies. Similarly, the survey's goals, the commitment of top management, the survey's general visibility, and a clear plan for the follow-up processes are supporting elements that are critical. Actually, the entire preparation phase of the ES can be seen under a TDM perspective: One can evaluate all decisions from the respondents' subjective cost-benefit perspective.

5.13 Prognosis Questionnaires

When presenting the results of an ES to management or to other groups, one often hears that the results are "not surprising", "as expected" or even "trivial." The impression of obviousness is not necessarily a defensive reaction. Rather, the recipients truly feel this way and, therefore, often are not very interested in these rather boring results. A strategy to reduce this effect is to ask the recipients to forecast the results of

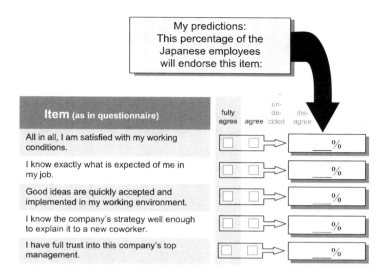

Figure 5.12. Excerpts from a prognosis questionnaire.

the survey, and then show them their prognoses in comparison to the actual findings. It can be shown experimentally that this works to make the survey results more interesting and get more attention of the audience (Borg & Hillenbrand, 2003).

One can ask the recipients for predictions on the spot during the presentation of the results, but it is better to systematically collect some predictions in writing before the survey. For that purpose, one needs a special questionnaire. An excerpt of such a prognosis questionnaire is shown in Figure 5.12. Its first two items repeat items from the questionnaire in Figure 5.10, except using a different answer scale: The respondent here is asked to predict the percentage to which some group of employees (here: the Japanese employees) will endorse the respective item.

A prognosis questionnaire can be short and ask for predictions on only a dozen items. A good selection is to use the overall satisfaction items (because they are ideal candidates for external benchmarking too), and a set of items that are particularly interesting to management, especially those where management is directly responsible such as trust in management or clarity of the company's strategy.

Using only a few items also enhances the chance that all top managers fill out this survey, although getting high participation rates (usually close to 100%) is typically not a problem in practice if this prognosis survey is given to management as an *integral part* of the survey project. A brief explanation suffices: "The prognoses are needed to compare beliefs with reality; the comparisons will be shown to top management only, and not to any other group of employees or to the works council[21]; all

---

[21] If the works council agrees, then one should also collect prognoses from this group. Another group that could make prognoses is the ES coordination team. Empirically, one finds that the prognoses of the works council are not superior to those of management even though the works council is usually

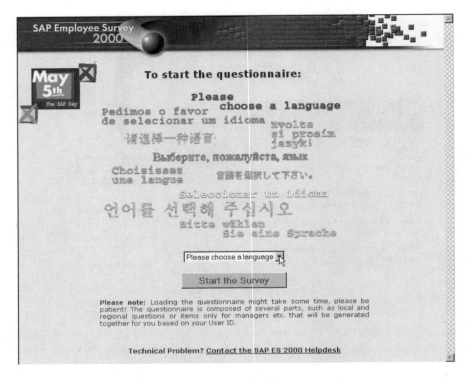

Figure 5.13. The welcome page of an electronic questionnaire.

individual prognoses will remain anonymous (managers who are interested to check the accuracy of their own prognoses are asked to save a copy of their forecasts)."

5.14 Electronic Questionnaires

Electronic questionnaires are the norm in North America today, and they are becoming more popular in Europe too, because wherever possible an ES today is run in an online mode to save costs and time. The design of an electronic questionnaire typically does not differ much from the paper version discussed above, although it allows, in principle, many additional features that make it much more flexible and adaptive.

Figure 5.13 shows a sample page from one of the first world-wide employee census surveys ever conducted in any company. The figure exhibits the "welcome page" of the questionnaire, where the respondent is asked to choose the language of the questionnaire.

---

convinced that they know the employees better than management does. Management is often overoptimistic about the employees' satisfaction, while the works council is typically too pessimistic.

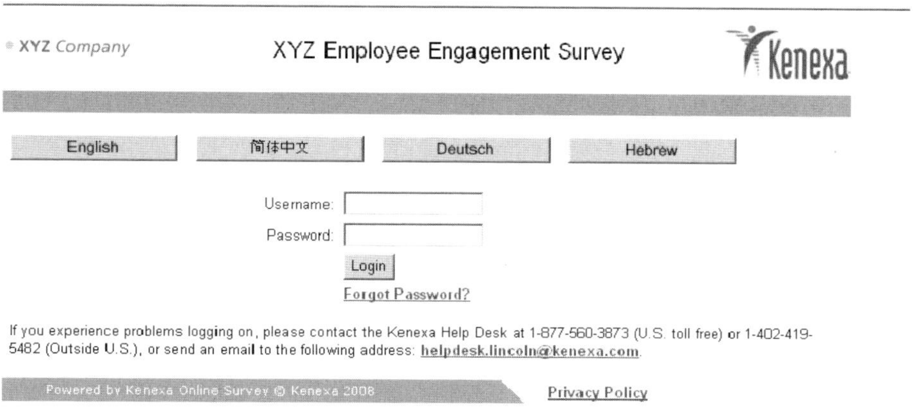

Figure 5.14. Excerpts from an electronic questionnaire with choice of language and user access information.

Note that using many languages can quickly increase costs, especially when different sets of items are specific to organizational subgroups. Sometimes companies will have one global *master* language (English, mostly), and translate everything into this language. "Local" languages are also provided, but only for the global items and for the items that are specific for the country or region. However, not every local item is translated into all languages. Thus, for example, a French manager who temporarily works in the company's Japanese subsidiary may be forced to fill out the items specific for Japan in English, not in French.

Next, the respondent is typically asked to submit his or her access code, username, or password, etc. Figure 5.14 shows an example, where the access information is combined with the choice of language. When these questions are answered, the questionnaire is assembled and appears on the PC screen, with all the specific features and information relevant for the particular individual.

In companies where the survey is not confidential but truly anonymous, the respondents' usernames or access codes are never stored together with their answers to the questionnaire items. The identifier information is only used to pull important demographics from the personnel information system (e.g., org unit, job grade, country). Figure 5.15 exhibits an example, where some essential demographic items have been filled out automatically. The results are shown in full text. The excerpt from the questionnaire also shows two demographic items that the respondents are asked to fill out themselves. This information is nice to have but not essential. The essential information cannot be changed by the respondents[22]. However, the respondents can call

---

[22] If the respondents do not want that this information is stored together with their answers to the questionnaire, the only option for them is to quit the survey. Then, in an anonymous survey, no information will be stored at all.

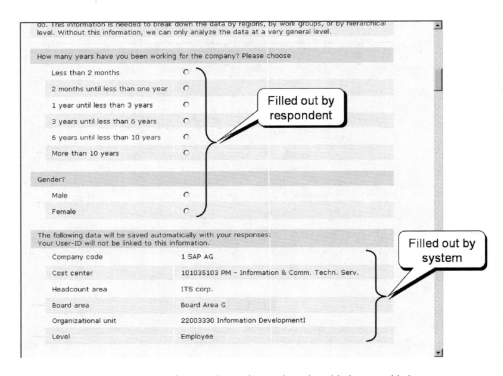

Figure 5.15. Excerpts from an electronic questionnaire with demographic items.

a help desk. These demographics would then be checked and fixed, if necessary, and the employee would be informed that a corrected/checked version of the questionnaire was ready.

Figure 5.16 shows a page with content items from an electronic questionnaire. The formatting of the items in this example corresponds closely to what one does in paper questionnaires (see Figure 5.10). For the user, the only difference is that he or she answers by clicking on a radio button, and not by writing an "X" in an answer box.

An electronic questionnaire can be constructed in a more person-specific way than a paper questionnaire. For example, rather than asking the respondent "How satisfied are you with your supervisor?", one can ask more specifically "How satisfied are you with your supervisor Karen Wilson?" This eliminates any guesswork for the respondent. It also helps to make data interpretation easier and less ambivalent. The name of the respective supervisor can be pulled from a data bank when the respondent calls the questionnaire with his or her access code or user number. Indeed, in matrix organizations or project organizations, one could even ask the respondent to rate several "supervisors"—one for each function or for each project, respectively—if this is relevant for the particular respondent. This eliminates the common argument against surveys conducted under such conditions that the employees "did not know who was meant by supervisor" or that they had "someone else" in mind when they answered these items.

An online survey, thus, allows one to construct tailor-made *adaptive* questionnaires. In the examples above, the computer filled out some demographic items, inserted the name of a supervisor into the respondent's questionnaire, or even offered the supervisor items several times for different supervisors. In addition, items specific for employees of particular organizational units, of a particular country, or for managers and for non-managers, respectively, could also be added to the questionnaire, to name just a few typical cases. This same technology can be used to substitute "my department" or "this business unit" with the actual names appropriate to each respondent. The questionnaire thereby becomes a *system of questionnaires*.

To generate such a variety of different questionnaires is not feasible with paper. It would simply drive up the costs and the complexity of the logistics too much, and increase the risk of errors (correctly designing so many questionnaire types, distributing the right questionnaire to the right person, responding to questionnaires with complex skip patterns, etc.).

Johnson & Johnson
September 2006

Section 1: Credo
The questions in this section ask your current opinions or perceptions about how well your Company is meeting its Credo responsibilities.

	Very Poor	Poor	Average	Good	Very Good
Overall, how would you rate your COMPANY on meeting its responsibilities to its:					
1 Customers	○	○	○	○	○
2 Employees	○	○	○	○	○
3 Communities	○	○	○	○	○
4 Stockholders	○	○	○	○	○
How do you rate your COMPANY on:					
5 Considering you as an individual	○	○	○	○	○
6 Respecting your dignity	○	○	○	○	○
7 Acting in just and ethical ways	○	○	○	○	○
8 Rate the extent to which management treats you with respect and dignity, that is, as a responsible individual.	○	○	○	○	○

Definitions
Frequently Asked Questions | J&J Privacy Policy | J&J Legal Notice | Contact Information

[<< Previous]   [Exit and Continue Later]   [Next >>]

Figure 5.16. Excerpts from an electronic questionnaire.

6 Processes of Questionnaire Development

Chapter 5 discussed item and survey construction from a technical perspective. This chapter examines processes to solicit conceptual input and involvement of the organization's stakeholders in the development of the questionnaire. Even when working with external consultants or standard surveys, a fair amount of customization is necessary to assure that the survey ultimately fits the organizational culture and fulfills the organization's purpose for the project. Iterations of meetings, pilot tests, and modifications are necessary to achieve the most appropriate questionnaire.

6.1 Developing an Early Version of the Questionnaire

An obvious and cardinal issue in any ES project is the development of the questionnaire for the survey: What topics should be covered? What topics should be avoided? How should one formulate the questions? What demographics are needed? Should the questionnaire be translated into other languages? How should one format the questionnaire?

One approach to answer these and related questions is to leave everything to the ES project team. Just let them start from scratch to construct the questionnaire in long brainstorming sessions and discussions. Yet better results can be attained if similar sessions are also conducted with different stakeholder groups, where results from various sessions are consolidated to create the final questionnaire. However, even then, the final product can end up as an odd home-grown questionnaire, based on unclear theoretical foundations and with unknown psychometric properties.

Creating survey content might seem easy to the novice, but the complexity of the process becomes apparent after one experiences pitfalls, mistakes, and shortcomings firsthand. Therefore, questionnaire development should start on the shoulders of those who have spent decades with employee surveys. One can do this by taking a close look at questionnaires used previously in other companies (e.g., Domsch & Ladwig, 2006; McConnell, 2003; Sirota et al., 2005), by searching the literature for scales that measure relevant issues (e.g., Cook et al., 1981; Fields, 2002), or by asking an experienced ES consultant to draft a first version of the questionnaire, which can then be modified to fit the particular needs of the organization. ES consultants also have many samples of questionnaires that they used in different organizations and industries. Hence, they are often able to build on that experience in developing a basic questionnaire that is fairly adequate from the beginning. For example, standardized items are often available that have an industry-specific focus while possibly even allowing for benchmarking the current company's ES results against industry norms.

When setting up a first version of the questionnaire, one should not only pay attention to the various technical requirements that good ES items must satisfy (Chapter 5), but also entertain a variety of questions: What content should be addressed? Are the respondents able to answer the respective items? Do they understand them? Do they have the information required to answer them? Are they willing to answer them? Are they too personal, too sensitive? Are the items consistent? Are they redundant or repetitive? Do they apply to all respondents? Are they understood by all respondents in the same way? Are the items psychometrically acceptable (not too extreme, enough variance, reliable, valid, etc.?)? Is the questionnaire easy to use? Can it be used in different modes (paper, online, etc.)? Is it cost-effective in terms of survey time?

The foundation for questionnaire content can be found in a variety of models (see Section 4.1) so that the ES comprehensively covers well researched topics necessary for post-survey decisions and actions. Most ES questionnaires, therefore, cover the same basic issues, but they must be trimmed to the particular company's needs, jargon, and culture. One should always assemble a solid first version of the questionnaire, rather than beginning with circuitous discussions of spontaneous ideas made by workshop participants. Such discussions have their role, but at the beginning they can be extremely time-consuming, opinionated, and political.

External consultants need to understand the particular organizational culture, the company's mission, vision and strategy, its products and clients, as well as its human resource policies and practices. This learning can be culled from written work about the various stakeholders and decision makers, observations of people and their work settings, analysis of printed reports and press releases about the company's business model and its strategy, examinations of available HR research data, and so on (Harrison, 1987; Harrison & Shirom, 1999). It is also crucial to form clear notions about the agendas—the official and the hidden ones—of the organization's stakeholders. Schiemann (1991) and Verheyen (1988) therefore recommend conducting interviews with these persons or groups to gain information as well as to place the ES project on their radar screens. The key organizational stakeholders—top management, in particular—may not only provide content input they deem important for the ES, but interviewing them also gives them the opportunity to ask questions about the ES project and to get to know the ES consultant. Interviewing middle managers or rank-and-file employees can have additional benefits. In many cases, such persons can give the expert additional perspectives onto the organizational culture.

However, one should not expect such interviews to yield the majority of final survey content. Questionnaires are largely based on theoretical and strategic considerations that do not simply surface in interviews, but have to be *systematically* pursued by the questionnaire design team. In most cases, interviews merely contribute to *refining* survey content or common topics. Furthermore, interviews are special situations that often yield fewer insights into the functioning of an organizational culture than observing members of the organization "from a distance" (e.g. how managers and employees interact in meetings or in the cafeteria) or even reading newsletters or information on bulletin boards (Neuberger & Kompa, 1987).

6.2 The ES Project Team's Role in Questionnaire Development

The ES project team plays an important role in designing the questionnaire. Given that a consultant provides a first draft of the questionnaire, three major tasks have to be accomplished.

Coordinating Language Adaptation and Translations

The first task to be accomplished by the ES project team is helping to adjust "off-the-shelf" items and other text sections of the questionnaire to the jargon that is typical for the particular organization. For example, some organizations refer to their training programs simply as "training", while other organizations use terms such as "employee development", and still others may use abbreviations. Similarly, what is the "immediate supervisor" in some organizations is called the "direct supervisor," the "immediate boss," the "team leader," or the "workgroup manager" in others. To ask "How satisfied are you with your direct boss?" may, therefore, make little sense to the survey participants, forcing them to speculate what the researchers really want to know. The ES project team must make every effort to formulate the questionnaire in a language that all participants understand in the same way. Moreover, items and other text passages should also sound as natural as possible to the normal employee, using language that is precise, but not artificial or stilted. This makes filling out the questionnaire easier and reduces the danger of controversial discussions about the meaning of the survey's results.

A related task is translating the questionnaire from its original ("master") language to other languages. The development of a second-language version can be necessary even if surveys are administered in only one country. For instance, in parts of the US, a Spanish version (suitable for Mexican or Latin American Spanish speakers) may be appropriate. In Canada, both English and French Canadian versions will be required. In Germany, both a German and a Turkish version may be needed. If possible, one should clarify what translations are needed early in the ES project: "In the past, at least in the United States, researchers often designed questions in English, then worried about ease of translation later. We know that if researchers think about how easy or hard it is to translate a particular question at the time of its initial design, the likelihood that questions can be comparable across languages in greatly increased" (Fowler, 2001, p. 53).

Identifying necessary language translations can be a tedious process affecting the interests of many stakeholders. ES project teams sometimes develop lengthy lists of languages deemed necessary to demonstrate to employees of different national origins that they are valuable contributors. Works councils can request or require even more translations. In one case, the works council in a large German company wanted an Ethiopian version of the questionnaire for a single Ethiopian employee. In other cases, management may require using just one language, without any translations, to stress that the company expects every employee to master one particular language; may this be English in the US or German in Germany.

After determining what languages are needed, one needs to pay attention to the "translatability" of a survey question. For example, one global retailer that is based in the US drafted a question in English that asked how well supervisors "deal with" poor performers. This vague verb was meant to include discussions, training, warnings, or even termination, but we learned that in China the question was best translated to how well supervisors "helped" poor performers. There was no easy way to capture the original broad concept that Americans would understand in a Chinese version without adding very specific examples—specificity that might have made the question controversial to employees.

For ES project teams, decisions on questionnaire translations can be hot topics that require diplomatic and pragmatic solutions. In some cases, the implementation of "information stations" staffed with bilingual employees can be useful in helping employees with insufficient knowledge of the questionnaire's language to understand the items at the time the survey is administered.

In other cases, translations of the questionnaire texts and items were developed and distributed in the form of raw text files that were supporting the one-language questionnaire, but not replacing it. This not only sends a message on what language is the official one, but it also reduces printing and administrative costs (e.g. data entry), while still allowing non-native speakers to use their native language text file (by having it next to the questionnaire they are filling out). An example for this approach is a world-wide ES conducted in a large IT company, where the "master" questionnaire was formulated in English. This master questionnaire was distributed to all employees, but it was recommended that each local survey coordinator produce PDF files with the items translated into the languages needed in their area. The decision (including the work and the costs) for the local translations was left to the local organization. Of course, the danger with local translations is that connotations and subtle meaning may be added or lost in any of the supplemental languages.

Translations tend to be expensive and, most of all, time-consuming. To assemble a list of translations that would be nice to have is one thing, but to implement the necessary translation work and to control its quality, to program or to even print the various questionnaire versions, and to make sure that the right questionnaire reaches the individual employee during survey administration is demanding. Therefore, the ES project team should always aim to keep the number of translations at a minimum. To accomplish this goal, the ES project team must make an effort to explain to all stakeholders and decision makers the strain many translations put on the ES project in terms of costs and time.

Coordinating the Development of Group-Specific Items

The ES project team also coordinates the inclusion of additional, group-specific items that complement the core questionnaire of items that is identical for every employee of the organization. The additional items are meant to address topics that are of interest to certain organizational units or groups only. For example, the subsidiaries of a company in different countries may want to use the survey to address their country-specific HR activities of the last years. The company's R&D function may also want to focus on some topics that are important or even uniquely relevant to researchers (e.g., advancing professional competencies needed to master future technologies), while the production function may have their own particular issues (e.g., safety at work, noise at work). Then, managers may want to have an opportunity to comment on the particular problems that a manager encounters in his or her role. Obviously, once one begins to ponder such group-specific items, the possibilities become excessive and the various crossings of country, function, position, etc. can make questionnaire construction very complex, especially if certain variations are needed in more than one language. The ES project team, therefore, has to generate a plan for what is really needed. The aim is to offer *some* group-specific items to *some* groups, but to keep everything as simple as possible. Usually, the number of group-specific items is limited to about 10 for all employees, and to 10 additional items for managers, to avoid excessive overall survey length.

For group-specific items to be valuable, local ES coordinators at the different sites need to be briefed on item writing and scaling issues. For instance, the use of certain standard rules (see Section 5.7 on item construction) and concrete examples of problematic items can help facilitate the development of useful, group-specific items. Carefully designed item-development training programs for local survey coordinators have been shown to be beneficial: The time invested here is easily made up for at later stages. For instance, if trainings are conducted successfully, less time has to be invested to discuss and modify the local survey coordinators' suggestions. ES coordinators can also be supported by assembling Q&A lists as shown in Table 6.1.

When designing group-specific items, the local survey coordinators need to make sure that they sufficiently involve the different groups. The HR directors of the respective sites are typically the most important agents for ensuring successful generation of good group-specific items.

Even if carefully designed item-development trainings are utilized and all precautions are met, the ES project team and its consultants still need to plan for ample time to discuss the various item suggestions. In many cases, changing survey items means substantial work for survey experts. All items proposed need to be read and carefully discussed before their formulations can be changed. Discussing items also requires respect and diplomacy, because those who propose items typically resist "arbitrary" modifications of their proposals. Thus, any item change needs to be done in a cooperative spirit and with convincing arguments that show that the suggested modifications lead to "even better" items. Dropping items (or issues) is even more difficult, because local ES coordinators often demand more and more group-specific items, leading to lengthy negotiations. Hence, rules for the maximum number of items must be made clear before any item proposals are generated.

Table 6.1. Some questions and answers for item writers.

- *Q:* Why are the items mostly/only closed items? *A:* To save time when filling out the questionnaire; to better protect the respondent's anonymity; to make statistical analyses fast and easy.
- *Q:* Why do the items use 5-point agree-disagree answer scales? *A:* That is common practice in employee surveys today. Most benchmarks are based on this answer scale.
- *Q:* Why use a middle category on the agree-disagree answer scale? *A:* Because there are issues where one can have a "mixed" attitude or opinion. The middle category can be labeled "undecided", "mixed", "partly agree, partly disagree", or similarly.
- *Q:* Why not use a "don't know" answer category? *A:* With few exceptions, items should be chosen such that they ask about something where every employee has an opinion, even if this opinion is only preliminary or insecure. Items can be skipped, too.
- *Q:* How do small changes in the item's wording impact the survey results? *A:* Usually there is little or no impact if the employee understands what you want to know. However, the exact wording can greatly impact the acceptance of the survey results and sometimes leads to long discussions.
- *Q:* Why not also provide "Anything else?" questions where every respondent can answer in his or her own words? *A:* Such questions often yield little additional information; they are also expensive and time-consuming to remove names, translate, and analyze; they threaten anonymity.
- *Q:* Shouldn't one also ask for "proposals" or "ideas?" *A:* Proposals are often made before the problem is clear. At this time, diagnosis is most important. Solutions can be proposed later in the follow-up processes.

Coordinating the Development of Demographic Items

The ES project team also needs to drive the development of demographic items. Usually, a survey expert first discusses the range of alternatives. They reach from setting up the minimum demographic variables that are absolutely needed to generate the focal reports required to run the follow-up processes in the planned width and depth. A minimum of demographic variables also helps to protect the individual respondent's anonymity. On the other hand, there may be special reasons to check if certain variables (e.g., gender, job type, performance rating) explain much variance in some or all items. In confidential surveys, the number of demographic variables is not restricted by anonymity concerns, but by practical questions such as collecting the answers in administering the questionnaire. However, this problem can be reduced or even eliminated if the demographic information for each respondent is filled out automatically in an online survey or by providing self-adhesive stickers (see Section 5.10) with this information taken from the personnel information system.

Obviously, deciding on demographic items is a complex issue. It depends on how the ES is positioned and on practical and technical considerations. Demographic items also determine what is and what is not possible in the follow-up processes. In order to arrive at optimal decisions, the ES project team must interact with a number of persons in different roles.

Local survey coordinators should be assigned the task of clarifying in their areas of responsibility what demographic variables are needed to get the follow-up processes going in the desired way. They can be instructed with a task outline such as this: "Arrange for a meeting with the survey sponsor (usually the HR director) in your area and discuss a general outline of processes needed when the survey data are in. Note that all follow-up processes have to be in line with the overall ES objectives. The exact nature of follow-up processes is not fixed from above, but leaves room for area-specific emphases and variation. However, the general format is a top-down approach that begins with presentations to top/senior management, to middle management, to the works council, and ends with discussions or workshops in the individual working groups. Thus, one should be able to generate not only general survey reports for all employees in your area, but also for special subgroups such as individual workgroups or the middle management in a particular division (function, subsidiary, etc.). Usually, what one needs is at least one (or several) demographic variable(s) that allows one to identify most individual working groups with whom one wants to discuss the survey results or for whom it makes sense to aggregate the survey results. Also, one wants to be able to distinguish employees by their job positions (e.g., rank and file, supervisor, middle manager, senior manager, top manager). It is your task to identify these variables and report them to the ES project team, or contact your support coordinator and ask for help on how to proceed."

The ES project team may also have to check with the HR department if the personnel information system (PIS) can be used for specifying the individual respondent's demographic profile. This information is needed to automatically fill out the demographic variables in an online questionnaire or for sending the respondents their individual demographic profiles (possibly in the form of self-adhesive stickers). In either case, it must be clarified first if and how the demographic variables can be extracted from the PIS. This is typically easy to realize in practice. However, the data quality of the PIS is often an issue. For an online survey, one must be sure that the PIS contains the correct information at the time of the survey, while for sending out demographic profiles to all participants, the needed information must be extracted and "frozen" in a data file at the latest-possible time t. This typically requires that the demographic profiles are extracted from the PIS some two weeks prior to time t, and then sent out to local survey coordinators for final quality control and corrections. The coordinators usually are not given direct access to the PIS, but rather give their feedback to a member of the ES project team for further processing. If everything works well, few relevant changes occur in the time period between freezing the demographic variables and survey administration, but some always do, and so rules have to be specified for this situation. One solution is to ask the survey participants to check their demographic profile and contact their survey coordinator by phone or email if this profile appears to be incorrect. The coordinator then informs the support coordinator if corrections are indeed needed in the frozen data file; finally, the participant is informed about the changes and asked to call the questionnaire a second time. This approach also ensures that survey participants are aware of the demographic information that is being collected, meeting a common ethical requirement of informed consent.

The ES project team should discuss the demographic items with the survey sponsor and key stakeholders. In addition to items that allow classifying the respondents into different organizational units and working groups, general demographic items such as gender, ethnicity, organizational tenure, hierarchical level, country, etc. may have to be collected as well.

For instance, personnel research may be interested in assessing the employee's organizational tenure. If so, an appropriate response scale has to be developed. Categories such as "less than 2 years", "2-5 years", "6-10 years", and "more than 10 years" may be useful in some organizations with traditional employment structures, while in more fast-paced environments more categories in the range of 1-5 years may be beneficial. At the same time, one must keep an eye on the stratification provided by relevant benchmarks. The categories should, therefore, be set up in such a way that they can be collapsed into those of the benchmark values. For example, if the benchmark data distinguish persons into "less than 1 year", "1-3 years", etc., then using the above scale leads to statistics that cannot be benchmarked anymore.

Tenure is, in a way, a particularly simple demographic item. It partitions all respondents perfectly into groups (i.e., it maps each respondent into exactly one group). Unfortunately, demographic items with such partitioning power are rarely available in practice. Rather, one often needs combinations of *several* demographic items (e.g., respondents in organizational unit X, but not those who belong to function Y or those in country B). Such combinations make ordering ES reports complex and error-prone. They occasionally lead to reports that make no sense. For example, in one case, the combination rule for a particular subgroup was set up with a top manager of a major high-tech company. When the report was delivered, it showed one respondent from Japan, and one from Argentina: They both satisfied the filter rule, but they definitely did not belong to the "competence center" of European, North American, and Indian employees that this manager wanted to select. To avoid such cases, and to make report ordering as simple as possible, it often pays if the ES project team generates "artificial" variables from the demographic items that later allow each survey coordinator to use simple filter rules where all or most organizational units of interest can be identified with one single code (such as "de4=78", selecting all persons with code 78 on the demographic item de4; see Table 10.4).

6.3 Involving Stakeholders into Questionnaire Development

If at all possible, construction of the ES questionnaire should involve more than just external consultants and survey coordinators. Important stakeholders such as top management, middle management, the HR function, and the works council should be involved as much as possible. However, involving stakeholders into questionnaire construction does not mean that each group can decide what should and should not be included in the final questionnaire. Rather, the last decision about the questionnaire lies with the survey sponsor.

Involving Rank-And-File Employees

Rank-and-file employees always play a role in the construction of an ES questionnaire. They are represented, to some extent, by the survey coordinators themselves. They also have an influence through those persons who serve in pre-tests of early versions of the questionnaire. The "average" employee can also be given a greater and more direct role in various ways. For example, some companies use email notifications sent out to all employees asking them to suggest items to be included in the survey. Clearly, this approach is risky business. The number of items suggested can be substantial, leading to a lot of work for the ES project team, and only a small selection of them can be considered for the final questionnaire. In addition rejecting item proposals can cause resentment and the feeling that employee opinions are not really valued after all. Instead of surveying employees to obtain a larger pool of items, conducting sessions with employee focus groups to generate ideas and to identify relevant topics is generally a better alternative. Such workshops also offer the opportunity to discuss, clarify, and refine all suggestions immediately. The members of the focus group can be selected randomly or in a quota way that guarantees, for example, that all major business areas are represented in the group. Note though that no item suggested by rank-and-file employees should be pushed directly into the questionnaire against management's (or other stakeholders') will. In case of conflict, a reasonable effort should be made to explain the role of a controversial item to all stakeholder representatives. Naturally, one should also make every effort to formulate the item in such a way that it serves its purpose without causing negative side effects. In the end, the ES sponsor must decide whether an item's benefits (for the goals of the ES) are worth some discomfort.

Involving the Organization's Executive Board

An organization's executive board is usually the official ES sponsor and the ultimate client for external consultants working on the ES project. The executive board needs to be provided with drafts of the questionnaire and needs to approve the final version before it can be used for data collection. In practice, this usually means that one of the top officers (often the HR director) takes over this role, but it can still be useful to sit down with some board members from time to time to actively discuss the ES project, given that there is enough interest. This also allows the ES project team to elaborate on the rationale used for questionnaire design (e.g., response scales, layout), the questionnaire's content and its relation to the ES project objectives, plans for data collection, analysis, and follow-up processes, etc. However, interactions with top managers must always be concise and to the point. Rarely can the questionnaire be discussed item by item—nor should that be attempted, because if top managers suggest items, they are typically poor ones that are, moreover, hard to change. What top managers are good at is to point out topics which add strategic momentum to an ES project. The ES project team can then draft questionnaire items that measure (or serve) these topics and then return with these items to discuss them with the survey sponsor. The Blue Sky session that we describe in section 4.1 provides a useful framework for working with executives.

In practice, one can approach top managers and ask them to suggest topics that are of particular importance to them and where they feel that the ES can serve as an instrument to accelerate the necessary change. Managers might answer this interview question by describing the strategic issues that they believe could be promoted with the ES. For example, they might say that "customer orientation needs to be strengthened at all levels and in all functions of the company" or that "the strategy needs to be implemented more quickly, much more quickly." They may also discuss issues that have no obvious relationship to the ES project team, but where the survey could help to prepare the climate that these issues receive more support (e.g., measures to cut costs).

HR executives always deserve special attention. They are typically quite conscious of the ES project and its potential. For example, in one case, the HR director intended to implement performance-based components in the company's pay and benefits systems. He thus suggested including the following item in the ES: "I support a stronger performance-based component of pay and benefits at company ABC." By suggesting the item, he was hoping for a large number of employees to endorse the item, supporting his plans further. However, one could ask whether it is likely that many employees will support this item, and what would happen to his plans if they don't. To speculate about such outcomes requires ES expert knowledge and it thus makes sense to include ES experts in such discussions. ES experts can also help reformulate items if necessary, suggest better items for a given purpose, or provide input on decisions other organizations have made in similar situations. However, managers want quick and targeted answers, and the ES expert can be in a difficult situation if she is not aware of the whole ES project and its positioning. Thus, it is essential to involve the expert in the entire ES project, including details about its positioning.

Involving the Works Council

In many western European countries, an organization's works council is likely to play a certain role in developing the survey instrument. One of the members of the ES project team often comes from the works council, or the works council is at least informed from time to time about the progress of the preparations for the ES. This does not automatically lead to extra work. What one can do is to invite the works council to send one or two representatives to participate in relevant sections of the workshops that the ES project team conducts with the local survey coordinators.

Care must be taken that the works council's involvement does not exceed a level that turns the ES into a works council's project. The works council should have a voice, but not a special voice, and other stakeholders are just as important. To keep the works council's natural tendency to claim the ES for itself under control, it sometimes proves useful if the ES project team offers to include one or two items that assess how the employees perceive and evaluate the works council itself (e.g., "I feel that the works council represents the employees' interests well."). The argument is that such items come with the risk of getting negative feedback. Management is willing to accept that risk. Thus, would it not be fair if the works council accepts the same risk? This question sometimes leads to lively discussions within the council, touching various issues. For example, some council members may question whether the data collected on council-related items should be made accessible for all employees. If one answers that items on the works council should be treated as any other item, and therefore be included in each report, and that the works council cannot be exempt from the evaluative component that an ES has for different persons, groups, and agents of the organization (e.g., managers or service functions), the works council often becomes more cautious with its demands. In organizations that have more experience with employee surveys, on the other hand, the works council often accepts that it too is up for evaluation in an ES, and it welcomes critical feedback and even asks for external advice on what to do with it.

Involving Middle Management and ES Advisory Boards

Other stakeholders can also be involved into constructing the ES questionnaire. One obvious group is middle management. It is possible to also conduct some interviews or focus groups with middle managers to find out if they have special concerns that could be included into the questionnaire. Often, ES questionnaires include a special section that focuses on managers' issues only. It addresses topics related to people-management, to support from above, to resources and decision making, to targets and bonus systems, etc.

Still further stakeholders can be considered, but obviously one cannot involve everyone. This would not only consume too many resources, but it would necessarily mean that many suggestions for the questionnaire would have to be rejected because there is simply no room to include everyone's items. Yet, what often proves a good solution is to set up an "advisory board" for the ES project where many stakeholders—middle management in particular—are represented. This board can meet with the ES project team from time to time to discuss proposals for the ES.

6.4 Pre-Testing and Pilot-Testing the Questionnaire

In a professional ES project, testing the quality of the questionnaire is mandatory (AAPOR, 1997). One form of testing is pre-testing, where *qualitative* "laboratory" methods (such as loud thinking, probing, or discussions) are used to evaluate if all survey items measure what they are supposed to measure. The other form of testing—which is the more traditional one—is pilot-testing, where the questionnaire is first given to a sample of respondents and their data are then analyzed for their *quantitative* (statistical) properties (such as each item's difficulty).

Pre-tests are a good investment in any ES project for two reasons. First, even the most experienced ES expert who follows all item construction rules and takes into account all contextual information cannot guarantee that all items are answered as intended. Second, and even more important: Pre-tests are crucial to protect the ES project against attempts to disqualify undesired results by arguing that the respondents did not understand the items properly. The authors know of ES projects that were stopped after data collection because important stakeholders challenged the meaning of the data to an extent where further work with the survey results would have had negative effects on the organizational climate. However, if the questionnaire were pre-tested with carefully chosen samples of respondents, and if the pre-testing results were documented together with all the revisions it led to in the questionnaire, the ES data would not be discredited that easily.

Pilot-testing is not that common in today's ES context. However, one often carefully analyzes the data of one ES in order to improve the questionnaire for the next ES.

A Simple Pre-Testing Approach for Employee Surveys

Pre-testing an ES questionnaire can be done with great sophistication (Willis, 2005). However, a simple pre-test is often sufficient. To conduct it, one selects a group of persons (often so that they satisfy some simple quota of gender, job type, or hierarchy), creates a realistic survey administration situation for them, and asks them to fill out the questionnaire as test persons "as if it was a real employee survey." The purpose is not to measure their opinions, but to test the questionnaire so that it can be fine-tuned into an optimal instrument that is used in the general survey of all employees: "There is no need to show how you filled out the present version to anyone. However, do not take this questionnaire version with you. After this session, all questionnaires will be collected and destroyed."

Then, while the test-respondents are filling out the survey, they can be observed from a distance to evaluate how long it takes to complete each of the survey's sections or individual items (particularly easy if electronic surveys are used, many programs allow detailed analyses on completion time of sections and items). Analyses of item and section completion times allow for recognition of potentially problematic areas that take respondents a lot of time.

After filling out the questionnaire, the test-respondents should be interviewed or participate in a focus group discussion. The researcher first asks them about their general reaction towards the questionnaire (e.g., "Did you like the survey altogether?", "How about the layout?", "Did you have difficulties with the font type?", "Did you find the questions interesting?", "Was it difficult for you to complete the survey?"). Next, the researcher works through the survey page by page, using probing questions such as: "Are the instructions easy or difficult to understand?", "Does the survey contain items that you find confusing or unclear?", "Are there items where you were concerned about being able to provide an honest opinion?" The use of these questions allows the survey development team to evaluate which survey components may need additional work or modifications.

During pre-test sessions, it makes less sense to ask respondents for their opinion on the survey's content. Usually, the survey has been developed with lots of attention to details, meaning that last minute changes to survey content would be unlikely to result in a better survey. However, if pre-test participants express that certain contents seem to have been intentionally omitted or avoided, modifying the survey might be necessary.

Although it is a good idea to ask respondents about their opinions, surveys should not be over-modified based on pre-testing feedback. In particular, while respondent impressions can be useful, respondents are unlikely to be good item developers (Fowler, 1995). Research supporting the notion of respondents being poor item developers (e.g. Hunt, Sparkman, & Wilcox, 1982) has found that few respondents were able to detect problematic survey items (e.g., items containing double-barreled statements, missing answer or response options). In addition, while some respondents can find deficient items, they are mostly unable to identify the items' specific problems or issues—resolving these issues is usually better left to experts.

Mangione (1995) also notes that respondents can have difficulty in voicing dissatisfaction or criticism towards interviewers whom they perceive to be survey experts. His findings suggest that providing participants with the feeling that their input is valuable can help alleviate these problems. Furthermore, asking respondents what problems they think "a coworker" might have in completing the survey can generate useful input without putting the respondent in the position of having to critique the survey or interviewer directly.

Cognitive Pre-Testing

Another approach towards pre-testing is asking respondents in one-on-one interviews to express their thoughts while going through the survey ("thinking aloud"). The respondent's comments can be recorded and used for later analyses.

This thinking-aloud approach towards survey pre-testing has been used successfully in opinion and market research. For instance, Loftus (1984) asked respondents about their recent doctor's visits ("How many times in the last 12 months did you see a physician?"). Her use of the thinking-aloud method showed that when asked, respondents were not likely to start from recent doctor's visits going back to visits about a year ago. Instead, respondents appeared to start at a date about a year ago and add up doctor's visits since then. Thus, reformulating the item asking "How many times have you seen a physician since May 1?" may be more in line with respondents cognitive processes than the original item. In contrast, Prüfer & Rexroth (1996) reported respondents averaging daily events to provide an estimate of their weekly activities (knowing this, respondents can be asked to provide estimates of daily activities right away, which can then be averaged for weeks and months).

Another technique used in cognitive pre-testing is *paraphrasing*. Paraphrasing requires the respondent to reiterate or restate the item's meaning to the interviewer in their own words. This allows one to detect interpretative difficulties at this stage of questionnaire development.

A related method is *probing*. This probing can be quite general ("Is there anything you did not understand?"), or focus on the answering process ("How did you arrive at your answer?"), or concentrate on particular issues or words ("Can you explain what the notion of 'XYZ' means to you?"). One could also use probing to check how the respondents understand certain formal properties of the questionnaire such as the middle category of the usual 5-point Likert answer scale: "Why did you check this answer box? What do you want to express by that?" The respondent's answer could be: "I checked the 'Undecided' category because I did not know what to say." If so, the answer scale is not used as intended—an "undecided" option should express a mixed opinion, not a "don't know"—and one should consider revising the questionnaire so that it becomes clearer (possibly by offering "don't know" answer categories in addition to the Likert scale).

Another example from practice is this. The questionnaire contained the item "My supervisor is very competent" (with an agree-disagree answer scale). Some test-respondents argued that they should have checked the disagree category because they did not feel that their supervisor is "very" competent, but just competent. This led to questionnaire design team to reformulate the item as "My supervisor is competent." The graded answer scale from "fully agree" to "fully disagree" still allows the respondent to express the "very" of the original item.

Cognitive pre-testing is not only interesting for improving the questionnaire, but also for getting an idea of what reactions managers and employees might have when receiving reports of survey results. Unclear items can thus be eliminated or modified to avoid communication problems with supervisors when ES results are being presented.

Thinking aloud or paraphrasing may, however, not model correctly how the respondent arrives at a judgment. Willis (2004) points out that cognitive pre-testing should be used only particular items, i.e. "those that involve processes that enter into consciousness, as opposed to those characterized by automatic, non-conscious processing of stimuli" (p. 28). Moreover, the tasks should be interesting and engaging; they should involve higher-level verbal processes that take more than a few seconds; and they should involve problem solving and criteria that people use in decision making. Hence, cognitive pre-testing should be used only for the more "difficult" items of the ES questionnaire. Most attitude items do not belong to this class.

How Many Pre-Tests?

Mangione (1995) recommends conducting at least 25 pre-test sessions if participant groups are used. Friedrichs (1973) suggests conducting a similar number of interviews with individual participants. Although these general guidelines may be useful, the exact nature of pre-testing has to be influenced by organizational characteristics. In organizations with complex structures and multiple languages, pre-testing has to be more extensive than in small organizations where no translated version has to be used. It should also be noted that merely increasing the number of pre-test sessions or participants is not an optimal strategy. Rather, pre-tests should be conducted in a *staggered* way. The results of an early set of pre-tests are first consolidated, and then an additional round of pre-tests is conducted with the improved questionnaire, and so on. Pre-testing is stopped if further pre-tests do not lead to new insights or real improvements. In the usual ES context, one does not need many such rounds because the first questionnaire is based on considerable experience so that its items and text passages typically only require modest adaption to the organization's culture.

In small organizations, pre-tests can also function as small interventions. Pre-test participants are likely to discuss their participation experiences with colleagues and report on their perceptions of the questionnaire's topics, the relevance of its items for the work context, the absence of sensitive items, etc. This lateral communication of the test-respondents with their peers can help to support the ES project, leading to higher response rates in the final survey.

Pilot-Testing the Questionnaire

Pilot-testing the ES questionnaire is the more traditional way to assess its quality. Pilot-testing was developed in the context of scale construction (Borg & Staufenbiel, 2007; DeVellis, 2003). The questionnaire is given to a small sample of employees that should be representative with respect to the demographic variables that are used in the ES (e.g., gender, job type, function, country). The sample size depends on the subgroups that one wants to compare (e.g., men vs. women; blue-collar vs. white-collar employees) in the sense that the smallest subgroup should be reasonably large for reliable statistics. What is "reasonably large" is not clearly defined, but in practice, sample sizes of 100 to 200 are often considered acceptable (Spector, 1992). The test persons fill out the questionnaires, and their data are then analyzed statistically.

Two statistics are most important. One of them is the percentage of persons endorsing an item ("item difficulty"). Items that are endorsed by all persons (or by no one) obviously yield no information on personal differences. Such items should be reformulated so that they differentiate among respondents. For example, the item "I deeply hate my supervisor" is so extreme that few if anyone would agree to it, while the item "I like my supervisor" is much more likely to produce endorsement in all categories of the agree-disagree answer scale, producing more variance. This variance can be better used to study how liking one's supervisor is correlated with other variables of interest, such as turnover intention, absenteeism, or productivity.

The other statistics of interest are the intercorrelations of the items, in particular the intercorrelation of those items that should all measure one particular issue ("internal consistency"). In other words, items that form a scale should be positively intercorrelated among each other. This is the core information in Cronbach's coefficient alpha. The common rule of thumb cutoff value is that alpha should be greater than .70. Items with an alpha of greater .70 are considered "reliable" in the sense of internal consistency. Items with low alphas need to be reformulated or eliminated: An index formed from averaging such items would have no clear meaning, because it averages "apples and oranges."

Factor analysis and multidimensional scaling are also useful for studying the structure of the questionnaire items. Both methods can guide the questionnaire design team in locating items that are candidates for revisions.

In practice, quantitative pilot-testing is not used that often in the ES context today. The core of an ES questionnaire is usually relatively standard, and its special items gain more from careful cognitive pre-tests than from statistical analyses of pilot-test data. Items that are too extreme, for example, can—and usually are—also recognized in a qualitative pre-test. Also, scales do not play a big role in employee surveys, and the properties of the items used to form scale scores or indices can also be tested when the survey data are in. What one should always do is to study the statistical properties of the questionnaire items in the data that result from an ES, and then use these analyses as input for possible improvements of the questionnaire of the next ES.

7 Sampling

One of the most prominent decisions in the design of an employee survey concerns the question of whether to administer a *census* surveys or a *sample* survey. In a census survey, all employees are invited to participate, while in a sample survey, only a (typically small) group of employees is targeted. When first confronted with this decision, most laypeople believe that a sample survey is easier and cheaper to run. However, as we will see below, this is not quite true: A sample survey can be quite difficult to construct, less reliable in generating reasonable return rates, and more complicated to analyze and to interpret. Moreover, in a census survey, the resulting data can be broken down to the smallest organizational unit so that every manager and every organizational unit gets a report of "their" data. To collect the data and to generate the necessary reports is usually not a major cost factor, particularly when administering an online survey. In today's practice, both census and sample surveys are used. A census is optimal for regular in-depth studies of the employees' attitudes and opinions, while a sample is preferred for occasional or interim "pulse surveys" that estimate trend statistics for larger organizational units without causing too much commotion and follow-up.

7.1 The Population

Any survey must define the group of persons it attempts to measure. One definition of such a *target population* is this: "All persons who work at ABC with a work contract of at least one half year." This excludes, for example, all short-term substitutes or apprentices. It includes, on the other hand, employees who are on a special leave of absence such as a sabbatical or a maternity leave.

Whether certain groups of persons should or should not be invited to participate is not only a statistical but also a psychological question because it sends the signal "You belong" or "You do not belong." To survey temporary employees is, on the other hand, typically not reasonable because such persons have no long-term commitment to the organization, and they may not provide thoughtful answers. Including or excluding certain groups requires one to consider very practical questions such as how easily such persons can be reached and how much it would cost. The target population normally either invites managers at all levels as well as non-managers, or it focuses on particular managers only. Surveying only non-managers is rarely done in practice. Likewise, the target population sometimes excludes unionized employees, usually because certain survey topics, such as compensation, are unique to this group.

Once the target population is defined, one needs to clarify how the employees who belong to this population can be identified. In the simplest case, the personnel information system (PIS) contains all the necessary data such that a list of the chosen persons can be generated with address, position, and organizational unit.

In practice, however, this is not always as easy as it may appear. It is almost always true that the information in the PIS is not completely up-to-date, containing data that are not accurate anymore. If one relies on such data in an employee survey, the *sampling frame*—that is, the particular database that is effectively used for sampling—as it is defined by the PIS may lead to (a) sending survey material to persons who do not work for the company anymore (*overcoverage*) or to (b) omitting persons who recently joined the company but are not yet listed in the PIS (*undercoverage*). Hence, such sampling frames define, in effect, a *sampling population* that is not equivalent to the target population.

Overcoverage and undercoverage effects are often hard to control. For example, when running an online survey, employees who never check their e-mail during the time when the survey is running are automatically excluded from the final sample. Thus, the final sample is drawn from an *inference population* that does not include "lazy e-mailers." The sample, thus, only allows statements about non-lazy e-mailers. Other examples for undercoverage can easily be found. Some employees may be sick or on vacation during the survey, others may be on business trips, and still others may be difficult to reach such as traveling salespersons. Obviously, undercoverage may be a serious problem if the omitted persons differ systematically from those in the sample. The inferences are then *biased*. Overcoverage is, on the other hand, hardly ever important in practice, provided one excludes the possibility that an employee participates more than once.

7.2 Non-Random Samples

Random samples require that each person of the population is chosen with a certain probability p (>0) for the sample. In case of a simple random sample, the value p is the same for every person so that each person has exactly the same chance as every other person of being selected. For non-random samples, the chance of a person being included in the sample is unknown.

Convenience Samples

Non-random samples are not uncommon in organizational surveys. They can be pure convenience samples or they can be systematic. If you go to the company's cafeteria and ask someone whether he or she is willing to volunteer to participate in a survey, and if you repeat this approach until you have collected your target number of cases, then you have formed a sample of convenience. Opgenoorth (1985) reports two similar cases. In one case, a printed questionnaire was added to the company newspaper.

In another case, the questionnaires were stacked up by the bulletin boards so that any by-passer could pick one up at their discretion. Obviously, such methods do not lead to a systematically planned selection of respondents. One simply hopes that "many" will participate.

Given the sample, however, it is possible to check its properties. For example, does the sample contain managers and non-managers in proportions similar to those in the population? Needless to say: For convenience samples, this is most likely not the case. Hence, convenience samples will not model the population, in general. Such samples are therefore only good, at best, for collecting first impressions for later, more systematic studies.

Typical Cases, Extreme Cases, Experts

Systematic sampling means that it is decided "by design" which respondents you want in the sample and which ones you do not want. One example is to survey "typical" employees. Such an employee could be male, married, with kids, and more than five years of tenure. This person is typical because most other employees either have the same or at least very similar profiles. What one wants to know is what the typical employee thinks, feels, and plans to do, not some "marginal" person.

The idea of surveying "extreme" cases is different. Here, one asks persons, groups, or organizational units that have, for example, excelled in terms of performance. The survey should help to find out their particular set up. Other extreme cases may be opinion leaders, subsidiaries with special problems or challenges, or individuals who are leaving the organization ("exit interviews"). Experts are, in a sense, also extreme persons. To survey them can be useful to predict the future, for example ("Delphi surveys").

Cut-Off Samples

Similar to extreme case sampling is the cut-off sample. It surveys only those cases that exceed on some important criteria. For example, one may select all subsidiaries that make more than x million dollars, or not survey all those subsidiaries that contribute less than $x\%$ to the total earnings of the company.

Snow-Balling

In some instances, surveys are conducted within social networks (e.g. in project groups). In these cases, the surveying process is started with one individual, who is asked to forward the request to participate and possibly pass on a link to an online survey to other relevant individuals who then in turn contact other relevant persons. Snow-balling is particularly useful for populations that do not make up a large part of the overall population (e.g., alcoholics), or for groups that are difficult to reach otherwise (e.g., employees who work in the field).

Table 7.1. Quotas of margins do not guarantee proper quotas of cells.

	(a) Population				(b) Sample 1			(c) Sample 2		
	A	B	N		A	B		A	B	
Managers	a	b	100		10	0	10%	0	10	10%
Non-managers	c	d	900		60	30	90%	70	20	90%
N	700	300	1000		70%	30%	100%	70%	30%	100%

Quota Sampling

Quota sampling means that the sample is drawn such that its elements satisfy certain proportions. For instance, if an organization employs 80% men and 20% women, one may want a sample that also contains 80% men and 20% women. The sample, thus, truly represents the population's gender distribution.

Quotas in employee surveys typically focus on at least two characteristic: Managerial rank (executives, top managers, senior managers, middle managers, supervisors, non-managers) and major organizational units (departments, functions, subsidiaries, etc.). Table 7.1 illustrates the method. Consider a population of $N=1,000$ individuals, where 700 belong to organizational unit A and 300 belong to organizational unit B. Assume further that the population consists of 100 managers and 900 non-managers. Finally, assume that the *marginal* distributions of the population are as shown in panel (a) of Table 7.1. Using quota sampling, one assures that the marginal distributions of the sample correspond to the marginal distribution of the population. That is, 10% of the individuals must be managers, and 90% non-managers. Furthermore, one must make sure that 70% of the respondents in the sample belong to org unit A and 30% to org unit B.

Unfortunately, satisfying marginal quotas does not guarantee that the frequencies in the cells of the sample correspond to the cell sizes of the population. This is shown in panels (b) and (c) of Table 7.1. In both cases, the marginal quotas are identical. However, in Sample 1, all managers belong to org unit A, while in Sample 2, all managers belong to org unit B. Thus, in order to adequately represent the cells sizes in the sample, simply concentrating on the margins is not sufficient. Rather, each cell must be filled with respondents so that their proportions correspond to the proportions of the population.

In applied settings, however, quota sampling that relies on marginal frequencies is sometimes the only feasible method because the cell frequencies for the population are unknown or too difficult to derive. So, one may attempt to derive how many cases one needs in each cell from the population margins. For example, in Table 7.1, one computes $(700 \cdot 100)/1,000=70$ for cell a. So, under what conditions do quotas based on margins yield proper samples? In our 2×2 table, the estimate is correct if the equation $a:b = c:d$ holds in the population (i.e. that the proportion of managers to non-managers is the same in both organizational units). If one can assume that such constant proportionalities are (approximately) satisfied, then deriving sample frequencies for the cells by using the margins of the population is (approximately) correct.

Quota-based samples have led to substantial discussions in the social sciences (Diekmann, 1995; Gabler & Hoffmeyer-Zlotnik, 1997). Because they only require that certain quotas be satisfied, the final sample typically contains employees who were easiest to reach or more cooperative than others. Hence, inferences to the population become risky.

Thus, even quota-based sampling methods should attempt to introduce some notion of randomness into the selection process. This can be accomplished, for example, by matching a particular digit in the employee ID with a randomly selected number. For example, one can select employees whose ID number has a three in the fifth position. As long as this fifth position uses zero through nine in a random fashion (i.e., it is not a code for geography, department, or some other demographic), then the result is a random sample within the quota (see "stratified random samples" below). One can filter the list of employees using a spreadsheet application and invite employees from the top of the list down until the cell's required frequency is met. This selection approach becomes particularly simple if a spreadsheet can be created, including employees names, ID numbers, and email addresses. Note that one can approximate this random process by selecting employees whose names begin with a "randomly selected" letter of the alphabet (if no random digit exists in the ID numbers).

7.3 Random Samples

Random samples are statistically superior to systematic samples. For random samples, a statistical theory exists that allows one to assess the precision of the parameters computed from the sample. Non-random samples have to be evaluated newly in each single case, using subjective criteria. Hence, when practitioners rave about their "positive experience" with a particular non-random sampling method, one should be careful: Such impressions are ill-founded.

Applied researchers are also fond of another notion, i.e. *representative samples*. They often ask questions such as "How large does the sample have to be to be representative?" or "Is the realized sample representative?", and then expect that the statistician can answer the questions simply by saying "500" or "yes", respectively. However, the statistician cannot answer these questions, because they do not belong to the scope of statistical theory and demand the judgment of experts in the particular subject matter being studied. A representative sample for an ES is a sample of employees that are distributed with respect to "important" variables just as the employees in the population. For example, the sample may contain men and women in the exact same proportion as the population. Then, the sample is representative with respect this one variable, gender. Thus, a sample is, at best, only representative in a certain sense. One way to obtain representative samples is to select a random sample. A random sample is the more representative of *all* features of the population the larger it is. And in stratified random samples, one even makes sure, by construction, that it is representative with respect to certain variables (e.g., tenure or job type such as blue collar and white collar jobs), provided it has a certain minimum size.

Simple Random Samples

The simple (unconstrained) random sample is the prototype of all random samples. The sample is drawn from the population such that each element of the population and each n-element subset of it has the same chance to end up in the sample (Stenger, 1986). To assess these probabilities, one needs a complete listing of all elements of the population. Assume that we have a complete listing of all employees of the organization of interest, and that it comprises $N=8,500$ persons. For drawing a sample of $n=100$ persons from this listing, we first enumerate the entries of this listing from 1 to 8,500. Then, we randomly draw 100 natural numbers from the interval [1, ... , 8,500] by using an appropriate computer program (easily found on the internet by searching for "random number generator") or a printed random numbers table (often found in books on statistics or research design). Finally, we select the persons that correspond to these numbers from the list.

Systematic Random Sampling

In today's companies, it is usually easy to generate a data file with all employees. However, this is not always true. For example, in some recent employee surveys in Eastern European companies, there were only printed listings or card files of the employees. To avoid the extra-work of first enumerating all entries in such listings or files, one can employ some "systematic" selection procedure. For example, to select a sample of n = 100 people from a population of $N = 8,500$, we begin with person s, who is picked randomly from the first 85 employees on the list, where 85 is derived from the formula $k=N/n$ persons (with k rounded to the next integer). We keep s as our first person in the sample, and then add every k^{th} person from the list until we reach n. Alternatively, one could partition the full set of card files into 100 piles of 85 cards each and then randomly select a card from each pile.

Stratified Random Samples

Because one wants the sample to truly represent certain demographics of the population, the usual method of choice is a stratified random sample. This method begins just like quota sampling by partitioning the population into different *strata* and, thereby, into various cells. Then, in contrast to quota sampling, one draws random samples of a certain size from the resulting cells.

The advantage of this approach can be demonstrated by the following example. Assume that in function X of the company we are surveying no one plans to leave the company in the near future, while in function Y, everybody intends to quit his or her job. Assume further that function X has 50 employees, and Y has 12. Thus, the total turnover intention rate is 0% (for 50 of the 62 employees plus 100% for 12 of the 62, which equals 19.4%). If we draw a simple random sample, we get this value only if we happen to sample, by chance, employees of function X and function Y in the ratio 50 : 12. In a stratified random sample, in contrast, we can *guarantee* this ratio by design.

Of course, this example is an extreme case because the different cells of the population are all completely "homogeneous"[23] on the issue of interest. That is generally not true; even people of the same cell of the population almost always differ in what we want to know. However, as long as there is some relationship between the respondents' membership in certain cells and the issue of interest, using stratified random sampling controls some error variance. Only if there is absolutely no relationship (for all variables of interest), would simple random sampling be just as good as stratified random sampling. Because this condition is not known in practice, stratifying the sample on criteria where one believes to find differences is always a good idea—especially when these strata have very different group sizes.

In the usual employee survey, one would stratify the sample on at least the criteria of organizational functions (or departments, areas, countries, subsidiaries, etc.) and the positions of the employees invited to participate. To illustrate, assume that the company has three functions with A=300, B=700, and C=50 employees. If we want a 10% sample (105 persons), we would—in *proportional* sampling—randomly select 30 employees from the function A (300/1,050 · 105 = 30), and 70 and 5 persons from functions B and C, respectively. This would lead to a representative representation of the three functions in the sample, while a simple random sample may miss the small function C altogether. It is also unlikely that the simple random sample would pick managers from the three functions in the proportions in which they exist in the population. Indeed, managers from function C may be missing completely in the sample.

The small function C from our example, however, leads us to also consider *disproportional* samples. After all, five employees in the sample are hardly sufficient to draw conclusions about this function. Thus, in a case like this, one may want to *oversample* certain cells on purpose. For sample employee surveys conducted in small companies, one often oversamples managers and simply invites all managers to participate, while drawing a true sample of non-managers. This method is often operationally the simplest. When attempting to ascertain perceptions of top managers or board members, where true proportional sampling makes no sense, asking everyone to participate is by far the best approach. It also does not require statistical "estimation" techniques when analyzing the data, provided the return rate is perfect (or very high).

Yet, even in large organizations, overrepresentations are not uncommon. When the German railroads conducted an employee survey in 1996, it had about 320,000 employees. One of its areas ("stations"), however, was relatively small with only 7,000 employees. In a proportional sample, one would only draw some 2.2% of the employees from this area. In a total sample of 1,000 persons, this would mean that only 22 employees from this area are asked to participate in the survey. Even if all of them actually participated, 22 persons are too few to convince anyone that their opinions are sufficient to draw inferences about the 7,000 employees from that area. Thus, in

---

[23] If the case where all cells are perfectly homogeneous, one really only needs one person per cell in the sample.

that case, oversampling could be considered (e.g. by the factor 10 so that 220 persons would be selected). Naturally, such oversamplings must later be compensated for by down-weighting the data from such subsamples (here: with 1/10) when aggregating the survey data to compute overall company-wide statistics.

Cluster Samples

In public opinion surveys one rarely uses simple or stratified random samples. One reason is that they can identify persons as candidates for the sample who are costly to reach because they live in various, perhaps remote, places. Also, complete listings of the entire population are seldom available. Similar conditions can also hold for employee surveys. For example, assume we want to survey a sample of employees who work for multiple companies in the automotive supply industry. There probably is no such listing of these employees anywhere. However, we might be able to compile a listing of the major companies in this industry. These companies would then be considered our *primary sampling units*. These PSU's represent *clusters* of what we are really interested in, the employees in that industry. The cluster sampling, then, proceeds in two stages: By first randomly picking clusters, and then by randomly picking persons within the clusters. The number of persons picked per cluster is usually proportional to the size of the cluster (i.e. in large clusters many persons are selected, in small ones proportionally fewer).

Cluster samples are statistically inferior to pure random samples if the clusters are relatively *homogenous* within but *heterogeneous* between. The precision of the estimated parameters then depends a lot on which and how many clusters are selected in the first place. If one suspects that the within-between homogeneity-heterogeneity condition holds, one should pick many clusters with small N's rather than just a few clusters with many persons per cluster.

Cluster sampling can be an economical sampling method in organizations that are regionally scattered such as, for example, a company with many subsidiaries in many locations such as Wal-Mart or Sears. In such cases, one sometimes modifies the sampling by picking a certain set of clusters in one survey and then picks clusters from the rest in the following survey (rolling samples). Another modification is to make sure that major subsidiaries are always in the sample.

Multi-Stage Sampling

In large organizations one can often save costs if the sampling is done in a multi-stage way. Many stages are normal in public opinion survey research. For example, if one wants to survey "the voter", one often begins with a sample of voting regions. Then, a random sample of addresses of households is drawn in each selected region. This sampling is proportional to avoid that small regions (e.g., rural districts) become overrepresented in the sample. On the third stage, a person in each household is picked randomly out of the age-groups of the household members. The advantage of such an approach is that one only needs a listing of voting regions on the first stage. Such listings exist and are readily available, while household addresses are difficult to get and expensive.

7.4 Sampling Errors

Assume that a proportion of $p=20\%$ of the employees seriously considers leaving the company within the next 12 months. However, if we draw a random sample of employees from the company's workforce, it is not likely that the proportion of persons with turnover intentions in the sample, $\hat{p}$, is also exactly equal to 20%. This error is simply a consequence of sampling. The error we make when estimating the population value p by the sample statistic $\hat{p}$ is likely to become greater, on average, if the sample is small.

Sampling Errors in Samples of Different Size

Assume we draw a million samples of $n=200$ persons each from a very large population where $p=20\%$ is true. We can then expect that the mean of the million observed $\hat{p}$ values (i.e., the proportions in the sample) is equal to p, because some samples overestimate p, while others underestimate p, and because these errors should compensate each other over the huge number of replications. In each single sample, however, we should rarely expect finding $\hat{p}=p$. The difference $e = p - \hat{p}$ is called the sampling error. For $n>30$, the distribution of these errors can be expected to be normal with a standard deviation[24] of

$$s_e = \sqrt{p(100-p)/n} \, . \qquad (7.1)$$

Because in a variable that is normally distributed one can expect that 95% of its values lie within ±1.96 standard deviations of its mean, we can predict that the sampling error of our one million random samples lies within the interval

$$-1{,}96 \cdot s_e \leq p - \hat{p} \leq +1{,}96 \cdot s_e \qquad (7.2)$$

in 95% of the samples. The inequality also holds if we add $\hat{p}$ to all its terms. It then says that for 95% of the samples one can expect that

$$\hat{p} - 1{,}96 \cdot s_e \leq p \leq \hat{p} + 1{,}96 \cdot s_e \, . \qquad (7.3)$$

This interval is called the *confidence interval* or, more precisely, the 95% confidence interval[25].

To compute the confidence interval, one needs s_e and to compute s_e one has to know p. However, since p is not known (otherwise there would be no need to do any survey in the first place), one must either estimate its value somehow from the data or

---

[24] For n<30, one uses the t-distribution. This means that instead of 1.96 one must inset a somewhat larger value than 1.96 in equation (7.2). Its exact size depends on n, the sample size. For n=10, this value is equal to 2.23; for n=20, it is equal to 2.09.

[25] The confidence interval is constructed by convention for a probability of 95%. Occasionally, one also finds 99% probabilities. Here and in the following we will always assume a 95% confidence level.

Table 7.2. 95% confidence intervals for different percentage proportions in the sample ($\hat{p}$).

Size of sample (n)	Proportion in sample ($\hat{p}$)				
	5% or 95%	10% or 90%	20% or 80%	30% or 70%	50%
35	7	10	14	15	17
50	6	8	11	13	14
75	4	7	9	11	12
100	4	6	8	9	10
200	3	4	6	6	7
300	3	3	5	5	6
500	2	3	4	4	4
1,000	1	2	3	3	3
2,000	1	1	2	2	2
6,000	1	1	1	1	1

Legend. In a sample of size *n*, the true population percentage values are, with a probability of 95%, within the interval $\hat{p}$ plus/minus the value shown in the table. Note that more extreme proportions (e.g., if 85% believe their performance is above average, if 15% believe the merger was successful) have a smaller expected error than do proportions near 50%.

from assumptions. What is often done is to estimate *p* by $\hat{p}$, because with larger sample sizes, $\hat{p}$ converges towards its expected value *p*.

Let us assume we have found $\hat{p}=10\%$ in our sample. The bounds of the confidence interval could then be estimated as

$$\hat{p} - 1.96 \cdot \sqrt{\hat{p}(100-\hat{p})/n} = 10 - 1.96 \cdot \sqrt{10(100-10)/200} = 5.84\%$$

for the lower bound and as 14.16% for the upper bound. Starting with our sample parameter value of 10% in the sample of *n*=200 we would thus conclude with a certainty (or: confidence) of 95% that the true (or: population) proportion lies roughly between 6% and 14%. Because the confidence is not equal to 100%, a certain amount of uncertainty remains when making this statement. In the present case, this uncertainty is well-founded, because the true parameter value *p* is equal to 20%, and this value does not fall into the interval from 6% and 14%. The risk for such an incorrect inference is small, though, because it is quite unlikely to observe a proportion of 10% in a sample of 200 persons if the true value is 20%. Table 7.2 makes this clear. It shows that one can expect in 95% of all samples to find a value of $\hat{p}$ that lies between $20\% - 6\% = 14\%$ and $20\% + 6\% = 26\%$. One can even compute[26] that 99% of the sample parameters $\hat{p}$ can be expected to lie between 13% and 27%, and 99.9% be-

---

[26] To compute 99% or 99.9% confidence intervals, the value 1.96 in formula (7.3) has to be replaced by 2.33 or by 3.09, respectively.

tween 11% and 29%. Hence, to observe 10% if 20% is the true value is almost impossible for samples of size 200.

But let us return to computing the confidence interval. If one does not want to closely rely on estimating the standard error s_e by using the observed $\hat{p}$ as an estimator of the population p, one can proceed as follows. In Table 7.2 we note that the *error margins* (i.e., the lengths of the confidence intervals) are largest for proportions of 50%. Thus, if we estimate our confidence interval for this worst-case parameter value, we get the most *conservative* margins of $\pm 7\%$.

Table 7.2, moreover, shows some general effects of the sample size. One notes that larger samples lead to smaller confidence intervals. The effect is most pronounced for small sample and reaches an asymptote at about $n=2,000$. Beyond that point further increments of the sample size have hardly an effect on error margins. Of course, this lawfulness only holds for random samples.

Sampling in Small Populations

The above considerations are based on the assumption that the population size is infinitely large. In practice, this means that the population is "large" with at least $N=100,000$ elements (Rea & Parker, 1992). This is typically true in public opinion surveys but not always in employee surveys. For smaller populations, one needs to correct the error margins with the factor $\sqrt{1-n/N}$, where the quotient n/N is the sampling ratio (Stenger, 1986). For example, for a sample of size $n=200$, drawn from a population of $N=1,000$ persons, the correction factor is $\sqrt{1-200/1,000} = 0.89$. Hence, the error margins become substantially smaller.

Sampling Errors for Means and Other Statistics

Percentage proportions are typically by far the most important statistics used in employee surveys because what one almost always reports in the percentage of respondents who endorse each (Likert-type) item. However, confidence intervals can also be computed for other statistics following the same logic. We show this here for the mean of a variable X, denoted as $\bar{x}$. We first denote the true mean, as usual, by μ. The sampling error for the mean is then $e = \mu - \bar{x}$, and its standard deviation (standard error) is $s_e = \sqrt{(\sigma_x^2/n) \cdot (1-n/N)}$, where σ_x^2 is the variance of variable X in the population. Assume we used the item "Overall, I am satisfied with my pay" together with the usual 5-point Likert answer scale from 1=fully agree to 5=fully disagree. In a sample of $n=200$ respondents, we observe a mean of $\bar{x}=2.3$ on the answer scale. The confidence interval of this mean is given by

$$\bar{x} - 1.96 \cdot s_e \leq \mu \leq \bar{x} + 1.96 \cdot s_e, \quad (7.4)$$

a formula analogous to formula (7.3). The value of s_e is typically estimated by σ_x, the standard deviation of the observed rating scores. Another possibility is to use "typical" values based on experience in previous surveys. For example, hundreds of employee surveys in companies with the usual 5-point Likert items have typically led to standard deviations that were roughly equal to 1.00 for most items. If we want to assume, therefore, that $\sigma_x \approx 1$, then $s_e = 0.14$ by formula (7.4). Thus, the population mean μ of this item should lie between 2.16 and 2.44, with 95% probability.

Sampling Errors under Different Sampling Methods

So far, we have assumed that our samples are simple random samples. Yet, this is rarely true in practice, as we have seen above. What effects the type of sampling technique (systematic sampling, stratified random sampling, or cluster sampling has on the margin of error is a complex topic that cannot be covered here (Stenger, 1986; Kalton, 1983). Just a few remarks, however, should be made that give the reader some feeling for these effects. For example, when using systematic sampling, the error margins should generally not differ from those for simple random samples. In stratified random samples, on the other hand, the error margins are smaller than those for simple random samples if the stratification variables are correlated with the variables of interest (Wonnacott & Wonnacott, 1977). Thus, some form of stratification with variables that are likely to have an effect for many items is always a good idea in employee surveys. For example, to stratify the sample by a demographic variable such as the employee's position in the organizational hierarchy (e.g., non-manager, supervisor, middle manager, senior manager, above) should lead to more precise estimates of population parameter than simple random sampling because position is correlated with almost any employee survey item to some extent. Because the persons within a stratum tend to be somewhat more similar than those in different strata, one can use this property to reduce the sampling error. Hence, estimates for the population means of attitude and opinion items should be more precise if computed as weighted (by size) means of the means of the various strata and not as simple means over all respondents. The error margins should also be computed from the error margins of the strata (Entsprechende Formeln finden sich z.B. in Stenger, 1986.).

A disproportionate selection of strata or cells entails that the error margins in over-represented groups become smaller but those for the total sample become generally larger as compared to simple random samples. That is not true only if strata or cells with relatively large variance are overrepresented.

Cluster samples lead to larger error margins than simple random samples for variables that are more homogeneous in the clusters than in the population. The effect is larger if few clusters are used.

7.5 Sample Size

A question of particular interest for any sampling in practice is always the minimum size of the required sample. The answer to this question is closely related to the costs of the survey. One can derive an answer by reversing the considerations made above when deriving error margins. In principle, one begins by defining error margins that appear acceptable for the given purpose. Assume, for example, we want to estimate the proportion of employee with turnover intentions with a precision of ±3% (at the usual confidence level of 95%). Assume further our company has a total of $N=2,000$ employees. Then, the sample size should be—assuming the worst-case situation of a population proportion of 50%—at least $n=696$ (Table 7.3).

The values in Table 7.3 are derived as follows. We first request that the factor $1.96 \cdot s_e$ in formula (7.3) must not be greater than ±3%. Which n is required for that value? To give an answer, we set $3[\%] = 1.96 \cdot s_e$ which yields $n = p(100-p)(1.96/3)^2$ or, more generally,

$$n = \left[\frac{1.96\sqrt{p(100-p)}}{M}\right]^2. \quad (7.5)$$

In (7.5), M is the required error margin. In our example, we have $M=3$ [%]. We can choose the most conservative value for p (i.e. 50%), we get $n=1.067$. For an infinite population, therefore, we would need a sample with at least 1.067 persons to be able to estimate the population proportion with a margin of error of ±3% in the worst case where $p=50\%$—provided, of course, we draw a simple random sample. If we take into account that our population is not infinite but finite with $N=2,000$, we can expect that even smaller sample would be sufficiently large. Adding the correction factor to equation (7.5), we get

$$n = \left[\frac{1.96\sqrt{p(100-p)}}{M} \cdot \sqrt{1-n/N}\right]^2, \quad (7.6)$$

which yields

$$n = \frac{1.96^2[p(100-p)]N}{1.96^2[p(100-p)] + N \cdot M^2}. \quad (7.7)$$

Formula (7.7) is used to compute the values in Table 7.3. It shows that we need at least 696 persons in our sample.

Table 7.3 does away with the wide-spread fallacy that a good sample must comprise a substantial proportion of the population. What we see here is that for a population of 100,000 persons, a sample of only 383 of them suffices to estimate even the most difficult proportions with a 5% margin of error. Using formula (7.7) allows one to compute that the minimal sample size for a population of 10 million persons is just one person more (i.e., 384). Even for 100 million persons, 384 is sufficient.

On the other hand, Table 7.3 also shows that the minimal sample size for a small population is a substantial proportion of the population. If you want small error margins with high levels of certainty (even in the case of the most difficult to estimate true value of $p=50\%$), then the minimal sample size can be more than half the size of the population!

Rea & Parker (1992) and Edwards et al. (1997) recommend in such cases to draw a sample with only $n=N/2$ persons. However, the statistical rationale they provide for

Table 7.3. Minimal sample size (*n*), given populations of size *N*, to estimate a true proportion of *p*=50% and 80% (or 20%), respectively, within an error margin of ±*M* with 95% confidence.

	p=50%				p=80% (or 20%)		
N	±3%	±5%	±10%	N	±3%	±5%	±10%
200	168	132	65	200	155	110	47
300	234	168	73	300	208	135	51
400	291	196	77	400	252	152	53
500	340	217	81	500	289	165	55
750	440	254	85	750	357	185	57
1,000	516	278	88	1,000	406	197	58
1,500	624	306	90	1,500	469	211	59
2,000	696	322	92	2,000	509	219	60
3,000	787	341	93	3,000	556	227	60
6,000	879	357	94	6,000	601	234	61
7,500	934	365	95	7,500	626	238	61
10,000	964	370	95	10,000	639	240	61
50,000	1045	381	96	50,000	674	245	61
100,000	1056	383	96	100,000	678	245	61

this recommendation is not correct (Gabler, 1999). Because there is no lower fixed bound for the sample size, and because the sample that is needed can be larger than three quarters of the population, one should run a census survey in such extreme cases. This would save costs and make everything considerably simpler, including communications with employees and data analysis.

Another question is how to determine the minimal value of *n* with items that have extreme proportions. When comparing the minimal sample size needed to estimate proportions of *p*=50% and *p*=80% (or equivalently *p*=20%), respectively, with a fixed error margin, Table 7.3 shows that the *n* required to estimate the more extreme proportions is substantially smaller. Formula (7.7) allows one to derive minimal *n*'s for other proportions. For example, the minimal n to estimate a true proportion of 30% (or 70%) in a population of *N*=200 persons with an error margin of 10% with 95% confidence is just *n*=57. For *p*=10% (o 90%) this value drops even further to *n*=29 (i.e., to less than half the *n*=65 needed for *p*=50%). Extreme proportions, thus, can be quite reliably estimated even in small samples.

Finally, let us consider a question that is sometimes asked in practice in one way or another: „By which factor do we have to enlarge the sample size to cut the error of margin by half?" The answer can be found by formula (7.7). It shows that cutting the confidence interval to half its size requires—if *N* is large—to essentially quadruple the sample size because M^2 is inversely proportional to *n*. For smaller populations, smaller increments of *n* suffice to generate the same effect (see Table 7.3).

7.6 Response Rates and Nonresponse

A topic of major concern in any employee survey is the response rate (i.e., the proportion of persons invited to participate who actually return completed questionnaires). This is an important topic both in sample and census surveys[27]. In almost no employee survey is the response rate perfect (100%). Rather, typical return response rates are about 70% (Church & Waclawski, 2001), with a wide variance depending, for example, on the mode of data collection and the attitude of the work force towards the survey. Generally, though, it seems to be getting more and more difficult to achieve high response rates, partly due to oversurveying (Cook, Heath, & Thompson, 2000; Weiner & Dalessio, 2006). So, nonresponse is a problem that is likely to grow in the future, presenting not only a statistical problem, but also a credibility problem. Management typically interprets low response rates as an indicator of low commitment[28], while unions and works councils take them as a sign that the employees are dissatisfied.

Nonresponse Bias

When pondering nonresponse, one should first distinguish good-intentioned nonrespondents, who meant to participate but did not, from those who consciously decide not to participate (active nonrespondents). Sometimes, there are objective reasons that prevent a person from participating. For example, the person may be on vacation or on sick leave during the time of data collection. There may also be technical reasons for nonresponse if the questionnaire never reached the person (e.g., the person's address is not valid). Then, there are persons who want to participate, but they are too "passive" to actually do so. They might have forgotten to return the questionnaire on time, mislaid it, taken ill, or just did not get around doing it (Rogelberg & Stanton, 2007). Active nonrespondents, in contrast, do not want to participate for a variety of reasons. They may believe that the survey it a waste of time and that it will have no effects. Or they may even be concerned that it will have negative effects and that their responses will not be handled in an anonymous or constructive way.

Rogelberg & Stanton (2007, p. 6) conclude that "considering that the individuals who make up the passive nonresponse group seem, as a general rule, willing to participate in filling out the survey, it is not surprising that they generally do not differ from respondents with regard to job satisfaction or related variables." Rogelberg et al. (2003) reports a study with a very low return rate of 18%. However, they found that 83% of the nonrespondents could be classified as passive nonrespondents, and that these persons did *not* differ from respondents in their attitudes, opinions, and personality. Active nonrespondents, in contrast, showed some significant differences: They were less satisfied with some job dimensions, they had a higher turnover ten-

---

[27] In quota sampling, the issue of nonresponse is often covered up, because one simply continues with sampling until the desired sample size is reached.

[28] Occasionally, the opposite is also true, i.e. low response rates are also taken as an indicator of high satisfaction. The argument, then, is that highly satisfied employees have nothing to complain about and, thus, have no reason to fill out a questionnaire.

Table 7.4. Estimates of the proportion of persons with attribute X, given different return rates and given a certain percentage of persons with attribute X among the nonrespondents.

Return rate (%)	Percentage of persons with attribute X among the nonrespondents						
	10	20	25	30	40	50	75
90	27	26	25	24	23	20	19
70	31	27	25	23	19	14	4
50	40	30	25	20	10	0	-
30	60	37	25	13	-	-	-

Legend. The values in the table cells are the proportions of persons who plan leaving in the sample when the true proportion is equal to 25%.

dency, and they were also less conscientious. Yet, because active nonrespondents were relatively few, the survey results were *not biased*, even though the return rate was extremely low.

Low return rates lead to biased survey results if nonresponse is related to the issues that the survey assesses. Consider the following case. Assume that we run an employee survey in a company where 25% of all employees plan leaving within the next year. If there is no systematic relationship between not participating and a person's intention to leave, the sample should contain about 25% persons who plan leaving. If, however, persons who plan on leaving do not participate in the survey (e.g., because they see no purpose in this extra work), or if they are especially motivated to participate (e.g., because they want to voice their concerns and frustrations), the sample will be biased. Table 7.4 shows some possibilities. For example, if 50% of the employees who plan leaving do not participate in the survey, and the return rate is 70%, then the survey finds that only 14% plan to leave. This is a gross bias because the actual turnover tendency in the company is almost twice as high as the survey says. Hence, statistical bias and grossly erroneous conclusions about the population are possible, even if the overall return rate is "acceptably" high (Rogelberg & Stanton, 2007).

Table 7.4 shows, on the other hand, that if nonresponse is not related to the issue of interest, then the return rate does not matter: The estimates remain on target, although their error margins become wider. If nonrespondents are mostly passive ones, then this is the expected outcome and low response rates are, statistically speaking, not a problem.

Dealing with Nonresponse

The problem with the statistical reasoning above is that one does not know to what extent the nonrespondents are passive or active ones. Because the survey is anonymous or, at least, confidential, it is also not possible to interview nonrespondents to find out why they did not participate, apart from the fact that such interviews would be a sensitive issue indeed. Yet, one is not helpless. At the very least, one should run some data analyses to learn more about the nature of the nonresponses.

One method is to compare the distributions of the demographic variables with those of the population. Are, for example, managers over- or underrepresented in the sample? If so, one can expect a bias on certain variables. Hundreds of employee surveys have shown that managers tend to be more satisfied with most dimensions of their job than non-managers (see Figure 12.8 for some examples). Hence, if they are underrepresented in the sample, the overall satisfaction statistics for the company are likely to be too low. However, because managers typically are a small fraction of the workforce only, this effect should be small.

One can also study if persons who return a filled-out questionnaire early (i.e., on the first day or so) differ from those who answer later to the survey. Since later respondents are almost nonrespondents because they are close to missing the survey, one may hypothesize that they are similar to nonrespondents. Hence, if there is no systematic difference between early and later respondents, one can conclude that nonrespondents are predominantly passive ones. Borg (2001b) and Borg & Tuten (2003) report two large studies (in over a dozen countries each) where the respondents' job satisfaction and commitment scores, respectively, were not correlated with the time of answering the survey in any meaningful subsample. This finding renders additional support for the notion that most nonrespondents are passive ones.

Survey researchers sometimes deal with over- or underrepresentation by using compensatory weightings, often called redressment (Gabler & Hoffmeyer-Zlotnik, 1997). If one knows, for example, that 60% of the population are blue-collar workers, and if this group makes up only 40% of the sample, then the data of the blue-collar workers in the sample are weighted by 60/40=1.5 and the data of the remaining employees by 40/60=0.67. This leads to smaller error margins provided nonresponse is not related to the issue of interest. On the other hand, such statistical "tricks" can be hard to communicate to the employees when feeding back the results. Also, weights tend to lead an enormously more complex data analysis processes and seeming inconsistencies (due to rounding) when the data are broken down to small units. So, we recommend not using such techniques in employee surveys.

Another method that should be considered is enclosing a few items into the questionnaire that measure possible reasons for nonresponse. For example, employees often do not participate because they do not expect that the survey will lead to positive change. Or they may feel that management did not deal constructively with the data of the previous employee survey. If those employees who participate in the survey rate such issues poorly, one can use this information to explain low response rates. The information is also valuable in its own right and should lead to actions that change the conditions of future surveys.

A related method concentrates on issues that would cause passive nonresponse. As Rogelberg & Stanton (2007, p.7) suggest: "To conduct a passive nonresponse analysis, one should include questions on the survey that tap into factors related to passive nonresponse. So, if busyness is related to standing on the survey topic, response bias would be quite probable. If a relationship is detected, it may be possible to compensate by using the variable as a control variable".

Naturally, before the survey one should always work on getting high participation rates (see Section 9.7). However, response rates are not everything, and pushing the employees too hard to participate may harm the data quality. After all, the respondents can always pretend to participate and provide meaningless answers or simply not report their true opinions or attitudes.

Item Nonresponse

A second form of nonresponse is item nonresponse. In almost every ES, not all respondents answer each single item. Rather, some respondents skip some items so that there are "missing data" in the questionnaires they return. This item nonresponse behavior also leads to a number of questions.

In a poorly designed questionnaire, item nonresponse can be substantial for various technical reasons. For example, the respondents may not understand the question. Or the item is so ambiguous (e.g., "double-barreled"; see Section 5.7) that a simple rating seems impossible. Or the questionnaire contains skip patterns that never lead the respondent to a particular item.

However, even in a well-designed questionnaire, items may be skipped for various reasons. For example, the respondent may not have an opinion on the issue; she has no information to generate a judgment; she does not feel confident enough to provide an answer; she is concerned about survey anonymity and does not want to answer sensitive questions. Another reason is that the respondent simply misses some items erroneously by overlooking some pages of the questionnaire or because he wrongly believes that he has reached the end of the questionnaire.

Because there are so many different reasons, it is difficult to say what proportion of item nonresponse is acceptable. Obviously, we again have to distinguish active nonresponse from other forms of nonresponse. The former may lead to biased results if the nonresponse is motivated by a special attitude or opinion of the respondent towards the issue of the item. For example, if respondents do not answer because they are concerned that their answers may not remain anonymous, then the results are likely too positive (compared to the population values) because persons with very negative ratings should be more likely to skip such items.

Moreover, items are sometimes thrown into a questionnaire not to measure something but only to place an issue on the agenda. For such placement items (see Section 4.1) item nonresponse can be expected to be high. Similarly, for other items, higher levels of item nonresponse can often be attributed to lack of information. For example, items related to strategy typically have relatively high rates of nonresponse, simply because a typical blue-collar worker, for example, may not feel confident enough to rate such issues. In that case, not responding is really an honest answer.

Item nonresponse can also lead to biased results if it is motivated by a special attitude of the nonrespondents towards the issue assessed by the item. Sensitive items are always candidates for underrepresenting those who feel concerned to voice their opinions. As a consequence, the survey results tend to be too positive. What one should always do, therefore, is to check all items for missing data. Items that have many missing data should be studied closely for reasons of nonresponse. In most cases in practice, one can expect to find that the respondents simply could not reliably answer the item and, thus, skipped it.

Omissions on *demographic* items often have more serious consequences than those on *content* items. In particular, if a person does not tell which organizational unit he or she belongs to, this person's answers have no influence on the survey results of this unit. Borg (1991) and Borg et al. (2008) report some studies where demographic nonrespondents were systematically less positive about almost any facet of their jobs, in particular with respect to management in general. This outcome corroborates the notion that demographic nonrespondents do not answer some items in order to remain unidentifiable. They know that supervisors and managers often want to know exactly who gave particularly negative answers. Yet, if a supervisor finds out that he received very negative scores from a female, who has been with the company for less than 2 years, who works in unit 123, in subsidiary X, he might be able to tell from this profile that this must be "Jane Miller." (While anonymity rules can prevent this from occurring, employees may still perceive the threat of being exposed for an unfavorable opinion.) Persons who do not provide this demographic information avoid this risk. As a consequence, the reports for smaller organizational units tend to be too positive compared to the overall statistics for the entire company.

To avoid demographic item nonresponse, one has to make sure that the employees believe that the survey is truly anonymous or, at least, confidential. The rules and regulations that make sure that the data are protected must be communicated to everyone in a transparent and convincing way. One must also make sure that top management or even the CEO guarantees that any violations have dire consequences for violators. It should also be stressed that skipping demographic items means that the answers of these persons will be lost for more focus reports. Consequently, they cannot impact any local action planning.

Because item nonresponse can also be due to excessively complex items that often come at the end of the survey where respondents tend to be tired or not fully attentive anymore, one should also consider asking the really important demographic variables at the beginning of the survey. In an online survey, one may even want to go one step further and import this information directly into the questionnaire from a data bank when the employee opens up the questionnaire with his or her password (see Section 5.10). Some employees may then decide not to participate at all, but it is better to lose some respondents totally rather than to have many answers that cannot be allocated to the org unit or stratum where it came from.

7.7 Sample Construction in Practice

Sampling in practice often does not follow statistical principles only. Stratified random sample are sometimes not used because the information needed for constructing such samples reliably is not readily available or too expensive to obtain. In such cases, a multi-stage approach is better than not using any random sample at all. An even better solution is to update and clean up the personnel database before running the employee survey. Indeed, the people who work for HR sometimes complain that one of the main purposes of an employee survey is to force them to do just that.

Sampling in practice involves many features that are often more important than error margins or sample size. Consider an example reported in Weisberg et al. (1996). If one would have drawn a sample from the list of countries accredited at the United Nations in the 1970's by using systematic sampling for estimating the opinion within the U.N. on some issue, it would have been impossible to have the USA, the USSR, and the UK all in this same sample. However, without these opinion leading countries, the validity of the estimates would have been dubious. Similarly, in public opinion surveys in the USA, one makes sure that the sample *always* contains interviews conducted in the major urban centers New York, Chicago, and Los Angeles. In other words, inclusion of these cities in the sample is *not* left to a random selection process. This is also true in an employee survey in a large company, where subsidiaries, production plants, or regions that excel in one way or another (e.g., being the most profitable ones or the ones that make the largest revenues) are set to be included in the sample. Also, in a sample survey, all top managers are usually asked to participate, not just a random sample of them. This is simply easier, cheaper, and yields more convincing data if the results are broken down over the levels of the company's hierarchy.

Yet another example is a "rolling survey" that is sometimes used in companies with many subsidiaries. The method (randomly or otherwise) selects a certain subset of, say, one third of the subsidiaries for inclusion in the survey in year one, and then again one third from the rest in year two, and finally the rest in year three. In year four, one begins with a new cycle (Edwards & Thomas, 1993).

Many arguments beyond statistics influence such sampling decisions: Saving costs, getting more "convincing" data, including opinion leaders, giving every employee a chance to voice his or her opinion, or controlling the workload that the various parts of the organization have to handle when working with the survey data in the follow-up processes.

When considering samples in practice, one should always ask which organizational units are to get a report of survey results that focuses on "their" results, and how many respondents does one need to generate such reports so that their statistics can be trusted. For example, when predicting the outcome of the parliamentary elections in Germany, samples of just about 1,200 persons are used. This allows one to reliably predict the behavior of "the German voter." However, one cannot reliably break down this small sample anymore to predict the voting behavior of the citizens of Berlin. However, while the behavior of "the voter" is interesting and relevant in politics, such statistics are not that interesting in industrial organizations. What typically counts more is what the employees in particular problematic or key units perceive because there is usually variability in unit scores and therefore different post-survey responses necessary. In the end, one needs both overall statistics and statistics that are more focused on smaller subgroups, and it is the size of these subgroups that will ultimately determine the size of the sample that is needed.

Thus, the seemingly simple question about the required sample size turns out to be rather complicated. No simple textbook answer is ever possible. This is particularly true for employee surveys, which always focus on many different issues, not just one (as in the voting behavior example above). Additionally, money and time are always scarce. The question arises "is it better to invest more money into a better sample (i.e., larger N, more strata, better strata, high return rates, etc.) or into a better questionnaire (carefully constructed, pretested, good information for all employees about purpose, rules, etc.)? There is no one answer to this question. It is important to note that a large N by itself is not that important. Public opinion researchers agree that "samples can actually be more precise than census surveys" (Schnell, Hill, & Esser, 1995, S. 287). There are, on the other hand, limits on what one can expect from small samples, namely error margins that may become too large to build expensive decisions on the observed statistics.

In the end one might argue that the accuracy of the statistics is not as important as the process of inviting as many employees as possible to participate in a survey-driven change effort. The employee survey process is, of course, not just a diagnostic tool, but also an intervention in itself, sending messages as well as receiving them. The right decision regarding whom to invite to participate in the survey should address both statistical and strategic objectives.

8 Information Campaign Before Data Feedback

Any employee survey should be accompanied by an "official" information campaign. It conveys the essential features of the project's positioning; it motivates employees to contribute to the project's success; it inform the employees about the timing of the ES project, its goals and rules, its current state, its general results, further steps and workshops, and possible actions—in short about everything that they should know or that they might want to know about the survey project.

8.1 Phases and Steps of the Information Campaign

Informing employees and managers about the ES is a task that accompanies the entire ES project from its start to the end of the follow-up processes. To organize this campaign, it is useful to first distinguish three phases where the following issues should be covered:

Phase 1: Before the survey
  First announcements and general statements on the ES
  - First announcement of the ES by the executive board and the CEO
  - Supporting statements on the ES by the local management
  - Comments on ES by the works council (in Europe)

  Motivating to participate
  - Background information on the ES: Company newspaper, articles, memos on ES
  - Making the ES visible: Poster, banners etc.
  - Testimonials: Interviews on the ES (with "names" and "photographs")
  - Clarifications: Questions and answers on the ES
  - An evaluation of the ES process by the data protection officer

  Administration of survey (data collection)
  - Call for participation by the executive board, the CEO, upper management
  - Call for participation by the works council (in Europe)
  - Organizational issues: Who, when, where, how

Phase 2: Between the survey and the follow-up processes (bridging)
  - Participation rate, thanks for participating
  - First results: General trends
  - First reactions by the executive board, possible fields of action

- On the feedback processes: Who sees what, when?
- ES workshops: When what for whom?

Phase 3: Results and follow-up processes (see Chapter 16)
- General priorities of responses and actions
- Action plans for departments, subsidiaries, regions
- Information on implementation progress
- Evaluating results

8.2 Phase I of the Information Campaign: Before the ES

The first phase of the information campaign aims at informing employees about the forthcoming ES and motivating them to participate with engagement.

Informing Employees About the Survey

Informing employees about the survey in phase I of the information campaign consists of some first announcements about the ES project and in describing the administration of the survey. Information should be provided such that employees understand the purpose and the goals of this project, learn how the project will be conducted, and understand what they are expected to do to make this project a success. The project's positioning should be made clear and convincing to every employee so that he or she becomes motivated to participate in the survey and make a serious effort to answer the questionnaire fully and honestly.

Initial announcements serve to inform the organization that there will be an ES that is supported by top management (and hopefully unions and works councils) and is designed to attain multiple goals. These initial announcements should come at an early point in time, but not before a firm decision for the survey and its probable date has been made. These announcements should be brief, without much detail, but they should indicate when and how the employees will be informed about further details.

In later messages one may want to address in more detail the reasons for doing an ES. If such a survey is completely new in the particular company, it may be useful to inform the employees first about the history of such surveys, about the companies that are running such surveys and why they do it. Then, one should explain why this particular company wants to do a survey. To avoid abstract language, these messages can emphasize the benefits that the survey generates for different groups in the organization. Figure 8.1 shows an example for three different groups. Although this example is somewhat generic, it nevertheless rests on a survey project in one particular company. Hence, one can use Figure 8.1 as a starting point, but one must adapt it to the given context.

Highly important in many cultures is information on data protection, confidentiality, and anonymity. Hippler et al. (1990) have shown in an experimental study in Germany that one gets the best return rates if these issues are explained soberly and in a concise way. Return rates go down if nothing is said on these issues, but also if

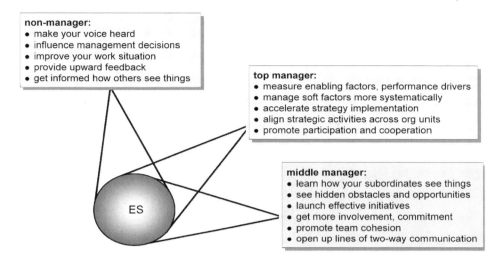

Figure 8.1. Utility of an ES from three perspectives.

the explanations are very detailed and broad. So, something should be said, but long explanations appear to lead to mistrust. What we have found effective is having some individuals—in particular, the CEO, the data protection officer, and/or the project leader, along with one person from the survey vendor—publicly commit themselves to handling the data exactly as specified in the project rules.

When the actual time of data collection approaches, an effort should be made to make every employee aware once more of the survey and its timing. Figure 8.2 shows how this was done in one German company, where banners were hung over each factory gate. They simply stated the motto of the survey ("Ihre Meinung zählt!" ="Your opinion counts!"), together with "Employee survey 1996" and the dates of the time window for survey administration. With such high visibility, an employee could hardly argue that she did not participate because she somehow "overlooked" the survey. See also Figure 9.10 for a similarly effective eye catcher.

Motivating to Participate

To motivate employees to participate, management should rely, first of all, on face-to-face communication. However, the information campaign should support these efforts by emphasizing confidentiality and trust, posting answers to frequently asked questions, and conveying the importance of the project. Often print media are used for these purposes. See, for example, Figure 8.3. It shows the title page of a special edition of a company newsletter of the German company on their ES. Note the ES logo and the ES motto on this page ("Wacker im Dialog"). This special newsletter informed employees not only about the positioning of the upcoming ES (goals, timing, milestones, rules, follow-up processes), but also contained articles by major company stakeholders on the ES project. For example, there were articles by the

Figure 8.2. Banner announcing ES over the factory gate of a German company.

CEO, by the head of the works council, and by the data protection officer. The first two explained why they supported the project and asked every employee to participate. The data protection officer, in turn, explained the measures taken to protect the individual respondent's anonymity. There was also a commitment by the CEO that he personally would see that all rules (data protection, who sees what when, etc.) of the ES project would be observed as announced, without exception. This was also a clear message to all managers. Furthermore, the special newsletter also introduced all members on the ES coordination team.

A further booster for positive attitudes towards the ES is informing the employees about the various persons who are responsible for designing, planning, and coordinating the ES project. It is important to describe these persons not just in terms of their names, roles, positions, or years of tenure, but also as human persons. Showing pictures of them individually as well as a picture of the entire ES coordination core team help make the staff "real." Consider communicating not just the team's educational background and professional experience, but also information about their families, their hobbies, or their predictions for upcoming sporting events. Including some statements about what they hope to accomplish through the survey and what they are doing to make it a success creates a sense of solidarity with these colleagues. The goal is to have employees feel that they should reciprocate these efforts: "These people are working hard for us in this project. The least I can do is filling out the questionnaire!"

Figure 8.3. Information on an employee survey in a special edition of a company newsletter.

Another approach to motivating employees to participate is to publicize what their coworkers and colleagues think about the ES. Figure 8.4 exhibits an excerpt from a folder developed for a German automobile company. The text (translated here from the German) says "We'll do our part!" The photographs show twelve workers interviewed at the plants' gates, together with what they had to say about the ES. These statements are real, not constructed, and range from very positive to conditionally positive ("I am supporting this survey, but it only makes sense if it leads to real improvement actions. If not, it would be a waste of money!"). The strategy in this approach is to foster the perception that most employees are going to complete the survey and its processes because they expect a constructive dialogue with management that possibly leads to improvements that are worth the effort.

It is usually not difficult to get employees to participate in such communication activities. Moreover, almost all employees are typically supporting the idea of an ES. However, they may not do so without adding some conditional "but" or "if" com-

Figure 8.4. Excerpts from a folder with testimonials on the employee survey.

ments. To print them, too, can actually be good for the ES project. For example, the expectations of the one worker cited above that "something must happen after the survey" is a common expectation, and printing it only reflects what most employees think. Moreover, it also helps to set the stage for management: They cannot simply forget about the survey after seeing the results and assume that this inaction will have no negative effects.

If, on the other hand, interviews with employees show a generally negative attitude towards the survey, then printing such testimonials would be counterproductive. In that case, one should first analyze the various caveats and arguments brought forward against the survey, and then find answers for them. This might result in the publication of a "Q&A" brochure or website that can address the concerns that many employees have.

An essential part of any motivating information is always a statement by top management, especially by the CEO and the HR director, asking each and every employee to participate. If the situation allows, such a statement may be more effective if the invitation becomes an expectation: "I expect each employee to participate" ra-

> by: [name]
> to: all employees in [subsidiary X]
> re: employee survey 2009
>
> Dear employees at the [subsidiary X]
>
> What makes us a successful company? Having a good product, satisfied customers, and a clear vision are all important. But it is our employees who create and support that product, work to exceed customers' expectations, and fulfill the company vision.
>
> To ensure our success, there will be a company-wide employee survey starting [date] and ending [date].
>
> The purpose of the survey is to understand how employees see strengths and weaknesses in how we do business. I am firmly committed to use this information to improve [subsidiary X] as much as possible.
>
> To accomplish this goal, we need honest information. The survey is not mandatory, and it is up to you whether to participate or not. However, I trust you will participate and support this common effort with your answers. Every opinion, positive or negative, is important.
>
> This survey will be conducted and analyzed by Y company, a leading employee research firm. No one at [subsidiary X] will know who answered or how they answered. Results will only be reported for groups of 10 or more respondents.
>
> For more information about the survey, please see [our intranet or current newsletter]. The results of this survey will be shared and discussed about 3 weeks after the end date. I look forward to what we can achieve together.
>
> With best regards,
> [Name]

Figure 8.5. Schema for a senior manager's announcement letter to employees.

ther than "I invite each employee to participate." In Europe the works council can also support the effort with a statement such as "You can say whatever you want to say, but say it!" In these public statements, the target should be 100% participation (although privately leaders should understand that adequate representation is possible with considerably lower participation rates). These statements can be communicated in the form of small articles in the company newspaper, for example. Some companies also choose to send out a personalized letter from the CEO to every single employee, often even to each employee's home address. Senior managers can send out similar letters too. See Figure 8.5 for a schema of such a letter.

ES information campaigns are sometimes overloaded with "sales" arguments. Many companies provide argument after argument on "what is in it for me." This is a dangerous strategy because it can lead to unrealistically high expectations on the side of the employees. The sales arguments can create the impression that the ES is some sort of wish list where one simply checks what management has to deliver. If it does not, one seems entitled to express disappointment ("led to nothing"). When in doubt, sales arguments should be cut in favor of simply providing clear information. Information is needed to communicate the essential features of the ES design and, thus, position the ES correctly in every employee's head to generate *informed commitment*. Indeed, what we have often found useful is to completely reverse the what-is-in-it-for-me argumentation by paraphrasing J. F. Kennedy: "Ask not what your company can do for you. Ask what you can do for your company!" Interviews showed that many employees first seemed surprised by this reversed argument, but, after some thinking, expressed that they liked the idea, especially if all other stakeholders were committed to do their best to make this project a success.

Slogans may also promise too much. One example we have seen reads: "How you can change the future of the ABC company in 30 minutes!" Even if taken with a grain of salt, this message is absurdly unrealistic. Also, be weary of the popular slogan "Your opinion is important to us," which makes one wonder who the "us" is. The typical interpretation is that this is top management. So, "they" want to know what "we" think. It suggests that "they" do not participate in the ES, which is usually not the case. Rather, *every* employee, *including top management*, is expected to participate. Not just top management, but the entire company needs the ES data.

Informing About Survey Administration

About two weeks before the actual data collection, the information campaign should also begin to focus on details of the actual survey administration: How to fill out the questionnaire? Where to get it or access it? When can I fill out the questionnaire? Details on that are described in Chapter 9.

8.3 Bridging the Time of "No Action" After the Survey

A critical time period for keeping the employees informed is the time shortly after the survey. It does not take much to generate the impression that the ES project came to a halt or even that it has been stopped by management. Consider this case from practice. A few years ago, the first author conducted an ES for the German railroads, a very large company. Only three weeks after the end of the data collection—just days before the results presentation to top management—the ES in this company was mentioned in a TV talk show. A viewer called in during this show and complained that "a long time ago" an ES had been conducted in this company but that everything has been "suppressed, probably because the results were so bad". Apparently, even such a short time lag is long enough to cause suspicious speculations. The anecdote shows how important it is to keep the employees informed about what is happening and why everything takes "so long." Hence, the time period before the top-down process reaches the shop floor or before employees see first overall results, should be bridged somehow.

One way of doing this is to report the participation rate shortly after the end of data collection, and send a thank you note to all employees from the CEO. If participation is low, one can possibly communicate not percentages but the absolute numbers

Figure 8.6. Impressions of the beginning of data collection at SAP.

of questionnaires sent out and returned. In large companies, the absolute number of participants can be quite impressive, even if the percentage value is low.

One can also report on the data collection itself. Figure 8.6 shows an example from an ES project at SAP. The poster exhibits a number of scenes of the "SAP day", as the day on which the ES began was called. Obviously, the pictures show a lot of good mood and a relaxed atmosphere.

8.4 Planning the Information Campaign

Planning an information campaign usually requires involving communication specialists. They should be familiar with the company's internal communication channels and media. In practice, therefore, the coordination of the informing activities is typically handled by a competent person from the company's communication department, often by the head of this department. This person acts as a subproject leader in close cooperation with the core team (see Figure 3.1).

In terms of media, a modern information campaign typically uses a mix of electronic media (intranet, voice message system, company TV), print media (company newspaper, posters, brochures), incentives (buttons, pens, etc.), "live" events and face-to-face activities, together with tool boxes for local managers that contain model letters to the employees and similar support material. In large companies, the campaign is coordinated from the company's headquarter. Some information is directly fed into company-wide communication channels, but most materials are only prepared so that the local coordinators can easily adapt it to their organizations' needs, given that they adhere to certain company-wide rules concerning style and content. For example, a poster as in Figure 8.6 can be prepared centrally, and then send out to the local coordinators for translation, print, and distribution in their organizations. Suggestions and models for staging live events, for example, can be collected by the ES core coordination team and then sent to the local coordinators to stimulate their thinking. The core team may even set up an electronic platform where local coordinators can suggest their ideas for the benefits of their colleagues in other parts of the organization or for further discussion.

8.5 Style of the Information Campaign

Best practice recommendations for ES information campaigns are difficult. Each organization has its style, and the information campaign should also be perceived properly by the employees. Consider the poster in Figure 8.7. Posters like that in Figure 8.7 were created, translated, and displayed in public places (cafeteria, entrance halls, etc.) across the company's many global locations. Figure 8.8 shows another example of such a poster, this time for an international IT company. One notes that both posters prominently display the survey administration dates as well as a slogan and "brand" for the survey itself. Indeed, it is important to have the survey fit the style of the organization. The first poster emphasizes the survey's role in assuring that business is run according to corporate values, appealing to employees' pride and sense of responsibility—a perfect match for a healthcare manufacturer famously built on ethical business principles. The second poster takes a less serious tone, playing on the

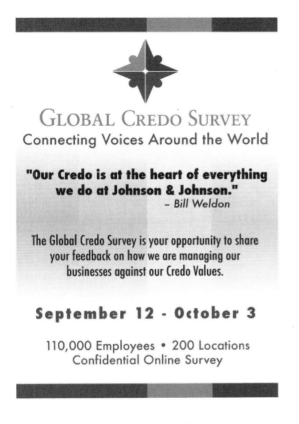

Figure 8.7. Poster for an ES at Johnson & Johnson.

company's name to ize the survey goals of "Satisfaction And Performance." The third poster presented in Figure 8.9. comes from an aerospace and defense company. It resembles a movie promotion and uses the principle of limited availability to increase employee interest and ultimately survey response rates.

As important as they are, ES information campaigns should not be overdone. The risk here is similar to excessive communication on anonymity, which can increase concerns instead of allaying them. As the default assumption for an ES, one should always adopt the notion (if there is no evidence to the contrary) that the ES, if designed and conducted properly, is a good thing for all stakeholders. Yet, if one keeps selling such a good thing with argument after argument, message after message, employees might get suspicious: If this is such a good thing, why do they have to sell it so hard? In the end, even their motivation to participate in the survey may change from "I want to participate" to "I want to participate because of the many incentives, promised outcomes, etc." Hence, one should aim at sending out a few strong messages rather than flooding employees with advertising, and one should also aim at informing them about the survey rather than selling the survey.

8.6 Typical Questions and Answers

Employee surveys always lead to many questions by the employees. Most of these questions are not new ones to the survey expert, and neither are the answers that can be given to them. In the following, we present a listing of such generic Q&A's.

Q: What is the purpose of the employee survey? *A:* Assess how employees see things; recognize strengths and weaknesses, and act to improve things on all levels and in all parts of the organization.

Q: When will the survey run? *A:* The survey will be conducted in the time from [date] to [date].

Q: How will the survey be conducted? *A (polling station):* The survey will be conducted by filling out a paper [online] questionnaire in a "polling station." *A (mail survey)*: ... by filling out a paper questionnaire that will be sent to your home [job] address. *A (online)*: ... by filling out an electronic questionnaire on your [a special] computer.

Q: Which topics are covered in the survey? *A*: Basically, there are two general topics, namely how satisfied and engaged employees are with the various aspects of their work, and how job conditions enable them to bring out their best performance.

Q: How are the survey questions formulated? *A*: All [or: Most] questions are formulated as simple statements (for example: "I am satisfied with the tools and the equipment I work with"). You answer by checking a box on an answer scale that ranges from "strongly agree" to "strongly disagree." [Are there other questions such as open-ended questions or "Anything else?" questions?]

Q: How long does it take to fill out the questionnaire? *A*: Pretests have shown that it takes about 20 minutes to fill out the questionnaire. [Pretest done?]

Q: Is it difficult to answer the questions? *A*: No. The questions have been carefully tested. We believe that you will find it easy to answer every question, but you can skip any question if you cannot answer it.

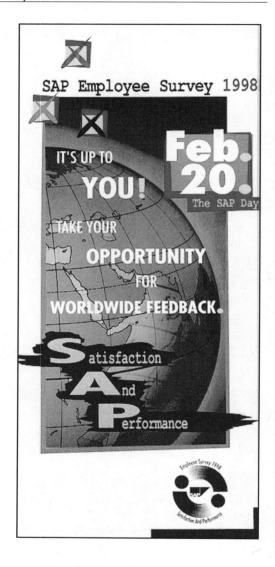

Figure 8.8. Poster for an ES at SAP.

Information Campaign: Before Data Feedback   203

Figure 8.9. Poster for an ES at L3 Integrated Systems.

Q: What if I feel uncertain about my answer to a particular question? *A*: It is okay to respond with your "first impression" even if you had not considered the matter.

Q: Can I give a "wrong" answer? *A*: Actually no. The questions assess only what you think, feel, or perceive. There are no wrong answers.

Q: Is participation in the employee survey mandatory? *A*: No. It is up to you! However, we rely on you. Please support this important project. The organization needs these data to make improvements.

Q: Will you know who completed the survey? *A*: The survey responses are anonymous to the company, but our survey vendor [or: the company] does track who participated to make sure that each employee submits only one response. Also, this knowledge allows us to send reminders only to those who have not yet participated. However, this list of participants will be destroyed when the survey administration comes to an end.

Q: Who are these guys at [survey vendor]? *A*: This is the company that runs and analyzes the employee survey for our company. All data go to them and are stored there. No one in our company has direct access to these data. They remain confidential. Any data report is generated by them according to the rules specified in the project positioning.

Q: Are other companies also running employee surveys? *A:* Yes, many, in all industries and in many countries. (Possibly mention some "big" names in your industry, such as GE, BMW, Johnson & Johnson, Dell, Deutsche Bank, Hewlett Packard, IBM, Microsoft, Philips, SAP, Siemens, Xerox).

Q: Will there be other employee surveys? *A (depending on positioning)*: Yes. The plan is to repeat such a survey annually [every 18 months, every two years].

Q: Is every employee in the company asked to participate? *A (depending on positioning)*: Yes, everyone from CEO to everyone on the shop floor.

Q: Why not ask a sample of employees only? *A (depending on positioning)*: We ask everyone because we want to break down the data to every part of the organization, so that every organizational unit can make improvements based on its results. Ultimately, every workgroup needs its own data for precise measurement and for effective follow-up actions.

Q: Given that everyone is asked to participate, does it really matter if I too participate or not? *A:* Yes and no. If a few employees do not participate, it will not affect the company-wide statistics a lot. However, your workgroup may not get a feedback report if fewer than [7] employees participated in the survey! Even if it does, it would not include your points-of-view.

Q: Is the survey anonymous? *A:* Yes. The survey does not ask for your name. It only registers your organizational unit and for your position because this information is needed to generate focused feedback reports. Moreover, the filled out questionnaires are send directly to the external survey vendor. The vendor will generate feedback reports only for groups where at least [7] persons participated in the survey. Your personal answers, therefore, are always combined with those of at least [6] other persons to create percentage values and other statistics.

Q: Is the survey confidential? *A:* Yes. Only the external survey vendor X has access to the data. They will only compute statistical analyses with these data that satisfy the rules specified in the survey's positioning. That is, only groups of employees will be analyzed that consist of at least [7] persons. Your answer, therefore, will become a building element of an overall statistic (e.g., an average value).

Q: What if fewer than [7] persons in my workgroup participate in the survey? *A:* Then, unfortunately, your workgroup will *not* receive a feedback report. Your data are then combined with the data of other workgroups.

Q: Why does the survey ask to which organizational unit I belong? *A:* Without this information, we would not be able to produce feedback reports that focus on your organizational unit. All data would then only lead to one big feedback report that fuses everything into a few lump statistics. Needless to say, this information would not be very useful.

Q: Why does the survey ask for gender? *A:* We want to see whether men and women answered differently to some items. The gender information will be considered only for large organizational units with at least [100] employees.

Q: What if I don't really know the present name of my organizational unit? *A (sticker method):* When you get your questionnaire, you will also get a self-adhesive sticker which contains the name of your organizational unit. You can use this sticker (recommendation) and attach it to your questionnaire. This saves time and makes it easy for you to complete the questionnaire. *A (online survey using HR feed):* When you enter the survey with your PIN, this information will be automatically embedded into your questionnaire. You can see it in your electronic questionnaire.

Q: What happens after the survey? *A (depending on design of follow-up processes):* The project then continues with the follow-up processes. First, the results will be analyzed and fed back to top management, then to senior management, in all market and business unit. They will discuss everything and decide on their responses and on possible actions. This will take a few weeks. The data will reach every workgroup at the shop floor for discussion and actions. You will be hearing and reading a lot about the various follow-up activities in the various communication channels.

Q: Will I be informed about the results of the survey? *A (depending on information politics):* Yes. Every employee will see the results of the whole company and the results of his/her department and workgroup (if more than [7] employees participated). You will *not* see what your colleagues in other workgroups said. Neither will they see the results of your workgroup. *Only* the manager who is responsible for *all* these workgroups is fully informed about similarities and differences in attitudes and opinions in these workgroups.

Q: Do I get a chance to discuss the results of the employee survey? *A (depending on design of follow-up processes):* Yes. Your manager will discuss things with you. [or: There will be a special workshop on the ES results and on what to do with them. These workshops will be facilitated by trained facilitators.]

Q: Will all this really improve things? *A (depending on positioning):* Most likely. This is the firm intention of top management. You will be kept informed about responses and actions.

Q: Who are these 'survey coordinators'? *A (depending on project architecture):* The survey coordinators are a group of company employees who were assigned to manage the survey project in all its parts and phases. The members of the coordination team work at company headquarters [and all business unit locations], primarily in HR. They steer the whole project, help to develop the questionnaire, design processes, bring about decisions, involve top managers, prepare tool boxes for managers, specify who gets what kind of feedback report at what time, and otherwise assure that the survey will help improve the company. Local coordinators do the same in your organization. You can read more about the survey coordinators in the publications on the employee survey. Please support these colleagues in this huge project!

9 Data Collection

This chapter discusses various approaches for conducting the actual data collection in an ES, such as filling out paper questionnaires in a polling station or answering online questionnaires on a personal computer. In each instance, the survey methodologists have to plan how the survey is to be administered to the respondent. They also have to plan the logistics of the entire data collection process.

9.1 Survey Administration and Survey Logistics

By survey administration we mean the way in which the survey questions are actually delivered to the respondent and how the respondent's responses are collected. Any particular survey administration also needs proper survey logistics to ensure that the right material reaches the respondent at the right time and that the completed questionnaire is properly collected and processed. The most common survey administration modes are the traditional paper-pencil method, where the questionnaire is filled out at the employee's work space or in a polling station, and the increasingly common online method, which can take place at the employee's computer of choice.

For paper-pencil surveys, logistical issues include getting the right questionnaires, a sufficient number of pens, envelopes, and instruction sheets along with ballot boxes, tables, and chairs to the respondents in time so that normal work flow is not disturbed. In organizations with tens of thousands of employees and different questionnaires tailored towards the needs of different workgroups (possibly in multiple languages), getting this material to the respondents and getting the filled-out questionnaires back quickly is often a major challenge.

Online surveys can reduce or eliminate the challenge of paper surveys, but online data collection has logistic issues as well. Because some employees will not have access to their own computers, there needs to be kiosk terminals made available in numbers large enough to handle entire groups of workers, particularly in manufacturing locations, which lose money for each minute the line is shut down. For the most part, logistic issues for online surveys involve the IT department. Technicians have to assure emailed invitations will not be filtered out as "spam" email and that the web survey will display properly on older software (particularly when using languages that use very specific characters such as Hebrew, Arabic, or Chinese). While data collection is fairly automatic using HTML coding, the data file being built in the background must be backed up and secure throughout the survey administration period. With increasingly complex online surveys asking different questions of different employees based on their demographic responses, there needs to be thorough testing to assure that the response to a specific question is recorded in the right data field. If the survey uses both paper and web formats, then there needs to be careful planning of how the data will be integrated. Obviously, any problems in this online process must be detected and solved before the survey is launched.

Administrative and logistical issues often lead to a host of questions. Should, for example, the data collection carried out at the employees' place of work, or in "polling stations", or is filling out surveys at home the best possible option? Should surveys be administered on company time or during the employees' free time? What time frame is needed for data collection? Obviously, data collection is a multi-faceted problem. It needs careful preparation that takes into account many considerations. Among them are feasibility considerations that assess what is possible in the given setting. Do the employees have the necessary skills, for example, for an online survey, and does the IT structure allow one to run such a survey in this organization at low costs? Another important criterion is defined by the costs of the data collection method. Printing, distributing, collecting, and entering/scanning paper questionnaires can be quite expensive. Also, each method comes with certain risks such as server problems in the case on an online survey or lost mail in the case of a paper survey. Then, of course, each method leads to psychological questions that may affect the return rate or the data quality. Do online surveys lead to more concerns about anonymity than paper questionnaires, and how would this affect the returns rate and the answers to the questionnaire?

9.2 Data Collection in Group Sessions

Collecting ES data in group sessions is most suitable for organizations where many employees work in a small number of plants or office buildings. Group sessions typically begin by having a person who is responsible for data collection (e.g., member of ES coordination team) schedule a 30-minute meeting with the group. In this meeting, he or she explains once more the objectives of the ES, distributes the questionnaires, supervises the completion of the questionnaires, and then ensures that questionnaires are sent to data entry. Group meetings of this sort generally lead to high participation rates. In addition, they allow for data collection within a couple of days or even within a single day.

The Polling Station Method

A very effective way of collecting data in groups is the polling station method (Borg, 1995). To illustrate this method, Figure 9.1 shows a picture taken in the survey polling station of a medium-sized German company. Notice the two people slipping their questionnaires into ballot boxes, and the two survey coordinators sitting at the desk, administering the distribution of the survey material to the employees. These coordinators hand out the survey material to the employees when they enter the polling sta-

Figure 9.1. Data collection in a polling station.

tion. At some organizations the survey coordinators will also record the names of respondents when they hand out the survey material or before the respondents put their questionnaire into the ballot boxes. This recording is often carried out by canceling names in an "electoral list" (e.g., a telephone listing). Checking names of respondents ensures (1) that no one returns more than one questionnaire, and (2) that follow-up invitations can be sent just to those who did not participate in the survey that day. This extra effort accommodates people who were absent that day; inviting them to participate afterwards (e.g., via a mailed questionnaire) is only fair and often significantly improves the return rate. Past experience with the polling station method shows that most employees perceive checking off their names after they return their questionnaires as a "normal" and necessary procedure if they understand and accept the usual rules of a democratic election. This analogy should be explained in advance to address the argument that recording names is incompatible with a voluntary survey. Naturally, the listing of who participated in the polling station and who did not should be kept strictly confidential and should be destroyed when data collection is over.

The background of Figure 9.1 displays employees taking the survey. When entering the polling station, they picked up the questionnaire along with a blank envelope, an instruction sheet, and a pen (that they got to keep as an incentive for participation in this particular setting) from the survey coordinators. They then chose their own place to sit down and fill out the questionnaire. Experience shows that while filling out surveys, employees tend to sit by themselves, often at some distance from other

Figure 9.2. Data collection in an electronic polling station (German production site).

employees. Cases of two or more employees filling out the surveys together are rare. Indeed, survey participants often cover the completed parts of the survey to further protect the confidentiality of their responses. In order to help employees achieve the highest level of confidentiality possible when filling out their surveys, additional visual barriers can be implemented at the polling station that further enhance employees' survey participation privacy. A different method of offering employees the maximum level of privacy can be achieved through arranging small desks with only one chair throughout the polling station room. Figure 9.2 shows an example for this type of arrangement from an electronic polling station.

Almost any room can function as a polling station. If rooms cannot be converted into polling stations, data collection can be accomplished similarly at employees' respective workspaces. Figure 9.3 displays an example from a German automotive manufacturing plant, where desks and chairs were added to the workspace to allow employees to complete their surveys there. In addition, various "information points" (displayed in Figure 9.4) were set up in the plant to allow workgroups to pick up their surveys and drop them off after completion. Staffing the "information point" with an employee with sufficient knowledge about the ES project let employees raise concerns and ask questions (e.g., "What is meant by this item?" or "My supervisor is new. How should I answer the questions on supervisor?").

Non-participation of employees who are present the day of the survey administration is rare if a group-session collection method is used. Group-session methods create a certain social pressure to participate. If an employee does not take the survey while the rest of the group does, then this individual isolates him- or herself and

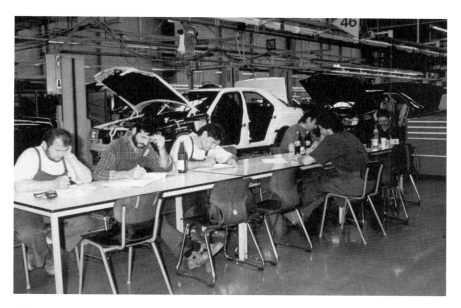

Figure 9.3. Data collection next to the assembly lines in a German automotive production site.

seems to defy the group's commitment to the company. He or she may thus be seen as non-cooperative, as not helping the workgroup or the company to improve. The pressure can be increased by communicating ahead of time that participation is discretionary but "expected" from any (committed) employee: "You can say what you want, but please do speak up!"

The above examples should make clear that data collection in a polling station typically leads to high visibility for the survey—it would be difficult for an employee to argue that he or she overlooked the opportunity to fill out the questionnaire. The mere stopping of the assembly lines for half an hour so that every worker has the opportunity to fill out the questionnaire is a major signal for the employees in this production site that the ES is indeed important. However, it is clear that such an unusual and expensive event must be well prepared so that everybody understands why the assembly lines stop when they do.

More generally, data collection can always be embedded into an event which creates a positive atmosphere that can help to increase survey participation. For example, in one global IT company (called ABC here), the first day of data collection was turned into a world-wide "day of the employee." On that day, various HR activities took place involving all workgroups in all countries. In some countries, the employees from certain functions were invited to a brunch party with live music, while in other countries the employees from the field were invited to headquarters to meet their colleagues from administration. The emphasis was on getting together and feeling as one ABC family rather than collecting information, although management may consider using such a platform to communicate and discuss strategy and future issues.

Figure 9.4. Info point to support the data collection shown in Figure 9.3.

However, one must carefully consider whether such activities go along well with the ES, or whether they are perceived by the employees as an attempt to influence employees to generate "better" scores. If the event activities do lead to truly positive effects and more informed and engaged employees, then "better" data would only be valid. If the employees are skeptical, then they may react by giving more negative survey answers than they would have without the event activities.

Turning data collection into an event can enhance the visibility of the survey so that all employees (including supervisors) become more aware of the pivotal role the survey has for the organization. In addition, this process ensures that all stakeholders take the ES seriously. In fact, a selling point for survey participation can be the fact that each employee's opinion weighs more heavily in employee surveys than in government elections because the number of participants in elections is typically much larger. As data from employee surveys are typically broken down to the workgroups at the shop floor level, hopefully resulting in changes at that level, employee surveys can be promoted as a feedback activity where literally every vote counts, in contrast to a national election where one vote is usually irrelevant.

Organizing a Polling Station Setting

The responsibility for organizing data collection using the polling station method is best given to the ES coordination team. The ideal set-up of a polling station for survey data collection depends on a number of circumstances, particularly on whether the regular work process can be interrupted by administering a survey.

In general, one cannot simply open up a polling station and then wait for employees to show up there for survey participation. This would almost always lead to traffic jams in the polling station around noon and to empty polling stations at other times. It is better to design a system of time slots where each slot is assigned to only a small set of groups for participation. For some workgroups, there may be two or three such slots, so that these groups can make sure that crucial business activities continue to be covered when a certain fraction of its employees are in the polling station.

In many organizations, the polling station is reserved for 1-2 hours per workgroup or per particular group. The ES coordination team determines the date and time each department is assigned with the departmental coordinators or supervisors. Two or more reserved times may be necessary for survey administration if departments cannot fully discontinue work to complete the survey (e.g., units in hospitals need to be staffed all the time). Employees are informed about their particular time windows, and assigned to time slots. One employee of each department is made responsible for informing everyone in the department once the time slots for survey administration arrive. Having employees go to the polling station together can further enhance the effectiveness of organizational norms on employees' participatory behavior.

A polling station also requires at least one member of the ES coordination team to be present at all times. For some workgroups, it may be advantageous to send an external consultant to the polling station to serve as an independent "observer" who guarantees that all rules of data collection are strictly adhered to. This person must be recognized as the independent overseer—for example by wearing a prominent name tag (e.g., "Bill Jones, XYZ Institute") and by sitting next to the ballot boxes. In European countries, work councils sometimes request that they be given the role of observers, but this request should not be granted. Rather, works council members should play the same role as managers do, participating by coming to the polling station to fill out their questionnaires. Indeed, politically minded managers often use this opportunity and make their participation quite visible (as politicians do) by having someone take a picture when they cast their questionnaire into the ballot box.

Then, rooms have to be found that can serve as polling stations. They must be reserved and be supplied with desks, chairs, and (if privacy is an issue) possibly equipped with polling booths. A sufficient quantity of questionnaires and name lists must be available for each time slot. Similarly, sufficient quantities of envelopes, pens and ballot boxes, and packaging supplies need to be brought to the polling station in advance. These things may appear obvious for survey administration, but it is exactly for this reason that they are sometimes overlooked, leading to a chaotic survey experience.

Polling Station Data Collection and Other Group Sessions

The polling station method is but one variant of collecting data in group sessions. It differs from more informal sessions by closely imitating an election setting, which most employees are familiar with. Thus, the rules of this approach do not have to be explained or justified in detail. Often, it suffices to simply point out that this format is "just like an election."

For other less formal group sessions—such as collecting data in a group meeting, for example—Dunham and Smith (1979) recommend paying attention to the following points:

- Each session should be planned in a way that at least 25 employees are participating at the same time so that feelings of anonymity can be strengthened.
- The atmosphere should be relaxed, the meeting should be solely devoted to data collection, and no other topics should be covered or addressed during the data collection meeting.
- "Questionnaires should either be placed on seats of chairs before employees enter the room or picked up randomly by employees as they enter. Seating arrangements are determined by employees themselves to alleviate employee concerns about secretly coded questionnaires" (Dunham & Smith, 1979, p. 86).
- The manager or survey coordinator responsible for conducting data collection introduces the ES and explains how the surveys are to be filled out. Furthermore, he or she answers possible questions on how to fill out the questionnaire, on the survey's purpose, on follow-up processes, etc.
- If the presence of the manager is disruptive of data collection efforts, he or she leaves the room. Otherwise, the manager remains at the end of the room, but should not be walking around during data collection.
- Completed questionnaires are to be deposited into ballot boxes or cartons in proximity to the room exit. The cartons or ballot boxes are then sealed by two employees of an "employee mailing committee," and are labeled based on the organizational unit they are from (e.g., with stickers). The surveys are then transported to the organizations' postal unit, from where they are sent to the external data entry facility. Surveys should not be collected or be posted by the manager as this may harm the credibility and trust employees may have in the surveying efforts.

A number of additional recommendations can be made. Most importantly, managers should not be made responsible for data collection in their own workgroups since most surveys contain items pertaining to the manager himself or herself. Hence, if managers control and oversee the data collection, employees may perceive this as a means to influence them to give more "positive" answers. Instead, one person can be selected per workgroup and asked to motivate survey participation and to coordinate all activities (such as going to the polling station in the assigned time slot) needed for complete participation.

Special Participation Requests for Unavailable Employees

If the organization is checking names from a list as employees participate at the polling station, then the coordinator has the opportunity to contact those employees who did not participate for whatever reason (e.g., travel, absence, temporary leave, vacation). These employees can receive the questionnaire in a different manner, such as by mail. A survey packet can be sent to them with a personal letter explaining why this is being sent, an instruction sheet (how to fill out, when to return, etc.), and a stamped return envelope addressed to the data entry office.

Occasionally, employees who expect to be on business travel or on vacation during data collection ask to obtain their survey in advance. Opportunities to have these employees fill out surveys can be granted at designated rooms. However, experience shows that finding specific arrangements for each employee's situation can be difficult and cumbersome.

The extent to which the administrator should accommodate special requests depends on both the expected response rate and the need for reliable data from this person's department, function, job type, or individual demographic grouping. Note that a low response rate does not automatically reduce the accuracy of scores. Rather, this is only true if the attitudes and perceptions of those who respond to the survey are different from those of non-respondents. Research shows that this is true for those non-respondents who intentionally do not participate in the survey, but not for "passive" non-respondents who intend to participate but ultimately do not for one reason or another (see Section 7.6). Active non-respondents have relatively low scores on commitment, job satisfaction, conscientiousness, and agreeableness (Rogelberg et al., 2003). Hence, if one portion of the population is invited to participate in groups (e.g., assembly workers, machine operators), while others are surveyed by methods that exert less social pressure to participate (e.g., office and clerical, staff positions, management), then the results are likely to differ somewhat because the group method will also capture persons who would otherwise be active non-respondents. Thus, special accommodations and personal invitations are most needed for employees who are not surveyed within group sessions.

Likewise, special accommodations make sense when reports need to include scores from certain units, groups, jobs, or demographic groups that are relatively small within the organization. For example, if management expects to see survey results for the IT group, which represents only 1% of the organization, then it is worthwhile for the survey administrator to make extraordinary arrangements to increase the response rate for that group or else risk an IT sample that is too small for survey results that are reliable enough for decision making and action taking. An even more extreme example is the executive board, which is not only relatively small but where extraordinary arrangements are often considered normal practice.

Monitoring Response Rates and Using Reminders

Like all forms of data collection, group sessions require careful monitoring of response rates. Ideally, the managers who are responsible for data collection have access to current response rates so that they can offer alternative opportunities to participate for departments that are lagging behind. Employees might be offered a second time slot or provided with pre-stamped envelopes to participate by mail.

Motivation to participate can be increased through the local survey coordinator or through the person responsible for data collection in the unit. Often workgroups are motivated to participate when they are told what their response rate is compared to those from other groups. The competitive nature of most Western countries usually results in pressure to avoid "losing" to other units. Note that this competition can become counterproductive when managers nag their employees to raise an already high participation rate in order to be the best. Not only does this notion focus on the wrong metric (response rate instead of improving survey scores), it also aggravates employees who have already participated, especially if the survey is promoted as a voluntary behavior. Rather than fostering competition to have the highest response rate, managers should foster competition to achieve a specific goal (e.g., at least 85% participation where group administration is being used).

Another motivational strategy is to communicate that response rates below a certain minimum value will prevent a unit from receiving a report with survey results. Typically surveys use an anonymity rule (e.g., minimum group size of seven) to protect the identities of participants from small groups. Employees usually appreciate this protection, yet they also want to have their perceptions and suggestions associated with their organizational unit so that the issues may be addressed. For groups with fewer than 10 employees, achieving a response count of seven is no guarantee. So, one can make the case that maximum participation will assure a local report and enhance anonymity for the good of the entire group. This way, the workgroup is positioned to benefit from the survey process.

Finally, it should be pointed out that motivating employees to participate in the survey is almost always best accomplished by "walking around" and talking to the respective workgroups face-to-face. If done well, managers can greatly increase participation by simply asking each employee "Did you already participate?" Positive responses should receive the manager's appreciation and a reminder that results will be reviewed soon after reports are released. For employees who say that they have not participated, managers can reply, "Please do. The company benefits greatly from learning employees' opinions, both favorable and unfavorable. It doesn't take much time, and we need your help. About 65% of us have taken the survey. I hope you decide to participate, too. Okay, thanks." This type of friendly invitation with a brief explanation should be received well as long as managers respect employees' right to avoid participation—there should be no threats of retribution from corporate, HR, or anyone else! Emphasizing that the majority of coworkers have already participated will capitalize on the power that perceived social norms have on human behavior while still acknowledging that the employee is in control.

9.3 Data Collection by Postal Mail

Setting up polling stations is not always feasible and can be far too costly and complex. This is particularly true for very large organizations with many locations that are spatially scattered over huge regions. The German rails, for example, employ over 200,000 people in thousands of locations all over Germany, including mobile locations on 30,000 trains daily. In cases like this the best method for data collection is through postal mail. Note that mail surveys also can be run through the internal com-

> ***Personal letter to each employee***
> - Use official stationary
> - Sender should be the CEO, speaking on behalf of the enire executive board
> - Keep letter concise, one page only
> - Must be easy to read for any employee
> - The first sentence should be catchy enough to motivate the reader to read on
> - The letter should address the following issues:
>   - What are the goals of the employee survey?
>   - Why are these goals important?
>   - Why a survey at this time?
>   - Who will see what results when? And what then? (some milestones)
>   - Who will profit from the survey? (everyone, in principle: the opinions of the employees are needed improvements)
>   - Participation is discretionary but why it is important that every employee who is invited to participate takes this opportunity to speak up
>   - The answers of the individual employee will remain confidential or even anonymous
>   - Filling out the questionnaire is easy, will take only some [20] minutes
>   - The CEO and the executive board are committed to the survey's goals and rules
>
> ***Instruction sheet***
> - How the data will be collected (online, paper and pencil, ...), and reasons why
> - How to fill out the questionnaire
> - How to submit the questionnaire, where to send it and why

Figure 9.5. Some tips and issues for personal letters (with instruction sheets) inviting an employee to participate in an employee survey.

pany mail system, but this approach to data collection may threaten perceptions of confidentiality.

In a mail survey, a packet with survey material is sent out to the individual employee's company or home address. This packet contains at least these items:

1) a personalized letter from the survey's sponsor (often the CEO) stating the purpose of the survey, explaining its rules and milestones, and motivating the employee to participate (see Figure 9.5)
2) instructions explaining how to fill-out the questionnaire
3) the questionnaire itself
4) a free return envelope (stamped or "postage paid by receiver")

Often, this material is augmented by:

5) a self-adhesive sticker that shows essential demographics of the individual employee (see Section 5.10)
6) an "I have participated" postcard (see Figure 9.6)

The major advantage of the mail survey data collection is that the complete data collection process can be outsourced. There exist companies that specialize in data collection by mail. They can produce and send out tens of thousands of personalized

> I have participated in the employee survey and returned a completed questionnaire by mail. I will not need a reminder or another questionnaire.
>
> Name:
> Address:

Figure 9.6. Prototype for an "I have participated" postcard.

packets generated from an electronic database. They can also provide exact and legally binding cost estimates that specify all services rendered—making costs of data collection transparent without binding labor resources within the organization.

One disadvantage of the mail survey method is that it yields relatively low response rate. Published research estimates response rates to mail surveys to be around 20 to 30% (e.g., Paul & Bracken, 1995). However, such estimates are difficult to interpret because of the many context factors. For example, if the survey packet is sent to the employees' private addresses, the employees are thereby also asked to fill out the questionnaires in their spare time and not during work hours. This not only means an extra-investment of the employee, but it may be interpreted as a sign that the survey is not important enough to be conducted during work hours. From the authors' experience, one can generate substantially higher response rates (up to 70% or even more) even in mail surveys. However, you do not get such response rates just by sending out a survey packet. Some of the natural disadvantages of mail surveys have to be compensated for by extra efforts. For example, a mail survey obviously lacks visibility in comparison with a polling station. So, one has to work harder on making the survey and its data collection time window known by every employee. Extra efforts are also required to keep track of return rates so that one can focus follow-up activities to generate higher participation.

Monitoring Response Rates and Using Reminders

Monitoring response rates when using the mail survey method is comparatively difficult. It takes time for the completed questionnaires to physically reach the data entry address. This is particularly true if the survey is run internationally. To keep more control over returns, it may be necessary to have the questionnaires sent to local data entry facilities that then electronically send data files. This would also substantially lower mailing costs.

Completed questionnaires should be entered or scanned on a daily basis so that return rates can be computed in near real-time. This information is fed back, for example, to a member of the ES coordination team who is responsible for reminder activities and notes. However, even with daily data entry, the procedures are almost never completely up to date due to slow mailing, weekends or holidays, or other unpredictable events such as union strikes. This makes controlling returns in mail surveys complicated and risky, and makes the availability of the best-possible information on return rates essential for possible ad-hoc interventions such as searching for lost mail.

Another method for controlling response rates and reducing unnecessary costs is to use "I have participated" postcards (Boek & Lade, 1963). In the survey packet, the employee receives a postcard such as the one shown in Figure 9.6, possibly even with name and address already printed onto it to make the process as simple as possible for the employee. The instructions for using this postcard could be as follows:

> *Once you have filled out your questionnaire and sent it off to data entry, please also send the enclosed postcard to the data entry firm. The firm then knows that they are no longer required to send you reminder mails, which provides for cost-saving. The anonymity of your responses is in no way affected by you mailing your postcard. The only organization that will keep track of the postcards is the data entry institute. The data entry institute treats all postcards as confidential and destroys them once the survey data collection is completed."*

"I have participated" postcards can save a lot of money because no reminder mailings or even complete survey packets have to be sent out to all employees, but only to those who have not responded yet.

Mangione (1995) studied the obvious concern that employees tend to return only the postcard, and not the actual survey. The results do not indicate that this is the case. Rather, on average, more surveys are returned than reminder postcards. Hence, some employees tend to forget about the postcard while others may not send them for other reasons such as, for example, to protect their anonymity.

Practical experience also demonstrates that in some cases, use of the postcard method is not worth the effort. If employees are informed in a timely manner about the response rates and if organizational units are compared on their response rates, then this is usually sufficient to motivate employees and particularly managers to participate and encourage others to participate as well. Communication of low response rates within the organization frequently leads to managers encouraging their employees to participate in order to avoid "coming in last." In most cases, managers take action by discussing the ES efforts with their employees in person, and by emphasizing the importance of the ES project.

Even without information about individual responses, postal reminders can still be sent to all employees. However, sending reminder notes with full survey packets is inefficient because the full set of materials is sent to employees who have already responded. To avoid the impression that the project wastes money, this "wave" approach (although common in public opinion surveys) should be avoided for employee surveys.

In an anonymous mail survey, one cannot know who did and did not respond. So, reminder notes cannot be addressed specifically to individuals who have not responded yet. In that case, all that is possible is a reminder such as this one:

Your [org unit] has a response rate of 50% so far. If you have not filled out a survey yet, please do so now. As you may know, in order to protect anonymity, we have agreed that reports will be generated <u>only</u> for groups of people where <u>at least</u> [seven] persons participated. Thus, if your [org unit] does not make this cut-off value, it will get no report. In that case, your responses will be integrated into the statistics of higher-order org units only."

9.4 Online Data Collection

Today, most large companies use an online survey administration for some or all of their employees to participate. Online data collection is increasing as the web has become prevalent in public and private locations in most industrialized nations. In the US, more than 65% of families have access to the web from their homes, indicating that the majority of the workforce is sufficiently tech-savvy to participate in online surveys. While earlier electronic means of collecting employee data included handing out disks with data files for employees to complete on their workstation PCs, these methods have become outdated and are now rarely used.

General Advantages of Online Surveys

Online surveys have multiple advantages in comparison to traditional paper-pencil surveys. Advanced web-survey development tools available for low fees allow for questionnaire development by survey coordination team members with little technical expertise, making use of web-survey development programs comparable to the development of paper-pencil surveys in word-processing programs.

Many web-survey development tools also provide server space to host survey data, allowing organizations to store ES data away from their own servers (and thus prohibiting unauthorized access of ES data from within the organization).

Centralized and quick administration reaches all employees with active email accounts within minutes. This may be particularly useful in large organizations employing predominantly white-collar workers who access their email accounts frequently.

If participation invitations do not reach the intended respondent, the emails "bounce" back to the ES coordination team and allow for quick follow-up or for development of alternative means of delivery. Current information on response rates can be traced in real time, even in large global organizations.

Online data collection is accomplished much more quickly than data collection using traditional paper-pencil surveys. Past experience shows that the majority of responses to web-based surveys usually occur within one or two days after initial invitation emails are sent out, with few responses coming in after more than a week if no reminders are sent. Automatic and individualized reminders can be sent from a central administrative unit. Data entry becomes unnecessary, allowing organizations to obtain results more quickly and without data entry errors while reducing the cost of production and distribution. Web-based surveys can be designed to allow an employee to complete the survey over multiple sessions, with data entered earlier being recorded for later completion. The survey can be designed to use a unique password (or PIN) for each employee so that he or she can only submit one completed set of responses, or the survey can use a universal password to avoid the perception that the company is tracking individual responses.

In addition, online questionnaires have the following advantages over paper-pencil based versions:

- Ability to create "adaptive" questionnaires that ask different questions to different employees (e.g., a set of questions for managers if the respondent is identified as a manager).
- Ability to program the questionnaire in different languages so that the respondent can pick his or her preferred language.
- Flexibility of managing the release of the survey questions so that last minute changes can be made without the need to reprint questionnaires (Mangione, 1995)

Challenges of Online Employee Surveys

Although the use of online employee surveys has various advantages, different challenges need to be faced when online surveys are chosen over paper-pencil versions.

- Computers need to be accessible for all employees
- The server needs to accommodate for high volumes of responses at certain times (e.g., right after the survey is sent out)
- Employees have to be sufficiently familiar with computers and web-browsing to fill out online surveys
- Issues of data protection need to be adequately addressed. Technical and organizational measures need to ensure that anonymity or confidentiality of responses are not at risk
- Employment and data protection laws in different countries have to be carefully scrutinized for conflicts with electronic ES data collection and storage
- For groups of employees with little previous exposure to computers, help desks and polling stations with computer access may have to be implemented

Online Data Collection and Anonymity

Do paper-pencil and online administrations lead to the same results? Various studies (Edwards et al., 1997; Rosenfeld, Edwards, & Thomas, 1993; Kuhnert & McCauley, 1996) demonstrate that there are few systematic effects of using electronic means of survey administration if anonymity concerns can be successfully addressed. Particularly when studies are administered through web-based systems, processes need to be made transparent and communicated credibly to all stakeholders. Figure 9.7 demonstrates an example. The employee first receives an invitation email to participate in the survey (step 1). The invitation email contains the URL link to the questionnaire (step 2). After starting the survey (step 3), he or she is informed about any demographic information that is drawn from the personnel information system and stored with his or her survey answers. The employee can then move on to answer the ques-

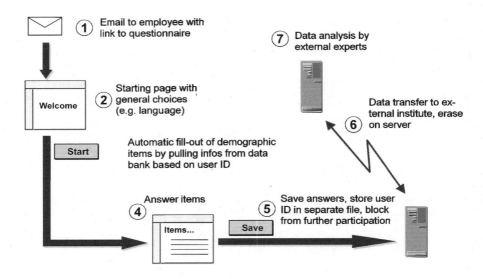

Figure 9.7. Steps of an online employee survey.

tionnaire, or can stop participation at this point. If he or she continues, then responses are stored locally until the submit/send button is pressed that initiates data transfer to the server (step 4). What is stored (in the set-up described here) is (a) the demographics of this respondent, (b) his or her responses to the items, and also (c) the respondent's username/login. The latter, however, is saved in a *separate* file and not together with (a) or (b). The (c) information is needed only to prevent persons to respond more than once and possibly also for sending out reminders to those who have not yet responded. Server access needs to be limited to as few administrators as possible. Data stored on the server can be encoded in regular intervals in order to prevent individuals who gain access to the server from gaining access to employee data.

A problem arises when it comes to interrupting an online survey, because in this case the respondent must be able to continue in "her" questionnaire at a later time and, hence, her answers must be stored temporarily together with her access code. If the respondents do not want that this information is stored together with their answers to the questionnaire, the only option for them is to quit the survey. Then, in an anonymous survey, no information would be stored at all. This, however, also means that the respondents cannot answer the questionnaire cumulatively in several sittings. One must either accept this situation for the sake of anonymity, or offer a solution such as the following provided in Johnson & Johnson's credo survey:

> *"If you cannot finish the survey in one sitting, click the 'exit and continue later' button, which allows your data to be saved. The software will assign you a unique 'return key' code (case sensitive), which you must use to reenter and*

complete your survey. A new 'return key' is assigned every time you exit to complete later. If you lose this code, you will not be able to access your saved data. Write the new return key down and keep it in a safe place. Once you complete the survey, the key will be detached from your survey making it impossible for you to be personally identified."

Concerns about anonymity can be reduced by providing transparent information about the various steps of the online data-collection process: What information is collected, what is saved when, what the respondent can do in this process. However, it is important to complement this "technical" information with "soft" facts, in particular with public commitments of the ES coordination team and the data protection officer that all rules will be strictly adhered to. These persons should *personally* assure the employees that everything has been done to make sure that the data collection can be trusted and that no unauthorized persons have access to the data. This information should be communicated to all employees within the information campaign, for example in the format of short testimonials which also show pictures of the ES coordination team and the data protection officer. This helps to build trust, because it is the people behind the measures that make the difference.

There are many ES vending companies who can develop and administer online surveys. Using a third party vendor not only eliminates the need for specialized skills and equipment, but also reduces the employees' concerns over confidentiality. If anything, the ease of providing an ES service has created the need for a company's survey director to be savvy in selecting a vendor that can handle the necessary complexity (e.g., translations, integration with paper data collection, report generation).

Publicly communicating the role of the internal data protection representative or the external vendor's confidentiality policy can enhance employee trust. By using organizational documents, the company intranet, and corporate newsletters, the survey's process is openly shared with employees and procedures for assuring confidentiality are made clear to employees and management. Ultimately, statements from the data protection representative, system administrators, and executives communicating a personal responsibility for data protection may contribute more to trust than communication of technical and organizational detail.

When online surveys are to be utilized in global surveys, cultural and national differences in accessing the internet and using computers as well as privacy concerns have to be taken into account. For instance, while the majority of production workers in the USA will have experience using personal computers and the web, this is not true in Eastern European countries, for example. In addition, privacy concerns and concerns about anonymity are often stronger in Western Europe than in other Western nations.

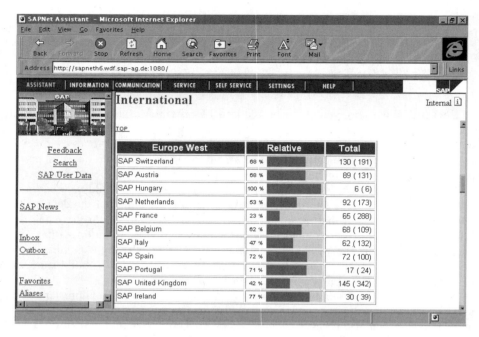

Figure 9.8. Response rates in real time in an intranet employee survey.

Monitoring Response Rates and Using Reminders

One major advantage of online employee surveys is the ability to compute real-time response rates and to inform the employees accordingly. Figure 9.8 shows an example from a global ES. In this case, all employees had continuous access via the corporate intranet to the current response rates for major organizational units. Each employee could see that, for instance, the current response rate in France was lower than the one in the UK, a subsidiary of about the same size. This comparative information itself can be sufficient to motivate employees in France to participate. In addition, the information can be used by local ES coordinators, works councils, or managers to communicate to employees that participation in the ES is important and, indeed, that it is "a matter of pride" not to come in last. However, most companies make response rates available only to survey coordinators. While pride and competition may encourage participation, they can also lead managers to apply inappropriate pressure on employees, practically forcing them to take the survey. Thus, it is often better to report which units have achieved the target participation rate (e.g., 85%).

Individual follow-ups can also be sent out via email. They can be simple reminders as in Figure 9.9, but they could also be individualized messages that basically say, "You have not yet participated. Please do!" However, one should carefully consider whether reminding each employee individually in a way that conveys "We know that

Data Collection 225

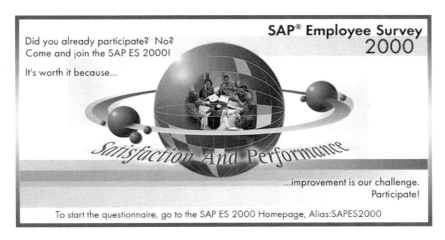

Figure 9.9. An unfocused electronic reminder

you have not participated yet" would harm the survey project. In organizations where anonymity is an issue, this approach can lead to suspicion that someone checks who did and who did not participate and that this information may be passed on to managers or coworkers. If individual reminders of that sort are considered at all, they should always be generated by a computer program ("Hi. This is a reminder, automatically generated by the survey program...").

Combining Online and Traditional Methods of Data Collection

In many companies it is possible to administer an ES exclusively online, but some organizations have production units without available computers or employees without necessary computer skills. Until online access is pervasive throughout entire companies (in all countries), employee surveys frequently have to be administered in a combination of online and paper-pencil modes. The question that is often discussed in this context is whether the individual employee should be given a choice in which mode he or she wants to complete the survey. In almost all projects, such an option is eventually not pursued because it becomes difficult to know whether an employee has participated more than once. Some companies trust that their employees will not sabotage the survey or believe that any attempts will not substantially change results. However, for those companies that are more concerned about guaranteeing only one completed survey per employee, providing a choice of online or paper formats would greatly complicate tracking efforts. In these situations one should decide on one mode only for each larger organizational unit. The larger these units the easier it is to centrally plan and control data collection.

In a mixed mode, employees who get "only" a paper questionnaire sometimes complain that they are treated as "second-class citizens." It appears that the company is doing everything it can to deliver the survey to the air-conditioned offices of the white-collar employees, while production workers are given the "cheap" paper questionnaires. But, indeed, from the perspective of what it costs, just the opposite is true: The paper-pencil mode is typically more expensive. Thus, it is important to communicate that the company is using paper questionnaires despite the fact that they are more costly than online data collection because the survey should be accessible to all employees, no matter what their work environment is.

9.5 Alternative Methods of Data Collection

The data collection methods presented so far are prototypes that are modified in various ways in practical applications. Opgenoorth (1985) reports, for example, that within the German Bayer AG, the ES questionnaires were distributed with the corporate newspaper as inserts. In some branches, they were simply piled up next to the bulletin boards to be picked up there by the employees. While such methods may be cheap to run, they have the disadvantage that they do not give the survey a lot of visibility and let it appear as a mere "reader's survey" that is of minor importance. Thus, such approaches tend to be quite unsuccessful in obtaining high response rates, with many projects reaching no more than 12%. For instance, Pittner (1997) reports on various employee surveys conducted at Lufthansa, a large German airline. Surveys were distributed through the internal mailing system, or they were delivered in conjunction with the company newsletter. If delivery was accomplished with the company newsletter, response rates were found to be very low (less than 10%).

Claassen (1985), on the other hand, reports on a variation of the group session method that he used within the headquarters of a German insurance company. He first selected some 20 employees "with good knowledge about the organizational structure" as responsible for data collection. These persons then had to (a) mark each questionnaire with a code for the particular organizational unit of the employee; (b) distribute the questionnaires in the org units they were assigned to; (c) resolve problems and questions during survey administration; (d) return two hours later to collect the questionnaires in sealed envelopes; and (e) make a list of employees absent at the time of data collection. With this method, data collection could be accomplished within a day. Employees on vacation or on sick leave had four weeks to mail in their surveys. In the end, an 81% response rate was achieved. This success was not only due to the group session approach, but also due to the personal rapport that was established between the employees responsible for data collection and the participants.

Other variations of the methods presented above are discussed by Pobel & Mueller (1995), Klann & Pobel (2000) and Hunsdiek (1991). Pobel & Mueller (1995), for example, report on a mail survey conducted at a large German manufacturing firm. They implemented a phone line where employees could ask questions about the ES project and get answers from HR personnel, the workers council and from the external consultants supporting the ES project. Although most employees never actually used these phone lines, they still seemed to help promote a climate of trust.

The telephone can also be used to collect data via computer-assisted telephone interviewing (CATI). This method is occasionally used for employee surveys of relatively small samples of selected employees, such as senior managers or field representatives who are frequently traveling. Employees may be called by interviewers or they can dial in at their convenience during the survey administration. In fully automated systems, the employees only interact with a recorded voice message that guides them through the survey. The interviewer or computer system asks employees if they agree to participate and then reads the questionnaire question by question, recording answers acoustically or via touchtone buttons. While use of this method had been waning, advances in Interactive Voice Response (IVR) technology is reducing the costs involved while improving the end-user experience. Nevertheless, telephone-based data collection is not commonly used.

Klann & Pobel (2000) reported on a world-wide survey project conducted for a large chemical company. Survey packets were mailed to the respective plants in the participating countries. The plants were then responsible for distributing this material to the employees invited to participate. Every respondent received a return envelope addressed to the data entry institute in Germany. Respondents could thus either return their surveys directly or they could drop them in ballot boxes placed at different sites within their plant.

Hunsdiek (1991) reports on an ES conducted at a large media corporation headquartered in Germany. There, the questionnaires were distributed by supervisors, and were collected by members of the works council or could be sent by mail to the president of the works council. The works council then delivered the questionnaires to the external data entry institute. Although this approach was successful in this company, it obviously cannot be used everywhere. It also remains problematic in principle since it blurs the roles of supervisors and works council. In general, neither supervisors nor works council should get active roles in running the data collection. Rather, their roles should be to inform the employees and to motivate them to participate.

Various other modifications of the data collection strategies presented above can be found in the literature. In most cases, they are designed to fit the specific organizational structures and constraints regarding cost efficiency at the company conducting the ES project.

9.6 Summary Comparison of Data Collection Methods

The data collection methods presented in this chapter have different advantages and disadvantages. They are compared in Table 9.1 with respect to different criteria. The assessments in this table assume that no particular means are utilized to compensate for the natural weaknesses of the respective method. For example, the polling station method will automatically generate high visibility for the survey, while the mail survey in and by itself will not. However, one can compensate for this natural handicap of a mail survey by extra communication efforts.

Table 9.1. A comparison of four data collection methods on different criteria

Criterion	Group	Mail	Online	CATI
Expected return rates	very high	low	medium	High
Visibility	high	low	low	low
Anonymity concerns	low	moderate	pronounced	moderate
Social pressure	high	none	none	high
Controlling distribution	costly	easy	very easy	easy
Controlling returns	difficult	delayed	real time	immediate
Follow-ups, reminders	complicated	costly	cheap, easy	(n.a.)
Costs of printing	high	very high	none	none
Costs of programming	none	none	low (Internet)	low
Data entry	after survey	daily	automatic	by interviewer
Time to data analysis	long	long	short	short
Internal coord. effort	very high	low (if home)	low (if PIS ok)	low
Admin in working hours	almost always	maybe	choice of em.	typically yes
Logistical challenge	very high	low	low (Internet)	low
Central administration	very difficult	medium	easy (if PIS ok)	easy
Last-minute changes	difficult	difficult	easy	easy
Tried and tested	often	often	growing	medium
Robustness	high	medium	rather high	high
Adaptive questionnaire	no	no	yes	yes
Employee skills needed	low	low	high	medium
Samples	census/cluster	any	any	n<3000

9.7 Measures to Increase Response Rates

Achieving high response rates is a basic priority for each ES. When response rates are high, there is no need to discuss an issue that is otherwise almost unavoidable, i.e., how those employees who did not respond would have changed the survey results. There is no simple answer to this question, and major acceptance problems can result from low participation. Thus, we should carefully consider measures that organizations can take to increase response rates. On the other hand, pushing too hard for high response rates can damage the data quality. If a person feels pressured to fill out a questionnaire, he or she may still effectively avoid the survey by providing meaningless answers such as checking "undecided" on most items or—even worse, because difficult to detect—by giving answers that are socially desirable or simply "positive".

What Response Rates can be Considered High Response Rates?

According to the literature and to our survey experience of some 20 years, the response rates for employee surveys have an enormous range: They lie between 7% and 100%. Yet, these values are extremes not likely to be encountered in a real survey project. Edwards et al. (1997) propose that each ES should aim at reaching at least a 50% response rate. They base this target on their literature review of response rates that mostly lie between 35% and 80%. This 50% target, however, does not take the administration mode into account. If group data collection methods are utilized, response rates of 50% are poor; values around 90% are normal (Dunham & Smith, 1979; Borg, 2003). For mail surveys, the response rates typically range between 50% and 75%, but they can easily be substantially lower if the survey is not properly marketed. For online employee surveys, the literature reports response rates that are somewhat higher. From our experience in online ES projects, we use a value of 80% as a rule-of-thumb target.

Response rates cannot, however, be attributed to the survey administration mode alone. First, companies that run online surveys typically differ from companies that run paper-pencil surveys in their workforce composition (white vs. blue collar), technology, and location (USA vs. Eastern Europe, for example). Second, each mode comes with a host of other factors that are more or less correlated with them such as the survey's visibility, the social pressure to participate, seeing others participate, and so on. For example, when Johnson & Johnson recently changed their ES to a 100% online administration, manufacturing locations were given nearly nine months' notice so that they could plan for the creation of kiosk computers for the survey. Later, their communication department began developing a new survey logo, posters, and audio messages for voice mail systems. With these efforts Johnson & Johnson companies were now encouraged to use a unified "brand image" for its Credo Survey, which had moved from a collection of local data points throughout a two-year cycle to a global, annual, autumn event. In survey programs like this, it is the quality of planning and effort that determines the response rate much more than the particular way of data collection or, indeed, the way a questionnaire is filled-out or answered. In addition, many other "random" factors influence the response rate such as the particular executive team's public commitment to the survey, the general organizational climate towards surveys, resistance of particular groups (e.g., middle management) against the ES, or the quality and impact of the information campaign that accompanies the survey. Hence, to expect a particular response rate just because one uses a particular mode is unrealistic.

Persuasive Positioning

To achieve high response rates one must first position the survey persuasively. Individual employees will only participate in the survey if the anticipated costs (invested time, brain work needed to answer the questions, risk of being identified as the one who gave negative answers, etc.) are at least outweighed by the anticipated benefits (e.g., changing things for the better, feeling good about contributing to one's organization, experiencing a sense of camaraderie when participating with peers, etc.).

Thus, when promoting employee surveys, one should present the survey as having a large benefits-to-cost ratio for the organization and the individual employee. Hence, one may argue that it takes only some 20 minutes to fill out the questionnaire; that everything has been done to make this task as simple as possible; that there are no "right" or "wrong" answers (rather, what one wants to know is the employee's opinions); and that similar surveys are conducted in many other organizations with the majority of employees participating. The perceived risk can also be reduced by clearly explaining, in particular, how the respondent's anonymity is safeguarded.

When it comes to benefits, a common mistake is to promise too much. For example, one large German car manufacturer marketed its ES under the slogan: "How you can influence your company's future in 30 minutes..." If taken literally, this is certainly a promise that is grossly exaggerated. However, when selling an ES to employees, the communication specialists often compile long lists of answers to the generic question "What is in it for me?" Such lists easily promise too much and without management's involvement, making strategic priorities for post-survey responses potentially seems hypocritical.

A good method to avoid such risky promises altogether is to turn the "What is in it for me?" question around when conceiving the marketing concept for the ES, much as US President John F. Kennedy did in his inaugural address: "Ask not what your country can do for you, ask what you can do for your country." This approach often offers an intriguing and convincing platform for launching a survey. However, such calls for "organizational citizenship" may not work everywhere, and so they have to be carefully adjusted to the organizational context. At one company where employee cynicism was particularly high, we were able to use their mistrust of management as a call for them to get involved and make the change happen for themselves.

The best approach to increasing survey response rates is to make clear what follow-up activities are scheduled. Hopefully, one can point to an ongoing history of the company using the survey as the first step in a systematic improvement process. Survey data should be shown as the first necessity in this process. One also should be emphasizing that improvements help both the company and its employees—the survey is a win-win opportunity, and management is committed to providing win-win outcomes.

In addition, the ES project should be positioned in a way that supervisors are made responsible for promoting the ES to their subordinates. Promotion does not mean that these managers are also held accountable for low response rates in their organizational units. However, when a manager is asked by his or her superior manager what was done to get employees to participate, he or she should have "good" answers.

In many European countries, it is also of crucial importance to obtain the works council's commitment to the project as early as possible. In many places unions' active resistance against employee surveys can make the project's success very unlikely. In the end, an ES cannot be run against the expressed will of the works council. If the works council publicly announces that it is against the survey and recommends not participating, the survey project has no chance to be successful. Under these circumstances, one should not run the survey. Rather, one needs to negotiate with the works council the conditions of the survey until an agreement is reached that is acceptable for management as well as for the works council.

Reducing Anonymity and Confidentiality Concerns

An important feature that may prevent employees from even looking at the questionnaire is concerns about the anonymity or confidentiality of their responses. What needs to be convincingly communicated to all employees is how anonymity or confidentiality is guaranteed, both technically (e.g., by setting up rules for reporting only statistics based on not fewer than seven respondents and rules for processing and storing ES data) and personally (e.g., by defining accountabilities for data protection and by formulating rules for managers about the information they are entitled to ask for and information that is off limits). As important as these messages are, one should take care not to overemphasize this aspect of the survey else employees begin to wonder why such excessive attention needs to be devoted to this issue if there is nothing to worry about. Indeed, Hippler et al. (1990) have shown that communicating excessively is just as bad for response rates as not addressing anonymity at all.

To raise employees' level of trust in the process, someone should publicly accept responsibility for the anonymity and confidentiality of the survey data. Often, this is the CEO, but it also helps if the data protection officer reports in the company newsletter or intranet on the measures taken to protect anonymity. This might be done in a small article, preferably with a picture of this person to give a more face-to-face appeal.

Concerns about anonymity and confidentiality can also be reduced through hiring an external survey vendor to accomplish data collection, data processing, entry, storage, and analyses. Most importantly, the raw data are to remain with this vendor so that no one in the company has access to them. Data analyses and reports are only done by the vendor, and only in full agreement with the rules for such analyses. The employees should be informed about the vendor, know who their key consultants are, and what the vendor's previous experience with employee surveys is.

Transparency and Visibility

The more transparent the steps of the survey process, the more likely it is that employees are willing to participate. In particular one should frequently communicate the processes that follow data collection. It is important for employees to see that the survey is not finished with them answering the questionnaire, but that clear plans with exact dates exist to work with the data on all levels—plans that cannot be easily changed because of their intricate interlocking of activities on all levels. It also helps if the employees have a role in the follow-up processes. Employees should understand what consequences their participation or non-participation will have for the follow-up processes.

In addition, each employee should be contacted, in writing or via email by the CEO, and motivated to participate (see Figure 9.5 for some hints). Such contact demonstrates the important role the survey plays in advancing the company and, of

Figure 9.10. Balloons to signal that the survey is now open

course, helps to enhance the visibility of the survey, as few employees ever receive personal letters or emails from the CEO.

High visibility of the survey can also be reached by simple methods such as clearly signaling the beginning of survey administration (Figure 9.10) or by structuring data collection as a "corporate event" (see Figure 8.6), depending on the culture of the organization. For instance, organizing a party or putting up banners and posters can enhance visibility as much as sending postcards with little thank you notes and small incentives (e.g., candy bars or pens). In addition, motivating supervisory personnel to explicitly discuss the ES project and the data collection with their employees can lead to increased commitment and understanding among employees: They not only feel committed to participate to help the survey efforts, but they also feel they can live up to their supervisors' expectations by participating.

Incentives

Incentives, particularly monetary ones, are often proposed as a means to increase participation rate. Research on monetary incentives typically leads to the conclusion that providing a small incentive to the employee at the point in time when questionnaires are distributed is most effective, increasing the response rate by about 10 percentage points (Brennan, Hoek, & Astridge, 1991; Church, 1993; James & Bolstein, 1990; Rose, Sidle, & Griffith, 2007), while rewards following returning the questionnaire are not. Incentives provided at the time questionnaires are completed lead to a feeling of reciprocity or social obligation—"They gave me this, so I will return the favor by participating." Few would simply cash the incentive and not participate, because this would be considered unfair. Hence, not surprisingly, research in the USA also suggests that providing these incentives as checks and not as cash may be particularly effective and efficient—employees view the check as a reason to reciprocate by participating. However, those employees who do not participate seem to feel guilty about cashing checks without fulfilling their part, and thus cash the check only in rare cases. In other words, using checks instead of sending cash can further enhance response rates while keeping costs low. In European countries where paper-checks are not as prevalent as in the USA, the use of coupons or gift certificates may work similarly.

The effects of monetary incentives or rewards on ES participation rates are rather intricate. First, almost all research discussing response rates in relationship to monetary incentives is based on public opinion surveys or consumer surveys, neither of which have the same circumstances and context of an ES. In a sense, the employee and the employer are not complete strangers, but part of an existing relationship that should not necessitate extrinsic incentives for attempts to improve the organization for everyone's benefit. Secondly, the effectiveness of monetary incentives is not based on compensating for participants' time, but on showing a token of appreciation for participants' efforts. Dillman (2000) suggests that if employees *perceive* the incentives as pay for extra work, they may not appreciate small monetary incentives. Tokens of appreciation, on the other hand, lead to certain reciprocity effects so that the potential respondent feels "morally" compelled to pay back this positive behavior by doing what the survey administrators want him or her to do, namely fill out the questionnaire (Diekmann & Jann, 2001; Porter, 2004). Hence, sending one dollar with the survey is typically more effective than sending ten dollars because one dollar clearly is not a payment for the time and effort, while ten dollars may be interpreted as payment and, for that matter, as one that is rather low.

Providing large monetary incentives can also be problematic for other reasons. It can destroy the employees' intrinsic motivation to participate (Deci, 1972). Without monetary incentives, employees will justify their participation by their motivation to contribute to the company's wellbeing by voicing their opinions, while monetary incentives can lead to perceptions of participating in order to receive the monetary incentive or because "I got paid to do it." Non-monetary incentives may function similarly.

Another undesirable assessment of incentives is when they are seen as wasteful. This is particularly bad if the company is simultaneously suggesting that costs have to be cut by all means. Hence, pens with ES slogans may be perceived as nice tokens of appreciation, but also as a waste of company resources. Thus, pilot-testing of employees' perceptions of the incentives used is mandatory for all organizations considering the use of incentives.

Many organizations consider the use of lottery incentives (e.g., weekend getaways, gift certificates or books). However, such incentives require registering each individual participant. This may be seen as a problem by some employees because it destroys the anonymity of participation and the respondent has to trust the survey administrators that this information is not made public. If anonymity is an issue, then this may have the opposite effect of what was intended (i.e., employees stay away from the survey.) Moreover, research findings (mostly reported by survey vendors) pertaining to the effectiveness of raffle incentives do not indicate that this is an effective method. Some researchers found no increase in response rates if non-monetary raffle incentives were used. Other studies did find large monetary raffle incentives to contribute to higher response rates, while a larger number of smaller monetary raffle incentives was less effective in increasing response rates.

In most cases enhancing the employee's motivation to participate deserves more attention than providing extrinsic rewards. Simple arguments that emphasize the relevance of employee's contributions to employee and company well-being can be more effective than most incentives. Thus, focusing on employee surveys as opportunities for employees to voice critical opinions and influence corporate policies should be given priority. One should also communicate that participation is not just an opportunity but rather an obligation of every "good organizational citizen." Furthermore, another danger involved in the use of incentives is employees' expectations for future survey efforts—usually employees will expect at least the same amount or incentive for a current ES than what was awarded in the past.

While past research has extensively investigated the consequences of incentives for response rates, little has been done to research the effects of incentives on the actual opinions and attitudes assessed in the surveys. For instance, it is possible that incentives lead employees to respond to questions more politely than they would without the incentive. On the other hand, it is also possible that the incentives could lead to more negative evaluations, particularly if the incentives are experienced as wasteful or as attempts to "bribe" for positive opinions.

Finally, we have seen creative techniques for motivating survey participation that do not involve any extrinsic reward. For example, a large US entertainment and media company created an animated video that employees would see once they completed the online ES. This video featured "bobble head doll" caricatures of the three top executives in the company singing a song about the company values. This amusing video was used to create "a buzz" throughout the company, and it brought the company's style and culture to what might have been an uncharacteristically *ordinary* company event. The video did not cheapen the survey process, but made it fun in accordance with the company's mission as an entertainment company. One could imagine other companies using symbols of their own folklore, stories, or recent victories over the competition to enhance participants' sense of camaraderie and organizational identity.

Monitoring Response Rates and Reminders

In most employee surveys that collect data by allowing its employees to respond within a two-week time window, response rates are usually highest within the first days after data collection starts, and then decrease exponentially to reach a lower asymptote after some two weeks. If the total return rate at that point is not satisfactory, the survey coordination team often considers extending the time window. Yet, announcing that the survey data collection is extended is problematic for many reasons. It clearly signals "no success," and it jeopardizes the planning of the often complex follow-up processes. Most of all, it typically does not lead to a significant increase in the return rate unless combined with major additional efforts to motivate the employees.

If the additional time period is seen as an extra "wave," one can use the practitioner formula for predicting the additional returns in this extra wave as follows. Assume that at the end of "wave 1" we have 30% returns. We assume that 30% is the characteristic return rate for this company within this period of time, and we would predict getting another 30% of the employees who have not participated so far in wave 2 (i.e., 30% of the remaining 70%, or some 21% of the total company (Hippler, 1988; see also Figure 9.11). However, this formula assumes repeating the whole process so that every employee receives a second survey packet (personal letter, questionnaire, etc.). Simply announcing an extension does not lead to any significant returns, as many companies learned the hard way when they did just that.

For all modes of conducting an ES, the use of reminders is an important means of increasing response rates. Survey researchers in general argue that "even under the best of circumstances you will not achieve acceptable levels of returns if you do not send out reminders" (Mangione, 1995, p. 66) and that "without follow-up contacts, response rates will usually be 20-40 percentage points lower than those normally attained, regardless of how interesting the questionnaire or impressive the mail-out package" (Dillman, 2000, p. 177).

The different reminder notes mailed out over time should differ from each other in content and form. For instance, Mangione (1995) recommends sending the full survey packet in the first and third reminder mailing, but using postcards only for the second and the fourth reminders. Dillman (1978) recommends similar procedures for the first and second reminders, but emphasizes that beyond the second reminder, phone calls and more explicit means may be appropriate. For instance, the use of an elaborate letter explaining the importance of the ES efforts in the beginning, followed by a "friendly reminder postcard" and another note emphasizing anonymity and the importance of having a certain number of responses for each unit to reach meaningful results. Last, another note indicating that the "last opportunity" to participate is about to pass can be sent out.

If mail surveys are used, reminders should be sent out in intervals of 10 to 14 days per wave. However, using these reminders is based on the time frame for data collection not being too firmly defined initially. For instance, if employees are informed that data collection will be conducted between March 1 and March 14, then additional reminders may be perceived as awkward and as a sign of data collection and the ES effort being unsuccessful. When conducting employee surveys it may also be relevant to be aware of past research's findings that indicate firm timeframes for data collection and strict dates for completion do not increase response rates (Roberts, McCrory, & Forthofer, 1978).

Using written or email reminders should always be the second choice—in most cases, personal reminders have been found to be more effective. Members of the ES coordination team, the works council, or managers can be very effective in increasing response rates through encouraging employees personally to participate. When "personal" reminders are used, it needs to be emphasized that participation is still voluntary, and that non-participation will not have negative consequences. Respondents who consciously decide to not participate are usually the exception, the majority of non-respondents do not respond due to forgetfulness or procrastination and not due to not wanting to participate—and these people can be reached using the reminder systems described above. Personal reminders create personal accountability and feelings of not wanting to "embarrass" one's department with low response rates or not wanting to cause additional work for those promoting the survey until a certain response rate is achieved.

Altogether, reminders can be effective means of increasing response rates. However, the benefit derived from *slightly* increasing response rates needs to outweigh the costs of the necessary effort. Because past research shows that individuals who respond to surveys after multiple reminders do not differ in their attitudes from individuals who respond right after the first invitation, the cost of increasing response rates beyond a certain threshold may not be justifiable in many organizations.

Questionnaire Design and Personal Invitation Letter

One obvious way to influence response rates is the design and layout of the questionnaire and its items. The questionnaire should not be too lengthy. It should look professional and stand out visually from other mail, but it should not appear expensive or flamboyant for the company's culture. Items should be relevant and refer to aspects of work that are relevant for each respondent. Strong emphasis needs to be put on phrasing all items in ways that allows *all* employees to fully understand item content. In the USA, if employees on all organizational levels are surveyed, items should not be phrased beyond a 7th grade reading level. Several internet websites provide tools for reading level analysis of text, making design of items on appropriate reading levels easier. Response scales should not vary too frequently throughout the survey. The use of five-point Likert scales (ranging from "strongly disagree" to "strongly agree") has been found appropriate for most survey items (except demographics). Survey instructions should also be checked for appropriate reading level, and they should be comprehensive and pilot-tested for misunderstandings. Altogether, the objective is to make participation as easy as possible by all means. This includes such convenience measures as providing stamped return envelopes for mail surveys or self-adhesive stickers that exhibit the demographics of individual employee.

Less obvious influences on participation include the effects of type of stamp used on return envelopes. Dillman (2000) found that return envelopes with "real stamps" led to higher response rates than those indicating "no postage necessary if mailed in the US" or their international equivalents. Using special issue stamps further increases response rates. The reason seems to be that such stamps make the survey more personable. The respondent recognizes that actual people are involved in making the project a success versus seeing the ES as another automated effort. Hand-signed invitation letters seem to have similar effects, although its impact on response rates is relatively small.

More important than this is the content of the invitation letter. The letter should come from the CEO. He or she should invite the individual employee to participate, point out why participation is important, and what will be done with the data. Also, the CEO should commit him- or herself to personally take responsibility that all rules of the survey project will be strictly adhered to, and follow-up processes will be conducted as planned. In other words, the data will not be put aside in some file drawer, but will be used to generate actions as planned. Such a letter should also show middle managers clearly what is expected of them in the survey process (i.e., to motivate their subordinates to participate).

9.8 Data Entry and Data Coding

If traditional data collection modes are used, then the data have to be transferred from the paper questionnaires to electronic data files. Historically, this was done by manual data entry, but optical scanning devices have today become commonplace for that purpose. Scanning requires that the scanning program knows what data are where on the questionnaire. Hence, in order to speed up an efficient and reliable scanning of questionnaires after data collection, the questionnaires should be designed in cooperation with the scanning vendor. If done properly, the questionnaire satisfies certain format constraints, and the scanning program can be set up and tested before the real questionnaires come in.

For surveys where the number of participants is small, where there are many open-ended questions, or where there are many marked or wrinkled questionnaires, manual data entry may still be simpler, cheaper, and organizationally more flexible. Theoretically, any program can be used for data entry, although database programs such as MS Access provide additional comfort and pre-defined data entry sheets allowing for initial checks of data consistency and for avoiding data entry errors. In addition, entering data into database programs also provides the advantage that simple frequencies can be displayed right after data entry is accomplished. These frequencies can then be used to plan reminder emails and follow-up workshops. Entering "late" data is not problematic if manual data entry is used—most data entry sheets are available on most PCs.

Scanning processes have to be planned more thoroughly. First, certain dates have to be designated as scanning dates. On those dates, all data collected up to then is scanned at once, and the process is repeated multiple times until all data scanning is completed. Second, survey design needs to consider the way data entry will be conducted. If data is to be scanned, then open-ended questions are a problem because scanning can, for example, lead to replacements of words with more common ones, or to inadequate "translations" of handwriting content. Moreover, handwriting that is undecipherable can make the scanning device stop, and a human data typist has to take over and enter the proper text by hand. Thus, whenever open-ended questions are used in employee surveys, awareness is needed that data entry has to include some manual component of editing.

Generally, even if scanning is not used for data entry purposes, open-ended questions still pose the most challenges when it comes to data entry. One example is the following item: "Which educational and training programs would be most helpful to you in your professional development?" If respondents are granted the opportunity to provide an open-ended response, then in practice hundreds of "standard" answers are given (such as "English courses" or "product training"), but also hundreds of very special answers, many of them highly idiosyncratic ones that occur only once in the sample. In principle, all these answers should be coded into a set of sensible categories. Multiple codes would even be more desirable, as they can later be used to group and stratify the answers in different ways. However, all this coding requires substantive understanding to generate reliable codes that serve a particular purpose. Then, the coders have to learn the code scheme and apply it intelligently. In almost all organizations, this is a task impossible for any coder because the respondents always generate comments that are completely obscure to the coder, or that the coder misunderstands. For example, when running an ES in the research & development function of a software company, a question that asks about needed trainings will generate lots of completely cryptic responses to almost any outsider, making coding impossible. But even in more ordinary companies, comments are often miscoded because the coder does not have the context information that makes the comment understandable.

In any case, reasonable coding schemes need to be developed when answers to open-ended questions are to be analyzed or simply counted and sorted. Individuals coding the answers into categories need to be well-trained and agreement on coding answers needs to be reached prior to conducting the coding. Coding needs to be conducted by conscientious individuals who have the cognitive ability to accomplish coding and some knowledge about the industry or organization the data is originating from. If coding is conducted, abbreviations and "corporate slang" need to be understood by coders. One way of deriving categories for coding is to ask multiple subject matter experts (e.g., members of ES coordination team) to review a random sample of, say, 300 open-ended answers to the same question. The subject matter experts are then each asked to propose categories for the responses. Discussions of the proposed categories are used to clarify and eliminate discrepancies in coding schemes, and further samples may be used to test how well the schemes allow one to reliably classify the respondents' comments. Once the coding schemes are defined and tested by the subject matter experts, data entry personnel are instructed to code accordingly.

9.9 Data Cleaning

The last steps that need to be followed before data is ready to be analyzed are data checks and data cleaning, particularly for the demographic items. If the demographics were collected by asking the respondents to check answer categories in the questionnaire or by providing answers in writing, errors are bound to happen. The simplest such error is when the respondent checks the wrong answer category—which is not impossible in a questionnaire where many small answer boxes are provided. Other errors occur if the employee does not know the answer. For example, in cases where restructuring has been accomplished shortly before data collection, employees may not know whether they should report their organizational unit's old or new name.

With organizational restructuring occurring so frequently in businesses these days, the current official name of an organizational unit may not be well known by respondents.

Similarly, questions pertaining to an employee's position in the organization's hierarchy are difficult to answer for many employees. For example, it is a typical finding that more employees classify themselves as supervisory or management personnel than warranted by their organizational status. Some employees may be trying to protect their anonymity, while others consider it "funny" to claim in their survey that they are members of the executive board. Indeed, almost all employee surveys find that more employees consider themselves members of the executive board than there are actual members of the executive board. If data or results based on these errors are presented to the executive board, the credibility of the results is at stake. Data cleaning needs to be taken seriously, especially in cases where just a few coding errors can lead to misrepresentation of results (e.g., small group sizes).

Data cleaning and eliminating data errors is tedious, detail-focused work, comparable to detective work. For instance, if we find that too many individuals have classified themselves as members of the executive board, then looking at the organizational units these individuals are from may be the next step. If two or more members of the executive board classify their organizational unit as marketing, for example, then we should know that at least one of the records is incorrect. Furthermore, if we know that the executive board member for marketing is a woman, then all male respondents who claim to belong to the marketing function and also to the executive board must be wrong. So, we should replace the male persons' answer to the position-in-hierarchy item with the missing data code. This is correct only, of course, if the answer "male" was correct and not an error. However, we may want to assume that the gender item does not pose any risk for anonymity, nor that offers itself as a category where giving an incorrect answer could be considered "funny." Yet, in the end, the recoding remains speculative.

Data cleaning often has to be accomplished in a collaborative effort of the data cleaners with the ES coordinators. The data cleaner, for example, has to obtain the objective information he or she needs for detecting errors as in the case discussed above (executive board member, marketing, female). This information must reflect the true workforce statistics at the time of data collection. Any practitioner knows that this personnel information system is almost never completely correct, and so an extra effort must be made to copy the most accurate version of the PIS at the time of data collection and save it for later use.

Another important data check pertains to the coding. If data entry sheets or masks for scanning contain errors, data cannot be entered appropriately. For example, one project conducted in the past miscoded two departments by simply swapping their codes. Only when results were presented did it become clear that something had gone wrong. Thus, it is generally best to scrutinize data as strongly as possible and to double-check data entry masks before entering or analyzing data.

10 Standard Data Analysis

Analyzing ES data typically requires satisfying a host of criteria. Not all of these criteria are also important for scientific data analysis. ES data analysis, for example, has to be quick so that the data remain "hot" and the momentum of the survey can be carried over into the follow-up processes (Kraut, 1996). ES data analysis, moreover, is geared towards a target audience that in its vast majority has little theoretical-substantive or methodological know-how. This audience is not interested in scientific discourses, but in results that can be applied to promote progress in the work environment. Then, for an ES to be really effective, every organizational unit has to get the results of "its" employees and not just the average statistics of a large potpourri of employees for which no one feels truly responsible. That means that data analysis has to produce not just "a few" reports, but typically thousands of reports. Such large-scale productions can only be accomplished—with speed and with accuracy—by setting up automated production systems that generate reports by programmed *algorithms* on the computer. We call the data analysis that belongs to this category *standard data analysis* (SDA). Because SDA is generated by the computer, it cannot contain true data "interpretation" in the form of structured arguments in prose form. Rather, it only describes the results statistically and offers a set of benchmark values that support the reader in interpreting the results.

10.1 Elementary Analysis of ES Data

The first questions that are carried to ES data are always simple ones. Thus, we first study how to report the results of the elementary building blocks of the survey, its items.

Survey Results for Single Items

For any given group, how can we describe employees' answers to a given survey item in such a way that it becomes *easy* to *correctly* understand the result? One answer is to report how many or what percentage of the employees within the particular focal group of the report has chosen each option from the answer scale. The reporting can be done in the form of tables, but graphics—at least in a supporting role—are often requested for presentations, especially when the audience has to digest many numbers at one time or if one score is compared to several other scores.

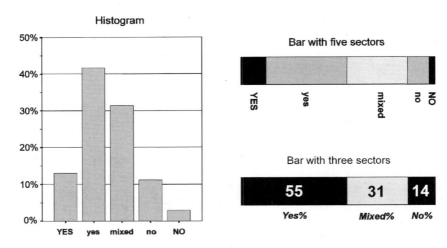

Figure 10.1. Three graphical representations of an ES item's answer distribution.

The textbook way to represent an answer distribution of an item is to plot its *histogram* (Figure 10.1, left-hand side). Yet, for most practical applications, histograms are too fine-grained and too space-consuming. They lead to voluminous survey reports that do not lend themselves to efficient usage. Moreover, experience has shown that paging through such reports easily gives the impression that all items are similar (i.e., "normally" distributed). A much thinner report can be generated by using *stacked horizontal bars* to represent the distribution graphically (Figure 10.1, upper right-hand corner). These graphs are often simplified further by collapsing the categories of the answer scale to only three "boxes", as shown in Figure 10.1 (lower right-hand corner).

Special names are given to these summary percentages. In particular, one calls the percentage of respondents who endorse the item (by checking either "fully agree" or "agree" in case of the usual 5-point Likert item) the item's "agreement percentage" or "*Yes%*." Another name for this statistic is "percent favorable" (Edwards et al., 1997; Folkman, 1998; Rogelberg, Church, Waclawski, & Stanton, 2002), a term often used in North America[29]. Reporting agreement percentages is common practice in both US and European companies.

In academic research, in contrast, it is more common to report item *means*. Means require one to first numerically code the categories of the answer scale (e.g., as "fully agree"=5, "agree"=4, ..., "fully disagree"=1), and then compute the arithmetic average of the categories checked by the participants.

---

[29] The "percent favorable" labeling is useful if more agreement indicates more positive attitudes or judgments of the respondents. This is often true for typical ES items. For example, more agreement to the item "I am committed to the company" is more desirable than less agreement. However, some items, such as "I am seriously considering leaving the company," should be reverse-coded to preserve this interpretation, because here disagreement is "favorable."

The mean aggregates more information than the agreement percentage because it is based on all responses, not just a part of them. However, the mean is not that easy to understand. The recipient must know, for example, how the answer scale was coded. This coding could range from 1 to 5 or from 5 to 1, for example. Both codings are possible. The first one is often found in Germany, because this coding mimics the grade-point scale used in German schools and, thus, brings in a useful connotation that helps interpreting the results: A "1" in a German school is the grade given for a "very good" performance, "2" means "good", "3" means "satisfactory", "4" means "sufficient", and "5" means "not sufficient." Unfortunately, this interpretation does not carry over to other cultures. In the USA, for example, a grade point of "4" is typically considered best, while "1" is the lowest score. In other cultures, still other grading scales are used, so that in cross-cultural surveys pointing out that the 1-to-5 coding corresponds to the German grade-point scale is not only useless, but most likely leads to confusion and misunderstanding.

In any case, the recipient of a report that shows mean scale values for the items must at least know the *polarity* of the scale. Moreover, the meaning of the mean depends on the number of categories of the answer scale. Since not all surveys use 5-point answer scales (but, for example, 3-, 7- or 9-point scales), this can lead to additional confusion. It also makes it difficult to compare the results of different surveys.

For these reasons, means are rarely used in employee surveys. Typically, what is reported is the percentages of persons who endorsed an item; who responded by checking the middle category; and who rejected the item, respectively (Control Data Business Advisors, 1986; Opinion Research Corporation, 1986; Macey, 1996; Edwards et al., 1997). This is also true for the big ES consortia, such as the Mayflower Group or the ITSG (Kraut, 1996; Church & Waclawski, 2001), which report their primary benchmarks in the form of favorable, mixed, and unfavorable percentages.

Some practitioners even recommend reducing these statistics to only reporting the percent agreement scores (Bergler & Piwinger, 2000; Bruennecke & Canisius, 1991; Borg, 2000). This *Yes%* scoring system is common, easy to understand, and ultra-compact. Yet, one can argue that these advantages come at the expense of throwing away potentially useful information. Percent agreement statistics ignore the employees who answer in the middle category and in the unfavorable categories. They also ignore if a respondent answers with "strongly agree" or with "agree." Thus, if 60% of the employees were "satisfied" with their supervisor, for example, they could all be "extremely satisfied" or just "satisfied."

Rogelberg et al. (2002), who consider agreement percentages as "extremely problematic," propose using means that are rescaled to resemble metrics that the audience is familiar with. One such rescaling is to map the mean onto a grade-point scale from 4 to 1, but this scale would be useful to Americans only. Another proposal is to map means onto a "test score scale" where 0 is the minimum and 100 is the maximum. Yet, such transformations, apart from being cross-culturally problematic, do not necessarily lead to an intuitively clear meaning of an item such "I am seriously considering leaving the company." Assume that the score for this item on a test scale score is 30. What can we learn from this score? How many employees plan to leave the company? Such natural questions obviously cannot be answered directly with this scale

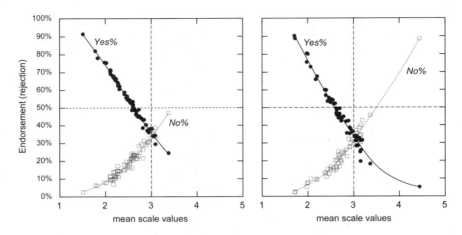

Figure 10.2. Empirical relation of *Yes%* (*No%*) and mean scale values for 94 items and 67 items, respectively, in two employee surveys.

score. An additional problem is that 100-point scales are often misinterpreted as percentage scales in practice.

Since agreement percentages are both common and easy to interpret, one can look at the empirical relationship of the *Yes%* and mean statistics. Figure 10.2 shows two cases from two different companies. In these plots, each point represents one item. The coordinates of each point are the item's *Yes%* and *mean* (dots), or the item's *No%* and *mean* (squares). One notes that both statistics are almost perfectly linearly related to each other, with some curvature only for very extreme items. In other words, the *more* persons endorse an item, the *stronger* the average endorsement. One even notes, for example, that a *Yes%* of 50 corresponds closely to a mean of 2.5. Because 2.5 is the midpoint between the scale category 2="agree" and 3="undecided" (on the 5-point scale), this suggests that an item that is endorsed by 50% of the respondents is an item where 50% of the respondents position themselves to the left of the point on the latent agree-disagree continuum where the scale's meaning changes from "just agree" to "just undecided."

We can therefore conclude that—at least in the two surveys reported in Figure 10.2—there is practically no loss of information when using agreement percentages instead of means. Rather, agreement percentages and means can be converted into each other almost like degree Celsius into degree Fahrenheit, and vice versa (e.g., 80% agreement corresponds to a mean of about 1.9 on the 5-point answer scale with 1="fully agree"). Deeper analyses show that this conversion depends on a number of statistical conditions that are usually satisfied by the items of an ES: The answer distributions of the items must be essentially single-peaked so that they can be interpreted as compressions of a latent normal distribution onto the categories of the answer scale (Borg, 1989; Borg & Gabler, 2002).

While we therefore recommend reporting agreement percentages instead of means, we do caution readers about using these statistics with small groups (fewer than 10 persons), because these values will be substantially affected by just one person changing sides. We also recommend always producing a plot (as in Figure 10.2) that demonstrates the relationship of the two kinds of statistics for the data of the particular organization under study.

The above considerations and findings are also relevant for another statistic that incorporates favorable, mixed, and unfavorable responses into one score. This statistic is the marketing researchers' Net Promoter Score (NPS), which is based on the responses to the item "Would you recommend [company X] to a friend or colleague?" (with a response scale from 0='not at all likely' to 10='extremely likely'). To calculate the NPS, the percentage of participants who gave "negative" responses (i.e., 0 through 6) is subtracted from the percentage of participants who gave highly positive responses (i.e., 9 or 10). Phrased differently, NPS examines the difference between the percentage of "detractors" and the percentage of "promoters." Similarly to the mean, it seems that the NPS statistic is more informative than simply reporting the percentage of promoters or detractors, but one notes from Figure 10.2 that computing the difference of *Yes%* and *No%* does not yield a more informative statistic than simply using *Yes%* (or *No%*) alone, because these two percentages are almost perfectly correlated with each other.

Comparisons of the Focal Group with Other Organizational Units

A natural first approach to interpreting ES results is to compare them with benchmarks. There are many forms of benchmarks; some of them are difficult to obtain (e.g., external benchmarks from other companies), others are always available. An important specimen of the latter is comparing the results of the focal group X with the results of some larger organizational unit to which X itself belongs ("upward comparison"). For example, we may benchmark the results of workgroup X with the results of the entire company. The recipient of the report can thus assess how this group is doing in comparison to what is "normal" in this company.

In practice one often uses several upward comparisons. For example, one can compare workgroup X with the department to which it belongs, and also with the results of the country where X is located, and finally with the results of all employees in a particular market area. Upward comparisons need not be hierarchically nested, but they often are.

Upward comparisons can be made more informative by adding some information on the scatter of the results. The common statistical measures (such as the standard deviations) are, however, often not that useful in practice, because few people are really familiar with their meaning. Simple alternatives are to report the smallest and the largest statistical values, or the average of the two largest or smallest values (to reduce the risk of reporting extreme outliers). Even more informative than this is the distribution of all organizational units that are comparable to the focal group in one way or another. Figure 10.3 shows an example, where the focal group's results for one particular item (i.e., "Suggestions are supported") is shown in comparison to 23

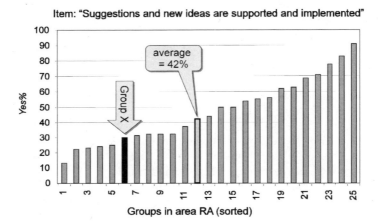

Figure 10.3. Yes% statistics of group X compared to results of 23 other groups from the same organizational area ("RA").

comparable groups within the same department ("RA") and in comparison to the average value of all 24 groups[30]. As in this example, it is common practice to keep the various groups anonymous in order to avoid exposing "poor" workgroups and prevent finger-pointing, but also to prevent workgroups from being put on a pedestal only because their "numbers" look good. The sole purpose of the plot is to aid the recipient in interpreting the results.

A plot as in Figure 10.3 is nice to have, but for SDA it often requires too much preparational work. Filtering out comparable groups from the data file is often not possible by simply using the categories of just one demographic variable and one constant selection rule. Rather, one needs to set up selection rules that require many ad hoc considerations which, in turn, depend on the expertise of HR professionals or other experts who are familiar with the intricacies of the organizational structure and the work of the various workgroups. To program such rules ahead of time for SDA is often too demanding.

Placing Absolute Scores in the Context of Several Standards

Managers unfamiliar with employee surveys often assume that if they rank the item scores from highest to lowest, the "top 10" are strengths to be maintained and the "bottom 10" point to concerns that should be addressed. This simplistic approach focuses on the absolute scores, but ignores relative comparisons and prioritization by what is important for desired outcomes (e.g., improved employee retention). Relative comparisons and importance weightings usually provides a much different and more accurate interpretation than does item ranking by absolute scores. For example, one

---

[30] A simple upward comparison would, in this example, only show that the focal group X lies below the global value for department RA. Adding min-max information would inform the reader that the other workgroups scored between 13% and 91%.

Table 10.1. Focal group's percent favorable scores in 2007, with differences to three comparisons; asterisks mark items classified as critically (**) or strongly (*) important.

	Focal Group 2007	Company 2007	External Norm	Focal Group 2006
Career Advancement Index	49	1	2	-2
How do you rate this company on your opportunity for advancement? **	41	-1	1	-1
How satisfied are you with your opportunity to get a better job in this company? **	46	1	3	1
The procedures for considering employees for job openings are fair. *	47	1	5	1
How do you rate this company on providing you with a sense of security in your job?	52	0	-5	-4
How do you rate this company on the fairness and consistency with which policies are administered?	52	0	1	-1
I am kept well informed about job openings.	55	0	5	2

might consider a score of 53% favorable to be low because it is barely past the *midpoint of the possible range* of the score (0% to 100%). Further, if we told this manager that this score has remained *unchanged* over the past two years, then she might conclude that she has a problem. However, if we told her that *most companies* score 45% favorable on this item, she would realize that *everyone* has a problem with this particular issue, and in fact she is doing better than most. Her interpretation would change further if she understood that this particular item is not as *strongly related* to employees' intentions to stay as most other items on the survey. This additional piece of information suggests that taking action on this item would not be prudent, even if it were the lowest ranked score in the report. The need to consider multiple perspectives suggests that reports include more than just current scores for a focal group. Table 10.1 shows how one unit's scores can be displayed together with several standards to provide a larger context for interpretation.

Naturally, for SDA, the information displayed in Table 10.1 is quite demanding. External norms, particularly good external norms, may not be available. And historical (or: backward) comparisons may be difficult to compute because the consistency of the focal group has been changing. Most difficult is to classify items in terms of their importance for a particular goal. In principle, importance can be based on the data, for example, by correlating each item with a criterion item or index, and then deciding which correlations are above certain magnitudes (see discussion below). Yet, a much simpler and also more transparent approach is to decide on importance on the basis of research evidence and theory before running SDA. The asterisks in

248 Chapter 10

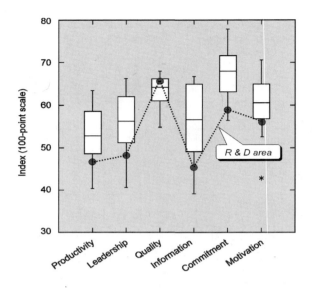

Figure 10.4. Boxplots showing the distribution of various org units on five indices; trace line connects index values of org unit "R&D."

Table 10.1 would then be added manually to the item texts, and not computed from the survey data.

Items, Indices, and Indicators

In an effort to simplify reports, one often displays an aggregation of selected items in the form of an *index*. An index is usually just the average of the answers that the respondents generate on a battery of items measuring one particular issue (*summative index*). For the index to be interpretable, its items must all be reflected in the same substantive sense. For example, an index on affective commitment to the company could be based on two items: "I am proud to work for this company" and "I seriously consider leaving this company within a year." Given a 5-point agree-disagree rating scale (coded from 1=agree to 5=disagree), a person who answers 1 to the first item and 4 to the second item would get the index value of $[1+(6-4)]/2=1.5$, where the term 6-4 represents the reflected score on the second item. To facilitate comparisons and interpretation, such a mean value can be mapped onto a convenient scale (e.g., a scale from '0=worst' to '100=best').

In principle, there are other ways to construct an index than averaging item scores. One example is using a *promotion rule*: If k of n ($k<n$) core indicators are below an acceptable level, then the index is set on "fail"; if not, an additive function is used to determine the "average grade." Such an index simply says that once the score falls below a certain level on k critical subscales, this deficit cannot be compensated anymore by even the best scores on other facets.

Indices condense the information of many items to one super-measure. This is particularly useful for comparisons and for trend analysis. Consider an example. Figure 10.4 shows the distributions of six important indices in one plot. The distributions of these indices for various organizational units of one company are shown here as *box plots*[31]. The plot exhibits, in a compact form, that the unit 'R&D' has relatively poor

---

[31] The upper/lower lids of the boxes represent the 75 and the 25 percentage quartile; the line in the middle of the box shows the median of the distribution; the whiskers emanating from the boxes towards the ceiling and the bottom of the plot generally reach to the greatest and the smallest observed

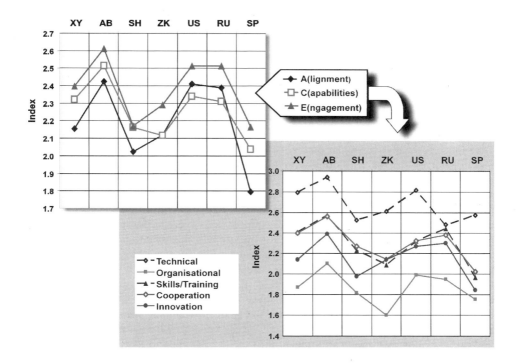

Figure 10.5. ACE indices for seven subsidiaries of an international company (upper left-hand corner), with the C-component (lower right-hand corner) broken down into its five constituent components.

scores on all major issues, except quality where all organizational units have relatively good scores.

Indices can also be constructed from other indicators than individual items. One possibility is to aggregate *subscale* scores. To illustrate, consider the ACE triple of indices in Figure 10.5. The C(apabilites) component of this index is based on five subscales (Technical, ..., Innovation), and each of these subscales is based on a set of items. For example, Technical is composed of items that measure how the employees assess the quality of their work tools, the maintenance and the support of these tools, or their physical working environment. The hierarchical nature of this system of indices (see the ACE hierarchy in Figure 4.3) helps to structure the survey findings into meaningful packages of super- and subcomponents. If one starts at the main dimensions, one notes that the various subsidiaries of this international company differ substantially with respect to the level of A, C, and E. One notes further that

---

index value, except in cases where this would make them longer than 1.5 times the length of the box; in that exceptional case, "outliers" are exhibited by stars.

E(ngagement) is relatively high everywhere. A(lignment) and C(apabilities) seem to be more problematic, and drilling deeper into C(apabilities) shows that it is organizational issues (bureaucracy, clarity of work processes, etc.) that have poor scores in all subsidiaries. The technical working environment, in contrast, is assessed comparatively positively by the employees, even in SP(ain) were all other ("soft") C-dimensions show relatively poor scores.

Indices, thus, condense the information of many items or item batteries into a few (hopefully meaningful) measures. This is particularly useful for comparisons and for trend analysis. Indices, moreover, can also be more robust than single items against sampling errors and response errors, because averaging item scores irons out measurement error ("noise"). In other words, an index is a "smoother."

Indices are typically constructed either based on statistical criteria or on judged similar content. The *statistical approach* combines the answers to a set of items that (a) seem to measure the same dimension and (b) that also exhibit certain formal properties that support that assumption. One example is to average the scores of all survey items on the employees' supervisor (e.g., how friendly this person is, how competent, how clear, how reliable, etc.). Empirically, one finds for such supervisor items that they typically are positively correlated among each other, with relatively high correlation coefficients, and hence can be seen as indicators of one common dimension. In other words, the employees tend to assess their supervisors in a rather "one-dimensional fashion" (i.e., from "poor" to "good", whatever the issue; Liu et al., 2004).

For SDA, however, one cannot wait until the data are in and then conduct statistical analyses to determine the statistical properties of the items. Rather, SDA needs to be prepared in advance so that it is ready to begin producing ES reports immediately after the survey administration is complete. Therefore, if one wants to construct indices on statistical foundations, one should analyze old data (assuming no major changes in survey content), or use standard scales from the research literature. The statistical properties of the indices thus constructed can later be checked with the new data.

An alternative to statistically constructing indices is to base them on *content* considerations. First, one specifies the defining characteristics or facets of a particular construct (Borg, 1992a), and then one culls those items from the questionnaire that (a) satisfy these criteria and (b) seem to evenly cover the construct. These items are then aggregated into an index. Note that while the statistical approach will create unidimensional indices, the content approach can combine qualitatively different variables that are not all positively intercorrelated—a *portfolio* index. So, for a content-based index I that includes two items, a and b, the score for I will be high if scores for both a and b are high. (Likewise, I will be low if a and b are low.) However, if I has a medium score, then it may be the case that a is very low and b is very high, or vice versa, or both a and b have medium scores. This situation cannot occur with a one-dimensional index because all of its components measure essentially the same concept. This non-uniqueness of medium scores for a portfolio index is not a serious handicap, however, if the various components of the index matter less than the overall score.

Using Interrelationships among Items to Determine Importance

In a set of ES items, it is reasonable to assume that some items are more important than others for achieving a particular end, such as commitment, engagement, or customer service. One way to estimate importance is to study correlations. If, for example, one is using the survey to improve employee retention, then one can assess whether answers to the survey item assessing intention to stay is more strongly related to items pertaining to immediate supervision, pay, belief in organizational strategy, etc. For example, it is often the case that perceptions of immediate supervisors show the largest range of responses in an ES, but employees who indicate low satisfaction with their boss may or may not have lower intentions to stay than those indicating high satisfaction with their boss. Thus, the importance of perceptions of the immediate supervisor as a possible driver of retention can be "bootstrapped" from the pattern of survey answers.

Similarly, SDA reports sometimes include the correlation of each item in a block of items with a summary item for that block. For example, the questionnaire may ask a set of questions on facets of pay (e.g., competitiveness, fairness, clarity) and conclude this set with the item "Overall, how satisfied are you with your pay?" Correlating each facet item with the overall item shows how well each facet item statistically explains the overall item or, going even further, how much the particular aspect of pay addressed by the item "drives" overall satisfaction with pay. Scharioth (1992) concludes that the higher an item correlates with the overall item, the more important it is for the employees' satisfaction with this job dimension. (One should quickly add the warning, though, that this interpretation requires not only a certain statistical relationship, but also sufficient substantive and theoretical arguments that support such an interpretation.) By correlating an item with different criteria (such as items or indices on overall job satisfaction, organizational commitment, or customer alignment), one should also be able to show how important the item is for different outcomes.

More complex statistical procedures (e.g., Structural Equation Modeling, Relative Weight Analysis, multiple regression) can also be used to determine the importance of survey items for one or more intended outcome (i.e., ultimate purpose or dependent variable). However, including the actual weights and statistical coefficients is dubious for reports that should be easy to understand and intended for action rather than analysis. We recommend a simplified display such as the "Nine Box" in Table 10.2, which shows survey items ordered on two axes: relative comparison (either upward, historical, or normative) and relative importance. Managers can quickly ascertain that if their unit has relatively low scores on items that are considered critically important for the purpose of the survey, then their top priority is to respond to those issues (as compared to other relatively low scores). This display works equally well when importance is determined through some other technique, such as qualitative analysis of interviews with senior leaders.

Table 10.2. A "Nine Box" display of survey items sorted by relative comparison and by importance, where top priorities are in the upper left box.

Division X compared against Total Company

		Clearly Below	Same	Clearly Above
Importance of issue addressed by item	Critical	• Feel there's opportunity to get promotion • Given opportunity to improve my skills	• On my job I have clearly defined goals • Have the resources to do my job well	• Cond. in job allow me to be productive • Good maintenance for equipment I use
	Strong	• Performance review accurately reflected performance	• Immediate supervisor treats me with respect • Immediate supervisor values individual differences • Performance review helpful in improving performance	• Immediate supervisor shows appreciation
	Moderate	• Company's benefits program meets personal needs • Satisfied with total bene-fits program	• Have good understanding of benefits • Satisfied with the amount of pay	

10.2 Standard ES Reports

A typical ES requires hundreds or even thousands of reports. Ideally, each workgroup or organizational unit where at least n (e.g., $n>6$) employees participated in the survey should get a *focal report* of "their" data. Ideally, managers should be empowered to efficiently and effectively work with these reports. This means that the survey coordination team must define content and structure of the standard ES reports a long time before data collection so that realistic "demo reports" can be produced before data collection.

For standard ES reports, many different designs are conceivable. The reports that are generated in practice, however, often do not differ that much (on closer inspection and apart from their graphical appearance). In the following, we will discuss some examples and prototypes that should be sufficient to gauge the reader in designing his or her own report.

The traditional form of a report is a printed and bound booklet. Today, reports are often produced in PDF format only. The PDF report is then either directly sent to each individual manager as an email attachment, or the individual manager is simply informed that he or she can download his or her report from a server. This manager can actually print the report or use it electronically only.

Other common forms of reports are Excel or Powerpoint documents. An Excel report, in particular, can be set up in such a way that the reader can "play around" with the statistics. For example, the reader may want to sort all items to see which ones receive the highest or the lowest endorsements, respectively, or which items differ most from certain benchmarks provided in the report. With Excel reports, it is also easy to generate simple graphics (e.g., bar charts) for particular items for usage in meetings in the follow-up processes.

The form in which the report is delivered must not, however, jeopardize anonymity agreements or lead to employee concerns that the statistics were manipulated by any manager. In cases where reports are delivered by an external survey vendor, it is easy to eliminate such concerns by producing bound booklets that use special paper with printed logos, for example. In case of an electronic report, it is more difficult to prevent abuse. One way to do this is to always deliver one version of the report as a document that cannot be changed. This could be done by always providing a "capsuled" PDF version, one that can only be looked at on the PC screen or printed. In addition, one should always stress that the rules for data analysis are mandatory for everyone. Hence, trying to find out what a single individual said, for example, is against the rules.

Recently, some vendors have begun to offer the possibility not to produce complete reports anymore, but to provide the managers with "online reporting" software that allows them to generate their own report or to at least view their data in a data bank of ES statistics (Barbera & Young, 2006). This has many obvious advantages such as speeding up the feedback process and reducing costs, but it also leads to new challenges such as training the managers to use the necessary tools and, above all, making sure that every manager gets the same data feedback and the same benchmarks. In Europe, this method has not received much acceptance from managers primarily for the reason that managers did not like doing simple "mouse-click work" themselves. Rather, they preferred to have someone else work out a meaningful report and deliver this report to their desk, ideally in a way that would allow them to quickly make the needed decisions and take proper actions.

10.3 Focal Reports

A focal report can be constructed in different ways. In the following, we present one prototypical structure that should serve as a starting point for the reader.

The General Introduction of a Focal Report

A focal report always begins with a cover page. It can show some deco material or the logo of the ES, but most importantly exhibits the name of the focal group of this report. The name of this focal group should also appear on each page of the report

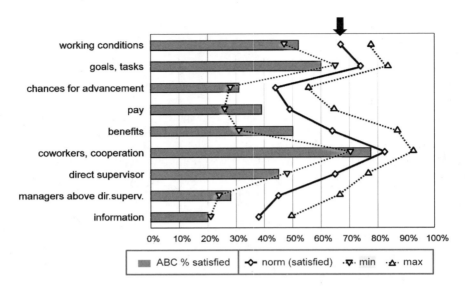

Figure 10.6. Results for nine overall satisfaction items in company ABC in comparison to external German industry benchmarks (norms=*Yes%* values).

(e.g., in the page's headline as shown in Figure 10.8), at least in a short form. This helps to give the report a character of uniqueness and authenticity.

The substantive part of a focal report begins with a general introduction that sets the stage. Employees as well as managers are typically not only interested in the results of their workgroups, but also in the results of the company's major organizational units. To report such outcomes also helps to build a sense of "we are all in this together."

The first issue in such a general introduction that deserves mentioning is the overall participation rate and the participation rates of major functions, departments, or countries. Then, turning to content, the natural question that comes up in practice is whether the results are generally "good" or "bad." One answer to this question is to report results on items that measure the main dimensions of employee satisfaction. Figure 10.6 shows an example from a large German company. The plot exhibits, as bars, the percentages of employees who checked the "fully agree" and "agree" categories for items that asked "Overall, I am satisfied with [X]", where [X] stands for working conditions, goals and tasks, and so on. It also shows three external benchmarks (average German blue-chip industry *Yes%* values, and minimum and maximum *Yes%* values). Figure 10.6 makes clear that this company has relatively poor satisfaction scores. Indeed, it sets new negative records on some dimensions (direct supervisor, for example). However, we also see that satisfaction with pay and satisfaction with benefits, although both relatively low, are actually this company's strongest job facets.

It may also be of interest to report some additional break-downs of the satisfaction data, such as contrasting the results of female and male employees, or stratifying sa-

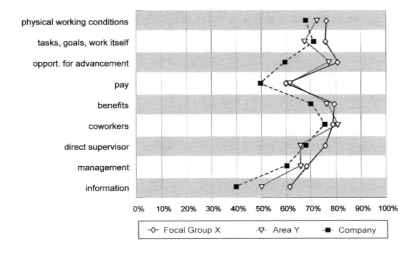

Figure 10.7. Percentage of employees satisfied with different facets in focal group X, Area Y, and total Company, respectively.

tisfaction by position in the organizational hierarchy (from non-managers to top managers; see Figure 12.8). However, such break-downs need to be annotated with some comments on what is normal. Managers, for example, are almost always more satisfied with every dimension of their job than non-managers. This is, in a way, as it should be, because they make more money, have better working conditions, and so on. However, women also tend to be more satisfied than men, at least in German companies. Yet, this finding relates more to the fact that women tend to work in different jobs (i.e., for example, more in office jobs than in production) than men. If one controls for kind of job, the gender difference disappears. Hence, some comments on what is normal should prevent the reader from jumping to premature conclusions, but getting this information on demographical effects can also help the reader to arrive at a more sophisticated understanding of the results of the focal group.

Turning to the Focal Group

A natural way to proceed in the introduction is to carry the benchmarking from Figure 10.6 to within the company by comparing the focal group to the company values and to the values of other groups of the company. Figure 10.7 shows an example for such a comparison from a different company. The chart plots the *Yes%* satisfaction statistics for nine "All in all, I am satisfied with [X]" items as lines for the focal group itself, and also for two comparison groups (i.e., the area to which the focal group belongs and the whole company). One notes that the focal group is relatively high on satisfaction, particularly with respect to information. The group is also very satisfied with its opportunities of advancement, but here the entire area to which the focus group belongs is clearly above the company average. Comparisons such as these help the reader to evaluate the results of the focus group against what one finds elsewhere in this company.

If data from previous surveys are available, they can be particularly interesting as benchmarks. However, it may be difficult to provide proper statistics. Even in relatively stable organizations, historical comparisons typically require a considerable recomputing of old statistics. For example, one may conclude that focal group X can be compared to the old group X but one needs to take out the employees in branch office Y because they now belong to another group. To define reasonable comparison groups for previous surveys and to specify how to identify these groups with the available demographic information usually involves a lot of work for the ES coordinators and the responsible group managers. In any case, the information needed for historical comparisons has to be available at the time when SDA begins, so the survey coordinators must decide on possible historical comparisons as early as possible to allow for enough time to program SDA accordingly.

Tables of the Focal Report

The main part of a focal report is the section that exhibits the results of the various items and item blocks. Usually, this reporting is done in the sequence in which these items appeared in the questionnaire. This makes it easy for the reader to check the results for completeness. It also facilitates recognition.

Figure 10.8 shows a section from a focal report that exhibits the results for a block of items on working conditions[32]. For each item, there is a graphic and a numeric representation of the respondents' answers. The figure displays the results of three groups: the focal group, called "Team X" (see the upper right-hand corner where this group is specified); and two upward comparisons, i.e., the results for "Dept. X" (to which Team X belongs) and the total company ("ABC AG").

Displaying the number of persons who answered each item is important, because there is almost always a certain fraction of employees who skip one item or another. Item nonresponse is particularly likely for items on managers above the immediate supervisor, for items on the company in general, or for items on strategy, where non-response rates may be as high as 30% (Treder, 2002). The reader should know about such missing values.

Mean values should also be reported in focal reports, in particular if such reports show the results of small groups. If the n is small, any percent statistic becomes quite discrete in its behavior. That is, if only one person moves from an "agree" to a "disagree", the *Yes%* may jump by 10 percentage points or more. Mean values behave more smoothly. Also, mean values provide additional information in case of extreme percentage values. If a percent favorable score is 100, for example, the mean value informs the reader to what extent the respondents merely agreed or even fully agreed to the item. However, the reader should know that for a first screening of the results it

---

[32] It should be noted that analyzing ES data and preparing focal reports is not easily possible with standard statistical software because it would involve quite a bit of hand work. When producing thousands of reports, this is neither fast nor reliable enough, apart from being too expensive. Survey vendors typically have their own tailor-made software.

3.1 My working conditions

Focal group: Team X

Question/Item	Yes%	?	No%	mean	N
I have the tools and the equipment I need to do a good job.	75	20	[5]	1.9	18
Dept. X	83		17	2.0	1467
ABC AG	78	18	[4]	2.0	12341
My work place satisfies the necessary requirements (e.g., space, lighting, ventilation, furniture).	67	33		2.1	18
Dept. X	70	23	[7]	2.2	1464
ABC AG	72	21	[7]	2.1	12340
I am satisfied with the health and safety standards in my working environment.	50	33	17	2.6	18
Dept. X	57	26	17	2.5	1468
ABC AG	65	23	[12]	2.3	12330
Overall, I am satisfied with my physical working conditions.	72	17	[11]	2.3	18
Dept. X	74	19	[7]	2.2	1465
ABC AG	76	19	[5]	2.1	12321

Figure 10.8. Excerpt from a page of a focal report showing the survey results for four items on working conditions.

suffices to concentrate on the *Yes%* statistics only, because *Yes%* values and mean values are generally highly correlated (see Figure 10.2).

Alternative Ways to Organize the Items in a Focal Report

Organizing the tables of focal reports in the way in which the items were sorted in the questionnaire (working conditions, work itself, advancement, pay & benefits, etc.) is a common way to structure the results. However, it is by no means the only way, nor is it always the best way. What speaks for reports organized in the structure of the questionnaire is that it needs no special justification. It also does not require additional considerations and it is, therefore, ideal for routine generation of standard reports. On the other hand, the usual item blocks in ES questionnaires normally correspond to the basic facets of job satisfaction (working conditions, work itself, pay, supervisor etc.): This makes it easier for the employees to reliably answer the questionnaire, but it does not necessarily help to interpret the data. The main draw-back is that the job satisfaction facets rarely suggest particularly convincing approaches for structuring the results into a hierarchy of indices and items. To illustrate the point, consider the ACE and the RACER notions introduced in Chapter 4. They offer three or five main categories, respectively, for displaying survey results, and then subcategories to structure each category in turn, before one turns to the items. Figure 10.5 shows this beginning with a display of the A-, C-, and E-indices for the main subsidiaries of an international company, followed by the components of the C-index over the same subsidiaries. This display could then the complemented by tables showing the results for the items on which the components of C are based. The reader could thus decide to only drill down into those C-components that seem problematic such as "feedback" and "organizational (conditions)", just like a doctor who wants to know more about symptoms that look conspicuous. Hence, to structure a report in such a hierarchical way makes it easier to read the report without getting lost in numbers and charts.

Since the RACER formula is a simplification of the PS motor, one may even consider an entirely different display of the survey results that maps the statistics into the graph of the PS motor. This is illustrated in Figure 10.9. The example shows the *Yes%* statistics for items that measure the functioning of the component that refers to technical-organizational working conditions. The text field also shows backward benchmarks, i.e., the results of this focal group for the same items in the last survey. The text field itself could be colored automatically by the computer (in green, yellow, or red, for example) depending on how the results compare against benchmarks (such as upward-comparison norms or external norms). In addition, each individual item can be marked or underlined (as the item "Excessive rules..." in Figure 10.9) if its result deviates from the norm by, say, more than one standard deviation, or if it changed by more than a certain amount relative to the previous survey. For a complete report, one would produce a variety of such displays, where each single one concentrates on one particular component of the PSM (e.g., goals and tasks; material rewards; or perceived fairness of rewards) or on a feedback loop or a link ("if ... then"), and on the items that measure this element of the PSM.

The advantage of such displays is that they not only show numbers and norms, but also make clear what these findings mean for performance and satisfaction, and where one should fix or "tune" the PS motor. Thus, provided the reader understands the theory of the PS motor, it offers a simple approach for answering questions on the implications of the results for the functioning of the work force or for evaluating the importance of the survey results for the desired outcomes.

Reporting Demographics in a Focal Report

Any focal report should also report the demographics of the persons who returned filled-out questionnaires. The persons who belong to the focal group can only be identified by their values on one or more demographic variables. If, for example, the selection of the person hinges on a particular value of the variable "cost center," then showing that all statistics in the focal report are based on persons who have exactly that score on this demographic variable demonstrates that the report contains the correct information (to the extent that the variable "cost center" contains reliable scores). In practice, this demonstration may be essential if the data are not accepted because they "don't appear to make sense." Then, one needs to prove that the data indeed come from persons who belong to the focal group, and only from such persons. Additionally, the demographics may show that certain subgroups (men or women, for example) of the focal group are over- or underrepresented in the data. This information is particularly relevant if the participation rate is low because knowing that the demographic variables in the sample are distributed as they are in the population can reduce concerns about bias in the results.

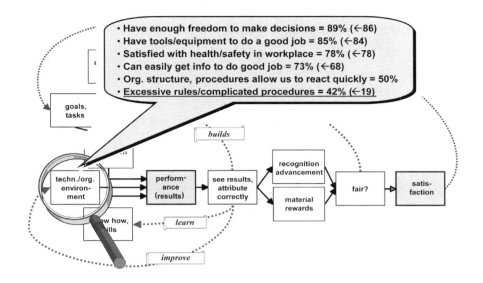

Figure 10.9. Survey results displayed within the PS motor (*Yes%* values; values to the right of "←" are historical values of focal group).

Appendices of a Focal Report

Focal reports in most organizations go to readers who are no experts in statistics. Hence, one should add an appendix to such a report that explains the statistics used to summarize the data. One may also consider adding a second appendix that gives a few hints on how to read and interpret the statistics. For example, some basic hints could be: "First, list the areas where your scores are most above and most below the total company's scores. Then, list where your scores have most improved and most declined. How do these lists of strengths and concerns bode for your unit's business goals and problems?" One may also choose to add the recommendations in Tables 11.1-11.3 to every focal report. The recipients of such reports are usually grateful for any simple recommendations on how to work with the material they get.

10.4 Cross-Comparison Reports

Managers who are responsible for several organizational units are typically less interested in overall results for their area of responsibility but rather in a systematic comparison of the different workgroups within their area. What they want to see is a cross-comparison (CC) of workgroups that shows where these workgroups differ among each other and where they are similar. Most of all, they want to be able to quickly identify poor performers.

Any demographic variable and sometimes combinations of demographic variables (e.g., women in administration vs. women in production) could also be used as a basis for cross-comparisons. Some such comparisons may be important for persons in special functions, such as diversity management, in order to see whether men and women are given the same opportunities for professional advancement, for example. Hence, cross-comparisons of the survey results of men and women would be crucial information for this person. There may even be items in the questionnaire that directly addresses the issue of "equal opportunity," fairness in personnel decisions, respectful treatment, or diversity of thought. Checking how the answers to these questions differ by gender, tenure, and ethnicity (where allowed by law) can be informative for certain human resource managers.

Cross-Comparison Tables

Cross-comparisons can be represented in different ways. One version that has proven useful in practice is shown in Table 10.3. It exhibits the results of 17 workgroups (A...Q) on seven items on the direct supervisor. The numbers in the table are *Yes%* statistics. Hence, 83% of the respondents of workgroup L endorsed the item "My direct supervisor recognizes good performance", while only 47% endorsed this item in workgroup Q. This, obviously, is interesting information for the manager who is responsible for all these workgroups. It suggests, for example, that he or she should discuss this finding with the supervisor of workgroup Q.

In Table 10.3, the workgroups are sorted on the last item of this CC table, i.e. on overall satisfaction. One notes that workgroup L is most positive about its supervisor, and Q least positive.

The results of some work-groups are suppressed ("x'ed out"), because fewer than the minimum number of respondents answered these items. The x'ed out workgroups are omitted in the sorting so that their scores cannot be inferred from their position in the rank order.

To make the table easier to read for those managers who want simple poor-average-good classifications ("traffic light codings"), the *Yes%* statistics are placed in colored cells. Cells marked in grey contain values that fall into the middle range of the distribution ("the box"), while black cells mark values at the low end, and white cells those at the high end. The rule used for the colorings in this example is as follows: Values within plus or minus 10 percentage points of the average *Yes%* value are marked in grey; the rest is black or white, respectively. The reasoning behind this rule is that many employee surveys have shown that, when using 5-point Likert items, two thirds of the respondents tend to give answers that fall into a scale range that corresponds to plus/minus 10 percentage points of the *Yes%* value.

One could also use other decision rules. One possibility is the logic of box plots (Tukey, 1977) to construct the coloring. In that case, workgroups with *Yes%* values that fall into the range from the 25th to the 75th percentile of all (or a particular set of) workgroups would be marked as grey. The rest is black or white, depending on whether the value falls below the 25th percentile or the 75th percentile, respectively. This rule would capture somewhat fewer respondents in the grey category, in general, and one may ask whether it serves a desirable purpose to categorize so many groups as "exceptional" ones. Also, with this rule, we would get roughly the same number of black, grey, and white groups for any item, even if the item's scatter is very small. Since the rule uses a different range for every item, this is also more difficult to explain to the reader.

In the context of the above supervisor assessments, the codings mark "white knights", "grey mice", and "black sheep", as managers sometimes like to call these categories. Note, however, that this interpretation is *based on statistics only*. It does not represent a true content interpretation made by an expert with open eyes and background knowledge. Yet, it is exactly this statistical nature of the codings that allows using the coloring scheme in SDA, because the decision rule can be programmed into the data analysis algorithm and applied *mechanically* without human intelligence.

Table 10.3. Excerpt from a cross-comparison report.

	Superv. recognizes per-	Superv. gives good feed-	Superv. supports ad-	Superv. keeps me in-	Superv. encourages new	Supervisor listens	Overall satisfied with su-
Dept. L	83	73	61	80	80	75	94
Dept. A	83	75	67	87	75	82	89
Dept. K	71	60	69	71	58	68	78
Dept. E	71	56	65	70	54	66	77
Dept. G	67	52	66	68	63	67	76
Dept. N	73	61	68	70	59	80	76
Dept. B	65	45	61	65	58	72	75
Dept. J	67	56	66	72	57	65	74
Dept. D	69	54	67	65	57	69	74
Dept. F	70	58	66	70	62	70	73
Dept. C	67	55	62	65	58	63	70
Dept. M	67	53	63	68	50	67	69
Dept. I	63	51	62	69	51	56	69
Dept. H	62	35	47	56	58	58	61
Dept. Q	47	27	43	33	27	50	47
Dept. O	×	×	×	×	×	×	×
Dept. R	×	×	×	×	×	×	×
total (*Yes%*)	62	52	64	66	58	68	74

A CC table allows the reader to quickly form a first impression where action is needed. In this example, it is easy to see at a glance that the supervisor of workgroup Q is having a problem. This supervisor's scores are clearly at the bottom end of the distribution. One also notes that the scores on *all* items of this item block are in the black range. The opposite tends to be true for the supervisors at the top. Hence, the different items are positively intercorrelated.

Who Should Get Cross-Comparisons?

Cross-comparisons are not without risk. Experience shows that they can cause senseless over-analyzing, where managers annotate their reports with zillions of minor differences, so that, in the end, they get lost in detail and do not see the big picture. Moreover, managers with "good" scores tend to lean back and point at the "losers," while managers with "poor" scores frantically search for reasons that are outside their control to justify their scores. Hence, cross-comparisons are not for everyone. Rather, they should be produced *only* for those managers to whom the various group's managers report directly. In other words, any second-level or higher manager should normally receive a cross-comparison report of the groups managed by his or her direct reports (see rules in Section 2.5).

We also recommend limiting the CC reports of a particular manager to the groups of his or her direct subordinate managers, but not compare groups further down in the hierarchy (i.e., subgroups of these groups). The reason for this restriction is that it prevents top managers to look down deep into the hierarchy and see the results of even the smallest workgroups without having to involve the managers responsible for these groups and giving them a chance to explain the results. Nevertheless, executives sometimes request this information anyway. They might even ask for one rank-ordering of all workgroups in their area of responsibility, particularly on items where employees assess their managers. Such a rank-ordering is easy to produce, but it should be clarified ahead of time whether this should be admissible. For executives, this may be in order, but then an expert has to stand by for consulting, or some written advice should be given on how to work with such data[33].

Cross-comparisons are typically not given to the managers of the groups that are being compared. This prevents peer comparisons. However, for higher management levels in particular, one may discuss later in the follow-up processes whether all managers, including their superior manager, agree to make this information available to this group of managers.

Cross-comparisons do not have to be produced in a separate report. Rather, it is better to include them routinely in the focal report that goes to a manager who is responsible for *at least two* workgroups. One way of doing this is to insert a cross-comparison page after each page that shows the results for the entire organizational unit (as in Table 10.3, for example).

10.5 Prognoses Reports

Sometimes, prognoses on the survey results are collected, primarily to involve management concretely into the survey issues and to control the impression of "I knew it all along" by contrasting results and prognoses. The prognoses questionnaire typical-

---

[33] Executives often tend to react spontaneously to such rankings. Here is an example. One manager when seeing the workgroups at the bottom asked: "What should I do? Should I fire the managers of these workgroups?" He was also disappointed to see that his "best managers"—all of them responsible for larger organizational units—had only "medium scores." The expert should prevent a manager like him from prematurely firing subordinate managers, and should advise him that managers of large units are less likely to receive extreme scores than managers of small workgroups. Likewise, scores tend to be lower for certain job types and countries, leading to underlying "biases" in cross comparisons of units.

ly asks the respondent to predict the percentage of employees (of organizational unit X and/or of the entire company) who will endorse an item. The prognoses reports simply show the averages of the predicted scores for particular groups (e.g., executive managers, top managers in the function "marketing", all managers in country X). These predicted scores are compared with the actual ES scores from those groups' employees.

One can also report some measure of variance of the prognoses, such as the standard deviation or the range of the predicted values. This is important because prognoses are sometimes quite accurate on the average, but any one individual manager may still be far off target. Because each manager acts on the basis of his or her own beliefs, merely indicating that there is a lot of scatter and that "some managers" are quite wrong in their predictions, often suffices to eliminate the impression of obviousness even if the average prognoses are on target[34].

Prognoses reports should be given only to those individuals who generated the prognoses. Of course, cross-comparisons make little sense because prognoses are not collected to show someone how far off target he or she is, or to find out who "really" knows the employees and who does not. Rather, their sole purpose is to support a more effective use of the survey data. From a position of "I knew it anyway," the data do not have much impact and are hardly remembered for very long. One should avoid revealing which manager or group of managers were most or least accurate—such games are a distraction from the purpose of the prognosis report.

10.6 Standard Reporting of Answers to Open Questions

Open-ended items pose a particular challenge for SDA. Managers often expect that the answers to these items are somehow condensed and that "typical" or "particularly interesting" answers are reported. SDA with its mechanical approach cannot satisfy this expectation because it requires reading and intelligently processing the answers. All that can be done in printed reports is to display the answers directly. A simple approach would be to select the comments given by the members of each focal group and include them *verbatim* in the respective focal report. However, this is not optimal for a number of reasons.

If comments are reported verbatim, then some employees will complain that they thought that the survey was anonymous and that they expected that comments would somehow be summarized, but not simply reproduced. Reporting comments verbatim can jeopardize the anonymity of the individual respondent because managers or coworkers often can tell who wrote which comment. People tend to have their own way of expressing things, have a preference for certain words or issues. For this reason, if verbatim comments are included in reports, there is usually a minimum number of respondents necessary in order for comments to appear in a given focal report.

---

[34] One should also recommend to every manager to keep a copy of her prognoses in her desk for later reference. Experience shows that quite a few managers actually do that to later compare their own prognoses with the actual survey results.

	01. What one thing would you do to improve the company?
1	To set budget goals to a realistically obtainable goal and provide a directly related associate <u>bonus</u> incentive program for each individual facility.
2	<u>Pay</u> our workers more. Gas prices - $3.00/gallon. Electric prices - 40% increase. Our insurance (healthcare) will be major expense.

Figure 10.10. Output from a comment search that filtered responses according to the user's entry for words related to compensation.

Some comments may also be politically incorrect. Mechanically feeding back whatever was said is therefore risky because it may massively harm the work climate and it may even lead to legal problems. Hence, comments should be edited somehow in any case. Sashkin & Prien (1996, p. 393) even suggest that "open questions should never be fed back in their original unedited form."

One should alert employees and managers if comments will be edited to remove names and titles, or if comments will only be included in reports for managers at higher levels of the hierarchy. As a result some specific data will be lost at their point of origin in order to reduce the risk of exposing an individual respondent. Knowing this rule, employees may alter what they write to accommodate who will be able to read what. Also, managers may alter how they promote participation in the survey so they do not set expectations for improvement on data that they will never be privy to.

Comments can automatically be grouped in reasonable ways if employees were asked to write comments that relate to different item blocks (e.g., working conditions, pay and benefits, direct supervisor) in the questionnaire. Then comments can be automatically coded into these categories, making them more understandable.

For online reports it is now common to have a search feature where comments can be filtered based on a set of words, word combination, or phrases. As Figure 10.10 shows, a manager can search for comments that pertain to a given issue (e.g., compensation) by entering related words (e.g., pay, salary, wage, bonus, benefits). This feature is particularly handy for directors in charge of reviewing survey comments that deal with legal and ethical issues. Further, managers can be guided to search for comments that pertain to the quantitative (i.e., closed-ended) survey items that need to be addressed—a strategy that is far more efficient than attempting to read all comments in order to "really understand" what employees are saying.

Research shows that some 30% to 60% of the employees write comments if the questionnaire asks for that (Borg et al., 2007). Not only is this a subset of employees who took the survey, but a "biased" subset. Most comments are negative ones (complaints, critique, etc.), and the more negative they are, the wordier they tend to be. Some persons even write pages in response to an open-ended item so that the opinions of even one employee can outweigh the opinions of the majority in the eyes of the reader. Note, however, that this is not necessarily a mistake, because this one comment may make a complex problem understandable or because it makes a great suggestion for improvement. Hence, suggestions to count the number of comments on a particular issue, and take this as an indicator of the "importance" of this issue, are dubious. Moreover, research shows that the number of comments is not correlated with the respondents' ratings of importance. Rather, the number and wordiness of comments is negatively related to the employees' satisfaction (Borg et al., 2007; Jolton, 2005; Suckow, 2005). People comment mostly on issues they are not satisfied with, describing problems and hoping that they get solved.

Managers should be trained on how to read comments. In any case, one can reduce possible over-reliance on comments by delaying their presentation until after quantitative data have been interpreted. For example, managers can receive separate printed reports that are devoted solely to comments (and released after the focal reports described above), or for online reports, comments can be inserted after the quantitative data are available (e.g., a two week delay). Any comment report must separate the data according to relevant demographics, such as function or location. If not, many comments would lose their meaning because most comments tend to focus on rather concrete issues in the direct working environment (Borg et al., 2007). This information is useless on a global level, but needs to be fed back to a level where it is understood.

10.7 First-Results Reports for Employees

Finally, when preparing standard data reports, one may want to prepare "first-results" reports that can be directly distributed to the employees. Focal reports are certainly too detailed for this purpose as they are meant for managers first and for usage in later workshops or other follow-up activities as a source of detailed information. For a first feedback to the employees, a more compact summary is needed. It seems ideal to do this in a report that is quite readable, such as a company newsletter on the results of the ES. However, such articles require journalistic work—and, thus, time and resources. Moreover, they may not satisfy everyone. Employees may feel, for example, that the wrong things are getting too much attention. Still others might even get the impression that the priorities were set by management, and that the writers were following "orders" from top management to emphasize the positive outcomes at the expense of critical issues that management does not want to deal with.

The simplest solution to deal with this problem is to satisfy the employees' request for "uncensored" feedback by reporting "facts" and "data." For example, one may briefly repeat the survey's objectives, summarize when and how the data were collected, and report the participation rates of major organizational areas. Then, a sober listing of the results for all or a selection of the items is presented, without any annotations or interpretations. A leaflet as shown in excerpts in Figure 10.11 is entirely sufficient and does not reveal too much information either. That is, when reporting first results, one should avoid breaking down the survey results in all but some very coarse ways (if at all) in order to avoid uncontrollable gossiping and endless comparisons. This discussion should be postponed until its time has come in the follow-up

	Providence Location Percent Favorable	Difference from Northeast Division	Difference from Previous Survey
Engagement	**66**	**-3**	**-7**
I like the kind of work I do	80	-2	
Feel I am a valued member of my dept	61	-6	-9
Recommend my Co as a good place to work	62	-3	-14
My job makes good use of my skills	60	-2	-7
Overall rate company as a place to work	65	-3	
How satisfied are you with your job	67	-2	-10
I am proud to work for my company	65	-4	-16
Work gives a feeling of accomplishment	63	-5	-1

Figure 10.11. Excerpts from a first-results report showing percent favorable scores, as well as upward and historical comparisons.

processes (i.e., until higher-level management has studied the data and set up some guidelines for actions and others responses). Indeed, even the information shown in Figure 10.11 may be considered too much, and some companies might prefer to leave out upward or historical comparisons until top leaders can present their interpretation of results.

10.9 How to Organize Report Ordering

It is normal nowadays that for a typical ES, hundreds or thousands of unique focal reports are produced. The biggest challenge in this context is not the computing, because this can be programmed, but the specifications of each focal report. Unless it is possible to program the exact specifications, one needs a reliable system for ordering reports that allows the person to specify exactly what she wants, and one that gives the data analyst an unambiguous order on what to produce.

Specifying Selection Rules

Even in the largest employee surveys, the resulting data are always stored in one data file. This file is the basis for all statistical analyses and for all reports. To produce a focal report, one first needs to select the respondents from this file who belong to the focal group. This is done by a selection rule which specifies a certain demographic profile for these particular respondents. This profile is shared by all persons in the focal group, and only by them.

Table 10.4. Essential selection rules and syntax for specifiying ES reports.

Group A: Simple selection rules
- de1=3 ↔ Select all respondents who have the value 3 on item de1!
- de1=(1,3-5,7) ↔ Select all respondents who have a value of 1, 3, 4, 5 or 7 on item de1! (de1=demographic item #1)

Group B: Connectors
- "*and*", written as "&":
  de1=3 & de2=4 ↔ Select all respondents who have a 3 on de1 and, at the same time, a 4 on de2!
- "*and/or*", written as "|"
  de1=3 | de2=4 ↔ Select all respondents who have a 3 on de1 and/or a 4 on de2!

Group C: Order of operations
- Parenteses, written as "(...)"
  de1=1 | (de2=1 & de3=1) ↔ Select all respondents with a 1 on de1 and/or all respondents who satisfy both de2=1 and de3=1!

An example for a simple selection criterion is the requirement that all persons of the focal group must have the score "1" on demographic item "de1." To illustrate, de1 could describe the organizational function to which the respondent belongs, and if the respondent has the score "1" on de1, we know that this person belongs to area "marketing", say. In other words, we want to select all respondents who satisfy the condition "de1=1", and reject all respondents where we find that "de1=1" is not true.

Unfortunately, not every group of employees that one is typically interested in is that easily identifiable. Often, one needs several demographic variables, in some combination, to select the employees of interest. For such selection functions, one needs certain selection rules that are understood in the same way by both the person who orders the report and by the one who produces it. Such rules (see Table 10.4) may appear exaggerated, but in case of many demographics, in difficult combinations, and with the request to produce thousands of reports, the data analysts needs lists that can be used to control a computer program. Lists as shown in Table 10.5 can be produced and checked before the data come in. Once they are in, the computer program simply reads an order listing line by line, and generates a focal report for each line.

If selection rules are defined and survey coordinators are trained to use them, they can be used in standard order forms. Table 10.5 exhibits an example, where an Excel sheet is used to specify focal reports. The first (white) row of the form shows that a coordinator with the name "Hans Maier" orders a report that he calls "SS1" (for possible later reference in case Hans Maier later wants to talk to the data analyst about his order). In column C, Hans set a check mark. This means that he wants an Excel version of the focal report in addition to the default PDF version. Because he does not want a PPT version, he leaves column D blank. Column E specifies the text that should appear on the cover page of the report. Column F contains a short form for the focal group, to appear in the headline of each page of the focal report. Column G ex-

Table 10.5. Excerpts from an Excel form for ordering ES focal reports.

A	B	C	D	E	F	G
Ordered by	Code	Excel	PPT	Title for front page	Headline text	Selection rule
Hans Maier	SS1	x		Service & Support Germany/South	S&S DS	de8=3 & de1=12 & de3=(11-14)
Linda Jones	FM1	x	x	Storage, Dept. 2 (light bulbs)	St/D2	de12=234

H	I	J	K	L	M
Label for norm #1	Selection rule for norm #1	Label for norm #2	Selection rule for norm #2	Label for norm #3	Selection rule for norm #3
Dept. X	de8=3 & de1=12	ABC AG	de8=3		
Logistics	de12=(205-242)	Zentrale	de4=7		

hibits the selection rule for the focal group. Column H contains a text label ("Dept. X") which denotes the first comparison group (as shown in Figure 10.8), and column I specifies the selection rule for this comparison group. In columns J and K, Hans specified the second comparison group. Because Hans does not want a third comparison group, columns L and M are left blank.

Automated Report Ordering

Ordering reports by hand can be a lot of work and always leads to errors. Hence, the ES coordination team should carefully consider ways to generate at least the bulk of the focal reports by an appropriate algorithm. This requires one to work out a set of rules and a data file with certain properties. The following rules are common examples:

1) Each manager gets a report for his or her subordinates, provided that at least $n=10$ of them return filled-out questionnaires. (This rule may be extended to each item, i.e., statistical results will be shown only for items that were answered by at least $n=10$ respondents.)
2) Each manager who is responsible for at least two organizational units gets cross-comparisons of these units on all items; only units for which Rule 1 holds will be compared, and other units will be x'ed out in the CC tables.
3) Who is and who is not a "manager" will be decided on the basis of the information in variables $X, Y...$ of the personnel information system (SAP HR Org, PeopleSoft, etc.).

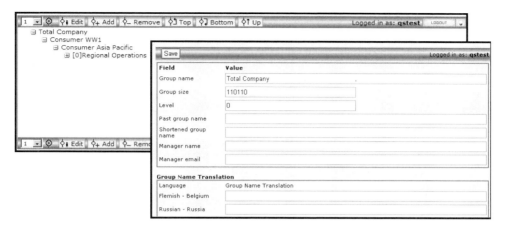

Figure 10.12. Screen captures of software that captures HR system feeds and allows users to add and delete units, modify details of all units, and provide language translations for subsequent reports.

4) As benchmarks for each focal group, the results of the next two higher-order organizational units to which the focal group belongs are used. These units are identified also on the basis of information in the personnel information system only.
5) All focal reports correspond in their structure to a certain prototype. This prototype is set up before the survey by the ES coordination team and decided by [survey sponsor].
6) Managers who do not get a report because of Rule 1 will be notified about the participation rate of their subordinate employees. Or: They will get a report where the statistics of their subordinates are x'ed out, but the statistics of comparison groups (upward benchmarks) are shown. Or: They may order a "special report" that combines his/her workgroup with other workgroups so that the $n=10$ criterion is reached.
7) The focal reports will be distributed to managers in the time from [date] to [date] via the company's intranet. Or: They can be downloaded from server X [specify]. The distribution is staggered according to position in the hierarchy: Top levels get their reports first.

The crucial element in these rules is Rule #3 (and to a lesser extent #4). A database that reliably shows who is and who is not a manager is often not available for the entire company, or if it exists, it is seldom up-to-date. What one can do in this case is to extract the relevant variables from the personnel information system, store it in an Excel sheet, and then ask each survey coordinator or local HR manager to check its validity shortly before or during the survey. Survey vendors typically use proprietary software to allow one to upload and edit an organization's hierarchy (see Figure 10.12). At time t, this information is "frozen" to serve as the database for report generation. This typically is much less work than hand-ordering reports using forms similar to the one shown in Figure 10.5. Also, this type of work does not only serve to run the ES program, but needs to be done anyway from time to time to keep the systems going[35].

For the special reports mentioned in Rule #6, extra rules can be set up. One such rule might be to require that a report combining two or more small groups[36] can only be produced if every manager who is responsible for one of these groups has given written consent for this focal report. Another rule is that exceptions to Rule #1 above may be possible if every employee in this group agrees to accept a smaller n than 10, provided $n>5$. The $n>5$ restriction is meant to avoid too much pressure on single individuals in very small groups to accept that a focal report is produced. In large organizations, however, such exceptions should be carefully considered, since they can lead to a lot of extra work. In our experience with such extra rules, we recommend not to use them. This also puts more pressure on employees and managers for high participation.

The entire set of rules should be set up before the data collection. All rules should be coordinated with the survey sponsors and, in Europe, the works council and the data protection officer. Once decided, they should be clearly communicated to all employees. Changing the rules afterwards is usually problematic.

---

[35] One manager once remarked that one of the best results of the employee survey in his company was that it forced HR to clean up the personnel information system and, indeed, the clarity of the organizational structure on which it rests.

[36] Such a combined report may not be very useful because the resulting group can be so mixed in terms of the work that these groups do that the results become difficult to interpret.

11 Designing Follow-Up Processes

At some point in any ES project, one has to find an answer to the question how to proceed after the survey. An ES project is almost never over by presenting the survey results to the executive board or by handing out survey reports to the project's sponsor. Rather, employee surveys are typically followed up with a series of more or less well-planned activities such as presentations of results to certain management groups or workshops with non-managerial employees. Such activities are meant to somehow put the survey findings to work, to utilize their potential for actions and improvements.

11.1 Basic Components of the Follow-Up Processes

By follow-up activities of an ES we mean all activities related to feeding back the survey results to the organization and making further use of them. The beginning of the follow-up processes is almost always the presentation of the results to the organization's executive board. Following this presentation, there are different ways to proceed.

Actions and Busy Work

Practitioners as well as writers on employee surveys (e.g., Church & Waclawski, 2001) unanimously require that something needs to be done after an ES. Expressed drastically, Viteles (1953) compares a completed survey to a defused hand grenade which obviously one cannot ignore or put away into the desk drawer. Indeed, actions[37] are usually considered the ultimate success criterion of any ES: "The success of an ES depends only and fully on the actions that are derived and implemented after the survey" (Trost et al., 1999, p. 6). Consequently, all activities of the follow-up become concentrated on defining and implementing actions.

Always asking for actions is, however, a dangerous position to start from. An organization, first of all, is never inactive. Hence, rather than automatically going for actions, one should first ask whether it appears necessary to set up actions *in addition* to those that are under way already. It may suffice, for example, to correct the actions that are in place given the new information from the survey. Indeed, one may find

---

[37] Actions are particular courses of *systematic* interventions that have a beginning and an end. They always aim at bringing about particular changes, moving something from A to B.

that no additional actions are needed since the survey shows that everything is running smoothly or that the actions that are currently in place are yielding the desired outcomes. In this case, extra activities are superfluous and most likely also wasteful.

If one insists on actions as the proper form to respond to the results of an ES, extravagant busy work may result with actions that only serve to demonstrate that the action's owner is doing something to keep his or her ex- or implicit promises. It is easy to see that the number of actions and, indeed, even the quality of actions should not be equated with the success of an ES. What is important is that the survey results have an *adequate* impact on the behavior and the decisions of the organization's managers and non-managers, respectively—just as data from other sources such as market research or the controlling function.

To avoid wrong expectations on the side of the employees, and useless pressure on managers to come up with highly visible activities, one should always make clear that *responses must follow the survey*, but not necessarily *actions* which are but one particular type of response.

Monday Morning Actions: Starting Small

In our experience action planning is often anxiety provoking. One reason may be that the tendency to seek the root causes of a problem implies that an action must solve that problem at a systemic level. Managers may come to the conclusion that the problem lies beyond their scope of influence or that the situation is too complex for them to risk publicly committing to a solution. Indeed some problems will require integrated, cross-functional actions that require coordination and planning at a high level of the organization. Nevertheless, complexity is no excuse for a manager at any level to ignore the little things can be done right now to improve the situation. We refer to these small responses as "Monday morning" actions, and we see them as the initial phase of a manager's follow-up process.

As many organizations are attempting to do more work with fewer employees, managers in the US are particularly resistant to engage in activities that do not "add value" to their core performance. Action planning sessions, focus groups, and other attempts to elicit participatory problem solving may not be well received by employees who already feel overwhelmed with job demands. A less burdensome response might be a short "Monday morning" meeting where a supervisor asks what he or she can do this week or this day to improve the problem that the survey results have brought to light. To the extent that supervisors are held accountable and are empowered to creating quick fixes for their direct reports, this approach can be used to quickly address an area of concern. If such conversations were repeated throughout the management chain, recurring actions would become apparent and provide top leadership the feedback for traditional top-down change efforts (to be discussed later in this chapter).

To be clear, we are not suggesting that responses be limited to superficial changes. Rather, we suggest that starting with small responses allows management to show a quick response to employees' calls for action. At the same time careful monitoring of these small responses helps shape a more long-term solution. Even failed efforts at this preliminary stage can help clarify a more extensive solution.

Avoiding Unnecessary New Initiatives or New Goals

Another phase of action planning that should precede or even substitute for new activities is a review of current or previously existing initiatives. Resurrecting old recommendations and action plans that resulted from earlier survey follow-up processes provides an historical context for action. What was done before? Why was the initiative not continued? Are there pieces from this previous effort that can be modified and reintroduced? To what extent are there existing resources and budget held over from this initiative that can be applied to the current issue that is being addressed?

When receiving the results of the ES, every manager should first study them from the perspective of his or her given goals: What do these results suggest in terms of actions that would help to reach these goals more efficiently and effectively? An ES should not lead to additional work and to extra goals against which the managers are somehow measured but that are *not aligned* with the rest of their objectives, targets, and rewards. For example, in practice it is quite common to use items where a team responded negatively for setting a goal. This is not necessarily bad, but such goals are often set in addition to the agreed goals and targets, and without clarifying what their achievement means for a manager's rewards or for the company's strategy. To avoid this problem, it is possible to even require from the start that *all* responses must promise to promote *given* goals.

These goals need not be restricted to what is defined in yearly goal agreements. Rather, they could also comprise basic necessities and principles of successful management behavior or strategic leadership (e.g., treating subordinates politely and with respect, or being clear on what one expects from the subordinates). In any case, all responses would then be evaluated in terms of the extent to which they contribute, directly or indirectly, to these goals. This requirement makes sure that responses that serve purely political goals are avoided. It also prevents that managers view the ES project as an intervention that eats up lots of their resources without necessarily making a positive contribution to their strategic and operational goals. Rather, the survey might identify issues that, if changed or if kept in their presently good shape, will make it easier for them to be successful.

One way to encourage using the survey results as a leadership tool rather than an HR tool is to require that goals use an objective based on a metric other than the survey. For example, managers frequently use items where a team responded negatively for setting a goal (e.g., "In the next survey, we expect that your employees will rate this issue at least 10 percentage points more positively."). We caution against this approach because it reinforces a means-end inversion. Rather than specifying a change in procedures or behaviors, a goal based on improving survey scores calls attention to changing perceptions. In rare circumstances this focus on perceptions is advisable; communicating results of an industry salary survey, for example, can counter incorrect perceptions of employees being underpaid. However, most situations call for more than a communication campaign. Setting goals based on survey scores can also encourage unscrupulous attempts to improve survey scores, such as managers who meet with their direct reports before the survey to assure that the group's next survey scores are favorable.

We also recommend that action plans use measurable definitions of success using metrics that are external but logically related to survey scores. If a group's survey scores suggest that they fear reprisal for reporting ethical violations, then a goal for action might be to create three new avenues for reporting ethical concerns. Likewise, if a group's survey scores suggest that sales professionals have less intention to stay with the company than in previous years, then a goal for action might be to improve employee retention by 5% by next year. The results from a well-designed survey should also provide insight into how the plans should proceed. Perhaps new methods for reporting ethical violations should sidestep immediate supervisors because scores suggest a lack of trust at that level. Perhaps attempts to improve retention within the sales team should focus on holding supervisors accountable for getting their team training opportunities because scores show satisfaction with compensation but not utilization of skill development programs. To the extent that the survey administration is an HR process, ownership of survey follow-up processes should be a leadership process.

Types of Responses to ES Results

Putting a strong focus onto actions bears the risk that other types of responses are overlooked or, in any case, not systematically screened. To avoid such tunnel vision, we distinguish three types of responses to an employee surveys:

Individual responses. Employee surveys can lead to important insights for any employee, especially for managers. They may serve as a springboard for individual responses that typically are not communicated to anyone. A manager may realize, for example, that some of the assumptions that he or she had about the attitudes of the subordinates are incorrect, and that this leads to ineffective management. Bringing one's assumptions in line with reality may have consequences that are far more beneficial than the effects of many highly visible actions.

Dialogical responses. A second type of response is a dialogue of a manager X with one of his/her subordinate managers Y about the survey results. Such a dialogue is almost mandatory if Y's subordinates provided poor ratings on issues that Y can control or influence. In a private face-to-face encounter, X and Y discuss the reasons for these results, and what can be done about them. It often is a good idea to also conduct such discussions in case Y's employees generated very positive ratings to identify "best practices," for example, which could be models for other groups. Comparing positive and negative groups may also help to understand better why some groups are so negative in their attitudes and opinions.

Official responses. Responses to the survey results that have an official character in the sense that they are communicated by management and have management's commitment for implementation are almost always considered the ultimate goal of a successful ES. Their most conspicuous type is the usual action plan with its goals, milestones, names of persons responsible for doing the work, etc. ("On this issue, we

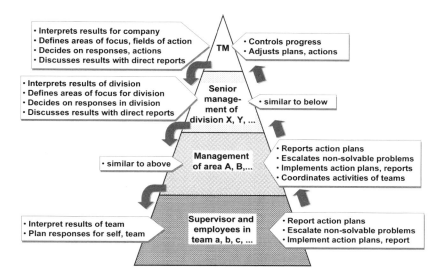

Figure 11.1. The top-down approach to follow-up processes.

decided to do this: Here is the plan...".) A second type of an official response is communicating a decision *not* to do anything about a problem field ("Regarding this issue we will not do anything: Here is why..."). Thirdly, a common type of official response is defining *areas of focus* or even *fields of action* that are passed down from upper management to lower levels of the organization as guidelines or tasks for further activities ("Regarding issue X, we expect that you and your team will make a positive contribution. Please report by [date] what you intend to do on [details].").

11.2 Approaches to Designing Follow-Up Processes

In any ES project, the results must be fed back into the organization in one way or another. The usual beginning of this feedback is presenting the results to the company leadership. It has to understand the results so that it can work with them. From there on, one can proceed in different ways. The choice depends on the goals of the ES, the financial and time resources available for further activities, the experience of the organization with conducting follow-up processes efficiently and effectively, and the size and structure of the organization.

The Top-Down Approach

The approach for organizing follow-up processes that is ideal in many respects is the top-down approach illustrated in Figure 11.1. It is speedy, economical, and makes it easy to align all follow-up activities along strategic trajectories. The top-down approach begins by presenting the survey results to the executive board. The officers see and interpret the results: "What are the main findings? Are they good or bad? What do they mean for our organization? Do they indicate need for action? Do they suggest opportunities for promoting strategic or operational goals?" On this basis, the officers then define a few (usually one to three) areas of focus that will be passed on together with the survey results to the rest of the organization, thus guiding further activities in certain ways. An example for such an area of focus is this: "The survey shows the employees do not sufficiently understand and/or endorse our strategy. We therefore ask every manager to pay particular attention to this issue when discussing the survey results and when considering what actions should be taken."

A stronger version of focusing the organization's attention to a particular issue is to make it a field of action, where action is mandatory. In the above example of weak acceptance of the organization's strategy, the officers could simply request all managers to deliver pertinent action plans: "The strategy must be better communicated and sold more effectively to all employees. Every officer will report to the board by [date] on the actions that are implemented in his or her area of responsibility." This touches off a top-down chain of activities initiated by each of the officers on the executive board and aiming at actions on all levels in their respective divisions of the organization. The individual board members must continue to control these processes. Otherwise, he or she will risk not having anything concrete to show when it comes to the date when actions are reviewed within the executive board (where competition is always high).

Besides defining areas of focus or fields of action, it is recommended in a top-down approach to systematically plan dialogues within and between management groups. This includes one-on-one dialogues of a superior manager with each of his or her direct-report managers, and also workshops of entire management teams from certain areas and/or levels that focus on "things we have to do as a team, otherwise they do not get done" (see below, two-phase management workshop design).

The process repeats itself on the next lower level of the organizational hierarchy, and then cascades further down the management lines. Thus, managers at lower levels do not only get the survey results, but also additional guidance through management dialogues and through areas of focus or fields of action.

The sequence of arrows on the right-hand side of the pyramid in Figure 11.1 shows that the cascade is eventually reversed when in the process of reporting action plans (their design, their progress with respect to milestones, and the success in accomplishing their goals). Indeed, rather than simple arrows it may be more appropriate to visualize the processes here by double-headed arrows, because reporting is usually not just a one-way street but a ping-pong interaction between managers at different levels in the hierarchy.

The top-down approach does not drive the follow-up processes through an ad-hoc project team. Rather, it utilizes the given management hierarchy and its well-established tools and processes. The managers thereby have control over what happens and remain responsible for achieving results. However, it is possible to support them, if necessary, through external consultants, coaches, or moderators. For example, it can be beneficial to ask an external facilitator to feed back the survey results to the employees of workgroups where it is obvious from the survey statistics that the group's supervisor is a major source of dissatisfaction. The facilitators are, however, never responsible for planning and implementing responses and actions.

The Bottom-Up Approach

The top-down approach, although the preferred approach for follow-up processes today, is by no means the only design for follow-up processes. An obvious alternative is to reverse the process, starting at the bottom and proceeding to the top. The only exemption in this reversal is the presentation to the executive board, which typically comes first in any approach. But after this presentation one immediately jumps to the workgroups "at the lowest level possible" (Edwards et al., 1997, p. 144). These workgroups discuss their survey results and draft proposals for actions which are directly implemented or, if necessary, passed on for decision to higher-level managers (Hinrichs, 1991).

Ideally, problems that can be solved directly in the workgroups can thus be tackled directly, so that higher-level managers are not bothered with them and, thus, can concentrate on larger, strategic issues. In practice, however, the bottom-up process can be extremely wasteful, because big common issues—which almost always exist in real-world organizations—are discovered time and again by team after team. They are fed back in various formats and frames to upper management, where they have to be interpreted, sorted, and consolidated. For example, in a large German automobile production plant, virtually every workgroup at the shop-floor level complained, in one way or another, about not getting enough performance feedback from its supervisor. The issue, however, was obvious from the survey statistics, and so it could have been picked up directly at a higher level. The workgroups could have concentrated on other issues instead, particularly on those that pertained to the respective workgroup only, because the wider issues automatically belong to higher-level managers anyway. Discussing them at length in each workgroup is not efficient[38].

The bottom-up approach also has another problem. If upper management does not commit itself on some lines of interpreting the survey and what must be done about it, the teams further down in the hierarchy tend to feel insecure on what they are entitled to do and what not. Moreover, there often is a feeling of deceit: "They first ask for our opinion, and now they hand all the work back to us without committing themselves to anything."

Also, without guidance from above, middle managers easily end up in a defensive position in case they want to pursue tough actions that mean work for everyone. They have no backup from above, and, indeed, they do not even know if their decisions will fit into an eventual master plan. In the worst case, the reporting on actions leads to finger-pointing and escalates only hygiene issues driven from below, combined

---

[38] It also puts enormous strain on the facilitator, because encountering the same issue over and over again can easily lead the facilitator to attempting to short-cut this issue ("I know, I know. Just what the other workgroups said."), a behavior that is often resented as arrogant and disrespectful ("We deserve a fresh approach, a new analysis, no premature generalizing from other workgroups.").

with the expectation that top management must deliver to the fullest ("democracy from below"). Any attempt to force tough performance- or strategy-related topics down the line may then prove difficult, because it appears that management is distorting the problems so that they fit into its agenda. The bottom-up approach makes it generally difficult to align the follow-up activities along strategic trajectories, because top-management is the *last* group to influence these activities.

However, when working in an organization that has fairly autonomous units, a certain degree of bottom-up action planning may be a necessary process that arguably produces better manager support. A corporate decision, for example, may be perceived as out of touch with the unit that exists in a different geographical location or industry than the rest of the organization. By allowing individual units to assess their results and develop their own solutions, their sovereignty is maintained. Nevertheless, one still needs to foster communication among these autonomous units to allow common problems to be recognized (along with their potential solutions) by upper management.

Some modifications of the bottom-up approach may alleviate these deficits. Borg (1995) suggested to first turn to the workgroups at the bottom, addressing all issues that can be solved by these groups directly, and then jump back up to the executive board with the remaining general issues. What these issues are must be determined by the ES coordinating team. The executive board can then decide on some general lines of action and ask middle management to pick up the rest. This approach often works well in smaller organizations, but care must be taken to avoid putting middle management in a "sandwich position" where they end up being responsible for implementing plans from the top and from the bottom. Middle management is frequently a difficult group to motivate in planned change efforts because they do not control organizational policies, they are not "in the trenches" executing the plan, and yet they are held responsible by top leadership for making the plan come to life.

Another variant of the bottom-up approach works better. The facilitators who conducted the first series of feedback sessions get together in a meeting to discuss their experiences, consolidate the results that the sessions produced, and draft some models for action plans that focus on common issues. This information is then passed on to those facilitators who run the next series of workshops to reduce their workload and to make better use of the available time by preparing them with schemes that they can offer to the respective teams as preliminary solutions if the same issues should pop up again.

For example, in some company the ES had found that the employees felt that their performance criteria were too vague. The HR manager and the external survey consultant agreed that there was need for action on this issue. A simple prototypical action plan was set up with the help of experts in performance management. This plan was given to the workshop facilitators to be used as a suggestion for solving this issue. Having such a plan at their disposal helped the facilitators to accomplish more in the following feedback workshops, because everyone was glad to have a reasonable action plan to start with. This is true in general: Most teams and managers are glad if they do not have to come up with their own solutions for every single problem.

The Task-Force Approach

The task-force approach begins with top management interpreting the survey results and deciding on certain fields of action. For each of these fields of action some "champion" is identified as the leader who is competent enough to be made responsible for working out, proposing, and finally implementing an action plan together with an ad-hoc project team, the task force.

This approach is economical because it does not require involving many employees, particularly at the beginning of the process. On the other hand, it may be risky for the very same reason: The success of many actions depends heavily on the commitment of those who are affected by them, and this commitment in turn depends on whether they were involved in planning the actions in the first place (Burke, 1987). Thus, if a task force does not merely set the goals, but also defines how to proceed in detail to achieve them, then these actions may not penetrate very deeply into the organization. Moreover, a task-force approach often has the drawback that an accountability hierarchy is set up next to the usual line of management, where the task-force manager competes, out of an ill-defined power position, with line management for resources.

Task forces are good in situations where top or senior management wants to plan and possibly even implement an action in a centralistic or top-down way. Not every issue should be addressed in the workgroups at the bottom of the hierarchy. The survey may show, for example, that the entire performance and bonus allocation system needs to be overhauled. Obviously, such a systemic change must be planned centrally by specialists. The individual line manager comes in only later when the new system has to be explained, trained, and applied.

Likewise, there are some situations where line management is a part of the problem, and then the creation of a separate task force is advantageous. At one company the survey had shown that the employees felt poorly informed and uncertain about how they could obtain needed information. Top management decided that this should be a field of action, and following a top-down model, they had lower levels of management create and execute the plan for change. The next survey showed that nothing had been accomplished. Upon further review, the executive board realized that line management was itself part of the problem. Therefore, they set up a "creative team" that started as a focus group composed of employees of all levels and divisions. The team's task was to intensively discuss the issue across divisions, and then to suggest what to do. Their proposals led to action plans that were implemented both centrally and locally.

The task-force approach, thus, is a good method for complementing, but not replacing, the top-down approach for the follow-up process. Task forces typically come as creative teams, as focus groups, as action planning teams, or as technical teams that work out detailed action plans. They should be considered teams of specialists working out specifications and side constraints for further action planning or implementation. Generally, one should consider combining a top down change effort with a task force to remove issues from the process that should not be left to line management (e.g., changing the compensation system or the organization's IT system).

The Big-Bang Approach

There are some instances when the results of an employee survey cannot be remedied by any of the follow-up approaches we have discussed. Under these circumstances a "high-profile move" (Barmash, 1993), a "big bang," or "dropping the bomb" is required. As an example, one company's survey had shown that the employees at all levels of the hierarchy were sharply critical of the executive board's competency and integrity. This critical attitude was reinforced in subsequent fact-finding focus-group discussions on the reasons for the survey findings. Finally, the supervisory board stepped in and replaced almost the entire executive board with new managers. It would have been entirely useless to deal with the issue in a top-down approach, for example. Moreover, it did not even make sense to start top-down processes with the new executive board in place: The new managers set out to change so many processes that any micro-evolutionary fine-tuning appeared to be nothing but a waste of time and money.

Under such a paradigm shift, even the survey results themselves become obsolete or at least dubious. The follow-up process in this case is restricted to a massive and *disruptive* intervention ("revolution"), followed by the "long march" (Kanter et al., 1992) of *continuous* change and improvement processes. Until the dust settles from the major disruption, none of the typical survey and response processes are likely to be meaningful for the organization.

Soft Varieties of the Top-Down Approach

The biggest risk with a top-down approach in practice is that some upper management group does not deliver its directive inputs for the follow-up processes on time. This leads to many problems. One of them is a psychological one, because in a top-down approach managers are first asked to remain disciplined and not move ahead until they have received signals from above in terms of areas of focus, fields of action, directives, task assignments, etc. If they do abide by this rule and upper management does not deliver, things come to a halt. Yet, often those managers who really want to put the survey results to work and get things done, begin with "preliminary" activities anyway. Soon, the activities become unsynchronized, and no one is able to tell where the follow-up processes are in terms of the original time plan. This not only leads to uncertainties, confusion, and frustration, but also to a waste of resources and to missing opportunities. Moreover, the disciplined managers tend to end up at the short end of the stick, often also receiving blame for being too passive or, of course, for eventually not coming up with better performance results.

Not delivering directive inputs on time often has good reasons. When the survey results are presented to the company's officers, they tend to be reluctant to quickly decide on particular courses of action before they have not carefully studied the results for their own area of responsibility. They want to make sure first that global actions really pay off for them too, not just for the organization as a whole or for other areas only. To avoid such non-alignment problems, one can modify the strict top-down approach to a *soft top-down approach* as illustrated in Figure 11.2. As usual, top management begins the process at time t_0, and then is given a head start until time

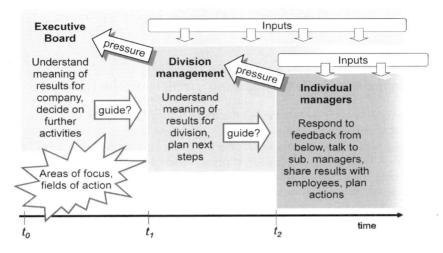

Figure 11.2. A soft variant of the top-down approach.

t_1 to come up with its inputs to guide the follow-up processes at the next level ("division management" in Figure 11.2). If no areas of focus, fields of actions, guiding interpretations, task assignments or the like are defined and communicated by time t_1, the next-lower level is entitled—indeed, expected!—to move on with its follow-up activities. While top management might still influence the follow-up process with inputs at a later time, the baton is passed to the next level of management. They too will have so much time to provide alignment of activities before the next level is held responsible.

The risk of the soft top-down approach is that the activities at lower levels of the hierarchy remain unaligned with one another or with strategy. If this is so, the various responses must later be corrected to some extent or even stopped completely, which can create a de-motivating and wasteful situation. This risk of poorly aligned action, however, is known to any manager from his or her daily work. Managers should know the general directions, goals, and strategies and always calculate the risk of having to correct decisions at a later time by keeping an eye on the bigger picture.

In practice, the soft top-down approach has additional advantages. Managers at lower levels are often more immediately responsible for ES results. They are also closer to non-managerial employees so that they also tend to be closer to their points-of-view and problems. Hence, it may be easier for them to set up responses that satisfy the needs of the general work force.

For top managers, in contrast, an ES usually means measurement, above all. So, if lower managers begin with concrete responses and actions before top management has delivered its inputs, a certain pressure builds up on top management to deliver their contributions to the follow-up processes. If, for example, the survey shows that the employees do not understand the company's strategy, then this pressure may mean that lower management asks that the strategy is communicated more convincingly from above. Hence, it is conceivable that lower levels influence or "guide" what top management finally decides to do. Insofar, the soft top-down approach also carries with it some advantages of the bottom-up approach.

11.3 Communicating the Organization's Official Response to ES Results

In this next section, we wish to revisit the three types of responses that we discussed earlier in this chapter: individual responses, dialogue, and official responses. Now, however, we will consider them in reverse order, moving from macro level behavior to micro level behavior. Indeed, official organizational responses (macro level) *must* come from top leadership, and we believe that a strong official response sets the tone for dialogue and individual responses (micro level).

The successful follow-up process requires not just execution of an official plan, but also communication and inspiration. Top level managers have to explain to all stakeholders the various official responses being made and how they interrelate. Yet, being understood is not enough: Stakeholders have to believe that the organization's official responses will bring about the desired outcome. As an example, using a strict top-down approach, these responses would be rolled-out as shown in Figure 11.3. The roll-out begins with presenting the survey results to the executive team, who can respond as follows:

1) *Decisions on actions.* The executive board notes a particular need for action. No further information seems necessary and, thus, the executives respond with a decision on what will be done. This decision on a particular action is communicated without much delay: "That is what we will do: ...." In practice, the decision often means that some task force is established which works out proposals for solving a particular problem. "The survey made clear to us, the executive team, that too many employees are considering leaving the company within the next year. We have assembled a task force [details] that will work out a proposal by [date] how the employees can better participate in the company's success. Your survey responses suggest that improvements in this area will strongly affect intention to stay with the company."

2) *Decisions on areas of focus.* The executive board decides that a particular issue will be the area of focus that all (or some) groups must closely study in the coming follow-up processes. This area of focus creates one target "desired state," but does not stipulate *how* individual groups must take action. "The employee survey has shown to us that cooperation among teams is perceived as a critical issue. You are asked to pay close attention to this issue when analyzing your survey results, when discussing them, and when considering appropriate responses to these results. If your group's scores on these items are below [benchmark], we expect you to report your initiatives and activities by [date]."

3) *Decisions not to act.* The executive board notes that the survey points to a problem (e.g., an issue with which the employees are dissatisfied). The executive board decides, however, not to act on this issue, except for communicating exactly this decision and the reasons for it. Example: "The survey has shown that the

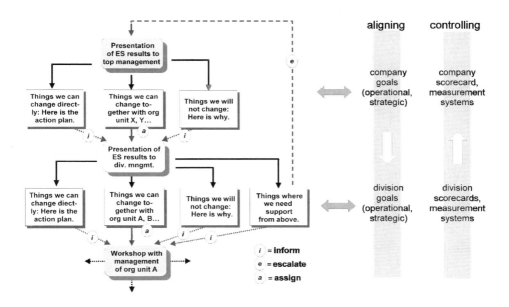

Figure 11.3. Types of decisions in a top-down design of follow-up processes.

employees are not satisfied with our business software X. Yet, X has been introduced only recently at substantial costs. At this time, we neither have the resources nor the time to change this software once more. Rather, we must come to grips with this software for the time being."

These decisions are passed on as information or as task assignments to the next-lower level of management who will proceed analogously (see Figure 11.3). The only additional element on lower levels is the possibility to escalate[39] issues where help from higher management levels is needed. This case most typically occurs when the lower level does not have the resources to carry through with certain plans. For example, they may need additional financial resources.

By proceeding top-down, such decisions and actions automatically become coordinated to the extent that top management itself is accountable for the response. Yet communicating the process for initiating actions is perhaps even more important when some other follow-up model is being used. By publicly announcing how the survey results are being interpreted and acted upon, an unspoken contract is formed where top leaders implicitly promise that changes will occur. If action planning begins with some other level of management, the failure to put senior leadership's weight behind the initiatives can send the nonverbal message that responding to the

---

[39] This escalation, practically speaking, is more a dialogue, a ping-pong process of delegating things back to upper levels and possibly re-delegating them back to the manager below in one way or another, after having discussed what is possible and what is not.

survey is not important. In fact we recommend that senior leaders continue communicating the "survey to action" process at multiple times throughout the year.

In working with senior leaders, we sometimes frame the survey as a 365-day process; the survey administration may last just a few weeks, but responding to the employees is an ongoing task. As one survey director at a Fortune 10 company proclaimed, our high response rate makes us, the corporate leadership, ethically responsible for addressing the employees' concerns. Unfortunately, too many organizations treat their ES as an event rather than a process. Posters and newsletters abound just before the administration of the survey, but after the results are communicated, the survey is forgotten until the next planned administration date arrives. Those organizations with a strong survey program, however, call attention to follow-up activities on a regular basis, pointing out wherever actions were taken as a direct result of the employees' voicing their opinion through the survey. Open, ongoing communication about responses to survey results is critical for the survey process to fulfill its potential as a tool for continuous improvement. Make the official response obvious and convincing.

11.4 Creating Dialogue as a Response to Survey Results

If the official response provides the destination for change, then honest dialogue between manager and direct reports provides the road map. A manager's survey results might create that dialogue, but a comparison of results from units led by that manager's direct reports is very likely to start that dialogue. Such cross-comparisons make it easy to see similarities and differences among the org units[40]. If, in addition, one recommends to first comparing the results on items on management and supervision, most managers realize quickly that what they have here is an easy-to-use entry point for a performance-related discourse with direct reports.

It pays to clearly demonstrate the potential of such cross-comparisons in the initial presentation of the survey results to the executive board. A recipe that almost always works in this regard is to show the distribution of percent favorable statistics for particularly important items for all organizational units at different levels of the organization. For example, for the item "Satisfied with supervisor", one typically finds that the percent favorable scores scatter essentially from zero to hundred in the different workgroups (see Figure 13.3 for a real example). Seeing this has two effects. First, executives almost always want to know first who the outliers at the lower tail of the distribution are. Second, the quickly notice that even without these outliers there is tremendous variance among the org units, and that a 100% satisfaction score may really be too high, unbelievable, exotic, or odd. Once managers have seen this, they

---

[40] In American companies, it is often assumed that the variance among such org units must somehow satisfy a normal distribution. Empirically, however, this by no means always true. The distribution may be skewed, exhibit extreme outliers, or may even be U-shaped or multi-modal. The normal distribution can, therefore, be considered a notion how things should "normally" be and thus can serve as a model that guides action.

become very interested in getting their reports so that they can see how their units are doing and how they compare against each other. They also become interested in clarifying what led to the tremendous scatter in the ES results. This interest serves as a useful energizer for the coming follow-up processes.

There are dangers associated with such cross-comparisons, however. If managers are not properly coached, they may fall prey to knee-jerk responses. The urge to see cross-comparisons as a competitive contest obscures what we know about survey data. For example, there are consistent patterns across organizations where employees from HR and sales score higher than the company total; likewise, employees from manufacturing and IT typically score below the company total. If units are organized by function, it is very unlikely that manufacturing will ever outscore sales. There are also typical global patterns of survey scores. Job types being equal, we would expect more favorable results from Latin America than we would from Japan (where most employees refrain from responding with extreme scores). One multinational chemical company had a high-scoring plant plummet on their survey once a newer, more modern location was built and touted by senior leaders. For these reasons, any "competition" among unit managers is done with unequal playing fields. A relatively old manufacturing site in Japan is not likely to have "best in class" survey scores even with the best leadership in the company. Likewise, the HR department in Latin America may appear to be "best in class" despite average leadership there.

One way to avoid distracting competition is to display only anonymous comparisons. If the names of these units were identified, the managers who were directly responsible for these units would not have a chance to comment on the results. Managers typically fear upper management looking only at survey results without necessarily understanding the context. To avoid this situation, many companies agree ahead of time that managers will only be given cross-comparison data that focus on units that directly report to them (see Section 2.4). Also, some survey consulting firms can provide similar group comparisons, such as the difference between HR employees in your unit versus HR employees throughout the company. Given such information a manager might discover, for example, that even though the high percentage of manufacturing employees is lowering his unit's scores, his manufacturing employees are scoring well above other manufacturing employees throughout the company.

A typical rule for who receives cross-comparison data is that only managers with at least two units (that each has a minimum number of respondents) get this view. This rule is often supplemented with an additional restriction: *Only this manager gets this report.* That means, in particular, that managers above this particular manager would not get this report, because it would allow them to look "through" this manager into details deeper down in the organization, comparing the survey results of org units without the responsible manager being able to comment on them. That does not prevent the more senior managers to also compare smaller org units, but it would require the managers in charge of these units be present when such comparisons are made.

Cross-comparisons, moreover, should *not* lead to simple rankings of org units or managers, in general. ("This ain't no beauty contest!"). Their purpose is to help the manager of an area see what is going on in his or her area of responsibility, how the org units differ, and where they are similar. They should also stimulate dialogue between this manager and his or her subordinate managers (if there are any). In such dialogues, the first thing to do is to "re-contextualize" the survey results by adding other information, such as information on recent changes in the particular sub-area, in its goals and tasks, in its people, etc., or information on personal conflicts, on known problems in the team's resources (including work overload, lack of skills, money, tools and machinery, lack of support, problematic cooperation with other teams, etc.). Moreover, the manager of the workgroup may also point out problems that he or she had in getting the support that is needed from the employees, lack of respect, bad discipline, etc., in particular if this position is a new assignment for him or her. Additional information that helps to properly interpret the ES results is any kind of performance data, customer satisfaction ratings, or statistics on training and learning within the team. Thus, to cut it short, the ES results should *not* be considered *in isolation*. When an evaluation is finally accomplished, it always leads to the question "What should be done?" or, better, "What should *we* do?", because poor results in smaller units also negatively affect the statistics of larger units and, hence, may have a negative impact on the bonus of the senior manager, for example.

It has proven useful to give managers some hints and how to conduct such dialogues. Some important ones are collected in Table 11.1. They are usually gladly accepted in practice, even though they may appear pedestrian at first sight. However, certain managers under harsh scrutiny will respond to "poor" ES results of their subordinate managers with rather quick and radical decisions ("Who is this person? I am going to fire him/her!"). The various tips and hints serve to lead the manager to a more tempered judgment and, consequently, to better decisions.

11.5 Cultivating Individual Responses to Survey Results

Almost all survey projects overlook that individual employees—managers, in particular—may also arrive at certain conclusions and plans for themselves on the basis of the survey results. Generally, little to nothing is done to make sure that the survey leads to such consequences on a large scale. The reason for not paying much attention to this issue may be that such thinking tends to remain *private* and *covert*. However, that does not mean that it is insignificant. A manager may, for example, arrive at the conclusion that his or her subordinates see things differently than expected, and that this must be taken into account when managing these people. Such insights and the subsequent changes in the manager's behavior may have an important impact on the group's performance and satisfaction. A new point-of-view on key issues may lead to a complete reevaluation of all principles and criteria of work behavior. Hence, the impact of this micro-level, private change may be much greater than the effect of any overt, official change.

Yet, a manager can make major mistakes by using unsophisticated interpretations of the survey results or by jumping to decisions based on only a subset of data. Experience has shown, however, that such problems can be avoided or at least reduced if

Table 11.1. Some hints for managers on dialogues with subordinate managers on ES results.

- Avoid quick judgments on subordinate managers that are based on the survey statistics only.
- Get other measurements and information on subordinate managers such as business data, performance scores, indices on customer satisfaction, etc.
- If employees come up with negative ratings in the survey, it is not always the manager's fault: He or she may have to implement unpopular changes, there may be a difficult environment to cope with, the manager may try to bring a reluctant team back to high performance, etc.
- Avoid exposing managers whose teams were particularly negative in the survey: If you do, it makes it hard for these managers to achieve positive change.
- Clarify the circumstances under which the employee survey data were collected in a private one-on-one discussion with the manager who is responsible for the particular group.
- For managers of groups with particularly positive survey results, you may want to consider some form of public recognition. However, be careful with unearned praise: First clarify whether other performance measurements (business statistics, customer satisfaction, etc.) justify such praise.
- Make it clear to subordinate managers that you cannot accept if they get negative ratings from their direct reports survey after survey. Eventually, they have to resolve conflicts and controversies, and create a reasonable working atmosphere, even if other performance measurements are OK.
- Discuss with your subordinate managers goals for improvement (specific, motivating, achievable but challenging, time-related) and arrive at a written goal agreement with each manager.
- All efforts for improvement should ultimately be instrumental for the given operational and strategic goals.
- Actions that are focused on generally improving satisfaction, mood, atmosphere, and the like should be avoided. Rather, concentrate on actions that improve conditions which make it possible for employees to be successful in their work and that reward them for good work.
- Offer your support to those managers who have problems (coaching, mentoring, regular meetings and discussions, additional training, etc.).

those who read the ES reports get more than just the statistics. What they should get, in particular, is coaching from a survey professional, interpretation training, or at the very least, a set of guidelines. Even basic hints such as those shown in Tables 11.1 to 11.3 can better prepare managers to work with results. It also helps to reduce their tensions and their belief that they must quickly produce highly visible solutions. In a business world that increasingly relies on "virtual" training and conference calls, we find that face-to-face, on-site workshops provide better understanding and more confidence among managers. Training and coaching sessions are usually welcomed by line managers, who may feel insecure with respect to such "soft" data.

Coaching is particularly helpful in a situation where a manager received exceptionally negative ratings and needs to resist becoming defensive about the feedback. This manager needs to focus on how the data can be used to promote his or her goals.

Table 11.2. Hints for managers on how to read, interpret their ES reports.

Reading your survey report
- Try to see the "big picture", and do not get stuck on details.
- Concentrate on central response tendencies of the group, and do not speculate about which person said what. In particular, do not attempt to find out where isolated negative ratings came from.
- Feedback uttered in a survey is often not very differentiated and rather emotional.
- Do not automatically reject any negative feedback. First, listen!
- On the other hand, you do not have to blame yourself for every negative feedback ("It is all my fault!").
- Try to see the issues and problems behind the emotions.
- Do not over-analyze everything: The big issues are almost always easy to see.

Interpreting survey results: Fallacies and mistakes
- "Only opinions!" True, but they allow one to predict "hard" criteria such as performance, absenteeism, sickness rates, or turnover behavior.
- "Objectively wrong!" Maybe so, but irrelevant. Perception is reality: People act on the basis of how they see things.
- "Answers are just random!" Wrong: The statistics exhibit structural patterns that are highly consistent and substantively significant; would be impossible for random data.
- "Answers are negative on purpose!" Not likely: Benchmarking confirms similar values and patterns in hundreds of companies.
- "Knew it all along!" Only true in hindsight: Comparing results with prognoses shows that this impression is not correct. It is a common fallacy.

Feedback by employees regarding you as a manager ("Person perception")
- Do not be surprised that others see you differently than you see yourself: This is normal.
- It is also normal that others see you less differentiated as you see yourself.
- It is normal that when it comes to others, one attributes the causes for problems to the person (too dumb, too lazy, ...), while when it comes to oneself, one sees the circumstances.

This coaching is typically not too difficult. It often suffices if a neutral consultant sits down, in a private meeting, with this manager to review the results in a constructive manner. The main task of the consultant is to reduce the manager's uneasiness and concerns about this form of feedback from below. One way of doing this is to make suggestions as in Table 11.2, pointing out what other managers have done in similar situations, and assuring the manager that these data must not be interpreted in isolation. Yet, one should not allow negative results to be interpreted away by such background data. Rather, the focus must always remain on finding responses that will elicit positive outcomes pertaining to this manager's goals

Even managers with scores that are not that negative often react quite strongly to survey feedback, in particular if they are not used to receiving feedback from below. It is human nature to consider any trace of criticism as a personal attack. Managers often exhibit signs of resentment, frustration, anger, bitterness, and other emotions that make it hard for them to soberly consider the potential for improvement. The

> Table 11.3. Hints for managers on how to respond to ES results.
>
> *Quick responses*
> - Remain calm. Do not overreact. Take your time.
> - Sleep at least one night before you come up with any public response.
> - Do not attack anyone (or the group) for negative or for "wrong" feedback.
>
> *Planning responses*
> - If you plan actions, restrict them to only a few issues (1 to 3).
> - Only focus on solutions that have very attractive consequences.
> - The consequences should serve your operational and strategic goals.
> - Perfect solutions are rarely needed; aim for solutions with good cost-benefit ratios.
> - Set measurable goals for your responses.
> - Make a milestone plan for more difficult actions.
>
> *Communicating responses*
> - Explain to your subordinates what you want to do and what not.
> - Explain why you want to do it, and how it relates to the survey results.
> - Communicate the essentials of your milestone plan and its timing.
>
> *Implementing responses*
> - Don't be fooled by quick success: It is difficult to make change stay because old habits keep coming back.
> - To make change last, change work structures and work processes.
>
> *Changing the image that others have of you*
> - You must know that it is difficult to change your image.
> - To really change it, you must change your behavior (not your "attitudes").

problems are often exacerbated when the ES results are discussed with their superior manager (see Section 11.4). Hence, if possible, some coaching should be available to supervising managers before they attempt to dialogue with direct reports.

11.6 The 7+7 Approach for Rolling-Out the Follow-Up Processes

The following "7+7" approach has proven successful in rolling out responses to survey results. However, there is no need to implement the plan exactly as it is presented here. Rather, the approach can be modified and extended as long as the order of the various processes is maintained. The design is structured in seven steps that serve to trigger the general follow-up processes in the organization, and seven steps for each manager receiving a survey report. We start with feeding back the results to the executive board.

(1) Present the survey results to top management
- Discuss the results in a pre-presentation with the survey sponsor and the CEO
- Revise the presentation based on questions, additional issues, weightings of topics, requests for further in-depth data analysis, etc.

- Present the survey results to the executive board, showing external benchmarks (where available) and cross-comparisons of the big areas of the organization
- Discuss, interpret results with the executive board; the executive board may set up areas of focus, fields of action, or other input to be communicated in the remaining feedback processes

(2) After the presentation, give each executive board member the ES report for the area of the organization for which he/she is responsible
- Each such ES report benchmarks one area's results against the results of the whole organization and contains cross-comparisons of the area's large org units
- Advise on possible responses and follow-up processes
- Answer questions, possibly add additional data analyses afterwards if requested

(3) Within each area, run a (2-phase) workshop on the survey results with all higher-level managers of this area
- First phase: A few managers of the area analyze the results, identify items where area management should act ("otherwise problems will remain or opportunities will be missed")
- Intermission: Suggestions of first phase are discussed with manager in charge of area
- Second phase: A survey consultant presents the results for the area; the manager in charge of area interprets the results, presents action items from first phase; all participating managers begin to work on action plans

(4) Rest of all managers of the area get their ES reports (if their survey return rates are high enough)
- Reports focus on employees within each manager's unit/function
- Reports include one or more upward comparison to the total company, total division, or "parent" group at the next higher level
- If the unit/function has two "subunits" that meet a minimum size and report to the owner of this report, there is a cross-comparison of scores these groups
- Communicate hints on how to read and utilize the reports
- For manager with very negative results, reports should be delivered by a coach; otherwise, see Section 11.7

(5) Each manager conducts one-on-one dialogues with each direct report
- See Section 11.4
- Manager and direct report clarify context, identify what to do, set goals and targets, sketch action plan
- Manager offers support, coaching

(6) Communicate survey results to all employees in all units/functions
- In a special information session (e.g., Town Hall meeting)
- or: in regular communication meetings
- or: in a special workshop (see Chapter 13)
- or: in writing (briefly, descriptively, no interpretations)
- Often brief communications are sent out as quickly as possible, followed by more detailed and two-way communications

(7) Connect survey scores to other organizational metrics for as many units/functions as possible

- Make sure survey results remain available for future decision making
- Suggest metrics external to the survey that are particularly related to areas of focus (e.g., linking customer focus group data to employee survey items measuring the climate for customer orientation)

This general sequence of events is one that we have found effective for generating interest in understanding survey results, creating thoughtful plans of action, and executing these plans to achieve actual (not just perceived) change in the organization. Starting with the general presentation of the survey results to top management, for example, motivates managers at lower levels to see how their results compare: "Are we a part of the problem?" Seeing scatter diagrams like the one in Figure 13.3 has managers asking whether the outliers belong to their areas and how the groups within their units are distributed. Having reports at all levels follow the same template of graphs and tables, fosters this comparison of "our group" to the whole company. Standardized reports, presentations, and processes are key to achieving an aligned change effort.

This effort is further reinforced when top management clears the path for one-on-one dialogues between managers and direct reports throughout the management chain. It is highly unusual to have all levels of management, down to the lowest front line supervisors, create action plans and "official" responses. Supervisors may not have the time, experience, or capability to effectively develop and implement a formal course of action. However, it is not too much to expect that dialogues occur down to the lowest supervisory level. This outcome is likely if one can create a domino effect: a manager who went through such a dialogue with his or her boss can easily model this behavior to create a similar dialogue with his or her direct reports. Senior leaders, thus, premiere the post-survey dialogues and then hold their direct reports accountable for conducting meaningful dialogues with their direct reports.

11.7 Response Sequences for Individual Managers

When an individual manager receives his or her survey report, the logical first step is reading this report. However, how to proceed from there on is not always clear for the occasional user of such data. To avoid having each manager come up with home-grown follow-up processes, we suggest a generic process. The seven-step approach in Table 11.4 can serve as a prototypical schedule. It makes sure that nothing important is forgotten and that the different steps remain ordered in a logically and psychologically sensible way. The details for a particular organization and a particular follow-up process will likely vary, but it is important to create such a schedule, give it a "reality test" with line managers, gather support for the process, and make sure that every manager who needs to know the process does in fact understand expectations. The person responsible for administering the survey and distributing results needs to make sure that each phase of the survey process leads all managers to respond according to this schedule. In other words, we strongly suggest that survey process

Table 11.4. The individual manager's steps of responding to survey results

No.	Step	Comments
1	Read your report and interpret the survey results: What do they tell you?	See hints in Table 11.1
2	Ponder how you want to respond to the results personally: What do you want to do?	See hints in Table 11.2
3	Discuss the results with the entire team of the managers who report to you (if you have any), and plan actions with this team.	Pay attention not to expose individual managers. Simple rankings are almost never useful. Concentrate on things that "we have to do; otherwise they do not get done". A good model to follow is the two-phase workshop (see Section 11.6, No. 3).
4	Talk "privately" with each of the managers who directly report to you (if you have any) about the survey results in their areas of responsibility.	Conduct such discussions at least with those managers where the survey results are relatively negative. It is better, however, to talk with every manager. See Table 11.3 for hints.
5	Inform all the employees in your area of responsibility about the survey results.	Choose a proper way, e.g., like a special info session or a compact summary in writing.
6	Respond to the results with "official" actions and decisions, and make sure that these are communicated to all employees.	See Section 11.3. The actions and decisions must be well explained to the employees: Reasons, goals, success criteria, milestones, accountable persons, and persons involved.
7	Systematically implement your action plans (if you decided to have actions) and keep your employees informed about their status.	Employees normally feel that *nothing* happened after a survey. You must, therefore, actively sell (but not oversell) such actions and/or involve employees in the actions.

owners consider the follow-up processes first. Otherwise the survey content, the distribution of reports, the depth of data, the interpretation training and other facets of the process may not enable managers to act as they are expected to act.

11.8 Criteria for Planning and Evaluating Follow-Up Processes

Follow-up processes have many facets. They are not trivial to plan, but some planning is unavoidable, because failure to do so at the beginning of any ES process will jeopardize the desired end goals of the project. These end goals can be articulated—as part of the total package design of the ES—in terms of particular effects. That is, the ES should make a difference in the decisions and the behavior of managers, nonmanagers, and workgroups that will eventually have a positive impact onto the company's the bottom line (see also Chapter 17 for many specific criteria).

The desired effects, in turn, require that certain content topics must be addressed in the questionnaire so that the follow-up processes can utilize specific measurements. For example, if "more innovation" is an overall goal, then there must be items that ask how new ideas are embraced in the organization or what hinders being more innovative.

The end goals also provide criteria for planning and evaluating the follow-up processes. They can be assessed in terms of the effects they have on reducing bottlenecks, preserving and further strengthening strong points, accelerating strategic change, measuring progress on specific strategic topics, or adjusting and fine-tuning goals and directions given information on the attitudes and cognitions of the employees.

All of these effects depend on people. They can be change catalysts, change agents, or those whose behavior at work is changed. Top management is typically the change catalyst by leading (directing, driving, coordinating) change into a certain direction. Middle managers often have to see that change is systematically implemented so that it really shows in the company's hard and soft factors. Rank-and-file employees have to live the change in their daily work behavior, or it will not impact the company's bottom line. It can be useful to think about these different roles when planning the follow-up processes, and communicate the ES results with these roles in mind. For example, one should plan the presentation of the ES results to top management in such a way that it helps these managers to define areas of focus and fields of action for other persons or groups to pay attention to or to execute.

One should also consider the various psychological modalities and the role they play in the follow-up processes. If, for example, the survey aims at strengthening the employees' commitment to the organization, then the questionnaire must contain items that assess the relevant emotions. Otherwise, one would not have the data to construct reasonable commitment indices. However, measurement itself is typically not the only goal. Change and commitment to change issues, for example, is often an additional objective. In order to be successful here, one would want to involve the employees actively into the follow-up processes (e.g., in feedback workshops and action planning) so that this involvement drives commitment.

If, on the other hand, the survey is meant to essentially only provide measurements to complement the company's strategic scorecards with soft-factor indices, one should concentrate on the cognitions of top and senior management in the follow-up processes. All items, statistics, and presentations, then, must aim to increase this group's understanding of where the company is with respect to its soft factors. Therefore, in this case, the follow-up processes must aim at the heads, not the emotions of these managers.

An important additional criterion of success is the cost-benefit ratio of the measures taken to generate the desired effects. Follow-up processes often unnecessarily consume many resources, because they are rolled out rather mechanically following some "proven" path advocated by a commercial vendor, or because they are planned with a 100% quality goal in mind where an 80:20 solution would do. For example, in one huge German company, the HR division took over the follow-up processes, conducting hundreds of feedback workshops, only to discover that these workshops led to an insight that had been clear from the survey statistics already (i.e., employees said that they had many ideas on how to be more productive), without delivering anything in addition (i.e., a listing of concrete ideas). A differently designed array of workshops—workshop clusters with intermediate sessions for consolidating results, and with stopping criteria—would have been a much better way to proceed (see Chapter 13), but too little time was invested in carefully planning the follow-up processes to adequately serve the particular purposes at that time.

12 Nonstandard Data Analysis

While standard data analysis (SDA) is defined as that type of data analysis that can be programmed to run automatically on the computer once survey data are available, nonstandard data analysis (NSDA) is always done "by hand." It requires human judgment, intelligent insights, deep statistical and substantive know-how, and a lot of experience. SDA cannot interpret the meaning of survey results, except in a rigid way. But knowing that some result is, say, two standard deviations below some norm, is not the same as evaluating this results within the structure of all other data, embedding it into scientific theories, viewing the statistics from the organization's operational and strategic goals, and considering the general context in which the survey was conducted (e.g., recent changes in the organization, customers, competitors, economy). This evaluation is so complex that it cannot be programmed into an algorithm that grinds out answers mechanically. That is not to say that this has not been attempted. Indeed, some ES vendors promise to deliver powerful interpretations instantaneously, but this is more like attempting "instant science" ("Just add data to our algorithms!"), a presumptuous undertaking.

12.1 Interpreting ES Results

Standard data analysis does not truly interpret the statistics it generates. Yet, when presenting survey results, the audience expects more than just numbers or bar charts. What it wants are competent—possibly even challenging—answers to questions such as these: Are these results good or bad? In which sense are they good or bad? What do they mean? What do they predict? How do they compare to what one normally finds in such surveys? What do we need to do? What opportunities for action do these results suggest?

None of these questions can be answered by SDA. Indeed, the item statistics of an ES are merely *indicators* of variables and relationships in systems that generate them. This is illustrated, symbolically, in Figure 12.1. When interpreting these indicators, one attempts to make intelligent and reliable inferences onto the constructs and relations that *underlie* these observations. To do that, one has to enrich the data with different forms of a priori knowledge. For example, one can check to what extent the observed data fit into a particular pattern that was observed before in a similar context or in other companies. One example is that the higher the job grade of a person, the more likely is it that this person is satisfied with every facet of his or her work. Or, one may know from scientific research that extra-role performance depends, in part, on trust in management, and so one can use this knowledge to assess the importance of trust scores derived from the survey.

An ES expert always strives for more ambitious goals than just feeding back *data* or *information*. The least he or she aims for is some form of *understanding*[41]. Indeed, even more is desirable, namely judgment that brings everything into perspective and evaluates what is important and what is possible with respect to a complex goal system ("wisdom").

To interpret ES data, a number of different approaches can be chosen.

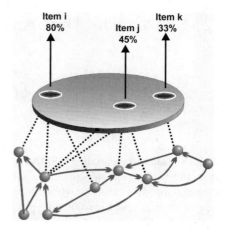

Figure 12.1. ES data as indicators of a latent network of variables.

Ideally, they should all complement and support each other in a methodological triangulation, leading to a robust story that implies clear directions for action:

1) *Experience-based hypotheses*: The results are assessed in terms of one's experience: "Do these findings confirm what I know, or do they contradict my experience?"
2) *Benchmarking*: The results are compared with those from other companies or from previous surveys in the same company; or the results of different organizational units or strata are compared among each other: "Are the results relatively good or bad? Are they better or worse than in previous surveys?"
3) *Scientific theories*: The results are embedded into well-confirmed and well-understood "if-then-given that" systems of hypotheses. For example, the results are evaluated in terms of what they say about the functioning of "the performance-satisfaction motor" outlined in Chapter 4. This also answers questions on what is important and what not, and in what sense.
4) *Deep statistical analyses*: Deep statistical analyses are not necessarily complicated analyses. Rather, they carefully study special questions that are carried to the data, or they check hypotheses that arise in the course of data analysis. For example, management may be particularly interested in the employees' tendency for turnover, and one then searches for drivers, moderators, and mediators of turnover tendency by multivariate statistical analyses.

---

[41] We here refer to the notion that data is not information, information is not understanding, and understanding is not wisdom (Ackoff, 1989). This can be further differentiated into the "D-I-MES-to-wisdom" partial order, where D=data, I=information, M=mechanical understanding, E=engineering understanding, S=scientific understanding (Borg, 2005).

5) *Business-related frameworks*: Under this perspective, the results are mapped into a framework of business scorecards in an attempt to systematically analyze what the results mean for the given goals and the strategy; or what they mean from an investor's point of view in terms of strengths and weaknesses; or vis-à-vis foreseeable business risks and opportunities.

12.2 Experience-Based Hypotheses and ES Results

If the feedback that managers get about an ES is nothing but a set of simple item statistics such as mean scale scores, item by item, they have no choice but to interpret these results on the basis of what they know from experience about the issues addressed in the survey. They then typically search for confirmation, and reject evidence to the contrary as not that relevant or as exceptions, or even re-interpret the statistics ("What the employees really want is ..."; "They only said X in order to get Y...."). The main problem is that interpretation by experience is usually not a systematic verification strategy. Rather, the interpreter arrives—in non-obvious ways—at conclusions that he or she quickly accepts as true without critical assessments. Even if asked "Do you really want to bet your money on that?," interpretations-by-experience do not disappear easily, because "most executives are not aware of the specific ways in which their awareness is limited" (Bazerman & Chugh, 2006, p. 90) and because "of the failure to seek information ... when decision makers are motivated to favor a particular outcome" (p. 92). Hence, one may want to test these interpretations—in particular in the absence of contradictory evidence—more aggressively with a suitable de-biasing method such as, for example, the "consider the opposite" technique (Lord, Lepper, & Preston, 1984; Mussweiler, Strack, & Pfeiffer, 2000).

The survey expert who is responsible for correctly communicating the ES results should make sure that interpretations do not become opinionated. The problem is that such prejudices may also affect the expert's own judgments. Prejudices easily build up from doing survey after survey, from an uncritical consumption of simplistic management literature, but also from an overly close attachment to certain stakeholders in the organization. Hence, the expert may, before giving a results presentation to management, present everything to a critical audience of colleagues who are not involved in this particular survey project and whose role it is to detect weak points in the presentation, in particular conclusions that cannot be convincingly *derived* (or at least supported) from the data and/or from established theory. In addition, the expert should never cease actively searching for arguments that *contradict* his or her interpretation of the data.

It seems that one should recommend a similarly critical attitude to the recipients of the presentation. However, there is no real need for that, because they usually come up with many counter-arguments against the interpretation of the expert anyway (see Chapter 13). These counter-arguments are, in part, attempts to check the validity of the results and the interpretations offered by the expert. To test management's own interpretations, it helps to compare its predictions of the survey results against the actual results. Borg & Hillenbrand (2003) have shown that this is a good method to reduce overconfidence in one's own beliefs and also helps to diminish the apparent obviousness of the results.

12.3 Benchmarking

The question that almost anyone asks when seeing a result such as "The survey shows that 60% of the employees are satisfied with their pay" is this: "What does one normally find on this issue?" If the answer is 50%, then one has a first standard for evaluating the finding as "good." The comparison value is called a benchmark. Benchmarks are typically the average values found in other companies for common issues such as overall satisfaction with pay. Ideally, these other companies used the same item or scale to assess the issue. These companies should also be comparable to the company of the survey. For example, one may require that they should all be of the same industry and of the same country[42]. Moreover, the survey data from these companies should not be too old either.

Types of Benchmarks

Comparing ES results to those of other companies is not the only way of benchmarking. Figure 12.2 shows a "mapping sentence" (Borg & Shye, 1995) that distinguishes $3 \times 4 \times 3 \times 4 \times 2 \times 4 \times 4 \times 4$ types of benchmarks and shows how they can be assessed with respect to their effectiveness for four different purposes. The many types of benchmarks make clear that one cannot simply "benchmark the results." Rather, one should first think about the purpose of benchmarking, and then pick a particular type of benchmark that is good for this purpose. To illustrate, consider two cases. A manager once asked us: "Do you have benchmarks on how satisfied middle managers in the IT industry in South-East Asia are with their pay?" This manager was interested in a particular external benchmark[43]. The CEO of another company had something completely different in mind when he asked this: "Can you compare our results to benchmarks from the best companies only? The benchmarks must be truly challenging, because this is what I need to motivate my managers to get their asses in gear!" These cases illustrate how benchmarks can serve different purposes.

Picking a benchmark involves many decisions. The most obvious one is related to specifying the focal unit of the organization. It could be the whole company, or a particular subgroup of the company (e.g., the research & development function,

---

[42] Ideally, of course, management would be most interested to know the values of their main competitors. If they ask for these values, and if you as a survey expert should have them, you should never reveal them. This would be against professional ethics. In case the competitors ask you the same question, you would not be willing to tell them either.

[43] The benchmark, in this case, was supposed to show whether the relatively high dissatisfaction of these managers was "normal" or not. The answer was: The values in many other IT companies were quite similar. The relatively low pay satisfaction, therefore, was quite normal and not specific for this company.

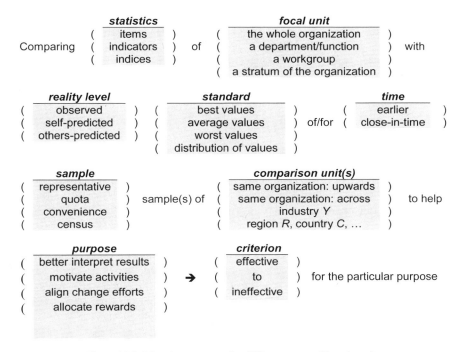

Figure 12.2. Mapping sentence for different types of benchmarks.

night-shift workers), or a particular stratum of the organization (e.g., women, new employees). Another one is what was discussed above: Best-in-class benchmarks, average statistics, minimum statistics, with or without variance measures, or other statistics. Then, one can benchmark against real data, but also against prognoses that management (or some other group) made on the outcomes of the survey. Matching the survey results against these prognoses helps reduce the audience's typical belief that the results are obvious and not surprising.

Picking an optimal benchmark is rarely trivial. Consider again the example where the CEO wanted best-in-class benchmarks to motivate his managers to act. Whether this goal is really achieved by showing such benchmarks is not necessarily true. It may be true that seeing the results of the best can be stimulating and show what is possible. However, such top values could also de-motivate management, because they may appear out of reach or because one cannot really compare such companies with the given company for various reasons. On the other hand, using averages as benchmarks can easily lead to complacency ("Here we are at benchmark. No action required.")

An alternative to an *external* benchmark is an *internal* benchmark. Of particular interest in this regard is comparing the survey results with those from previous surveys in the same company. Such *backward* (also called *historical*) comparisons, just as external benchmarks, require that one has access to the relevant statistical values (if they exist). If that is not the case, one can always resort to using internal *cross-comparisons*. For example, it is common practice to compare the results of different areas of the company to show where they are similar and where they differ. An even more popular type of benchmarking is *upward* comparisons, where the focal group is compared with the values of larger organizational units to which it belongs (see Figure 2.4).

Benchmarking Single Items and Indices

Benchmarking is mostly done for *items*. If similar items do not exist, one may still be able to construct comparable *indices* for selected topics. In the simplest case, such an index is just the average value for a set of reasonably homogeneous items (also called a "parcel"). The items, then, form a scale, and the average is the scale value of the topic that they all measure.

Indices may even be compared if their items do not form a scale as in case of an inflation index, where the many items that measure inflation are usually different in different countries, because these items are supposed to measure what is in the typical consumer's normal basket of consumption goods. Indeed, using different items in different companies to measure the same topic may even be superior to constructing comparable items. Consider the case of a German benchmarking consortium that consists of companies from vastly different industries such as coal mining, IT, and insurances. The only thing that these companies have in common is that they are all "blue chip" companies. When measuring how employees view their technical working environment, for example, one could ask a relatively abstract question in all these companies (e.g., "I have the tools and the equipment I need to do a good job."). However, as Scheuch (1993) suggests, more abstract concepts have a greater likelihood of producing unintended differences in meaning and should therefore be avoided. Just as an inflation index is computed differently in the USA and in Russia, it may be more meaningful and informative to compute a technical working environment index from items that are more specific for each particular group of respondents. What one wants is that the index is *functionally* comparable, and that does not require that the "basket of its issues" must have the same dimensionality or that the items use the same words.

Figure 10.6 shows an example that is typical for a first benchmarking of ES results using item-based benchmarking. What is being compared here are the *Yes%* statistics of company ABC for eleven items on job satisfaction with the results observed in other companies. One notes that ABC's results closely match the pattern of the industry benchmarks. However, their levels are quite different. For example, satisfaction with advancement at ABC is relatively low. Also, satisfaction with management and with information/communication is relatively low. On the other hand, satisfaction with direct supervisor and with benefits is comparatively high.

On the Validity of Benchmarks

Information about comparison levels is interesting and useful. It avoids becoming too complacent or, conversely, setting unrealistically high expectations on what is possible[44]. They also lead to discussions. In case of company ABC in Figure 10.6, it is easy to predict that higher-level managers, in particular, would ask critical questions about the *source* of the benchmarks[45]: "Which companies are behind these benchmarks? In which industry do these companies have their main business? In what shape are these companies? How large are they? When were they surveyed?" Discussing such questions often helps to better understand one's own data.

No survey expert and no survey vendor have good benchmarks for everything, even though some vendors have huge data bases from client surveys and from representative general-population surveys. To have access to more specific benchmarks, a company may therefore consider applying to become a member of an ES *benchmarking consortium* such as the Mayflower group or the ITSG (IT Survey Group), for example. The member companies of such consortia commit themselves to conducting employee surveys regularly, using a certain number of items from a fixed set of consortium items in their questionnaires. The data, or a consolidated form of the data, are then fed back to an external vendor who computes benchmarks and informs the members of the consortium about the resulting norms. Benchmark consortia are usually organized in divisions, where a division represents a certain industry such as IT, chemistry, or logistics. Consortia that consist of companies that are just all "big" or "global players" are the exception.

When using external benchmarks, one should be aware of a few basic caveats. First, no organization is completely comparable to any other organization. This is often used as a "counterargument" when the ES results look relatively poor. The argument is valid, to some extent, but external benchmarks are still useful as a first approach to the data. Then, external benchmarks are often based on millions of data, but they are rarely *representative* in any strict sense. Rather, the data are based on *convenience* samples, not on a carefully constructed random sample of organizations with a certain profile. In case of consortia, though, the sample of companies can cover all key players of a particular industry, and then the benchmarks are strong in that sense. Yet, even then, the various surveys which give rise to the benchmarks are most likely never conducted all at the same time. External benchmarks, therefore, should only be taken to guide a first approach to the data, but they should not be interpreted too closely.

Benchmarks from Different Countries

Comparing ES results becomes particularly difficult if a company has subsidiaries in different countries. Figure 12.3 (Lück, 1997) shows how the respondents in various

---

[44] Apparently without considering such benchmarks, Martin (1981) requires that "any question or item where the employees' response is less than 75% positive is normally considered negative." Benchmarking shows that such an absolute standard is unjustified. In Germany, for example, a satisfaction level of 75% positive on coworkers is a sign that there may be conflicts or problems in the work teams. In contrast, 75% satisfaction on (higher) management is a very good (i.e., very rare) score. Benchmarks also show what is possible. The idea that one can reach 100% satisfaction on all job dimensions is unrealistic.

[45] Such questions are, of course, entirely sensible. Management wants to know what these benchmarks are worth: Are they reliable, valid, and relevant? Do they show need for action?

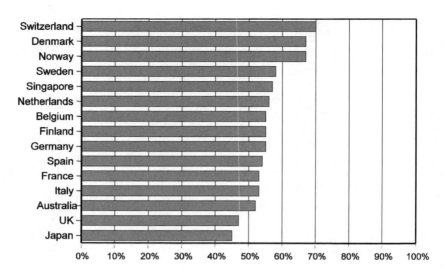

Figure 12.3. General job satisfaction (*Yes%* values) in numerous employee surveys in 15 countries (Lück, 1997).

employee surveys (conducted by ISR of Chicago) in 15 different countries responded to an "overall job satisfaction" item. The Japanese, apparently, are least satisfied, and the Swiss most satisfied. However, this conclusion may be premature, because the differences can also be caused by cultural differences in response style such as the "courtesy bias" (Jones, 1963) which leads to socially desirable responses, or "acquiescence," the tendency to agree to an item whatever its content. Harzing (2006, p. 252) reports, for example, that respondents "from Spanish-speaking countries show higher ERS [=extreme response style] and high acquiescence, while East Asian (Japanese and Chinese) respondents show a relatively high level of MRS" [=middle response style]. Hence, the low satisfaction scores of the Japanese in Figure 12.3 may be caused by their tendency towards the middle categories of the rating scale, and so it is difficult to decide whether the Japanese are "really" less satisfied than the Swiss[46] (see also Spector & Wimalasiri, 1986; Spector et al., 2002; Ryan, Horvath, Ployhart, Schmitt, & Slade, 2000). On the other hand, Figure 12.3 also shows that, apart from the extremes, the differences among the various countries are not that big. In most countries, the proportion of employees who rate themselves as overall satisfied with their job lies between 52% and 58%.

When studying less global attitudes, one finds similar results. The differences among most countries are generally moderate. Figure 12.4 shows the proportions of employees in 15 countries who are satisfied with management, direct supervisor,

---

[46] The question is actually scientifically meaningless. Science always looks at "if X then Y, given Z" relationships that involve more than just one variable (Guttman, 1981). Thus, one should ask if job satisfaction—assessed in a particular way—has the same correlation to performance, for example, in Japan and in Switzerland.

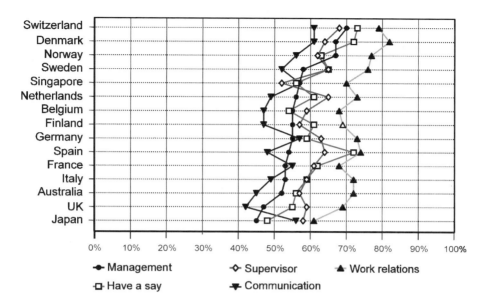

Figure 12.4. Percentage of employees with positive attitudes towards different aspects of their work (Harding & Radford, 1994).

working relations, codetermination, and communication, respectively (Harding & Radford, 1994). For countries that correspond to those in Figure 12.3, one notes that they are ordered similarly in terms of satisfaction in both graphs. Switzerland and the Scandinavian countries tend to be on top in every respect, while the UK is always at the bottom. Hence, there seems to exist a general ordering in the sense that the working relations, for example, are assessed more positively than the direct supervisor, and the direct supervisor more positively than management or communication.

Representative population surveys—where one potentially also asks farmers, coal miners, taxi drivers, college professors etc., i.e. just anyone who works for an income—on job satisfaction often show considerably *more* variance among countries (z.B. Kaase & Saris, 1997; Kenexa Research Institute, in press). East European countries (Hungary, Bulgaria, etc.), Japan and Sweden, for example, have been constantly low on pay satisfaction (with *Yes%* values of about 30% or less), while Canada and the US have scores that are almost twice as high (Wiley, 2008; Kowske, in press). The similarity of the country norms in Figure 12.3 may, therefore, be related to the fact that all these companies have a number of important features in common: They are all big, global players and they all conduct employee surveys. It may well be that this leads to a particularly homogeneous sample.

Benchmarking Against Industry and Job Norms

Frequently, senior leaders want to compare the company's scores to external norms, and often they assume that these normative data vary greatly by industry (e.g., that the survey scores from the IT industry differ from those from manufacturing). However, Eldridge's (2005) analysis of representative data from the US workforce indicated that industry explained an average of just 1.2% of variance among 39 survey questions. By comparison, job type explained an average of 1.5% of variance. In fact, job type was the demographic that explained the most variance in 18 of the 39 questions, while industry explained the most variance in only 7 questions. In terms of percent favorable scores, the average standard deviation of items across eight job types was 6 percentage points, while across 10 industries the average standard deviation was just 4 percentage points. These data suggest that survey scores vary more by the type of work that employees perform than by the industry in which they perform that work. Benchmarking by job provides a better statistical explanation of scores than does benchmarking by industry.

Analysis from a global medical equipment company suggests that job type actually explains more variance in survey scores than does business unit or location. This study revealed that job type explained an average of 5% of variance across 22 indices, while unit explained an average of 4% and location explained an average of 2%. Again, results suggest that survey scores differ more according to the type of work that employees do rather than the unit or location where they do the work.

Given these findings, we recommend that comparisons be made within like jobs, such as the company's sales professionals versus only sales professionals in the normative data. These *similar-groups comparisons* provide an improved evaluation of a group's scores relative to external (or internal) norms.

To be clear, the low percentages of variance that demographics explain, *on average*, in the above studies should not lead one to conclude that demographic variables are unimportant. Indeed, if one proceeds in a more theory-guided way, studying how particular constructs are related to particular demographics, one finds stronger effects (10% and more) and even lawful relations. For example, various facets of job satisfaction are related in a *monotonic* way to job grade: Satisfaction goes up with the employee's position, from rank-and-file employee to executive (see Figure 12.8). Tenure and age, on the other hand, are related to job satisfaction in a *U-shaped* or, more precisely, in an inverted *J-shaped* function: New employees are highly satisfied; satisfaction then drops sharply for the 2-3 year category; and then it slowly recovers with longer tenure, but not to its original high level (Bruggemann, Groskurth, & Ulich, 1975; Gibson & Klein, 1970; Schulte, 2005). Thus, we will see below that one can use such lawful patterns for benchmarking purposes.

Benchmarking by Cross-Comparisons within the Organization

A standard question in any analysis of ES data is to what extent the overall trends and findings hold for particular subgroups of the organization. Hence, one form of benchmarking that is always needed is comparing the various parts of the organization among each other. To illustrate, Figure 12.5 exhibits how three items come out in eighteen regional subsidiaries of a large German logistics company. The plot shows a number of things: (a) The endorsement of the three items is almost everywhere ordered in the same way—that is, agreement to "goals/tasks are motivating" is

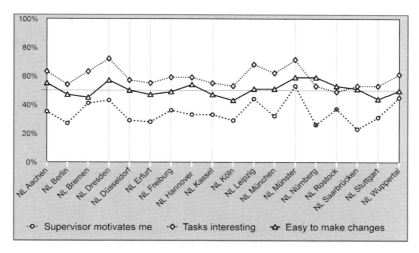

Figure 12.5. Yes% values for three items across different subsidiaries in a German logistics company.

highest, and "supervisor motivates" is lowest, with "anyone can bring about change around here" in between; (b) the subsidiaries differ up to 30% points among each other (e.g., "supervisor motivates" has a lowest score of 22% and a highest score of 53%); (c) the items are positively correlated, i.e., if X goes up, then Y goes up too, and vice versa.

Upward and Backward Benchmarking

The organizational units that are compared in Figure 12.5 are all on the same level of the organization. Such same-level comparisons must always be done with care in order to avoid conflicts that arise because managers may feel that their unit has been undeservedly exposed as a particularly negative one without considering the circumstances. The usual benchmarking for standard data analysis is *upward* comparisons, comparing an organizational unit (such as a subsidiary in Figure 12.5) to the average of similar organizational units (such as: all subsidiaries).

The other standard comparison is to match an organizational unit's results to the results obtained in previous surveys (see Figure 12.6 for an example). When making such historical comparisons, one should always carefully check to what extent such comparisons are really meaningful. Organizations change all the time, and even though the survey items may be similar or even formally equivalent, they measure attitudes and opinions of different people in a different environment: The organizational structure may have changed in the time interval between the surveys, most employees may be new to the unit, or the management of the unit may have changed, for example—to name just a few internal elements of normal change. All these factors make historical benchmarking particularly complex and almost always rule out a simple "here we have improved" and "here we have gone down" type of interpreta-

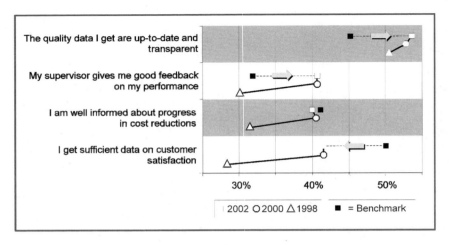

Figure 12.6. Comparing the results on four items on quality management over three consecutive employee surveys.

tion. The comparability can be enhanced, however, if one also has historical external benchmarks, because they can show general trends in the industry, for example, so that one can see if the own company follows the same pattern.

Benchmarking Against Prognoses

Another form of benchmarking is comparing the empirical ES results with predicted results. Two examples are shown in Figure 12.7. The forecast represents another form of assumed "normality," and results that deviate from the predictions can be taken as evidence that corrects these assumptions.

Benchmarking Correlations and Patterns

Benchmarking usually means comparing measures of central tendency such as the mean or the *Yes%* value of an item to the average mean or the average *Yes%* value of that item in the industry. Occasionally, one also compares the variance of items, but rarely ever the correlation of item X and item Y with the correlation of these items in the reference sample. It is not clear why this is not done more often, because correlations can be much more relevant than means. It would be interesting to note, for example, that commitment is "driven" by other variables in one's own company than in most other companies of the industry. Or, that commitment in one's own company is *not* correlated with the usual drivers of commitment. Or, consider a case from practice. We found that an item that assessed to what extent the individual had ideas for improvement was "strangely" uncorrelated—compared to what was found in other companies—with the individual's optimism for advancement, with being satisfied with performance appraisal, or with knowing what the supervisor wants. In later discussions it became clear that employees of this company were not rewarded for good ideas in the sense that they positively impacted their performance appraisals. Rather, ideas belonged to "the suggestion box" which was bureaucratic and not geared towards the individual's immediate work environment.

It can also be useful to compare certain patterns—such as the differences in job satisfaction among employees in different age groups or in different job grades—to normal patterns. This is best explained by an example. Figure 12.8 shows the satisfaction values for a number of basic job dimensions in three different companies. The two plots on top are from two large companies with deeply structured hierarchical organization charts, ranging from executive managers in six major steps to rank-and-file employees. The third plot shows comparable satisfaction values from a third large company with a very flat hierarchy (three levels only). The top plot exhibits the normal staircase pattern: satisfaction goes up monotonically on any job facet the higher the job grade, i.e., rank-and-file employees are least satisfied (with their working conditions, for example), while executives are most satisfied. The company at the bottom shows the same regular staircase pattern, although at a much higher level. The company in the middle, in contrast, is different. Here, one notes a remarkable—and "unusual"—gap between non-managers and lower managers on the one side, and upper to top management on the other. In the company at the bottom, top management was pleased to see that the spread of satisfaction ratings among the three levels was relatively small. Indeed, they argued that keeping this spread small had always been one of their management objectives. The executive board of the company in the middle panel, in contrast, found their non-normal staircase pattern alarming and called for action.

12.4 Using Theory to Interpret ES Data

Most companies want to know which actions can be recommended on the basis of ES results. Since management is ultimately focused on performance, theories of performance behavior and performance management are always interesting as guidelines for interpretation. Simple practitioner theories are often useful for this job. As an example, consider the following "formula" for employee performance (Stewart, 1986): *performance* = $f(SOME)$, where S = skills, O = opportunities, M = motivation, E = environment. This formula helps to take a systematic look at the ES data from a particular perspective. That is, one can ask to what extent the conditions for high performance are given in the company, and where the survey points at deficits, by checking the items that speak to the state of S, O, M, and E, respectively. For example, if one finds that employees complain about the training in the company, one may have found a reason for low performance or, expressed differently, an opportunity for actions that lead to higher performance.

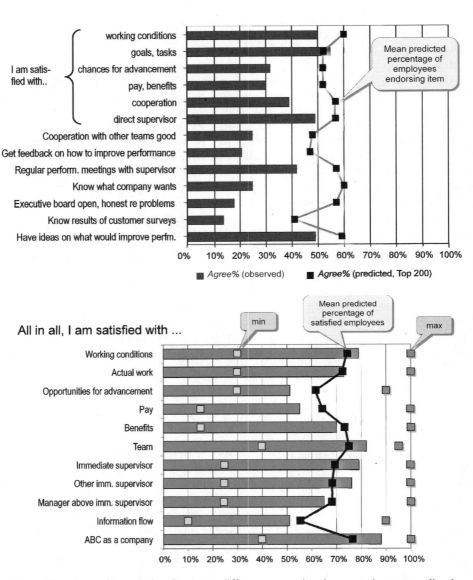

Figure 12.7. Some item results, from two different companies, in comparison to predicted endorsement values and min-max values (in lower panel).

Similar, and more recent, formulas are the ACE and the RACER notions discussed in Chapter 4. Figure 10.5 gives an example for using the ACE formula in standard data analysis. Yet, simply presenting such a diagram, and drilling further down into the C component as shown in Figure 10.5, is not the same as embedding these statistics into a compelling story. Formulas such as ACE are useful guidelines for data interpretation, but the final story must be delivered *in prose*, not in numbers or charts. For example, we notice in Figure 10.5 that one subcomponent of C, called "organizational conditions," is quite low for org unit X. First, one should explain what items underlie the index "organizational conditions," and then one should explain what the consequences are of the problems thus measured, and how they compare in terms of priority to other issues where actions seem necessary or promising. Also, one may want to discuss possible solutions and their feasibility in terms of costs or in terms of the organization's readiness.

The simple formulas above offer only limited support for constructing a compelling story. The implications of having weak and strong results on different issues are made more tractable in a systemic theory such as the performance-satisfaction motor (see Figures 4.5 and 4.6). The PS motor is a roadmap that allows one to go through much of the survey, ty-

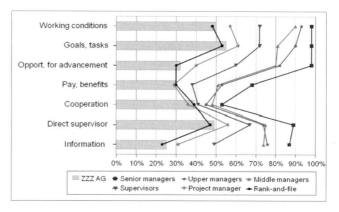

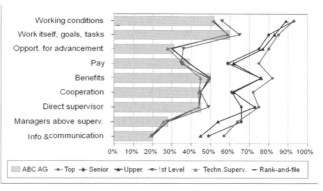

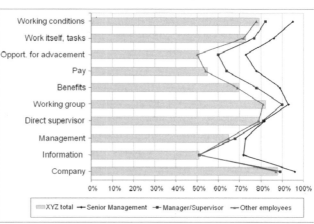

Figure 12.8. Satisfaction values (*Yes%*) of employees on different levels in the organizational hierarchy in three companies.

ing together the various pieces of information into a meaningful network. What is and what is not a "good" value can be assessed, for example, by benchmarking. In this way, the PS motor can be used as scaffolding for standard data analysis (see Figure 10.9). However, a deeper meaning of "good" can be derived from the role that the particular issue plays in the network of all other issues, and this, then, is NSDA because it requires human intelligence, not just computer programs. Good actions, in any case, need more than just data or information: They rest on understanding and on wisely assessing risks and potentials of interventions in systems.

An ES usually yields information on most elements of the core version of the PS motor (Figure 4.5), and missing information can usually be interpolated from what one has. The extended version of the PS motor (Figure 4.6), in contrast, is almost always under-measured by the survey in the sense that for many of its components and loops there are no specific measurements. What is usually missing is fine-grained information on the various elements that drive extra-role performance (e.g., trust in management, perceived integrity of management, system trust, fairness; see the elements in the lower right-hand corner of Figure 4.6). To measure all this in detail is not possible in an ES, but one can collect all the items that somehow relate to fairness, to being treated with respect, to management keeping its word, and so on and derive an overall index that assesses the condition of this cluster of issues as a whole. These issues are typically positively intercorrelated anyway, and even though they may not be truly one-dimensional, they nevertheless all load on a common second-order factor so that they, in combination, can be used to predict extra-role performance.

12.5 Deep Statistical Analyses

The PS motor helps to interconnect the many results of an employee survey on the basis of a theory. A second approach for looking at the structure of the items is using the statistical relationships observed in the data, in particular the intercorrelations of the items.

The Psychological Map of the Respondents

There are various methods for analyzing correlations among items. However, only few of them are useful in the sense that they help non-statisticians to intelligently interpret the item structure. They also avoid dubious assumptions[47]. One of these techniques is *multidimensional scaling* (MDS; Borg & Groenen, 2005). To see how MDS works, consider an example. We are looking at the 351 intercorrelations of 27

---

[47] Structural equation modeling, for example, can be a useful technique, provided one does not fall into a simplistic "causal" thinking. What one needs here are strong theoretical arguments in favor of a particular model specification. This is often forgotten in practice. On the contrary, "experts" communicate such modeling efforts in a causal language and managers eventually wonder why actions based on these causal implications do not yield results.

variables from an ES in a German IT company. The variables are 27 questionnaire items and two indices derived from two different batteries of items. What (two-dimensional) MDS does is shown in Figure 12.9[48]. It represents each variable by a point in the plane such that the distance between any two points corresponds (as closely as possible[49]) to the correlation of the variables that are represented by these two points. That is, the closer two points in this *psychological map*, the higher the correlation between the variables, and the farther any two points are apart from each other, the smaller (or the more negative) the correlation. Since any two variables in this data set are correlated non-negatively[50], one can simply say that large distances represent essentially "no" correlations, while small distances represent high correlations. Expressed differently, sitting on any point in Figure 12.9, one can predict that respondents who endorse the variable strongly (relative to the variable's mean value), also tend to support the neighboring variables strongly (relative to their mean values), and vice versa. For example, the MDS plot shows that a respondent who supports the company's strategy also tends to trust management, and vice versa. On the other hand, knowing that a respondent is satisfied with her working conditions does not allow one to predict whether he or she is satisfied or dissatisfied with the quality of trainings. Causal speculations are also possible, of course, using theory and sheer logic. For example, knowing the strategy can be interpreted as a cause or driver for trust in management, and not vice versa. Indeed, in one company, it was predicted that "pulling up" the psychological map like a handkerchief in one particular point (such as making the strategy clearer to employees) would also lift up the points in the neighborhood of this particular point. The next survey showed that these predictions did work: Providing better information about the company and explaining the strategy more carefully to everyone—as the MDS plot suggests—led to a major improvement in trust in management.

An MDS only represents the correlations of the variables, but one can display further statistics of the variables in the plot. This is shown in Figure 12.9 for the various overall satisfaction items (shown as circles), where *Yes%* statistics are added to the respective points. This can help finding issues where actions appear most promising because the results leave enough room for improvement.

The MDS configuration in Figure 12.9 is additionally structured by white patches. These patches cluster items that are substantively related into geometrical regions. What the regions demonstrate, quite clearly, is that the respondents did not answer the questionnaire in a random fashion. If they would have, all items would be randomly mixed, and regions of similar content would not show. The MDS thereby also helps to demonstrate that the answers of the respondents have to be taken seriously in the sense that they are highly structured in a meaningful way.

---

[48] The plot is a simplification of an MDS plot with 55 variables, representing 1485 (!) correlations with a stress of .19, an excellent fit to the data.

[49] It is not always possible to represent the correlations of that many variables in a plane, not even approximately. This is possible only if the correlations are highly structured.

[50] Non-negativity of the intercorrelations is typical for most items of an employee survey--provided the items are all reflected in the same positive-negative sense. This reflects a general affective halo in all answers, which makes MDS particularly simple.

312   Chapter 12

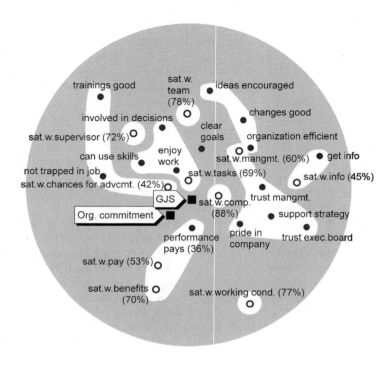

Figure 12.9. MDS structure of 27 ES variables.

The regions show, moreover, how the respondents structure the various meta-topics. One can simplify this structure even further by distinguishing three intersecting "spheres" of attitudes and opinions (Figure 12.10): The individual's immediate working environment (including work itself, co-workers, supervisor), the company (including management, strategy, information), and the systems (comprising the pay system and the working conditions). The simplified sphere model helped to approximate the findings for general communication in this company. It also indicates that the sphere "company" spins around managers, while the sphere "my working environment" spins around the supervisor. Whether this is so or not, and what it means can at least be discussed, and managers, apart from using the MDS item plot to guide their action planning, like to explore such MDS plots for additional meaning.

Dependent Variables within MDS

Figure 12.9 contains two particular points that represent variables of particular interest: General job satisfaction (GJS) and organizational commitment. They can be interpreted as dependent variables that are to be explained by the other (independent) variables in this plot. Both dependent variables are measured through aggregating the results of a set of items. In case of GJS, an index is constructed by averaging the responses over various items that measure satisfaction with pay, supervisor, co-workers, advancement, etc. Commitment is measured by aggregating such items as "I am proud to work for ABC."

The GJS point lies, not surprisingly, at the center of the plot. Indeed, it corresponds to the centroid of the points that measure the various job facet satisfactions and that show the level of satisfaction (*Yes%* values) in parentheses. From the position of GJS in

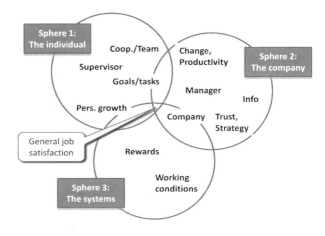

Figure 12.10. Meta-stucture of MDS plot in Figure 12.9.

the plot, one can derive—actually "see"—what is most highly correlated with general job satisfaction. This information is sometimes taken as evidence for what is and what is not so important (for GJS). This interpretation is valid, but only in a correlational sense. Working conditions are poor predictors of GJS (in this company), for example, but that does not mean that working conditions are not relevant. It only happens in this case, that the respondents did not differ much in their evaluation of the working conditions: They were all satisfied. Thus, closeness to GJS only shows where generally satisfied and generally dissatisfied respondents differ most, and this can be valuable information for follow-up activities.

Commitment was of particular interest in this survey, because of a high turnover tendency among employees. The MDS plot says that high vs. low commitment were most correlated with endorsement or rejection of the items "performance pays," "satisfied with advancement," and "satisfied with tasks."

External Dependent Variables and Linkage Research

In many employee surveys, management brings its own questions to the data, as in the case illustrated above. Such questions always deserve particular attention and deeper statistical analysis, often with regression methods. The dependent variable need not be an item or an index that comes from the survey itself. It can also be an *external* variable. This is often called *linkage research*. For example, in one automobile production plant, a major issue was the high sickness rate of its workers. Management was hoping to learn something about its reasons from the survey.

The problem with an issue like this is that the survey is typically anonymous (not just confidential). So, one does not know to what extent each *individual* respondent is actually absent and so one cannot relate individual attitudes and opinions to how of-

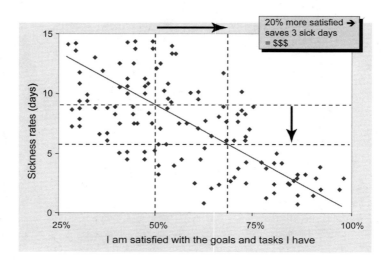

Figure 12.11. Relating the sickness rates of workgroups (points) to the average endorsement of one particular ES item.

ten a respondent calls in sick[51]. The only way to address the issue is by looking at *average* values of *groups* of employees, even though employees are known to differ substantially with respect to their sickness rates. In the case of the above automobile plant, sickness statistics were available for 125 workgroups. Regressing the means of the survey items for each workgroup on the workgroup's sickness statistics showed that the item that best predicted sickness rates ($r=-0.51$) was: "Overall, I am satisfied with the goals and tasks I have." Although more sophisticated analyses are possible (e.g., considering moderators such as commitment), it was decided that this finding had so much practical usability that it was cast into the slide shown in Figure 12.11. Each point in this scatter plot represents one particular workgroup.

The regression line was used to discuss a model of "behavioral accounting" (Cascio, 1982): If one is willing to assume that low satisfaction with goals and tasks *causes* higher sickness rates, then one can compute to what extent the sickness rate would go down if this satisfaction was improved from its relatively low average value of 56% satisfied by, say, 20% on the average so that it reaches a normal level. The answer is easy to find: The reduction in the sickness rate would be more than three days, a tremendous cost reduction.

---

[51] One way to circumvent this problem is to ask the respondents about absenteeism in the survey. The item could be this: "How many days of work have you missed in [in time period *X*/since time *Y*] because of sickness?" (Johns, 1994). Research shows that self-reported absenteeism is objectively too low, but that matters little for correlation research. On the other hand, the item measures a sensitive topic, which may lead to lower participation rates.

Less speculative, but very practical is another aspect: Since each point represents one workgroup, one could take this chart and talk with the supervisors of these workgroups, pointing out this relationship and searching for improvement actions. The chart legitimizes and focuses these discussions. It also makes clear how relevant attitudes can be for bottom-line variables. One could also study how the "good" workgroups differ from the "poor" workgroups. Indeed, this was done in this plant, and it was found that the good workgroups had set up their work differently, i.e., they worked more as a team assembling complete cars rather working individually on assembly lines.

Figure 12.12. The High Performance Model linking soft and hard facts.

Linkage research as in the example shown in Figure 12.11 has a lot of power to generate actions. However, it usually is not easy to find the necessary hard data to build linkages. But, then, one does not have to reinvent the wheel again and again, and one should check what science has to offer on this matter. Some basic laws of linking soft to hard facts are consolidated, for example, in the *High Performance Model* (Wiley & Campbell, 2006), depicted in Figure 12.12. It integrates "all previously published linkage research findings to produce an understanding more comprehensive than could be provided by the results of any single study. The model suggests that the more visible and present certain organizational values and leadership practices are in a given work environment, the more energized and productive the workforce is. In turn, the more energized and productive the workforce, the greater the satisfaction and loyalty of customers and, with a time lag, the stronger the long-term business performance of the organization" (p. 151). Meta-analytic research has shown, for example, that the more leaders emphasize quality or the better the training employees receive, the higher the employees' engagement and, in turn, the higher customer satisfaction. One can use this model at least as a demonstration of what various ES results on leadership and engagement mean for business, without having to prove with new data over and over again that this is true (given obvious side constraints and other conditions such as a good strategy, competitive products, etc.).

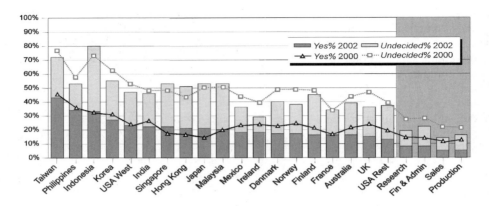

Figure 12.13. Turnover tendencies (in 2002 and 2000, resp.) in various subsidiaries (left panel) and functions (right panel) of a global company

Relating Internal Dependent Variables to Demographic Information

One of the first questions that comes to mind when studying variables of particular interest is to what extent they can be explained by the demographic information collected in the survey. Figure 12.13 shows an example of a global company. The item here is "I seriously plan leaving the company within 12 months." The X-axis shows various countries and, to the right in the gray part, the functions within the company's European headquarters. The Y-axis shows the endorsement of this item. The bars exhibit the percentages of employees who endorsed this item in 2002, and (stacked on top) the percentages of the employees who answered with checking the "undecided" (middle) category of the Likert scale. The lines depict the respective agreement and undecided values, respectively, found in a previous survey in 2000. The graph makes clear that turnover tendency is quite different in the various organizational units of this company. Also, while turnover intention went down in the European countries, it had an upward tendency in countries outside of Europe.

Further breakdowns of this item by other demographic items such as position in the hierarchy, years of tenure, function, etc. are possible and may be interesting. However, a note of caution is due for such analyses: They can easily lead to premature interpretations in the sense that the particular demographic predictor is taken as the *cause* for the different responses. For example, in German companies one often finds that women are more satisfied with most job aspects than men. Seeing this a few times, one begins to feel that this is not only some kind of lawfulness, but that this is "as it should be" for this or that reason. However, when testing this hypothesis in surveys that are representative for the working population, no gender effect can be found for job satisfaction (Antoni, 1999). When going back to ES data, one quickly notices that the gender effect is an artifact, because once one controls for other demographic differences—in particular, once one compares women who work in white collar or blue collar jobs with men in similar jobs—no systematic gender differences

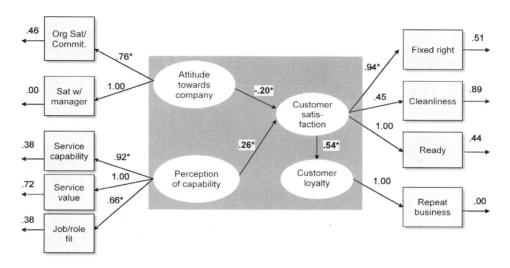

Figure 12.14: A more positive attitude towards the company correlates negatively with customer satisfaction (Lezotte & McLinden, 2003).

remain. Hence, the typical German gender difference on job satisfaction issues is a *spurious* correlation, a fallacy. The lesson for data analysis, therefore, is that one should always check whether the *effect* of a particular demographic variable X on a content variable Y remains essentially the same if one or more *additional* demographic variables are used besides X as predictors at the same time. If not, the effect of X on Y is spurious.

Interpretations and the "More is better" Fallacy

Interpretations of survey results should eventually be condensed into a simple story. Managers often ask for extremely compact indices, preferably in the form of a simple listing of the main points together with a traffic-light coloring that indicates what is good, what is bad and requires action, and where one needs to be alert. Values clearly above the benchmarks are typically considered "green." However, this automatic assignment can be quite wrong. To show this, consider a case. Lezotte & MacLinden (2003) found in a census survey in a large American automotive services company that the employees' responses could be explained by two latent factors. These were attitude towards the company, with organizational satisfaction, commitment, and satisfaction with manager as indicators, and perception of capability, the employees' assessment of the company's quality of services delivered to the customer (Figure 12.14). Concurrent to the ES, a customer satisfaction survey was run. Linking the attitudes and perceptions of the employees to the customer satisfaction data revealed that perception of capability was positively correlated with customer satisfaction ($r=.26$), but attitude towards the company was negatively correlated ($r=-.20$). So, a more positive attitude towards the company does not automatically mean that the customer is more satisfied. Indeed, this attitude may become too positive in the sense that all attention is turned to the inside and the customer gets out of focus. The lesson from this example is simple: One should keep the whole system of variables in mind (as, for example, in the PS motor), with possibly *U-shaped* relationships among its variables, and even relate this system to critical dependent variables that drive business. It does not mean that one cannot arrive at a simple traffic-light categorization of major findings, but one should be careful not to improve "red" issues beyond their *point of optimum*.

12.6 Business-Oriented Frameworks for ES Data Interpretation

Managers typically want to know what the results of an ES mean for their operational and strategic goals. If one can show this convincingly, the ES will have impact and its follow-up processes are taken seriously. If not, management listens and then delegates further activities to lower-level management or to HR. In Figure 12.11 we have shown one simple example that typically does impress management because it links the survey data to a variable that clearly impacts the bottom line (i.e., sickness rate which means costs, low productivity, possibly even low quality, problems to stay on time schedules, etc.). Indeed, in some companies where a proper linkage analysis was not possible, we have shown just this slide "as an example from another company" to make the point that attitudes and opinions can be powerful predictors of important business variables.

ES Data and the Balanced Scorecard

Almost all companies use some kind of scorecard to keep track of their vital statistics. One popular version is the *Balanced Scorecard* (BSC) that measures the company's strengths on four fields such as finances or customer. These fields are mostly assessed in terms of a set of outcome indicators, most of them "objective" ones. For example, financial strength is measured in terms of the company's earnings before interests and taxes (Ebit), by assessing the company's return on investment (ROI), and by other such indicators. Customer strength is measured by customer satisfaction, by the number of complaints, by market share, and so on. Managers (and analysts) typically follow these performance indicators of a company closely and regularly.

It is easy to see that all of these indicators are somehow influenced, if not even generated, by the company's employees. Hence, it is only natural to ask what the employee survey has to say about the BSC. Figure 12.15 shows an example where three different ES items are associated with each of the four measurement fields of the BSC. It also exhibits the results for these items from an ES in a major utility company. The results in white boxes were considered "good" (by a set of criteria such as external benchmarks and considerations on what seems achievable). The grey boxes show "average" results and the black boxes shows items where action seems necessary.

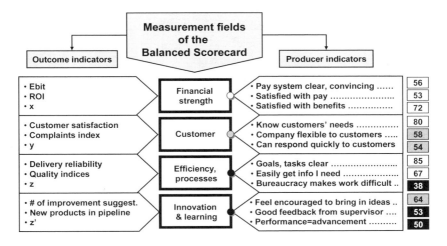

Figure 12.15. A BSC with ES items and results (*Yes%* values) to the right.

One can easily see the power of such a display by viewing these results from the perspective of an investor. If you assume that you were considering buying stocks from this company, then knowing, for example, that an unusually large proportion of the employees are dissatisfied with their pay would make you look differently at good financial indicators, because this dissatisfaction is a latent risk factor for the company's financial strength. In any case, a BSC plot such as the one in Figure 12.15 is easy to produce and often stimulates useful discussions because it links the ES results to important categories of management thinking. One typical consequence is that management realizes that the ES results should be treated as "confidential" information that must not be freely distributed outside the company. They, therefore, understand that the ES results are important business data.

SWOT Analysis

The results of an employee survey can also be interpreted using other familiar management methods. One such method is a *SWOT analysis* which looks at the company's current strengths and weaknesses vis-à-vis the foreseeable opportunities and threats that come from "upstream" towards the company. Upstream events are things that are not under the control of the company such as, for example, consumer optimism, tax rates, environmental protection legislation, or the emergence of new markets. Strengths and weaknesses, in contrast, are internal conditions such as the organizational structure, systems, skills, etc., and also opinions, attitudes, and the employees' behavior that impacts positively or negatively on the business. The SWOT question then is this: "Assume that everything in the company remains as it is now. How likely is it then that the company can take advantage of the foreseeable opportunities, and master the probable threats?"

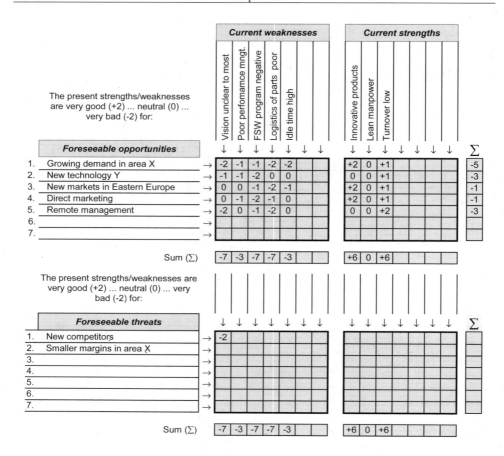

Figure 12.16. Excerpts of a 3SA matrix.

One can answer such a question by using the 3SA procedure (Borg, 1995). It works by filling out and then analyzing a matrix as illustrated in Figure 12.16. One begins by specifying the most important strengths, weaknesses, opportunities, and threats. Then, each strength and each weakness is rated relative to its impact on seizing each opportunity and repelling each threat.

Finally, one sums up the ratings over columns and over rows, respectively. Large column sums hint at strengths and weaknesses with great potential. They mark strengths that should be preserved or weaknesses that should be reduced.

Special attention should be given to columns that sum to about zero while having a large variance of their rating scores. In such cases, the column entry may be multidimensional and too inhomogeneous for consistent ratings. Splitting the weakness or strength into two or more components often leads to simpler results.

In summary, one notes from this example that it requires deeper knowledge about the particular company and its business environment than the survey expert can be expected to have in general. Hence, a reasonable SWOT analysis for ES results can only be done in cooperation with partners from within the organization where the survey was done. Such partners may come from the ES coordination team, for example, or it may be the survey sponsor. Another possibility is to prepare only a "tentative" SWOT analysis and then work on it with management in a follow-up workshop after the results of the survey have been presented.

12.7 Triangulation and Other Views onto the Data

The five different perspectives onto the data discussed above are by no means the only ones that are possible, although they do represent the major categories of looking at ES data. Consider, for example, Schiemann's (Schiemann & Morgan, 2006; Kostman & Schiemann, 2006) concept of *people equity* and its three basic dimensions—alignment, capabilities, and engagement (ACE). These authors suggest to aggregate the survey information into an *ACE triple index* for each organizational unit, from the global enterprise down to each workgroup, and map these triplets onto the tree diagram of the organization to see where "trouble" and where "strength" are located, or where things are simply "OK." The diagnosis is supported by coloring the elements of the ACE triple in different ways if they exceed or do not exceed certain pre-defined cut-off values that serve as benchmarks. The ACE chart thus constructed yields a compact but sufficiently differentiated picture of the state of the organization. It combines benchmarking with a theory-based aggregation approach, and it also shows the scatter underneath the main trends.

Another look onto the data results from studying the data in an effort to find answers to a central management question such as "Why don't employees do what they are supposed to do?" Fournies (1999) discusses a set of reasons why they don't do it. These reasons can be formulated in different ways, for example, as follows:

- They don't know what they are expected to do (e.g., because goals, directions, or the strategy are unclear to them).
- They don't endorse these expectations (e.g., because they believe that they don't make sense, will not work, cannot be done, set the wrong priorities).
- They don't believe that these expectations are taken seriously by management ("only on glossy paper").
- They don't understand what these expectations mean in terms of their work behavior (e.g., because they are too abstract, they are not broken down to their work) .
- They don't understand why they are expected to behave this way (e.g., because they don't see the implications for business success or for job security).
- They think that they are doing it (e.g., because they do not get proper feedback).
- They do not know how to do it (e.g., because training is poor).

- They cannot tell whether they are doing it or not (poor feedback, no proper performance appraisal).
- There are no positive consequences if they do it (e.g., because rewards do not depend on reaching the right goals or showing the required behaviors).
- Doing it has negative consequences (e.g., is socially not accepted, does not fit the culture) or is perceived as risky (e.g., fear of failure and its consequences).
- Not doing it has no negative consequences (e.g., supervisor looks away).
- Not doing it is positively rewarded (e.g., is rewarded by peers, workers' hero resists management's demands).
- There are obstacles they cannot overcome (e.g., in the working environment).
- Their personal limits are reached (e.g., too difficult, burnout, work-family tensions).

Given the "why don't they do it" question and the various prototypical answers, one can look for evidence in the survey. For example, what does the survey tell us about clarity of strategy, goals, and work performance expectations? If employees say, for example, that they do not really understand what their supervisor wants from them, we have one answer to our question. If managers feel that the company's strategy is just a window dressing and that careers really depend on other things, then we have another explanation for our basic question. In general, an employee survey should give at least a partial answer to each answer category.

Each particular perspective onto the survey data (benchmarking, theory, particular questions, etc.) corresponds to one set of queries. The answers that each such query extracts from the survey data may be independent but complementary, or they may support each other, but they should not be contradictory. If they are, one should reconsider one's interpretations. It just may be the case that one has over-interpreted the data in one way or another or that one has moved too far away from the empirical evidence. Hence, different perspectives onto the data can be seen as a triangulation method that helps to cross-check the validity of one's conclusions.

13 Presenting Survey Results to Management

The follow-up processes of an ES typically begin with the presentation of the survey results to top management. The success of this presentation is decisive for the success of the entire ES project. Powerful presentations of ES results require a lot more than simply reading number after number to the audience. Rather, what is needed is a story that interweaves survey statistics, theory, and interpretations into a network of arguments and conclusions that promote business goals by sparking effective activities. If everything works well in a presentation, it succeeds to (1) inform management about the survey results so that they see both the big picture as well as important details, and not get lost in statistics; (2) arrive at valid interpretations that go beyond general good-bad categorizations and that relate to specific business goals; (3) make management aware not only of needs for action but also of opportunities that the data suggest; and (4) motivate and empower management to make the right decisions.

13.1 Structuring an ES Presentation

Any presentation of ES results needs to be structured in one way or another. The simplest possible structure is to follow the categories of the questionnaire. This typically means that one begins with items related to 'working conditions', and then proceeds with 'work itself', 'coworkers', 'advancement', 'pay and benefits' and so on. Such an ordering of topics has the advantage that it does not require an extra rationale or justification. However, for higher levels of management, it also leads to a presentation that will likely fail to inspire effective action. Leaders want to focus on managerial issues, and they want insightful recommendations for action.

There are different ways to structure an ES presentation. What is optimal has to be decided within the context of the particular ES project. Still, it may be helpful to consider one prototypical set-up for such a presentation. Table 13.1 outlines an approach using some of the models and statistical analyses that we have presented elsewhere in this book. We have found this structure useful across many different companies, adjusting for different models, statistics, and circumstances along the way.

Introduction of an ES Presentation

A useful way to begin an ES presentation is to briefly recall the goals of the survey project, as they were formulated in the project's positioning. Then, one can show

Table 13.1. Prototypical structure of an ES presentation.

1	**Introduction**
	• Goals of employee survey
	• Overview of phases, steps, and milestones: Where are we? (Figures 1.4, 3.2)
	• Participation rates
	• Data quality
	• Reminder of questionnaire, items: Format, answer scale (see Figure 5.10)
	• Statistics: Which statistics will be used, why, how to interpret (see Figure 10.2)
2	**Results**
2.1	Results by facets/dimensions of the organization climate
	• Organization as a whole
	• External benchmarking (Figure 10.6)
	• Results from previous surveys
	• Results vs. prognoses (Figure 12.7)
	• Differences among major org. functions, regions, etc. (similar to Figure 10.7)
	• Differences among managers and non-managers (Figure 12.8)
2.2	Results within a framework, e.g., the performance-satisfaction motor
	• Explain core of PS motor (Figure 4.5)
	• Link various items to boxes and/or connectives in the PS motor (Figure 10.9)
	• Introduce (lower right-hand corner of) extended PS motor (Figure 4.6)
	• Report results on commitment, trust, contextual performance drivers
2.3	Empirical/statistical structure of items, e.g., Multidimensional Scaling (MDS)
	• Explain MDS structure of items (Figure 12.9)
	• Show position of variables of particular interest within MDS plot (Figure 12.9)
	• Discuss influences, what drives what
2.3	Special topics
	• Items that show progress and decline since the last survey
	• Hot topics given current business context
	• Items for managers only
2.4	Business perspectives onto the ES data
	• ES data in the Balanced Scorecard (Figure 12.15), SWOT analysis, etc.
	• Linkage analysis (Figures 12.11 to 12.12)
2.5	Some Monday morning platforms for actions (Figure 13.3)
3	**Ending**
	• Summary of results
	• Recommendations for global areas of focus
	• Recommendations on next steps, time line

where the project is situated on its time line, and what the next steps are. To do this, it suffices to use simplified displays as in Figures 3.2 or 1.4 (if the latter is annotated with a few concrete dates). The goal of this introduction is to set the stage for the presentation. Management, in particular, should understand that after the presentation there needs to be some decision on how they will respond, culminating in a detailed timeline for the follow-up activities.

Next, one begins with feeding back the results of the ES. The first information is always the global participation rate and the participation of important parts of the organization (e.g., functions, major subsidiaries, blue vs. white collar). If participation is low, one should clarify to what extent the results may be biased. Most often, the bias introduced by nonresponse is unsystematic or mild, as general survey research shows.

It can also be useful to mention at this time that the items were pretested and that the pre-tests make it likely that the items were correctly understood by every employee. The survey statistics support this finding if the number of non-responses is small for each item, and if the items exhibit meaningful patterns (e.g., scalability).

Then, before turning to the survey's items, it is useful to remind the audience of the structure of the questionnaire. An excerpt of the questionnaire that shows, for example, the item block on "working conditions" is sufficient. What one needs to do is to remind the audience of the way the questions were asked and scored (i.e., usually as Likert items). In case of a paper questionnaire, one can also distribute original copies of the questionnaire.

The demo block of items can also be used to show how the data will be aggregated to item statistics (*Yes%*, *Mixed%*, *No%*, and/or means). Practical experience has made clear that one needs to point out at this point that responses in the middle category of the Likert answer scale ("mixed") should be interpreted, first of all, as ambivalent answers and not as that "Don't Know" answers (see Figure 4.8). Also, one should demonstrate with the data of the actual survey that it is sufficient to concentrate one's attention on the *Yes%* values. There is hardly any loss of information when examining the percentage of employees who responded with a 5 or 4 compared to the statistical mean (Figure 10.2 shows a nearly perfect correlation between the statistical mean and *Yes%*).

Facets/Dimensions of the Organization Climate

In the next stage of the presentation, we provide an overview of major strengths and weaknesses by showing a reduced set of scores (i.e., not all the item scores). One way to achieve this simple overview is to display just index (category) scores that represent the major facets or dimensions included in the survey. Another option is to present a representative item from each of these major facets. If the survey is designed with an "overall satisfaction" item for each facet, then one might begin with a presentation of the results for these items, showing a stacked graph that displays their *Yes%*, the *Mixed%*, and the *No%* scores.

In later charts of this kind, one should consider *not* presenting *Yes%* and *Mixed%* and *No%* for each item. This only leads to informational overload, and no one can remember that many values later on. Also, after having shown that *Yes%* values closely correspond to mean values (as in Figure 10.2, for example), it would be a contradiction to continue exhibiting all these statistics all the time. The purpose of showing the three types of percentage statistics on the initial chart only serves as an opportunity to stress that not all respondents who did not endorse an item automatically rejected it. Rather, the rejection percentage is usually quite small, and only occasionally does it make sense to show it explicitly on the slides. Moreover, all the details are in the SDA reports for anyone who wants to know them.

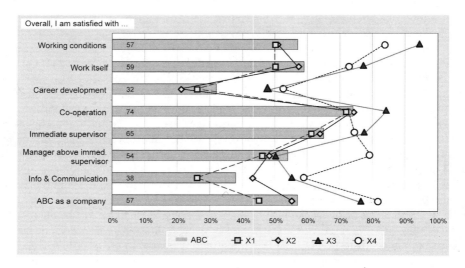

Figure 13.1. Satisfaction with various job facets in company ABC and in its four major functions X1, ..., X4.

External benchmarks (as in Figure 10.6) provide a necessary complement to these *Yes%* scores. If no such benchmarks are presented, management will likely ask what scores are considered "normal" or "typical." However, these benchmarks need not be of a specific type (e.g., benchmark values for a particular industry). Top management is typically satisfied with "some" benchmark information if the data are accurate and appropriate. One should point out that benchmarks are only one part of the data interpretation process. Likewise, internal benchmarks help provide a relative context for managers to understand their survey scores.

At this point in the presentation, one can compare management's predictions of survey scores with the actual findings. One chart is usually sufficient. It should show management's mean prediction values and how they differ from the results, and then also the scatter of these predictions (e.g., high and low values; see lower panel in Figure 12.7). One such chart suffices to reduce the (false) impression that the results are "obvious." If the mean predictions are on target, the presenter may add some comments on the scatter of the predictions and point out that each manager acts on the basis of his or her own convictions, and that different convictions imply different managerial behaviors.

A natural question that pops up at this time is how the survey results differ among major parts of the organization, most importantly among its main functions or market units. This can easily be shown by overlaying line plots onto the bar chart as demonstrated in Figure 13.1. One notes in this figure that the function X1 is generally producing the lowest survey scores, and X3 and X4 the highest. As usual in such comparisons, the overall trends are quite similar, except for some "outliers": For example, X3 has relatively low scores on satisfaction with 'manager above immediate supervisor', while X4 has a similar dip for 'co-operation'. Without going into further details, such a chart suggests right at the beginning of the presentation that the results of different functions of the organization cannot be simply compared on an absolute scale, but that a certain overall "additive constant"—often predictable by the different types of jobs—must first be taken into account.

Another important question is how managers and non-managers differ in terms of survey scores. The benchmarking here is not comparing the values against normal values but rather the *pattern* of the values against the normal "staircase" pattern (see Figure 12.8). The aim is to check whether the pattern is normal in the respective organization or whether some levels of the hierarchy deserve special attention.

Similar comparisons can also be made for other strata of the organization, such as levels of tenure. Here, one usually finds that new employees are most satisfied with all dimensions of their jobs. For older employees, job satisfaction drops substantially to reach a bottom level at about 3-5 years of tenure, and then recovers slowly with longer tenure. This inverse J trend has also been described repeatedly in the academic literature (Bruggemann et al., 1975; Neuberger & Allerbeck, 1978).

These "rules of thumb" should be understood to determine what is normal versus abnormal. Normative data from the US suggests that (compared to average) survey scores are 11 points higher for management, 4 points higher for first-level supervisors, and 7 points higher for first year employees (Johnson & Mastrangelo, 2008). The presenter should, however, only use such benchmarking data to detect symptoms that need further study and not jump to causal interpretations (e.g., "New employees are more satisfied because they are younger!").

The Performance-Satisfaction Network: Core and Extension

After discussing the ES data from an overview or satisfaction perspective, one should find a way to move on to specific topics that are of more direct interest to management. Yet, rather than opening a completely new chapter, one needs to preserve–and possibly deepen–insights gained earlier. One way to do this is to use an overarching framework of organizational culture or a comprehensive theory that links satisfaction to performance. For example, the core of the PS motor (Figure 4.5) is sufficiently detailed to serve as robust scaffolding for presenting many items within the performance-satisfaction context. An example for how to do this is shown in Figure 10.9.

Given a topic such as the technical-organizational working environment in Figure 10.9, one can possibly add further information to such a chart by inserting (in an animated way) supplementary tables or charts. For example, the one item identified as critical in Figure 10.9 ("excessive rules") may not be such a hot issue everywhere in the organization, and so some statistics on how this item is scored in the organization's major divisions is important information. Management, after all, should decide at the end of the presentation whether such an issue has to lead to a *common* field of action to which every part of the organization must contribute improvement actions.

A Simpler Alternative: ACE or RACER Structuring

A graphics- and network-based presentation as the one suggested in Figure 10.9 can be too complicated. Some managers also prefer to work with simpler graphics and in a more index-oriented way. Fortunately, there are ready-to-use approaches for this situation too, in particular the ACE or the RACER formulas (see Chapter 4). If they are employed in a more hierarchical way (Figure 4.3), one arrives at charts as in Figure 10.5. They lend themselves to structure a presentation in such a way that the presenter and the audience can ping-pong between super- and sub-topics: If a super-topic (such as "C", for example) shows some peculiarities (e.g., generally low scores, much variance among org units), the presenter may drill down into the components that underlie the big categories. Alternatively, if previous analyses have shown that on lower hierarchical levels there are elements with extreme values, attention could be focused on them too. The presenter, thus, is in a position similar to a medical doctor who looks at large symptoms, special findings, results from the laboratory, etc. All this must be considered and integrated into a coherent diagnosis, and one method to do this is to *alternate* back and forth between the various levels of analysis, between big symptoms and small pieces of evidence. If nothing is "wrong", there is no need to discuss the issues at length. Rather, it suffices to simply state that X or Y are just fine. When looking not for problems and weaknesses but for strengths or potentials for improvement, one can proceed in the same fashion, i.e. by moving up and down the hierarchy in an attempt to discover interesting pieces of information. The formulas, and the concept hierarchies linked to them, prevent that one gets lost.

Further Break-Downs of the Statistics

The presenter should be careful not to overload the presentation with "interesting" statistics that serve no clear purpose. Such statistics are, in fact, counter-productive because they divert attention from what *is* important. Moreover, when asking managers after the presentation for details that they can remember, they will recall very few statistics, if any. Details are needed only for the critical building blocks of the survey's story. For them, management always needs to know to what extent they hold throughout the company. Hence, the presenter should provide an answer by checking at least the differences among major organizational divisions and among hierarchical levels, respectively, to name just the two "standard" points-of-view.

Consider the example in Figure 12.5. It shows three items, each of them broken down over the major subsidiaries of company X. Given this plot, one can discuss whether the issue "motivation through supervisor" should be considered a universal problem issue or just one that is locally important. In the given case, it seems that the scores are relatively poor in all subsidiaries so that this issue is a viable candidate for a company-wide field of action.

Figure 12.5, moreover, also demonstrates that the three particular items are empirically correlated: Wherever the scores of one item are good, the other two items also tend to be good, and vice versa. If the presenter points out to the audience that the various line plots run essentially in a parallel fashion up and down on the chart, then everyone can *see* that and how the items are correlated. There is no need for correlation coefficients.

If one cannot resist including statistical coefficients, we suggest putting them in an "appendix" section, which should be referred to only if the audience wants more detail. Often presenters with statistical skills overemphasize the details of the analytical method instead of stressing the results and their implications for the audience. Heath and Heath (2007) call such errors "the curse of knowledge," meaning that once a person knows something, it is difficult to imagine what it was like to not know it. They suggest that the key to making a point memorable is not in proof via statistics, but in using as many "SUCCESS" elements as possible: Simple, Unexpected, Concrete, Credible, Emotional, Stories. While statistics may seem to contribute to making results credible, they should be used in the context of a larger story.

Empirical Structure of Items

Often statistical procedures are helpful in detecting the relationships among survey items. If a presenter can sidestep the complexity of the procedure itself, the outcome of the procedure can often help simplify the interpretation of the survey results by reducing the number of content issues to its basic components and prioritizing those items that are most related to key metrics (e.g., performance, engagement, turnover). While a variety of statistical procedures can be used, the key is to use a visually appealing presentation of its output. One example is the "psychological map" of the items in Figure 12.9. This MDS map can serve as a basis for some (data-based) *causal* speculations that help to plan actions. It also gives some answers to the question what is important for what. Moreover, it clearly demonstrates that the employees' responses to the survey are not just random but highly structured.

Special Topics

Most employee surveys contain some very specific items that are not always easy to integrate into the general issues, such as dimensions of job satisfaction or performance-satisfaction networks. It is often best to present them in a few extra sections in order not to disturb the above balanced schemas with inserts. Special topics usually require various breakdowns over demographic variables. The data analyst should systematically check all such breakdowns, but only show those in the presentation that really contribute to the ES story.

Business Perspectives

At this point of the ES presentation, managers often seem a bit tired of statistics and of psychology. To bend the story back onto business issues, one should therefore present some analyses on what the data mean in the categories in which managers think. One recipe for doing this is to look onto the ES results from a Balanced Scorecard perspective as shown in Figure 12.15. Another possibility is to use a SWOT point-of-view which, however, needs careful preparation with an expert from inside the organization. A third possibility is to present some linkage research as in Figure 12.14. Linkage research is usually most effective in communicating to managers that the ES data are not just soft measures that belong to HR. Yet, linkage research is also difficult because "outside" data that could be matched to the ES data of reasonably small organizational units are often not accessible. In that case, one may simply show a chart from one's archives to make the point that attitudes are correlated with hard business variables. Indeed, in one large company, the CEO asked us to simply show Figure 12.11 in the ES presentation, and comment verbally on its meaning.

Monday Morning Action Platforms

Before ending the presentation with general conclusions that always require time before they lead to concrete actions, one should identify some platforms that offer the individual manager a chance to make use of the survey results without much additional planning, complex coordination, or deep thinking. One recipe that always works in this regard it to drill down from the overall trends to smaller organizational units in order to make clear that there is considerable variance underneath these statistics. Even if everything looks fine on average, one will usually find poor results for single subgroups. The reverse is also true—poor overall results do not imply that all subgroups have the same poor scores. Demonstrating the existence of such scatter for a few important topics often stimulates managers to carefully study their reports to find such cases, and then discuss with subordinate managers why certain subgroups in their areas of responsibility are "so good" or "so far behind" (see Figure 13.3 for a case).

Summary and Recommendations

To end an ES presentation, one can simply summarize the survey's findings (participation rate, satisfaction values, important performance bottlenecks and opportunities, etc.). In fact, one should consider finishing each of the above sections with a brief summary and even with a tentative conclusion of what these findings mean for the company. This also helps to more clearly structure the presentation for the audience in terms of topics.

Survey presentations always implicitly suggest or discourage certain fields of action by way of the analyses, the interpretations, and the theorizing that they make or that they do not make, respectively. But should one also make an *explicit* suggestion on what to do? Recommendations are sometimes requested by management. In the simplest form, they come at the end of the presentation: "What would you recommend to do?" When asked ahead of time to conclude the presentation with recommendations, the expert should be cautious. He or she is not a manager, and recommendations should promote specific operational and strategic goals that are, in the end, known to the managers only. To reduce the risk of recommending something that is not fitting, the expert should discuss his or her recommendations with the CEO, the survey sponsor, or the HR director before presenting it to the entire management group. The recommendations can thus be made more differentiated, possibly supported with more data analysis, and better linked to the particular business objectives. But then the recommendations become, at least in part, the recommendations of the respective managers, and it would be proper for the expert to only present the analyses *and then hand over the discussion to these managers*. It is quite risky for the expert to present these recommendations as his or her own conclusions, because they never follow directly from the survey results.

Moreover, it may be quite sufficient to identify a few (one to three, say) issues that seem the most promising areas of focus for actions. Indeed, the entire presentation should converge on such areas so that these recommendations appear completely natural and obvious. To actually recommend concrete actions, in contrast, is quite risky, unless these recommendations have been carefully discussed with the survey sponsor or the CEO before the presentation. An alternative is to prepare such recommendations together with a key manager, and then let this manager propose these actions at the end of the presentation. This also helps to see where the "research project" ends, and where management has to take over.

Any recommendation must, of course, be solidly anchored in the survey data. In addition, they should be action-oriented. Hence, a recommendation such as "Improve communication" is quite poor because it does not offer any hints on how to accomplish this goal, nor does it specify exactly what the goal is. On the other hand, recommending to "make use of the ideas that employees have on how to be more productive" is more useful. With this recommendation, any experienced manager would know to discuss this issue directly with subordinates.

An ES always allows many recommendations. Some of them are almost always valid (such as "improve communication") and, hence, trivial in a way: One need not run an expensive survey to arrive at such insights. So, one should always search for at least one hidden performance driver, even it is likely that management will not easily accept it and ask many critical questions before seeing its value. Usually, such hidden performance drivers are detected not by looking at single items, but at a network of items and their structure. For example, one company's survey results revealed that items on suggesting improvements and proposing new ideas were not meaningfully correlated with items on performance appraisal and supervision. Because innovation was critical for this company, management decided that actions should be taken that would make being innovative and suggesting improvements an integral part of the notion of high employee performance.

What is most useful and stimulating in presentations to managers is to point to what "others" (other companies, other plants, other managers, etc.) have done when they encountered similar situations, if possible. Such cases always lead to a more concrete discussion. Managers check whether the reported solution is applicable for them too, or how it could be fitted into their context. Or they find reasons why this solution does not work for them, but this too helps them to focus on proper actions.

One recommendation that the survey expert can always make is on the process that should be used to review the data and turn them into actions. If the presentation has been introduced in the context of systematic follow-up processes, closure can be achieved by returning the audience to specific recommendations that address how important findings can be highlighted in staging the management response.

Still Other Forms of Structuring an ES Presentation

The methods discussed above for structuring an ES presentation are, of course, not the only ways to set up such a presentation. One can use them as prototypes, as starting points, and change them according to what seems most promising in the given context. For example, it sometimes makes more sense to begin with recommendations, and then state that the rest of the presentation will be conducted as a data-based and theoretical explanation of these recommendations.

Another principle to structure the presentation is to base it on the project goals as they are written down in the project's positioning. This sometimes can be a safe retreat if, for example, a new HR director takes over during the ES project. Such a new manager often wants to change things, and so he may endlessly criticize directions and details that appear to stem from his predecessor. If this threatens to stalemate the project, a safe fall-back position is to structure the presentation along the goals that were defined for the project by the executive board.

Still other forms are possible. In one large automobile production site, management asked to organize the items of the questionnaire not along the usual job satisfaction dimensions but in categories that were derived from their new vision statement. That is, rather than addressing working conditions, pay and benefits, direct supervisor and so on, the questionnaire placed the items into item blocks labeled as openness, quality, innovation, etc. Naturally, because management wanted to get employees to think in these categories, they also wanted to structure the results in this fashion. Hence, it was asked in the ES presentation what the survey had to say about the employees' attitudes and opinions most relevant for openness, quality, innovation, etc.

13.2 The ES Presentation Process

Good slides and a convincing story are important for the success of an ES presentation, but they are not sufficient. One must also hold the presentation so that management "buys in", and one typically needs to coordinate the presentation with a number of key players from within the organization.

Aligning the Final Presentation with Key Managers

ES experts can usually prepare a solid ES presentation on the basis of substantive know-how and experience gained in many survey projects. However, before actually holding the presentation, one must often pass a number of important gatekeepers before getting the permission to present a particular presentation to management. Even if the presenter is given unconditional access to management, it often pays to test the intended presentation with some key managers before actually staging it before the executive board. Feedback should be sought on how convincing the presentation's story line is to management, where more or deeper statistical analysis is needed, and where the presentation tends to get boring for managers. For example, in one case where the presentation was shown and discussed with one top manager, it became apparent that the executive board was particularly interested to see whether employees with different types of contracts also differed in their opinions and attitudes. Hence, all items were scrutinized for such differences and the findings were included into the presentation. In another case, our "test manager" repeatedly asked how the results related to trust in upper management and how they differed from those of other companies. This was important information for bettering the presentation in this respect by searching for appropriate benchmarks and by studying how management trust was related to other items in this and in other companies.

Testing the presentation also allows one to discuss tactical issues. Benchmarks, for example, can be chosen in different ways. In one company, we discussed the presentation with the CEO. He wanted benchmarks from "high performance" companies only to set high goals and to fight complacency. Another example is agreeing on how to present the conclusions and recommendations. That is, where the presenter should normally end his or her part, and where and how the CEO or some other top manager should take over the agenda. One may even plan the staging of key moments in the presentation. For example, the CEO may ask certain questions at time t, and the presenter then responds "spontaneously" with relevant statistics or even with recommendations that the CEO, in turn, can use as a stepping stone for his or her agenda. A similar agreement should be reached on what to do after the presentation of the survey results, in particular on the time-line of decisions and actions. If these are not well prepared, experience shows that either the entire structure of the follow-up processes is at risk or that management decides on "something" rather spontaneously just to keep things going.

Another purpose of such a pre-presentation is, of course, to simply inform key managers ahead of time about the main findings so that they are not surprised in the main presentation by the results. They are also given a chance to think about the results and the time line of the follow-up processes. So, when it comes to the main presentation, they are much more in control of things, having at least an idea of what they consider appropriate responses to the ES results.

Pre-presentations, however, also carry considerable risks that one should be aware of. The persons in the "test audience" sometimes want to change or even distort the results. For example, they may insist that certain negative results are "not important" and that they should not be presented; that the results are generally presented too negatively; or that the conclusions should be aligned with what management wants to do anyway. A particularly difficult person to deal with in pre-presentations is often the project manager: He often wants to act as a final decision maker, changing the presentation in various ways because "management" would not understand or would not be interested in certain arguments. However, this person is rarely ever a top manager or an ES expert him- or herself. Thus, one has to find a way to preserve the presentation's professionalism. In one particular case, the project manager argued that using a presentation structured along the PS motor would be too complicated for management, but when we used it anyway, management greatly appreciated this approach and asked for similar presentations at lower levels. Additionally, new managers and HR directors are often critical of goals and directions that one has set with their predecessors, claiming that they are irrelevant or not fitting with the "new" perspectives. This can make life very difficult for the ES presenter. Sometimes, the only rescue in this case is to fall back onto the "official" goals formulated in the ES positioning. They can always be used to structure the presentation.

Some of these risks can be reduced by carefully explaining the purpose of the pre-presentation to the test audience. This is always necessary vis-à-vis the ES project manager, because this person has to arrange for the meetings with the relevant test audience, the CEO, or other top managers.

Global Management Decisions as Input to the Follow-Up Processes

An ES presentation always converges onto a point where management has to make some decisions on its own responses to the survey results and on areas of focus assigned to managers and organizational units. In the typical top-down follow-up processes, these decisions are important for different reasons. First, when reporting survey results in organizational units further down in the hierarchy, employees typically want to know what their management, in particular the executives, had to say about these results and what they decided to do about the findings. Second, areas of focus are task assignments for managers, because they are expected to study the relevant issues and, if necessary, respond with actions. Hence, a top-down design for the follow-up processes usually assumes that the next-lower level must not begin its activities before some guiding decisions have been made by upper management (see Figures 11.1 and 11.2).

The problem is that top management is often slow in its decision making. It also does not want to be pressured to make decisions at the end of an ES presentation on the spot. Rather, most top managers usually want more time to think about the results, study their own reports, and possibly discuss everything once more before supporting any global decision—often without agreeing on a clear time line. This is, to some extent, a rational strategy because each manager first wants to know what benefits for his or her goals are likely to result from any global decision before supporting it.

Even during the presentation, some managers tend to be inquisitive in that they always want to know precisely to what extent any overall result also holds for "their" parts of the organization. The presenter can either point out that everyone of these top managers will get a detailed report with all this information immediately after the presentation, or one can distribute to each manager a report where all items are cross-compared over divisions and/or levels as part of the presentation material before the presentation so that they can look up such statistics during the presentation. With this material, managers typically ask for fewer details, and they tend to feel less "manipulated" towards particular conclusions by the presenter.

Overcoming Typical Psychological Barriers

Few managers are experts on psychology. It is normal during presentations that they pull all kinds of counter-arguments that challenge the results and their interpretation, in particular if the results are "negative." If the expert does not succeed in answering them well, the presentation will have no impact. Here are some common examples, together with generic answers:

1) Argument: "What the employees said is objectively wrong!" (Or: "The employees do not know what really counts.") Answer: "The employees' perception

is their reality[52]—they will act based on what they perceive to be real. ES data reliably predict certain behaviors. For example, scientific research has found that job satisfaction is a good predictor of absenteeism, and this is objectively measurable! If it is not true what the employees believe, then you may have a communication problem."

2) Argument: "The employees did not understand these items!" Answer: "Not likely. The questionnaire was carefully pretested. If you are interested, you can have the report of these pretests."

3) Argument: "The employees did not take the survey seriously. They randomly checked the answer boxes." Answer: "Not likely. The survey data exhibit many form of internal consistency that also make sense. For example, one can predict a person's response to item X from his or her response on item Y. Random variables are not (systematically) correlated among each other."

4) Argument: "Trivial. I could have told you this in advance." Answer: "Maybe true in your case, but management's mean prognoses of the survey results are off target for many items. The predictions of different managers also scatter substantially. Moreover: Now you know what you only assumed so far."

5) Argument: "More analysis is needed!" Answer: "Do not fall into the paralysis-through-analysis trap. We have seen this often in practice: The main issues are usually clear, and more and more analyses do not change the picture." (But also: Show some typical data breakdowns ahead of time, such as tenure groups, or functions. This information is useful to avoid simplistic conclusions.)

6) Argument: "There is nothing we can do. It's the circumstances, the market, and other things beyond our control." Answer: "It is important to see the whole picture, but it is hardly ever true that management cannot do anything."

7) Argument: "The employees' responses are extra negative on purpose, so that we give them what they really want: More money." Answer: "The results show no outliers from the normal benchmark patterns. That makes strong distortions in certain domains unlikely. Also, the item intercorrelations would be affected by local distortions, but deeper data analyses show that the data are highly consistent and interlocked in patterns that are so complex that no one would be able to generate them by consciously producing particular answers."

8) Argument: "I'd like to know who said that! Can you identify these persons?" Answer: "We just focus on trends, not on single individuals. A few outliers do not affect these trends very much. Also, remember that we guaranteed to treat the data confidentially. All statistics are based on at least N persons."

9) Argument: "It is all so terrible. I am deeply depressed." Answer: "Do not get stuck in depression. Focus on what you can do. The employees are less interested in your feelings than in your actions."

10) Argument: "There is an error in your Table X. How can we know that there are not more errors? Come back some other time with a more professional analysis!" Answer: "Attacking the messenger is no solution. We checked everything, but

---

[52] One often says that "perception is reality.". This means that "peoples' level of motivation, affective states, and actions are based more on what they believe than on what is objectively true" (Bandura, 1997, p. 2).

the presentation slides are made 'by hand', and so an error may occasionally occur. The computer-generated reports are 100% error-free." (Recommendation: Check and double-check everything. Even minor formatting or spelling errors can massively damage the effect of the presentation. What counts, in the end, is your credibility and your track record in the company. If they are good, minor errors become 'exceptions' of no significance.)

13.3 Adding Punch to the Presentation

Presentations of survey results can be quite boring, reporting one percentage value after another. They can also be a firework of gimmickry, exhibiting impressive statistical modeling in animated multimedia displays, for example[53]. In both cases, little is typically accomplished in terms of enabling and motivating management to set up a set of effective responses to the survey. We here describe a few recipes that have been developed and tested successfully in numerous presentations.

Positioning the Presentation in the Context of the Follow-Up Processes

Presentations typically accomplish little if management does not clearly understand the plan of the follow-up processes and its role in them. In particular, they should see the general design of these processes (as shown Figure 11.1, for example) and the plan of the feedback presentations at the next-lower levels, together with concrete dates. In large companies, there can be dozens of such presentations that involve an immense planning effort. For example, in one large supply company, the ES presentation to the executive board was followed with a similar presentation to the group's international works council the next day and with local presentations to its six major market units (each with an executive board presentation, a senior management workshop, and a presentation to the works council) within two weeks in different countries and languages. Then, within another three weeks, similar clusters of presentations (some combined with workshops and additional support activities) were given to some 30 business units within these market units, all in different locations. The executive management should know this plan to understand that it cannot easily be changed. Also, at least one key manager must be a strong supporter of sticking to this plan.

Avoid Wasting Time on Side Issues

The time allotted to a survey presentation is always too short. Yet, a long presentation would not necessarily be more effective. The solution is focusing. The presenter must

---

[53] Any information that is *not* important for the particular audience should be avoided because it contributes to information overflow. This not only means that one should carefully consider what to report, but also how to report it. Often, presentation slides are highly artistic, with many colors, fonts, animation effects etc. This may look pretty, but it often clutters the charts and makes them more difficult to read (Wilkinson, 1990).

avoid getting sidetracked with minor issues. A typical time waster is the return rate of the survey. If the return rate is high or normal, congratulate the survey's sponsor and management to having such an engaged workforce, and then turn to the survey results. Only if the return rates are low should some time be allotted to this issue, but it should be as short as possible. The pending question is to what extent the results are representative: "Is this what the employees really feel and think?" Or, expressed differently: "Are the results biased?"

A partial answer is provided by comparing the sample's demographics with the demographics of the population. This may show that nonresponse is higher among certain subgroups so that these subgroups are underrepresented in the results. Such information can help in estimating the bias of overall results. For example, if blue collar workers are underrepresented, then the overall results should be too positive, because blue collar workers are normally less satisfied than white collar employees. However, such a bias effect is not likely to be very pronounced (see Table 7.4), although that is difficult to compute with precision.

Low response rates can lead to radical proposals such as throwing away the whole survey. In one case, only 36% of the employees participated in the ES. On the other hand, those who responded still added up to some 110,000 employees. So, one can ask whether it would be wise to simply ignore what that many engaged employees said. After all, a presidential election is not invalid just because many citizens did not bother to cast their votes: The ones who did determine the course of the future, and to build actions on data provided by those employees who cared to voice their opinions seems not only fair but also appropriate. Hence, one should point out that how one wants to respond to low response rates in the ES context is to a large extent a political decision.

As to the statistical aspects of low response rates, it important to note what Rogelberg et al. (2003) found: Most non-respondents are simply too passive to participate, but have the same attitudes and opinions as respondents. Only some 15% of the total sample consisted of purposeful ("active") non-respondents. And it is only them who differ somewhat from respondents (their attitudes are slightly more negative, and they are slightly less conscientious, for example). Also, early respondents do not differ from later respondents (Borg & Tuten, 2003): As later respondents are almost non-respondents, this too indicates that biases, if they exist, are likely to be small.

Item non-response is a related problem. Employees who skip some of the demographic items in an ES assess management more negatively, for example (Borg et al., 2008; Borg, 1991). Yet, although significant, the differences are not very pronounced. Item non-response in content items shows no systematic relation to other content items (Borg & Treder, 2003). Thus, from what we currently know, the bias induced by non-response is not large enough to warrant lengthy discussions.

There is also no simple interpretation of the return rate as such. To see this, consider two opposing interpretations from one company. The CEO took a low response rate as a sign that the employees are highly satisfied ("There was no reason for them to participate."), while the work's council concluded just the opposite ("Voting by refusing to vote"). It should suffice to point out such findings, and then proceed with the presentation, concentrating on the data one has, not speculating on the meaning of data one does not have.

Comparing return rates across organizational units is not that simple either. What must be taken into account is the mode of the survey. Different modes such as a mail survey sent to the employee's home address or a survey administered in a group session have different typical response rates (Borg, 2003; Borg & Faulbaum, 2004). What also matters is the type of employees surveyed (blue/white collar, education, gender, etc.) or the country, but also technical matters (e.g., correcting or not correcting for "net" return rates) and psychological factors such as the respondents' experience with previous surveys or their personalities (Dillman, 2000).

Another element that tends to consume too much time in a survey presentation is benchmarking. Initially, benchmarks are often interpreted rather naively. First, there are many types of benchmarks (global mean values, top scores, means of best-of-class companies, $x\%$ thresholds, minimal values, etc.). Second, what matters a lot are the samples on which these values are based (what companies, which industries, what countries, when surveyed, etc.). Benchmarks in organizational surveys are never representative in a survey sampling sense, even if based on very large samples. Once such issues are pointed out to management, benchmarks are typically taken for what they are worth: They offer a first and simple way to approach data interpretation.

Avoid Over-Interpretation

Presenters of survey results often make mistakes that can easily be avoided. One such mistake is to excessively use evaluative labels such as "good" or "bad." The problem with such labels is that the presenter rarely knows with certainty what is good or bad for a particular company. Consider the case of one ES where employees very much supported the item that their job will change a lot in the future. This seems "good" because everyone knows that change is the only constant thing in these turbulent times. However, top management did not agree with this evaluation at all because they said the work of most employees would not change for many years to come. Hence, if the employees expect a lot of change which never comes, they may feel that management is not doing its job or that their job is at risk. In another case, 10% of the employees felt that bureaucracy was a problem in their work environment. By German benchmarks, this seems like a "good" sign, but is it necessarily good in terms of business success? Not necessarily, because bureaucracy may actually be quite high in this company, but the employees are used to it and consider it "normal."

When it comes to the interpretation of the ES results, the owners of the data should always have the last word. The owners are the persons who generated the data and the persons who are responsible for transforming the results into responses and actions. These data are "their" data, not the expert's data. The expert has benchmarks, theories, methods, and experience with similar data, but he or she is not an expert on the insides of the company. Thus, the expert can only suggest certain interpretations, and hope that discussing them with the data owners makes them meaningful and useful.

Interpretations, moreover, are never unique. Managers, works councils, shop-floor employees, and many other groups can interpret the statistics differently. Even comparing these statistics with those of other companies does not change the situation because whether the statistics look "good" or "bad" often depends on which companies generated the benchmarks (and at what times). Even comparing the results to those of a previous survey can be quite difficult upon closer scrutiny. It often turns out that so much has changed—organizational units are regrouped, the business has changed, the markets are up/down, the strategy has been modified—that one must be very careful comparing actual with old data. Similar context effects need to be taken into account in any evaluation. If some 60%, say, of the employees trust their executives in a situation of downsizing the company, then this would be a truly impressive result, while the same 60% in times of rapid growth should be considered rather normal.

13.4 Motivating Managers to Act

One goal of any ES presentation should always be to motivate managers to "do something with the data" and to spark actions, in particular. There is no fail-safe method to accomplish this, but experience has shown that a few tricks almost always work.

Motivating Managers to Get Involved

A powerful element in a management presentation is to show at least one example that relates survey results to hard business data. We illustrated such a linkage example in Figure 12.11 where the sickness rates of various workgroups were plotted against their responses to an item from the ES. The relationship is obviously strong, and invites managers to speculate causally what drives what. Such relationships can be made even more impressive if they are formulated in terms of dollars. In the words of one manager: "This is when I realized how hard the soft factors really are!" This manager also knew what to do: Go to the various workgroups, find out what they did in the high/low workgroups, and then act on it.

To find hard data that can be used to demonstrate such relationships is not always easy. Anonymous survey data, for example, cannot be broken down to the individual level. Moreover, performance data are rarely available for smaller workgroups. However, it usually suffices to demonstrate the soft-hard relations *with just one example* to convince management that the survey data are serious information.

Another recipe to generate more involvement is using prognoses. We always ask top managers before the survey to predict the results of the survey for some important items. Some of these predictions are typically quite wrong, but even if their means are on target, their scatter is always substantial. This scatter usually makes an even bigger impression on managers. The main function of predictions is that they reduce apparent obviousness of the survey results. Indeed, just seeing the predictions of other persons has the effect that survey results appear more interesting and less obvious. They are also better remembered by those who make predictions (Borg & Hillenbrand, 2003).

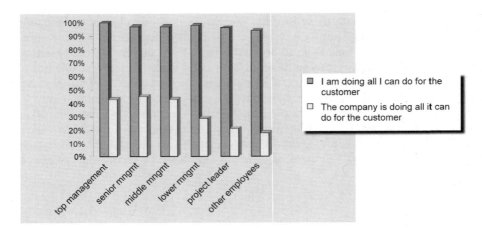

Figure 13.2. *Yes%* statistics for two items and six hierarchical strata in a German logistics company.

Yet another motivator in survey presentations is to confront management with some of their own results. Figure 13.2 shows a striking example from a large European logistics company. Two items are compared here: "I am doing all I can do for the customer" and "The Company is doing all it can do for the customer." Not surprisingly, the employees at all levels of the hierarchy endorsed the first item strongly, but not the second one. What is surprising is that the endorsement of the second item is equally low at all levels of the hierarchy, from rank-and-file employees all the way up to top management. When this result was shown to top management, confusion set in: "Who is the company?" However, this confusion and discussion was generated intentionally as part of the presentation plot. The plot continued by providing an answer to this seemingly odd result. Further data analysis showed poor scores on a variety of cooperation issues, so that it became clear that this company suffered from a common productivity paradox: Non-alignment of efforts. The presentation was set up not only to show this problem in numbers, but also to demonstrate to management that they were part of the problem.

Managers can also be motivated by reporting what other companies have done in similar situations. Indeed, managers often ask this question, sometimes in terms of "best practices". This does not mean that they want to copy the responses of others. Rather, such input serves to stimulate their thinking: What is the basic idea of these responses? To what extent can we learn from this? How successful was this response anyway? What can we do to make this work in our environment?

Building Platforms for Immediate Actions

Analyses and interpretations as those discussed above should converge on a few (i.e., one to three) topics that suggest powerful actions or at least promising responses.

However, rarely do they also give the individual manager a concrete hint on what to do with the ES results on "Monday morning." The responses that top management considers first have to be discussed in more detail, and action plans may have to be developed, coordinated, and decided. The first presentation of the ES results typically does not lead to more than a few preliminary decisions on some rather general fields of action.

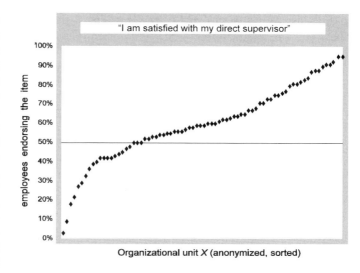

Figure 13.3. Satisfaction with direct supervisor in 76 (anonymized) organizational units.

If, however, the presentation contains a plot such as the linkage chart in Figure 12.11 and if the manager is in charge of some of the workgroups depicted in this chart, he may know what to do on Monday morning, namely have a meeting with subordinate managers on this finding, or meet with the manager of each workgroup one-on-one to discuss these results and to agree on actions. Yet, such a diagram is difficult to produce and often takes time.

Fortunately, there are simpler ways to analyze the ES data with the goal in mind to give the individual manager a platform for action on Monday morning that speaks for itself and that motivates him/her to do something with the data. One recipe is looking at the statistical scatter below the main trends (i.e., the variance among different groups). Consider Figure 13.3. The chart exhibits the percentages of those employees in 76 different workgroups who are satisfied with their supervisors. A chart like this automatically triggers certain reactions from almost any manager. The most obvious one is noticing the unit at the low end of the distribution (i.e., the one where almost no employee is satisfied with his or her supervisor). Managers first ask: "What workgroup is this one? Who is this supervisor?" and then possibly also "Should I fire this supervisor?" When looking more closely, they may also wonder about the workgroups where the satisfaction with their supervisors is at extremely high levels. Certainly, 100% seems a bit too high. Then, some discussion sets in about the workgroups with such extreme scores, and often also about the context of these results ("How comparable is this? What other data are there?"). In any case, the plot makes managers eager to get their own reports to check how the workgroups in their area of responsibility rate their supervisors. The plot, thus, motivates them to study and discuss the ES results, and to do something with them. The survey expert should show how this motivation can be used efficiently and effectively, and what mistakes should be avoided (see Section 11.4). In the end, managers typically decide to discuss the ES results with all subordinate managers in one workshop, and also with each direct report individually in order to set goals for improvement and plan appropriate actions. This is "normal" leadership behavior, and the scatter plot in Figure 13.2 directly leads and supports such behavior by providing a particular motivation and focused data.

Comparisons are, of course, also sensitive information and should be handled with care. The guiding principle is that the responsible manager should be present when it comes to his or her workgroup and should be given a chance to explain the context of the data. He or she should also see the results for his or her unit prior to the superior manager to have a chance to digest this report. If not, comparisons can easily lead to defensive behavior and to bitterness ("unfair") that stalemates all further processes. If these conditions are not satisfied, then comparisons should be made without identifying the units (as in Figures 10.3 or 10.4).

One final recommendation for inspiring post-survey activity is to plan for the inclusion of a survey item such as: "Please describe the action taken since the prior survey: (1) Results were not discussed; (2) No action was taken; (3) Action failed to address key issues; (4) Action somewhat addressed key issues; (5) Action directly addressed key issues; (6) I don't know/NA."

Among companies who have used such a survey item, a consistent pattern emerges where surveys scores are increasingly more positive as responses to this item increase from 1 through 5. This strong positive correlation may not necessarily prove that good actions were planned, executed, and communicated to employees, because employees with positive attitudes might perceive, remember, or even create examples of action addressing key issues (see Chapter 17). Regardless, the message to leaders is straightforward: Managers who do nothing will most likely not receive better scores. Moreover, just knowing that actions will be evaluated in the next ES automatically leads to relevant activities.

14 Employee Survey Workshops

Employee polls and benchmarking surveys normally end by presenting the results to top management. In other types of employee surveys, one wants to continue working systematically with the data. The main work horse for doing this is the "feedback workshop," (Nadler, 1977; Morgan, 1993) which typically does a lot more besides feeding back the results of the ES to the employees. Almost always, these results are discussed and sorted so that action planning can begin. We, therefore, prefer to use the more general term "ES workshop" for such sessions. In smaller companies, ES workshops often cover the entire workforce. That is, each workgroup conducts such an ES workshop. In larger companies, ES workshops often are conducted with representative samples of the total population. In any case, ES workshops are a considerable investment of staff and resources—they should be carefully designed.

14.1 Foundations of ES Workshops

There are a variety of ways to design an ES workshop, and they tend to be run differently in the US as compared to Europe. Yet the fundamental purpose of the ES workshop remains constant across most situations: namely, to clarify the gap between the current state and the ideal state. The survey is used as the catalyst for dialogue with employees to reveal specific definitions and examples of what "ideal" looks like. Figure 1.3 shows a scene from an ES workshop in a German company. The person standing at the front side of the room is the facilitator. He is presenting the results of the ES, and helps the group in discussing and structuring the issues related to them. The workshop participants typically all belong to the same workgroup.

The Basic Goals of an ES Workshop

The basic goals of the workshop facilitator are these (Figure 14.1):

1) Together with the workshop participants, answer the question "Where are we now?" Begin by feeding back the ES results to the participants. Facilitate a discussion of the results that aims at clarifying the issues and sorting them into substantive clusters so that meaningful *problem stories* can be identified. The participants have to re-contextualize the survey statistics by complementing them with qualitative information that makes clear what exactly the problem is, who is responsible, why it is important, etc.

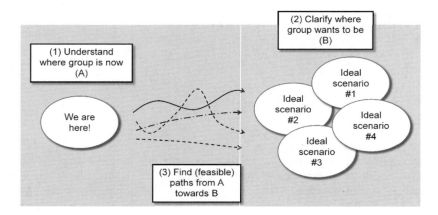

Figure 14.1. Basic goals of an ES workshop.

2) Identify *ideal scenarios* for the various issues. Given the problem stories, the workshop group develops ideas on where it wants to be. These ideas should be formulated without paying attention to side constraints such as money and time. Their sole purpose is to generate goals that guide later action planning. For example, if the workshop concludes that the employees do not get the information they need to do a good job, any action planner must understand what would be "ideal" in this regard. It would help to know that the employees consider the situation ideal when information is simple, updated weekly, sorted by content, weighted by strategic importance, and always available in the intranet by hitting the "F7" key.

3) If the present situation is clear and if ideal scenarios are available, action plans can be worked out that move things in the desired direction as far as this is possible under the given side constraints of time, money, and quality requirements.

Feedback, Discussion, and Explanations

ES workshops should be designed in such a way that they make the transition from the survey results to powerful actions as easy as possible. This requires, first of all, that the "voice of the employees" becomes as clear as possible. Hence, an ES workshop's primary task is to discuss the survey results and make them as understandable as possible by *adding* specific context and concrete details to the survey's statistics. After the workshop, the participants should have a clear and common notion about the present situation.

ES workshops are the most effective form of feeding back the ES results because they do not simply pour statistics onto the employees, but they invite them to get actively involved in understanding and even improving this information by adding explanations and details. The survey may show, for example, that the employees are relatively low on satisfaction with their chances for advancement, but what exactly this means for the members of a particular workgroup, function, or culture is not that clear. Other items and further data analysis may give some answers, but asking the employees directly to explain this finding can yield the most convincing information. In other cases, asking the employees is, in fact, the only way to better understand the survey results. The employees, for example, typically indicate that they could be much more productive "given certain changes in their working environment." To find out what these "certain changes" are, one simply has to ask them. Such a probing into the reasons for the statistical results not only leads to further data and insights, but discussing these inputs in the group also leads to shared understanding and convergence of the various ideas and points-of-views of the group members. In the end, the ES workshop should make clear how "the group" perceives the situation and not just every single individual. The open discussion, together with visible recordings of the group's inputs, also means that the workshop's outcomes take on an "official" character that sets a reliable starting point for planning actions.

Proposals for Solutions

Although some authors recommend using ES workshops to discuss solutions or to ask the participants to make proposals for solutions (Dunham & Smith, 1979; Hellriegel et al., 1992), our experience shows that looking for solutions before carefully considering problem definitions can create ineffective responses. Consider that even the term "solution" can lead to a narrow focus on problems where action is needed. This, in turn, encourages a repair mentality, a near-sighted search for fire extinguishing. It would be better to search for *opportunities* where actions—whether they solve a problem or whether they take advantage of chances—are most promising in terms of the given operational and strategic goals.

Folkman (1996, p. 40) adds another important consideration that also deals with premature attention to solutions: "Often people find the issue that appears most negative and conclude it is the most important issue to change. This is faulty logic. Issues that are most negative or most complained about are simply the ones that are most noticeable. Evaluating what issues to change ought to be a completely separate decision-making process, independent from how negatively people react to issues."

Another reason to avoid asking for solutions is that solutions are often made before it is clear exactly what issue they are supposed to solve, how this issue is interconnected to other issues, what other issues need to be taken care of, and what resources are available. A simple example from practice is the following. The employees in one workgroup requested larger hard disks for their personal computers. When the computers were checked, however, it turned out that all of them were overloaded with unneeded files. Thus, what seemed necessary was better data management and software support rather than new hardware. However, things need not be that obvious. Porras (1987, p. 143f.) reports the following example: "Often a situation in which costs are out of control may be stated as 'Need a system to control costs'. This way of presenting the problem is simply a solution—a cost control system—disguised as a problem statement. Put in this manner, the normal action would be to create a new cost control system. Other alternatives, some of which may be more appropriate to the situation, exist, but are essentially blocked out because of the way the problem has been stated. If, on the other hand, the problem was described as 'Costs are out of control,' then this would open up a new set of possible actions, only one of which is to create a cost control system. It is safe to say that the great preponderance of inappropriately stated problems is of this form. Organization members are so action oriented that they often see problems in the form of preconceived solutions and are not aware of the limitations this places on their abilities to generate the best solution for any given situation."

One final consideration in determining the amount of ES workshop time devoted to potential solutions is the degree to which the survey results were expected. Occasionally, survey scores call out a problem that is both well known and understood by management. In this case spending time discussing the problem would not be as meaningful as discussing what, if anything, can be done to improve the situation. However, such a discussion needs to include management's priorities for action given limited time and resources. Ending any ES workshop with a list of proposed solutions can generate expectations that they will be implemented as quickly as possible. Under these circumstances, any change or delay will likely exacerbate the problem as employees wonder "Why doesn't management do what we suggested to do?" For all these reasons we typically recommend separating feedback of results from proposed solutions.

Alignment

Another function of ES workshops is to align the different ES processes. If every workgroup focuses on "its" problems only, and each group can decide what to do when, the ES follow-up processes are not likely to have real impact for the organization as a whole. This can be true even if each workgroup works hard on improvements because each group may pull into a different direction. ES workshops should therefore be coordinated in some way. The most effective method is that top management defines certain fields of action as task assignments for all organizational units. Each of the units (or their managers) must then plan, implement, and report appropriate improvement actions. A milder requirement is that each org unit must turn its attention to certain areas of focus—usually issues where the ES resulted in very poor results—and consider actions in case that the unit's results are as poor as they are in general. This at least forces each unit to carefully consider that issue, and thus helps to align the organization's focus of attention.

Alignment, however, can be oversimplified. For example, if a software company's executive team selects innovation as its top priority for post-survey action, one might expect to see all units across functional areas paying careful attention to employee responses to the innovation and risk taking questions in the ES. Yet a better way to coordinate efforts across units would be to consider each unit's *unique potential* to improve the company's innovation. For the HR function to contribute, its managers may focus on the speed and execution questions in the ES so that they can improve recruitment and selection of new R&D talent. For the sales and services functions, their managers may focus on the questions pertaining to customer feedback so that the company can develop more relevant, sellable products. Given this specific desired outcome for the company, perhaps only the R&D employees would spend a tremendous amount of time discussing results from the innovation and risk taking questions. Alignment, therefore, does not necessarily mean identical action areas.

14.2 Typical Design of an ES Workshop

The following section outlines a general approach for conducting ES workshops. Yet, we realize that what constitutes a typical ES workshop in Europe is not the same as in the US. Likewise, a common format in one organization may not be the norm in another organization. Therefore, our "general" approach sometimes includes alternative techniques and philosophies. As always, one should choose or blend approaches that are most appropriate for his or her situation.

The optimal design for an ES workshop depends on a number of side constraints, such as the maximal time that is available to run the workshop; restrictions on what can be spent for the workshop (to hire an external facilitator, to book a room etc.); the organizational feasibility to gather the particular group of participants at a given time in a certain location; the level of skills and know-how of the participants to successfully conduct a particular type of workshop; the organizational culture that implies certain expectations and success criteria for the workshop; or the quality of the facilitator who is available for running the workshop.

Some large organizations in the US use broad communications (e.g., a memo, newsletter, video conference) to relay overall survey results, and then rely on a series of workshops taking place down the organizational hierarchy, potentially down to the first level supervisors. Under this scenario, the survey director may work with the communication department to create a "meeting in a box" template, which consists of graphs, tables, company-wide priorities, and specific language to be used when explaining results and soliciting feedback. This approach works well when a limited amount of time can be spent with employees (perhaps 90 minutes or less), but it focuses more on sending out a consistent message than on collecting clarifications.

There is usually at least some subset of units where it is desirable to create more employee participation both as a means to improve management's understanding of the results and to create commitment to the subsequent changes necessary to improve the unit. This more elaborate workshop typically requires three hour's time and, to assure uninhibited dialogue, is usually facilitated by someone other than the immediate manager of the group. Indeed, the workshop design might include an additional 15 minutes to provide feedback to the manager of that group. The workshop itself can be organized into four phases. This is shown schematically in Figure 14.2 and described in more detail in Tables 14.1-14.4.

Phase I: Introduction

In the beginning of the workshop, the facilitator briefly introduces him- or herself to the participants, and explains the role of the facilitator as a catalyst for progress. The

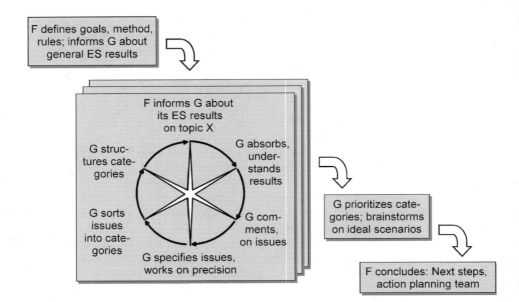

Figure 14.2. Phases and steps of a traditional ES workshop (F = facilitator, G = group of participants).

goals of the ES as they were communicated in the information campaign should then be highlighted to make clear that the workshop is but an element in a chain of activities that serve a clear purpose. It also helps at this point to show an overall project plan so that every participant sees where the workshop lies within the overall project plan. The goals of the workshop can then be defined within this context. They are to inform the participants about the survey results, discuss these results and improve them with additional information, identify where one could or should act, and prepare everything so that later action planning starts on an optimal foundation.

The facilitator then agrees with the participants on the rules for the workshop. Figure 14.3 shows an example for such rules. They are typically written on a poster that is hung on the wall so that it remains visible for everyone throughout the workshop. It also allows the facilitator to point at these rules if necessary (e.g., if a person consumes too much time with overly verbose comments). Additionally, a rough time table should be sketched that complements the rules. Time estimates for the workshop's phases are provided in Tables 14.1-14.4.

In the second section of the introduction phase, the facilitator presents the results of the survey that focus on the company as a whole and on large org units to which the workgroup belongs (e.g., subsidiary, department, function, or country). One typically begins by reporting the participation rates and some statistics on job satisfaction, morale, or commitment of the employees of these parts of the company. Other indices (e.g., perceptions of future success, top management, career development) can also be shown graphically as in Figure 10.6, which exhibits the proportion of em-

Table 14.1. A facilitator's check list of the introduction phase of an ES workshop.

Phase I: Introduction
Introduction (15 min.)
☐ Introduce yourself (Name, position, department; role in workshop: "I will lead you through this workshop").
☐ Time plan of ES project: Where is the ES project today?
☐ Explain goals of workshop.
☐ Explain and get agreement for rules of workshop. Hang poster with rules on the wall.
☐ Present time plan for workshop, ask one participant to act as the time keeper.
☐ (Ask one participant to record the discussions substantively.)
Feedback on general ES results (15 min.)
☐ Reminder: When was the employee survey conducted?
☐ Inform: Participation rates (global, major org units)
☐ Reminder: Format of items; answer scales
☐ Explain the statistics used to report the results (*Yes*%, mean…)
☐ Inform about ES results for "Overall, I am satisfied with [X]" items for the company as a whole and for the department to which the group belongs
☐ Inform about the ES results for the "Overall, I am satisfied with …" items for some strata of the organization (e.g. men vs. women, different functions, managers vs. shop-floor).
☐ Inform about top management's general responses to ES results, in particular about areas of focus and/or fields of actions (where this group must deliver), and other decisions (e.g., on global actions)

ployees satisfied with various main dimensions of their jobs (pay, supervisor, work itself etc.), together with some benchmarks.

However, one should choose this initial visual display carefully as it sets the stage for the rest of the workshop. At one global conglomerate based in the US, the corporate survey director was frustrated by the amount of time HR managers spent discussing the work-life balance index. Even though the score for this index had been consistent for 20 years (even before the use of fax machines, email, and cell phones) and was above external benchmarks, these managers insisted on giving high action priority to this topic. In retrospect we realized that we had been promoting the use of a graph that ranked the survey's many broad indexes by the percentage of favorable responses. Because of the wording used in the survey, the work-life balance index was always the lowest score on the list. Indeed, some survey topics will always produce lower favorability scores than others; in the US pay satisfaction is rarely above

> **Rules of the employee survey workshop**
> - Be brief, to the point, precise, clear, concrete, focus on facts
> - Do not use more than 3 to 5 key words per index card
> - Write legibly
> - Diagnosis comes first, proposals for solutions _may_ come later
> - Active involvement is desirable, but not mandatory
> - Time is limited: Everyone be brief, give others a chance too
> - Use time for important topics, not for side issues
> - Keep an eye on the time plan
> - Issues that do not get recorded will not be used in future discussions or planning
> - When discussing the survey results on the supervisor, the supervisor leaves the room
> - Comments on the supervisor must remain in this room
> - The participants are responsible for the results of the workshop, not the facilitator
> - Role of facilitator:
>   - Leads group through workshop
>   - Drives discussions through questions, suggestions (summaries, interconnections)
>   - Remains neutral, does not take sides
>   - Follows an "everyone must win" strategy
>   - Is not a technical specialist, no solution provider, but only a catalyst, a helper
> - Additional rules: _____

Figure 14.3. Poster with typical rules of an ES workshop.

55%, but positive perception of workgroup productivity is usually above 75%. Hence, a lower absolute score does not necessarily mean that an index should be interpreted as poor. However, nearly everyone who saw this graph assumed that the bottom index must be the worst score, and employees were quick to generate examples that supported this erroneous conclusion. Thus, our choice of a graph used to conduct feedback sessions had been inadvertently spreading a false message that work-life balance was terrible and deserved attention.

In order to call attention to more deserving survey topics, we focused on visual displays that ranked indexes by importance (i.e., their correlation with desired outcomes). Likewise, if top management decided on certain areas of focus or task assignments, then these decisions were communicated and integrated into the ES workshops. With this approach workshops get a certain common alignment, and the participants' contributions know what management expects them to do. Also, the participants are always interested to hear how management viewed the results and, in particular, what management intends to do.

Phase II: Discussing and Structuring the Results

In the main phase of the ES workshop, the participants concentrate on "their" results (i.e., the results of the particular focal group to which they belong). A simple way to proceed here is to work through the various item blocks or indices. Alternatively,

Table 14.2. Check list of discussion phase of an ES workshop for facilitator.

Phase II: Where are we?
Show results of group, discuss, clarify (1 hour + 45 min.)
☐ More to results of group: Inform about group's participation rate.
☐ Explain the benchmarks used for this group.
☐ Show results of group on overall satisfaction items. Possibly indicate what areas of focus they seem to suggest.
☐ Decide in which sequence item blocks should be discussed. Normally, proceed in the sequence of the questionnaire, block by block.
☐ Agree on time plan for rest of phase II. If items are discussed in order of questionnaire, use about 30 minutes for the item blocks "working conditions" to "workgroup and co-workers", then another 30 minutes for items on "supervisor", then another 30 minutes for rest.
☐ Use topic grinder: Work through item blocks in agreed order: Show results, discuss, make topics more concrete, clarify topics, collect comments that help to better understand results, order comments in content categories, structure the categories.

items that are most strategic to the organization's overarching improvement goals can be used to create a storyboard for the review of the survey. The facilitator begins by presenting the survey results (see Figure 14.4). The group then discusses these results, adds qualitative explanations if needed and if available, and finally sorts and structures its input. The topics and their survey results are processed through a "topic grinder" in order to lift them to a level of information that serves as a springboard for planning effective actions. Often charts that show the results for "overall satisfaction" questions or "outcome" questions (e.g., engagement, customer alignment) are useful as a summary of how the focal group fits into organization-wide trends and where it seems to have particular strengths or weaknesses.

The group then decides in which order the various topics should be presented and discussed. The default approach is to proceed from the more concrete, directly observable topics (working conditions, tasks and goals, recognition, etc.) to the more abstract topics (company as a whole, strategy, execution, etc.). This order is particularly useful when participants have seen this topic order in the ES questionnaire. They also find it easier to discuss the more concrete topics first. These topics, moreover, typically profit the most from additional qualitative input. For example, if the survey shows that the employees are critical about the tools they need for being productive, one must clarify what exactly these tools are and what exactly is wrong with them. This requires additional information that is specific and highly concrete. It is the responsibility of the facilitator to clarify the problem situation to an extent that persons who later get this information are in a position to directly begin work on action plans that are fully on target. In other words, action planners should not have to say: "I do not quite understand what the problem is. Let's ask the employees what they had in

Figure 14.4. Presenting ES results in an ES workshop.

mind and what they want." No questionnaire used in a general ES can ever collect this information by itself, not even if it contains specific open-ended questions. Topics that come later in the questionnaire such as strategy, on the other hand, typically do not profit much from such in-depth discussions. For example, if the survey says that the employees do not really understand the strategy or that they do not endorse it, not much information is gained by discussing this problem at length. On the contrary, such discussions can easily be counter-productive, ending with nothing but finger-pointing at "those managers up there who are too distant from the real business."

If the workshop works through the topics in the order of the questionnaire, it will typically consume about 45 minutes for the topics preceding "direct supervisor." Then, the workshop can focus on the direct supervisor for some 30 minutes, and finally address the rest of the topics in another 45 minutes.

In central Europe, the common way to organize such discussions is by using the card method. Its characteristic feature is that the participants write their comments onto cards which are then pinned onto boards (see Figure 14.5). At the beginning of the workshop, each participant gets a stack of such cards, plus a big felt-tip pen. The facilitator asks the participants to write their comments and explanations onto these cards (one card per comment, maximum three lines, written legibly, etc.). The cards are collected, repeatedly, by the facilitator, and sorted roughly by content. The facilitator then shows these cards, one by one, to the group (Figure 14.5). He or she also reads the card to the participants. Sometimes, the facilitator also asks what the card means, pointing out that the comments should be so clear that later action planners

Figure 14.5. Discussing ES results using the index card method.

know exactly what needs to be done. Finally, the facilitator pins the card to the board in a cluster of cards that all focus on the same issue. Headlines can be written for these clusters, and cards and clusters can be regrouped if better categories seem possible. In the end, the participants sort the resulting issues in terms of their importance (see Figure 14.6; after Oyler & Harper, 2007).

Normally, quite a few cards have to be re-written because their comments are too vague, ambivalent, illegible, or unintelligible. Figure 14.5 exhibits such a case. The facilitator here shows a card where someone wrote the comment "Peter principle." The facilitator—not understanding what that means or pretending not to understand what the comment is supposed to mean—asks the participants for help regarding this comment: "I don't understand. What does that refer to? Can we make this more concrete so that everyone who will later work with this information will understand it?" Often what happens then is that the person who wrote the card speaks up: "I wrote this comment. What I meant is this: ..." The facilitator then can ask the participant to re-write the card accordingly: "The clearer your comments, the better."

A good facilitator can achieve a lot using the card method. The trick is to drive the group to write and re-write cards that are as precise as possible, and by grouping and re-grouping the cards into clusters with headlines that are griping and that succinctly characterize a real issue. To express it differently: A facilitator has not succeeded if the workshop produces a potpourri of vague comments under ambiguous headlines, since this type of information does not serve as a solid foundation for action planning.

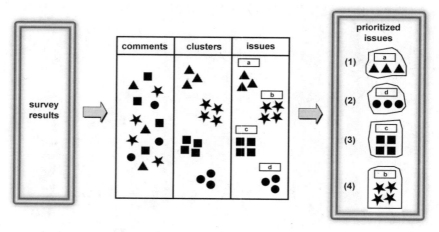

Figure 14.6. From survey results to prioritized issues.

To drive and motivate the participants to do their best is not an easy task. The facilitator must be highly awake, concentrated and critical, but also diplomatic in tone so that he or she is perceived as a person who is really working hard for the sake of the group. At the same time, the facilitator should strictly avoid making public his or her own ideas on what the problems "really" are or how to solve them. This sounds easier than it is, in particular if a facilitator runs a whole series of workshops. In that case, it becomes likely that the facilitator is tempted to suggest short-cuts or solutions for problems encountered before. The participants often view such suggestions as arrogant if they are not introduced properly as just suggestions that may be helpful.

Phase III: Action Fields and Ideal Scenarios

On the basis of a clear understanding of the topics, the workshop should turn towards actions. One needs to pay attention, though, not to confuse actions with extra activities or to focus actions on problems only. Often, the data show that everything is on course so that no extra activity is needed, except the activity that consists of reinforcing the given course. Moreover, the data may suggest opportunities for actions that were not anticipated. For example, the employees may say in the survey that they have many ideas on how to be more productive or how to better serve the customer. Managers often respond to such survey findings rather cynically: "That is what they always say! But if you ask, there is nothing concrete." Experience shows that this is indeed often true, but not always. (Good ideas, after all, are rare events.) Finally, certain fields of action may be given to the workgroup from above so that the workshop must prepare responses to these requests. For any kind of action field—problems that need to be attended to, opportunities for positive change, or specific action tasks from above—the last step before turning to planning actions should always be formulating visions of where one wants to be.

Table 14.3. Consolidating and concluding a traditional ES workshop.

Phase III: Action fields and ideal scenarios (III)
Action fields (20 min.)
☐ Inform group about top management's assigned areas of focus or fields of action (if there are any), establish connection to ES results of group. Remind group and its manager they must deliver on fields of action, and must be ready to justify their responses on areas of focus.
☐ Identify needs/chances for group-specific actions. Not more than 3 to 5 action fields, possibly cluster action fields under common headings.
Ideal scenarios (20 min.)
☐ Brainstorm on the group-specific action fields: Group should articulate what ideal scenarios they have in mind (costs, resources are irrelevant).
Phase IV: Next steps
Next steps (5 min.)
☐ Inform group on the next steps of the follow-up processes.
☐ Suggest to group to form an action team (with supervisor and employee X, Y...).

A practical approach to finding visions that can guide action planning is to brainstorm with the workshop participants ideal scenarios for the action fields. The starting point is the given situation as it is characterized by the survey data and the additional information gathered in phase II of the workshop. The group then concentrates on a particular topic and generates concrete descriptions of how the world *should* be like—without paying attention to the question how one could possibly get there and at what price. It is left to the action planning team to think about feasible solutions that will move the present situation into the desired directions.

Consider a typical case. Employee surveys often convey the complaint that employees are not properly informed about the company's strategy. Obviously, before planning an action on "better information" one must know what exactly the employees want to know and which ways of information delivery they have in mind. The question for a brainstorming session about the ideal scenario of being informed about the company's strategy could then be formulated as follows: "Imagine an ideal state of affairs where everything is perfect. What would then be true concerning 'information about the company's strategy'? What type of information would then be delivered to you in which form? What information would be accessible to you, and how? What are you dreaming of?"

Table 14.4. Finalizing a traditional ES workshop.

Phase V: Immediately after the ES workshop
Documentation
☐ Photograph posters with cards; pictures remain with person who takes the minutes.
Feedback for supervisors (30 min.)
☐ Facilitator informs supervisor about the discussion inputs of the participants. In case of several supervisors: inform one by one.
☐ The feedback of the participants is the perceptions of the group, not objective facts. Names (who said what) will not be reported.
☐ Begin with positive feedback.
☐ Then, negative feedback, critique, requests for improvements.
☐ Advise supervisor to thank group for feedback; tell them that she/he understands; that she/he will concentrate on one to three issues, etc. Hand out list with tips and hints (see Box 10).

Phase IV: Outlook on Next Steps

Finally, the facilitator brings the workshop to an end by giving a brief outlook onto what lies ahead. The natural next step is to think about responding to the given data situation. Decisions must be made and actions may be planned and implemented. An action planning team could be set up consisting of some participants of the workshop and the focal group's manager. Since the participants often do not want to commit themselves spontaneously to such extra work, the facilitator could directly ask particularly engaged (and constructive!) employees of the workshop to get together "next week" with the manager to define an action planning team. Another successful approach is to ask the group to nominate peers to work with the manager; the facilitator selects a representative group from this list and assures that those nominated are willing to serve. In practice, this defining team often becomes the action planning team, with a few possible additions or cancellations.

Phase V: Wrapping Things up After the Workshop

After the workshop, the facilitator or a particular participant of the workshop should document the results of the workshop. This is an easy task these days: All one needs to do is to take photographs of the various pin boards or the posters with their comment cards glued to them. These pictures can be uploaded to a computer and supplemented with a few notes about the workshop (date, time, participants, brief description of how the workshop went, special events during the workshop, etc.). The poster and comment cards should then be *completely removed* and not be left in the room.

Persons who did not participate in this workshop should not have a chance to see these notes.

Finally, the facilitator should sit down with the focal group's direct supervisor in a one-on-one session and inform this person about what the participants said about him or her personally during the time interval when this supervisor was not present in the room. Some hints on how to communicate this information is given at the end of Section 14.7.

14.3 The Participants of an ES Workshop

The participants of a typical ES workshop all belong to the same workgroup and all report to the same supervisor. If possible, the entire workgroup participates in the same workshop. If this is not possible, a random sample or a subsample that "represents" the workgroup employees in one way or another can run the workshop. In cases where the workgroup has a heavy workload, such a set-up may be the method preferred by both employees and managers. Even a selection of those employees who have the time for such an extra activity may be sufficient and accepted: What counts, in the end, is the effect the workshop has on the workgroup's working conditions, not the number of participants.

In many larger organizations, focusing on natural groups when organizing workshops may not be possible. The pilots of an airline, for example, typically do not form workgroups. Yet, different groups of pilots (within certain regions and functions, or just random groups of pilots) are likely to generate similar results in the workshops, because the working conditions of different pilots should not differ that much in general. Thus, from a sheer cost-benefit point-of-view, running many workshops would be a waste of resources. In any case, if one runs a few workshops with different groups of pilots, it would be easy to check to what extent the results resemble each other. So, it would be possible to stop further workshops if the workshops produce nothing really new anymore.

In some cases, the participants of ES workshops are only managers such as, for example, the managers of all subsidiaries of a company in a certain region. This group does not form a natural workgroup either. They all report, however, to the same manager. They should also share a common set of problems and concerns that suggests that an ES-results-based discussion with all of them will improve the conditions for effective action planning. When facilitating a managers' ES workshop, some special conditions should be considered (see Section 14.9), but the basic design of the workshop can remain unchanged.

14.4 The Facilitator of an ES Workshop

Choosing a good facilitator is decisive for a productive ES workshop. Yet, as it is always true when exceptional quality counts, it is not easy to find such individuals.

The easiest solution seems to hire external experts. They can be very experienced in facilitating workshops. In contrast to internal experts, they are also neutral and not blinded by what appears normal in a given company. On the other hand, not every good workshop facilitator is also an expert on employee surveys. The ideal facilitator, of course, should also know how to interpret ES results (e.g., interpreting results in the context of external norms, internal norms, and historical trends for the group). Moreover, the ideal facilitator should know the design of the ES project with all its phases and steps. Finally, it would be desirable to have a facilitator who knows the company and its business so that the workshop participants do not waste time explaining the meaning of comment after comment to an uninitiated facilitator.

It is easy to see, thus, that ideal external facilitators are not easily found. Moreover, given limited scheduling options or a limited budget, it can be difficult to get them to run certain workshops at a certain time in a certain place. Thus, ES workshops are often led by "internal externals" (Lipp & Will, 1998). Such individuals are employees of the company who work for different workgroups or even for different departments or functions than the participants of the workshop. For example, such a facilitator could come from the sales function while the participants come from research & development. The internal externals are often experienced managers who are properly trained for their task as a workshop facilitator. In the US internal organization development specialists, often from the HR department, will facilitate workshops across functions or units.

Some companies have opted not to automatically pick persons from HR as facilitators, but prefer middle-level line managers. The idea is that participants will expect more of an action-oriented session rather than a chance to "let off steam" with someone with a sympathetic ear. Indeed, one wants to avoid having the workshop end up in moaning and groaning, endless philosophical considerations, irrelevant side issues, etc. Whether or not a facilitator from HR is advantageous, choosing line managers as internal externals does have positive side effects: These persons learn something about the points-of-view and the problems of other org units of the company. That experience can help reduce the proverbial silo thinking of many managers. It can also help these managers in their careers by looking across the fence.

The supervisor of the participants is rarely a good choice for a facilitator. This person is partially responsible for the present problems and conditions. He or she is also not ideal to facilitate a discussion that is focused on the important topic of the supervisor him- or herself. The supervisor may be defensive and partial on that issue. He or she also "knows" how to interpret what Jim or Mary says, why they say it, and what they intend to accomplish saying it. Most likely, such comments will also be remembered, in particular negative ones. The participants, in any case, may feel that it is risky to be critical and, thus, they will not say much or will say whatever they want to say in an indirect and cautious way. Thus, no real insights can be expected here.

A good facilitator must possess the social skills to adapt his or her moderating style to the particular group of participants. The facilitator must also be able to listen carefully to what the participants say. In other words, persons who have strong opinions and who are used to promote their own points-of-views are poor choices for facilitating ES workshops. On the other hand, the facilitator should not simply accept any comment as is. Rather, he or she must often question a comment, but the goal should always be to make the comment more precise and clearer—without offending the person who contributed the comment but in a way that this person feels that the dialogue with the facilitator and the other participants led to a better comment.

The simple technique of working with comment cards is easy to learn from the many books that describe it in detail (e.g., Hartmann, Rieger, & Pajonk, 1997), or from carefully studying this chapter. Even more effective is it for the future facilitator to participate in an ES workshop as a co-facilitator. The time invested into such co-facilitation activities in workshops conducted by seasoned ES facilitators can be considered an excellent investment into management skills (Sperling & Wasseveld, 2002).

A good facilitator succeeds in engaging the participants in a lively and constructive discussion that produces an optimal starting point for later action planning. In addition, the participants should experience that the workshop was worthwhile. For example, after a successful workshop they often say something like this: "With your help, we managed to really advance a number of important issues. Without you, we would probably not have come that far in weeks, if ever!" In larger workshops, it often makes sense to have two facilitators. Their roles could be different, with one facilitator recording statements and ideas while the other focuses on content, clarifications, and even nonverbal communication in the room.

Facilitators can succeed only if they are not trying to impress the participants as a person. They should not act as a preacher or teacher who knows best. Modesty is a desirable attitude when facilitating a workshop. Facilitators should always suggest that the group knows best, but that they are attempting, on purpose, to bring in a critical and analytical way of thinking that is generally more difficult to pursue for those who are within the group. They may be blinded by habits, by what seems normal, etc. The sole purpose facilitators have in mind when asking seemingly "dumb" questions is to clarify things as much as possible. After the workshop, action planners should never run into ambiguities where they say: "Let's ask the group members what they meant by this."

The facilitator, moreover, follows an "Everyone must win" strategy as much as possible. That means, in particular, that the facilitator should never take sides with a particular subgroup or person as, for example, the supervisor of the participants, the works council, or the executive board. Such one-sidedness typically leads to counterproductive emotions. The facilitator should also never promise that a particular topic will be solved in later action planning. He or she is in no position to make such promises.

14.5 Organizing and Preparing an ES Workshop

ES workshops must be well organized and carefully prepared. If not, expensive chaos can result that can easily burn a lot of working time.

Participants, Time, Location, and Invitation

The size, time, and place of the workshop should be coordinated with the schedules of the target group for the workshop, in particular with the group's supervisors or managers. The number of participants for a normal ES workshop should be restricted to not more than 25 persons. Larger groups are possible too, but they require multiple facilitators and special designs with a mix of plenum work and break-out sessions.

Once the time and the place of the workshop are clear, an invitation is send to all participants. This message also briefly informs the participants about the purpose of the workshop (feedback of survey results, discuss and clarify the results, identify areas for action) and how the workshop will be run (roles of participants, facilitator, agenda). If available at the time of inviting the participants, one could also inform them about important global results of the ES such as, for example, the participation rates and the satisfaction scores of the company as a whole and of its major organizational units. They can help to generate interest in the workshop. On the other hand, the ES results of the group itself are usually not sent out before the workshop to avoid an uncontrollable spreading of possibly sensitive information.

Room

The room for the workshop must be large enough for the participants to move around freely. There should be enough space for working with flip charts or pin boards, for writing and collecting worksheets or comment cards, and also for water and refreshments. If the room is too small, working becomes difficult and the participants get tired more quickly. The typical rule is to have a minimum of about two to three square meters per participant.

The room should allow a sitting arrangement that enables every participant to see any other participant from where he or she sits, plus the facilitator and workshop materials. The ideal arrangement of chairs, therefore, is a U that opens up to the front where presentation materials are placed. The facilitator will work most of the time from the mound of the U, which can be formed with tables or chairs that have foldable writing tables.

Materials

To conduct an ES workshop with comment cards, you ideally have three to four pin boards and at least one paper poster for each side of the pin-board. You also need at least 25 comment cards and 25 pin needles, one thick felt-tip pen for every participant, two big felt-tip pens for the facilitator to draw lines around the comment clusters, mark the cluster headlines, and so on. Glue sticks come in handy for attaching the comment cards onto the posters. Then, of course, you need an overhead projector or a beamer, together with a pointing device, and a projection screen. What is also needed is a digital camera for recording the resulting comments and comment clusters.

Most workshops in the US would include the use of a projector and some printed material, such as a workbook for participants to take notes. Many companies take advantage of online action planning systems, which can be accessed and projected for the team to populate.

The facilitator should bring the following content material to the workshop: (a) A printed copy of the questionnaire (with items, headlines, intro text etc.) in order to be able to answer questions on the questionnaire quickly; (b) some slides that can be used to show how the questionnaire pages were formatted; and, of course, (c) slides that show the results of the survey for the target group, or a power point presentation on a laptop with such slides, or just an access code to such a presentation if it should be accessible on a server elsewhere. What one also needs are (d) appropriate slides for introducing the workshop (such as a slide on the ES project plan with major milestones as, e.g., in Figure 3.2), slides that explain the agenda of the workshop, a slide that explains how the data will be presented, etc.

Experience has shown that it often pays to prepare some simple forms and checklists for ES coordinators and facilitators. For example, a form for the participants of the workshop with fields for their names, for their signatures, and for the cost centers they belong to. Such a list can help to document the workshop properly and make sure that the workshop's costs are allocated to the correct sources. Other forms are checklists of the materials that the facilitator and the ES coordinator, respectively, must bring to the workshop or that these persons must arrange or prepare for the workshop. Often, dozens or even hundreds of workshops are conducted after a survey, and it can therefore save a lot of time if such forms and checklists are produced by the ES coordination team. The problem is that each such detail is rather obvious or even trivial, and for exactly this reasons it can be overlooked in preparing the workshop. However, the workshop's success depends on many such simple factors, and each of them can cause considerable damage.

Preparing an ES Workshop: the ES Coordinator's Role

The task of planning ES workshops is usually assigned to the local ES coordinator. This person's main task is to coordinate such workshops in terms of who should participate when in what workshop, to find appropriate facilitators, to make sure that all employees are properly involved in the planning, and possibly even in monitoring the workshop rollout. The exact nature of the coordinator's task depends on what is requested by the total ES design.

In smaller organizations, it is not uncommon that every workgroup is expected to conduct an ES workshop. Hence, the coordinator must sketch a realistic plan (who, when, where, how, with facilitator X, etc.) and then talk to the various supervisors to involve them early into the planning and to get their agreement.

In larger organizations, complete coverage of the workforce with ES workshops seldom makes sense and is, therefore, rarely mandatory. What is often requested is that subunits of the organization report either their responses to the ES results (decisions, actions) or the completion of a number of steps in the follow-up process (informing every employee about the survey results, planning actions, etc.).

In either case, the ES coordinator should approach the managers—possibly through or with the support of the local HR director—with a suggestion on what ES workshops appear optimal in terms of cost and benefits for the given goals. The respective managers must then decide what they want. To be successful in these tasks, the coordinator must be properly trained to know enough about ES workshops (time, participants, purpose, method, etc.) to make the right decisions or to draft good proposals. The responsibility for this training lies with the ES coordination team.

A Facilitator's Personal Preparation for the ES Workshop

When preparing for an ES workshop (see checklist in Table 14.5), the facilitator should first read the group's focal report to form a (tentative) impression of how the group views the various issues addressed by the ES. It often helps to mark those results where he or she feels that more discussion, illustrative concrete cases, further details etc. are needed to clarify the issues to an extent where action planners know what the problem is. The second substantive preparation should concentrate on the areas of focus defined by top management as issues that each group must at least carefully study when discussing the results. The facilitator should have an idea whether these areas of focus are completely irrelevant for this group or not. The first case is not very likely because areas of focus are usually based on conspicuous overall trends and, thus, should be relevant to most subgroups too. Yet, the particular group may attempt to "reject" an area of focus as not relevant for them. The facilitator should be prepared to sense evasive behavior early, and then explain in more detail in what sense an area of focus defines a task assignment for this particular group: "If you meet the CEO in the elevator and he or she asks you what you have done in the assigned area of focus, you better have a convincing answer right away!"

The facilitator should also contact the group's supervisor before the ES workshop. She should introduce herself, explain her role in the workshop, and ask for the supervisor's agreement to that role. The goal is to get the supervisor to say something like this: "OK, I understand how you want to run the workshop. I see why, and this is fine with me."

An issue that requires diplomacy is that the usual rules require the supervisor to leave the workshop while the results of the items on the direct supervisor are reported and discussed. For all issues before and after this item block, the supervisor should be present. Immediately after the workshop, the facilitator will sit down with the supervisor and explain the results of the discussion on the supervisor items. The facilitator may also want to point out that she will do everything that the discussion on this (and all other) topic remains objective, fact-oriented, balanced, and constructive. Her goal is always to make the results as precise and as concrete as possible.

Facilitators with little experience are sometimes concerned that a supervisor might not leave the room easily when it comes to the supervisor items. These concerns are rarely justified. Most supervisors get rather positive scores from their subordinates and those who do not can be easily identified before the workshop by simply studying the group's focal report. When talking to the supervisor, the facilitator can then stress that the rules that govern the ES workshop are all official ones, signed off by the ES sponsor. In other words, there is no room for discussing these rules.

Table 14.5. A facilitator's checklist for preparing an ES workshop.

	Activities	when
☐	You will receive from your ES coordinator: The name of the focal group you have to support by facilitating an ES workshop; a suggested time period for the ES workshop; presentation material (standard ES report of focal group, general slides on ES, and checklists for ES workshop).	[Date]
☐	Call the manager of the focal group and arrange for a meeting, where you introduce yourself, explain goals and steps of the ES workshop, your role and the manager's role in this workshop. Get manager's agreement on process and rules (if not, he/she should contact the ES coordinator). Agree on a date for WS.	Soon after [Date]
☐	Make sure or check with responsible person that the workshop room is booked and appropriately equipped (chairs, tables, overhead projector, beamer, flipcharts, posters, pens, paper etc.).	When date for WS is fixed
☐	Make sure that a proper invitation to the participants is send out (who, when, where, why, how).	As soon as possible
☐	Prepare, sort slides (physical or electronic) to be shown in WS.	1 week before WS
☐	Clarify with your ES coordinator whether top management has made any decisions or any new decisions that should be communicated in the WS (global actions, fields of action, or areas of focus).	1 week before WS
☐	Check whether the hardware and software in the WS room works so that you can present your slides.	2-3 days before WS
☐	Read the group's standard ES report. You should develop a rough idea about the group's attitudes and opinions. Check, in particular, how good or bad the group's ES results are on the issues that belong to top management's areas of focus or fields of action. This is where the group must respond or act, respectively. Also note major "problem areas" of the group.	1-2 days before WS
☐	Prepare two posters, one with the rules of the workshop (similar to Figure 14.3), and one with the phases, steps, and time plan of the WS.	1-2 days before WS
☐	Read the tips and hints for facilitating this WS (see Section 14.7 or as they were provided to you by your ES coordinator).	

14.6 Discussing ES Results

The main phase of an ES workshop serves to feed back the survey results to the participants and to discuss and further clarify these results if necessary. There is no failsafe method to achieve these goals optimally, but to proceed systematically avoids chaos and keeps things under control.

Workshop Activities for a Particular Item Block

The following steps can be used to roughly organize the work on each item block from the survey or index used in reports:

1) You, the facilitator, can begin by showing the slide(s) with the results of a particular item block. Two examples are shown in Figures 14.7 and 14.8, respectively.
2) Ask the participants to "explain" the results for the issues that you feel are not self-evident or where they want to add something. Ask them to make comments or to write them on cards (as described above). Questions to initiate discussion might include "What exactly did you have in mind when answering this item? Could you please describe this? Can you briefly describe a significant illustration, case, incident, or event for this issue?"
3) If using cards, all participants should be encouraged to participate and to write cards simultaneously without any established maximum. Collect the cards from time to time. Roughly sort the cards by content. You can do this by thinking aloud: "On issue X, there is one card. Let me see if there are more." Read and show each card to the participants as in Figure 14.8, working through issue by issue.
4) Try to work on ambiguous comments by asking the participants for explanations. Again, thinking aloud often helps: "I am not sure how to classify your comment. What exactly does that mean?" The comments are the main product of the workshop. Their quality and precision should be as high as possible. When better comments surface after a discussion, ask a participant (often the one who submitted the comment in the first place) to please restate the comment. Having participants (rather than the facilitator) write comments (on cards, paper, flip-charts, etc.) will keep the workshop moving along quickly.
5) If using the card system, pin the cards that are deemed good into a preliminary cluster that has as its headline simply the name of the item block of the questionnaire.
6) If time allows, it is important to note changes and developing intricacies in ideas as they occur during the workshop. The initial comments often are a potpourri of related but different issues. By repeatedly discussing how to regroup the comments/cards into truly meaningful substantive clusters, you better facilitate the discussion and better capture information. Along with the re-groupings, also think about labels or headlines for clusters. Good labels can, in turn, stimulate new or sharper comments.

An Illustrative Item Block

Figure 14.7 shows an example for the ES results of a focal group X in a German production plant for medical instruments. The item block contains some items on the topic "Goals and tasks, work itself". The item texts are shown in full length as they appeared in the questionnaire so that questions such as "What exactly was the ques-

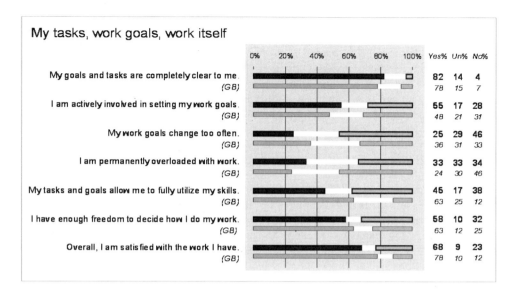

Figure 14.7. Example of a chart with ES results.

tion in this case?" become superfluous. The slide also shows the percentages of respondents who endorsed the item, who answered undecided, and who rejected it, respectively. Below the statistics of the focal group for each item, one notes benchmark values. These are the results of a larger org unit to which the focal group belongs (called "GB" here).

How should the facilitator work with such a chart? The least efficient way is to read it item by item, beginning at the top. A better way is to examine the topic as a whole by reviewing the index score or any overall evaluation item in this block (e.g., "Overall, I am satisfied with the work I have."). What we see for that item in Figure 14.7 is that the focal group is somewhat less satisfied overall with the work they have than the comparison group GB. This is important information, because work itself is typically the main driver of job satisfaction and an important aspect of employee engagement. Hence, you as the facilitator should be motivated to find out more clearly what problems there are in this domain. You begin by looking at the other items in Figure 14.7, learning from the first item that the clarity of goals is not an issue in this focal group: 82% are satisfied, 4% are dissatisfied, and the rest perceives a mixed situation. Do not allow for long discussions on the 4%, but rather stress that the goals do not appear as a topic that is worthwhile to be discussed at length in this workshop. On the contrary, one can summarize that "everyone" felt that the goals and tasks are quite clear. Hence, it does not make sense to waste time on that issue.

The second item tells a different story. About half of the survey respondents feel that they can participate in setting their work goals, but about one third does not endorse the item. The facilitator might consider (if there is enough time) asking the group how this one third feels about it: "Is participating in goal settings important for you or not?" What the facilitator should not attempt to clarify is who belongs to the 28% of respondents who answered the item "negatively".

Work overload does not seem to be a big topic, even though the participants might feel the contrary and that something should be done about this work load. The essentially three times one third distribution on the over-load to under-load scale seems to indicate that the work load is just right. It is possible, though, to clarify whether overload, for example, is seen as a chronic or as an occasional problem, whether it is attributed to poor planning and management, to an inefficient org structure, to bottlenecks in certain capabilities within the workgroup, etc.

The next item shows that less than half of the respondents feel that they can make proper use of their skills and competencies at work. If this is true, it is likely that they are wasting their time with work they are overqualified for. Hence, the facilitator as a person who is interested to detect promising springboards for responses that will promote both satisfaction and performance, could spend some time to answer the usual W questions (who, where, when, why, what for, etc.).

Finally, the message of the last item may benefit from some discussion and clarification. After all, about one third of the respondents said that they do not have "enough freedom to decide how to do their work." What does that really mean? Can this be illustrated with some concrete cases? Or is this more a general feeling that, maybe, is related to the supervisor? Answering questions like these would be helpful as a prerequisite for improving the working conditions of the employees by giving them more decisional power or by explaining carefully where and why their freedom to decide must be limited (e.g., for security reasons).

Another Illustration with Items on the Supervisor

Figure 14.8 exhibits another block of items focusing on the supervisor of the group. Again, one can begin by looking at the overall index score or any "overall" item in the set. In this example, the overall item shows that the group is generally quite satisfied with its supervisor, a common finding in employee surveys. Only 15% are not satisfied. Why they are not satisfied with their supervisor may become clear from the other items in this item block. The facilitator, therefore, should turn to these items first before collecting any comments that further explain the group's general satisfaction with their supervisor.

Jumping back to the top of the item block, one first notes that "recognition" is not an issue for this group. The second item shows that the supervisor's feedback behavior is slightly above the average of the department ("GB"). However, comparisons are not the only thing that is important: One should also evaluate the results on absolute scales and ask whether there is room for improvement—whatever the relative score is! When discussing the item's message, one should also begin with reading the item's wording carefully. The second item says "on *my* performance." This is important when discussing the workshop results with the supervisor after the workshop, because supervisors sometimes argue that they do give good feedback, but their feed-

ES 2001: Focal Group XYZ

Direct Supervisor		Yes%	No%	mean
I am satisfied with the recognition that I get for excellent work from my direct supervisor.		80	6	1.65
	GB	(68)	(12)	(2.07)
My direct supervisor manages to motivate me with good feedback on my performance (specific, close in time, clear).		54	24	2.46
	GB	(46)	(38)	(2.75)
My direct supervisor supports innovation, suggestions, and new ideas.		41	0	2.66
	GB	(58)	(0)	(2.85)
My direct supervisor keeps me sufficiently informed about issues I need to know for doing a good job.		58	32	2.22
	GB	(63)	(25)	(2.4)9
When making decisions, my direct supervisor seriously considers what the people think.		92	0	1.47
	GB	(88)	(0)	(1.67)
Overall, I am satisfied with my direct supervisor.		72	15	2.24
	GB	(65)	(16)	(2.56)

Figure 14.8. Example of a table with ES results.

back is more general on the workgroup as a whole. This is not what this item focuses on. As a facilitator, you could possibly drill deeper into the feedback issue: "What could be improved? Is the supervisor's feedback too general? Is it too negative? Is it on time? Or is it too frequent?" Yet, since the item's rating is relatively good, such questions should only be pursued if there are not more important issues that need careful attention. The item also shows that the facilitator walks a fine line: He or she should always stick closely to the items and the survey statistics and not attempt to follow his or her personal interpretation attempting to make an issue of the 22% negatives while 62% are explicitly positive. In the end, the data are the property of the respondents, and so is their interpretation.

A result in this item block that is difficult to understand for the outsider is the item that asks about the supervisor's support for new ideas. The percentage of respondents who endorsed this item is substantially lower than the benchmark value. At the same time, no one answered the item negatively. This needs to be explained. One possible explanation is that new ideas do not really matter in this workgroup. Another interpretation is that new ideas belong to a suggestion system and not to the supervisor. Perhaps the employees want to avoid innovations and new ideas, but it is not really clear how the respondents interpreted the notion of new ideas. Hence, this item illustrates a case where further discussion in the workshop could be very helpful.

Altogether, the results of this item block are normal in the sense that the direct supervisor is quite positively assessed by his or her subordinates. This will certainly please the supervisor. There is no urgent need to extinguish a fire or to fix a major problem. However, this information does not help much in terms of improvements. The facilitator should, therefore, always look out for issues that potentially offer such opportunities. This could even be defined as one of the main goals of the ES workshop, and facilitators who are also good management consultants will always be able to detect issues (and possible solutions) that are interesting to a supervisor.

14.7 Tips and Hints for Facilitating an ES Workshops

In the following, we list a number of practical tips and hints for facilitating ES workshops. They are based on the experience collected in hundreds of workshops that we facilitated ourselves in companies around the world. Reading these recommendations can also help to anticipate how such workshops normally run and to set one's expectations accordingly.

Timing

- Make sure that the workshop does not run out of time. The time intervals for the workshop's phases and steps must be closely observed. To avoid being perceived as rigid or someone who rushes the group too much, have the group agree on a time table at the beginning of the workshop. This time table should be sketched on a poster and hung up on the wall. It becomes part of the workshop rules.
- Possibly also ask one participant to act as the time keeper of the workshop. If the group spends too much time in a phase or step of the workshop, the time keeper should send a signal to make everyone aware of the problem and motivate the participants to conclude the topic and move on.
- The time intervals in Tables 13.14.1-14.4 are just recommendations that serve as a starting point when planning the workshop. You should replace them with real time markers (such as 14.00 or 2 p.m.) that also take the total maximal length of the workshop into account.
- If there is little time for the workshop or if you want to minimize the risk of running into time problems, you should consider reviewing item blocks in terms of importance rather than simply starting at the top of the list. Importance might be predetermined by statistical analyses or by upper management. Alternatively, importance can be determined by the facilitator or by the group itself in a preliminary discussion. Make clear to participants that time may not allow a review of all topics, and display the ranking of topics by importance early on.
- Item blocks that cannot be discussed because time is too short can be moved to later, regular meetings of the participants attending the workshop. If so, the facilitator should calm participants not to panic about topics being lost or suppressed. Another option is to reserve a few minutes for participants to comment on any topic that did not get discussed because of time constraints.
- If time is too short, you may also decide to skip phase III completely. The action planning team or the supervisor together with one or two subordinates, for example, may then develop ideal scenarios after the workshop.

Role and Behavior of the Facilitator

- Let the participants know that the facilitator is not there to solve the group's problems. The facilitator only helps the group to run the workshop so that it becomes as clear as possible where action is needed or where it appears promising.
- The facilitator should never make any promises on later actions. This is not under the facilitator's control. His or her job is done when the workshop is over.
- The facilitator serves many customers at the same time, and it is easy to get confused about his or her role in this job: Who is the client? Is it the participants or is it their supervisor? Or is it not, in the end, the survey sponsor or the executive board? Ultimately, it is all of them and others, too (e.g., works council, dotted line leaders). No conflict arises if you as the facilitator follow an "Everyone must win" strategy. That means, for example, that you should stop discussions that become excessively one-side or simple-minded as, for example, when the participants find that "everything" is really management's fault.
- The facilitator should make clear what he or she expects from the participants. Namely, the participants ...
  o must abide by the workshop rules
  o must accept a certain responsibility for the tangible results of the workshop: By simply sitting there and letting the facilitator do all the work and all the thinking, the result will most likely be suboptimal
  o remain responsible for the quality and the quantity of the comments; the facilitator can only try to improve this input
  o must know that the discussion can (and often needs to) be open and critical, but it must remain politically correct at any time
  o should please accept the fact the facilitator is not an expert on everything so that he or she sometimes may ask "dumb" questions
- The facilitator must always remain neutral on the issues. The facilitator should never attempt to sell or to even impose his or her personal attitudes or opinions onto the participants. Rather, it is better not to let the group know what you personally think about these issues. Leave your ego at home.
- It is not important that the group likes you, the facilitator, as a person. Do not try to become "popular" with the participants. Rather, concentrate on facts and on clear results.
- Be careful when you "criticize" a participant's comments. Critiquing ideas, in any case, should only serve one purpose: to better discriminate what is good and what is not so good or what was meant and what was not. Critiquing comments is, thus, questioning the contribution with the intention of generating information.
- As a facilitator, you are sometimes attacked personally, even viciously. You do not have to accept such attacks. Stay calm and make clear that you are facilitating this workshop for the company and that you are reporting, ultimately, to the survey sponsor. Indeed, internal facilitators often do this work on top of their normal workload in order to support a common effort of improvement. They do their best to come to a good result, but go home when the workshop is over. The problems of the workgroup, however, remain with the workgroup.

Presenting the Survey Results

- Do not read every item and every statistic. It takes too much time, and it is also boring. It suffices if you "screen" through the items and characterize their content briefly. The participants can read the full text of the items themselves if they are interested.
- You may evaluate the statistics in a straightforward way as "about on benchmark level", "apparently no big issue here", "relatively positive", etc.
- When reporting statistics, concentrate on the *Yes%* (or percent favorable) statistics. They are easy to understand and to memorize. The *No%* (or percent unfavorable) statistics are only occasionally important. Normally, the information contained in the Yes% is sufficient to see the main response trends.
- Often, the results for the middle response option (i.e., mixed or neutral) are not reported explicitly (see Figure 14.8). If so it typically holds that $Yes\%+No\% \neq 100$. The delta is the percentage of respondents who answered by checking the middle category. Notice that this does not mean that they do not have an opinion on that item. Rather, their attitudes are "mixed", or their opinions are "undecided."
- Occasionally, the participants find the results obvious and trivial ("Why waste time on all that? This is all known anyway!"). If so, cover some results and let the participants guess the statistics. They will notice quickly that the results are not nearly as obvious as they appear to be.

Discussing the ES Results

- Time is rarely sufficient to discuss everything. Often, participants want to discuss every topic at length in the beginning of the workshop, even if the topic is not particularly important and even if it concerns only one or two participants but not the majority of the group. You should try to keep the workshop on course. Concentrate on the big issues. It is better to make real progress with the big issues only than to spend time on all issues.
- You might want to point out the 80-20 rule (Pareto rule). This "rule" says that identifying the 20% most important problems and solving only them (and no other problems) means that you achieve 80% of the possible positive effects.
- The comments are memory cues for the action planners. They should be concise and unambiguous. Cards should be legible and have no more than 3 to 5 words.
- The comment cards that make it to the pin boards should not duplicate an issue. If cards with similar content are written by the participants, the facilitator should ask the group whether they denote the same thing. If that is not clear, the cards should be re-written in less ambiguous terms. The number of cards, in any case, should not indicate a topic's importance. Also, not the number of cards, but their quality counts.
- In the end, it is the group of participants (not the facilitator) who decide which cards makes it to the pin board and which ones do not.
- If you as the facilitator want a decision from the group (e.g., on whether a topic has been discussed sufficiently so that one can move on to the next topic), it is often convenient to let the participants vote by raising hands. Do not always rely on

the nods from a few participants or your ability to read facial expressions correctly.
- Comments that repeat the results of the survey are useless. If, for example, the survey has shown that the focal group is dissatisfied with the company's information, then a comment card that says "Information is poor" does not add any information. The facilitator should work on that issue with questions such as: "Which information do you mean? By whom? When? Are the info channels and media ineffective? If so, what exactly is the problem? Can you describe these problems with some concrete cases?" The facilitator must ask such questions in a diplomatic way. The participants should be convinced that it is the facilitator's intention to make everything as clear as possible. The questions should never be a cross-examination of the person who made the comment.
- Special attention is needed when it comes to issues that the facilitator does not understand, but where the participants appear to agree. Often, if you probe a little into such seemingly clear issues, you find that there are many different interpretations of the key notions. If so, you as the facilitator can always act "dumb" and ask for "help" on that issue from the participants. If one participant then explains what it means, it often happens that others disagree with what this person says, which results in a discussion.
- Avoid mock structures of comments with vague "miscellaneous" headlines. For example in Figure 14.5, there is a headline "Information and Communication," with begs for a specific structure within this large topic. In a case like this one, the facilitator should drive the group to work harder and to split the cluster into meaningful components. If, however, the group is not able or willing to produce a better result, then the facilitator must leave it there.
- Extremely fine-grained clusters are not desirable either. Although it would be easier to place every issue in its own cluster, there is value in looking for overlap and relationships among issues. Attempt to integrate a narrow issue within a larger category of issues.
- Work both on clusters *and* on super-clusters, not just on clusters. It often helps if the issues in a big topic such as the above "Information and Communication" domain are sorted into a number of sub-categories. Typically, one should not have more than about seven such sub-categories. If more are needed, one can break up a sub-category into further subcategories. However, keep the purpose in mind, namely to get effective actions for the really important problems. Thus, keep it as simple as possible!
- To visually structure the card arrangements on the pin boards, you can use different colors for the cards with the headlines. You can also simply underline the headlines.
- Do not ask for solutions in the ES workshop. Rather, point out clearly at the beginning that solutions are not the goals of this workshop. The task is, first of all, a sharp diagnosis of the present situation with its problems and opportunities. The action planners then think about solutions. If participants suggest solutions anyway—some always will because they communicate about problems by suggesting one (vague) solution after another ("management should act", "one should be

more attentive to the customer", etc.)—collect them and pass them on to the action planners.
- When discussing an item block, there is often no linear path of progress. Rather, the activities jump back and forth from writing comment cards to discussions to asking what this means to re-writing cards etc. As long as progress is made, this jumping around is perfectly alright. If this circular pattern does not yield progress, however, the facilitator should stop the discussion by, for example, suggesting a tentative summary of the results for the item block. The group thus will at least realize that the item block must be brought to a conclusion.

Behavior of the Participants in the Discussions

- All participants in an ES workshop are invited to actively participate in the discussion, but active participation is not mandatory. You as the facilitator should, nevertheless, encourage passive participants to make their voices heard. This could be done by asking them directly: "What do you think about that? " Often, they add a verbal comment, and then you could ask them to write their comment down on cards. This may entice them to write more comment cards later on. Even if they do not, it often seems sufficient for participants if they have just one comment card on the pin board to feel that they were involved in a common effort where they made a little difference.
- Try to stop lengthy verbal discussions in the plenum by pointing out that time is short. If a point has been made, it does not need to be reiterated over and over again.
- Verbal discussions are time consuming. Writing comment cards in a parallel fashion is more productive. You should, therefore, remind the participants repeatedly to write comment cards. (Admittedly, one gets tired doing that but it improves efficiency.)
- To entice the participants to actually write cards, explain—after presenting the survey results of the first item block—how to work with comment cards and then add: "I now give you three minutes to write comments on these issues. Please begin now!" In the next three minutes, turn away from the group doing something else (e.g., reading the focal report) and leave the group alone.
- Always observe whether the discussion is moving forward. If it gets stuck or goes in circles, you could ask: "Can we conclude this issue now? Are there important points that we have not covered yet? If not, I would like to move on to the next issue." If necessary, you could ask the participants to vote on whether to move on to the next topic or not.
- From time to time, it pays to remind the group of the time schedule. Simply point to the poster on the wall that is part of the workshop rules and ask: "Where are we now and what must be done?" The ES workshop should cover the most important topics. Minor topics can be addressed in later meetings.
- Discussions should remain focused. They sometimes tend to become too general, with everyone leaning back and discussing the world in philosophical terms. You cannot accept this. Time is too short. It is also expensive, because it is working

time. Remind the group that this is a concerted effort, paid for by the company that must lead to results that can be used to plan improvements.
- General complaining or whining is not helpful. While it may be necessary in some cases to let a group start out with some "venting" of emotions, the facilitator has to bring the group beyond that level.
- Motivate participants who make verbal comments to be brief and to the point.
- If some participants keep acting in negative or uncooperative ways, you may want to interrupt and point out the purpose and the rules of the workshop. This workshop is part of a program implemented by the executive board. It is conducted during paid working time. It thus is an investment of the company that *must* generate tangible results.
- If survey results are presented that threaten the participants' positive self-images they often respond defensively by criticizing the validity of the findings. You should get the group to accept the survey results as data that have to be utilized for positive change. Endless counter-arguments[54] that attempt to discredit the data are not bringing about positive change. So, in the end, such arguments are preventing progress and hurting the group.
- You as the facilitator should, however, not simply reject such counter-arguments, but interpret them as legitimate attempts to test the validity of the survey results. Because almost all such counter-arguments have been used hundreds of times before in similar workshops, it is easy to answer them with standard arguments.
- If a group is in a particularly bad mood, the facilitator must try to lead the group back to a fact-oriented and constructive path. The workshop is an opportunity to promote progress, but the participants must make a concrete contribution here. Lamenting will not lead to improvements.
- Never allow speculations about who said what in the survey. First, the survey is, and should remain, anonymous or confidential. Second, what counts is the trend, the group's attitudes and opinions, and not the answers of single individuals.
- Stop speculations about the respondents' intentions when filling out the questionnaire. For example, some people sometimes speculate that the respondents answered particularly negatively or positively on purpose (e.g., to get more money or to prevent change in their working conditions). Although that may be true occasionally, research has shown that ES data allow one to reliably predict behavior that really matters (e.g., sickness rates, turnover rates, performance on the job, conflicts). Thus, these data should better be taken seriously.

Discussing the Items on the Direct Supervisor

- When discussing the items on the direct supervisor, the supervisor should leave the room.

---

[54] Examples for such counter-arguments are: "The respondents did not understand the question", "what they say is objectively wrong", "possibly an error in data analysis", "too few employees participated", "these benchmarks are not relevant for us", "we cannot influence this", "it is all management's fault."

- For these items, the facilitator (or a helper) should write or re-write all comments in order to prevent that the supervisor identifies the source of the comments from the handwriting.
- When discussing issues that relate to particular persons, the discussion must stay politically correct. What this means in each instance is not always easy to tell. For example, calling the supervisor "stupid" cannot be tolerated, but if the group feels that this person is "arrogant", then this is important feedback because it relates to behavior that can be changed. However, emotions must be controlled and the comments that make it to the pin boards should be written in such a way that they promote positive change.
- If the supervisor is harshly criticized, you as the facilitator should ask the group to also name some strengths of this person. There are no persons who have no strengths. Such comments will make it easier to overcome defense mechanisms when talking with the supervisor after the workshop.
- Do not attempt to turn the workshop into a comprehensive feedback session of subordinates on their supervisor. An ES should not degenerate into a tool that represents one source of 360 degree feedback. Its scope is *much wider*, and personal feedback to the supervisor should be restricted to the main points. The supervisor should not automatically become the dominating issue of the ES.
- After you are done with discussing the items on the supervisor, cover the pin board posters with the comment cards on that issue, and invite the supervisor back to the workshop. Continue with the next item block without interruption.

Brainstorming on the Fields of Action

- Fields of action are task assignments to the org units from above (management). The org unit *must* respond with an action. Brainstorming on these fields of action serves to make sure that (a) everyone understands that the requirements and (b) it generates visions that guide action planners.
- The facilitator should make sure before the workshop that there is a clear description of what deliveries are expected by management regarding a field of action. This requires a description such as the following: "The focal group is expected to work out an action plan for at least one of the topics A, B, or C. The action plan must be such that the plan's goals can be reached by activities that the focal group can deliver itself. If the group does not see any possibilities for action, then it must at least deliver a concrete description of ideal situations of A, B or C, and explanations why these situations are ideal. It must also explain why it feels that it cannot do anything to better the situation. The results of the planning must be reported to the next-level manager by [date] for further decision making. Expect that meager reports will be delegated back to the group."
- When brainstorming, one first concentrates on quantity. There should be as many inputs as possible, and as many aspects as possible (divergence). Exotic and crazy ideas are welcome. They should not be commented, discussed, or challenged. Simply collect them and encourage the participants to build on what others said before (Kaner, with Lind, Toldi, Fisk, & Berger, 2007).

- When brainstorming, verbal discussion can replace written cards. If people utter their comments verbally it becomes more likely that their ideas trigger off related or contradictory ideas of others. If the acoustic chaos becomes excessive, the facilitator can bring in more structure by, for example, switching to a carousel sequencing of inputs.
- If the group is very structured and if there is enough time, the brainstorming results could be clarified, sorted into clusters with appropriate headlines, and interconnected as in a normal item-block discussion.

Behavior of Managers in ES Workshops

- Few managers are experts on HR issues. Their judgments are, therefore, intuitive and based on their own personal experience. In spite of their lack of systematically acquired and scientifically based expertise—or, maybe, because of it—they often defend their opinions rather emotionally. One way of doing this is to attack the facilitator ("You have no real management experience!"). Another argument is to refer to what has been found to work "in practice", not "in theory." You as the facilitator should not get involved in discussions of that nature. Your role is to facilitate the workshop. The rest is up to the participants and management.
- Managers often question the quality of the survey data with various "counter-arguments." These arguments serve two purposes. Many managers want to better understand the validity of the data and whether they can be taken as a solid foundation for decisions or not. Other managers, however, do not like the survey results and their implications. Their counter-arguments, thus, are attempts to discredit the data to avoid annoying consequences such as a loss of reputation or additional work.
- Counter-arguments by managers need to be answered convincingly by the survey consultant. Fortunately, this is usually quite easy, because these arguments tend to be the same in every company. Standard answers to ten standard counter-arguments are provided in Section 14.2.
- Almost every manager has a naive (private, non-tested, non-scientific) theory on the relationship of satisfaction and performance. Most often, this theory says that that satisfaction drives performance. You as the facilitator should question such simplistic notions, because they are often a road block for effective actions. If satisfaction is assumed to be the driver of performance, then actions often focus on how to make the employees more satisfied. The goal to develop employees as entrepreneurs, for example, is thus easily missed.

Giving Feedback to the Supervisor after the ES Workshop

- You are successful as a feedback provider if the supervisor accepts the comments of the participants as their perceptions, and if the supervisor accepts them as useful information for positive change.
- Avoid discussions about who said what.
- Avoid discussions about the objective truth of the comments. You do not know the facts, and to discuss this with the supervisor is a waste of time. In any case, the

comments reflect the participants' perceptions, and these perceptions guide their behavior.
- Note that no one likes to be negatively criticized. Hence, it is only natural that supervisors will try to defend themselves against negative feedback. To do this, they use an array of standard arguments. Most of them can be discarded easily (see above).
- Supervisors not used to feedback from their employees can be quite surprised that not everyone loves them and that not everyone assesses them as super-competent. Even if 80% of the employees indicate that they are satisfied with them, they may turn pale and want to find out exactly who criticized them. Use benchmarks to demonstrate what is normal and concentrate on the items.
- Negative feedback on the supervisor should always be seen within its proper context. Sometimes, supervisors are fiercely attacked because they are serious about fundamental changes that are necessary to stay competitive. This can damage a cozy situation for the employees. So, negative feedback is sometimes unavoidable, and the supervisor must live with it for some time. However, eventually, the supervisors and their subordinates should strive to return to a less stressful way of interacting.
- Supervisors who receive lots of negative (or positive!) feedback should be prepared that their direct managers will want to discuss the survey results with them. In order to do this optimally, they should identify the main characteristics of the present situation, including customer satisfaction, necessary strategic changes, performance measures etc. However, they should not do this in a defensive (or aggressive) way, but in a data- and fact-oriented way. Their problems are also the problems of their direct managers, and together they have to bring about the required changes.
- The facilitator should make sure that the supervisor does not lose sight of the survey results. The comments generated in the workshop only complement these statistics. If the statistics get lost, one is back at square one: All that is left are singular comments and anecdotes.

14.8 Variants of the Traditional ES Workshop

The traditional ES workshop described above is designed for participants who all belong to a natural workgroup. It also assumes that there is sufficient time and a good facilitator. For other groups and for more limiting side constraints, one may need to modify the traditional approach, or choose a different design.

ES Workshops with Managers Only

The literature on employee surveys says little about feedback workshops with groups that consist of managers only. Rather, the idea of feedback workshops is usually seen as a way to involve the shop floor to make the most of its own results. The only other group that is usually given a special role in working with ES data is top management.

Yet, this group is often just informed and not integrated into a comprehensive design where every group is planned to deliver actions or decisions. Senior and middle management is often ignored altogether. Supervisors, on the other hand, participate in the usual ES workshops, but if and how they discuss their particular issues as a group is ignored in the usual follow-up process design.

Conducting feedback workshops with middle and higher-level managers can have positive effects above and beyond improving the problems that concern these persons themselves. These managers also learn how such feedback workshops run. This makes it easier for them to optimally inform and motivate their subordinates, in particular managers who report to them. They also know that they will be receiving feedback from below just as they are giving feedback to the managers they report to. Each one of them can see that he or she will eventually be in the role of a recipient of feedback, not only in the role as a feedback provider. This makes it easier to convince everyone of the usefulness of abiding by the rules of politically correct—indeed, constructive—feedback. Then, to see that every level of management goes through the same feedback processes, may also help to reduce the wide-spread fear of feedback (Jackman & Strober, 2003).

ES workshops with managers can follow the same principles and the same basic design as the traditional ES workshop. First of all, one needs a special data analysis that focuses on the survey results of the participating group of managers and possibly also on the issues of their subordinates. The guiding principle when preparing the presentation of results for such a management workshop is what this group of persons must know and discuss or else it will be lost or never be clear. The goal is to get the actions that only this group of persons can deliver.

ES Workshops under Tight Time Constraints

An ES workshop that requires three hours or more is often not feasible. For example, in a production site, one cannot stop production for such a long time interval. Hence, the workshop must either be conducted before or after the normal work hours, or it must be designed differently. Usually, this means that the workshop must be split into sections that can be run separately at different times. Another possibility is to shorten the workshop and concentrate on discussing the two to three most important issues.

A short ES workshop version can be prepared by giving the participants a printed report of the survey results before the workshop. The participants also receive instructions on how to read this report in a way that sets the stage for the ensuing workshop. That is, they are asked to form an impression of the main trends and issues, possibly think about cases and details that re-contextualize the statistics so that the problem situation becomes as clear as possible. A short description of the workshop, including the usual rules, the name and role of the facilitator, and other how-when-where details can also be handed out in printed form to save time in the workshop itself. The facilitator should prepare the workshop similarly, identifying what appear to be the most prominent topics, but also taking into account possible tasks assigned by top management. This will lead to a priority list of topics for the workshop that can be used as a starting point. The workshop can then begin by deciding on these priorities and by agreeing on how the remaining topics will be covered in other meetings. It is important that the participants do not perceive concentrating on a few important issues as a trick to avoid or censor certain issues.

Concentrating on the most important topics can be an effective strategy for ES workshops in general. Folkman (1996, p. 40) remarks that "in the real world, people face limitations in terms of how many issues they can successfully address at a time. A guaranteed way to fail in making change based on feedback is by trying to change too many things all at the same time. Our research shows that people *cannot* make five major changes at the same time. Whenever people try to change more than one, two, or three things at once, they end up making no change at all." In practice, employee surveys seldom lead to more than a few major actions. If they focus on key issues, this can indeed be better than to lose focus with zillions of minor activities. Moreover, the key issues typically are those that are, directly or indirectly, interconnected to many other issues.

To make the ES workshop as efficient as possible, one must also prepare the feedback material in such a way that it exhibits the important survey results under a few relevant headlines. A standard data report that feeds back the survey results in the format of the questionnaire is suboptimal in this regard, because it can force the workshop to skip through different slides to gather the relevant information needed to process a particular topic. If the participants have a standard data analysis report, feedback in the sense of reading number after number is not needed anyway. Rather, the facilitator or the (core) coordinators (in cooperation with the external expert) can prepare a few slides that are much more task-oriented such as, for example, the slide shown in Figure 14.9 below. Another (or an additional) possibility is to prepare slides that embed the various issues in a network of interconnections as in the PS motor in Figure 10.9.

14.9 Alternatives of the Traditional ES Workshop

With a good facilitator, the traditional ES workshop is usually an effective design for bridging the gap between survey data and actions. However, it is not the only and seldom the most efficient way to proceed. Alternative designs should, therefore, always be considered by the ES project team.

In some companies, survey feedback is completely left to supervisors and managers. There is no particular design for how such feedback should be conducted. Other companies promote survey feedback workshops that resemble the design discussed above with the exception that the supervisor of the participant is the default facilitator. Because most supervisors receive relatively positive scores from their subordinates (see benchmarks in Figure 10.6), this is a solution that is emotionally viable and that greatly simplifies organizing such workshops. In case of supervisors that have a less positive relationship with their subordinates, an external facilitator could do the job.

Table 14.6. Two alternatives for the traditional ES workshop.

Action-oriented ES workshop:

step	activity	min.
1	Facilitator explains goals, method, rules of workshop	15
2	Facilitator informs about general ES results	15
3	Facilitator explains common fields of action, tasks	20
4	Screen which items, results are relevant for common fields of action; clarify, structure present situation: where are we now?	40
5	Brainstorm on ideal scenarios: Where do we want to be?	30
6	Brainstorm on possible actions	30
7	Sketch most promising actions	20
8	Who reports what, when and how to responsible manager?	10

ES workshop with representative focus group:

step	activity	min.
1	Facilitator explains goals, method, rules of workshop	15
2	Facilitator informs about general ES results	15
3	Screen items, results for *common* topics	60
4	Study, discuss, structure common topics: Where are we now?	60
5	Prioritize topics re their potential for the given operational and strategic goals	10
6	Brainstorm on ideal scenarios: Where do we want to be?	10
7	Who reports what, when and how to responsible manager, to co-workers?	10

Yet, supervisors as facilitators are not ideal. Supervisors (as well as their subordinates) are not likely to come up with new points-of-view, new insights, or new solutions. They also tend to "know" each other, or, worse, assume to know each other and to understand what the other says or "really" means by what he or she is saying. The external facilitator, in contrast, is not blinkered by habits and culture, and thus often notices immediately when there are problems or that proposed solutions are bound to fail. External facilitators are also in a position that allows them to ask "dumb" questions and ask for explanations, poke into the meaning of any input, and challenge any suggested solution. Indeed, this is required behavior of a facilitator. What counts are the results and the facilitator is expected to focus on these results (without, of course, being too harsh on the individual participants).

Sometimes management insists that ES workshops should not simply "discuss" various issues but they should begin to work out action plans. To run a workshop that delivers such outcomes (see Table 14.6 for a possible agenda) requires considerable care because solutions are often suggested prematurely before the problem is really clear. Moreover, many persons tend to habitually propose their favorite solutions whatever the problem may be (Porras, 1987). Hence, the facilitator must make sure that solutions are postponed until the diagnostics are completed. The workshop design should make sure that this is indeed accomplished by setting up a clear first-this-then-that approach. In any case, if actions plans (or first considerations of such action

Table 14.7. Two-phase ES workshop for managers.

Step	Phase 1: Preparing the workshop with seniors	min.
1	Facilitator explains goals, approach, and rules of workshop	15
2	Facilitator informs participants about survey results in general and in the particular org unit	45
3	Identifying the topics where management should act (max. 3-5)	15
4	Specifying the action tasks (reasons, goals, side constraints)	45
5	Finding persons who should drive the different actions; talk to them after workshop (once org unit managers gives a "go")	15
6	Planning of next steps, in particular a meeting with the manager of the org unit to decide, fine-tune the action tasks	15

Step	Phase 2: Workshop with all managers of function/department	min.
1	– same as step 1 above --	15
2	– same as step 2 above --	45
3	Manager of org unit explains how he/she sees these results	15
4	Spokesperson of the preparation team from phase 1 explains what this team has identified as action tasks for this group of managers and who was identified (and is willing) to serve as an action manager	15
5	Find first ideas on actions in break-out sessions	60
6	Spokespersons of break-out teams report first ideas in plenum	15
7	Final discussion; facilitator informs about next steps	15

plans) must be produced, the phases and steps of the traditional workshop have to be reduced in both scope and depth to make room for these additional activities.

Another variant of the traditional ES workshop does not work with a natural group of participants but with a random (or quota) sample of employees who are "typical" for some type of employee (e.g., for an airline pilot or for a nurse in geriatric care). Experience shows that it is often possible to identify and discuss most of the topics that are really important for most employees in such *representative* focus groups (see Table 14.6 for a possible agenda). Since there are hardly ever more than a few actions that are really pursued with sustained engagement anyway, it means that conducting such sample workshops rather than a workshop with every single workgroup can greatly reduce the costs of the ES workshop phase. That does not mean that local issues have to be ignored, but preceding generic workshops can substantially reduce the workload for the individual workgroup.

The design for representative focus groups can also be used for workshops with managers. However, for managers in particular, another design has been found to be even more efficient and effective, the *two-phase* ES workshop (Table 14.7). This workshop is typical for managers relatively high in the organization's hierarchy, often those who report directly to executive or senior managers. This group of managers is

> **Issue: Vision & Strategy (ABC AG, Sales Division)**
>
> Why? ES shows that the employees do not know or understand the strategy. They only they support it out of a general emotional commitment at best. This leads to a loss of trust in management, uncertainty, turnover tendencies.
>
> Your task is to find answers to the following question:
>
> What do <u>we</u> have to do so that the strategy ...
> - ... is clearly and correctly understood
> - ... gets accepted
> - ... is assessed as correct, convincing ("That's it!")
> - ... leads to positive excitement ("Wow!")
> - ... is supported through the work of our subordinates
>
> Who? M. Krueger, H.J. Werner, S. Miller, ...

Figure 14.9: Example case of an action field as input for stage two of a manager ES workshop.

usually much too large for one single ES workshop. It is also rarely possible to assemble them all in one workshop, because of their overfull appointment calendars and because they would generally not be willing to set aside the time needed for such a workshop. Yet, to properly involve this group into the survey results is decisive for the momentum of the follow-up processes in general.

The two-phase workshop begins with a preparatory phase where only a small group of hand-picked managers (senior spokespersons, high potentials, seasoned warhorses, etc.) assemble to screen the results in an effort to answer the questions "What do we have to do?" and "Who should coordinate and drive these actions?" Typically, the number of such actions is restricted to not more than three.

Consider a case. Figure 14.9 shows an example from a German computer company. The ES had shown that the employees did not understand the company's strategy. The participants in the preparatory workshop had concluded that this required action with a particular set of goals. They had also identified a number of individuals who they felt were particularly able and motivated to coordinate and drive actions aiming at solving the I-do-not-know-the-strategy problem. After formulating the slide in Figure 14.9 (and two more such slides covering two other topics), they presented their ideas to the executive manager responsible for the entire area. After some fine-tuning, they then prepared a final version of the slide and approached the persons identified as action managers to get their agreement. In the main phase of the workshop (see Table 14.7), all senior and middle managers of the area were invited. (The workshop was embedded into the agenda of a regular manager's meeting day.) This workshop began with an external ES expert presenting the survey results. Then, the responsible executive positioned himself with respect to the results: "This is how I see the results: First, ..." Then, the work from the preparatory phase was presented by a spokesperson of the participating managers. Although this work presents clear tasks, it is almost always gratefully accepted by the participants: A group of respected colleagues already invested time and effort to promote the things that have to be done. The participants were then asked to identify which one (only one!) of the topics they wanted to support with their own ideas and contributions. They then immediately spread out into break-out sessions where they began to work—under the supervision of the preselected action managers—for one hour on first ideas of action plans for their respective problem and task. Finally, they all came back to the plenum, where they reported their ideas and on how they wanted to proceed. The executive manager then concluded this workshop.

Experience shows that the two-phase workshop is well-accepted by managers. It does not waste time with endless discussions but focuses on tangible outcomes. It also shows who is in charge in which way. The survey expert remains the survey expert, and the executive manager can be seen as the decision maker. The problem task managers drive the actions, and every manager is involved in conceiving one action. Every manager, moreover, may be responsible to implement all actions in his or her area of responsibility.

14.10 Planning Batteries of ES Workshops

In practice, an ES workshop hardly ever comes as a single event. In many organizations it used to be tradition to conduct hundreds of such workshops, often with all workgroups of the shop-floor. Workshops with managers, on the other hand, are not that common. Yet, things have changed, and many companies have reduced the number of ES workshops with shop-floor employees drastically, while running considerably more manager workshops on all levels. The main reasons for this shift is that shop-floor workshops tend to rediscover the same issues over and over again (usually those that are already addressed in the areas of focus defined by executive management), while managerial involvement into the ES follow-up processes is crucial for effects that last. ES workshops, in any case, remain a substantial investment of the company. Hence, all possibilities to optimize their cost-benefit ratio should be considered.

A typical mistake is to conduct too many workshops in a parallel fashion. With parallel workshops, there is no transfer from one workshop to the other. A sequential arrangement of workshops over time is often more productive. For example, one may first conduct one workshop and then carry its (non-sensitive, not person-related) results into the second workshop as suggestions for where to start further discussions. This often leads to superior results (more precise, more suggestive, deeper, interconnected, etc.), because the later workshop stands on the shoulders of the previous one. However, the sequential approach also carries its risks: If the previous results do not properly characterize the situation of a later workshop group, then these results can slow down progress, because the participants of the second workshop must first overcome the wrong seed. The mistaken assumptions may even go unnoticed.

A better design, thus, is to be more careful with the seed information in the second workshop. One should first run a set of ES workshops in a strictly parallel way with different facilitators. When they are done, the results of these workshops are consolidated and, in particular, carefully sieved for commonalities. In case of doubt, one may conduct a few additional workshops. It is only these commonalities which are then carried into a second cluster of parallel workshops. When they are completed, the results are again checked for common topics. This *cumulative* approach can be terminated when convergence is reached in the sense that nothing new is discovered anymore. The common topics should then be clear and no further workshops are needed. The remaining topics are local ones, and they can be addressed in regular meetings of the respective workgroups. Experience shows that the theoretical possibility that series of workshops do not lead to any common topics is unrealistic. Often, the opposite is true: The common topics typically are also the important topics.

A case that deserves special attention when planning workshops is a focal group that assesses its supervisor negatively. "Poor" scores on the supervisor should be noticed by the facilitator and by the supervisor's manager before there is a workshop with the supervisor's employees. In that case, one should, prior to the workshop, arrange for a one-on-one meeting of this supervisor with his/her manager as described in Section 11.4. Under no circumstances should the supervisor be forced to facilitate the workshop him- or herself. Neither should such supervisors be left in doubt about how their managers view the situation, and what they intend to do about it.

14.9 Additional Follow-Up Work on ES Workshop Results

The results of an ES workshop can often be improved by further work after the workshop. For example, the comments may lead to hypotheses that can be studied statistically in the survey data; additional theory can be consulted to answer substantive questions; or the various issues can be interrelated in causal networks.

Additional Statistical Analysis of the Survey Data

Additional statistical studies of hypotheses generated in the workshops can be done in many ways. A simple case is the hypothesis that a certain issue is perceived differently by different strata or subgroups of the workforce. For example, bureaucracy can be a problem for blue-collar workers in certain subsidiaries, but it may be irrelevant for white-collar employees in general. Statistically breaking down the data can show the boundaries for generalizing certain diagnostic insights. Knowing such boundaries helps to avoid actions that are not needed. Other hypotheses can require deeper statistical modeling. For example, the workshops may have generated the hypothesis that persons who intend to leave the organizations do so because they feel that their chances for advancement in this organization are limited. Regression analysis, MDS (see Figure 12.9), or structural equation modeling (see Figure 12.14), can then be used to study such hypotheses, while discriminant analysis would show the major differences of persons with high and low turnover intentions, for example.

Consulting Additional Theory in the Literature

ES workshops sometimes lead to topics where additional theory can help. For example, in one company the survey and the ensuing discussions of the results identified 'trust in top management' as a problem issue. One could search for good predictors of trust in the data, but the variables may not lend themselves to answer this question very well. A better or, in any case, a complementary approach is to consult the research literature on trust. Science often provides excellent answers to such questions, and there is no need to reinvent or rediscover the wheel over and over again. This means, however, that experts on substance—not only on statistics—are needed at this stage.

Understanding Opportunities

ES results often contain various opportunities for powerful actions and important decisions. However, seldom are such opportunities very obvious. Consider, for example, the case where the survey shows that the employees are dissatisfied with their supervisor's feedback on performance. A rather direct response to this finding is to make performance feedback an action field. However, one could also use this finding to launch a general discussion on performance and on performance management (goals, target, criteria, expectations, consequences and rewards, outlooks, etc.). The ES results certainly legitimize such a response. However, one should not take that road before it is clear what its potentials and risks are and what needs to be done to reach an optimal end result.

Cause-And-Effect Analyses for Problem Areas

If the ES identifies problem areas, they usually require some form of cause-and-effect analysis. Statistical analyses provide one type of answer, but one can also attempt to fit the survey data and the workshop results by logical reasoning and substantive arguments into various forms of causal networks. For example, the problem area 'low trust in top management' was studied by a focus group for its "drivers." The result is the diagram in Figure 14.10. It shows that 'management by walking around' would definitely not solve the problem. Rather, the causal network suggests to first work on the company's logistical problems, involving employees with particular competence.

Cause-and-effect diagrams are not easy to generate, even though there are some proposal that may help to get started. For example, fishbone diagrams are schemas where the head of the fish represents the problem and the bones the problems that generate it. Substantive suggestions such as the *five M's* (materials, methods, manpower, machinery, maintenance; Peratec Ltd, 1994) may help for an initial problem sorting. Similarly, stream analysis (Borg, 1995; Porras, 1987) suggests to first sort the problems into four problem streams assumed to represent the basic dimensions of any socio-technical system; issues that appear to be root problems are placed towards the top, and issues that flow from the root problems at the bottom of the streams; the issues can be shifted when they are interconnected (see Figure 14.11). The consistency of the network is repeatedly tested by the problem stories it implies: If they are con-

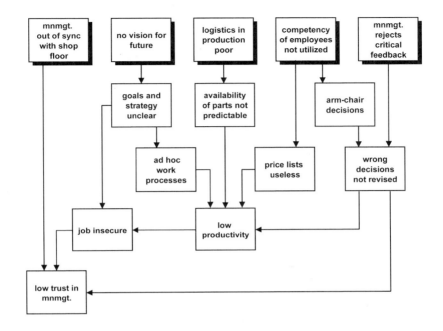

Figure 14.10. Example of a cause-and-effects diagram generated by a focus group for the issue "low trust in management"

vincing and can be summarized under griping titles[55], one has a useful foundation for communication and for action planning.

Even if no detailed cause-and-effect diagram is worked out in the end, the mere attempt to construct a diagram can be worth the time and effort. It induces at least a disposition to think in networks and interdependencies, and not in isolated actions. In practice, it often does not take long to see what the root problems are. Once this is clear, detailed analyses the effects and their interactions that flow from these root problems are not needed anymore.

Testing the Strategic Value of Possible Areas of Action

Another useful activity after the survey and the ensuing ES workshops is to check the strategic value of possible areas of action. Management often feels under pressure to quickly deliver actions so that the employees notice that management appreciates

---

[55] An example for such a problem story is "fire extinction thinking", where planning is understaffed (O stream), where people who manage crises get most recognition (S stream), where machines and computers are designed so that they can easily handle extra loads (T stream), and where open offices (P stream) make it difficult to thinking about complex plans. This should lead to symptoms such as "always behind plan", "no rewards for being on time", and "information always too late".

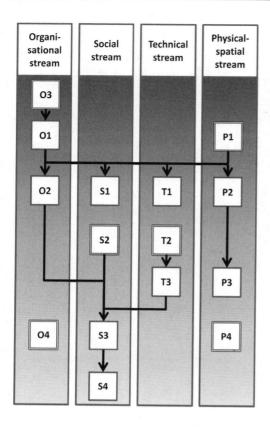

Figure 14.11. Symbolic stream analysis diagram.

their input and indeed "acts" as promised. Yet, such actions can easily be strategically useless or even a waste of resources that should better be invested differently. Indeed, they can be counterproductive if nothing of real substance follows. What is strategically valuable can be found out by SWOT analysis, where the action is evaluated vis-à-vis its role in promoting apparent opportunities (O) and reducing likely threats (T) by building necessary strengths (S) and reducing obstructive weaknesses (W).

Summarizing how Workshop Participants Interrelate the Topics

Top management sometimes asks the facilitator of an ES workshop (in particular one for managers) to report to them how the workshop went and what it produced. Before answering such a request, the facilitator must first clarify what the rules say about communicating such information. Clearly, one should never report what particular individuals said in the workshop. The facilitators should also think twice before they report their personal impressions about the "mood" during the workshop, the "cooperativeness" of the participants and so on. Only experienced facilitators should dare to walk on such thin ice. They can always ask themselves what would happen if the participants of the workshop knew what they are reporting to top management. Would they agree that this is a proper description of the workshop? And would they accept that the facilitator is reporting information that belongs to the group? Asking questions like these results in reports that are more descriptive than impressionistic, and predictions on the participants' future behavior should always be complemented by warnings about the speculative nature of these hypotheses.

Top managers sometimes actively attempt to influence the workshop by picking a facilitator who they expect to really "challenge" the participants in their habitual ways of thinking. For example, a facilitator who is a stereotypical no-nonsense action-oriented manager rather than the stereotypical empathetic HR manager is often their favorite. After the workshop, they are then interested to hear how the partici-

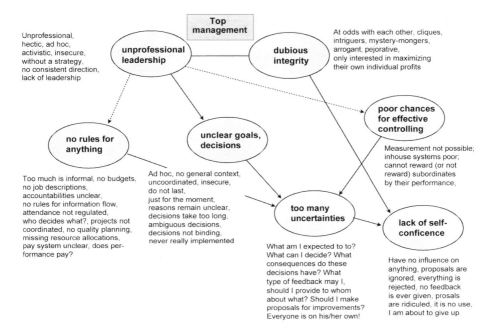

Figure 14.12. Example of a facilitator-perceived cause-and-effects structure of the comments produced in a managers' ES workshop.

pants responded when they had to deal with someone who does not easily accept lamenting, vague comments, ambiguous finger-pointing, or simple laziness. The facilitator, thus, is often expected to write up his or her general impressions on these meta-topics.

The participants may also want the facilitator to summarize or even further develop the results of the workshop. Indeed, the participants may even be grateful if the facilitator offers that he or she will attempt to sort and structure the comments collected after the workshop—and return the result to them for their approval. The time of the workshop is often not sufficient to work out substantively convincing clusters, concise and powerful headlines, or even plausible causal relationships that interconnect the various issues. The results of such additional brain work after the workshop can then be presented to the participants or some representatives of them for their information, approval, or possible fine-tuning.

Figure 14.12 shows an example of a facilitator's work that summarizes the results of a series of workshops with middle managers in an IT company. The facilitator here sorted the comments into a hierarchical network that summarizes what he sensed to be the participants' thinking behind the comments they made during the workshops. Note that this is not a theory about facts but about the psychology of the participants. It shows a number of topical clusters (ellipses) and various paths that interconnect them (closed = B depends on A; dotted = A influences B). In this example, the facilitator felt that the middle managers ultimately attributed all the listed problems to the small group of top managers. This is interesting information for top management, even though this is just the facilitator's hypothesis on the cause-and-effect relations in the minds of the workshop participants[56]. On the other hand, if the facilitators are experienced consultants, they can often diagnose a problem situation quickly and reliably. Moreover, if they know before the workshop(s) that such reports must be produced afterwards, they can test and retest their judgments during the workshop(s) until they arrive at reliable problem stories.

---

[56] There are various ways to validate such theories (Coffey & Atkinson, 1995). In the given case, the network shown in Figure 14.12 was presented to a random sample of the participants of the workshops for their feedback and approval.

15 Action Management

The quality of an ES project depends on its contributions to the goals of the organization. The ES and the momentum that it generates should normally result in actions that affect employees' and (in particular) management's behavior. Actions are special activity patterns implemented to reach certain goals. They differ from routine activities by having both a start and an end point, and by aiming to bring about a particular change. Actions can vary a lot in their scope and complexity, ranging from small measures (e.g., moving a printer from office A to office B) to huge projects consisting of a network of interlocking activities that involve many employees, functions, and departments over a longer period of time (e.g., reorganizing the sales force).

The ES literature usually strongly recommends conducting an ES only if it leads to actions. Yet, little is said on exactly what actions are envisaged and how one should construct them. If these actions are not generated systematically, experience in many ES projects shows that even highly motivated organizations do not produce more than alibi actions at the top or an unaligned potpourri of actions at the shop-floor level.

Systematic action management requires, for example, clearly defined tasks that specify the action's goals, its side constraints, and the roles and authorities of all people involved and affected by the action. Good action planning should also include plans for controlling the action's implementation. One way to do this is to rely on the action's milestones where evaluation of progress and reporting is natural. Then, action planning must pay attention to the human side of action management. The people involved in the actions should want to work on the action, and they should have the capabilities, energy, and resources to do the job. Those people affected by the action should be kept informed about the action, its goals and benefits, and its status of implementation.

15.1 Developing Ideas for Actions

Before any action planning can begin, one first has to bridge the gap from an ES presentation and some areas of focus to specifying certain ideas on what should be done. If the ES has shown, for example, that the employees do not really understand the company's strategy, "good understanding of the strategy by every employee" may become an area of focus. One can then—as it is often done in practice—assign this

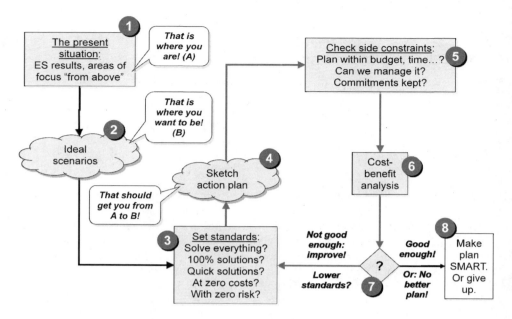

Figure 15.1. Steps for developing action ideas.

area of focus to an action manager with the following task: "Plan and implement actions that improve the common understanding of the company's strategy." This may be sufficiently precise for an experienced manager to generate some first ideas, but it leaves too much open for any more concrete action planning. For example, what "improvement" is deemed sufficient, or how much money may be spent for information measures?

Moreover, there is rarely a one-to-one correspondence of areas of focus and actions. Actions typically have *multiple* consequences, direct and indirect ones, impacting a number of different content areas. For example, if the ES finds that the supervisors' performance feedback to employees is poor, then an action that trains supervisors to give better performance feedback should not only lead to higher employee performance, but it may also improve vertical communication, promote the workgroup's productivity, build trust in management, and improve organizational commitment. Actions, thus, can serve many different goals. Conversely, one particular area of focus can be addressed by several different actions, directly or indirectly.

When considering particular actions, one must also develop an idea of what appears realistic in terms of costs and time, and what goals should be formulated for the actions. The many considerations that are required when specifying what actions should be pursued can be organized in a structured process as shown in Figure 15.1.

Its starting point is the status quo "after the survey" as defined by the ES survey results and its areas of focus. With this information, a group of persons (e.g., the ES project team with the support of some managers, specialists, and experts) can run a workshop that aims at specifying ideas or concepts of actions that can then be assigned as tasks for further work.

1) In the first step of the workshop, clarify where the organization is (status quo, situation "A"). Are there, in particular, general areas of focus and, if so, what exactly is their present condition? How bad or good is this condition? Are there any areas of focus defined by top management?

2) Then, given the situation as it is, answer the question what would be an ideal situation ("B")? For example, if employees say that they do not understand the company's strategy sufficiently well, an ideal situation may be one where every employee always has access not only to the strategy in general, but also to information on what all this means for his or her individual work, simply by hitting "F7" on their computers or by asking their direct supervisors. Such ideal scenarios describe where one wants to be. Note that ideal scenarios are best derived by *not* paying close (or any!) attention to what is feasible in terms of costs and other resources. Rather, they should be "dream" conditions.

3) Set standards for any feasible action from A to B. For example, such actions should certainly not take "forever." Yet, how quickly should the action reach its goal? A very demanding requirement would be: Immediately! Indeed, "forever" and "immediately" define the logical bounds for a time standard. Similar standards can be set for criteria such as costs, quality, and risks. To begin with, one may simply define a very tight "solution quadrant" for actions by requiring: time=immediately, costs=zero, quality=100% and risks=none. These standards can later be lowered to more realistic levels, but to get started, tight requirements are better than loose ones.

4) Sketch ideas of action plans that get you from A to B (or at least closer to B).

5) Check whether these first ideas of action plans are feasible: Do they satisfy the standards defined in Step 3? Do they also satisfy further criteria that one needs to keep an eye on; for example, are they in agreement with promises made earlier to those affected by the actions? And are the action plans realistic, for example, in terms of time?

6) Sort all action plans in terms of their cost-benefit ratios, where "costs" lump together every input that goes into the action (man days, money, risks, collateral damages) and where "benefits" summarize all the action's likely output (effects on business goals, productivity, customer satisfaction, work climate, quality of products, etc.).

7) Decide if the action plan that is best in terms of cost-benefit is "good" or at least "acceptable". If so, pursue this plan further. If not, give up completely, or conduct another planning cycle, beginning with Step 3, where you possibly want to lower your standards to more realistic (but still acceptable) le-

vels. Then, draft new actions, or modify the old ones, check whether they satisfy the constraints for the action plans, etc.

8) Once a decision on a particular action has been made, this plan can be further specified in "smart" terms before it is assigned to the action director. Smart action plans are S=specific (they focus on specific goals, criteria, and constraints); M=measurable/motivating (they indicate how to measure success; set challenging goals); A=aligned (they make sure the action is aligned with strategy and operational goals); R=realistic/reasonable/relevant (they concentrate on what appears possible and what degree of perfection makes sense; they are relevant for achieving the particular goals); and T=time-related (specify an end date for the action).

A perfect action reaches all its goals and satisfies all side constraints. Such actions, however, are typically hard to find so that one has to search for an acceptable compromise by loosening the constraints on budget, time, risk, etc., and/or by lowering the demands concerning the action's goals (=B). For example, rather than looking for a perfect solution, a work-around or fix may be all that can be accomplished within the given time and budget. Indeed, not going for an almost perfect but for an 80:20 solution may be an optimal strategy within the system of given operational and strategic goals. On the other hand, one may also find that it is better not to pursue a given area of focus at the present time. It is often true that concentrating on a few—sometimes even on only one—area of focus yields better overall effects than splitting up one's resources on many unrelated actions. Note that "one action" does not necessarily mean that only "one issue" is being addressed. Rather, good actions typically have a deep structure and lead to multiple effects.

15.2 Organizing Actions

Successful action planning requires solving a number of organizational issues such as clarifying which persons are involved in the action and in which roles, or deciding on how the work required for the action is to be coordinated with normal work.

Level of Action

Most ES follow-up processes contain not one but many—often hundreds or thousands—of actions. In the early days of ES projects, actions were almost completely restricted to activities at the shop floor. Moreover, these actions usually focused on local issues where action was "needed," where a problem had to be fixed or a fire had to be extinguished. Today, one attempts to align all actions along strategic directions. This requires coordinating actions in a multilevel approach that distinguishes:

- *Company-wide actions* such as, introducing a performance-related pay system or informing employees about the company's strategy

- *Area-wide actions* on the level of functions, departments, or areas such as, for example, re-organizing the sales force in the company's Scandinavian subsidiaries
- *Local actions* at the shop-floor level such as moving some employees from one office to another

Roles in Action Management

Most actions involve different people or groups of people in three basic ways: Some are involved in planning and implementing the action, others are merely affected by the actions. For the rest, the action is irrelevant. Those who are involved in the action can be involved in one or several of the following roles:

- *Customer.* Person or group who orders the action. This important role often remains unclear in practice. A striking example is the customer of the ES project itself: It is often initiated by the HR department, but the HR department is rarely the customer. (Most often, the executive board is the customer of the ES—sometimes without knowing it.)
- *Beneficiary.* Person or group who, by design, profits from the action.
- *Sponsor.* Person or group who supports the action by providing needed resources such as money, people, time, or power.
- *Promoter.* Person or group who actively supports running the action.
- *Decider.* Person or group who, at various points of the action's course, decides on which alternative to take (e.g., when specifying the action's goals, when setting dates for milestones, when planning the budget, when setting quality expectations, repair measures if the action runs into problems).
- *Action director.* The person who is given the responsibility for coordinating the action and for driving the action's progress. The action manager reports to the decider at specified points in time or when decisions concerning the project are needed.
- *Action team member.* Larger actions (such as the ES project) are run by action teams. Such a team is either a natural team (e.g., the executive board) or a group of persons who are assembled just for the purpose of running the action. The action team can be structured into a core team and various satellite teams or persons, some of them with temporary assignments only. The action team plans the action and coordinates the action, and often also does most of the work.
- *Action part manager.* A member of the action team who is responsible for a part of the action such as accounting or communicating to persons affected by the action.
- *External action contributor.* Person or group who contributes to the action without being members of the action team. Examples are experts or specialists on various issues such as, for example, an advertising agency that works out a media plan for communicating the action to outsiders.

Selecting Action Directors and Action Team Members

Action directors should be selected so that one can be reasonably sure that the action will reach its goals within the bounds of the given resources. An additional criterion is that the action should be managed such that the action manager's normal duties suffer as little as possible. Moreover, the action directors must be skillful enough to manage the action so that it does not lead to collateral damages on organizational climate or on the future cooperation among employees or groups. In terms of competencies, this means that a good action director should not only have technical skills regarding the issues that the action focuses on, but also good management skills, including social skills. If the action is a complex project, then at least some project management experience is required. Project management expertise can possibly be improved by outside experts, but the action director must be the type of person who is resourceful and determined enough to see that the action is led to success in spite of all the obstacles and problems that inevitably pop up sooner or later in any project. This not only requires maintaining the action team's cohesion, but also using or building the needed social capital, i.e., a network of good relations to the various persons and groups involved in and affected by the action.

Similar criteria can be used to select the people needed for an action team, but the emphasis is more on technical and methodological expertise, and less on managerial skills. In the end, the action team should assemble a good mix of people with different competencies, skills, and experience. In addition, the various people should get along well with each other. Thus, when assembling an action team, care must be taken not to select people with unsettled conflicts or people who do not want to participate. This would only lead to problems later on, to endless mock discussions on side issues without rational solutions. Similarly, people who indicate they do not have the necessary time should not be considered. Ideally, all team members should *want* to participate in the team for example, because they are interested in the particular issues that the actions focus on or because they see their work in the team as an opportunity to gain project experience.

Action team members need not all come from inside the organization, but the action director should always be an insider who knows the organization well, and who has a network of social connections. When persons from outside the organization become members of the action team, they usually first work out and sign a contract with the action director that makes sure that both sides understand their responsibilities and deliverables.

Action Management vs. Line Management

Actions are special assignments that typically require people from the given workforce. In principle, there are three approaches to deal with this issue for the action members:

- *Hierarchy*. Action team members work only in the action, and stop working in their normal jobs. Sometimes, they even physically move to a special action bureau. The action director has full authority over these persons.
- *Matrix*. The persons in the action team remain in their jobs and take over action responsibilities on top. They have two managers to report to, their team supervisor and the project director.

- *Influence.* No particular structure is defined. The action director simply coordinates work on the actions, but she gets no formal authority over the action team members. The only power she has is her personal influence on line managers and action team members.

In ES projects, one almost always uses a matrix approach. One reason is that an action team that only works on the action itself quickly begins to see everything from the action's perspective, while in the matrix the action team members remain involved in their usual job environment and the feedback that comes from this environment. It enables action team members to communicate with their colleagues in the base organization and bring their suggestions back to the action team. The matrix, moreover, is more flexible. It avoids under-utilizing people at times, and it allows temporarily making use of those key people with special capabilities who are often the busiest people in an organization. The line managers of these specialists must agree to release them to the action team and provide cover to do their work in the meantime. This becomes a lot easier if these special people are only involved in the action at times but not for weeks or months.

A matrix, however, has a basic problem too. There is always a latent conflict between the action team and line management for resources that can easily lead to open or covert resistance of the line against the action. Line managers, for example, do not pass on important information or they play an I-am-difficult-to-reach tactic when action team members want appointments with them. This problem can be reduced if line managers understand that the action is to their benefit, too. It also helps if they are kept informed about the action's progress and if they are invited to discuss the action plans.

The Action Mission Contract

A typical reason for poor actions is the absence of a charter that specifies the action's goals and scope. The action's mission needs to be negotiated between the customer and the action director until it becomes sufficiently clear to both sides. In the end, both sides should agree on an action brief in the form of a signed mission contract, as shown for the example "reduce night work" in Figure 15.2. This contract specifies various conditions that help planning and evaluating the action. To work out such a mission contract, the customer may begin by specifying a few key requirements (e.g., dates or goals) and then ask the action director to work out a first draft of the mission contract. This proposal is then discussed, fine-tuned, and closed by signing it.

The mission contract form in Figure 15.2 is, of course, just an illustrative model case. It can be modified, extended, or simplified to fit the particular action. What one wants to specify in the end depends on how "big" the action is. Actions that consume a lot of resources typically need to be more carefully defined than little actions. Yet, one should avoid the common mistake to assume from the start that everything is clear anyway, and that no mission contract is needed. Even if this is true, it does not guarantee that the customer, for example, later remembers exactly how the action was specified.

goals	description	criterion	benefit	input	musts	risks
Super goal	Increase productivity					
Action goal	Reduce night work				Total production must rise	
Sub-goal 1	Work processes clear to all employees	Everyone knows processes	Employees know what to do	Workshops, trainings		
Sub-goal 2	Deadlines are met in internal processes	Deliveries are on schedule	Reduced times of over or under capacity	Costs for planning, controlling		
Sub-goal 3	Supplies are top quality	Number of defects very small	Reduced costs for rework	Time for quality control		Compulsive zero defect thinking

| End of planning: Apr 2, 2006 Customer: H. Meier Action team members: X, Y, .. |
| Action start: Apr 29, 2006 Decider: E. Schmidt |
| Action end: Aug 2, 2006 Action director: K. Ullrich |

| Date: Mar 27, 06 | Signature customer: *Hans Meier* | Signature decider: *E. Schmidt* | Signature action director: *K. Ullrich* |

Figure 15.2. Example of an action mission contract.

Some specifications in the form in Figure 15.2 may seem unnecessary. Defining a super-goal for the action is one example. Yet, explicating such a super-goal often helps to motivate the members of the action team by showing them that they contribute to an important objective. Similarly, thinking at least once about the benefits of the action helps to align the action with business goals and strategy.

The "musts" column defines what is critical for evaluating any action plan as a possible solution or not. For example, a must for new software in department X may be that it can read data files generated with the software presently used.

The column "risks" may also be important (e.g., if the action has implications on safety at work or if meeting a particular deadline with the action is an absolute must). In such cases, all foreseeable risks should be listed and assessed in an X-Y diagram where Y="consequences of event" and X="probability of event." For the most consequential and/or the most likely events in this risk portfolio one should conceive of if-then emergency measures (repair plans, escalation measures, plan "B" alternatives, etc.) as supplementary parts of the action plan.

Defining the Action Director's Action Space

In any action, the action director and the action team members must know the parameters of their action space, i.e., their tasks, responsibilities, and authorities. These

tasks	responsiblities	authorities
• Defines goals, success criteria of action with decider • Plans milestones and activities • Plans needed costs, resources • Proposes action team members, substitutes to decider • Assigns work to action team members (incl. vacation) together with line managers • Manages action team such that goals are reached • Regularly conducts should-is assessments on action's progress, side constraints • Reports major should-is (real, likely) deviations to decider • Documents action process • Checks action's risk regularly	• Keeps action within budget • Keeps action on time • Makes sure that milestones are reached • Keeps decider informed about action • Informs employees affected by action • Finds solutions to problems in action's progress • In case of major problems (real, likely), informs decider early	• Has disciplinary authority over action team members • Has substantive authority over action team members • Decides on budget • Can veto selection of action team members • Decides on solutions, proposals that go to decider • Can veto any decision of action team members • Has access to all information relevant for action • In matters of the action, reports to decider only, not to line managers

Figure 15.3. Defining elements of the action space of an action director.

definitions must be worked out anew for each action. Often, the action director is first assigned an action with rather vague specifications, and then it becomes the action director's responsibility to *actively* ask for more precision. To do this, he can work out a proposal as shown in Figure 15.3 and then discuss it with the decider. Often, a few iterations are needed before these specifications are both comprehensive and clear enough to run the action. The typical problem in a definitional framework as in Figure 15.3 is that the action director's authorities remain ill-defined or are simply so weak that personal influence becomes the only power at the action director's disposal.

When to Begin Action Planning

The action director should not begin work on detailed action planning before the action's goals and side constraints have not been made sufficiently clear—in writing. That sounds easier than it is, because the action director walks a fine line when he keeps asking for more precise definitions. The action customer may get angry that the "stupid" action director does not seem to understand what is clear to "everybody." Fact is that it often is not clear to anybody, not even to the customer him- or herself. Yet, as we saw in Figure 15.1, it is not that easy to work out a precise idea of an action and its many side constraints that unambiguously define the task of the action director. So, a realistic strategy for both the action customer and the action director would be to attempt definitions that are as clear as possible to get started, but *remain open* for possible modifications later on when actual planning shows problems or opportunities that were not noticed before.

15.3 Foundations of Action Planning

When the concept of the action and its conditions are clear, the action can be planned concretely and in more detail. This is best done if certain general principles are observed.

Planning Actions Hierarchically

Action planning in practice is often concentrated on the level of specifying detail after detail, and then, to save space for communication, cramming everything with special terminology and acronyms. There are often no *master plans* that give an overview of the major elements of the action in a language that everyone can understand. This not only makes it difficult to communicate the action plan to outsiders, but outsiders easily get the impression that they cannot contribute anything to the plan. Hence, there is no discussion on the action plan, and consequently there is little involvement in the plan or even resistance against it. Moreover, overly detailed plans are difficult to control in their implementation phase. On the other hand, having an action plan that is very broad in scope may be too vague to actually manage progress. The solution is to draft plans *on several levels at the same time*. The minimum level should be two levels: a plan at the milestone level for guidance and overview, and one on the activity level for task management.

Milestones mark points of transition in an action plan. A milestone describes what, according to plan, is true at time t. Two special milestones are condition A (the starting situation) and B (the goal situation) in Figure 15.1. Other milestones are the intermediate points that lie on the way from A to B (see Figure 15.6 for examples). They break down the path from A to B into a series of steps and stages. Milestones are critically important for keeping track of action progress.

Activities consist of what is done to move the action ahead from one milestone towards the next milestone. They often get most of the attention when discussing an action plan, and they are often the only components of an action plan that are described in more detail. Figure 3.2 shows an example of a coarse master plan that shows only the outline of activity strings. There are eight types of activities, shown as horizontal bars over the time axis. The milestones would be descriptions of what is the case at the end of each bar or section of a bar.

When drafting an action plan, one often begins with one or two particular milestones (e.g., in case of the ES project plan in Figure 3.2); pivotal events for the plan are the timing of the data collection and also the date of results presentation. The former must be positioned so that it does not fall into a vacation period. Ideally, it should come shortly before this period, so that data analysis can be conducted while the employees are away, and the feedback processes can begin shortly after they are back.

If there are many (i.e., far more than ten, say) milestones and many activities, master plans tend to become cluttered and potentially unstructured. The solution is to break up the master plan onto several layers. It is like writing a book, with title, chap-

No.	What? [action]	Why? [benefit]	In which way? [activities]	With what? [resources]	Who? [name]	When assigned?	When done?
1							
2							
3							
4							

Figure 15.4. Example of a simple W form for action planning.

ter headings, section headings, and subsection headings. Care must be taken, however, to use only a minimal number of layers (not more than three at the most).

The Timeline of an Action

Experience with action planning and implementation has shown that it rarely makes sense to consider actions that extend over more than four months (Porras, 1987). If an action's final goal is too far away, people involved in the action easily get the impression that, since so much time is left, there is no need to begin work immediately. The action, thus, is set on a low priority and action team members fill their time with other activities or with ineffective work. Moreover, when the time span of the action gets long, then it becomes more difficult to control progress. As the intervals between milestones become longer, small planning errors and unforeseen problems tend to accumulate without anyone noticing that the plan begins to run out of time. Only when the date of the next milestone is close, the action team notices—in panic—that time is running out and that the available time buffers may be too tight to catch up. Finally, in today's turbulent times, a long time span for an action always implies the risk that by the time the action approaches its end, the original goals are not that important anymore. However, there is no rule that specifies an optimal planning horizon. Actions that focus on "eternal" topics, for example, are not in danger to become obsolete before they reach their end (e.g., actions that focus on improving people management). What one should do in such long-range planning cases, though, is not go into a lot of fine-grained activities planning and date fixing for parts of the action that are scheduled far ahead in the future, because when the plan gets there, one often has to redo this planning.

15.4 Simple Action Planning Tools

Many organizations (industrial companies in particular) have their own methods and standard forms for planning actions. Usually, such methods are relatively simple, but nevertheless useful tools similar to what we now describe.

"W" Action Forms

The most popular action planning tools are variants of what can be characterized as a W action form. They are simply spread sheets or printed forms as illustrated in Figure 15.4. The purpose of such forms is to make sure that at least some specifications of the action plan are documented in writing, without going into a lot of detail. What the form asks are a number of important "W" questions in sentences such as "What should be done, and why, and in which way, by whom until when?"

- *What?* What is the name of the action? What is it concerned with?
- *Why?* What are the goals of this action? What is it trying to accomplish? Who are the beneficiaries of this action?
- *In which way?* By what activities is the action proceeding? In which way does the action intend to reach its goals?
- *With what?* With what resources (budget, people, support) can the action work?
- *Who?* Who is responsible for managing the action? (action director, possibly also other relevant people such as decision maker or customer)
- *When assigned?* When was the action assigned to the action director? [date]
- *When done?* When is the action planned to come to an end? When does it reach important milestones? [date]

Not all of these questions have to be addressed in a W action form. In practice, the minimum is 'What', 'Who', and 'When done.' Saying something about 'Why' is desirable, though, because its forces the action team to come up with a written statement on the action's purpose and its beneficiaries rather than with a shallow "That is obvious anyway!"—which often is not true after all.

Specifications on the 'Why' are sometimes expressed in terms of dollars, man days, or other productivity measures. In some companies, there even exist long lists with productivity variables that one can use for that purpose.

W forms are particularly useful at the shop-floor level because most actions at that level are rather simple ones. They often consist of just one or two activities that are described in sufficient detail by answering a few W questions. The information captured in such a form is, in any case, better than not documenting anything about the action in writing.

"W" Action Forms with Status Indicators

W action forms as the one in Figure 15.4 are sometimes extended by adding a column that shows a status indicator. Two examples—both from the German automobile industry—for such an indicator are exhibited in Figure 15.5. The indicator on the left-hand side shows that the action is in its "planning phase," while the action on the right-hand side is "in an analysis phase," using the terminology of the respective companies.

When posting W action forms on public blackboards, the employees thus not only see who works on what actions, but they also get some information on the action's progress. In case of W action forms with status indicators, one may choose to mark

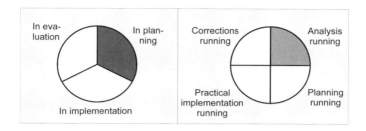

Figure 15.5. Two simple action status indicators.

the sectors of the status circles cumulatively. That is, for example, when the analysis phase in the action on the right-hand side of Figure 15.5 is over, one then simply leaves the W action form where it is but checks the next sector ("in planning") in addition. The last checked sector of the status indicator thus shows where the action is. This makes it easy to see at a glance that the action is nearing completion, an advantage when several action plans are exhibited (as, for example, in Figure 15.5). When the wheels begin to fill, this is also a nice signal of success.

15.5 Planning Complex Actions

Action planning tools of the W form type are too simple for planning and implementing large actions. Even for simpler actions, one should consider incorporating some features of more complex planning methods into the action plan.

Planning Milestones

Any action planning should begin with milestones, in particular with a clear definition of the action's desired outcome. Not only is it true that "if you don't know where you are going, you probably end up somewhere else," but any planning also gets inefficient if the goal is unclear.

Milestones in between the start and the goal result from segmenting the action into steps. These steps need not all lie on one single path. Rather, the more complex the action, the better it is to work simultaneously on different components that are linked in a network with common knots. This speeds up the action overall.

Milestones should generally satisfy a few requirements. They should be expressed in a language that is natural for the expertise of the people who are working on the action; positioned on important decision points that lend themselves to controlling action progress; measurable in terms of sub-goals[57]; limited in number (not more than

---

[57] A milestone such as "a proposal is worked out" is measurable in the sense that one can decide if this proposal is or is not available at the critical point in time. However, "a proposal" does not say anything

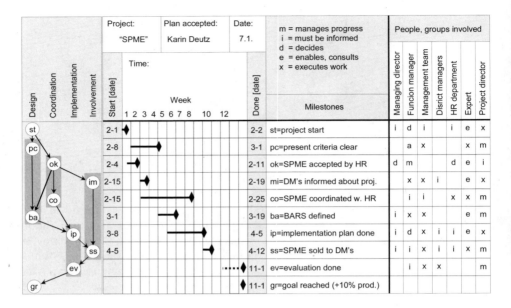

Figure 15.6. An example of a milestone plan for a project called "SPME."

10, otherwise break the action down into parts); and spaced in time intervals that are short enough to keep the action controllable.

An example for an action plan with milestones is shown in Figure 15.6, where each milestone is marked by a solid rhombus (♦) and the activities that lead to it with a horizontal fat line. The objective of this plan is to develop and implement a system for productivity measurement and enhancement ("SPME") for district managers of a computer company. The milestones are, for example, the project start (st) or the milestone "pc" which is characterized by the requirement that, at that point in time, the present criteria for productivity measurement of district managers are "clear" (i.e., fully collected, hierarchically structured, reliably prioritized, written up in an accessible way, etc.).

Figure 15.6 also exhibits an example of a milestone network plan in the panel on the left-hand side. It shows, for example, that milestone "ip" logically requires that both the milestone "co" and also milestone "ba" have been passed. In addition, this network plan organizes the different milestones into four strings of activities (design, coordination, implementation, and involvement).

The plan also shows the roles (based on the *MIDEX* scheme of Table 3.2) that various people or groups have in the different parts of the action. These roles are often not made clear enough in practice. Coarse role assignment such as "Mr. X is 'responsible' for the action" can easily lead to mistakes that can be avoided by more transpa-

---

about reaching the intended goals because no specifications about the quality of this proposal are formulated. This milestone is, therefore, substantively quite useless.

Man days	Start [date]	Time: day 1 2 3 4 5 6 7 8 9 10	End [date]	Activities	Managing director	Function manager	Mnmgt. Team	2 Reps of DM's	Expert	Projekt dorector	Project part man.
				Milestone: "ba" from: Hans Meier to: Brigitte Schmidt Plan accepted by: H.M. on 3-1 m = manages progress i = must be informed d = decides e = enables, consults x = executes work Persons, groups involved							
2	3-8		3-8	Explain concept, methods, process	i	i			x	m	i
1.25	3-8		3-8	Present old (=present) system	i	i			x		m
1.25	3-8		3-8	Explain structure of old system	i	i			x		m
5	3-9		3-9	Construct qualitat. criteria hierarchy	d	x			e		m
5	3-10		3-12	Quantify criteria hierarchy	d	x			e	i	m
2.5	3-12		3-12	Discuss role of base criteria	d	x			e	b	m
10	3-17		3-18	Formulate BARS (1)	d	x	x		e		m
3	3-19		3-19	Formulate BARS (2)	i	d	x	x	e	i	m
2.5	3-19		3-19	Define contingencies		d	x	x	e	i	m

Figure 15.7. Activities plan for activities leading to milestone "ba" in milestone plan of Figure 15.6.

rent planning. For example, a typical mistake in many actions is to simply forget to inform certain people or groups systematically about the action's progress.

A person or group can take on several roles simultaneously in any part of the action. Indeed, the simple "is responsible for" assignment that is typical for W action forms is one example. Yet, when planning actions it often pays to carefully consider focusing on main responsibilities and assigning them to one person or group only. If an action director is expected to do everything him- or herself all the time, then further role assignments are not needed.

Planning Activities

A milestone plan as in Figure 15.5 requires one to think about the activities that are needed to reach the respective milestone. To construct a first milestone plan, it suffices to work with lump notions of these activities. An expert typically has enough experience to reliably say that one can get from A to B, under normal circumstances, in some six weeks, say. Detailed planning of the required activities can be postponed for later. They, in turn, may lead to adjustments in the original milestone plan. Hence, milestone planning and activities planning remain closely related.

Very detailed planning of activities is typically only needed for the activities of the coming four to six weeks. This approach can save a lot of wasted work because plans for activities that come later often have to be adjusted when their time arrives. Exceptions to this recommendation are all activities that involve participation of top managers, because their appointment calendars tend to have a long planning horizon.

All activities should be broken down into parts that lead to measurable results. This makes it easy to control progress when carrying out an activity. Indeed, statements such as "80% of the work is done" only make sense if progress can be measured in this way.

Figure 15.7 shows an activities planning form. It describes the activities within the two-week activity bar leading to milestone "ba" in Figure 15.6. Most of the activities specified here are meetings of the function manager and his management team, together with the expert, where they specify what BAR (=behaviorally anchored rating) scales they want to use to measure a district manager's productivity. Only after they have worked out what they want, two representatives of the district managers are involved into fine-tuning these scales.

The planning form also shows a column where (internal) employee days are estimated. The first activity ("Explain concept, methods, process"), for example, is calculated to consume two employee days altogether. Such estimates can be made in different ways. If, for example, we assume that this activity needs one meeting of two hours with the function manager and four members of the management team, then this adds up to 5 persons × 2 hours = 1.2 employee days. Additionally, we here assume that instructing the action director and the action part manager through the expert will take 3 hours, adding another 6 hours or 0.8 employee days. In the end, the time consumed by the activities directly preceding milestone "ba" add up to 9.5 employee days.

Smart activities planning should also specify some time buffers because activities often run into unforeseen or unpredictable problems. Time buffers are particularly important if the dates for deliverables are crucial and if the various activities are complex, risky, and involve many persons. If time buffers become excessive, however, then an action may appear "dead" for the outsider, while it is actually just idle.

15.6 Controlling Action Implementation

A common pitfall in action management is to assume that once an action plan has been constructed it only needs to be "implemented." Practical experience shows that it is normal that even the best plan is hardly ever implemented as planned, in particular in complex actions. A plan, after all, is only a plan. It rests on a set of assumptions that may not be completely accurate or realistic. Some resources, for example, may not be available in the expected quantity or at the time when needed, and some activities may run into resistance by those who are affected by them. And, of course, events in the larger environment (e.g. power failures, mail strike, or heavy snowfall) may lead to serious delays. This all means that the action team must systematically control the action's progress so that it recognizes *as early as possible* when special interventions or adjustments of the plan are needed.

Principles of Action Controlling

Without controlling, actions are always endangered to peter out because they keep being pushed aside by unforeseen events and by the requirements of normal work which is the basis of an organization's reward system. Dates are postponed, people that are needed are not released because of "urgent" matters, or money is used up for other purposes, for example. The action director often notices these problems, but does not report it to the decision maker because the action's deviation from the plan appears correctable or because the action director does not want to appear incompetent in solving problems alone. Yet, not reporting the problems carries the risk that they grow to become uncontrollable. In that case, the decision maker will certainly ask why he or she was not informed about them earlier. To avoid constantly thinking about reporting or not reporting the action's status to the decision maker, status reports should become part of the action plan. That is, reporting is scheduled for certain milestones or dates, irrespective of how well the action is advancing.

Requesting systematic action reporting is often encountered with resistance in practice. Reporting can be seen as bureaucratic extra-work and even as a method to police the action director. Hence, one must show the advantages of action controlling to an action team, and explain its principles carefully:

- *Make the action plan binding.* Implementing an action must follow the action plan, and reporting on action progress must refer to this plan. The action plan, however, can be adjusted or changed—but only for good reasons and only "officially" in agreement with the decider. If so, then this new plan is binding. If this principle is dropped, the plan is not worth much because no one will take it seriously. The dates in the plan, for example, are not taken seriously, and people will not deliver input needed for the action's progress on time.
- *Define the criteria for progress before implementation.* Milestones should always be described with certain standards regarding quality, costs, and time. Such standards make progress reporting less arbitrary and simpler, often reducing it to going through a check list. Moreover, clear criteria also set clear goals, and clear goals make success more likely ("You get what you measure!").
- *Set the dates for (normal) progress reporting before implementation.* The action team should report on an action plan's progress at dates that are fixed before action implementation and that are part of the implementation plan. At the level of activities, reporting should be scheduled at intervals of 1-2 weeks, while at the level of milestones, reporting is usually done when the milestone is due or when it has been reached.
- *Require reports in writing and discuss them.* Written reports of individual action team members are, by themselves, insufficient for controlling action progress. They only serve to document the action, but they should be discussed in the action team. The discussion should assess the action's progress, its risks and problems, possible adjustments of the plan, preventive measures to keep the plan on course, measures if the plan goes astray, etc. Such discussions, moreover, motivate action team members to provide precise progress reports. It also informs everyone about the current overall state of the action.

- *Make controlling a part of the action plan.* The whole controlling system should be worked out before the action is implemented. It should be accepted by everyone as an integral part of the plan. To introduce controlling after action implementation is on its way already can be perceived as a signal of no trust.
- *Control action progress on all levels of the action plan.* Controlling should be done on all levels: master plan, milestone plans, activities plans, and all sub-plans. Often, different people are responsible for different plans, and each plan has its own goals, time horizons, and side constraints.

Reporting

Effective action controlling requires some written documentation of an action's progress on the various levels of the action plan:

- *Status reports.* Regular reports on action progress at fixed time intervals such as, for example, on the first Monday of each month.
- *Milestone reports.* Reports on reaching a milestone, in particular the very last milestone (final report). Milestone reports are usually edited by the action director and sent to the action's customer and decider. They should show, in a compact form, where the action is and whether it runs according to plan.
- *Activity reports.* Reports on the activities within the action. They are written by the persons responsible for the actions and sent to the action director.
- *Change reports.* Reports on changes of the action plan (goals, conditions). Change reports are sent from the action director to all action team members and to the decider to document his/her decision on changes.

Simple Reporting Forms

For many actions that follow an ES, simple action monitoring is sufficient, provided it is done systematically. Some forms should be worked out for that purpose. A model for such a form is shown in Figure 15.8. It exhibits the status of the action on four criteria—time, costs, people, and quality—on a three-point scale that ranges from "good" over "OK" to "critical." The categories of this scale are here marked with faces. An alternative would be a traffic light ranging from green over yellow to red. The idea is to use a form that shows at a glance if the action is in trouble. If it is not, then it takes only one glance to notice that. If there are "red" lights, then the action director should explain in the comment field what the problem is. For example, in case of a red light on the criterion "people," the problem may be that certain specialists who are needed in the action were not released by their line managers on time.

Reporting in Complex Actions

Systematic reporting is especially important to keep track of complex actions. Reporting here starts at the activity level where the actual implementation work is done. Figure 15.9 shows a reporting form for the activities in Figure 15.7. The panel in the lower left-hand corner of the form repeats the description of the activities and their

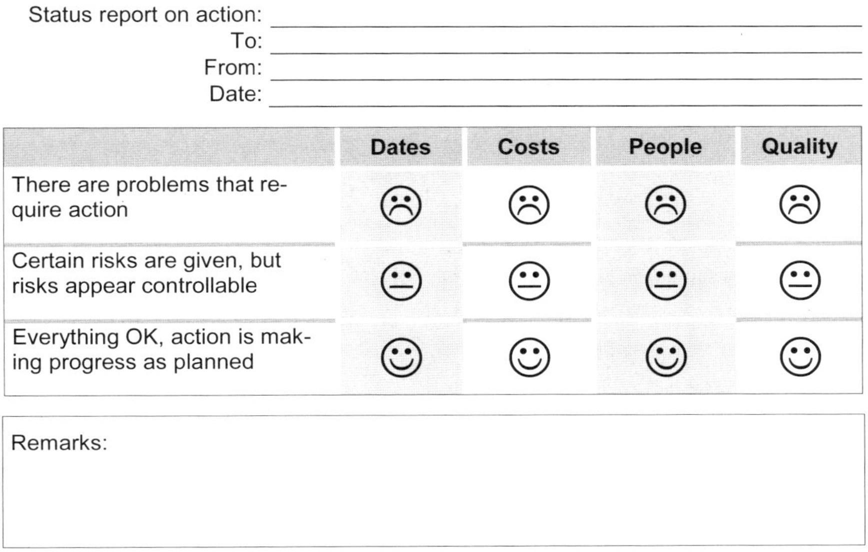

Status report on action: _____
To: _____
From: _____
Date: _____

	Dates	Costs	People	Quality
There are problems that require action	☹	☹	☹	☹
Certain risks are given, but risks appear controllable	😐	😐	😐	😐
Everything OK, action is making progress as planned	☺	☺	☺	☺

Remarks:

Figure 15.8. A facial schema for a status report.

starting dates from the plan in Figure 15.7. The panel in the center assesses the status of these activities on a number of criteria (time, quality, budget, etc.). The ratings can be done by writing Y(es) or N(o), for example, into the respective boxes. In Figure 15.9, all Y(es) ratings are skipped to simplify the reporting as much as possible ("reporting by exception"). In case of an "N" rating, the problem must be briefly described, as illustrated in Figure 15.9. No ratings simply indicate that everything runs (essentially) as planned.

Milestone reports are typically less formal and detailed. Figure 15.10 shows an example that assesses the SPME project at the time when milestone "ba" is scheduled. The left-hand side of this form simply replicates the left-hand side of the milestone plan in Figure 15.6. The reporting here is done "in words" in the panel on the right-hand side. The form does not require the action director to rate the action on a set of quality criteria—it can be done in his or her own words. However, one can easily combine this form with the "traffic light" form in Figure 15.8 by, for example, adding additional columns on the right-hand side.

Adjusting an Action Plan

Monitoring is necessary for successful action management but it does not, of course, guarantee that an action will reach its goals. The progress reports have to be read and discussed, and special efforts may be necessary to keep the action on track. An alternative response is to adjust the plan itself. Adjusting the plan should not be seen as a sign of failure, as the action plan is just a plan. However, adjustments should not be

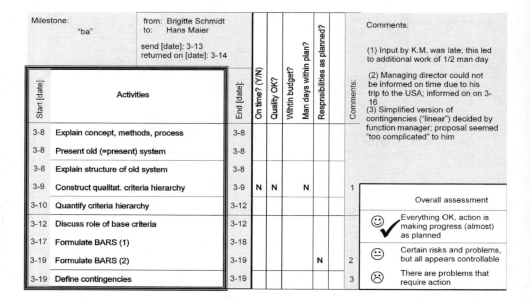

Figure 15.9. Activity reporting plan for activities leading to milestone "ba" in the activities plan of Figure 15.7.

done in passing either because if a plan is changed all the time, few will feel that it is binding. For adjustments, one can consider a variety of alternatives:

- *Reorganize work.* Sometimes, the people required for implementing the plan are not available as planned, and those who are do not have the necessary competencies. This requires reorganizing the work that needs to be done.
- *Invest more.* The plan is found to require more resources than planned. Additional resources are needed or those in the action team have to work harder.
- *Postpone milestones.* Postponing is an option that may be very consequential in a complex action that has tight time buffers. It often entails that the rest of the plan has to be redone completely. Should be chosen only as a last resort. However, reaching the action's goals is ultimately more important than sticking to an end date that is often rather arbitrary.
- *Downgrade standards.* Implementing the action plan may show that the standards are so high that they can be reached only by an excessive input of resources. Then, standards should be lowered to 80-20 solutions.
- *Stop the action.* Actions that have a long time horizon sometimes are planned under conditions that become obsolete during the action's life span. In that case, the action should be terminated.

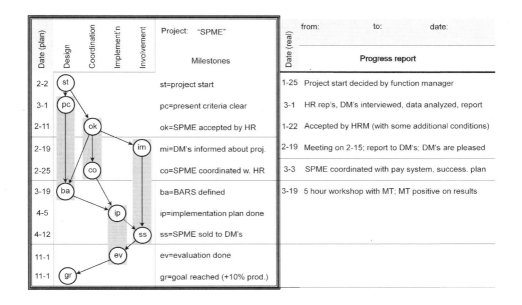

Figure 15.10. Milestone reporting plan for milestone plan of Figure 15.6.

Online Action Planning Tools

With the development of online survey reporting systems have come integrated online action planning tools. Such systems not only provide a common format for entering goals, details, milestones, and responsibilities (see Figure 15.11), but also reinforce communications from senior leaders regarding priorities for action. Survey topics related to organizational level goals can be highlighted for each manager's consideration for action. However, the biggest advantage of an online action planning system is its ability to display the content and current status of all plans throughout the organization. Thus, senior leaders, OD specialists, and action directors have the ability to monitor planned activities and current progress. Presumably, managers are more likely to be held accountable for the execution of their plans when the plans are entered into a searchable database. In practice, the efficacy of any post-survey actions has as much to do with "soft" factors as they do with technological ones.

15.7 Soft Factors in Action Management

In the sections above, we have repeatedly pointed out the importance of soft factors in action management. In the following, we complement these remarks.

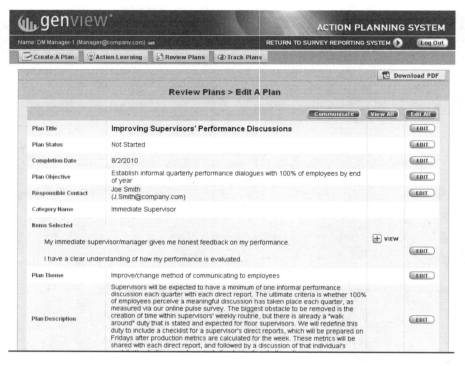

Figure 15.11. An online action planning tool integrated with survey reports.

Selecting the Right People

The key success factor in action management is capable people. Nothing is more important in running an action than to select the right people for the action team. The action director should assemble the best possible team in terms of technical competence; people that have the time and energy to do the work; people who can systematically plan, clearly organize, and reliably control their work; people who are resourceful and conscientious; people who can work in a team, inspiring others; and people who are motivated to work in the action.

Often these selections can be made after first asking employees to nominate a pool of individuals for the action team. Peer nominations have several advantages over hand-chosen and volunteer processes. First, all employees in the group have a say in how they are represented, usually nominating respected, well-spoken individuals. Second, these employees are more likely to ask for updates and to provide feedback because their nominations end up reflecting informal networks. Third, those who ultimately become members of the action team feel a responsibility to the employees who nominated them. The action director need not treat this process as an election where whoever gets the most votes "wins." Rather, he or she should select the best candidates who also represent geographies, departments, functions, levels, and/or shifts.

Delegating Actions Away

Action management is an issue where often few people in an organization have a lot of expertise and experience. Moreover, few like to work on actions because it means "extra work" that has no positive impact on their rewards. Hence, actions sometimes get delegated away with some rhetoric that explains why that particular person has been chosen ("hand-picked," "key potential," "opportunity to advance management skills," etc.). The person who ends up with the actual work is often neither particularly competent nor motivated. Hence, customers and deciders of actions should not be too quick in assigning an action task to just anyone. Alternatively, the action should be assigned to a capable action director who has been given enough support so that he or she can build an action team and a support organization that does most of the operational work.

Remaining Open to Clarify the Action's Goals and Conditions

A particular problem is that in practice the objectives and side constraints of many actions are still fuzzy by the time the action team begins working on an action plan. This can lead to frustration and conflict later on. Yet, asking for clarification before work is begun is not easy. Customers and deciders may feel that goals and side constraints are obvious; that the action director is or acts "stupid;" or that the action director should come up with attractive definitions him- or herself. It is important to keep the definitional issue open for some time because crystal clear definitions are hardly ever possible at the beginning. Definitions, moreover, may have to be adjusted when the action plan shows more clearly what can be accomplished, at what costs, and in what time. Hence, customer, decider, and action director should view defining an action more as a *process* that eventually *converges*, but that needs a few rounds of discussions.

Accepting and Endorsing the Action Plan

Technical know-how of action team members alone does not guarantee that an action will be successful. The persons who drive the action must also believe in the action plan, including its methods to control action progress. If they are convinced that the reporting system, for example, is just a bureaucratic nuisance, then the utility of this system must be more carefully explained, or the system must be simplified.

Insisting on Discipline

A certain amount of discipline is necessary to run any action successfully. What is specified in the plan must be adhered to as much as possible—or the plan must be adjusted! All action team members must agree that without such discipline no reliable cooperation is possible. Discipline is in the interest of each single action team member. To get this discipline, the action team should be involved in working out the action plan so that they develop a sense of ownership and understand the reasons for the plan's specifications. Part-time team members should also know the master plan so that they see the meaning of their contributions for the whole action. Finally, all team members should take part in team building activities so that they also feel responsible, to some extent, for their colleagues in the team.

Leading Action Team Members

An action director must find the right balance between closely controlling the team members' work, and giving them enough freedom to work according to their own rules. It must be clear, though, that "non-delivery" can have negative consequences for the individual action team member, in particular if it comes unannounced. If an action team member runs into serious problems, he or she must inform the action director as early as possible, so that the problem can be solved on time. On the other hand, an action director who is looking away and hopes for the best when she sees problems is not doing her job. Indeed, an action director should, to some extent, not naively believe all the positive feedback that she keeps receiving from her action team members. For example, when filling out a progress report, some action team members tend to say that everything is on schedule, even if it is not, because they feel that they can catch up.

Planning Realistically

Action plans that are written by people with little project experience tend to be overoptimistic. They overestimate their own capabilities and capacities, and do not take into account that the circumstances for running an action are never ideal. For example, some 20% of the time is almost always lost due to unforeseen problems such as illness, late input from outsiders, or tardiness of line managers. Another example is that any action plan omits or forgets some activities. Moreover, customers and deciders tend to exacerbate the problems, because, whatever the plan, they always insist that it must be possible to do the work more quickly and cheaply. The inexperienced action director is not in a position to argue away these additional pressures. Thus, in the end, an action plan is grossly unrealistic. To avoid the problem, experienced project planners should be consulted before finalizing the plan, and inexperienced action planners should be warned about overly optimistic planning.

Controlling Action Progress Constructively

Written progress reports are needed in all but the simplest actions to document an action's course. They should not, however, be perceived as policing devices or as instruments to identify those who can be blamed for problems. Those people may indeed exist, but to simply point at them and blame them does not help the action. Rather, solutions must be found and repeated problems must be avoided by proper measures. The worst measure is to simply hope for the best, the most radical one is to replace the wrong-doer by a more capable and more reliable person.

Yet, written reports are not sufficient. They often do not contain "soft" information such as impressions, hunches, perceptions, and attitudes. People also do not like to write down any little problem, in particular if these problems cannot be objectively proven. For example, if a line manager seems tardy in releasing resources needed in the action, reporting this as a "problem" is risky because the line manager is likely to challenge this as pure fiction. A better way to capture such information is, therefore, a meeting or even a one-on-one discussion between the action director and the particular individual working on the action.

Thinking About the Politics of the Action

Politics are always involved in actions, and the action director should think about the context they form at least to some extent. It often helps to first identify those persons or groups who benefit most from the action, and those who do not. Then, different persons or groups may actually pursue goals that have nothing to do with the "official" goals of the action. For example, an action (or resistance against this action) may aim at simply damaging someone's sphere of influence, or serve to make a particular person more visible. In that case, rational arguments can be entirely useless. What helps are tactics, getting opponents of those who are against the action together in a coalition that helps their latent goals, and presenting a mock surface rationale.

Another dimension of politics is to establish who is engaged in an action, in which role, at what time. Although everyone usually agrees that this is an important precondition for successful action management, Frame (1987, p. 47) remarks: "I have never had a group that systematically attempted to identify their full roster of actors affected by the project, or a group that consistently took account of the actors' motivations, or a group that spent any time trying to uncover the hidden agenda implicit in the project situation. Rather, what the groups typically do is to immediately commence offering solutions to the problem as stated in its most superficial form. It is usually apparent that these early solutions are woefully inadequate, so the groups spend most of their time refining and reworking their original efforts."

Turning the Action Team into a Team

An action team often has the problem that it is not a real team, but a group of persons that meets occasionally to work on an action. Roles and tasks are assigned to the different members of the action team, some discussion takes place, and then everyone returns to their normal work locations. Hence, it takes an extra effort to turn this group into a real team. Some team-building is always needed. The various people should get to know each other to some extent—their competencies, skills, and positions—but also their personalities, interests, and values to build trust and help informal collaboration. Such team-building often does not require much more than a common dinner or a grill party, but can also involve a "retreat" away from the regular work activities and locations. If possible, important promoters of the action (the customer, the decider, the supporter) should drop by, thank the team members for their work, wish them all the best, and demonstrate their commitment to the action.

Keeping Technical Gimmickry Minimal

People like to show off their technical skills. For example, in one ES project, one member of the ES project core team was an expert with a particular computer program for project management. He convinced the team to run all planning and controlling in this program rather than using "old-fashioned" paper and pencil methods. In the end, all planning became so complex that the team members privately went back to simpler methods of planning, such as an appointment calendar. The lesson is that the action director should always encourage techniques that everyone is familiar with, and introduce new technology only if it definitely means a major improvement.

Showing Commitment to the Action and its Tasks

An action director who does not clearly demonstrate that he is completely behind the action and that he is serious about the assigned tasks will soon find that it becomes hard to keep the action on track. The action manager, in other words, must exert some pressure on the team to be successful. Success needs to be a must, not a maybe. Some managers also tend to assign task after task to those who are in reach, without ever keeping track of such assignments. Unfortunately, a rational response to such assignments is to do nothing until the manager remembers. Often, this does not occur. Indeed, a member of an action team once said when asked why he had not delivered on time: "I was waiting to be reminded."

16 Information Campaign on ES Results and Responses

In chapter 15 we described reporting as an element of action management, where the purpose was to promote the action. Such within-action reporting is, however, not sufficient, and those involved in the actions are sometimes surprised to learn that not *everybody* knows *all* about their projects. In this chapter we discuss a second type of reporting that is needed to keep all employees informed about the follow-up processes in general. Without it, employees often overlook real accomplishments. When asked about actions from previous surveys, employees frequently remark "Yes, there was some action planning, but I do not know what eventually became of it" or "There was some momentum initially, but then everything petered out." If employees have no reason to believe that the survey process benefits employees or the company, then the survey itself becomes a source of frustration, and future survey participation is likely to decline. Although there are some horror stories of organizations failing to act on survey results, this is the exception rather than the rule. Change often occurs, but *seems* illusive because it occurs gradually. Alas, we look the same in the mirror each day, but quite different in pictures from a few years ago! Hence, change has to be traced closely to make it obvious.

16.1 Information on Results and Management's Responses

Employees need to be informed about the results of the ES and the corresponding organizational response. This communication can be done in various ways:

- *By print media*, such as a printed folder where the results are reported as shown, for example, in Figure 10.11
- *Live*, through face to face communication with the employees' direct supervisors or via special "town hall sessions" as shown in Figure 2.3
- *Electronically*, by placing articles or presentations into the organization's intranet or by distributing results reports as pdf attachments to everybody's email address

Most often, a mix of different approaches is chosen. For example, one may want to send out general feedback relatively early in the follow-up processes. This can be done by both distributing this information as email pdf attachments to all employees, but also, at the same time, by placing printed material on bulletin boards. The latter has the advantage that bulletin boards are located in places where employees congregate; as a result the results and post-survey activities become the topic of conversation. Then, one can invite the employees to participate in a local information session, where either an external survey specialist or a member of the coordination team first presents the general results and the results that are more specific to their part of the organization. Next, a senior manager reports what management has to say about the results and what it intends to do about them. This manager, in particular, should be in a position where he or she can make reliable statements on management's decisions and plans regarding the ES results. Finally, the employees will be informed by their direct supervisors about the results of their workgroups. This information can be given within the normal communication meetings, or in a special ES workshop. Such a cascading information plan is easy to construct, but perhaps because it is so obvious, it is not often implemented properly in practice.

Typically, the step that either comes too late or fails to occur is informing all employees about the general results of the survey as soon as top management has seen the results. Failing to provide quick feedback means missing an opportunity for *systematic* communication—one should not leave everything to grapevines and gossip. And yet, this initial communication need not go into details or interpretations, and it does not have to present any concrete decision by management. In Figure 16.1 for example, the CEO of a manufacturing company thanks employees for their participation in the survey, calls out both strengths and concerns that were raised, and sketches upcoming post-survey activities. Even in a more specific communication, it suffices to present just a graph of scores, probably relative to some benchmark comparisons (e.g., scores most above the norms down to most below the norms), along with a timeline of next steps.

Obviously, communicating general results and upcoming activities requires that the various information measures are planned as parts of an information campaign for the follow-up processes. When planning such a campaign, one should take into account that the first feedback of survey results often comes at a time that is perceived as "late" by most employees. Hence, having an information plan, and communicating this plan and the reasons for its timing *before* the survey is even administered will reduce the impression that information is being held back by management.

16.2 Information on Actions

One important aspect of the information campaign within the follow-up processes is keeping employees informed about actions that result from the ES. What is needed is an overview of the main trends of these actions, not about details. A listing of hundreds of little actions is not only useless to most employees, but it also looks defensive: If one cannot report any major action, then an endless list of minor activities and decisions does not compensate. Indeed, employees may get suspicious as to whether all of these activities were really caused by the ES or whether management or the ES coordination team are simply reporting what has been in the making anyway.

To ACME Employees:

I want to personally thank you all for your participation in the recent ACME's Your Voice employee survey. About 80% of ACME employees completed the survey this year, and it is such involvement and dedication that helped make this survey a success.

The survey results are in and there are many positive things you have shared and a few issues that we need to consider. In general, results indicate that you find ACME a good place to work and enjoy your contributions to the company. The data verifies that our employees are committed, hard-working, and quality-oriented individuals who put forth a real effort to help us achieve our standards and objectives. Many of you feel good about your supervisors and workgroups, the training you receive, and the ability to be productive and successful in what you do.

Some employees expressed concerns related to pay, understanding how performance is evaluated, and feeling free to share concerns with management. We hear your concerns and will investigate ways to address them as we move forward. Several of you took the time to share your comments and thoughts with [COO NAME] and me. Many of these comments contain ideas and directions that we will consider as we continue to make ACME a great place work.

The survey may be completed, but the process is just beginning. Over the next several weeks reports will be distributed to department heads, and workshops will take place to help them properly interpret and share the survey results. Throughout the first quarter of 2009, we expect employees to see more specific details of the survey results for both the total company as well as for your department. Together we can celebrate the positive things you have to say about ACME and define actions that will allow us to build on our strengths and become an even stronger company.

Once again, I thank you for your participation, and look forward to continuing this important process with you.

Sincerely,

CEO SIGNATURE

Figure 16.1. A generic letter from the CEO of a manufacturing company (labeled ACME here) thanks employees and highlights strengths and concerns.

Reporting only a string of details rather than a big picture also conveys the impression that all these actions may not be properly aligned towards the given operational and strategic goals of the organization. Rather, they appear to be ad hoc measures, often geared towards hygienic goals and mainly driven by local management and HR. This impression can backfire on the evaluation of the ES in general.

Presenting the big picture means that one has to show a few (i.e., one to three) main conclusions from the ES, and how most of these actions focus on these issues. Details can be reported in the sense of illustrative cases, but the specific actions for each part of the organization need not be reported in the general information campaign. This campaign, in any case, should also be somewhat entertaining and journalistic, and not a controller's Excel sheet. Figure 16.2 shows an example from the German railroads. The tabloid style of this company newspaper is chosen on purpose. It matches the type of newspapers that many employees in this company read. What are reported here are actions that were already implemented ("Things that were done already!"), and common areas of focus of the different market units of this company ("All market units focus on improvements"). Moreover, the paper shows a letter of the CEO to all employees ("Dear employees…"), and an appeal of the head of the works council ("The balance sheet at half time").

Style and content of this information make clear that this newspaper is not a piece of controlling, but rather that it intends to show what has been done and what will be done. The typical questions to be addressed in such general pieces of information are, for example: What does management say on the survey results? What has management decided to do or not to do? Why exactly this, why not that? What rationale lies behind these decisions? What do they want to accomplish? What is management's commitment to these decisions? What priority do they have? Who will be doing what in the near future? Who is responsible for all that? What are the major milestones of actions? What are the next steps of the follow-up processes? Will I be informed about further steps? Do I have a chance to discuss the ES results? If so, when and how? If not, why not? What can I do to support further activities? What is the role of middle and lower management in the follow-up processes?

The employees are often not just interested in reading about what is happening in their own part of the organization, but also about what others are doing. An ES offers a great opportunity to strengthen this interest by providing some comparative information. This can also lead to a healthy competition, because seeing that others are working on important action fields, employees in general and managers in particular may not want to appear uninvolved and passive. Also, seeing what others are doing may make managers aware of how the ES results offer a great opportunity for improvements. Likewise, publically promoting post-survey activities sets the expectation that all groups should be taking action, and if a manager is not meeting the expectations of his or her direct reports, then this manager risks looking bad.

Another issue worth reporting is information on which steps of the follow-up processes have been carried out where. For example, it can be of interest to report how the employees have been informed about results and actions, and how this information was delivered (in writing, via supervisors, in special info sessions, etc.);

where special ES workshops have been done or will be done; whether there were special workshops for managers; where presentations were given to top management groups, and by whom. To communicate such an information plan ahead of time to management can be a potent motivator for them to actually see that important process steps are implemented rather than just considered and "postponed" until a more convenient time comes along.

In general, a publication like the one in Figure 16.2 can help to revitalize the follow-up processes. It shows to everyone in the organization that the ES remains a significant intervention that is still receiving a lot of attention. This attention, in turn, helps to drive responses to the ES results.

16.3 Planning and Organizing the Information Campaign

A publication as the one shown in Figure 16.2 is based on journalistic work that needs to be planned and organized in advance.

Architecture and Roles

The entire information campaign within the follow-up processes is best planned and coordinated by the team that also designed and led the information campaign before data feedback. This information team must be led by a member of the ES core coordination team, and its major decisions must be signed off by the HR director or even the CEO. It should also involve some specialists from the organization's own communication, marketing, or advertising department, and possibly complement its expertise with external experts.

Continuing with the same information team in the follow-up processes has many advantages. For one thing, it is economical, because one does not have to explain all features of the ES project to project novices from scratch. The members of the information team have also made their own experiences in the early phases of the information campaign, thus seeing what flies and what does not. They have built a network of interpersonal connections (e.g., with local coordinators) that they can use to collect the information they need regarding post-survey activities. Also, continuing with the same team, means that the information campaign continues in the same style. Most importantly, one team can design and plan the entire information campaign as an integral whole and with features that are part of the ES project positioning.

The job of the information team in the follow-up process is more difficult than the job before data collection. Now, the team has to communicate what is planned and what has been done by *various* parts of the organization and not simply report things that the ES core team largely controls itself. This requires a lot of research and data collection. Also, getting statements from stakeholders such as the CEO, top management, the HR director, union leaders, the works council, or various managers requires a lot of planning to keep all publications on time and up to date.

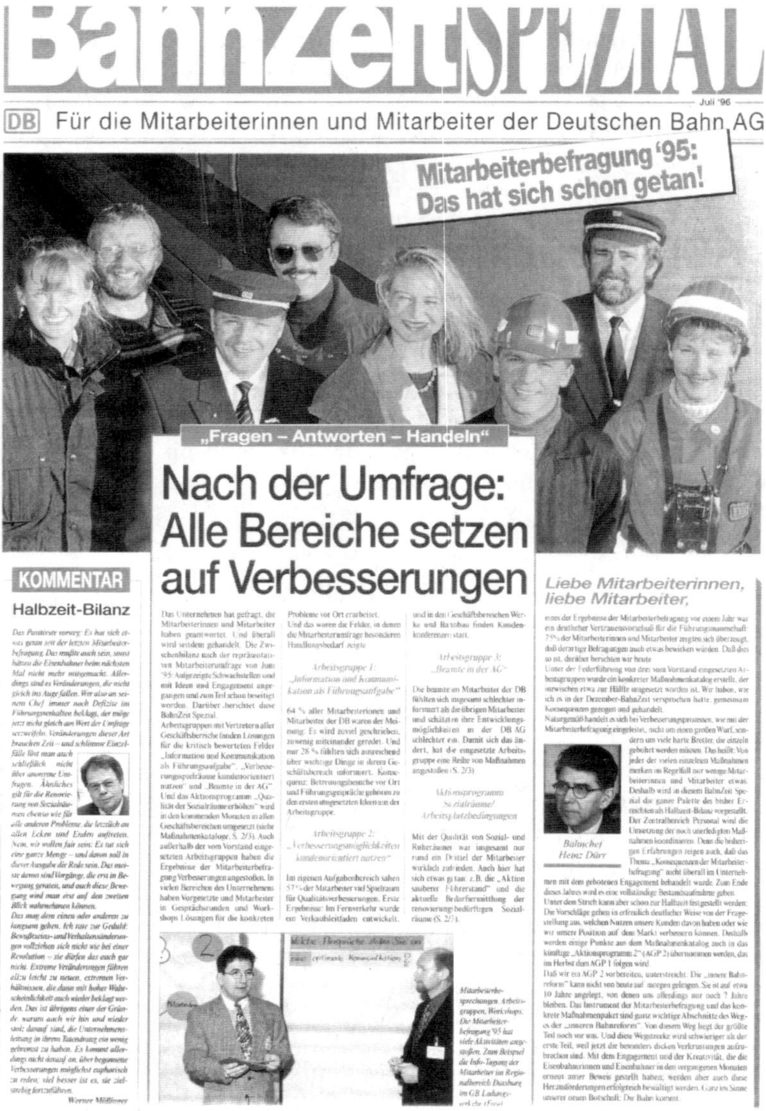

BahnZeit SPEZIAL

Juli '96

DB Für die Mitarbeiterinnen und Mitarbeiter der Deutschen Bahn AG

Mitarbeiterbefragung '95: Das hat sich schon getan!

„Fragen – Antworten – Handeln"

Nach der Umfrage: Alle Bereiche setzen auf Verbesserungen

KOMMENTAR

Halbzeit-Bilanz

Das Positivste vorweg: Es hat sich etwas getan seit der letzten Mitarbeiterbefragung. Das mußte auch sein, sonst hätten die Eisenbahner beim nächsten Mal nicht mehr mitgemacht. Allerdings sind es Veränderungen, die nicht gleich ins Auge fallen. Wer also an seinem Chef immer noch Defizite im Führungsverhalten beklagt, der möge jetzt nicht gleich am Wert der Umfrage verzweifeln. Veränderungen dieser Art brauchen Zeit – und schlimme Einzelfälle löst man auch schließlich nicht über anonyme Umfragen. Ähnliches gilt für die Renovierung von Sozialräumen ebenso wie für alle anderen Probleme, die letztlich an allen Ecken und Enden auftreten. Nein, wir wollen fair sein: Es tut sich eine ganze Menge – und davon soll in dieser Ausgabe die Rede sein. Das meiste davon sind Vorgänge, die erst in Bewegung geraten, und auch diese Bewegung wird man erst auf den zweiten Blick wahrnehmen können.

Das mag dem einen oder anderen zu langsam gehen. Ich rate zur Geduld: Bewußtseins- und Verhaltensänderungen vollziehen sich nicht wie bei einer Revolution – sie dürfen das auch gar nicht. Extreme Veränderungen führen allzu leicht zu neuen, extremen Verhältnissen, die dann mit hoher Wahrscheinlichkeit auch wieder beklagt werden. Das ist übrigens einer der Gründe, warum auch wir hin und wieder stolz darauf sind, die Unternehmensleitung in ihrem Tatendrang ein wenig gebremst zu haben. Es kommt allerdings nicht darauf an, über begonnene Verbesserungen möglichst euphorisch zu reden; viel besser ist es, sie zielstrebig fortzuführen.

Werner Mößinner

Das Unternehmen hat gefragt, die Mitarbeiterinnen und Mitarbeiter haben geantwortet. Und überall wird seitdem gehandelt. Die Zwischenbilanz nach der repräsentativen Mitarbeiterumfrage von Juni '95: Aufgezeigte Schwachstellen sind mit Ideen und Engagement angegangen und zum Teil schon beseitigt worden. Darüber berichtet diese BahnZeit Spezial.

Arbeitsgruppen mit Vertretern aller Geschäftsbereiche fanden Lösungen für die kritisch bewerteten Felder „Information und Kommunikation als Führungsaufgabe", „Verbesserungsspielräume kundenorientiert nutzen" und „Beamte in der AG". Und das Aktionsprogramm „Qualität der Sozialräume erhöhen" wird in den kommenden Monaten in allen Geschäftsbereichen umgesetzt (siehe Maßnahmenkataloge, S. 2/3). Auch außerhalb der vom Vorstand eingesetzten Arbeitsgruppen haben die Ergebnisse der Mitarbeiterbefragung Verbesserungen angestoßen. In vielen Bereichen des Unternehmens haben Vorgesetzte und Mitarbeiter in Gesprächsrunden und Workshops Lösungen für die konkreten Probleme vor Ort erarbeitet.

Und das waren die Felder, in denen die Mitarbeiterumfrage besonderen Handlungsbedarf zeigte:

Arbeitsgruppe 1: „Information und Kommunikation als Führungsaufgabe"

64 % aller Mitarbeiterinnen und Mitarbeiter der DB waren der Meinung: Es wird zuviel geschrieben, zuwenig miteinander geredet. Und nur 28 % fühlten sich ausreichend über wichtige Dinge in ihrem Geschäftsbereich informiert. Konsequenz: Betreuungsbesuche vor Ort und Führungsgespräche gehören zu den ersten umgesetzten Ideen aus der Arbeitsgruppe.

Arbeitsgruppe 2: „Verbesserungsmöglichkeiten kundenorientiert nutzen"

Im eigenen Aufgabenbereich sahen 57 % der Mitarbeiter viel Spielraum für Qualitätsverbesserungen. Erste Ergebnisse: Im Fernverkehr wurde ein Verkaufsleitfaden entwickelt, und in den Geschäftsbereichen Werke und Bahnbau finden Kundenkonferenzen statt.

Arbeitsgruppe 3: „Beamte in der AG"

Die beamteten Mitarbeiter der DB fühlten sich insgesamt schlechter informiert als die übrigen Mitarbeiter und schätzten ihre Entwicklungsmöglichkeiten in der DB AG schlechter ein. Damit sich das ändert, hat die eingesetzte Arbeitsgruppe eine Reihe von Maßnahmen angestoßen (S. 2/3).

Aktionsprogramm Sozialräume/ Arbeitsplatzbedingungen

Mit der Qualität von Sozial- und Ruheräumen war insgesamt nur rund ein Drittel der Mitarbeiter wirklich zufrieden. Auch hier hat sich etwas getan: z.B. die „Aktion sauberer Führerstand" und die aktuelle Bedarfsermittlung der renovierungsbedürftigen Sozialräume (S. 2/3).

Mitarbeiterbesprechungen, Arbeitsgruppen, Workshops: Die Mitarbeiterbefragung '95 hat viele Aktivitäten angestoßen. Zum Beispiel die Info-Tagung der Mitarbeiter im Regionalbereich Duisburg im GB Ladungsverkehr (Foto)

Liebe Mitarbeiterinnen, liebe Mitarbeiter,

eines der Ergebnisse der Mitarbeiterbefragung vor einem Jahr war ein deutlicher Vertrauensvorschuß für die Führungsmannschaft: 75% der Mitarbeiterinnen und Mitarbeiter zeigten sich überzeugt, daß derartige Befragungen auch etwas bewirken würden. Daß dies so ist, darüber berichten wir heute.

Unter der Federführung von drei vom Vorstand eingesetzten Arbeitsgruppen wurde ein konkreter Maßnahmenkatalog erstellt, der inzwischen etwa zur Hälfte umgesetzt worden ist. Wir haben, wie ich es in der Dezember-BahnZeit versprochen hatte, gemeinsam Konsequenzen gezogen und gehandelt.

Naturgemäß handelt es sich bei Verbesserungsprozessen, wie mit der Mitarbeiterbefragung eingeleitet, nicht um einen großen Wurf, sondern um viele harte Bretter, die einzeln gebohrt werden müssen. Das heißt: Von jeder der vielen einzelnen Maßnahmen merken im Regelfall nur wenige Mitarbeiterinnen und Mitarbeiter etwas. Deshalb wird in diesem BahnZeit Spezial die ganze Palette des bisher Erreichten als Halbzeit-Bilanz vorgestellt. Der Zentralbereich Personal wird die Umsetzung der noch unerledigten Maßnahmen koordinieren. Denn die bisherigen Erfahrungen zeigen auch, daß das Thema „Konsequenzen der Mitarbeiterbefragung" nicht überall im Unternehmen mit dem gebotenen Engagement behandelt wurde. Zum Ende dieses Jahres wird es eine vollständige Bestandsaufnahme geben.

Unter dem Strich kann aber schon zur Halbzeit festgestellt werden: Die Vorschläge gehen in erfreulich deutlicher Weise von der Fragestellung aus, welchen Nutzen unsere Kunden davon haben oder wie wir unsere Position auf dem Markt verbessern können. Deshalb werden einige Punkte aus dem Maßnahmenkatalog auch in das künftige „Aktionsprogramm 2" (AGP 2) übernommen werden, das im Herbst dem AGP 1 folgen wird.

Daß wir ein AGP 2 vorbereiten, unterstreicht: Die „innere Bahnreform" kann nicht von heute auf morgen gelingen. Sie ist auf etwa 10 Jahre angelegt, von denen uns allerdings nur noch 7 Jahre bleiben. Das Instrument der Mitarbeiterbefragung und das konkrete Maßnahmenpaket sind ganz wichtige Abschnitte des Weges der „inneren Bahnreform". Von diesem Weg liegt der größte Teil noch vor uns. Und diese Wegstrecke wird schwieriger als der erste Teil, weil jetzt die besonders dicken Verkrustungen aufzubrechen sind. Mit dem Engagement und der Kreativität, die die Eisenbahnerinnen und Eisenbahner in den vergangenen Monaten erneut unter Beweis gestellt haben, werden aber auch diese Herausforderungen erfolgreich bewältigt werden. Ganz im Sinne unserer neuen Botschaft: Die Bahn kommt.

Bahnchef Heinz Dürr

Figure 16.2 Company newspaper on ES results and actions.

The information team, thus, has to reach out to the local coordinators and ask them for help as follows: "Please systematically research all actions in your part of the organization that were planned (or changed, or reinforced) in reaction to the results of the ES. Report to the ES core coordination team in writing by [date] on what you found: (a) Number of actions, (b) main focus of these actions, and what they intend to accomplish, (c) the present status of the actions or action plans, (d) next steps and major milestones down the road, (e) any peculiarities in this context that may be worth publishing in the entire organization." This task assignment to the local survey coordinators comes ultimately from the survey sponsor (i.e. a member of the executive board or even the CEO). It means, practically speaking, that the local coordinator must collect this information from local management, either by interviewing managers directly or by asking other employees to provide the needed information. To accomplish this task, it usually means that the local coordinators must seek the support of the local HR directors or even the lead managers at these locations. This support is almost automatic if it becomes clear that this information will be brought to the attention of the entire company and to the company's top management in particular. It also provides the risk of hyperbole: reporting too much too positively. Thus, the coordinator should point out that it is not the number of actions that matters, but their quality and how they are related to business goals. Even currently disappointing outcomes are worth promoting as long as the planning and execution were clearly well received and continue to be supported.

The information team, in addition to this company-wide information task, has to manage a second assignment, namely providing models for decentralized information activities. In large organizations, there are often various regions, countries, or subsidiaries that need to complement any information that comes from company headquarters with specific information on what is going on in their part of the organization. Even the central information may have to be adapted or simply translated. How all this can be done is best discussed when the entire coordination team meets for one of its regular meetings. The ideas of local coordinators can be collected, discussed, and then integrated by the information team into a campaign that has a common thrust, but that allows for local changes and additions. The information team can support local coordinators by providing models, templates, graphic files, and the like for information sessions, workshops, posters, brochures, and newsletters that can be adapted to local needs within certain limits. Again, such centralized coordination assures that a consistent and coordinated message goes out.

Publications and Time Line

Figure 16.3 shows a prototypical publication plan for informing employees after the survey. The plan here has four phases. In the first phase, general results of the ES are reported along with any high priority focus areas that top management has decided upon. This information should be continued with statements by senior management who announce their responses with respect to their parts of the organization. Employees are also interested in how the follow-up processes will continue. A simple schema as the one shown in Figure 16.4 is often sufficient to show that[58].

---

[58] The example shows that "central" information that comes from the organization's headquarter must be complemented with local information later on. The central information only serves to show the general direction and to align the various processes.

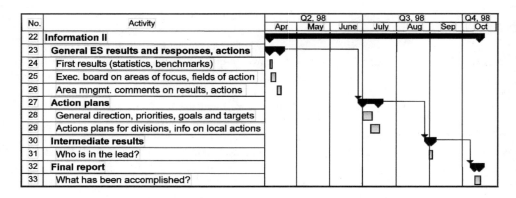

Figure 16.3. A plan for the info campaign within the follow-up processes.

In the second phase, major action plans are presented with their goals, major milestones, and responsibilities. What is most important here is to describe what is planned with respect to areas of focus, if there are any. Departmental and local action plans should only be reported in a coarse way so that employees see the main directions, similarities, and differences of these activities.

In the third phase, this information plan communicates what has been achieved by the action plans. Again, this central information should not go into details but only show that things are moving. Figure 16.5 shows an example for such a report from a smaller company which stresses comparisons among its functions ("Marketing is in the lead!") [59].

The last phase of the information plan in Figure 16.3 provides for a final status report on actions. Because most ES projects do not have a clear ending—rather, the follow-up processes are gradually absorbed into the normal line management—this final summary is really just another status report. It often comes with an outlook on the next ES that will evaluate what has been accomplished.

This prototypical plan is but one possible example for the information campaign after the survey. Indeed, this post-survey campaign is less standardized than the campaign before the survey. Communications regarding results and activities necessarily must pay a lot of attention to the particular context of the organization and to the particular decisions and plans in this environment. However, what can be said for any information campaign within the follow-up processes is that it should not be planned as a "daily" stream of information. Change is most effectively communicated by taking snapshots and by comparing the current situation to what existed at the time of the original survey. If the information plan is designed early as part of the ES project positioning, it too should be communicated as an element of the project design. This also helps to make management aware what they are expected to deliver.

---

[59] The example is from 1989. We show it here to demonstrate that it is not the glossy graphics that are important but rather the message. In this case, the comparative exposition led to much discussion.

Figure 16.4. Info on next steps (ES workshop, action planning team, implementation).

Communication Politics

The various communication tools can be constructed in many different ways. They leave lots of freedom for creativity, but it must be kept within the limits of the official communication politics. The formal part of it concerns using or not using certain logos, slogans, and design elements. Such rules are usually explicitly available in the organization's communication department. Then, all publications in this information campaign must adhere to the rules of serious journalism. The style can be casual, but the substance must be well researched, the representation must be precise and well balanced. Most of all, the information must be *neutral*. The information team is not a

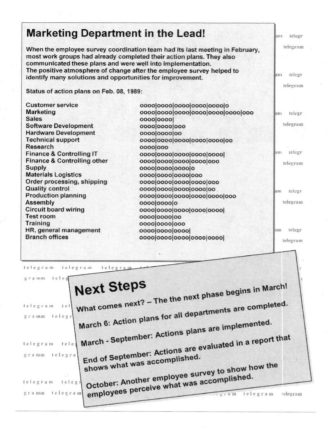

Figure 16.5. A page from an intermediate report on action implementation.

censor or evaluator, but simply a *reporter*. Thus, the team should not provide an overly positive portrayal of events that might, for example, attempt to sell action on side issues, non-aligned activity bursts, or lack of decision making as "successful." Employees are wary of communication that appears to have too much public relations spin and not enough straight talk. The reporting, therefore, needs to be realistic, but it should not be de-motivating. Indeed, one does not want to be so truthful that parts of the organization feel they are being called out as failures. In Figure 16.5 ("Marketing department in the lead!"), the progress that departments had made to date was displayed graphically. A public report card such as this might not work at all companies. At this company, the departments that were supposedly trailing responded with protest. They started a discussion on what types of actions were actually being implemented across departments, and they concluded that most completed actions to date were "easy" while they were attacking more difficult problems, requiring more time and effort. Yet some of these "lagging" departments actually felt motivated by this public recognition of their activities. Top management felt that this was a worthwhile discussion, and that the arguments of this discussion should also be reported to employees.

The point we want to illustrate is that the information team must always consider what is acceptable within the organizational culture or even the country culture. Global organizations, where post-survey activities are reported across countries and societies, must pay particular attention to how progress is communicated. A proposal by Porras (1987), for example, to inform employees about action plans by hanging them on bulletin boards and asking employees to write comments on them may not work across all cultures. In some locations, one might end up with lots of graffiti and "funny" remarks, while in other locations there would be no comments written at all.

16.4 Communication as Part of Planned Change Management

The desired outcome for all post-survey communications is to demonstrate a continuous process of improvement that should invite each employee to personally commit to the desired change. By sharing survey results openly, the post-survey information campaign sends the message that the survey will be used to make changes. By outlining general milestones for the process, the campaign sets expectations and leads to a psychological contract between management and employees for what should be done by when. By communicating only a general definition of focus areas, the campaign communicates that senior leaders will seek additional input in specifying problems and opportunities as well as best courses of action. By sharing initial actions being taken, the campaign shows that change is not only possible, but that it is happening—akin to a "proof of concept" that should inspire more effort. The "easy" actions, "low hanging fruit," or "quick wins" are celebrated (modestly) in order to gain more employee support for the next wave of change efforts related to this area of focus.

Creating Perceptions of what most People are Doing

Communication of coordinated progress is in itself a necessary part of the successful intervention. A long line of social psychological research from Cialdini (e.g., Cialdini, 2007; Schultz, Nolan, Cialdini, Goldstein, & Griskevicius, 2007) indicates that people align their behaviors with what they perceive others to be doing (behavioral norms) and what they perceive others should be doing (injunctive norms). One can position the role of the post-survey information campaign as the conveyor of these norms. By highlighting multiple instances of employees engaging in new processes and behaviors aligned with pre-established organizational goals, the campaign creates the perception that most employees are experiencing change and are actively involved with creating change. Likewise, the campaign creates the perception that managers should be encouraging similar discussions and coordinated activities to match the success seen elsewhere in the organization.

For these reasons, it is critical for senior leaders to identify at least one group or process that will receive immediate, but also ongoing attention and resources in order to generate initial successes that will start a domino effect throughout the organization. The activities produced in this one targeted area will become the raw material for the information team to build persuasive communication throughout the organization.

Communicating what Employees are Ready to Hear

To maximize their persuasive effect, the makeup of these communications should be tailored to what employees are ready to hear. In applications of the Trans Theoretical Model of Behavioral Change (TTM) to organizational change, elements of the message to be communicated are aligned with employees' progression across identified stages of change: Precontemplation, Contemplation, Preparation, Action, and Maintenance (Mastrangelo, Prochaska, & Prochaska, 2008; Anderson, Gantner, & Hanson, 2006; Prochaska, DiClemente, & Norcross, 1998). For employees who have yet to contemplate a behavioral change, persuasive communication regarding that change should focus on why it would benefit the organization and each individual member. For employees who are contemplating the change, but have yet to prepare for the change, communication should focus on what the desired behavior is exactly. For employees who are preparing to change, but have yet to fully do what is being asked, communication should focus on what the first steps are in the desired behavior. Facilitating progression through each of these stages requires indentifying and promoting personal reasons why employees should make the change (i.e., pros) while realistically preparing for, preventing, or otherwise eliminating the reasons why employees should not make the change (i.e., cons).

What survey experience shows, however, is that organizational members are typically at various stages of change for any specific focus area. So, while it may be reasonable to have initial post-survey communication start with "Why", while subsequent messages progress through "What" and "How," there are likely to be some employees ready to act early into the process while other employees will remain unprepared even well into the process. Nevertheless, post-survey decision making usually does follow the path of: (1) Why we should make this area a priority; (2) What exactly we define as success; and (3) How we will start this journey.

We recommend that post-survey communications progress through these messages so that the first 2-3 weeks of messaging address why senior leaders are calling for changes in a specific area of focus. Then, as mid-level managers discuss what should be done to address these areas of focus, more specific definitions of the desired outcome should be publicized, and these definitions will likely vary by function or location. Not every organizational element should be expected to act in the same way in order for the organizational system to achieve its goal (e.g., supporting the goal of "Decreasing product development time to market" would require different changes from Research & Development, Operations, HR, IT, and Sales). Finally, the details of how employees should start working in a different manner would be worked out and communicated later into the process, likely at the workgroup level[60].

By emphasizing how employees at all levels are progressing through the stages of change, how they are benefitting from these changes, and how they have overcome obstacles to these changes, the information team applies evidence-based psychological science toward the planned change initiative.

---

[60] At the same time that this top-down process is taking place, local level actions that address locally identified areas of focus are also being planned and executed. Publicizing these local activities may or may not be a part of the same coordinated storyboard.

17 Evaluating Employee Survey Projects

The final step in a survey project is an evaluation of what has been accomplished and at what cost. What one wants to know is the extent to which the project has reached its goals; whether quality, cost, deadlines, and risks of the project were adequately managed; and how various stakeholders judge the project's progress and outcomes. The main objective of most evaluations is to provide the project manager and supporting staff with guidelines for similar projects in the future.

17.1 Project Evaluation and Learning

In some organizations, managers are satisfied if projects are completed on time and within budget. In these organizations, project evaluation is usually not emphasized. Managers feel that the project was assessed before it was started, so they see little sense in evaluating the project after completion.

Evaluating a project has various components that can contribute to organizational development and change management. For example, no complex project is ever implemented as planned, and it may be important to know when, why, and how the plans had to be corrected; whether there was resistance against particular modifications of the plan; whether the plan was sufficiently transparent and clear to everyone involved or affected by it; or whether all stakeholders were committed to the plan. The insights from such questions can be used to improve the management of future ES projects and perhaps other projects within the organization.

There are always assumptions of how a project should lead to certain outcomes or effects. These assumptions often rest on armchair reasoning or on common, everyday experiences. For example, many managers believe that the more satisfied employees are, the better they perform. Others believe that commitment to the company assures high job involvement. Such beliefs are what psychologists refer to as "folk theories" or "naïve theories" because they are not subjected to rigorous testing (Geary, 2005; Heider, 1958). From a scientist's point-of-view, they are mere hypotheses or conjectures that require empirical validation before they guide managers' behavior. Frequently, however, these untested assumptions do influence managers either because they believe the assumptions need no validation or they are unaware that they are making the assumptions. While these assumptions may be effective, they are often not as effective or enduring as evidence-based theories.

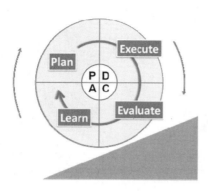

Figure 17.1. The Deming wheel.

It seems wise, therefore, to check the validity of one's assumptions from time to time. Plans should not only be executed, but they should also be evaluated so that improved plans can be constructed if necessary. The cycle of planning, executing, evaluating, and learning is shown in Figure 17.1. It comes in various forms (Shewhart, 1939; Scholtes, 1998) such as the "Deming wheel" or the "PDCA cycle" in quality management, where one wants to keep improving the quality of an organization through first planning business process components that improve results (P=plan); next implement the plans and measure performance (D=do); then assess the measurements and report the results to decision makers (C=check); and finally learn and act to make the necessary corrections in your results, assumptions, and tools (A=act).

The Deming wheel can be used to distinguish two types of learning. The first type is adaptive and operational learning. It focuses on improving planning and execution, but it never questions the assumptions on which the plans rest. The second type is strategic learning (Grundy, 1994), which keeps an eye on the possibility that the plan's underlying assumptions could be wrong. Argyris (1994, p.8) describes these learning types as follows: "Whenever an error is detected and corrected without questioning the underlying values of the system ...., the learning is single-looped. ... The thermostat is programmed to detect states of 'too cold' or 'too hot', and to correct the situation by turning the heat on or off. If the thermostat asked itself such questions as why it was set at 68 degrees, or why it was programmed as it was, then it would be a double-loop learner." Obviously, single-loop learning is sufficient if the planning assumptions are correct, but many organizations found out that taking prior recipes of success for granted can be dangerous in days of rapid change.

17.2 Evaluating ES Projects

The Deming wheel represents a general framework for evaluating ES projects. We now turn to some more practical considerations.

Positioning the Evaluation of an ES Project

Evaluating an ES project is a project in itself that needs to be properly positioned as a total package. In particular, the evaluation's goals should be made explicit, and the usual side constraints (budget, time frame, quality criteria) should be specified. Only then can one begin to design the evaluation's methods and processes.

A major objective that any ES project evaluation pursues is documenting the project results so that they can be communicated to the organization's stakeholders.

This is often necessary because the follow-up processes of an ES project can be so lengthy that the project has no clear end. An ES project typically does not end with a "big bang." Rather, it "fades away" by being gradually absorbed into the organization's daily routines. For example, when the organization turns to action planning and implementation, line management takes over most or all activities. Supporting action management by providing tools, advice, or trainings may still be considered part of the ES project, but action implementation is not. Hence, unlike other projects, ES projects rarely have a clear end-point. As a consequence, employees and managers frequently get the impression that the ES project somehow petered out without achieving much. Likewise, slow and gradual change is likely to go unnoticed, leading many to believe that nothing has changed at all. If you have ever visited your home town after years of absence, you probably noticed a lot of change. However, for the people who lived there all their lives, it seems to be just as it always was. ES projects often function in a similar way, with steps in "long marches" rather than highly visible "bold strokes" (Kanter et al., 1992).

Another standard goal of almost any ES is finding proof for positive change prompted by the ES in order to use it to boost management and employee commitment in future surveys. Naturally, one has to be careful fabricating shallow jubilance reports. Rather, objective assessments of what went well and what did not is needed.

It even helps to announce evaluations during the early stages of the ES project. Managers feel more accountable for their actions, and thus increase their efforts to follow all the rules, to communicate constructively with their subordinates about the results, and to plan and implement meaningful actions. The underlying logic is "You get what you measure," or—expressed conversely—things that are not systematically tracked and measured are perceived as not so important. The rational person concentrates on things that "count."

Evaluations benefit from giving the employees an active role in the follow-up processes. The employees, then, evaluate everything not from the perspective of outside observers, but as authors and producers. This may lead to (irrelevant) consequences, such as "better" ratings of whatever was accomplished, but it can also generate objectively better outcomes: Knowing from the beginning that all actions will eventually be evaluated helps to focus all agents on results, not just on activities.

Evaluation Criteria

Evaluations are assessments on certain criteria. Thus, positioning an evaluation always requires specifying these criteria. The most important criteria for evaluating an ES project are the following:

- *Process Goals.* Every ES pursues basic, but fairly explicit goals regarding measurement, alignment, involvement, and the like. Senior leaders often want the survey to provide an external benchmark to evaluate employee engagement, using identical questions throughout all locations, while attaining at least 80% employee survey participation. Evaluation, therefore, might be a matter of verifying a checklist of these process criteria. Some elements may be evaluated through multiple means. For example, employee involvement can be measured by survey response rates, by the extent to which the results were discussed in follow-up workshops, and by percent of employees participating in action planning.

- *Secondary goals.* Most ES projects also pursue a variety of secondary goals, which are important to particular stakeholders. For example, HR may want the ES to get managers and non-managers systematically communicating, while senior leaders may want to insert company values into day-to-day business. Such secondary goals can also lead to evaluation criteria, provided they are not incompatible with the project's main goals (as, e.g., some hidden political goals).

- *Hard side constraints.* All projects pursue their goals under a number of side constraints such as cost efficiency, adherence to delivery dates, 100% quality requirements, or avoiding excessive risks. Hence, one can ask to what extent the ES project satisfied these constraints (at time t). For example, one can assess which costs have been created through the ES project overall or through one of its processes (e.g., the information campaign) at time t, and how these costs compare to the costs estimates in the ES plan.

- *Soft side constraints.* The various "minimal requirement" rules set up in the project's positioning define a second set of side constraints. A typical criterion of that sort pertains to every employee being given the opportunity to obtain information about the results of the ES. Thus, when evaluating the ES project, one can identify and assess the measures that were taken to ensure fast, open, and honest communication of relevant information.

- *Quality of planning and aberrations from the plan.* Another evaluation criterion is the quality of the ES project plan itself, and to what extent this plan was implemented in practice. This leads to questions such as: "Was the overall project plan followed or were there major deviations from the initial plan? Who or what was responsible for deviations from the plan? What were the consequences?" The answers to such questions can provide valuable insight pertaining to future ES projects (e.g., the plan was too simple/complex, unrealistic; conflicts among stakeholders arose; costs and resource planning was inadequate; the project goals were too vaguely defined or remained controversial; the necessary personnel resources were not available; the communication between the project team and decision makers was too slow; the project team did not have enough power; top management showed too little interest to "push" the project).

- *Performance of project agents.* An ES project always contains a large number of people who are involved in the project in different roles (see Table 3.2, *MIDEX* roles). The roles and responsibilities of these project agents within the different parts of the ES project are sometimes defined in detail (see, e.g., Tables 3.3a-d). This automatically establishes a set of criteria for measuring their performance. If their roles are less well-defined, one may still be able to rate their performance on an overall good-to-poor scale, or identify critical incidents in their behavior that help to assess what went well and what did not.

- *Impact and change.* An obvious criterion for an ES project is to assess its impact, meaning the change that it caused: Did the organization's climate change? Are communication processes better than they were before the start of the project? Have action plans been created for the really important topics, or for just for easy-to-solve side issues? Where does the organization stand in terms of implementing the action plans? Some of these questions may be difficult to answer, and the answers one receives to the majority of them may be vastly dependent on the respondent. As a consequence, questions of this sort are frequently posed to more than one individual and to different stakeholders ("How do you assess this criterion?") by conducting focus groups or even by running an anonymous survey in a stratified random sample.

- *Criteria specific to repeated employee surveys.* In cases where employee surveys are conducted repeatedly (e.g., annually, biennially), more recent surveys are, in a way, evaluations of earlier ones. The recent ES results are compared to earlier results to check whether significant change has occurred on items or factors where actions were taken. Response rates for surveys can rise or decline in part because of how visibly prior surveys yielded improvements. One can also include items in the questionnaire that ask the respondents to assess the quality of the follow-up processes after the prior survey or the extent to which their supervisors used prior ES results constructively to promote improvements.

Objective Business Criteria

The official goals of an ES project are usually only instrumental goals, not business goals that affect the bottom line. Management, therefore, sometimes wants to know how much an ES project contributed to these goals. For example, in one case, the president of a mid-sized German company asked directly: "To what extent did the ES boost productivity? You promised you would not just ask about employee satisfaction, but focus on performance!" This question, however naïve it may be, expresses what management is really interested in.

To measure an ES project's contribution is a difficult problem. What makes it so difficult is, among other things, that many business criteria are "fuzzier" than what one might expect. For example, productivity can be defined in many different ways that are not only theoretically, but also practically relevant (Borg, 1992a). There is a host of such criteria (e.g., customer loyalty, sustained profitability, innovation rate, competitive edge), and they often imply different time perspectives. For example, downsizing may positively influence profitability in the short run, but jeopardize delivery reliability and, thereby, harm customer loyalty in the future. The many indices of business success, moreover, are based on numerous assumptions, on estimates and experience, and on rather arbitrary composition rules. Naturally, such problems cannot be solved along the way when conducting an ES evaluation, and so the "dependent variables" of the evaluation can be ambiguous.

Another difficulty when assessing an ES project's impact on business objectives is to distinguish ES effects from the effects of other internal activities and external events (e.g., economic downturns, changes in exchange rates, changes in executive board membership). There is, in general, no mono-causal relationship between an ES project and business outcomes. In other words, "everything" depends on "everything else."

Another complexity in linking survey projects to business criteria is that the ES assesses many practices that are better classified as strategic means than strategic outcomes. The effects of an ES project often influence what the European Foundation for Quality Management refers to as "enabling factors." Actions that result from an ES can serve to extinguish a current fire, fix what is broken, or create conditions necessary for future business performance. These conditions should not be judged as relevant or irrelevant because of changes in temporary business indices. For instance, a survey may assess whether employees know what performance is expected of them or what the consequences are for high or low performance—these questions are relevant *regardless* of subsequent changes in profitability, market share, or revenue growth. Clarity about individual work goals and deliverables is a *necessary* (but not sufficient) condition for sustained business performance, and there is actually no need to show how this clarity is related to the current bottom line.

One should not conclude from these considerations that hard evaluations of employee surveys make no sense. However, an ES project should be evaluated in line with the project's goals and strategic objectives defined during project positioning. The evaluation should not attempt to prove that an ES is a useful intervention in general. The utility of the ES in general has already been empirically established in the organizational sciences (see chapter 4, section 1; see Figure 4.2). Rather, the evaluation of the survey project within an organization should demonstrate exactly what happened and what one has learned for future projects.

Finding the Right Time for Evaluations

Most projects are evaluated when they are completed. Project completion is usually equivalent to the delivery of project results to the ordering party. In the old days, delivery of ES project results meant that the survey results were presented to the sponsor or the executive board. In modern ES projects, this presentation is only the first of numerous systematic follow-up processes, and these follow-up processes generally have no clear-cut end.

Finding the right time for ES project evaluation, therefore, is not easy. The responsibilities in an ES project gradually shift from the ES project team to line managers during the follow-up processes. Moreover, there are typically many responses to the ES results, at different levels of the organizational hierarchy, and with different time horizons and various possibilities for fine-tunings and corrections. This makes it difficult to tell whether an activity is really still part of the ES project, or whether it is already a line-management project in itself. Even at the beginning, the organization does not start at square one. Rather, it is in motion all the time, and many projects and programs are running already when the ES becomes effective. Thus, it typically is not easy to decide what was really caused by the ES or if the ES simply influenced certain action tendencies that existed before a survey was even considered.

Altogether, if the ES sponsor, for example, wants to have an evaluation of the ES project, or if he/she must report on the project, then an "artificial" date has to be identified. In practice, one often sets this date some 4-6 months after the beginning of the follow-up processes. Most actions will be underway, and simpler actions that are designed to show "proof of change" (see chapter 16, section 4) should be completed by then.

17.3 Evaluation Methods

The methods used to evaluate ES projects can be categorized into five groups: Analysis of the quality of the survey data, studying documentation materials, collecting observations about the ES, interviewing stakeholders, and surveying employees and managers about the ES. In most cases, a mixture of these methods is used.

Analyzing the Quality of the Survey Data

Any ES is automatically evaluated to some extent when the quality of the survey data is assessed. The list of questions that can be asked in this context is long, and many such questions are described in detail in standard textbooks on social science methodology. We here mention a few issues that particularly focus on employee surveys:

- *Survey participation*: Is the response rate normal for the particular type of ES? Is the response rate high enough to warrant reliable and valid data interpretation (Rogelberg et al., 2003)? Are certain subgroups or strata over- or under-represented in the data?

- *Nonresponse bias*: Can one expect that the groups that are underrepresented in the data would change the results significantly? (Rogelberg & Stanton, 2007)

- *Demographic item nonresponse*: Are there many missing responses in the demographic items? Do those who skip some or all demographic items differ in their attitudes and opinions from those who answer all demographic items? (Borg et al., 2008)

- *Evidence of response styles:* Do the data (or some particular items) show strong evidence of response styles (e.g., social desirability, acquiescence) or many missing responses that make their interpretation dubious? (Harzing, 2006)

- *Consistency of items* that measure the same topic (scales): Do the items generate the expected factor structure or interpretable, contiguous regions in an MDS analysis (see Figure 12.9)? (Borg & Groenen, 2005; Borg & Staufenbiel, 2007)

- *Measurement equivalence* of scales: Are the statistics comparable across different groups, or do these groups differ so much in the way they structure their perceptions that comparing them leads to an apples-oranges dilemma? (Vandenberg & Lance, 2000; Vandenberg, 2002)

- *Normality of patterns*: Do the data behave normally? Do they show the patterns that are typical for employee surveys? (see Figure 12.8, for example)
- *Content validity*: Do the data form patterns that correspond to theoretical expectations and that reflect item content properly?
- *Predictive validity*: Is there evidence that the "soft" survey data predict "hard" variables such as performance or sickness rates? (see Figure 12.11)

Studying Documentation Materials

An ES project should always be documented in some way. This documentation is more than just a preliminary step for evaluating the project: Collecting, categorizing, analyzing, and describing what happened (processes) and what was accomplished (results) requires the project agents to make many decisions on what information is important, and what can be ignored. It also helps to make corrections in the project while it is being developed and implemented ("formative evaluation").

We recognize that creating, collecting, and reviewing documentation is time consuming and easily deferred or forgotten. Nevertheless, maintaining a "lessons learned" file throughout the survey process is invaluable for improving future ES projects. The information collected in the documentation can pertain to the following topics:

- *ES processes and activities.* Documents that focus on objective and quantitative elements of the ES processes:
  o Response rates and the build-up of the final response rates during the time period of survey administration, in particular conspicuous patterns such as poor initial participation, or gaps due to technical problems in administering the survey.
  o Adherence to delivery dates of all persons and groups involved in the ES project.
  o Number of reports, information on who received what report when, problems in ordering reports, quality of reports, problems in delivering or downloading reports.
  o Number and kind of survey results presentations delivered to management groups, works councils, working groups, etc. (who, when, where, by whom), including a summary of the "reports" the presenters wrote on how these meetings went.
  o Number of action plans, and the topics covered by these action plans.
  o Status of the actions plans (percentage completed), future milestones, ways to keep all stakeholders informed.
- *Critical incidents.* Documents about critical incidents that influenced project management. The agendas and minutes of the various meetings of the core coordination team (see Figure 3.1) should contain much information that is valuable in this

regard. Additionally, critical incidents can be found by reviewing the communications between the ES coordination team (ES project team) and the external vendor, between core team members and specialists involved in organizing the ES, and between support coordinators and area coordinators.

- *Unexpected problems.* Notes documenting unforeseen events and their influence on time frames and deadlines can be useful.
- *Unexpected positive events.* Notes about project successes and special contributions made by certain employees or groups should be screened. Documentation of cost effectiveness and evidence for sound decision making (e.g., "thank you" letters from managers).

The ES project manager should start to assemble such documentation materials as early as possible in the ES project and in a systematic way. One way of setting this up is to make documentation a definitional part of each project milestone. It is also important to repeatedly instruct all coordinators that they should regularly document the project status in their area of responsibility *in writing*, take notes of particular events, and collect and file all ES-related mails and minutes.

The documents should be summarized in some type of final report. Even if this report is not requested by top management or the ES sponsor, it often proves invaluable for follow-up questions or for the development of future ES projects. The report can contain both non-confidential and confidential information. For example, organizations may be interested in the contributions of each ES coordinator to project success, but also in the behavior of line managers (or other stakeholders) during the project.

Collecting Observations on the ES Project

Observations are always one possible data source of an ES project evaluation. All stakeholders of the ES project make multiple observations during the project. These observations are typically not made intentionally, and when asked about them, they are often reported in the form of anecdotes or as vague subjective impressions. The anecdotes can be rather drastic in nature, exaggerating grossly what really happened. Moreover, they often focus on things that did not go well. The quality of these reports also depends on the observer's talent and experience. External consultants with lots of project experience and a more neutral attitude towards the organization can frequently make important observations, while the usual employee who is personally affected by the events may be too involved to arrive at sober judgments. Also, employees are often blinded by the habits and the culture of their particular organization. They may overlook what is really important, reporting mostly those events that were highly emotional. Observations, therefore, should always be accepted with caution. If at all possible, one should ask whether they are mere impressions—which is important information too!—or whether they correspond to objective facts.

Using observations as a method for evaluating an ES project need not rely on collecting what happened to be observed and remembered. Rather, observations can also be made systematically, using methods that range from observing participation in the field to observing the effects of certain interventions in experiment-like situations such as assessment centers. For example, one may want to evaluate the ES-induced action "Supervisor gives better feedback on subordinate's performance." To check this, one could simply observe this supervisor in his or her day-to-day interactions with subordinates, or create particular situations where performance-feedback is essential, or observe the supervisor in simulated performance appraisal settings, etc.

If observational methods are not very structured, observers have to be well trained and competent to arrive at meaningful information. Structured observations are more objective, but they tend to lack detail and depth. In any case, extensive observations can involve a lot of effort, and cost time and money. As both time and money are usually scarce resources when ES projects are evaluated, observations are not used that much for ES project evaluation as other methods.

Interviews to Evaluate the ES Project's Results and Processes

Interviews of managers, employees, ES coordinators, or any other stakeholder are a popular method for evaluating an ES project. They often produce a wealth of data, with lots of detail and contextual information. On the other hand, this specificity can make it difficult to determine how much the interview data can be generalized.

Interviews should best be seen as instruments to measure perceptions of the interviewees. Perceptions can be objectively wrong, but they are still important to know, because "perception is reality" and people base their behavior on how they perceive the world around them. Assessing the *objective* outcomes of an ES project by interviewing managers or employees is difficult. Experience shows that frequently even those who were deeply involved in a project feel that nothing has really changed or even that nothing was done. Objectively, this impression is often wrong. For example, the members of the executive board in an organization were interviewed one by one about their own actions after an ES. Their answers were recorded, sorted, and documented. When the documentation was presented to the executive board, the board members were pleasantly surprised about the number of issues that were addressed or triggered by the project. The opposite effect is also possible. If interviewed, employees may feel that the ES project has led to many improvements in particular problem areas, even though *no* specific actions were implemented at all. It seems that if the ES and its processes are generally perceived in a positive way by the employees, then positive but objectively incorrect opinions are generated out of the employees' "gut feelings" (Borg, 2003). When an interviewee is asked about positive change, the answer may boil down to "How do I feel about it?" rather than an objective review (Schwarz & Clore, 1983).

Interviews for evaluating an ES project can be designed in different ways. The interview itself can be highly standardized, using a structured questionnaire. It can also be conducted in an explorative way, where the interviewer is free to follow any cue that promises to lead to interesting insights (Oppenheim, 1992). The interviews can be conducted individually or in a group of up to about a dozen persons. The mode of the interview is mostly face to face, but interviews are frequently also conducted via telephone to save traveling time. The interviewees can belong to all levels of the hierarchy (from rank-and-file employees to the CEO); they can work for different functions of the organization (R&D, sales, etc.), subsidiaries, etc.; they can also represent different stakeholders (middle managers or works council member, for example).

Junior interviewers should only conduct standardized interviews that use interview questionnaires with questions that have to be read exactly as they are formulated. Only the answers to these questions are recorded. If the interview is well-prepared, the questionnaire may even provide answer categories that can be checked. Expert interviewers, in contrast, better work with interview guidelines that only list the topics to be covered—in some order and by any questions that seem appropriate. They thus have enough freedom to pursue, in more depth, particularly interesting issues that emerge during the interview.

If interviewers are conducting a large number of interviews, they need to be trained to ensure data quality and, in particular, continued impartiality. The first interviews can quickly make an unprepared interviewer "opinionated" in the sense that later interviews only support the "insights" that he or she gained in early interviews. In that case, the early interviews strongly determine what is found in later interviews, making them essentially worthless.

When planning who should interview whom, one should consider possible interviewer effects. Interviewees may, for example, tailor their answers to what they think would satisfy or please the interviewer (social desirability). Interviewees may also be intimidated if they are interviewed by someone with great power (expertise, formal, or otherwise). Moreover, certain features of the interviewer may make certain answers more likely. For example, if the interviewer obviously belongs to a minority group, he or she should not conduct interviews that focus on minority issues. Thus, different interviewers and a careful interviewer-interviewee matching should be used to reduce the risk to arrive at biased results.

The interviewees have to receive a careful explanation of the interview's objectives, and a clear rationale as to why they and not other persons were chosen to participate (e.g., random selection). Moreover, the interviewer must inform the interviewee about the rules that govern the use of the interview data. The interview data must not, for example, be shown to the interviewee's direct supervisor without the interviewee's explicit consent. Generally, interview data are summarized in some way to show main trends or "typical" comments. Individual comments that are particularly interesting should be reported only in an anonymous way (similar to open-ended items in an ES).

Interviews must also be organized properly. The choice of the interview place should be guided by efforts to protect the participant's confidentiality. Employees' regular workspaces are usually not good places for conducting interviews: They provide little privacy, and interruptions (e.g., phone calls, colleagues) are likely to occur. Also, interviewing dates and times should be coordinated with the employees' supervisors to avoid scheduling conflicts.

A crucial factor in ensuring successful interviews is choosing the right questions. Typical questions geared towards an ES project evaluation are the following:

- *Goals:* Which of the ES project goals have been accomplished? What were your expectations for the ES project? Were these expectations met?

- *Efficiency:* From your perspective, are the costs of the ES project justified in light of the project's outcomes? What is your assessment of the psychological effort invested in the project (e.g., sheer work, conflicts, aligning stakeholders)? What problems were there? What could/should have been done differently?
- *Data collection:* From your perspective, how did survey data collection go? Were you or your colleagues concerned about anonymity? Could all of the anonymity concerns be eliminated? Why were the response rates in unit [X] relatively low? Was the information about the ES project sufficient? Did all stakeholder groups support the ES project?
- *Questionnaire:* Do you think that the questionnaire covered the important issues? Were there questions in the questionnaire that you feel shouldn't have been there? What other comments have you on the questionnaire?
- *Acceptance of the survey results:* What were your co-workers' reactions towards the survey results? Were the results embraced by everyone as valuable information? Were the results discussed in a constructive spirit? Did everyone fully understand the ES survey's results? How did your supervisors/superiors respond towards the ES results? Did the employees blame themselves for poor results, or was blame solely attributed to others (e.g., supervisors, top management)?
- *Action planning:* Was action-planning understood as a joint effort meant to lead to real improvement? Did employee ideas and comments receive sufficient consideration when actions were planned? Were action plans communicated clearly? Was the general direction of all action plans clear? Did the actions focus on the truly important topics in a balanced way? Did all actions fit together, or did they contradict each other? Were the priorities underlying the actions plans clear and accepted by everyone? Were there actions that appear unjustified or unnecessary? Do you think that the actions were caused (or at least reinforced) by the ES project, or would they have come anyway, with or without the ES?
- *Implementation of actions:* Did the implementation of actions follow a clear set of guidelines? Did everyone receive sufficient information about the state of the actions? Are all efforts helpful for the same overall goals? Are different groups pulling in different directions? Is everyone's involvement in line with their expertise and skill level? What resistance has been encountered in the efforts to implement follow-up actions? What other problems have come up? Is there real progress or do the same old problems resurface again and again?
- *Results and side effects of actions:* What influence did the actions have on the organization's climate? Has mutual trust between employees and the organization been improved? Was the ES project perceived as a joint effort of all stakeholders? What results has the ES project had for leadership styles, participation, listening, effectiveness, productivity, customer service orientation, performance appraisal and merit-based compensation, ethics, involvement, commitment and employee empowerment, etc.? Has the basis for future ES projects been successfully created (e.g., has the ES eliminated employee concerns about anonymity and misuse of data)? Are project outcomes worth the effort? Do the employees feel that an ES is generally worthwhile?

Surveys to Evaluate the ES Project's Results and Processes

Besides studying documentation materials or conducting interviews, one can also use surveys to evaluate an ES project. Surveys have a number of advantages: They can be completed and analyzed in a short time period; they are relatively inexpensive; they can collect data from an arbitrarily large sample of respondents; and the sample can be carefully structured to represent important subgroups and strata, where it does not matter where the respondent is physically located (e.g., in New Zealand). Moreover, surveys are standardized, asking the same questions to everyone at the same time. This makes comparisons easier. The disadvantage of surveys is that one must invest heavily into constructing good questions. Unclear answers cannot be clarified by discussing an issue in more depth. However, one could employ some open-ended questions to at least pick up issues that were missed by the closed items (e.g., "What comments do you have on the ES project?"; "What could be done to improve the next ES?"; "From your perspective, what are the major results of the ES project?").

A central question in survey-based evaluation pertains to sampling the right individuals. Partially, this question can be answered on the basis of the ES project's positioning. If solely an estimate of overall parameters is needed, then a small random sample is sufficient. If the evaluation is supposed to be informative with respect to different departments, for example, then samples become necessary that are large enough to yield reliable information for each subgroup of interest (see chapter 6).

17.4 The Practice of ES Evaluations

Evaluating an ES project is not as common as it used to be in the early days of employee surveying. The reason is that it has become rare to run an ES as a stand-alone project. Today, employee surveys are almost always repeated in regular time intervals and, hence, the next ES can be used to evaluate the previous ES. Formal evaluations that use more than just a few interviews or some screening of the project's documentation have become the exception. However, if an organization starts a series of employee surveys and if it wants to learn as much as possible from its early surveys, a deeper form of evaluation can be a good investment. In practice, this almost always means that an evaluation survey is used, because a survey allows one to involve a larger number of employees than the use of any other evaluation method. Still, evaluation surveys pose a number of challenges, which we will briefly discuss next.

Sample

Evaluation surveys often use quota samples because they are cheaper to draw than (stratified) random samples. However, if a reliable personnel information system exists, a random sample can be easily drawn by a statistician who knows sampling methods. Small organizational units are typically oversampled, and managers at higher levels are all invited to participate in this survey. This has the advantage that the total sample size can be kept small. On the other hand, oversampling requires weightings in data analysis to make the overall statistics unbiased.

The sample size for evaluation surveys is a function of various considerations. A common fallacy in this context is the notion that a sample has to have a certain size to be representative. The answer is that the sample size has nothing to do with "representativity." Indeed, representativity is not even a statistical term (Diekmann, 2007). The size of an (unbiased) random sample only determines the margin of error for the resulting statistics. One would also hope—or make sure via stratification—that certain distributional properties of the sample (e.g., the proportion of men vs. women) match the respective properties of the population. If so, the sample is representative— in this regard! Hence, the main criterion for the sample size is the number of respondents needed to generate statistics with an error margin that seems acceptable. Formal answers are given in Chapter 6, but one must also speculate about the participation rate and possible bias effects due to nonresponse. In the end, the required size of the sample depends on statistical considerations, but also what one intends to do to avoid nonresponse behavior.

To invite all members of upper management to participate in an evaluation survey is usually a good idea. Top management is usually a small group that is of high importance for the overall project success, and to get population statistics rather than just estimates for this group is therefore important. There is no need to explain estimates or margins of error, and running a census surveys in a small population is also easier and cheaper than sampling.

Oversampling in small organizational units may be required to keep the budget for an evaluation survey within limits. For example, organizational units usually differ substantially in size. If organization unit A consists of only 500 employees, and organizational unit B consists of 10,000, and if one wants to survey at least 30 individuals per 500 employees, then proportional sampling would require surveying a total of 630 persons, where 30 are from unit A and $[(30/500) \times 10,000]=600$ from unit B. If only overall trends are of interest for both A and B, respectively, one does not need that many persons in the B sample, and oversampling in A may be substantially cheaper. On the other hand, oversampling can have some psychological drawbacks: if small units are oversampled, members of larger units may wonder why smaller units are receiving that much more "attention" and weight than larger units. Thus, it is always advisable to carefully inform employees about the rationale for sample construction.

Organization

Data collection for evaluation surveys is most easily realized using a centrally organized, postal-based mailing of the questionnaires. In organizations where most employees have computer access, the use of web-based surveys provides an even more cost-effective mode. When evaluation surveys are sent out, one has to assume right from the beginning that various follow-up postcards and other reminders will be needed to achieve the necessary sample size. Experience shows that obtaining high participation rates in non-census surveying is more difficult than in census surveys. In some cases, it may also be crucial to assign data collection responsibility to local coordinators who are present in the respective organizational units. These coordinators can then attempt to stimulate response rates by emphasizing the importance of the evaluation survey by various local activities—most of all by face-to-face interactions—with employees.

Items and Survey Design

The development of evaluation survey items has to ensure that all topics discussed earlier are accounted for. Usually, an evaluation questionnaire contains:
1) An introductory part (similar to Figure 5.8)
2) A section with demographic items (similar to Figure 5.9)
3) Two to three item blocks pertaining to:
   a) Opinions on the survey itself and its follow-up processes (feedback, workshops, action planning and implementation, communication etc.)
   b) Opinions on the outcomes of the ES project
   c) Open-ended or semi-closed questions about the ES project ("Anything else?", "Other things I wanted to say", etc.)

Figure 17.2 displays some items of an evaluation survey. The items are formulated in the same format as the items in the questionnaire used in the ES. Hence, we here assume that the ES questionnaire used 5-point Likert items. These items should be familiar to most respondents, allowing them to fill out the questionnaire more quickly and reliably.

The second part of the questionnaire addresses the ES project's results. The simplest items that can be used to evaluate such effects ask the respondent directly for an overall judgment: "Altogether, the ES has led to positive results"; "Altogether, the ES has initiated a significant amount of positive change"; or "Without the ES project, many changes would not have occurred at all or would have occurred much later than they did."

Although such general evaluations may be useful, the ES sponsor and other stakeholders are typically more interested in measuring more specific effects. For instance, they may want to evaluate whether the ES project's goals have been achieved, or whether the actions taken in response to the ES successfully promoted the topics they were supposed to improve. Figure 17.3 shows some items meant to measure such more specific effects. Note that these items are not formatted as Likert items. Instead, the respondent has the opportunity to rate each issue on an improved-to-deteriorated scale. We advise against the use of items that allow the respondent to rate only improvement, because some respondents may perceive this as an attempt to manipulate the survey into a "positive" direction.

Items of the improved-to-deteriorated type always have to be carefully interpreted, though. If, for example, the respondents in a particular workgroup had no complaints about the clarity of their supervisor's expectations regarding their work, then a "no change" result would be just fine. Therefore, "change" items should always focus on issues where change was deemed necessary, in general.

The employee survey	Fully agree ⏪	Agree ◀	Unde-cided ⏸	Dis-agree ▶	Fully dis-agree ⏩
I always felt well-informed about the employee survey and its processes.	☐	☐	☐	☐	☐
I was concerned that my answers to the employee survey would not remain anonymous.	☐	☐	☐	☐	☐
The workshops that followed the employee survey were conducted in a constructive atmosphere.	☐	☐	☐	☐	☐
An employee survey should be conducted regularly in this company.	☐	☐	☐	☐	☐
The employee survey caused or supported a lot of positive change.	☐	☐	☐	☐	☐

Actions taken in response to the employee survey	Fully agree ⏪	Agree ◀	Unde-cided ⏸	Dis-agree ▶	Fully dis-agree ⏩
A serious effort was made after the employee survey to identify the topics where action was needed.	☐	☐	☐	☐	☐
During action planning, I felt encouraged to contribute my own ideas and suggestions.	☐	☐	☐	☐	☐
I know the action plans sufficiently well.	☐	☐	☐	☐	☐
I am confident that the actions will lead to important improvements.	☐	☐	☐	☐	☐
I can easily get sufficient information about the implementation of the action plans.	☐	☐	☐	☐	☐

Figure 17.2. Excerpts of an evaluation questionnaire (part A).

Another way of assessing change is to use relevant items from the ES questionnaire (i.e., those that measure issues where action was taken) a second time and then check the differences between the respective survey results. However, when comparisons of this sort are made, it is important to compute margins of error to see if any observed differences are statistically significant. For example, if the ES generated 30% agreement to an item, we would need at least 39% in the evaluation survey to be reasonably confident that real change occurred (assuming $N=1,000$ for the census ES and $n=100$ for the evaluation sample survey; using Formula 6.6).

Change after the employee survey	Clearly improved	Somewhat improved	No change	Somewhat deteriorated	Clearly deteriorated
The support and the service of the IT department for my work environment	☺	○	😐	○	☹
The clarity of what my supervisor expects of me	☺	○	😐	○	☹
The opportunities to voice my opinion on decisions that directly affect my work	☺	○	😐	○	☹
The quality of communicating of our workgroup with other workgroups that are important for our work	☺	○	😐	○	☹

Figure 17.3. Excerpt of an evaluation questionnaire (part B).

The issues in evaluating an ES project are generally less standard and less predictable than the issues addressed by a regular ES. Standard items focus on general project outcomes or on the functioning of the ES processes, but actions in response to an ES are always specific for the particular organizations and things that did not work well are even more specific. Thus, in addition to close-ended items, one should also add some open-ended questions that allow the respondent to focus on topics of his or her own choice. These items often provide interesting information on issues that had not been expected by the ES project team. Figure 17.4 shows an example for two open-ended items. The item asks about the issues (up to 2 only) where the ES had a particularly positive and negative impact, respectively. Obviously, other open-ended items are also conceivable, such as a very generic question asking for "additional comments you may have about the ES project." Sometimes, open-ended questions may also be useful to complement blocks of closed items ("Anything else on that topic?").

Data Analysis and Interpretation

The analysis of an evaluation survey follows essentially the same logic as the analysis of ES data. All statistics should be easy to comprehend for everyone; they should show similarities and differences among different organizational units; and they should allow one to aggregate the information into meaningful indices.

For items pertaining to change as in Figure 17.3, it is usually easiest to describe the percentage of respondents who felt that there was positive or negative change, respectively. A presentation of means for these ratings is good supplementary information. Comparisons across organizational units (Figure 17.5) allows for interesting discussions about the project and its outcomes.

Interpreting the results of evaluation surveys, however, always requires extra care. For example, Figure 17.5 shows that the respondents in the department "DV" felt that

> Please briefly describe up to 2 issues where the employee survey had really *positive* impact:
>
> _____
> _____
> _____
>
> Please briefly describe up to 2 issues where the employee survey had really *negative* impact:
>
> _____
> _____
> _____

Figure 17.4. Excerpt of an evaluation questionnaire (part C).

there was only little change in regarding their opportunities to voice ideas. The meaning of this finding, however, depends on whether this issue required action or not: If the employees in DV were generally satisfied with the opportunities to voice their ideas, then 25% additional endorsement would be a remarkable improvement; if they were highly dissatisfied, then 25% change would be meager. Thus, change statistics always have to be made evaluated against the context from which they come.

Furthermore, any change should also be evaluated in conjunction with the "circumstances" and the difficulties the respective units may have encountered in trying to implement change. It is easy to change some things, but difficult to change other things. Moreover, it may be even more difficult to make change last. All this should be considered when evaluating the snapshot information provided by an evaluation survey.

In the example in Figure 17.5, one also notices that positive change seems to outweigh negative change. Results of this sort are rather usual in applied settings. Occasionally, employees even feel that in areas where *no* actions had been implemented, positive change has occurred! The reason for such judgments is unclear. One theoretical rationale that has been proposed pertains to a halo effect. When halo occurs, a positive evaluation of different issues leads to a spillover of affect to unrelated topics. For example, the vast majority of employees (often more than 90%) typically support running employee surveys. Furthermore, ES projects typically improve internal communication, in particular if the survey is followed up with workshops and discussions conducted in a cooperative spirit. Moreover, the individual may also learn something from the survey that can lead to a positive effect in his/her own behavior, feeling, or thinking. Thus, if this causes a halo, then merely conducting an ES can lead the individual to frame all aspects of work more positively and perceive positive change where, objectively speaking, nothing happened.

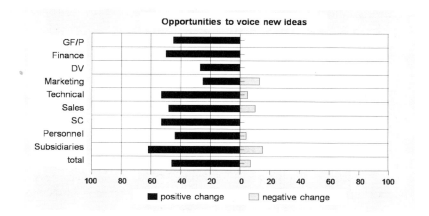

Figure 17.5. Percentage of persons in different departments who said that "opportunities to voice new ideas" had changed in a positive/negative way after the last employee survey.

No evaluation ever succeeds to clearly prove *causal* relationships: Did the ES or a particular action really cause a certain result, or did other factors bring about the effect? An ES is never the only project or the only pattern of activities in an organization. Still, most textbooks today still promote the classic model of organizational change that conceives of change as a three-stage process comparable to unfreezing an ice block, changing it, and refreezing it (Lewin, 1951). Yet, the model is wrong, at least for today's organizations: There is no ice block in the first place. Rather, the organization and its elements are constantly in motion, adapting to a changing environment, setting new goals and modifying old ones, initiating new directions, learning what works and what does not, etc., and the ES is but one of many interventions.

An ES project, moreover, usually extends over a period of several months, and many things can change during that time: An unexpected surge of the markets, the loss of major accounts, a crash in the stock market, etc. One case that demonstrates the confounding effects of other events is the case of a company where the executive board decided shortly after completion of the survey to revoke its previous decision to close down a plant, but rather to invest heavily into this plant so that it could produce a new line of products. It should be obvious that this decision had a major impact on the mood of the employees in this plant so that one can safely assume that repeating the ES would have led to far "better" results across all content areas. An evaluation survey, therefore, would have been rather useless, because the context had changed so dramatically that it would make no sense to try to track the positive impact of isolated actions or ask for a general evaluation of the ES.

If a lot of organizational change is happening while the ES project is being conducted, then the visibility and impact of the ES project can become rather small. The employees then sometimes feel that the ES did not lead to much, even though one can show that it led to a number of important actions that were all implemented according to plan. Hence, asking employees for their evaluations always reflects their perceptions. If these perceptions are negative, management may have to do a better job communicating what was done—or the perceptions may indeed be right and not much was done.

Under certain circumstances, even change in a negative direction has to be interpreted positively. For instance, in a German company with a long tradition, 30% of the employees complained about the organization's excessive bureaucracy. The topic "excessive bureaucracy" was then extensively discussed and addressed in various workshops after the ES. When an evaluation survey was later conducted, 40% of the employees complained about the organization's bureaucracy. Interviews conducted after this survey revealed that this change of assessment merely indicated that many employees had previously not even noticed that bureaucracy had been excessive, and the discussions succeeded to make them notice it. Management was pleased with this finding, because they argued that perceiving that bureaucracy was "excessive" was the first step in becoming more efficient.

References

AAPOR. (1997). *Best practices for survey and public opinion research and survey practices AAPOR condemns*. American Association for Public Opinion Research, May.

Ackoff, R.L. (1989). From data to wisdom. *Journal of Applied Systems Analysis, 16*, 3-9.

Adler, P.S., & Kwon, S.-W. (2002). Social capital: Prospects for a new concept. *Academy of Management Review, 27*(1), 17-40.

Ajzen, I. (1988). *Attitudes, personality, and behavior*. Chicago: Dorsey.

Allen, N.J., & Meyer, J.P. (1990). The measurement and antecedents of affective, continuance, and normative commitment. *Journal of Occupational Psychology, 63*, 1-18.

Alper, S.W., Pfau, B.N., & Sirota, D. (1986). Successful employee attitude surveys. *The President, 22*(4), 1-2.

Amabile, T.M., & Conti, R. (1999). Changes in the work environment for creativity during downsizing. *Academy of Management Journal, 42*, 630-640.

Amabile, T.M., Conti, R., Coon, H., Lazenby, J., & Herron, M. (1995). Assessing the work environment for creativity. *Academy of Management Journal, 39*, 1154-1184.

Andersen, E.S., Grude, K.V., Haug, T., & Turner, J.R. (1984). *Goal directed project management*. Worcester, England: Kogan Page.

Anderson, K.T., Gantner, S.M., & Hanson, T.F. (2006). A change model for healthcare organizations. *OD Practitioner, 38*(3), 42-48.

Antoni, F. (1999). *Funktionale Beziehungen der Arbeitszufriedenheit mit arbeitsbezogenen Meinungen, Einstellungen und demographischen Variablen*. Master's thesis, FB 06 Psychologie, Universität Gießen, Germany.

Argyris, C. (1994). *On organizational learning*. Cambridge, MA: Blackwell.

Ashford, S.J., Lee, C., & Bobko, P. (1989). Content, causes, and consequences of job insecurity: A theory-based measure and substantive test. *Academy of Management Journal, 32*, 803-829.

Bandura, A. (1997). *Self-efficacy: The exercise of control*. New York: Freeman.

Barbera, K.M., Beres, R.K., & Lee, W.C. (2007, April). Survey stakeholders: An outside view. *Paper presented at the 22nd Annual SIOP Conference*. New York.

Barbera, K.M., & Young, S.A. (2006). Online reporting: Real time, real impact, real opportunities. In A.I. Kraut (Ed.), *Getting action from organizational surveys: New concepts, technologies, and applications* (pp. 213-237). San Francisco: Jossey-Bass.

Barmash, I. (1993). Employee attitude surveys: More substance than style. *Across the Board, May*, 43-45.

Bazerman, M., & Chugh, D. (2006). Decisions without blinders. *Harvard Business Review, Jan*, 88-97.

Bearden, W.O., Netemeyer, R.G., & Mobley, M.F. (Eds.). (1993). *Handbook of marketing scales*. Newbury Park, Ca.: Sage.

Becker, G. (1997). Mitarbeiterbefragungen im TQM-Modell. In W. Bungard & I. Jöns (Eds.), *Mitarbeiterbefragung: Ein Instrument des Innovations- und Qualitätsmanagements* (pp. 214-223). Weinheim, Germany: Beltz.

Bergler, R., & Piwinger, M. (2000). Die Mitarbeiterbefragung als Instrument der Entwicklung von Strategien der Unternehmensentwicklung bei Vorwerk. In M.E. Domsch & D.H. Ladwig (Eds.), *Handbuch Mitarbeiterbefragung* (pp. 73-102). Berlin, Germany: Springer.

Bishop, G., Hippler, H.J., Schwarz, N., & Strack, F. (1988). A comparison of response effects in self-administered and telephone surveys. In R.M. Groves, P. Biemer, L. Lyberg, J.T. Massey, W.L. Nicholls, & J. Waksberg (Eds.), *Telephone survey methodology* (pp. 321-340). New York: Wiley.

Block, P. (1999). *Flawless consulting: A guide to getting your expertise used* (2nd ed.). New York: Pfeiffer.

Boek, W.E., & Lade, J.H. (1963). Test of the usefulness of the postcard technique in a mail questionnaire study. *Public Opinion Quarterly, 27*, 303-306.

Borg, I. (1986). A cross-cultural replication on Elizur's facets of work values. *Multivariate Behavioral Research, 21*, 401-410.

Borg, I. (1989). Zur Präsentation von Umfrageergebnissen. *Zeitschrift für Arbeits- und Organisationspsychologie, 33*, 90-95.

Borg, I. (1991). Sind Personen, die sich in Umfragen nicht identifizierbar machen, besonders kritisch? *Zeitschrift für Sozialpsychologie, 22*, 123-129.

Borg, I. (1992a). Facetten des Produktivitätsbegriffs. *Paper presented at the conference "Leistungs- und Produktivitätsmanagement"*. Bad Homburg, Germany: Institute for International Research.

Borg, I. (1992b). Überlegungen und Untersuchungen zur Messung der subjektiven Unsicherheit der Arbeitsstelle. *Zeitschrift für Arbeits- und Organisationspsychologie, 36*, 107-116.

Borg, I. (1994). Coping with the dilemma of high importance and low satisfaction. *Perceptual and Motor Skills, 78*, 833-834.

Borg, I. (1995). *Mitarbeiterbefragungen: Strategisches Auftau- und Einbindungsmanagement*. Stuttgart, Germany: Verlag für angewandte Psychologie.

Borg, I. (1997). Mitarbeiterbefragungen im Rahmen des Auftau- und Einbindungsmanagement-Programms (AEMP): Entwicklungen und Erfahrungen. In W. Bungard & I. Jöns (Eds.), *Mitarbeiterbefragung: Ein Instrument des Innovations- und Qualitätsmanagements* (pp. 59-73). Weinheim, Germany: Beltz.

Borg, I. (2000, October). From mind maps to mapping sentences. *Paper presented at the Fifth International Conference on Social Science Methodology (RC33)*. Cologne, Germany.

Borg, I. (2001a). Affective halo and the first law of attitudes. In D. Elizur (Ed.), *Facet theory: Integrating theory construction with data analysis* (pp. 7-14). Prag: Matfyzpress.

Borg, I. (2001b). Früh- versus Spätantworter. *ZUMA Nachrichten, 47*, 7-19.

Borg, I. (2002a). *Latenzzeiten bei der Beantwortung von MAB-Items*. Unpublished manuscript, FB 06 Psychologie, Universität Gießen, Germany.

Borg, I. (2002b). *Mitarbeiterbefragungen - kompakt*. Göttingen, Germany: Hogrefe.

Borg, I. (2003). Affektiver Halo in Mitarbeiterbefragungen. *Zeitschrift für Arbeits- und Organisationspsychologie, 47*, 1-11.

Borg, I. (2005, April). Story construction in employee surveys: From information to understanding. *Paper presented at the symposium of the ITSG*. Los Angeles.

Borg, I. (2006a). Arbeitswerte, Arbeitszufriedenheit und ihr Zusammenhang. In L. Fischer (Ed.), *Arbeitszufriedenheit: Konzepte und empirische Befunde* (pp. 61-79). Göttingen, Germany: Hogrefe.

Borg, I. (2006b). Unifying O'Reilly's organizational culture profile and Schwartz's value theory. *Paper presented at the biannual conference of the ISSWOV*. Tallin, Estonia.

Borg, I., & Braun, M. (1992). Arbeitsethik, Arbeitsinvolvement und Arbeitswerte als Moderatoren der Arbeitsplatzunsicherheit. *Zeitschrift für Arbeits- und Organisationspsychologie, 36*, 167-176.

Borg, I., & Braun, M. (1995). Trust in organizations. In J.J. Hox, G.J. Mellenbergh, & P.G. Swanborn (Eds.), *Facet theory: Analysis and design* (pp. 47-53). Zeist, NL: Setos.

Borg, I., & Braun, M. (1996). Work values in East and West Germany: Different weights but identical structures. *Journal of Organizational Behavior, 17*, 541-555.

Borg, I., Braun, M., & Baumgärtner, M. (2008). Attitudes of demographic item non-respondents in employee surveys. *International Journal of Manpower, 29*(2), 146-160.

Borg, I., & Faulbaum, F. (2004, March). Vor- und Nachteile von Online-Mitarbeiterbefragungen im Vergleich zur Wahllokal-, postalischen und CATI-Administration. *Paper presented at the DGOF Conference 2004*. Duisburg, Germany.

Borg, I., & Gabler, S. (2002). Zustimmungsanteile und Mittelwerte von Likert-skalierten Items. *ZUMA Nachrichten, 50*, 7-25.

Borg, I., & Galinat, W.H. (1987). Ist man mit wichtigen Aspekten seiner Arbeit zufriedener als mit unwichtigen? *Zeitschrift für Arbeits- und Organisationspsychologie, 31*, 63-67.

Borg, I., & Groenen, P. (2005). *Modern multidimensional scaling. Theory and applications* (2nd ed.). New York: Springer.

Borg, I., & Hillenbrand, C. (2003). Prognosen als Methode zur Reduktion der Offensichtlichkeit von Umfragebefunden: Ein Pilotexperiment. *ZUMA-Nachrichten, 52*, 7-19.

Borg, I., & Noll, H.H. (1990). Wie wichtig ist "wichtig"? *ZUMA Nachrichten, 27*, 36-48.

Borg, I., & Shye, S. (1995). *Facet theory: Form and content*. Newbury Park, CA: Sage.

Borg, I., & Staufenbiel, T. (1992). Productivity management by combining HISYS and ProMES. *Proceedings of the Third International Congress on Work and Organizational Values* (pp. 273-282). Karlsbad, CR.

Borg, I., & Staufenbiel, T. (2007). *Theorien und Methoden der Skalierung* (4th ed.). Bern, Switzerland: Huber.

Borg, I., Staufenbiel, T., & Pritchard, R.D. (1995). Hierarchies of objectives in productivity management: Combining features of HISYS and ProMES. In R.D. Pritchard (Ed.), *Productivity improvement strategies and applications* (pp. 312-324). New York: Praeger.

Borg, I., & Treder, C. (2003). Item-Nonresponse in Mitarbeiterbefragungen. *ZUMA-Nachrichten, 53*, 77-95.

Borg, I., & Tuten, T. (2003). Early versus later respondents in Intranet-based, organizational surveys. *Journal of Behavioral and Applied Management, 4*(1), 134-147.

Borg, I., Zuell, C., & Beckstette, C. (2007). Kommentare in Mitarbeiterbefragungen: Welche Themenfelder werden von wem wie kommentiert? *Zeitschrift für Personalpsychologie, 6*, 49-59.

Boyett, J.H., & Conn, H.P. (1995). *Maximum performance management*. Lakewood, CO: Glenbridge.

Bradburn, N.M., & Sudman, S. (1991). The current status of questionnaire research. In P. Biemer & et al. (Eds.), *Measurement errors in surveys* (pp. 29-40). New York: Wiley.

Brennan, M., Hoek, J., & Astridge, C. (1991). Effects of monetary incentives on the response rate and cost-effectiveness of a mail survey. *Journal of the Marketing Research Society, 33*, 229-241.

Brief, A.P., & Motowidlo, S.J. (1986). Prosocial organizational behaviors. *Academy of Management Review, 11*, 710-725.

Brislin, R.W. (1986). The wording and translation of research instruments. In W.J. Lomner & J.W. Berry (Eds.), *Field methods in cross-cultural research* (pp. 137-164). Beverly Hills, CA: Sage.

Brooks, S.M., Wiley, J.W., Hause, E.L., & Moechnig, K.R. (2002). The wake of disaster: Impact on the nation's workplace. *Paper presented at the Seventeenth Annual Conference of the SIOP*. Toronto, Ontario.

Brown, S.L., & Eisenhardt, K.M. (1995). Product development: Past research, present findings, and future directions. *Academy of Management Review, 20*, 343-379.

Bruennecke, K., & Canisius, E. (1991). Open Line - Eine Mitarbeiterbefragung der Hewlett-Parckard GmbH. In M. Domsch & A. Schneble (Eds.), *Mitarbeiterbefragungen* (pp. 95-107). Heidelberg, Germany: Physica.

Bruggemann, A., Groskurth, P., & Ulich, E. (1975). *Arbeitszufriedenheit*. Bern: Huber, Switzerland.

Buckingham, M., & Coffman, C. (1999). *First, break all the rules: What the world's greatest managers do differently*. New York: Simon & Schuster.

Bungard, W., Fettel, A., & Jöns, I. (1997). Mitarbeiterbefragungen: Verbreitung, Einsatzformen und Erfahrungen bei den 100 umsatzgrößten Unternehmen in der Bundesrepublik Deutschland. In W. Bungard & I. Jöns (Eds.), *Mitarbeiterbefragung: Ein Instrument des Innovations- und Qualitätsmanagements* (pp. 246-263). Weinheim, Germany: Beltz.

Bungard, W., Müller, K., & Niethammer, C. (2007). *Mitarbeiterbefragung - was dann...? MAB und Folgeprozesse erfolgreich gestalten.* Berlin, Germany: Springer.
Burke, W.W. (1987). *Organization development: A normative view.* Reading, Mass.: Addison-Wesley.
Cascio, W.F. (1982). *Costing human resources: The financial impact of behavior in organizations.* Boston, MA: Kent.
Church, A.H. (1993). Estimating the effect of incentives on mail survey response rates: A meta-analysis. *Public Opinion Quarterly, 57*, 62-79.
Church, A.H., Desrosiers, E.I., & Oliver, D.H. (2007, April). Can you add my item? Addressing the needs of multiple stakeholders through customization. *Paper presented at the 22nd Annual SIOP Conference.* New York.
Church, A.H., & Waclawski, J. (2001). *Designing and using organizational surveys: A seven step approach.* San Francisco: Jossey-Bass.
Cialdini, R.B. (2007). *Influence: The psychology of persuasion.* New York: Collins.
Claassen, J.J. (1985). Mitarbeiterbefragungen zur Analyse der Führungs- und Arbeitssituation bei den Hamburg-Mannheimer Versicherungsgesellschaften. In A. Töpfer & E. Zander (Eds.), *Mitarbeiter-Befragungen* (pp. 317-343). Frankfurt, Germany: Campus.
Clark, H.H., & Clark, E.V. (1977). *Psychology and language.* Orlando, FL: Harcourt, Brace, Jovanovich.
Coffey, A., & Atkinson, P. (1995). *Making sense of qualitative data: Complementary research strategies.* Thousand Oaks, CA: Sage.
Colihan, J. (1999). *Personal communication.* Minneapolis, MN: IBM International Employee Research.
Collins, J. (2001). *Good to great: Why some companies make the leap...and others don't.* New York: Harper Collins.
Conger, J.A., & Kanungo, R.N. (1988). The empowerment process: Integrating theory and practice. *Academy of Management Review, 13*, 471-482.
Control Data Business Advisors. (1986). *Employee surveys.* Minneapolis, MN: CDBA.
Converse, J.M., & Presser, S. (1986). *Survey questions: Handicrafting the standard questionnaire.* Newbury Park, CA: Sage.
Cook, C., Heath, F., & Thompson, R.L. (2000). A meta-analysis of response rates in Web- or Internet-based surveys. *Educational and Psychological Measurement, 60*, 821-836.
Cook, J.D., Hepworth, S.J., Wall, T.D., & Warr, P.B. (1981). *The experience of work.* London, UK: Academic Press.
Coombs, C.H. (1964). *A theory of data.* New York: Wiley.
Cranny, C.J., Smith, P.C., & Stone, E.F. (Eds.). (1992). *Job satisfaction.* New York: Lexington.
Deci, E.L. (1972). The effects of contingent and non-contingent rewards and controls on intrinsic motivation. *Organizational Behavior and Human Performance, 8*, 217-229.
Deitering, F. (2006). *Folgeprozesse bei Mitarbeiterbefragungen.* Munich, Germany: Hamp.
Delany, J.T., Lewin, D., & Ichniowski, G. (1988). *Human resource management policies and practices in American firms.* New York: Industrial Relations Center, School of Business, Columbia University.
DeVellis, R.F. (1991). *Scale development.* Newbury Park, CA: Sage.
DeVellis, R.F. (2003). *Scale development: Theory and applications* (2nd ed.). Newbury Park, CA: Sage.
Diekmann, A. (1995). *Empirische Sozialforschung: Grundlagen, Methoden, Anwendungen.* Hamburg, Germany: Rowohlt.
Diekmann, A. (2007). *Methoden der empirischen Sozialforschung.* Reinbek, Germany: Rowohlt.
Diekmann, A., & Jann, B. (2001). Anreizformen und Ausschöpfungsquoten bei postalischen Befragungen: Eine Prüfung der Reziprozitätshypothese. *ZUMA-Nachrichten, 48*, 18-27.
Dillman, D.A. (1978). *Mail and telephone surveys: The total design method.* New York: Wiley.
Dillman, D.A. (1983). Mail and other self-administered questionnaires. In P.H. Rossi, J.D. Wright, & A.B. Anderson (Eds.), *Handbook of survey research* (pp. 359-377). New York: Academic Press.

Dillman, D.A. (2000). *Mail and internet surveys: The tailored design method.* New York: Wiley.
Domsch, M. (1985). Das Konzept der Arbeitsgruppe "Mitarbeiterbefragungen". In A. Töpfer & E. Zander (Eds.), *Mitarbeiter-Befragungen* (pp. 109-126). Frankfurt, Germany: Campus.
Domsch, M., & Schneble, A. (Eds.). (1991). *Mitarbeiterbefragungen.* Heidelberg, Germany: Physica.
Domsch, M.E., & Ladwig, D.H. (Eds.). (2006). *Handbuch Mitarbeiterbefragung.* Heidelberg, Germany: Springer.
Downey, R., Wefald, A., & Whitney, D. (2007, April). Does the Utrecht Work Engagement Scale (UWES) scale measure engagement? *Paper presented at the 22nd Annual SIOP Conference.* New York.
Duffy, M.K., Shaw, J.D., & Stark, E.M. (2000). Performance and satisfaction in conflicted interdependent groups: When and how does self-esteem make a difference? *Academy of Management Journal, 43,* 772-782.
Dunham, R.B., & Smith, F.J. (1979). *Organizational surveys.* Glennview, Ill.: Scott, Foresman & Company.
Edwards, J.E., & Thomas, M.D. (1993). The organizational survey process. In P. Rosenfeld, J.E. Edwards, & M.D. Thomas (Eds.), *Improving organizational surveys: New directions, methods, and applications* (pp. 3-28). Newbury Park, CA: Sage.
Edwards, J.E., Thomas, M.D., Rosenfeld, P., & Booth-Kewley, S. (1997). *How to conduct organizational surveys.* Newbury Park, CA: Sage.
Eldridge, L.E. (2005, April). Have you ever wondered…Should you use industry norms? *Presentation at the 20th Annual SIOP Conference.* Los Angeles, CA.
Elizur, D., Borg, I., Hunt, R., & Magyari-Beck, I. (1991). The structure of work values: A cross cultural comparison. *Journal of Organizational Behavior, 12,* 21-38.
European Foundation for Quality Management. (1994). *EQA application brochure.* Brussels, Belgium: EFQM.
Farr, J.L. (1993). Informal performance feedback: Seeking and giving. In H. Schuler, J.L. Farr, & M. Smith (Eds.), *Personnel selection and assessment: Individual and organizational perspectives* (pp. 163-180). Hillsdale, NJ: Lawrence Erlbaum.
Fazio, R. (1989). On the power and functionality of attitudes: The role of attitude accessibility. In A. Prtkanis, S. Breckler, & A. Greenwald (Eds.), *Attitude structure and function* (pp. 153-179). Hillsdale, NJ: Erlbaum.
Feger, H. (1980). Einstellungsstruktur und Einstellungsänderung: Ergebnisse, Probleme und ein Komponentenmodell der Einstellungsobjekte. *Zeitschrift für Sozialpsychologie, 10,* 331-349.
Fields, D.L. (2002). *Taking the measure of work: A guide to validated scales for organizational research and diagnosis.* Thousand Oaks, CA: Sage.
Fischer, L. (1989). *Strukturen der Arbeitszufriedenheit.* Göttingen, Germany: Hogrefe.
Fischer, L., & Lück, H.E. (1972). Entwicklung einer Skala zur Messung von Arbeitszufriedenheit (SAZ). *Psychologie und Praxis, 16,* 64-76.
Fischoff, B. (1991). Value elicitation: Is there anything in there? *American Psychologist, 46,* 835-847.
Folger, R., & Konovsky, M.A. (1989). Effects of procedural and distributive justice on reactions to pay raise decisions. *Academy of Management Journal, 32,* 115-130.
Folkman, J. (1996). *Turning feedback into change.* Provo, UT: Novations.
Folkman, J. (1998). *Employee surveys that make a difference.* Provo, UT: Executive Excellence Publishing.
Fournies, F.F. (1999). *Why employees don't do what they are supposed to do and what to do about it.* New York: MacGraw-Hill.
Fowler, F.J. (1995). *Improving survey questions: Design and evaluation.* Newbury Park, CA: Sage.
Fowler, F.J., Jr. (2001). Why it is easy to write bad questions. *ZUMA-Nachrichten, 48,* 49-66.
Frame, J.D. (1987). *Managing projects in organizations.* San Francisco, CA: Jossey-Bass.
Freimuth, J., & Kiefer, B.-U. (Eds.). (1995). *Geschäftsberichte von unten: Konzepte für Mitarbeiterbefragungen.* Stuttgart, Germany: Verlag für angewandte Psychologie.
Friedrichs, J. (1973). *Methoden empirischer Sozialforschung.* Hamburg, Germany: Reinbek.

Fritz, H. (1992). Vermutungen, Illusionen? - Dann doch lieber Realitäten, auch wenn es Probleme schafft! *Personalführung, 92*, 69-70.

Früh, W. (2001). *Inhaltsanalyse: Theorie und Praxis* (5th ed.). Konstanz, Germany: UVK.

Fryxell, G.E., & Gordon, M.E. (1989). Workplace justice and job satisfaction as predictors of satisfaction with union and management. *Academy of Management Journal, 32*, 851-866.

Gabler, S. (1999). *Exakte notwendige Stichprobenumfänge bei kleinen endlichen Populationen*. Unpublished manuscript, ZUMA, Mannheim, Germany.

Gabler, S., & Hoffmeyer-Zlotnik, J.H.P. (Eds.). (1997). *Stichproben in der Umfragepraxis*. Opladen, Germany: Westdeutscher Verlag.

Gallup, G. (1988). Employee research: From nice to know to need to know. *Personnel Journal, August*, 42-43.

Geary, D.C. (2005). Folk knowledge and academic learning. In B.J. Ellis & D.F. Bjorklund (Eds.), *Origins of the social mind* (pp. 493-519). New York: Guilford Publications.

Genesee Survey Services. (2002). *The 2003 National Work Opinion Survey* (Technical report).

Gibson, J.L., & Klein, S.M. (1970). Employee attitudes as a function of age and length of service: A reconceptualization. *Academy of Management Journal, 13*, 411-425.

Gillet, B., & Schwab, D.P. (1975). Convergent and discriminant validity of corresponding Job Descriptive Index and Minnesota Satisfaction Questionnaire scales. *Journal of Applied Psychology, 60*, 313-317.

Globerson, A., Globerson, S., & Frampton, J. (1991). *You can't manage what you don't measure*. Aldershot, UK: Avebury.

Gomez-Mejia, L. (1994). Compensation practices in the Maquiladora Industry. *Paper presented at the Universidad Autonoma de Mexico*. Mexico City.

Grabner, G. (1985). Betriebsbefragungen bei der Hamburgische Electricitäts-Werke AG. In A. Töpfer (Ed.), *Mitarbeiterbefragungen* (pp. 232-258). Frankfurt, Germany: Campus.

Greenberg, J. (1990). Employee theft as a reaction to underpayment inequity: The hidden costs of pay cuts. *Journal of Applied Psychology, 75*, 561-568.

Grice, H.P. (1975). Logic and conversation. In P. Cole & J.L. Morgan (Eds.), *Syntax and semantics: 3. Speech acts* (pp. 41-58). New York: Academic Press.

Grundy, T. (1994). *Strategic learning in action*. London, UK: MacGraw-Hill.

Guilford, J.P. (1954). *Psychometric methods*. New York: MacGraw-Hill.

Guttman, L. (1981). What is not what in theory construction. In I. Borg (Ed.), *Multidimensional data representations: When and why* (pp. 47-64). Ann Arbor, MI: Mathesis Press.

Hackman, J.R., & Oldham, G.R. (1976). Motivation through the design of work: Test of a theory. *Organizational Behavior and Human Performance, 16*, 250-279.

Haire, M., Ghiselli, E.E., & Porter, L.W. (1966). *Managerial thinking: An international study*. New York: Random House.

Halamaj, J.S. (2007, April). Survey stakeholders: Senior managers, boards, and regulators. *Paper presented at the 22nd Annual SIOP Conference*. New York.

Hall, D.T., & Parker, V.A. (1993). The role of workplace flexibility in managing diversity. *Organizational Dynamics, 21*, 5-18.

Harding, S., & Radford, M. (1994). *Work values in cross-national perspective: Some observations from applied research*. WORC Paper 94.11.044/6, Tilburg University, the Netherlands.

Harkness, J. (2005). Questionnaire translation. In J. Harkness, F. van De Vijver, & P.P. Mohler (Eds.), *Cross-cultural survey methods* (pp. 35-56). New York: Wiley.

Harrison, D.A., Newman, D.A., & Roth, P.L. (2006). How important are job attitudes? Meta-analytic comparisons of integrative behavioral outcomes and time sequences. *Academy of Management Journal, 49*, 305-325.

Harrison, M.I. (1987). *Diagnosing organizations*. Newbury Park, CA: Sage.

Harrison, M.I., & Shirom, A. (1999). *Organizational diagnosis and assessment: Bridging theory and practice*. Thousand Oaks, CA: Sage.

Hartley, J., Jacobson, D., Klandermans, B., & Van Vuuren, T. (1991). *Job insecurity: Coping with job at risk*. London, UK: Sage.

Hartmann, M., Rieger, M., & Pajonk, B. (1997). *Zielgerichtet moderieren*. Weinheim, Germany: Beltz.

Harzing, A.W. (2006). Response styles in cross-national survey research: A 26-country study. *International Journal of Cross Cultural Management, 6*(2), 241-266.

Heath, C., & Heath, D. (2007). *Made to stick: Why some ideas survive and others die*. New York: Random House.

Heider, F. (1958). *The psychology of interpersonal relations*. New York: Wiley.

Hellriegel, D., Slocum, J.W., Jr., & Woodman, R.W. (1992). *Organizational behavior*. St. Paul, MN: West Publishing Co.

Higgs, A.C., & Ashworth, S.D. (1997). Organizational surveys: Tools for the assessment and research. In A. Kraut (Ed.), *Organizational surveys: Tools for assessment and change* (pp. 19-40). San Francisco: Jossey-Bass.

Hinrichs, J.R. (1989). Employee surveys as a catalyst for productivity. *Paper presented at the American Society for Personnel Administration National Conference and Exposition*. Boston, MA.

Hinrichs, J.R. (1991). Survey data as a catalyst for employee empowerment and organizational effectiveness. In R.J. Niehaus & F. Price (Eds.), *Applying psychology in business: The handbook for managers and human resource professionals* (pp. 640-652). Lexington, MA: Lexington.

Hinrichs, J.R. (1996). Feedback, action planning, and follow-through. In A. Kraut (Ed.), *Organizational surveys* (pp. 255-279). San Franciso, CA: Jossey-Bass.

Hippler, H.J. (1988). Methodische Aspekte schriftlicher Befragungen: Probleme und Forschungsperspektiven. *Planung und Analyse, 6*, 244-248.

Hippler, H.J., Schwarz, N., Noelle-Neumann, E., Knäuper, B., & Clark, L. (1991). Der Einfluss numerischer Werte auf die Bedeutung verbaler Skalenendpunkte. *ZUMA Nachrichten, 28*, 54-64.

Hippler, H.J., Schwarz, N., & Singer, E. (1990). Der Einfluss von Datenschutzzusagen auf die Teilnahmebereitschaft an Umfragen. *ZUMA Nachrichten, 27*, 54-67.

Hofer, M. (1985). Subjektive Persönlichkeitstheorien. In T. Herrmann & E.D. Lantermann (Eds.), *Persönlicheitspsychologie: Ein Handbuch in Schlüsselbegriffen* (pp. 130-138). Munich, Germany: Urban & Schwarzenberg.

Hossiep, R., Gudat, J., & Frieg, P. (2008). *Ergebnisbericht: Zum Einsatz von Mitarbeiterbefragungen in den 820 größten Unternehmen im deutschsprachigen Raum* (Technical Report). Bochum, Germany: Ruhr-Universität, Fakultät für Psychologie.

Howard, A., & Associates. (1995). *Diagnosis for organizational change*. New York: Guildford.

Hunsdiek, D. (1991). Mitarbeiterbefragungen als Element der partnerschaftlichen Unternehmenskonzeption bei Bertelsmann. In M. Domsch & A. Schneble (Eds.), *Mitarbeiterbefragungen* (pp. 33-61). Heidelberg, Germany: Physica.

Hunt, S.D., Sparkman, R.D., & Wilcox, J.B. (1982). The pretest in survey research: Issues and preliminary findings. *Journal of Marketing Research, 19*, 269-273.

Huselid, M.A. (1995). The impact of human resource management practices on turnover, productivity, and corporate financial performance. *Academy of Management Journal, 38*, 635-672.

Inglehart, R. (1977). *The silent revolution: Changing values and political styles among western publics*. Princeton: Princeton University Press.

Inglehart, R. (1995). *Value change on six continents*. Ann Arbor: University of Michigan Press.

Jackman, J.M., & Strober, M.H. (2003). Fear of feedback. *Harvard Business Review, 81*(4), 101-107.

James, J.M., & Bolstein, R. (1990). The effects of monetary incentives and follow-up mailings on the response rate and response quality in mail surveys. *Public Opinion Quarterly, 54*, 346-361.

John, K.A., & Mannix, E.A. (2001). The dynamic nature of conflict: A longitudinal study of intragroup conflict and group performance. *Academy of Management Journal, 44*, 238-251.

Johns, G. (1994). How often were you absent? A review of the use of self-reported absence data. *Journal of Applied Psychology, 79*, 574-591.

Johnson, S.M., Smith, P.C., & Tucker, S.M. (1982). Response format of the Job Descriptive Index: Assessment of reliability and validity by the multitrait-multimethod matrix. *Journal of Applied Psychology, 67*(4), 500-505.

Johnson, S.R. (1996). The multinational opinion survey. In A.I. Kraut (Ed.), *Organizational surveys* (pp. 310-329). San Francisco, CA: Jossey-Bass.

Johnson, S.R., & Mastrangelo, P.M. (2008, April). Have you ever wondered if survey "rules of thumb" are valuable tools for data interpretation? *Paper presented at the 23rd Annual SIOP Conference.* San Francisco, CA.

Johnson, T.P. (1998). Approaches to equivalence in cross-cultural and cross-national survey research. In J. Harkness (Ed.), *Cross-cultural survey equivalence* (pp. 1-40). Mannheim, Germany: ZUMA.

Jolton, J. (2004). Survey legends: Dispelling common myths. *The Genessee Dimension, 13*(3), 1-4.

Jolton, J. (2005, April). Have you ever wondered if people who make unfavorable responses on survey also write comments on the same topic? *Paper presented at the 20th Annual SIOP Conference.* Los Angeles, USA.

Jones, E.L. (1963). The courtesy bias in South-East Asian surveys. *International Social Science Journal, 15*, 70-76.

Joyce, W.F., Nohria, N., & Roberson, B. (2003). *What really works: The 4+2 formula for sustained business success.* New York: Harper Collins.

Judge, T.A., & Bono, J.E. (2001). Relationship of core self-evaluations traits–self-esteem, generalized self-efficacy, locus of control, and emotional stability–with job satisfaction and job performance: A meta-analysis. *Journal of Applied Psychology, 86*(1), 80-92.

Judge, T.A., Heller, D., & Mount, M.K. (2002). Five-factor model of personality and job satisfaction: A meta-analysis. *Journal of Applied Psychology, 87*, 530-541.

Judge, T.A., Martocchio, J.J., & Thoresen, C.J. (1997). Five-factor model of personality and employee absence. *Journal of Applied Psychology, 82*, 745-755.

Judge, T.A., Thoresen, C.J., Bono, J.E., & Patton, G.K. (2001). The job satisfaction-job performance relationship: A qualitative and quantitative review. *Psychological Bulletin, 127*(3), 376-407.

Jung, K.G., Dalessio, A., & Johnson, S.M. (1986). Stability of the factor structure of the job descriptive index. *Academy of Management Journal, 29*, 609-616.

Kaase, M., & Saris, W.E. (1997). The Eurobarometer - A tool for comparative survey research. In M. Kaase & W.E. Saris (Eds.), *Eurobarometer measurement instruments for opinions in Europe* (pp. 7-26). Mannheim, Germany: ZUMA.

Kagay, M.R., & Elder, J. (1992, 9. August). Numbers are no problem for pollsters: Words are. *New York Times*, p. E5.

Kahn, R.L., & Byosiere, P.B. (1992). Stress in organizations. In M.D. Dunette & L.M. Hough (Eds.), *Handbook of industrial/organizational psychology* (Vol. 3, pp. 571-650). Palo Alto, CA: Consulting Psychologists Press.

Kalton, G. (1983). *Introduction to survey sampling.* Sage university paper series on quantitative applications in the social sciences, series no. 07-035. Beverly Hills, CA: Sage.

Kaner, S., with Lind, L., Toldi, C., Fisk, S., & Berger, D. (2007). *Facilitator's guide to participatory decision-making* (2nd ed.). San Francisco: Jossey-Bass.

Kanter, R.M., Stein, B.A., & Jick, T.D. (1992). *The challenge of organizational change.* New York: The Free Press.

Kanungo, R.N., & Mendonca, M. (1992). Employee alienation, empowerment, and work design. *Proceedings of the Fourth International Congress on Work and Organizational Values.* Karlsbad, CR.

Kaplan, R.S., & Norton, D.P. (1996). *The balanced scorecard.* Boston, MA: Harvard Business School Press.

Katzell, R.A., Thompson, D.E., & Guzzo, R.A. (1992). How job satisfaction and job performance are and are not linked. In C.J. Cranny, P.C. Smith, & E.F. Stone (Eds.), *Job satisfaction* (pp. 195-217). New York: Lexington.

Kenexa Research Institute. (in press). *The 2008 WorkTrends^{TM} Technical Report.* Wayne, PA: Kenexa, Inc.

Kiresuk, T.J., & Lund, S.H. (1979). Program evaluation and utilization analysis. In R. Perloff (Ed.), *Evaluator interventions* (pp. 71-102). Beverly Hills, CA: Sage.

Klann, C., & Pobel, K. (2000). Befragung in internationalen Unternehmen & Befragungen zur Unterstützung der Globalisierung der Henkel KGaA. In M.E. Domsch & D.H. Ludwig (Eds.), *Handbuch Mitarbeiterbefragung* (pp. 133-166). Heidelberg, Germany: Springer.

Kostman, J.T., & Schiemann, W.A. (2006). People equity: The hidden driver of quality. *Quality Progress, May*, 37-42.

Kowske, B. (in press). What's pay got to do with it? *Evolve^{HR}, 2*(5).

Kraut, A.I. (1996). Planning and conducting the survey: Keeping strategic purpose in mind. In A.I. Kraut (Ed.), *Organizational surveys: Tools for assessment and change* (pp. 149-176). San Francisco, CA: Jossey-Bass.

Kraut, A.I. (2006). Moving the needle: Getting action after a survey. In A.I. Kraut (Ed.), *Getting action from organizational surveys: New concepts, technologies, and applications* (pp. 1-30). San Francisco: Jossey-Bass.

Kraut, A.I., & Freeman, F. (1992). *Upward communications: Programs in American industry* (Tech. Report No. 152). Greensboro, NC: Center for Creative Leadership.

Krippendorff, K. (2004). *Content analysis: An introduction to its methodology*. Thousand Oaks, CA: Sage.

Krosnick, J.A. (1991). Response strategies for coping with the cognitive demands of attitude measures in surveys. *Applied Cognitive Psychology, 5*, 213-236.

Krosnick, J.A., Holbrook, A.L., Berent, M.K., Carson, R.T., Hanemann, W.M., Kopp, R.J., et al. (2002). The impact of "no opinion" response options on data quality: Non-attitude reduction or an invitation to satisfice? *Public Opinion Quarterly, 66*, 371–403.

Krosnik, J.A., & Fabrigar, L.R. (1997). Designing rating scales for effective measurement in surveys. In L. Lyberg, P. Biemer, M. Collins, E. de Leeuw, C. Dippo, N. Schwarz, & D. Trewin (Eds.), *Survey measurement and process quality* (pp. 141-164). New York: Wiley.

Kuhnert, K., & McCauley, D.P. (1996). Applying alternative survey methods. In A. Kraut (Ed.), *Organizational surveys: Tools for assessment and change* (pp. 233-254). San Francisco, CA: Jossey-Bass.

Kulesa, P., & Bishop, R.J. (2006). What did they really mean? New and emerging methods for analyzing themes in open-ended comments. In A. Kraut (Ed.), *Getting action from organizational survey: New concepts, technologies, and applications* (pp. 238-263). San Francisco: Jossey-Bass.

Kunin, T. (1955). The construction of a new type of attitude measure. *Personnel Psychology, 8*, 65-77.

Lambert, S.J. (2000). Added benefits: The link between work-life benefits and organizational citizenship behavior. *Academy of Management Journal, 43*, 801-815.

Lawler, E.E. (1971). *Pay and organizational effectiveness*. New York: McGraw-Hill.

Lawler, E.E., III. (1981). *Pay and organizational development*. Reading, MA: Addison-Wesley.

Lepsinger, R., & Lucia, A.D. (1997). *The art and science of 360° feedback*. San Francisco, CA: Pfeiffer.

Levinson, S.C. (1983). *Pragmatics*. Cambridge, England: Cambridge University Press.

Lewin, K. (1951). *Field theory in social science*. New York: Harper & Row.

Lewis, M.W., Welsh, M.A., Dehler, G.E., & Green, S.G. (2002). Product development tensions: Exploring contrasting styles of project management. *Academy of Management Journal, 45*, 546-564.

Leymann, H. (2002). *Mobbing*. Hamburg: Rowohlt.

Lezotte, D., & McLinden, P. (2003, April). A test of a path model to determine climate-related antecedents of customer satisfaction and loyalty. *Paper presented at the 18th Annual SIOP Conference*. Orlando, Florida.

Likert, R. (1932). *A technique for the measurement of attitudes*. New York: Archives of Psychology.

Lipp, U., & Will, H. (1998). *Das große Workshop-Buch*. Weinheim, Germany: Beltz.

Litwin, G.H., & Stringer Jr., R.A. (1968). *Motivation and organizational climate*. Boston, MA: Harvard University.

Liu, C., Borg, I., & Spector, P. (2004). Measurement equivalence of a German Job Satisfaction Survey used in a multinational organization: Implications of Schwartz's culture model. *Journal of Applied Psychology, 89*, 1070-1082.

Locke, E.A. (1976). The nature and causes of job satisfaction. In M.D. Dunnette (Ed.), *Handbook of industrial and organizational psychology* (pp. 1297-1349). Chicago, IL: Rand-MacNally.

Locke, E.A., & Latham, G.P. (1990). *A theory of goal setting and task performance*. Englewood Cliffs, NJ: Prentice-Hall.

Locke, E.A., & Taylor, M.S. (1990). Stress, coping, and the meaning of work. In A.P. Brief & W.R. Nord (Eds.), *Meanings of occupational work* (pp. 135-170). Lexington, MA: Lexington.

Loftus, E. (1984). Protocol analysis of responses to survey recall questions. In T.B. Jabine, M.L. Straf, J.M. Tanur, & R. Tourangeau (Eds.), *Cognitive aspects of survey methodology: Building a bridge between disciplines* (pp. 61-64). Washington, DC: National Academy Press.

Lord, C.G., Lepper, M.R., & Preston, E. (1984). Considering the opposite: A corrective strategy for social judgment. *Journal of Personality and Social Psychology, 47*(6), 1231-1243.

Lowenstein, M. (2006). *"Mirroring" customers from inside the company: The wisdom and benefits of understanding how closely employee perceptions of value delivery reflect those of customers* (Technical paper): Harris Interactive.

Lück, H.E. (1997). Die Zufriedenheit deutscher Mitarbeiter in europäischer Perspektive. In W. Bungard & I. Jöns (Eds.), *Mitarbeiterbefragung* (pp. 399-406). Weinheim, Germany: Beltz.

Macey, W.H. (1996). Dealing with the data: Collection, processing, and analysis. In A.I. Kraut (Ed.), *Organizational surveys: Tools for assessment and change* (pp. 204-232). San Francisco, CA: Jossey-Bass.

Macey, W.H., & Schneider, B. (2008). The meaning of employee engagement. *Industrial and Organizational Psychology, 1*, 3-30.

Mangione, T.W. (1995). *Mail surveys: Improving the quality*. Thousand Oaks, CA: Sage.

Martin, W. (1981). What management can expect from an employee attitude survey. *Personnel Administrator, July*, 75-87.

Maslow, A. (1954). *Motivation and personality*. New York: Harper & Row.

Masterson, S.S., Lewis, K., Goldman, B.M., & Taylor, M.S. (2000). Integrating justice and social exchange: The differing effects of fair procedures and treatment on work relationships. *Academy of Management Journal, 43*, 738-748.

Mastrangelo, P.M., Prochaska, J.O., & Prochaska, J.M. (2008). How people change: The transtheoretical model of behavior change. *Master's Tutorial at the 23rd Annual SIOP Conference*. San Francisco, CA.

Mayer, R.C., & Gavin, M.B. (2005). Trust in management and performance: Who minds the shop while the employees watch the boss? *Academy of Management Journal, 48*, 874-886.

McAllister, D.J., & Bigley, G.A. (2002). Work context and the definition of self: How organizational care influences organization-based self-esteem. *Academy of Management Journal, 45*, 894-904.

McConnell, J.H. (2003). *How to design, implement, and interpret an employee survey*. New York: Amacom.

McGregor, D. (1960). *The human side of enterprise*. New York: MacGraw-Hill.

Mealiea, L.W., & Latham, G.P. (1996). *Skills for managerial success*. Chicago, IL: Irwin.

Meyer, J.P., & Allen, N.J. (1997). *Commitment in the workplace: Theory, research, and application*. Thousand Oaks, CA: Sage.

Meyer, J.P., Stanley, D.J., Herscovitch, L., & Topolnytsky, L. (2002). Affective, continuance and normative commitment to the organization. A meta-analysis of antecedents, correlates and consequences. *Journal of Vocational Behavior, 61*(1), 20-52.

Miller, G.A. (1956). The magical number seven, plus minus one: Some limits on our capacity for processing information. *Psychological Review, 63*, 81-97.

Mirvis, P.H. (1990). *Personal communication*. Munich, Germany: Human Resources Consulting.

Mirvis, P.H., & Lawler, E.E., III. (1977). Measuring the financial impact of employee attitudes. *Journal of Applied Psychology, 62*, 1-8.

Mobley, W.H., & Locke, E.A. (1970). The relationship of value importance to satisfaction. *Organizational Behavior and Human Performance, 5*, 463-483.

Moorehead, G., & Griffin, R.W. (1989). *Organizational behavior*. Boston, MA: Houghton Mifflin.

Moorman, R.H. (1991). Relationship between organizational justice and organizational citizenship behaviors: Do fairness perceptions influence employee citizenship? *Journal of Applied Psychology, 76*, 845-855.

Moorman, R.H., Blakely, G.L., & Niehoff, B.P. (1998). Does perceived organizational support mediate the relationship between procedural justice and organizational citizenship behavior? *Academy of Management Journal, 41*, 351-357.

Morgan, D.L. (Ed.). (1993). *Successful focus groups*. Newbury Park, CA: Sage.

Morrison, E.W., & Phelps, C.C. (1999). Taking charge at work: Extrarole efforts to initiate workplace change. *Academy of Management Journal, 42*, 403-419.

Mussweiler, T., Strack, F., & Pfeiffer, T. (2000). Overcoming the inevitable anchoring effect: Considering the opposite compensates for selective accessibility. *Personality and Social Psychology Bulletin, 26*(9), 1142-1150.

Nadler, D.A. (1977). *Feedback and organization development: Using data-based methods*. Reading, MA: Addison-Wesley.

Nagy, M.S. (2002). Using a single-item approach to measure facet job satisfaction. *Journal of Occupational and Organizational Psychology, 75*, 77-86.

Nelson, D.L., & Sutton, C. (1990). Chronic work stress and coping: A longitudinal study and suggested new directions. *Academy of Management Journal, 33*, 859-869.

Neuberger, O. (1974). *Messung der Arbeitszufriedenheit*. Stuttgart, Germany: Kohlhammer.

Neuberger, O., & Allerbeck, M. (1978). *Messung und Analyse von Arbeitszufriedenheit*. Bern, Switzerland: Huber.

Neuberger, O., & Kompa, A. (1987). *Wir, die Firma*. Weinheim, Germany: Beltz.

Newman, D.A., & Harrison, D.A. (2008). Been there, bottled that: Are state and behavioral work engagement new and useful construct "wines"? *Industrial and Organizational Psychology, 1*, 31-35.

Noelle-Neumann, E. (1970). Wanted: Rules for wording questions. *Public Opinion Quarterly, 34*, 191-201.

Noelle-Neumann, E., & Petersen, T. (1998). *Alle, nicht jeder: Einführung in die Methoden der Demoskopie*. Munich, Germany: DTV.

Nunnally, J.C., & Bernstein, I.H. (1994). *Psychometric theory*. New York: MacGraw-Hill.

O'Reilly III, C.A., Chatman, J.A., & Caldwell, D.F. (1991). People and organizational culture: A profile comparison approach to assessing person-organization fit. *Academy of Management Journal, 34*, 487-516.

Olve, N.G., Roy, J., & Wetter, M. (1997). *Performance drivers: A practical guide to using the balanced scorecard*. New York: Wiley.

Opgenoorth, W.P. (1985). Informationsbedarf in der Personalführung - Die Mitarbeiterbefragung als Instrument in verschiedenen Problemfeldern. In A. Töpfer & E. Zander (Eds.), *Mitarbeiter-Befragungen* (pp. 169-231). Frankfurt, Germany: Campus.

Opinion Research Corporation. (1986). *Organizational research survey programs and consulting services*. Princeton, NJ: ORC.

Oppenheim, A.N. (1992). *Questionnaire design, interviewing and attitude measurement*. London, UK: Pinter.

Organ, D.W. (1984). *Organizational citizenship behavior: The good soldier syndrome*. Lexington, MA: Lexington.

Oswald, M., & Wendt, D. (1993). The concept of trust in psychology: A facet approach. *Proceedings 4th International Facet Theory Conference* (pp. 351-360). Prag, CR.

Oyler, M., & Harper, G. (2007). The technology of participation. In P. Holman, T. Devane, S. Cady, & Associates (Eds.), *The change handbook: The definitve resource on today's best methods for engaging whole systems* (2nd ed.). San Francisco: Berrett-Koehler Publishers, Inc.

Pacific Gas and Electric Company. (1991). *Survey-guided development*. San Francisco, CA: PG & E.

Paul, K.B., & Bracken, D.W. (1995). Everything you always wanted to know about employee surveys. *Training & Development, January*, 45-49.

Pauli, O. (1992). Mitarbeiterbefragung - ohne den Betriebsrat geht gar nichts. *Paper presented at the conference "Mitarbeiterbefragung"*. Darmstadt, Germany: Institute for International Research.

Pawlowsky, P., & Flodell, C. (1984). Schwitzen nur noch in der Freizeit? *Psychologie Heute, January*, 39-45.

Peratec Ltd. (1994). *Total quality manangement: The key to business improvement*. London, UK: Chapman & Hall.

Pfeffer, J. (1995). *Competitive advantage through people: Unleashing the power of the work force*. Boston, MA: Harvard Business School Press.

Pierce, J.L., Gardner, D.G., Cummings, L.L., & Dunham, R.B. (1989). Organization-based self-esteem: Construct definition, measurement, and validation. *Academy of Management Journal, 32*, 622-648.

Pittner, P.M. (1997). Mitarbeiterbefragungen - Vertane Chancen? Eine Synopse von Befragungen im Lufthansa Konzern. In W. Bungard & I. Jöns (Eds.), *Mitarbeiterbefragung: Ein Instrument des Innovations- und Qualitätsmanagements* (pp. 284-293). Weinheim, Germany: Beltz.

Pobel, K., & Müller, G. (1995). Führungskräftebefragungen - von der quantitativen Erhebung zur qualitativen Wirkung: Führung und Unternehmenskultur gezielt gestalten. In J. Freimuth & B.-U. Kiefer (Eds.), *Geschäftsberichte von unten: Konzepte für Mitarbeiterbefragungen* (pp. 125-151). Göttingen, Germany: Verlag für angewandte Psychologie.

Porras, J.I. (1987). *Stream analysis*. Reading, MA: Addison-Wesley.

Porter, L.W., & Lawler, E.E., III. (1968). *Managerial attitudes and performance*. Homewood, IL: Irwin.

Porter, S.R. (2004). Raising response rates: What works? *New Directions for Institutional Research, 121*, 5-21.

Pritchard, R.D. (1990). *Measuring and improving organizational productivity*. New York: Praeger.

Prochaska, J.O., DiClemente, C.C., & Norcross, J.C. (1998). Stages of change: Prescriptive guidelines for behavioral medicine and psychotherapy. In G.P. Koocher, J.C. Norcross, & S.S. Hill III (Eds.), *Psychologists' Desk Reference*. New York, Oxford: Oxford University Press.

Prüfer, P., & Rexroth, M. (1996). Verfahren zur Evaluation von Survey-Fragen: Ein Überblick. *ZUMA Nachrichten, 39*, 95-115.

Quinn, R.P., & Mangione, T.W. (1973). Evaluating weighted models for measuring job satisfaction: A Cinderella story. *Organizational Behavior and Human Performance, 10*, 1-23.

Rea, L.M., & Parker, R.A. (1992). *Designing and conducting survey research*. San Francisco, CA: Jossey-Bass.

Reeve, C.R., & Smith, C.S. (2001). Refining Lodahl and Kejner's job involvement scale with a convergent evidence approach: Applying multiple methods to multiple samples. *Organizational Research Methods, 4*(2), 91-111.

Roberts, R.E., McCrory, O.F., & Forthofer, R.N. (1978). Further evidence on using a deadline to stimulate responses on a mail survey. *Public Opinion Quarterly, 42*, 407-410.

Robinson, S.L., & Rousseau, D.M. (1994). Violating the psychological contract: Not the expectation but the norm. *Journal of Organizational Behavior, 15*, 245-259.

Roccas, S., Sagiv, L., Schwartz, S.H., & Knafo, A. (2002). The Big Five personality factors and personal values. *Personality and Social Psychology Bulletin, 28*, 789-801.

Rogelberg, S.G., Church, A.H., Waclawski, J., & Stanton, J.M. (2002). Organizational survey research: Overview, the Internet/Intranet and present practices of concern. In S.G. Rogelberg (Ed.), *Handbook of research methods in industrial and organizational psychology* (pp. 141-160). London: Blackwell.

Rogelberg, S.G., Conway, J.M., Sederburg, M.E., Spitzmüller, C., Aziz, S., & Knight, W.E. (2003). Profiling active and passive non-respondents to an organizational survey. *Journal of Applied Psychology, 88*(6), 1104-1114.

Rogelberg, S.G., & Stanton, J.M. (2007). Understanding and dealing with organizational survey nonresponse. *Organizational Research Methods, 9*, 1-15.
Roosevelt Thomas, R. (1996). *The diversity paradigm: A framework for practice and inquiry.* Atlanta, GA: American Institute for Managing Diversity Inc.
Rose, D.S., Sidle, S.D., & Griffith, K.H. (2007). A penny for your thoughts: Monetary incentives improve response rates for company-sponsored employee surveys. *Organizational Research Methods, 10*, 225-240.
Rosenfeld, P., Edwards, J.E., & Thomas, M.D. (Eds.). (1993). *Improving organizational surveys: New directions, methods, and applications.* Newbury Park, CA: Sage.
Rosenstiel, L.v., Falkenberg, T., Hehn, W., Henschel, E., & Warns, I. (1983). *Betriebsklima heute.* Munich, Germany: Bayrisches Staatsministerium für Arbeit und Sozialordnung.
Rousseau, D.M., Burt, R.S., & Camerer, C. (1998). Not so different after all: A cross-discipline view of trust. *Academy of Management Review, 23*, 393-404.
Ryan, A.M., Horvath, M., Ployhart, R., Schmitt, N., & Slade, L.A. (2000). Hypothesizing differential item functioning in global employee opinion surveys. *Personnel Psychology, 53*, 531-562.
Ryan, A.M., West, B.J., & Carr, J.Z. (2003). Effects of the terrorist attacks of 9/11/01 on employee attitudes. *Journal of Applied Psychology, 88*(4), 647-659.
Salant, P., & Dillman, D.A. (1994). *How to conduct your own survey.* New York: Wiley.
Sashkin, M., & Prien, E.P. (1996). Ethical concerns and organizational surveys. In A. Kraut (Ed.), *Organizational surveys* (pp. 381-403). San Franciso, CA: Jossey-Bass.
Scarpello, V., & Campbell, J.P. (1983). Job satisfaction: Are all the parts there? *Personnel Psychology, 36*, 577-600.
Scharioth, J. (1992). Vom Kunden lernen. In C. Krebsbach-Gnath (Ed.), *Den Wandel in Unternehmen steuern* (pp. 103-126). Frankfurt, Germany: Frankfurter Allgemeine Zeitung.
Schaufeli, W.B., Bakker, A., & Salanova, M. (2006). The measurement of work engagement with a short questionnaire: A cross-national study. *Educational and Psychological Measurement, 66*, 701-716.
Scheuch, E.K. (1993). The cross-cultural use of sample surveys: Problems of comparability. *Historical Social Research, 18*, 104-138.
Schieman, W.A. (1991). Using employee surveys to increase organizational effectiveness. In J.W. Jones, B.D. Steffy, & D.W. Bray (Eds.), *Applying psychology in business: The handbook for managers and human resource professionals* (pp. 623-639). Lexington, MA: Lexington Books.
Schiemann, W.A. (1992). *Employee surveys in the United States: Tools for change.* Paper presented at the Symposium "Mitarbeiterbefragungen" of the Institute for International Research, Darmstadt, Germany.
Schiemann, W.A., & Morgan, B.S. (2006). Strategic surveys: Linking people to business strategy. In A. Kraut (Ed.), *Getting action from organizational surveys: New concepts, technologies, and applications* (pp. 76-101). San Francisco, CA: Jossey-Bass.
Schnell, R., Hill, P.B., & Esser, E. (1995). *Methoden der empirischen Sozialforschung.* Munich, Germany: Oldenbourg.
Scholtes, P.R. (1998). *The leader's handbook: Making things happen, getting things done.* New York: MacGraw-Hill.
Schulte, K. (2005). Macht Alter zufrieden mit dem Beruf? Eine empirische Analyse über die hohe Arbeitszufriedenheit älterer Beschäftigter. In L. Fischer (Ed.), *Arbeitszufriedenheit: Konzepte und empirische Befunde* (pp. 271-290). Göttingen, Germany: Hogrefe.
Schultz, P.W., Nolan, J.M., Cialdini, R.B., Goldstein, N.J., & Griskevicius, V. (2007). The constructive, destructive, and reconstructive power of social norms. *Psychological Science, 18*, 429–434.
Schuman, H., & Presser, S. (1996). *Questions and answers in attitude surveys: Experiments on question form, wording, and context.* New York: Academic Press.
Schwartz, S.H. (1999). A theory of cultural values and some implications for work. *Applied Psychology: An International Review, 48*, 23-47.

Schwartz, S.H. (2004). Mapping and interpreting cultural differences around the world. In H. Vinken, J. Soeters, & P. Ester (Eds.), *Comparing cultures: Dimensions of culture in a comparative perspective* (pp. 43-73). Leiden, the Netherlands: Brill.

Schwarz, N. (1996). *Cognition and communication: Judgmental biases, research methods, and the logic of conversation*. Mahwah, NJ: Erlbaum.

Schwarz, N., & Clore, G.L. (1983). Mood, misattribution and judgments of well-being: Informative and directive functions of affective states. *Journal of Personality and Social Psychology, 45*, 513-523.

Schwarz, N., Hippler, H.J., & Noelle-Neumann, E. (1989). Einflüsse der Reihenfolge von Antwortvorgaben bei geschlossenen Fragen. *ZUMA Nachrichten, 25*, 24-38.

Schwarz, N., Knäuper, B., Hippler, H.J., Noelle-Neumann, E., & Clark, F. (1991). Rating scales: Numeric values may change the meaning of scale labels. *Public Opinion Quarterly, 55*, 618-630.

Seibert, S.E., Kraimer, M.L., & Liden, R.C. (2001). A social capital theory of career success. *Academy of Management Journal, 44*, 219-237.

Shewhart, W.A. (1939). *Statistical method from the viewpoint of quality control*. New York: Dover.

Shirom, A. (2003). Feeling vigorous at work? The construct of vigor and the study of positive affect in organizations. In D. Ganster & P.L. Perrewe (Eds.), *Research in organizational stress and wellbeing* (Vol. 3, pp. 135-165). Greenwich, CN: JAI Press.

Silberman, M. (Ed.). (2002). *The consultant's big book of reproducible surveys and questionnaires*. New York: MacGraw-Hill.

Sirota, D., Mischkind, L.A., & Meltzer, M.I. (2005). *The enthusiastic employee: How companies profit from giving workers what they want*. Upper Saddle River, NY: Wharton School Publishing.

Smith, F.J. (2003). *Organizational surveys: The diagnosis and betterment of organizations through their members*. Mahwah, NJ: Lawrence Erlbaum.

Smith, P.C. (1992). In pursuit of happiness. In C.J. Cranny, P.C. Smith, & E.F. Stone (Eds.), *Job satisfaction* (pp. 1-19). New York: Lexington.

Smith, P.C., Kendall, L.M., & Hulin, C.L. (1969). *The measurement of satisfaction in work and retirement*. Chicago, IL: Rand-MacNally.

Spector, P., & Wimalasiri, J. (1986). A cross-cultural comparison of job satisfaction dimensions in the United States and Singapore. *Applied Psychology, 35*, 147-158.

Spector, P.E. (1992). *Summated rating scale construction*. Newbury Park, CA: Sage.

Spector, P.E. (1997). *Job satisfaction*. Thousand Oaks, CA: Sage.

Spector, P.E., Cooper, C.L., Sanchez, J.I., O'Driscoll, M., Sparks, K., Bernin, P., et al. (2002). A 24 nation/territory study of work locus of control in relation to well-being at work: How generalizable are western findings? *Academy of Management Journal, 45*, 453-466.

Sperber, D., & Wilson, D. (1986). *Relevance: Communication and cognition*. Oxford: Basil Blackwell.

Sperling, J.B., & Wasseveld, J. (2002). *Führungsaufgabe Moderation*. Munich, Germany: Haufe.

Spreizer, G.M. (1995). Psychological empowerment in the workplace: Dimensions, measurement, and validation. *Academy of Management Journal, 38*, 1442-1465.

Staufenbiel, T., Kroll, M., & König, C.J. (2006). Could job insecurity (also) be a motivator? In M. Braun & P.P. Mohler (Eds.), *Beyond the horizon of measurement: Festschrift in honor of Ingwer Borg* (pp. 163-173). Mannheim, Germany: ZUMA.

Stenger, H. (1986). *Stichproben*. Heidelberg, Germany: Physica.

Stewart, D. (1986). *The power of people skills*. New York: Wiley.

Strack, F., Martin, L.L., & Schwarz, N. (1988). Priming and communication: The social determinants of information use in judgments of life-satisfaction. *European Journal of Social Psychology, 18*, 429-442.

Suckow, K. (2005). Have you ever wondered whether comment providers differ from comment nonproviders? *Paper presented at the 20th Annual SIOP Conference*. Los Angeles, USA.

Sudman, S., & Bradburn, N. (1974). *Response effects in surveys: A review and synthesis*. Chicago, IL: Aldine.

Sudman, S., Bradburn, N., & Schwarz, N. (1996). *Thinking about answers: The application of cognitive processes to survey methodology.* San Francisco: Jossey-Bass Publishers.

Taylor, F.W. (1912). The art and science of shoveling. Testimony before a special committee of U.S. House of Representatives. Quoted in R.B. Dunham & J.L. Pierce (Eds.), *Management.* Glenview, IL: Scott, Forseman & Co.

Taylor, F.W. (1947). *Scientific management.* New York: Harper.

Thomas, K.W., & Velthouse, B.A. (1990). Cognitive elements of empowerment: An interpretative model of intrinsic task motivation. *Academy of Management Review, 15*, 666-681.

Thomas, L.T., & Ganster, D.C. (1995). Impact of family-supported work variables on work-family conflict and strain: A control perspective. *Journal of Applied Psychology, 80*, 6-15.

Thorndike, E.L. (1911). *Animal intelligence.* New York: Macmillan.

Töpfer, A., & Zander, E. (Eds.). (1985). *Mitarbeiter-Befragungen.* Frankfurt, Germany: Campus.

Tourangeau, R., Rips, L.J., & Rasinski, K. (2000). *The psychology of survey response.* Cambridge, UK: Cambridge University Press.

Townsend, P.L., & Gebhardt, J.E. (1992). *Quality in action.* New York: Wiley.

Treder, C. (2002). *Item Nonresponse in Mitarbeiterbefragungen.* Master's thesis, FB 06 Psychologie, Universität Gießen, Germany.

Trost, A., Bungard, W., & Jöns, I. (1999). *Mitarbeiterbefragung.* Augsburg, Germany: Weka Verlag.

Tsui, A.S., Pearce, J.L., Porter, L.W., & Tripoli, A.M. (1997). Alternative approaches to the employee-organization relationship: Does investment in employees pay off? *Academy of Management Journal, 40*, 1089-1121.

Tukey, J.W. (1977). *Exploratory data analysis.* Reading, MA: Addison-Wesley.

Van De Vijver, F., & Leung, K. (1997). *Methods and data analysis for cross-cultural research.* Thousand Oaks: Sage.

Van Dyne, L., & LePine, J.A. (1998). Helping and voice extra-role behaviors: Evidence of construct and predictive validity. *Academy of Management Journal, 41*, 108-119.

Vandenberg, R.J. (2002). Toward a further understanding of and improvement in measurement invariance methods and procedures. *Organizational Research Methods, 5*, 139-158.

Vandenberg, R.J., & Lance, C.E. (2000). A review and synthesis of the measurement equivalence literature: Suggestions, practices, and recommendations for organizational research. *Organizational Research Methods, 3*, 4-70.

Verheyen, L.G. (1988). How to develop an employee attitude survey. *Training & Development Journal, August*, 72-76.

Viteles, M.S. (1953). *Motivation and morale in industry.* New York: Norton.

Wallner, I. (2000). Die Siemens Mitarbeiterbefragung: Ein Instrument zur Weiterentwicklung der Unternehmenskultur. In M.E. Domsch & D.H. Ladwig (Eds.), *Handbuch Mitarbeiterbefragung* (pp. 39-64). Heidelberg, Germany: Springer.

Wanous, J.P., Reichers, A.E., & Hudy, M.J. (1997). Overall job satisfaction: How good are single-item measures? *Journal of Applied Psychology, 82*, 247-252.

Warr, P.B. (1987). *Work, unemployment, and mental health.* Oxford: Clarendon.

Warr, P.E. (2007). *Work, happiness, and unhappiness.* New York: Lawrence Erlbaum.

Weber, M. (1922). *Wirtschaft und Gesellschaft.* Tübingen, Germany: Mohr.

Weiner, S.P., & Dalessio, A.T. (2006). Oversurveying: Causes, consequences, and cures. In A.I. Kraut (Ed.), *Getting action from organizational surveys: New concepts, methods, and applications* (pp. 294-311). San Francisco: Jossey-Bass.

Weisberg, H.F., Krosnick, J.A., & Bowen, B.D. (1996). *An introduction to survey research, polling, and data analysis* (3rd ed.). Thousand Oaks, California: Sage.

Weiss, D.J., Dawis, R.V., England, G.W., & Lofquist, L.H. (1967). *Manual for the Minnesota Satisfaction Questionnaire.* Minneapolis, MN: University of Minnesota Press.

Whiteley, R.C. (1991). *The customer driven company: Moving from talk to action.* Reading, MA: Addision-Wesley.

Wicks, A.C., Berman, S.L., & Jones, T.M. (1999). The structure of optimal trust: Moral and strategic implications. *Academy of Management Review, 24*, 99-116.

Wiley, J.W. (2008, March). Understanding the Talent LifeCycle: Why employees join, stay, and leave their organization. *The Kenexa Research Institute WorkTrends Seminar Series*. Minneapolis, MN.

Wiley, J.W., & Campbell, B.H. (2006). Using linkage research to drive high performance. A case study in organization development. In A. Kraut (Ed.), *Getting Action from Organizational Surveys. New Concepts, Technologies, and Applications*. San Francisco, CA: Jossey-Bass.

Wilkinson, L. (1990). Cognitive science and graphic design. In L. Wilkinson (Ed.), *SYGRAPH: The system for graphics* (pp. 38-60). Evanston, IL: SYSTAT Inc.

Willis, G. (2004). Cognitive interviewing revisited: A useful technique, in theory? In S. Presser, J.M. Rothger, M.P. Couper, J.T. Lessler, E. Martin, J. Martin, & E. Singer (Eds.), *Methods for pretesting and evaluating survey questionnaires* (pp. 23-43). New York: Wiley.

Willis, G.B. (2005). *Cognitive interviewing: A tool for improving questionnaire design*. Thousand Oaks, CA: Sage.

Wilson, T.D., & Hodges, S. (1992). Attitudes as temporary constructions. In L. Martin & A. Tresser (Eds.), *The construction of social judgments* (pp. 37-66). New York: Springer.

Woehr, D.H., & Roch, S.G. (1996). Context effects in performance evaluation: The impact of ratee sex and performance level on performance ratings and behavioral recall. *Organizational Behavior and Human Decision Processes, 66*, 31-41.

Wonnacott, T.H., & Wonnacott, R.J. (1977). *Introductory statistics for business and economics*. New York: Wiley.

Wrapp, H.E. (1967). Good managers don't make policy decisions. *Harvard Business Review, September*, 91-99.

York, D.R. (1985). Attitude surveying. *Personnel Journal, May*, 70-73.

Author Index

A

AAPOR 163
Ackoff 296
Adler 97
Ajzen 118
Allen 79, 94
Allerbeck 3, 6, 23, 78, 327
Alper 19
Amabile 96
Andersen 69
Anderson 426
Antoni 316
Argyris 25, 428
Ashford 132
Ashworth 17
Astridge 232
Atkinson 388

B

Bakker 94
Bandura 98, 335
Barbera 30, 253
Barmash 280
Bazerman 297
Bearden 132
Becker 32
Beckstette 125
Beres 30
Berger 374
Bergler 243
Berman 99
Bernstein 132
Bigley 98
Bishop 121, 124
Blakely 98
Block 30
Boek 219
Bolstein 232
Bono 95, 98
Booth-Kewley 126
Borg 2, 8, 12, 18, 19, 22, 24, 44, 78, 82, 85, 99, 102, 103, 104, 105, 119, 125, 126, 128, 132, 138, 147, 167, 185, 187, 208, 229, 243, 244, 250, 264, 265, 278, 296, 298, 310, 320, 337, 338, 339, 384, 431, 433, 434, 436
Boyett 95
Bracken 218
Bradburn 12, 111, 122
Braun 19, 24, 99
Brennan 232
Brief 98
Brislin 128
Brooks 42
Brown 96
Bruennecke 243
Bruggemann 304, 327
Buckingham 18
Bungard 1, 2, 110
Burke 279
Burt 99
Byosiere 97

C

Caldwell 22
Camerer 99
Campbell 315
Campell 23
Canisius 243
Carr 42
Cascio 35, 314
Chatman 22
Chugh 297
Church 2, 48, 124, 125, 183, 232, 242, 243, 271
Cialdini 425
Claassen 226
Clark 111
Clore 119, 436
Coffey 388
Coffman 18
Colihan 106
Collins 80
Conger 97
Conn 95

Conti 96
Control Data Business Advisors 243
Converse 113, 128
Cook 94, 153, 183
Coombs 120
Coon 96
Cranny 6, 78
Cummings 98

D

Dalessio 132, 183
Dawis 6
Deci 233
Dehler 96
Deitering 2
Delany 1
Desrosiers 48
DeVellis 132, 167
DiClemente 426
Diekmann 173, 233, 440
Dillman 17, 141, 146, 233, 235, 236, 338
Domsch 2, 120, 141, 145, 153
Downey 94
Duffy 98
Dunham 98, 214, 229, 345

E

Edwards 126, 138, 181, 188, 221, 229, 242, 243, 277
EFQM model 32
Eisenhardt 96
Elder 57
Eldridge 304
Elizur 19, 24
England 6
Esser 189

F

Fabrigar 111
Falkenberg 3
Farr 92
Faulbaum 338
Fazio 117
Feger 118
Fields 94, 132, 153
Fischer 23, 78
Fischoff 118
Fisk 374
Flodell 22
Folger 98
Folkman 2, 42, 126, 242, 345, 378
Forthofer 235
Fournies 321
Fowler 131, 155, 165

Frame 413
Frampton 24
Freeman 1
Freimuth 2
Friedrichs 166
Fritz 19
Früh 126
Fryxell 98

G

Gabler 173, 182, 185, 244
Galinat 103
Gallup 1
Ganster 99
Gantner 426
Gardner 98
Gavin 98
Geary 427
Gebhardt 50
Genesee Survey Services 42
Ghiselli 7
Gibson 304
Gillet 132
Globerson 24, 36
Goldman 98
Goldstein 425
Gomez-Mejia 19
Gordon 98
Grabner 125
Green 96
Greenberg 98
Grice 101, 111
Griffin 17
Griffith 232
Griskevicius 425
Groenen 310, 433
Groskurth 304
Grundy 428
Guilford 114
Guttman 302
Guzzo 22

H

Hackman 92
Haire 7
Halamaj 30
Hall 99
Hanson 426
Harding 303
Harkness 133, 134
Harper 353
Harrison 35, 81, 82, 95, 154
Hartley 99
Hartmann 359

Harzing	19, 302, 433
Hause	42
Heath	183, 329
Hehn	3
Heider	427
Heller	25
Hellriegel	17, 345
Henschel	3
Herron	96
Herscovitch	94
Higgs	17
Hill	189
Hillenbrand	147, 298, 339
Hinrichs	11, 17, 19, 35, 277
Hippler	114, 192, 231, 235
Hodges	104, 117
Hoek	232
Hofer	21
Hoffmeyer-Zlotnik	173, 185
Horvath	302
Hossiep	1
Howard	95
Hulin	23, 132
Hunsdiek	226, 227
Hunt	19, 165
Huselid	36

I

Inglehart	22

J

Jackman	40, 377
Jacobson	99
James	232
Jann	233
Jick	95
John	93
Johns	314
Johnson	10, 132, 133, 134, 327
Jolton	125, 265
Jones	99, 302
Jöns	110
Joyce	80
Judge	25, 95, 98
Jung	132

K

Kaase	303
Kagay	57
Kahn	97
Kalton	180
Kaner	374
Kanter	95, 280, 429
Kanungo	97
Kaplan	88, 89
Katzell	22
Kendall	23, 132
Kenexa Research Institute	303
Kiefer	2
Kiresuk	45
Klandermans	99
Klann	226, 227
Klein	304
Knafo	25
Kompa	155
König	99
Konovsky	98
Kostman	321
Kowske	303
Kraimer	97
Kraut	1, 2, 12, 241, 243
Krippendorff	126
Kroll	99
Krosnick	112, 113, 137
Krosnik	111
Kuhnert	221
Kulesa	124
Kunin	6, 23
Kwon	97

L

Lade	219
Ladwig	2, 153
Lambert	92, 99
Lance	433
Latham	85, 88, 92
Lawler	22, 24, 35, 44, 92
Lazenby	96
Lee	30
LePine	98
Lepper	297
Lepsinger	95
Leung	133
Levinson	111
Lewin	445
Lewis	96, 98
Leymann	99
Lezotte	317
Liden	97
Likert	112
Lind	374
Lipp	358
Litwin	7
Liu	19, 82, 250
Locke	22, 85, 92, 97, 103
Lofquist	6
Loftus	165
Lord	297

Lowenstein 80
Lucia 95
Lück 23, 78, 301, 302
Lund 45

M

Macey 94, 243
MacLinden 317
Magyari-Beck 19
Mangione 103, 165, 166, 219, 221, 235
Mannix 93
Martin 119, 301
Martocchio 25
Maslow 22
Masterson 98
Mastrangelo 327, 426
Mayer 98
McAllister 98
McCauley 221
McConnell 2, 78, 153
McCrory 235
McGregor 21
Mealiea 88
Meltzer 44
Mendonca 97
Meyer 79, 94
Miller 111
Mirvis 35, 97
Mischkind 44
Mobley 103, 132
Moechnig 42
Moorehead 17
Moorman 98
Morgan 25, 82, 321, 343
Morrison 98
Motowidlo 98
Mount 25
Mueller 226
Müller 2
Mussweiler 297

N

Nadler 17, 42, 343
Nagy 23, 132
Nelson 97
Netemeyer 132
Neuberger 3, 6, 23, 78, 103, 155, 327
Niehoff 98
Niethammer 2
Noelle-Neumann 122
Nohria 80
Nolan 425
Noll 104
Norcross 426

Norton 88, 89
Nunnally 132

O

Oldham 92
Oliver 48
Olve 89
Opgenoorth 170, 226
Opinion Research Corporation 243
Oppenheim 436
O'Reilly III 22, 82
Organ 23, 98
Oswald 99
Oyler 353

P

Pacific Gas and Electric Company 17
Pajonk 359
Parker 99, 128, 179, 181
Patton 95
Paul 218
Pauli 1
Pawlowsky 22
Pearce 98
Peratec Ltd. 384
Petersen 122
Pfau 19
Pfeffer 97
Pfeiffer 297
Phelps 98
Pierce 98
Pittner 226
Piwinger 243
Ployhart 302
Pobel 226, 227
Porras 345, 379, 384, 399, 424
Porter 7, 22, 24, 98, 233
Presser 113, 122, 128
Preston 297
Prien 264
Pritchard 44, 95
Prochaska 426
Prüfer 165

Q

Quinn 103

R

Radford 303
Rasinski 104
Rea 128, 179, 181
Reeve 94
Rexroth 165
Rieger 359

Rips 104
Roberson 80
Roberts 235
Robinson 99
Roccas 25
Roch 92, 99
Rogelberg 183, 184, 185, 242, 243, 337, 433
Roosevelt Thomas 99
Rose 232
Rosenfeld 126, 221
Rosenstiel 3
Rousseau 99
Roy 89
Ryan 42, 302

S

Sagiv 25
Salanova 94
Salant 141
Saris 303
Sashkin 264
Scarpello 23
Scharioth 251
Schaufeli 94
Scheuch 300
Schiemann 23, 25, 82, 154, 321
Schmitt 302
Schneble 141
Schneider 94
Schnell 189
Scholtes 44, 428
Schulte 304
Schultz 425
Schuman 122, 128
Schwab 132
Schwartz 24, 25, 82
Schwarz 101, 111, 114, 119, 122, 436
Seibert 97
Shaw 98
Shewhart 428
Shirom 94, 154
Shye 102, 298, 434
Sidle 232
Silberman 94, 132
Sirota 19, 44, 126, 153
Slade 302
Slocum 17
Smith 2, 6, 23, 94, 124, 132, 214, 229, 345
Sparkman 165
Spector 19, 44, 78, 119, 128, 138, 167, 302
Sperber 111
Sperling 359
Spreizer 97
Stanley 94

Stanton 183, 184, 185, 242, 433
Stark 98
Staufenbiel 44, 99, 132, 167, 433
Stein 95
Stenger 174, 179, 180
Stewart 307
Stone 6
Strack 119, 297
Stringer 7
Strober 40, 377
Suckow 125, 265
Sudman 12, 111, 122, 137
Sutton 97

T

Taylor 21, 23, 97, 98
Thomas 98, 99, 126, 188, 221
Thompson 22, 183
Thoresen 25, 95
Thorndike 85
Toldi 374
Töpfer 2, 141
Topolnytsky 94
Tourangeau 104, 117, 137
Townsend 50
Treder 256, 337
Tripoli 98
Trost 110, 271
Tsui 98
Tucker 132
Tukey 260
Tuten 185, 337

U

Ulich 304

V

Van De Vijver 133
Van Dyne 98
Van Vuuren 99
Vandenberg 433
Velthouse 98
Verheyen 154
Viteles 20, 271

W

Waclawski 2, 124, 125, 183, 242, 243, 271
Wallner 78
Wanous 23, 132
Warns 3
Warr 92, 97, 100
Wasseveld 359
Watershed Liveware 375
Weber 21

Wefald 94
Weiner 183
Weisberg 114, 188
Weiss 6, 23, 78
Welsh 96
Wendt 99
West 42
Wetter 89
Whiteley 96
Whitney 94
Wicks 99
Wilcox 165
Wiley 42, 303, 315
Wiley 44
Wilkinson 336
Will 358

Willis 164
Wilson 104, 111, 117
Wimalasiri 302
Woehr 92, 99
Wonnacott 180
Woodman 17
Wrapp 80

Y

York 23
Young 253

Z

Zander 2, 141
Zuell 125

Subject Index

3SA 320
7+7 approach 289

A

ABB 6, 23, 78
absenteeism 36, 81
absenteism 314
ACE 83, 249, 257, 308, 328
ACE triple index 321
acquiescence 302
action
    measure of success of 274
action director 393
    action space of 396
    responsibilities of 397
action management 389
    vs. line management 394
action mission contract 395
action oriented 15
action planning
    of activities 403
    of milestones 401
    online tools for 409
    politics in 413
    reporting forms for 406
    soft factors in 409
    tools for 400
    W forms for 398, 400
action plans
    activities in 398
    adjusting 407
    hierarchical 398
    milestone network plan 402
    milestones in 398
    smart 392
    status indicators in 400
action team 393
action team members
    selection of 393
actionitis trap 67
actions
    area-wide 393
    company-wide 392
    complex 401
    consequences of 390
    controlling of 404, 405
    definition of 271, 389
    developing ideas for 390
    effects of 391
    informing on 416
    local 393
    Monday morning 272
    number of 392
    perfect 392
    reporting on 406, 418
    roles in 393
    time line of 399
    to promote given goals 273
    unnecessary 273
actions vs. busy work 271
actions vs. responses 272
additive constant 327
affective halo 116
agreement percentage 242
alignment 82
anonymity 52, 124, 142, 192, 221, 231
answer 137
    optimal 137
    satisfycing 137
answer scale 109
answer scales 114
answers
    inadmissible 101
Anything else? 123
area of focus 4, 275, 276, 282, 331, 346, 390
assimilation effect 123
attitude
    composition of 112
    crystallized 117
    judgment 117
    no 112

B

background variables 77
back-translation 133
balanced scorecard 318

Subject Index

banners 193
behavioral accounting 314
benchmark
    cross-comparison 300
    external 300
    internal 299
    upward 300
benchmarking 296, 298, 338
    and prognoses 306
    backward 305
    by cross-comparisons 304
    of correlations 306
    of indices 300
    of items 300
    of patterns 306
    upward 305
benchmarking ES 10
benchmarks 4, 6, 9
    country-specific 302
    external 326
    industry 303
    representative 301
    types of 298
    validity of 301
Bertelsmann 141
best practice thinking 19
biased inference 170
big bang 280
box plot 248, 260
brochures 196
BSC 88, 318

C

capabilities 82
card method 352
cause-and-effect analysis 384, 386
CC table 261
CCT 61
census survey 43, 57, 169
change
    continuous 280
    disruptive 280
change management 8, 16, 425
climate satisfaction 88
climate survey 7, 11
co-determination laws 55
coding 237
coding schemes 238
cognitive pre-testing 165
comment items 53
comments
    cleaning of 124
    coding of 127
    negative 125
    reporting of 124
    typical 126
commitment 35, 79, 313
    organizational 19
communicating ES results 49
comparability
    functional 300
comparing ES results 50
comparions
    anonymized 285
comparisons
    backwards 247
    cross- 259
    historical 247
    of comparable groups 246
    relative 246
    similar-groups 304
    upward 245
composition rule
    mathematical 7
confidence ratings 113
confidentiality 55, 192
consortium 3, 301
context effects 119
context performance 35
contrast effect 122
coordination team 61
coordinator
    sub-area 63
    support 63
coordinators
    selection of 64
    tasks of 63
core coordination team 61
correlation
    of items 306, 311, 328
    spurious 317
counterarguments 334
Cronbach's alpha 167
cross-comparison tables 260
cross-comparisons 259, 285, 342
    recipients of 261, 285
CT 61
customer satisfaction 36
cutoff value 52
cut-off values 54

D

data cleaning 238
data collection 42, 207
    as an event 212
    by mail 235
    comparing methods of 227
    in group sessions 208

Subject Index

information point 210
polling station method 208
data entry 237
data protection 192
data protection laws 55
data protection officer 223
data-information-understanding 296
data-protection officer 30, 56
demographic sticker 136
demographic variables 52
dependent variable 316
dependent variables 312
designs
    standard 28
    trade-offs in 29
dialogues
    as responses to an ES 284
DIMES-to-wisdom 296
disseminating ES results 49
DK category 113
Don't Know answers 130
Don't Know category 113, 141

E

Eastern Europe 44
effectiveness
    individual 82
EFQM 33
emotions at work 22
employee
    meaning of term 45
employee models
    naive 21
employee poll 8
employee survey
    interim 16
    measurement-oriented 15
employee surveys
    architecture of 61
    as interventions 7
    as OD tools 38
    benefits of 35
    content of 47
    costs of 37
    cross-cultural 19, 24
    cyclical 42
    dollar impact of 35
    for measurement and change 15
    general characteristics 5
    goals of 44
    in Eastern Europe 2
    initial reasons for 32
    logical reasons for 35
    phases of 71

politics of 40
potentials of 19
purpose 6
purpose of 56
risks of 19, 44
roles in 71
side constraints of 28
strategic 25
systemic 13
typcial cases 3
types of 8
usuage in industry 1
engagement 82
    aligned 82
equivalence
    cultural 18
error margin 179
ES
    integral 19
ES consultant 66
ES coordinator 66
ES core coordination team 420
ES master plan 68
ES project director 61
ES workshop 343
ES workshops
    action-oriented 379
    and supervisors 376
    batteries of 382
    brainstorming in 374
    design of 347
    discussing results in 363
    efficiency of 378
    facilitator of 357
    facilitator preparing for 362
    follow-up work of 383
    goals of 343
    managers in 375
    parallel 382
    participants of 357
    preparing an 360
    role of facilitator in 369
    side constraints of 347
    supervisor in 373
    timing of 352
    tips and hints for 368
    traditional 378
    two-phase 380
    varieties of 376
    with little time 377
    with managers only 376
    with representative focus groups 379
    with typical employees 380
ES/i 16

ES/m 16
ethnicity 53
exit interview 5

F

facet satisfaction 23
factor analysis 167
fear of feedback 40, 42
feedback workshop 343
field of action 275, 276, 327
fields of action 346
fire extinction thinking...............................385
first announcements 191
first-results report.......................................265
fishbone diagram...384
focal group 241
focal report...252, 253
follow-up activities 20
follow-up processes 68, 334
 big-bang approaches in 280
 bottom-up..277
 definition of..271
 design of...275
 for the individual manager 291
 planning of...292
 task-force approach in 279
 top-down 275

G

Gallup 18
global surveys 223
goal setting theory...85

H

hidden agendas...30
High Performance Model............................315
high-performance cycle 88
high-profile move 280
hints
 for conducting dialogues on ES 286
 for reading ES reports 286
 for responding to ES results 287
histogram 242
human side of enterprise 21

I

ideal scenario 344, 355
I-have-participated postcard.......................219
importance and satisfaction........................103
importance items...116
importance of item 251
importance of topic 105
incentives 232
 lottery 233

monetary 233
index
 individual effectiveness 35
 of strength 15
 one-dimensional.....................................250
 overall job attitude 35
 people-management 4, 36
 portfolio 250
 promotion rule.......................................248
 summative..248
index card method.......................................352
index construction.......................................248
 content-driven 250
 statistical approach for 250
indicator
 leading..89
indicators (of constructs) 82
information campaign
 after survey 415
 architecture of 419
 planning of...200
 politics of 423
 publications of..421
 style of 200
information station......................................156
information team...419
informed commitment 31, 198
informing about the ES 191
instant science...295
interpretation of ES results 295
interventions
 disruptive 280
invitation letter..236
involving top management..........................48
item
 action..90, 131
 debiasing 131
 function of.............................89, 102, 131
 importance of 350
 measurement 90
 placement 90, 131
 reminder 90
 single 23, 133
item importance 251
item nonresonse 114
item nonresponse 41
Itembatterie
 homogene 139
items
 actionable 100
 ambiguous 129
 batteries of...132
 bipolar 109
 blocks of...137

closed 109
comment 123
content 77
control 101, 130
demographic 77, 107, 135, 140, 158, 187
difficulty of 132
equivalent 133
extreme 129
factual 113, 120
focussed comment 126
for managers 106
formulating 128
group-specific 156
importance 7, 24, 103
inadmissible 57
industry-specific 154
job-related 57
Likert 78, 109
manipulative 130
mapping sentence for 101
on advancement 92
on benefits 92
on change management 95
on coworkers 92
on empowerment 97
on fairness 98
on goals and tasks 92
on information 93
on innovation 96
on job security 99
on job-related self-esteem 98
on justice 98
on management 93
on mergers 97
on mobbing 99
on networking 96
on new ideas 36
on OCB 97
on org. commitment 94
on organizational issues 94
on pay 92
on productivity 95
on project management 96
on psychological contracts 98
on quality 95
on restructuring 97
on strategy 96
on stress 97
on supervisor 93
on task-specific self-efficacy 98
on the company 93
on the customer 96
on trust 98
on trust in leadership 99
on work engagement 94
on workgroup 92
on working conditions 91
on work-life balance 99
open-ended 53, 123
order of 119
personal 57
pick-n 121
placement 186
ranking of 350
sensitive 100
single 132
sorting of 137, 138
structure of 329
technical rules 131
unipolar 109
ITSG 301

J

JDI 6, 23, 78, 132
job satisfaction 4, 8, 35, 81
    and job grade 304, 327
    and tenure 304
JSS 78

K

Kunin scale 6, 132

L

lateness 81
latness 81
law of effect 22
law of effects 85
legal department 30
Likert item 78
Likert response scale
    middle category of 111
linkage research 313
logic of conversation 111

M

magical 7±2 principle 111
mail survey 3
management
    scientific 21
margin of error 58
Mayflower group 301
MDS 311, 329
mean values 242
meeting in a box 347
mental representation 104
middle category (of scale) 112
minimal group size 54

models
  additive-compensatory 83
Monday morning action platform 330, 341
More-is-Better fallacy 317
MSQ 6, 23, 78
multidimensional scaling 167, 310

N

need hierarchy 22
Net Promoter Score 245
Nine Box 251
no opinion problem 12, 112
nonrespondent
  active 337
  passive 337
nonresponse 183, 184
  active 183
  dealing with 185
  demographic 337
  item 114, 186, 256
  passive 183, 185
  to demographic items 187
nonresponse bias 183
nonstandard data analysis 295
no-opinion option 112
norms 6
  external 247
NPS 245
NSDA 295
numerical scale values 114

O

obviousness problem 339
OCB 23, 88
official ES responses
  communicating 282
online surveys
  interruptions in 222
open-ended comments 54
open-ended questions
  coding of 264
  editing of 264
  reporting of 263
  typical results of 264
opinion polls 34
ordering ES reports 266
organizational change 4
organizational citizen 23
organizational climate 4, 8
outcome satisfaction 87
overall job attitude 81
overcoverage 170
over-interpretation 338
oversampling 175

oversurveying 183

P

paraphrasing method 165
participation 41
participation rates
  normal level of 229
  ways to increase 228
pay satisfaction 20, 44
people equity 321
percent favorable 242
perception is reality 335
performance
  extra-role 88
performance
  contextual 81
  discretionary 88
  individual 81
  in-role 81, 86
performance driver 331
performance-satisfaction motor 85
personnel information system 159
pilot-testing 164, 167
PIN 37, 52, 135
PIS 72, 159, 170
polling station
  electronic 209
polling station method
  organization of 213
population
  finite 181
  infinite 179
population parameter 58
positioning an ES 27
posters 191
postponing an ES 42
predictions 297, 326, 339
presentation
  aligning the 332
  counter-arguments in 334
  of ES results 323
  process of 332
  punch of 336
  risks of 333
  structure of 323
  tactics in 333
pre-testing 163
pre-tests
  number of 166
primacy effect 122
privacy violations 54
probing method 165
problem story 343, 384
prognoses report 262

PS motor 258, 309, 327
PSM 85
PSU 176
psychological contract 87
psychological maps" 311

Q

Q1 18
Q12 .... 18, 33
questionnaire
    adaptive 151
    cover page of 139
    electronic 148
    language of 149
    layout of 139, 141
    paper-pencil 140
    pretesting of 134
    prognosis 147
    standardized 7
    structure of 136
    tailored 7
    tailor-made 78
    thin 110
    translation of 134, 155
    used previously elesewhere 153
questionnaire development
    pre-testing in 163
    with advisory board 163
    with employees 161
    with executives 161
    with middle management 163
    with stakeholders 160
    with works council 162

R

RACER 84, 257, 308, 328
rankings of org units 285
readiness for an ES 38, 39
recency effect 122
re-contextualizing ES results 286
redressment 185
reliability 6
reminders 218, 219, 224, 234
report card 15
report ordering
    automated 268
resistance against an ES 45
response
    dialogical 274
    individual 274
    official 274
response criteria 115
response rate 183
    low 337

response rates
    monitoring of 215, 218, 224, 234
response scale
    categories of 111
response style 19
responses to ES results 274
return rate 337
    interpretation of 337
return rates 184
    comparison of 338
revolutions 280
rules
    for anonymity 53
    for comparing ES results 50
    of an ES workshop 347

S

sample
    convenience 170, 301
    disproportionate 175
    random 3, 173
    realized 59
    representative 173
    simple random 174
    stratified random 174
sample construction
    in practice 187
sample size 180
    minimal 181
sample survey 43, 57, 169
samples
    cut-off 171
sampling
    cluster 176
    confidence interval in 177
    multi-stage 176
    proportional 175, 176
    quota 172
    snow-balling 171
    systematic 171
    systematic random 174
sampling error 177, 180
sampling ratio 179
sampling unit
    primary 176
sandwich model 119
SAP 44
satisfaction survey 1
SAZ 23, 78
scale
    multi-item 6, 132
    single-item 6
scanning questionnaires 237

scorecard
  balanced 88
  strategic 88
scorecards 15
SDA 241
selection rules 267
self-confidence..88
sickness rate 86, 314
smart feedback 22, 86
smiley faces scale...6
solutions
  proposals for...345
SOME 307
stakeholders 30, 40
standard data analysis 241
standard ES report.....................................252
standard instruments 6, 78
standard questionnaire 17
standard surveys..18
steering committee 63
sticker method...204
stream analysis..384
subscales 82
SUCCESS 329
survey
  anonymous 149
  confidential 149
  representative 303
survey administration..........................43, 207
  by mail 216
  comparing modes of.............................227
  online..207, 220
  paper-pencil...207
survey feedback 7, 24, 416
survey logistics 207
surveys
  cross-cultural 243, 302
SWOT 319, 329, 386
SWOT analysis 80
system satisfaction 87

T

tailored design method 17
target population 169

TDM 17, 146
tenure 53, 160
testimonials...195
thinking aloud method 165
timing of an ES 41, 43
tokens of appreciation...............................233
top-down approach
  soft 280
top-down process..4
topic grinder..351
total design method 17, 146
total package design......................8, 27, 30
total package design method 18
TPD..30, 31
traffic light coding 260
translation 37
TRAPD 134
trust...20
TTM 426
turnover...36, 81

U

UIMP 12
undercoverage...170
unfreeze-and-involve management program 12
unions 30, 40
upward appraisal...5

V

vacations 41
visibility of ES 231

W

waves of data collection............................235
wish lists 20
withdrawal behavior 35
works council..................................30, 40, 147
workshops...7

Y

Yes% 242
Yes% vs. Mean...244